MW01031068

Utah in the Twentieth Century

Utah in the Twentieth Century

Edited by

Brian Q. Cannon
and Jessie L. Embry

A Project of the Charles Redd Center for Western Studies

Utah State University Press
Logan, Utah

Utah State University Press
Logan, Utah 84322–7800
www.usu.edu/usupress

Manufactured in the United State of America
Printed on acid-free, recycled paper

ISBN: 978-0-87421-744-5 (cloth)
ISBN: 978-0-87421-745-2 (e-book)

Library of Congress Cataloging-in-Publication Data

Utah in the twentieth century / edited by Brian Q. Cannon and Jessie L. Embry.
    p. cm.
"A Project of the Charles Redd Center for Western Studies."
Includes bibliographical references and index.
ISBN 978-0-87421-744-5 (cloth : acid-free paper) -- ISBN 978-0-87421-745-2 (e-book)
1. Utah--Social conditions--20th century. 2. Utah--History--20th century. 3. Utah--Politics
and government--20th century. I. Cannon, Brian Q. II. Embry, Jessie L. III. Charles Redd
Center for Western Studies.
  F826.U857 2009
  979.2'033--dc22
                            2009013985

Contents

Illustrations

Acknowledgments

As editors we owe a debt of gratitude to many who have assisted us over the course of this project. The authors whose essays appear in this volume deserve special credit for sticking with us through all the hard work of writing, rewriting, and proofreading. Some of their effort is rewarded with their work and names' appearance in print. But there were others who were not as visibly rewarded. At the outset of this project, Kris Nelson, the secretary for the Charles Redd Center for Western Studies, faithfully and efficiently arranged travel plans, coordinated schedules, and did behind-the-scenes logistical work in preparation for our seminar on Utah in the twentieth century. P. Jane Hafen, Jenny Harris, Richard Jackson, Ryan Paul, and Deidre Tyler shared their research at the seminar and provided feedback to those whose work appears in this volume. Thomas Alexander took time from his busy schedule to conduct an afternoon workshop at the seminar. John Alley, executive editor of the Utah State University Press, attended the entire seminar, where he met with each participant to offer constructive criticism and advice regarding their work. Following the seminar, John advised and assisted us, facilitating the process of revision, thematic organization, and editorial refinement of the manuscript. Jason Thompson, who manages the Redd Center office, cheerfully read page proofs, scanned images, prepared tables, and secured permission to publish many of the illustrations. Dean David Magleby of the College of Family, Home and Social Sciences; the administration of Brigham Young University; and members of the family of Charles and Annaley Redd have offered institutional and financial support for western studies at BYU over the course of this project. Finally, we thank our mentors who introduced us in our student years to Utah's history: Tom Alexander, Jim Allen, Leonard Arrington, Gene Campbell, George Ellsworth, Chas Peterson, and Ted Warner.

Introduction: Utah in the Twentieth Century

Pick up any map of Utah. Straight lines drawn at right angles demarcate the state, bisecting the landscape without reference to physiographic regions, mountain ranges, lakes, or rivers. Although those lines have a history, they reflect the intent or caprice of nineteenth-century lawmakers rather than the realities of the physical or cultural landscape. Often people have moved across the landscape as if the boundaries did not exist. Mormon settlers in northern Utah's Cache and Bear Lake Valleys did not turn back in their colonizing at the Utah Territory's northern border, nor did they create fundamentally different settlements north of it. Franklin, Whitney, Preston, and Paris—Mormon towns north of the border—possessed similar institutions, public buildings, and layouts to their Utah counterparts south of it like Lewiston, Richmond, Smithfield, Round Valley, and Garden City.

Despite the physiographic and, at times, social irrelevance of boundaries, states do possess distinctive histories and defining cultural and political characteristics. Over time, law and public policy within individual states create contrasting results. Ask the 14 percent of Utahns who cross the state line each year to purchase lottery tickets in Idaho or those who drive to Wyoming to buy contraband bottle rockets or beer with an alcohol content of more than 3.2 percent. Some of the differences seem minor or idiosyncratic. Others alter the social and economic structure more fundamentally. Consider the twin towns of Wendover, Utah, and Wendover, Nevada. West of the border, casinos flush with money pump tax dollars into infrastructure and public education. East of the border, poorly paid service-sector employees in the casinos—many of them immigrants from the Mexican state of Zacatecas—live in substandard housing and send their children to underfunded schools. State policy shapes the lives of residents from the taxes they pay to the schools they attend, the social services they are offered, and the restrictions on their behavior.

Boundaries have been consequential historically, too. After the Idaho legislature enacted a test oath in 1885 disfranchising members of any organization that advocated plural marriage, Mormons north of the Utah line could not vote. Neither Congress nor the Utah legislature took such a drastic step south of the border, although Mormon polygamists were disfranchised by federal law, as were all women in Utah. Such differences provide one significant justification

1

for examining the history of individual states as well as that of broader geopolitical regions.[1]

Within Utah's rich history, what are the most important elements? Educators and scholars struggle with this question as they organize, revise, and update their curricula. Confronted with limited classroom time, teachers of Utah Studies must choose which features of the state's past they will emphasize. Between 2000 and 2002, the State Office of Education established a core curriculum for Utah Studies classes in the fourth and seventh grades to guide teachers in their choice of what is most important. The fourth-grade curriculum used the past to understand the present and anticipate the future. It focused largely on the nineteenth century, emphasizing Utah's early inhabitants and the events leading up to statehood. The illustrative "important historical figures and historical sites" suggests the pre-1900 focus: "Fathers Dominguez and Escalante, Jim Bridger, Brigham Young, Heber Wells, Martha Hughes Cannon, This Is the Place, Promontory Point."

The seventh-grade course standards "particularly emphasize Utah from statehood to the present." Still, one of the three course standards with a substantial historical component concentrated largely on the nineteenth century and its legacy: "students will understand the contributions of native American Indians, explorers, and Utah's pioneers." The other two history-based standards treated economic development, religious and ethnic diversity, and immigration by looking broadly at the nineteenth and twentieth centuries. Twentieth-century themes singled out in the curriculum included the impact of military installations, heavy and high-tech industries, recreation and tourism, and labor unions.[2]

Like elementary and secondary schoolteachers, social scientists use professional standards to prioritize and assign significance to historical Utah topics. The subfields in which they specialize with their distinctive methodologies, scholarly canons, and questions, along with personal interests, direct them toward discrete time periods or topics. Archaeologists scrutinize pottery shards, arrowheads, and other vestiges of the first peoples from Paleo-Indians to the Fremont and Anasazi. Anthropologists and ethnohistorians study the cultures and lifeways of indigenous inhabitants. Historians schooled in the Spanish Borderlands tradition study intercultural contact in the American Southwest, including the first Spanish explorers and Catholic fathers who came to present-day Utah in the eighteenth century. Others specializing in the fur trade and exploration are particularly interested in the Euro-American traders and explorers who came to the Great Basin in the eighteenth and early-nineteenth centuries.

Scholars' expertise, training, and preferences also shape their depiction of the Utah story following 1847. Abundant documentation and cultural or ancestral ties predispose some historians to engage Utah's history beginning with the arrival of the Mormon pioneers in 1847 and focus on Mormon themes. Undeniably the Mormon presence shaped the experiences of most Utahns in the nineteenth century, but the degree to which that story should dominate

Theron Luke, a Utah County
journalist and historian.

Utah history has been hotly contested. Theron Luke, a longtime teacher of
Utah history at Utah Technical College in Provo, largely avoided Mormon topics in his classes. Some students chafed at Luke's artificial segregation of the
Utah and Mormon stories, but he felt that Utah history as it was commonly
taught was the quintessential insider story, marginalizing the voices and experiences of those who came before 1847 or lived outside the Mormon circle. As
Helen Papanikolas, a lifelong student of Greek immigration and life in Utah,
observed in her 1976 preface to *The Peoples of Utah,* "Utah has long ceased
being an agrarian society of a 'peculiar people.' Although still predominately
Mormon, many cultures have contributed to its unique essence in this lost
domain of the Indians." Luke and Papanikolas sought to move those other
stories toward the center.[3]

　　Whether they emphasize German-Jewish merchants, rough-and-tumble
mining camps, soldiers stationed at frontier army posts, or Brigham Young,
Mormon villages, and polygamy, many historians, along with the general public, gravitate toward the romance of the Old West. Did the 1890s, the demise
of the Old West, and statehood mark the end of Utah history? Of course not.
Utah celebrated one hundred years of statehood in 1996. But after the 1890s,
both Utah history and the broader western American history of which it is a
part have often been treated as anticlimactic. Among historians the most influential privileging of the years before 1900 is Frederick Jackson Turner's frontier
thesis, which did more than any other historical argument to establish western

American history as a respectable intellectual enterprise. Turner argued that the experiences of Americans on successive frontiers as the nation expanded westward had been the most influential force in shaping American democracy and society. Taking his cue from a report issued by the superintendent of the census, Turner proclaimed that the frontier had "closed" in 1890 because the West's isolation had declined and its nether regions had been populated. By linking the importance of the frontier so closely to the West, Turner implicitly diminished the importance of the region for the nation as a whole after the frontier closed. At the time he wrote it in 1893, the Turner thesis justified the full sweep of western history, but it made less sense as the twentieth century unfolded.[4]

Like Turner, many historians studying Utah also infused the pioneer era with special meaning. The pioneers themselves began the process of romanticizing the early years of settlement, much as they did throughout the West, exaggerating the hardships and accentuating their heroic responses to challenges. Their children and grandchildren deepened the romance as they lionized their forebears' achievements.[5] For chroniclers of Utah's history, the divide between the Old West and the new, the frontier and the postfrontier eras, was even more striking than for the larger region; it entailed not only the general forces of modernization noted by Turner and his disciples but also the Mormon majority's gradual renunciation of plural marriage, economic isolation, communitarian institutions, and theocratic government. Emblematic turning points, clustered around the turn of the century, included the Woodruff Manifesto of 1890, the discontinuation of the Mormon-dominated People's Party in 1891, Utah's admission as a state in 1896, the Smoot hearings of 1903–7, and the Second Manifesto of 1904.

The romance of the fur trade, the overland migrations in covered wagons and handcarts, the tempestuous tug-of-war between the United States government and the LDS Church, the fabulous mineral strikes and rambunctious mining towns, vigilante justice, the open range, and the Indian wars all belonged to the Old West of the nineteenth century. Those developments vibrated with so much drama and exoticism that even well into another century, many teachers and professors focused their Utah history classes almost exclusively on the region before 1900. As one eminent Utah historian, George Ellsworth, observed in his 1972 Utah history textbook for seventh graders, the state's history after 1920 held "little uniqueness" and, by implication, little intrinsic appeal, although Ellsworth added, "Even so, it is interesting to learn what life was like in the new age." For many people, the state's recent history lacked charm and seemed only to be a smaller-scale, duller version of regional or national history.[6]

In the field of western American history, a cadre of scholars rejected the notion inherited from Turner's frontier thesis that the West's history prior to 1890 mattered more than what came after. Some, including Patricia Limerick, argued that the divide between the frontier and postfrontier eras was artificial and that the same features that made the West significant in the nineteenth

Many Utahns, like this family on a pioneer float in Vernal, focused on the charm of the Mormon pioneer past and celebrated it in the late twentieth century.

century made it important in the twentieth. For one reason, the West was a preeminent case study in the processes of conquest and conflict. For another, it was the most ethnically and racially diverse region of the nation, the premier American case study of multicultural life. Other historians, including Donald Worster, focused upon the persistence of the region's most distinctive character-istic—its aridity—and argued that the West's fragile environment and civiliza-tion carried a burden for the nation at large, teaching vital lessons about the relationship between humans and their surroundings.[7]

In the same era that western historians like Limerick and Worster offered creative and compelling arguments for regionally based studies of the twenti-eth-century West, historians studying Utah also worked to interpret the twen-tieth century in meaningful ways. As Charles S. Peterson observed in 1977, historical work on the twentieth century had been "sparse and spotty" to that point in time, and S. George Ellsworth observed in 1972, "The social history of Utah in the twentieth century is a field barren of studies of much consequence with few exceptions." But in the late 1970s and 1980s, historians began to pay more sustained attention to interpreting the twentieth century. In 1977 W.W. Norton published Peterson's interpretive history of the state, *Utah: A Bicentennial History,* as part of its States and the Nation series. Peterson devoted a bit less than 40 percent of his volume to the years after 1890. He traced the process by which Utah between 1890 and 1977 was "thoroughly assimilated into the mainstream of American society." Peterson described Utah's rejection of self-sufficiency and its embrace of competitive capitalism, its evolution as a supplier of agricultural products and minerals for the nation, and its dependence upon external investment capital. The "nationalization" of Utah resulted partly from the influence of "other Utahs" that many historians had marginalized—the Colorado Plateau, the countryside, and ethnic and racial minorities. These agents of diversification "multiplied the points at which the local tradition interlocks with the broader American community."

Peterson characterized Utah's politics through the mid-1970s as centrist, for business and opposed to government regulation, and wedded to the status quo. In characterizing the years following World War II, he emphasized environmentalism, the growth of the defense industry, and tourism. Despite Utah's integration with the nation, Peterson noted that even in the 1970s, the state remained different on a less-fundamental level: "The Mormon–non-Mormon division cuts through and influences all other grouping arrangements." Utahns minimized the impact of the divide by withdrawing from political engagement and emphasizing conformity. Thus, reform movements generally lagged in Utah, and even on university campuses, debate was subdued, Peterson believed.[8]

In 1978 Utah historians compiled the first college-level textbook in Utah history, entitled simply *Utah's History*. Before that time, a typical text was Leonard J. Arrington's *Great Basin Kingdom*, which made no attempt to cover anything but the nineteenth century. *Great Basin Kingdom* was not written to be a textbook, however, but was the best and most wide-ranging scholarly study of Utah history at that time. The new textbook divided the state's history chronologically and then topically. Roughly 40 percent of the book was devoted to the twentieth century. In his introductory essay for the section on the twentieth century, Thomas G. Alexander suggested that "the decline of ecclesiastical domination of politics, society, and the economy and the rise of a secular life characterized by competition" was "perhaps the most important characteristic" of the state's history in the twentieth century. Thus, the core story for Alexander, as for Peterson, was "integration into the national economic, political, and social framework." Alexander identified urbanization as another noteworthy "aspect of twentieth-century life in Utah" and characterized its modern political history as "an extraordinary combination of the conservative and progressive."[9]

In 1987 Dean L. May completed a popular history of the state, *Utah: A People's History*. Perhaps because it was geared to a general audience, May devoted less than one-third of his volume to the seemingly less-romantic twentieth century, and he wrote little about events after 1945. May, too, discussed the "Americanization" of Utah but argued that it was "far more complicated and subtle than the simple Americanization of the Mormon population." Like Peterson, he emphasized the role of immigrants from southern and eastern Europe, Mexico, and Asia in diversifying the state politically and economically and making Utah "far more American in 1910 than she had been in 1880." May argued that America's international economic power, demand for American products abroad, and high defense spending placed Utah in an "advantageous position" economically until the late 1970s. Writing during the economic slump of the late 1980s, May emphasized Utah's precarious economic position, borne of its dependency upon consumers and politicians far removed from the state. Other significant characteristics of the state late in the twentieth century included the conservatism and probusiness sentiment of Utah's politicians and the power and importance of the federal government.

To a greater degree than Alexander or Peterson, May disputed the reality of Utah's integration with the nation; instead, he suggested, the state was becoming increasingly different from the nation. He argued that the economic and political presence and power of Mormonism had rebounded in recent decades, symbolized by its involvement in politics, its prominence in initiatives to revitalize downtown Salt Lake City, and the social polarization along religious lines in that city. "The Mormons, one suspects, are still a peculiar people, and the extent of their 'Americanization' more apparent than real," he contended.[10]

For Utah's statehood centennial in 1996, the Utah State Historical Society planned new historical studies. Thomas G. Alexander wrote a one-volume history, *Utah: The Right Place,* which covered the state's history to that time. In 2003 he revised the history, updating it to include more-recent developments, including the 2002 Winter Olympics. Roughly half of the book dealt with the twentieth century—a higher percentage than in any previous study. Alexander described integration between Utah and the nation as a process that began "long before 1890," the date of the Woodruff Manifesto, and "did not stop . . . in 1896" with statehood. But he supplemented the theme of integration with greater attention to Utah's economic evolution over the course of the twentieth century from a colony of Wall Street; to a colony of Washington, D.C., dependent upon defense spending; to an "American commonwealth," where Utahns owned and managed many of the largest businesses in the state. He charted Utah's emergence in the second half of the twentieth century as "an internationally renowned cultural oasis" for art, music, dance and sport. Another significant theme of the postwar era was the struggle for equal rights for minorities and women.[11]

In addition to their survey texts of Utah's history, scholars also focused upon twentieth-century themes in article-length studies. In 1995 John S. McCormick and John R. Sillito compiled a collection of previously published articles in an edited collection of readings in Utah history entitled *A World We Thought We Knew.* The editors lamented the relative neglect of twentieth-century history. They noted that the years from 1896 to 1939, for instance, "await additional scholarly attention." Nevertheless, the editors privileged the twentieth century by dedicating more than three-fourths of the volume to post-1900 topics. Although "the Mormon presence and experience is central to the

Utah story" and "the predominant concern of historians," the authors wrote, they wanted to avoid a "narrow and selective reading of Utah history" focused largely upon Mormons and the Mormon Church. Instead, they advocated a polyvocal approach, selecting articles that emphasized diversity and conflict. Acknowledging that Utah's history in the twentieth century intersected with many broader regional and national themes and currents, Sillito and McCormick rejected the notion that studies of the state's history had to focus on the distinctive to be instructive. Rather, they argued, studying events close to home could be a "fruitful ground for illuminating larger questions and patterns in American history and in the larger society of which it is a part."[12]

Unlike *A World We Thought We Knew*, this volume primarily showcases fresh, previously unpublished work. But it builds upon McCormick and Sillito's contention that the twentieth century deserves historical investigation partly because it can help us understand larger regional and national issues. It also proceeds from Charles Peterson's contention that Mormonism has continued to configure Utah's social landscape in manifold ways over the twentieth century. Several articles in this volume offer empirical support for Dean May's observation that Utah did not entirely shed its distinctiveness in the twentieth century and Mormonism's political and cultural power rebounded somewhat in the 1970s and 1980s, contributing to the New Right's political and cultural ascendancy across the nation. Thus, the state's development between 1900 and 2000, as explored in this volume, teaches us about both Utah's commonalities and its distinctiveness in the constellation of states.

This volume is designed to supplement and provide added depth to the information available in previously published surveys of the state's history. The articles in this book were originally prepared and critiqued at a seminar on Utah in the twentieth century sponsored in 2006 by the Charles Redd Center for Western Studies at Brigham Young University. Scholars studying Utah in the twentieth century were asked to contribute papers. Using the criticism and questions that originated in the seminar, the authors revised their papers for publication. The coeditors of this volume and John Alley from Utah State University Press arranged the articles thematically in four sections. The coeditors then wrote an introduction for each section to contextualize the articles.

The first section, "Getting to Know the Place: Image and Experience," examines images of the land and the people and the way they relate to Utahns' experiences in the twentieth century. Those dependent for a livelihood upon traditional extractive industries such as mining and ranching often viewed the land through different lenses than did recreation enthusiasts, tourists, and environmentalists. The balance of power in this contest shifted as the number of Utahns residing in metropolitan areas rose and the ranks of miners, farmers, and ranchers thinned. Meanwhile, the nature and defining characteristics of Utah's social and cultural landscape altered, with some Utahns applauding the changes brought by in-migration and diversification and others defensively resisting them.

The second section, "Connecting to the Nation: Utah and the U.S.A.," examines Utah's relationship to the nation in terms of warfare and national defense, commerce, economic development, and political participation. The articles in this part show that, while Utah followed many of the same patterns as other states—from the travails of the Great Depression and reliance upon the New Deal to increased dependence upon federal defense spending during World War II and the cold war—some elements—especially the presence and influence of the Church of Jesus Christ of Latter-day Saints—made the state's experiences unique.

The third section, "Voicing Government: Politics and Participation," looks at some of the political choices Utahns made in the twentieth century and compares them to political trends elsewhere in the nation. It explores the way Utahns exercised political power and used political processes to alter governmental structures, enfranchise some groups, and deny rights to others.

The final section, "Growing Challenges: People and Resources," discusses a major characteristic and challenge of the twentieth century, particularly the years after 1940—growth. How did the state and federal government and Utah residents deal with population increases that put greater demands on limited resources, including water, land, and education dollars?

Utah State University Press and the Charles Redd Center hope that this volume will be a valuable resource for students and teachers of Utah history. It should also be fruitful reading for anyone who desires to know more about key themes of Utah's history in the twentieth century.

Notes

1. *Deseret News*, August 14, 2004; June 26, 2005; *Daily Utah Chronicle*, February 22, 2001; Sarah Barringer Gordon, *The Mormon Question: Polygamy and Constitutional Conflict in Nineteenth Century America* (Chapel Hill: University of North Carolina Press, 2002), 153–54, 180, 225–28.
2. Utah State Office of Education, *Elementary Core Curriculum: Social Studies* (Salt Lake City: State Office of Education, 2000), 5–8; Utah State Office of Education, *Secondary Core Curriculum: Social Studies 7–12* (Salt Lake City: State Office of Education, 2002), 1–4.
3. Helen Z. Papanikolas, ed., *The Peoples of Utah* (Salt Lake City: Utah State Historical Society, 1976), 1.
4. On Turner and his work, see Allan G. Bogue, *Frederick Jackson Turner: Strange Roads Going Down* (Norman: University of Oklahoma Press, 1998).
5. Richard H. Jackson, "Righteousness and Environmental Change: The Mormons and the Environment," in *Essays on the American West, 1973–1974*, ed. Thomas G. Alexander, Charles Redd Monographs in Western History 5 (Provo, UT: Brigham Young University Press, 1975), 21–42; Richard H. Jackson, "The Mormon Experience: The Plains as Sinai, the Great Salt Lake as the Dead Sea, and the Great Basin as Desert-cum-Promised Land," *Journal of Historical Geography* 18 (January 1992): 41–58.

6.   S. George Ellsworth, *Utah's Heritage* (Santa Barbara, CA: Peregrine Smith, 1972), 197.

7.   Patricia Nelson Limerick, *The Legacy of Conquest: The Unbroken Past of the American West* (New York: W.W. Norton, 1987); Donald Worster, "New West, True West: Interpreting the Region's History," *Western Historical Quarterly* 18 (April 1987): 141–56.

8.   Charles S. Peterson, *Utah: A Bicentennial History* (New York: W.W. Norton, 1977), 159, 204, 202, 208; S. George Ellsworth, "Utah History: Retrospect and Prospect," *Utah Historical Quarterly* 40 (Fall 1972): 361.

9.   Richard D. Poll, Thomas G. Alexander, Eugene E. Campbell, and David E. Miller, eds., *Utah's History* (Provo, UT: Brigham Young University Press, 1978), 405, 406; Leonard J. Arrington, *Great Basin Kingdom: An Economic History of the Latter-day Saints, 1830–1900* (Cambridge, MA: Harvard University Press, 1958).

10.   Dean L. May, *Utah: A People's History* (Salt Lake City: University of Utah Press, 1987), 167, 194, 196.

11.   Thomas G. Alexander, *Utah, the Right Place: The Official Centennial History,* rev. ed. (Salt Lake City: Gibbs Smith, 2003), 218, 454, 459. In addition to Alexander's sweeping history of the state, the Utah Historical Society and county commissioners commemorated the state centennial by commissioning histories for Utah's twenty-nine counties and a one-volume history on Utah's Native Americans. Plans for more specialized histories of Utah, including two volumes covering the twentieth century, failed to materialize.

12.   John S. McCormick and John R. Sillito, *A World We Thought We Knew: Readings in Utah History* (Salt Lake City: University of Utah Press, 1995), 3, 6, 483.

I

Getting to Know the Place
Image and Experience

What do most people think of when they hear the word "Utah"? In 2007 Governor Jon M. Huntsman Jr. and the Utah Office of Tourism hoped that potential visitors and residents would relate to the new slogan, "Utah: Life Elevated, . . . a quick, easy way to remember what Utah does best: put you on high ground." But describing Utah in two words was challenging. "The colors are so diverse, the mountains so majestic, the desert so mysterious. . . .We are summer. We are winter. We are historic. We are cultured. We are modern and progressive, but we still have true, laid-back authentic charm."[1]

What is underneath these grand statements? What is Utah to those who live in the state, and how has it changed? What did it mean to Native Americans? How did their and others' views differ from those of the Mormon majority who dominated in the state during the nineteenth and much of the twentieth centuries? What did Utah mean to twentieth-century immigrants from different regions? There may be as many answers as there are Utahns. And where Utahns may agree, other Americans may have completely different opinions. Nevertheless, there are commonly held images of the land, the people, and the experience.

Images of the Land

Shoshonean-speaking tribes—Utes, Paiutes, and Shoshones—called Utah home for centuries before the first Mormon settlers arrived in 1847. Athabascan-speaking Navajos moved into southeastern Utah possibly as early as the seventeenth century. All of these indigenous groups resourcefully used rich arrays of plants and animals to support themselves in a relatively arid environment where few species were abundant. For instance, the Western Shoshones, who include the Gosiutes, used eighty-one species of plants from the Basin and Range

11

Province of western Utah and eastern Nevada for food. Their rituals, creation stories, and tribal lore demonstrate that Utah's Indians identified closely with the natural world, imbuing it with transcendent power and other sacred qualities. They had to know it well to harvest such diverse resources.[2]

For the early Mormons, the land was a gift from God. Their initial accounts described trees along the riverbanks and tall grasses. Later, Mormon leaders developed a story that the area had been a treeless desert that God and pioneer industry caused to "blossom as a rose" for His chosen people.[3] Views of the land as a resource to be exploited and made to flower for wealth and productivity remained strong in the twentieth century. New farming techniques and irrigation projects enabled Utahns to transform and reclaim more land more efficiently in the quest for greater wealth. Between 1890 and 1902, with the age of agricultural modernization and mechanization still looming on the horizon, Utahns increased the amount of land they farmed from 1.3 million to 5 million acres.[4]

Not everyone viewed land and nature as commodities to be developed economically and according to immediate needs, however. During the twentieth century, Utahns, like other Americans, witnessed the depletion of natural resources, and many demanded preservation or at least conservation through control of land use. State and federal governments created programs and agencies to save the state's beauty and conserve resources for the future. Near the end of the nineteenth century, the governments cooperated in establishing forest reserves in the Uinta Mountains and near Fish Lake. In 1903 an additional four million acres across the state received protection as national forests, allowing managed use instead of unlimited exploitation of their resources. Between 1908 and 1915, United States presidents established four national monuments in Utah, which provided stronger protection for areas especially valued for their natural and scenic qualities. Utah Senator Reed Smoot used his influence on the Committee on Public Lands to help push the National Park Service bill through Congress in 1916 and worked to create the first national parks in Utah. Other monuments and parks followed and are listed in table 1.[5]

Table 1. National Parks and Monuments in Utah

National Monument/Park	Year Created
Natural Bridges National Monument	1908
Mukuntuweap National Monument	1909
Zion National Park	1919
Rainbow Bridge National Monument	1910
Dinosaur National Monument	1915
Timpanogos Cave National Monument	1922
Bryce Canyon National Monument	1923
Bryce Canyon National Park	1928

Hovenweep National Monument	1923
Arches National Monument	1929
Arches National Park	1971
Cedar Breaks National Monument	1933
Capitol Reef National Monument	1937
Capitol Reef National Park	1971
Canyonlands National Park	1964
Grand Staircase–Escalante National Monument	1996

Most of these national parks and monuments were in Color Country in southern Utah, the red rock area that Stephen C. Sturgeon describes as "a landscape that is *in* Utah but not *of* Utah" in his chapter in this volume. The federal government owns this land, partly by default. Homesteaders attempted to farm and ranch parts of these areas, but many of them failed. Like Blue Valley near Capitol Reef, which Kristen Rogers-Iverson writes about in her chapter, they were places that offered promise but then proved too harsh. The same unusual geology that gave them special environmental and scenic appeal often made them unsuitable for farming.

Beginning later, Utah developed more than forty state parks between 1957, when the Division of State Parks and Recreation was established, and 2000.[6] Utah's state parks are situated not only amidst red rock canyons and cliffs but also in the lofty Wasatch and Uinta Mountains, with their quiet valleys, roaring rivers, and meandering streams. Some state parks and national recreation areas even celebrate man-made features on the landscape, such as the Bureau of Reclamation's dams and reservoirs. For example, Lake Powell on the Colorado River, designed for water storage and power generation, has evolved into a water playground. In the 1990s, this huge reservoir behind Glen Canyon Dam had more than two million visitor days each year (the National Park Service's way of calculating time spent at its sites).[7]

As population grew, open space diminished, and pollution imperiled vital elements of fragile ecosystems, some Utahns formed organizations to preserve open space and protect plants and threatened species. Congress provided the tools to do so on federal lands by passing laws, including the Wilderness Act of 1964, the Wild and Scenic Rivers Act of 1968, and the Endangered Species Act of 1973. Utahns joined national organizations such as the Sierra Club and formed their own groups, including the Utah Wilderness Association and the Southern Utah Wilderness Alliance, to protect the environment. A signal victory for the environmental movement in the state was the passage by Congress of the Wilderness Act in 1984, setting aside 750,000 acres across the state as wilderness.[8]

In the 1970s, '80s, and '90s, as more Americans and Utahns played in the outdoors at places like Lake Powell, the state acquired the image of an outdoor wonderland. The number of skier days (a skier day is defined as one person purchasing a lift ticket) first topped one million in 1972, the year after

Chester Olsen, director of the Utah Parks Commission, at Dead Horse Point State Park.

Snowbird, Utah's first deluxe resort, opened. Thereafter, skier visits rose fairly consistently, exceeding two million for the first time in 1979 and three million in 1996.[9] While the LDS Church's Temple Square in Salt Lake City remained the most visited spot in the state in the twentieth century, natural and other outdoor wonders increasingly shaped many people's image of Utah. The state government hoped an image of outdoor recreation also registered with those who saw a skier and "The Greatest Snow on Earth" slogan (first issued in 1985) or Delicate Arch (first issued in 1992) on license plates.

A desert example illustrates the shifting perceptions of Utah's landscape. The Bonneville Salt Flats near the Utah/Nevada border was always a forsaken place. Historically Native Americans avoided the area. Explorers and trappers learned of the harsh environment and then stayed away when they could. The Donner-Reed emigrant group took Hasting's Cutoff across the salt flats and suffered through the soggy mud and salt plains.

Does a place like the salt flats where nothing grows have any value? Amazingly, yes. Groups even disagree on their best use. Recreation and mining arrived in the early-twentieth century. Industries found a market for potassium chloride (a fertilizer popularly known as potash). Prices soared during World War I when German exports ceased, but after the war, a market remained for potash extracted through an evaporation process.

Ab Jenkins, who was elected mayor of Salt Lake City, without campaigning, became famous for racing his Mormon Meteor car on the Bonneville Salt Flats in the 1930s.

While the Donner-Reed party had to slog across the salt, automobile enthusiasts found it perfect for traveling quickly. Utahn Ab Jenkins raced a train to Wendover and won. He then set endurance records, driving twenty-four hours nonstop. After international and national racing commissions refused to accept his speeds, he invited British racers to set the land speed record (the fastest measured mile) on the salt flats in the 1930s. During the 1960s, Americans used jet engines to set new records. The salt flats became known worldwide as a place to go fast.

Uses of the salt flats moved beyond mining and racing. The movie industry discovered their stark beauty. *Independence Day* (1996) and *Pirates of the Caribbean: At World's End* (2006) are among movies set at the site. Artists and nature lovers appreciate the austere purity of an area where they can see the curvature of the earth. Can all these activities coexist? The salt flats are drying up. The land speed record can no longer be set there because the track is not long enough. The racers blame the miners. The miners credit Mother Nature. The Bureau of Land Management, which supervises the area, is working with both parties, and the mining company is returning salt to the track. The racers call the project "Save the Salt"; the mining company calls it the "Salt Laydown Project." The names reflect the different ways they perceive this landscape. This type of conflict among miners, ranchers, environmentalists, and recreationists is repeated throughout the state. [10]

How did the shift in uses and perceptions of the state's land take place? Partly it reflects a major shift in cultural values nationally and beyond, but a more-mundane, albeit major, factor was the automobile. Cars enabled people to travel widely and see Utah's amazing places. During the twentieth century, more visitors saw the state and found it to be a natural-wonder playground. A large and extensive tourist industry sprang up to support these activities. As Susan Sessions Rugh discusses, entrepreneurial Utahns established motels and other services to accommodate vacationers who took to the roads in record numbers following World War II.

The People: Changing the Image

Long before visitors came to see Utah's natural wonders, they came to experience the state's distinctive culture. Travelers to Utah in the nineteenth century were curious about Mormon polygamy, theocracy, and communitarianism. In the twentieth century, those distinctive features of Mormonism receded, but the perception of the religion and its culture as aberrant and bizarre persisted. Many visitors still associated Utah with the Mormon Church and expected the state to be different as a result. Like Samuel Taylor, who returned to Utah in 1953 after an extended absence, newcomers regarded Utah as a "physical island with its strange mental wall, in which a peculiar people live their religion as a way of life." Utah was "an island fairyland of enormous beauty, peopled by a unique brand of tightly-knit Puritans."[11]

That image endured throughout the twentieth century. A Connecticut transplant living in West Valley City wrote in 1995, "Living in Utah has been quite an experience, to say the least. Although it is a beautiful state with many outdoor advantages, I find it a very backward state in many ways—prejudice is very high, narrow-minded people and a very uptight society in general." University of Utah history professor Larry Gerlach observed in 2002, "In no other state does a single entity have such unquestioned control over public life as the LDS church in Utah . . . Mormonism is an omnipresent web of sensibility that seems natural and comforting to some, but embarrassing and exclusionary to others."[12]

Despite the persistent image of all Utahns as Mormons, the state's population profile changed during the twentieth century. While the Mormon influence remained significant, three major movements gave Utah a more-diverse population. First, workers came to the state's developing coal and copper mines and smelters during the Progressive Era. Many of these "new immigrants" differed culturally, religiously, and ethnically from previous waves of immigrants. Labor recruiters canvassed American cities, Europe, and Japan for employees. Thousands of Greeks, Italians, Japanese, Slavs, Mexicans, and other immigrants moved to Utah between 1900 and 1930 to work on the railroad, in mines and smelters, and on farms. Table 2 documents the magnitude of this immigration.[13]

Table 2. Origins of Key Groups of "New" Immigrants, 1900–1930

Foreign-Born Immigrants	1900	1910	1920	1930
Greek	3	4,039	3,029	2,197
Italian	1,062	3,117	3,225	2,814
Slav			999	1,108
Japanese	417	2,110	2,936	4,012
Mexican	40	145	1,083	4,012

Sources: See note 13.

In addition to in-migration during the Progressive Era, a second impetus for diversification was World War II. Thousands of soldiers, who reflected the religious, ethnic, and racial diversity of the nation, converged upon northern Utah as they trained or labored in the state's military installations. Hundreds of Jewish soldiers temporarily swelled the ranks of Utah's small Jewish community. Salt Lake's Jewish community eagerly accommodated the soldiers, renting rooms where they could socialize, arranging for Jewish services on military bases, and organizing celebrations for religious holidays. Nearly one million African Americans served in the military during the war, and many trained or worked at Utah's bases. Black soldiers who "were going overseas to kill for freedom" were determined "to have some freedom here before they went" and pushed back the color line. In Ogden black GIs "literally [tore] up" cafés and theaters whose proprietors refused to serve them. African American Nathan "Woody" Wright of Ogden believed that the soldiers "were the reason Twenty-fifth Street got desegregated." Following the war, jobs at defense installations continued to attract African Americans; the number of blacks in Utah rose from 1,235 in 1940 to 2,729 in 1950 and 4,148 in 1960. Hundreds of Mexican Americans and American Indians also migrated to Utah—especially from northern New Mexico and southern Colorado, having been recruited to fill wartime jobs in mines, factories, and defense installations .[14]

Most Japanese Americans were unique because they came to Utah under duress. More than five hundred West Coast Japanese averted forced relocation by moving on their own to Utah between the bombing of Pearl Harbor and the instigation of internment. Those forced to come later, more than eleven thousand, resided temporarily at the Central Utah Relocation Center, commonly known as Topaz, near Delta. Topaz consisted of thirty-four residential blocks containing hastily constructed 20-by-120-foot pine barracks covered with tar paper and heated with pot-bellied stoves. Each barrack included six apartments. Iku "Yukari" Umegaki Uchida vented her frustration at her barren surroundings in poetry: "Someone named it Topaz . . . . This land where neither grass nor trees nor wild flowers grow. Banished to this desert land, I cherish the Blessing of the sky."[15] After the war, some Japanese American

Japanese American internees at the Central Utah Relocation Center congregate near the entrance to greet new arrivals from California, ca. 1942.

internees remained. Utah's Japanese American residents numbered 3,060 in 1950—1,200 more than in 1940.[16]

The Immigration Act of 1965, along with a strong U.S. economy and Southeast Asian refugees displaced by war, provided the third impetus for diversification. By dispensing with the old quota system, which had favored Europeans, the law facilitated greater immigration from Asia, Latin America, the Caribbean, and the Pacific. Due to a large Mormon presence in the Pacific islands, Utah became a natural destination for Tongans and other Polynesians—Mormons and non-Mormons—desiring to emigrate. Relatives and friends followed the early immigrants, creating a chain of journeys to the Beehive State from the South Pacific. By 1999 5 percent of the students in the Salt Lake City School District were Pacific Islanders.[17]

During the 1980s, more than one million Mexicans entered the United States, but large numbers did not arrive in Utah until the following decade. At the end of the century, 57 percent of the state's foreign-born population had been in Utah less than ten years, and most of the recent arrivals were Mexicans who had come seeking economic opportunities and wholesome community life. Nine percent of the state's population was Hispanic. The percentage was even greater in some locations. Wendover was 75 percent Hispanic. One in four students in Salt Lake City's public schools spoke Spanish as their first language.[18]

As newcomers moved to the state in the 1990s, the proportion of Mormon residents fell. According to the *Salt Lake Tribune*, 66.4 percent of the state's population was LDS by 2000, down from 71.8 percent in 1990. Grand and San Juan Counties, which had small populations overall, also had the lowest percentages of Mormons. They were followed by Summit (reflecting the influence of the ski industry and tourism), Tooele, Salt Lake, and Weber Counties.[19]

By the turn of the twenty-first century, Salt Lake City was "the least Mormon place in Mormondom." Only about one-third of the city's population was nominally LDS, and nearly 20 percent of the population was Latino. One resident described it as "a bastion of social diversity and political liberalism," whose mayor, Ross C. "Rocky" Anderson, was a "liberal Democrat, divorced, ex-rock guitarist, former American Civil Liberties Union lawyer, and liquor-imbibing non-religious ex-Mormon."[20]

Culture: Image and Achievement

As the preceding quotation demonstrates, changing demography in the twentieth century did not eliminate Utah's atmosphere of cultural polarity. For many who liked the state as they had known and experienced it, criticism of its people, religion, and culture touched a raw nerve. They wanted their home state to be presented to the world in a positive light. In 1912, when several silent films lampooned the state as a bastion of religious violence and polygamy, Isaac Russell, a Utah native working as a journalist in New York City, observed, "The fever to welcome the tourist, to make him at home, to get him over certain old ideas . . . is a fiercer fever than anyone who has not felt it can realize." In Utah "boosters and boomers" vowed to "fight incessantly against everything in the West with which the outsider could find legitimate fault and against everything outside that [gave] a false impression" of the region.[21]

Utahns' inferiority complex and hypersensitivity to criticism became abundantly apparent when Bernard DeVoto, a native of Ogden and an American essayist and critic, complained in the 1920s that cultural life in Utah was insipid. As David Lewis explains in his chapter, DeVoto's criticisms put a bad taste in many Utahns' mouths, and they refused to accept him as one of their own. Yet maybe DeVoto was right. For example, according to historian Thomas G. Alexander, Utah did not produce any great cultural novelists during the 1920s. DeVoto argued that with its distinctive characteristics like polygamy eliminated, Utah became a rather dry, dull place.[22]

But did it remain that way? Over the course of the twentieth century, Utah developed an array of offerings in music, dance, drama, and sports comparable to those in other states with similar numbers of residents and produced fine literature and art. The best-known example is the Mormon Tabernacle Choir. The volunteer choir represents an early Mormon public-relations success from its appearance at the 1893 Chicago World Fair to its weekly *Music and the Spoken Word* program, started on CBS radio in 1929—the longest continually operating radio/television program. "America's choir" has toured nationally and internationally and performed for U.S. presidents and other world leaders.[23]

The Utah Symphony played just as important a role in promoting music within the state. Maurice Abravanel directed the symphony from 1947 to 1979 and made it into a world-class organization that toured the state, the nation, and the world.[24] Well-known professional dance companies were established including Ballet West (1963), Ririe-Woodbury Dance Company (1964) and Repertory Dance Theatre (1966), and Odyssey Dance Theatre (1999).[25] The state became home to professional regional theaters, including the Tony Award–winning Utah Shakespearean Festival in Cedar City (1961), the Utah Festival Opera in Logan (1993), Pioneer Theatre Company (1962), and Salt Lake Acting Company (1969) in Salt Lake City. Because of a small population, these arts organizations usually focused on the entire state for their audience and funding support.[26]

Utah also inspired literature and art. Some of the writers and artists were native born and then left the state. Others came from outside only to work. Their works paint in words and color the diversity of Utah's lands and people. Edward Abbey's greatest work, *Desert Solitaire,* was inspired by his work as a seasonal ranger in Arches National Park. Wallace Stegner spent his high-school years in Salt Lake City and considered Utah home. Both Mormons and non-Mormons praise his Utah classics, *Mormon Country* and *The Gathering of Zion.* Later in the twentieth century, Utah native Terry Tempest Williams moved preservationists with her *Refuge: An Unnatural History of Family and Place* about her family's experiences in Utah and the way the beauty of the Great Salt Lake sustained them through both good times and bad. Nationally acclaimed poet May Swenson spent her early years in Logan and often returned to visit Utah.[27]

Art followed much the same pattern as literature. In the nineteenth century a group of artists went on missions to Paris to study painting and then came back to work on murals in the Mormon Salt Lake Temple. These artists attempted to make a living in the early twentieth century in Utah but often had to leave the state. Mahroni Young, a grandson of Brigham Young, first studied under one of these missionaries, James T. Harwood, who set up a studio in Utah. Young later studied in New York City and Paris and lived most of his life in New York. Young painted working men and southwestern Native Americans. The *Seagull Monument* on Temple Square, the *This is the Place Monument*, and his statue of his grandfather in the nation's Capitol Building all demonstrate his continued interest in and appreciation for Utah and its history.[28]

Other artists came to the state because of the beauty. California-based Maynard Dixon (1875–1946) escaped his San Francisco studio for the quiet desert and did many of his paintings in southwestern Utah. His stylized paintings of the mesas show the sharp angles that are famous in the area.[29]

Later in the twentieth century, Utah's universities provided a place for other well-known artists to teach and paint. LeConte Stewart, for example, grew up in Sevier County at the turn of the twentieth century. He taught school to earn enough money to attend art school in New York City in 1913. When he returned, he taught in Kaysville and developed an art program in the Davis County School District. He headed the Ogden High Art Department from 1923 to 1938. He then became the chair of the art department at the University of Utah, where he worked until he retired. Stewart is best known for his Utah desert and rural landscapes. Trevor Southey grew up in Rhodesia and then attended art school in England. He came to Utah because of the Mormon

Mahroni Young was commissioned to carve a statue of Brigham Young for the United States capitol building. Young, a grandson of Brigham, was asked by the family to show a loving father figure and by the state to show a strong statesman. Young did both. On the profile, Brigham Young looks relaxed on one side and strict on the other. In this photograph, note the position of the hands, legs, and feet.

Church and studied and then taught at Brigham Young University. He left the university to paint full time and settled in Alpine, Utah. Although he later broke with the LDS Church, he continued to paint religious themes.[30]

Sports have also always been an important part of the Utah experience. During the first part of the twentieth century, the focus was on participation. After the advent of radio and television, though, the focus shifted to spectator sports, including baseball and boxing and, later, hockey and basketball. Most of Utah's professional teams have been regional and minor-league affiliates. But the Utah Stars in the American Basketball Association and then the Utah Jazz in the National Basketball Association have provided a national basis for sports and generated interest across the country. For a short time, Utah had a team in the Women's National Basketball League.[31] Colleges and universities have also sponsored teams that excelled in basketball, football, volleyball, track and field, baseball, gymnastics, and softball, among others.[32]

Summary

Is Utah really "life elevated?" Time will tell if the new slogan lasts longer than previous ones such as "The Greatest Snow on Earth" and "A Pretty, Great State," but there can be little doubt that the state's image continues to change. Land that was once seen primarily as a resource to exploit is now increasingly regarded as a precious, but fragile, lifeline for humankind. A population that in the nineteenth century changed from primarily Native American to overwhelmingly Mormon diversified over the course of the twentieth century, although a smaller Mormon majority remained and stereotypes persisted. Cultural activities were local at first, and these continue to be important, but Utah's cultural expressions and contributions have increasingly paralleled those of the rest of the nation and world and are no longer, if ever, limited by the state's artificial political boundary. Over the century, Utah was lampooned by some as a cultural backwater, but artists, authors, musicians, and athletes who have lived in and drawn inspiration from the state have made undeniably important contributions. The essays in this section illustrate the complexity of Utah as it was perceived and experienced, derided and promoted during the twentieth century.

NOTES

1. http://w.w.w. travel.utah.gov/logoguidelines/index.htm
2. Winona Holmes, *Newe: A Western Shoshone History* (Reno: Intertribal Council of Nevada, 1976).
3. Richard H. Jackson, "The Mormon Experience: The Plains as Sinai, the Great Salt Lake as the Dead Sea, and the Great Basin as a Desert-cum-Promised Land," *Journal of Historical Geography* 18 (January 1992):41–58.
4. Thomas G. Alexander, "Integration into the National Economy, 1896–1920," in *Utah's History*, ed. Richard D. Poll, Thomas G. Alexander, Eugene E. Campbell, and David E. Miller (Logan: Utah State University Press, 1989), 431.
5. Charles S. Peterson, "Natural Resource Utilization," in Poll et al., *Utah's History*, 660, 664–65; Thomas G. Alexander, "Red Rock and Gray Stone: Senator Reed Smoot, the Establishment of Zion and Bryce Canyon National Parks, and the Rebuilding of Downtown Washington, D.C.," *Pacific Historical Review* 72 (February 2003): 1–38.
6. Peterson, "Natural Resource Utilization," 665; http://www.utah.com/stateparks/
7. Jared Farmer, *Glen Canyon Dammed: Inventing Lake Powell and the Canyon Country* (Tucson: University of Arizona Press, 1999), 162, 187.
8. Thomas G. Alexander, *Utah, the Right Place: The Official Centennial History*, rev. ed. (Salt Lake City: Gibbs Smith, 2003), 424; Jeffrey O. Durrant, *Struggle over Utah's San Rafael Swell: Wilderness, National Conservation Areas, and National Monuments* (Tucson: University of Arizona Press, 2007).
9. Demographic and Economic Analysis Section, *Utah Ski Database: December 2006* (Salt Lake City: Governor's Office of Planning and Budget, 2006), 4.
10. For information on the uses of the Bonneville Salt Flats, see Jessie Embry and Ron Shook, "'Those Bloomin' Salt Beds:' Racing on the Bonneville Salt Flats," *Utah Historical Quarterly* 65 (Fall 1997): 355–71.
11. William Mulder and A. Russell Mortensen, eds., *Among the Mormons: Historic Accounts by Contemporary Observers* (Lincoln: University of Nebraska Press, 1973), 467.
12. *Deseret News*, February 6, 1995; Larry R. Gerlach, "Church and Games: The Mormon

Church and the Salt Lake Olympic Winter Games," *Olympica: The Sixth International Symposium for Olympic Research* 11 (2002): 14.

13. U.S. Bureau of the Census, *Fifteenth Census of the United States Taken in the Year 1930,* vol. 3, *Population,* pt. 2, "Reports by State Montana-Wyoming" (Washington, D.C.: GPO, 1932), 1104, 1094; U.S. Bureau of the Census, *Thirteenth Census of the United States Taken in the Year 1910,* vol. 3, *Population,* pt. 3, "Reports by State, Nebraska-Wyoming" (Washington, D.C: GPO, 1913), 877.

14. Leslie G. Kelen and Eileen Hallet Stone, *Missing Stories: An Oral History of Ethnic and Minority Groups in Utah* (Logan: Utah State University Press, 2000), 99, 168, 440.

15. Yoshiko Uchida, *Desert Exile* (Seattle: University of Washington Press, 1982), 121.

16. Sandra C. Taylor, "Japanese Americans and Keetley Farms: Utah's Relocation Colony," *Utah Historical Quarterly* 54 (1986): 344.

17. *Deseret News,* July 5, 2000; Institute of Public and International Affairs, *Mexico and Utah: A Complex Relationship* (Salt Lake City: University of Utah Institute of Public and International Affairs, 2006), 1.

18. *Deseret News,* November 13, 1997; September 25, 1999; July 23, 2000.

19. *Salt Lake Tribune,* July 21, 2005; September 1, 2005.

20. Gerlach, "Church and Games," 14.

21. Brian Q. Cannon and Jacob W. Olmstead, "'Scandalous Film': The Campaign to Suppress Anti-Mormon Motion Pictures, 1911–1912," *Journal of Mormon History* 29 (Fall 2003): 63; Isaac K. Russell to National Board of Censorship, January 24[?], 1912, box 4, folder 16, Scott G. Kenney Collection, L. Tom Perry Special Collections, Harold B. Lee Library, Brigham Young University, Provo, Utah.

22. Alexander, *Utah, the Right Place,* 265, 274.

23. For information on the Mormon Tabernacle Choir, see Heidi S. Swinton, *America's Choir: A Commemorative Portrait of the Mormon Tabernacle Choir* (Salt Lake City: Shadow Mountain and Mormon Tabernacle Choir, 2004).

24. Alexander, *Utah, the Right Place,* 393; http://www.utahvalleysymphony.org/history.php

25. Alexander, *Utah, the Right Place,* 393, 454; http://www.odysseydance.com/flashindex.html

26. http://www.ufoc.org/; http://www.infowest.com/personal/b/bakerhouse/shakespeare.html

27. Alexander, *Utah, the Right Place,* 454.

28. Alexander, *Utah the Right Place,* 273.

29. *Maynard Dixon: Art and Spirit,* documentary, available at http://www.maynarddixon-doc.com/about.html.

30. Rovert O. Davis, "Desert Bush and Oil: A Portrait of LeConte Stewart," *Ensign* (February 1985): 38–42; Trevor Southey, *Southey* (Salt Lake City: Utah Museum of Fine Arts, nd), back cover.

31. Alexander, *Utah, the Right Place,* 438–42. See also Jessie L. Embry and Adam Seth Darowski, "Coming Home: Community Baseball in Cache Valley, Utah," *Utah Historical Quarterly* 70 (Spring 2002):108–22; and Jessie L. Embry, "'The Biggest Advertisement for a Town:' Provo Baseball and Provo Timps, 1913–1958," *Utah Historical Quarterly* 71 (Summer 2003): 196–214.

32. http://www.utahutes.cstv.com/sports/; http://www.byu.edu/sports

1

The Disappearance of Everett Ruess and the Discovery of Utah's Red Rock Country

Stephen C. Sturgeon

When many Americans think of Utah, their frame of reference is Salt Lake City and the Church of Jesus Christ of Latter-day Saints (although they only know the church by its familiar name, the Mormons). When these people hear of the red rock country of southern Utah, they often picture the Grand Canyon and Arizona. In his essay, Stephen C. Sturgeon explains why that frequently happens. Southern Utah with its natural beauty and wilderness does not match the typical image of the state—Mormon cities and villages. Those who recreate in the national parks and monuments are often more liberal than many people in Utah and more likely to support the Sierra Club than the Eagle Forum. Sturgeon uses literature, personal essays, newspapers, and scholarly reports to explain that southern Utah is a great place to visit, to disappear into, and even to die in as baby boomers retire to the area. Sturgeon chooses the story of Everett Ruess, the first "ecotourist," as a framework to illustrate the struggle between environmentalists and land users in the area.

On November 11, 1934, a young man wandered into the wild country near Escalante, Utah, and promptly vanished—presumably meeting his death, either by accident or foul play. Such events, while perhaps less common in the 1930s, are not that unusual. A 2005 *New York Times* article, using a phrase from park workers, described what they called "the disappearance season," when young men (and it is almost always young men) venture out into wilderness areas on their own, without leaving any itinerary, and disappear. Sometimes their bodies are later found by search and rescue teams dispatched by concerned friends or relatives; often they simply vanish without a trace. Jon Krakauer's best selling book, *Into the Wild,* recounts the final trek of one such

24

young man, Christopher McCandless, who ended up starving to death in the wilderness of Alaska.[1]

What made the 1934 disappearance different was that the young man, Everett Ruess, left behind a substantial body of artwork and writings (mainly in the form of correspondence and journal entries) describing his quixotic treks through southern Utah and northern Arizona. His writings capture the almost rhapsodic reaction he had to the landscape. In a letter from Navajo Mountain dated June 29, 1934, five months before his disappearance, Ruess wrote, "The perfection of this place is one reason why I distrust ever returning to the cities. Here I wander in beauty and perfection. There one walks in the midst of ugliness and mistakes. All is made for man, but where can one find surroundings to match one's ideals and imaginings? It is possible to live and dream in ugly, ill-fitting places, but how much better to be where all is beautiful and unscarred." In his last-known letter, dated November 11, 1934, Ruess remarked, "A few days ago I rode into the red rocks and sandy desert again, and it was like coming home again." As a result of his artwork and writings, Ruess has been described as the "artist in residence" of southern Utah and the Kerouac of the canyonlands.[2]

Over time Ruess has somehow evolved into a somewhat mythical figure, a symbolic embodiment of wanderlust. Like James Dean or Buddy Holly, Ruess's untimely death means that he will be forever young, but unlike those two mainstream heroes, Ruess has become a larger-than-life antiestablishment figure—an icon in absentia. (N. Scott Momaday even goes so far as to draw parallels between Ruess and Billy the Kid as symbols.) A combination of factors has probably contributed to this elevated status: Ruess came from an educated and financially secure family in Southern California, yet rejected this life to head out into nature; he was apparently quite friendly and well liked by all who met him; and he was only eighteen years old when he set out on his journeys, despite not having any previous outdoor experience. By all accounts, he seems to have lived a carefree life—right up to his presumed death. His writings evoke the same spirit as those by Henry David Thoreau, John Muir, and the English romantics. His life story stands as a fulfilled fantasy for anyone who has dreamed of leaving it all behind and just heading out into nature.[3]

However, there is another continuing dimension to Ruess's legacy: his descriptions of and reactions to the landscape of southern Utah. As publisher Gibbs Smith puts it, "The enduring significance of Everett . . . is that in his writings is the first expression of what I see as a modern point of view regarding the red rock canyon desert." Ruess, in some ways, was the first ecotourist. His reactions to the landscape of Utah's red rock country have been echoed and amplified by the steady flow of explorers, writers, hikers, rafters, and tourists that have (literally) followed his trail. In the past seventy years, this region of Utah has gone from being a blank spot on the map to a major travel destination. Yet the tourism industry that has developed in this swath of land, stretching in a crescent from Moab (the unofficial capital of Utah's red rock country) to Zion National Park, seems to target a very un-Utah-like audience: largely well-to-do, out of state, and non-Mormon. The red rock country is a landscape that is *in* Utah, but not *of* Utah. This disconnect is underscored by a recent survey, which showed that when people living outside Utah were asked to identify the location of such red rock landmarks as Delicate Arch, most of them chose Arizona.[4]

Other better-known states seem to lack this disconnect. It is doubtful that most Americans would have trouble identifying the major landmarks of, say, California. While it is true that some states, such as North Dakota or West Virginia, may not register much in the public consciousness, that is not the case with Utah. Most people seem to have a well-defined image of the state in their minds, but frequently this image is a negative one. To many nonresidents, Utah conjures up diverse, and often misleading, impressions: everyone is Mormon, you can't get a drink there, it's the most conservative state in the country, and, of course, Mormons practice polygamy. These stereotypes are sufficiently embedded in the public's consciousness that Utah can be used as a shorthand punch line in programs such as *The Simpsons*. These types of (mis)perceptions have created a strange dichotomy, where a significant portion of Utah's territory has been embraced by nonresidents with an almost religious fervor, while these same people emphatically reject the state as a whole. A further twist is the fact that it has often been local and state tourism promoters who have marketed red rock country in a manner that helps create this dichotomy.

Everett Ruess, of course, was not the first person to notice the beauty of the southern Utah landscape. Early federal explorers and Mormon settlers in the late-nineteenth century frequently commented on the stark beauty of the region, placing the emphasis typically on "stark." One of the first places to garner sustained positive attention was the area that eventually became Zion National Park. In 1862 Joseph Black, a Mormon settler, settled in the lower part of Zion Canyon after first exploring its upper reaches. His descriptions of the beauty of the canyon were so glowing that cynics referred to the place as "Joseph's glory." It was two more decades, however, before the beauty of Zion came to the attention of the outside world. In an 1882 U.S. Geological Survey report, Clarence Dutton wrote, "Nothing can exceed the beauty of Little Zion Valley . . . . In its proportions it is about equal to Yosemite, but in the nobility and beauty of the sculptures there is no comparison."[5]

However, nearly thirty years passed before any formal steps were taken to help set aside and preserve the region. In 1909 President Taft signed a proclamation designating the area as a national monument (it was subsequently "upgraded" to a national park in 1919). Taft's action does not seem to have triggered the sort of negative backlash that subsequent similar presidential proclamations have engendered. The establishment of the national monument, according to historians Douglas Alder and Karl Brooks, changed southern Utah forever: "Gradually outside influences began to interrupt the peaceful isolation, the monolithic culture, the agrarian austerity that pervaded [Utah's] Dixie. . . . it was the beginning of a process that would eventually give Dixie its international reputation for scenic beauty and its largest industry—tourism."[6]

This process was extremely slow at first, given the relative isolation of Zion from the outside world. However, as the numbers of tourists began to increase, the National Park Service faced the dilemma of how best to provide services for the visitors. In response the Utah Parks Company, a subsidiary of the Union Pacific Railroad, approached the National Park Service about becoming an official park concessionaire to provide accommodations. This was a logical venture for the Union Pacific Railroad to undertake since it was in the railroad's own best interests to encourage tourism. More tourists, the thinking went, would translate into more rail passengers.[7]

The Union Pacific Railroad launched an aggressive advertising campaign in magazines on behalf of Zion National Park. One such ad in *Sunset* magazine read, "The World's Most Startling Loveliness Awaits You in Zion." The railroad also distributed booklets extolling Zion and the surrounding area. In one the desert was described as having "glorious, unbelievable color," while Zion was "decorated with an endless array of fantastic sculpturing." A later booklet described the scenery in the area as ranging from "friendly intimacy" to "awesome grandeur" and offering a "matchless geology of natural wonders."[8]

Lest potential tourists be suspicious of all the purple prose, the Union Pacific Railroad published a booklet entitled *They Say* in 1926, which featured comments from travelers to Zion and the surrounding area. One quote, describing Zion Canyon, used practically every color of the spectrum: "There were soft apricot and salmon tints, vague pinks and creams; lemon blending into deepest orange, with all gradations in between, and with here and there a haunting suggestion of pale mauve. Brilliant red spires stood beside domes of ivory white." Another visitor focused on the mystical: "Guide books describe in detail the coloring and the thousand weird features of the formation far better than it is possible here to do, but the lasting impression left upon my mind by Zion National Park is one of humble reverence, and I sincerely trust that the atmosphere of divine mystery which now ennobles the Park may always be preserved." These quotes show that the traditional nineteenth-century attitude of viewing the desert as a barren wasteland was giving way to a new (perhaps New Age) vision of the landscape as having therapeutic value.[9]

For the local population near Zion, and the other emerging tourist destinations in the red rock country, the most important color was green, and the chief value was financial. The rise of the tourist economy brought steadily growing amounts of outside money into what had been previously a limited local economy. "After years of exporting a modest volume of agricultural goods and struggling with a life of scarcity, [Utah's] Dixie residents had a new product: beauty." "Here was something that did not need to be shipped away; the consumers

Tourists view Zion Canyon in a sightseeing wagon, n.d. The rise of tourism reshaped the economy of southern Utah.

came to the source and, when they left, the beauty remained." Although there is a great deal of debate among scholars over the pros and cons of a tourist economy, Alder and Brooks see it as a definite plus. The Union Pacific Railroad, the State of Utah, and the National Park Service contributed "the outside capital that had long eluded county developers."[10]

The role of regional tourism promoter was not restricted only to the Union Pacific Railroad but included other entities as well, some of them located elsewhere, such as Salt Lake City. Even though some of these promoters were geographically at a distance, they nonetheless believed that they stood to benefit financially from tourism in the southern part of the state. In the 1920s, the Salt Lake City Commercial Club began distributing a brochure entitled *Salt Lake City—The Center of Scenic America,* which, among other things, made the not-so-practical suggestion that visitors to the "scenic wonderland" of southern Utah should make Salt Lake City their "headquarters" for their excursion.[11]

In addition to commercial groups, another source of promotion was newspapers. In 1923 the Salt Lake–based *Deseret News* hired Frank Gay to head the Deseret News Tourfinding Department with an assignment to travel by automobile around the region and report on the scenic wonders he saw. The articles, which were published in the automotive section of the paper, were intended to provide readers with detailed road descriptions while also promoting the notion of traveling by car. The newspaper editor who created this position, Elias S. Woodruff, a key state promoter who had a strong affinity for the red rock region, explained, "Utah had more south than north."[12]

Gay also shared his boss's passion for southern Utah. In an August 25, 1923, article, he rhapsodized about the "sacred precincts" of the region, describing them as places "where time must have retired from the rest of the world and gone into seclusion, there to work out an empire unlike any other region of the earth. Weirdly fantastic, wildly colored, grotesquely beautiful. This seemed to have been his [time's] secret workshop, his private laboratory from whence came the pigments to paint the heavens and gild the sunsets." The *Deseret News* did not limit itself simply to promoting the region through its articles; it also began publishing tour guides and even erected two billboards (one near Zion and the other near Moab), featuring maps with directions for motorists to find nearby natural wonders. Gay also was dispatched to places like Los Angeles to help promote tourism in Utah, often accompanied by Clarence Neslen, the mayor of Salt Lake City. This aggressive promotion of the wonders of Utah led Gay and Woodruff to join an effort with various civic leaders to found the Scenic Highway Association in 1923, which worked to improve road conditions and tourist amenities in southern Utah. As a result, the state road commission permitted the Auto Club of Southern California to erect road signs for highways in southern Utah. The *Deseret News's* rival, the *Salt Lake Tribune,* also engaged in its share of regional boosterism and promotion. The *Tribune* dispatched a reporter in 1935 to go in search of Everett Ruess while also providing readers with vivid descriptions of the area's landscape. William Rishel wrote extensively about the region for the *Tribune* and also was the author of a series of nationally known regional tour guides.[13]

These examples of outside promotion are not meant to suggest that the local folks in southern Utah were not actively boosting their own cause—far from it. While local promotional efforts, such as occurred with Zion National Park, date back to the early part of the twentieth century, large-scale efforts did not get under way until after World War II, when improved road conditions and increased automobile ownership led to a sharp rise in vacation travel by car. Groups such as the Zion Natural History Association and the Bryce Canyon Natural History Association, despite their scientific-sounding names, actively promoted the tourist industry in their areas through various publications, such as a 1962 glossy booklet entitled *Southern Utah's Land of Color!,* which extolled the scenic beauty of the region. The content of this booklet, which contained explanations of such Mormon practices as tithing and a strong denunciation of polygamy, clearly indicates that the anticipated audience for the publication was out-of-state, non-Mormon tourists. In a bit of unusual marketing, the publication actually encouraged people to bypass the better-known landmarks in search of undiscovered treasures. "There is a tendency today to look only for the obvious, the spectacular, and the already famous. Those who are content with this deprive themselves of much that is deeply satisfying."[14]

During the 1930s road conditions were often primitive in Utah's red rock country, as this Utah Writers' Project photo of an auto trip near Moab suggests.

While it might be easy to dismiss the purple prose of earlier promotional literature as simply the overwrought style of those times, more-recent examples show that this genre is alive and well. During the 1990s, an organization called the Utah Travel Corp., based in Draper, Utah, published a quarterly magazine entitled *Utah Highways*. Reflecting its title (a clear homage to the long-running tourist publication *Arizona Highways),* the publication chiefly consisted of glossy photo spreads of various outdoor tourist destinations with red rock country as a frequent subject of its articles. The 1996 issue, in particular, provided an in-depth focus on the region and featured an article on "The Towns of Color Country" along with a photo essay of the region. The publication, put together with extensive help from local travel organizations, strikes a tone not dissimilar from earlier tourist/booster efforts with its emphasis on the spectacular. The photo caption for a stunning sandstone formation in the Wave-Paria Canyon-Vermillion Cliffs wilderness area hearkens back to Everett Ruess: "If you are ever fortunate enough to find out how to get there and actually do find it, you will never be the same again."[15]

One major, and seemingly unique, challenge that tourism promoters in Utah had to contend with was balancing the secular and the sacred. Utah's Mormon past was well known if not well understood by most Americans, and, in fact, "Mormon tourism" to Utah (mainly consisting of members of the Church of Jesus Christ of Latter-day Saints) provided a major source of revenue for the state. The challenge became how to entice non-Mormons to visit Utah as well.

During the 1940s, state officials began developing an active marketing campaign to promote tourism in Utah. In seeking to create a unique brand image for the state, they made a conscious decision to downplay the Mormon aspect of Utah's past, which had featured prominently in previous promotional efforts such as the WPA travel guides. This choice was based on the fact that, while Mormon-related tourism was the dominant type in Utah, the state wanted also to lure more secular kinds of tourists, especially recreational ones, to increase and diversify Utah's tourism base.[16]

After initially using the slogan, "Utah, the Friendly State," state officials in 1948 selected "Utah: Land of Color" to emphasize the state's red rock region as well as its national parks. As the press release announced,

COLOR IS LIFE! UTAH IS THE LAND OF COLOR!
Every known color, tint and shade is seen in rich abundance within this area. When the traveler crosses the state's border, he enters a new world of vivid and startling color . . .
THIS IS UTAH, LAND OF COLOR!

In keeping with this theme, the state created promotional movies, which were loaned around the country for public viewing at schools and libraries and by media outlets. The films had titles such as *Crimson Cliffs* and *Adventure in Color*. The state also created a booklet featuring scenic photographs from around Utah. State tourism officials also attended travel expos, such as the California Sportsmen's and Vacation Show, to promote Utah. These efforts, however, were hampered by the small amount of money that Utah's government budgeted to attract tourists.[17]

In addition to promoting the state, Utah tourism officials also served as an information clearinghouse for potential travelers planning their trips. Here the aggressive promotion of red rock country ran into the reality that the area's infrastructure had not yet been developed extensively. One potential tourist in 1951, who expressed an interest in visiting Arches, Bryce, Zion, and Monument Valley, was warned, "Since the roads are unimproved you will not be able to travel fast. Take plenty of water and food and it is advisable to take a shovel . . . in case you should run into very bad roads as a result of a recent storm. If a flash flood occurs, seek high ground." Sometimes it seemed as if the travel conditions of the nineteenth century were not so far in the past.[18]

By the mid-1950s, the state had switched to a new, more ambiguous, and flexible slogan: "Utah, the Unique." This was followed in the early 1960s with "The Different World of Utah." While the slogans changed, the accompanying promotional material continued to give a prominent place to the red rock region. By the mid-1960s, however, state tourism officials began to focus actively on promoting winter tourism and the ski industry. "Ski Utah" and "The Greatest Snow on Earth" became the new slogans and quickly received broad national recognition. The chief incentive for the change in emphasis was

A tourist pauses at a Welcome to Utah sign in Washington County in April 1948. State tourism officials worked to achieve the right balance between sacred and secular symbols and slogans in their promotion of the state.

financial. Studies in the late 1960s determined that, while ski tourists might be smaller in number than summer ones, they stayed longer (an average 5.4 days) and spent eight times as much. Snow had become a cash crop.[19]

Utah's ski-centric tourism promotion continued for the next thirty years and scored its biggest public-relations coup when Salt Lake City hosted the 2002 Winter Olympics. By then, however, the state had shifted gears again. Techno-Governor Mike Leavitt launched the slogan "Utah! Where Ideas Connect" in 2001 to little acclaim, and it quickly sank without a trace. In March 2006 Governor Jon Huntsman unveiled a new slogan "Utah: Life Elevated," which seems to suggest a return to a more outdoor-oriented promotional effort. Huntsman described the slogan as "a simple phrase with deep meaning." While the first part of his statement is self-evident, the second part has yet to be determined. In general the slogan seems more evocative of the vague phrases used during the 1950s rather than the concrete "Ski Utah" slogan of the 1960s.[20]

While the state of Utah shifted away from a red rock oriented tourism effort in the 1950s, interest in the region continued to grow—often promoted by unofficial sources. Starting in the late 1930s and early 1940s, a new industry began to develop in southeastern Utah: river rafting. There had, of course, been previous boating trips on the Colorado River and its various branches (the most famous being John Wesley Powell's scientific expeditions in the late-nineteenth century), but river rafting was different because the people who signed up for these trips did so for recreation. The allure of the trip was to experience the wild white-water rapids and see the stunning scenery of the region. The emergence of this new industry helped to expand the public's awareness of the red rock country that existed beyond the southwestern corner of Utah (Zion and Bryce) and would over time lead this area to become a major tourist destination in its own right.

The unofficial founder of commercial river rafting was Norman Nevills, who guided his first trip down the San Juan River in 1936. Although that trip was less than a complete success (plagued by bad weather and insufficient food supplies), Nevills followed it up with more successful and well-publicized trips down the Green and Colorado Rivers in 1938 and 1940. After that, Nevills, who was a ruthless self-promoter, began offering multiple trips on various regional rivers each year. By 1949, when Nevills died in a plane crash, his company had grown rapidly, and this success had attracted a number of other competitors into the river-rafting business. (Many of these rival river rats had actually gotten their start working for Nevills, but for some reason, his personality had transformed them from friends into enemies.)[21]

One such protégé was Harry Aleson, whose own start in the business also faced some challenges. One two-week trip ended on the first day when Aleson got into a verbal fight with one of the passengers over the unsanitary conditions in the campsite. The unsavory reputation that Aleson and other river runners initially had was sufficiently negative that one periodical, *Desert* magazine, declined to accept advertising from Aleson, lest it sully the reputation of the publication. By the late 1940s, however, the river-rafting industry had found its sea legs and overcome any lingering "customer-satisfaction" issues.[22]

So what was it that drew an increasing number of people to rough it on the rivers of southeastern Utah? Nevills made the case in a letter to a potential tour customer: "It's the thrill of going where few have ever gone, or will, it's the thrill of seeing cliff walls too sheer and stupendous to describe—in myriads of colors—to be around a campfire at night and talk over the day's adventures—and those of past voyagers—Rainbow Bridge, Outlaw Cave, Mystery Canyon. And the [San Juan] River is absolutely unique. The boating itself is fascinating." In this description, the thrill of river rafting takes a backseat to the beauty of the surrounding lands and the ambience of the travel experience.[23]

While it might be possible to dismiss these comments as little more than advertising propaganda, the people taking these tours seemed to share Nevills's reaction. Echoing Everett Ruess's language, one passenger after her trip wrote, "I longed to be back on the rivers again—for the huge boulders, the sand waves, the sand bars and even the rapids. Most of all I longed for those long calm stretches through Glen Canyon where we floated down the river without a thought or care, feasting our eyes on the beauty all around us...." For travelers such as these, the trip clearly was more than a simple vacation.[24]

The river-guiding community during this period was a fairly small, eclectic group full of eccentrics and misfits. (Harry Aleson, for instance, was described as being to the political right of his friend Barry Goldwater and refused to ever file an income-tax return.) Yet by the mid-1950s, this group became unified and galvanized in its opposition to the proposed Glen Canyon Dam. Some of this opposition was clearly a response to the damaging commercial effect the dam would have on river rafting in the area, but it also seemed to be motivated by a deep love for the region and the loss it would suffer.[25]

The Glen Canyon Dam was part of the larger Colorado River Storage Project, which encompassed a half-dozen reclamation projects for the Colorado River watershed. Congress debated the project for several years until its passage in 1956. During these debates, most of the opposition focused on the proposed Echo Park Dam located inside Dinosaur National Monument. (See Adam Eastman's chapter, "From Cadillac to Chevy," for more details on this.) In exchange for dropping the Echo Park Dam, the Bureau of Reclamation lobbied instead for the inclusion of two new dams, one at Flaming Gorge (on the Utah-Wyoming border) and the other at Glen Canyon on the Colorado River in southern Utah. Environmentalists, fearing they would overreach the limits of their political influence, agreed not to oppose these two projects.[26]

In the aftermath of the approval of the Colorado River Storage Project, however, environmentalists began to have regrets as they learned more about Glen Canyon. (Ironically, the construction of the dam was a good thing in the short run for the river-rafting industry since more and more people began signing up for tours to see this place that was about to be lost.) David Brower, who famously and erroneously proclaimed in subsequent decades that he was responsible for the loss of Glen Canyon, once again led the vanguard in opposition to the dam in the hopes of getting Congress or the U.S. Department of the Interior to delay or abandon the project.[27]

One of the major "campaign tools" used by Brower was a glossy coffee-table book called *The Place No One Knew.* Published by the Sierra Club, the nearly two-hundred-page book contained large color photographs of Glen Canyon taken by Eliot Porter and accompanied by quotes from various authors describing the region. The book in many ways was an extended elegy since, by the time it was published in 1963, the fate of Glen Canyon had already been largely sealed.[28]

In his introduction, Porter uses almost-mystical language to describe the experience of visiting Glen Canyon:

> It is an intimate canyon. The feeling of intimacy comes partly from your being able to travel through it by boat. . . . The intimacy also comes from the calmness and congeniality of the river and the closeness of the walls. Life along the banks and bars is unhurried. Every bend offers a good campsite. At evening, in the glow of burnished cliffs, a quiet peace settles on the boatmen gathered close to their campfire, their subdued voices accentuating the faint gurgling of the big river slipping past its banks. With night spreading fast and stars appearing in the diminished sky, the canyon's dimly silhouetted walls give comfort and security.

Later, he discusses exploring the side canyons running away from the river: "Of all the phenomena of the side canyons, it is the light, even in the farthest depths of the narrowest canyon, that evokes the ultimate in awe. In somber, rocky caverns of purple and ocher stone into which the sun rarely strikes, shallow pools glitter brassily from sunlit cliffs high overhead. Wherever there is a damp cleft, maidenhair fern and scarlet lobelia and white columbine grow. Their drooping leaves turn a dusky cyan–green in the blue shadows, creating a subdued, almost funereal atmosphere."[29]

At the close of his essay, Porter paints a picture of Glen Canyon as the gateway to Nirvana:

> In the canyon itself the days flow through your consciousness as the river flows along its course, without a break and with hardly a ripple to disturb their smoothness. Problems fade from the forefront of your mind. The river supplies and in a sense supplants the need for a measure of time. The current becomes the time on which you move. Things happen and days pass. They exist simply in a heap of impressions and memories, all different and yet all of one kind. There is no more liberating or healing experience. It penetrates to the very core of being, scattering anxieties, untangling knots, re-creating the spirit.

While Porter does not use overtly religious language, his words and pictures clearly imply that the destruction of Glen Canyon is a modern equivalent of the expulsion from the Garden of Eden. Outside this enchanted realm, life is hard, and people suffer.[30]

It is this haunting sense of loss that keeps Glen Canyon alive as a symbol for the environmental movement. Decades after the completion of the dam, Brower and other environmentalists continued to call for its destruction and the resurrection of Glen Canyon. At times it is hard to decide whether this crusade is a noble quest for the Holy Grail or merely a pale imitation of Don Quixote tilting at windmills. But as Jared Farmer points out in his book, *Glen Canyon Dammed,* the destruction of the dam would not eliminate the sense of loss but rather, simply shift the burden onto others. For literally millions of people, Lake Powell, formed by Glen Canyon Dam, has become a sanctuary. What some see as plunder, others see as bounty. To drain the lake would please a few but upset many—not to mention economically devastate the region.[31]

This tension between the quest for economic security and the protection of the environmentally sublime has played out in other parts of Utah's red rock country as well. In the mid-1970s, a group of California and Arizona electrical utilities proposed building a 3,000-megawatt, coal-powered electrical plant on the remote Kaiparowits Plateau in southern Utah, a location that was within a hundred miles of Bryce Canyon, Zion, and Capitol Reef National Parks. The plant would have been the largest in the United States, would have employed between eight and ten thousand people (the majority of whom would work at the adjacent coal mine to power the plant), and would have necessitated building a new town to house twenty-five thousand people.[32]

Opposition to the project came from the usual suspects (the Sierra Club, Friends of the Earth, etc.) but also featured a new player as well—actor Robert Redford. The star of *Butch Cassidy and the Sundance Kid* had first purchased a place for himself in the mountains near Provo, Utah, in the 1960s. Slowly he acquired more land and steadily developed it into what eventually became the Sundance Resort. Redford's development of his own property notwithstanding, what had led him to purchase the place was its very lack of development: "I felt in love with this canyon the first time I saw it. To me it was special to the point of having mystical properties. There was no development to speak of. And I thought, 'This will be the last outpost. I'll be safe here for a long time.'"[33]

Redford spoke out publicly and visibly in opposition to the proposed coal-powered plant at Kaiparowits. In March 1976, this opposition was the subject of a story on the TV-news program *60 Minutes,* where Redford was interviewed by Dan Rather. Asked to explain his opposition to the project, Redford remarked, "when I think of it—the land we're talking about—of all the places to be putting a plant—that is so beautiful. If we remove the air quality surrounding the scenic parks, if we degrade the land with roads and transmission lines, then obviously, that space that has scenic value is gone, and we've just removed yet another spot for man to go and feel nature and feel space and feel in touch with himself." Whether or not Redford's contribution helped turn the tide, the plant project was cancelled shortly after the news segment aired. This action inspired its own counterprotest when the residents of Kanab, Utah (which had stood to benefit economically from the project), burned Redford in effigy. Some even lingered after the protest was over "to roast hotdogs over the glowing coals of the dummy." Redford was surprised by the personal venom expressed by the protestors and subsequently avoided being drawn into new environmental battles in Utah.[34]

Twenty years later it was time for a different telegenic Democrat to be attacked in Utah for his environmental actions. In September 1996, President Bill Clinton created the Grand Staircase–Escalante National Monument. The 1.8-million-acre (2,700-square-mile) federal reserve in south-central Utah included the location for the proposed Kaiparowits power plant. Although plans for that plant had been abandoned, a Dutch energy company continued to hold a lease for the massive coal deposits in the area. The establishment of the new national monument represented the culmination of a multiyear battle over the fate of public lands in southeastern Utah. During the previous year, the state's Republican members of Congress had tried to pass a bill that would have set aside as wilderness 1.8 million acres throughout the entire region. By comparison environmentalists had counterproposed setting aside 5.7 million acres. Public hearings and polling data in Utah suggested that residents of the state actually preferred the larger bill. Congressional Republicans, however, would not budge, and both bills eventually died.[35]

Much of the tension over the creation of the Grand Staircase–Escalante National Monument stems from the seeming incompatibility between the goals of economic development and environmental protection. Longtime local residents often view the surrounding landscape through commoditizing eyes. If you can't harvest it, log it, or dig it up, of what use is a bunch of "sagebrush on barren hills"? They often view not developing the land as a betrayal of their pioneer legacy. By contrast the call to preserve the land untouched often comes from outsiders, many of whom seem to ascribe an almost spiritual significance to this barren landscape. Nature writer Terry Tempest Williams (who occupies a unique niche as both a local and an outsider) expressed this attitude when she said, in response to the controversy, "If you knew wilderness in the way that you know love, you would be unwilling to let it go. We are talking about the body of the beloved, not real estate."[36]

Reacting to this latest environmental initiative, residents in southern Utah protested again. In Kanab citizens released black balloons and carried signs proclaiming, "Shame on You, Clinton." It was the turn of the folks in Escalante to break out the effigies and symbolically hang Clinton and Secretary of the Interior Bruce Babbitt. These protests, while economically motivated, were in many ways economically counterintuitive. By 1995 tourism was the largest industry in Utah, with the national parks in red rock country alone generating $200 million in outside spending and employing nearly five thousand people. This economic reality was not completely lost on the locals. Following the protest, one shopkeeper in Escalante told a reporter that she was planning on increasing her order for postcards, figuring that the new national monument would boost the number of tourists in her store. She even went so far as to comment, "Now we could use a couple of more bed and breakfasts, a few more guided tours."[37]

If there is one town in Utah's red rock country that best captures the extremes of a transition between an extractive and a recreational economy, it is Moab. The community experienced its first boom in 1952 when the discovery of rich uranium deposits nearby transformed the town of twelve hundred residents almost overnight. By 1957 Moab had grown fivefold. This boom continued for the next thirty years before collapsing in the early 1980s. Fortunately, during the boom years, local officials began to lay the groundwork for the eventual switch to a tourist-based economy. Some of these tourist features were the direct result of the uranium boom. Prospectors blazed trails in the surrounding countryside that tourists (hikers, bikers, and motorcyclers) later followed. The local infrastructure (hospitals, motels, better roads) built to support the mining economy became key elements in the tourist economy. Moab also benefited from outside actions. The decision by the Department of the Interior in the 1960s and early 1970s to create Canyonlands National Park and expand and upgrade Arches from a national monument to a national park brought increased national exposure to the nearby landscape.[38]

Perched on the edge of a cliff, a visitor to Dead Horse Point takes in a breathtaking view of the Colorado River near Moab.

Moab may have also profited from a trait peculiar to Utah. As a writer for *California Bicyclist* in 1988 put it, "Moab didn't feel like a classic Mormon Utah town where the locals give you the evil eye and little kids hurl invectives for coming out of the State Liquor Store with a package." His analysis, while stereotypical, is also accurate—Moab is not a "Mormon town." A *Salt Lake Tribune* article published in July 2005 analyzed demographic trends in Utah and estimated that the population that is LDS in Grand County, where Moab is located, is only about 32 percent. That makes Grand and adjacent San Juan County (where the LDS population is approximately 43 percent) the only two counties in the state where Mormons are in the minority—a land that is in Utah, but not of Utah.[39]

If Moab seems unique from other parts of Utah, over time it did not necessarily become different from other western tourist towns. The great variety and abundance of tourist-related events and options, coupled with the sheer number of tourists, appear to be taking their toll. Certainly the number of tourists visiting the area in the past half century has exploded. Annual visitation figures for nearby Arches National Park went from approximately fifteen thousand in 1950 to close to one million by the end of the 1990s. Even local boosters have begun to express their doubts. When a tourist asked about making the hike to Delicate Arch, one of the most famous sites in Arches National Park and a state icon, a worker at the Moab Visitors Center replied, "Delicate Arch is pretty. Delicate Arch is fantastic. But it's one of those things where there's always so many people there, and personally, when I go to a place like that, I want to be able to feel it. And with 100 or 200 people there, it's sometimes like, 'Alright, whatever.'"[40]

Author Page Stegner offered a harsher assessment, following a visit to the town in 1994: "I cross the bridge over the Colorado River into . . . Moab? I don't recognize it. Maybe I have never really noticed it before. The town seems to have multiplied. I don't remember all those T–shirt and gift shops, western-wear outlets, artisan co-ops, deli/bakeries, bookstores, ORV rentals, bike rentals, rafting companies, helicopter tours, realtors. I count seven realtors." The abundance of realtors reflects the rapidly growing real-estate costs in the area. The "Aspenization" of Moab means that it is increasingly harder for the working class, who staff the various tourist-related facilities and businesses, to actually afford to live there. As a result of the hike in housing prices, *Mountain Bike* magazine in 2001 explicitly excluded Moab (and Durango, Colorado) from its list of "The Ten Best U.S. Cities for Mountain Biking."[41]

This pattern of development (or overdevelopment in the eyes of some) is not limited to Moab but is also starting to appear elsewhere in the region. The small town of Torrey, located outside Capitol Reef National Park, is turning into an artist colony and is home to a southwestern nouvelle-cuisine restaurant that each year hosts a major fund-raiser for Utah Public Radio. A similar pattern is occurring in nearby Boulder, located on the edge of the Grand Staircase–Escalante National Monument. Even tiny Bluff, located in Utah's Four Corners, is shifting its chief economic focus from raising cattle to enticing tourists with events such as a hot-air balloon rally and a regional arts festival.

The biggest impact that development is having in red rock country, however, is in the area surrounding St. George in southwestern Utah. The type of transformation that St. George is experiencing, however, is distinctly different from what is occurring in the rest of the red rock region. Here the emphasis is less on recreation and more on retirement. Most of the new arrivals are looking for a place to live rather than just visit, and many are Mormons from Utah. As a result, the cultural dynamics in St. George are quite different from those in Moab. Utah's Dixie has become for Mormons what Florida is for Jews from

New York City or southern Texas for midwesterners: a place to retire in the sun while still surrounded by your own culture.

A strong irony emerges when issues such as the debate over development and commercialization intrude into the red rock country because the chief value that so many of the region's proponents tout is the ability the place gives a person to escape from worldly concerns. Numerous writers over the years have struggled to try and tangibly express this intangible quality. Amidst this flood of words, three authors in particular have stood out for their passionate descriptions of the region: Wallace Stegner, Terry Tempest Williams, and Edward Abbey. For Stegner the chief virtue the landscape possesses is its pristine emptiness: "It is lovely and terrible wilderness . . . harshly and beautifully colored, broken and worn until its bones are exposed, its great sky without a smudge or taint from Technocracy, and in hidden corners and pockets under its cliffs the sudden poetry of springs. Save a piece of country like that intact, and it does not matter in the slightest that only a few people every year will go into it. That is precisely its value." He continues that here a person "can look two hundred miles, clear into Colorado; and looking down over the cliffs and canyons of the San Rafael Swell and the Robbers' Roost they can also look as deeply into themselves as anywhere I know."[42]

Terry Tempest Williams's background is different from that of most other people who have written about the red rock country. Whereas many of the advocates for this region are non-Mormons from out of state, Williams is the descendant of a Mormon pioneer family and has lived all her life in Utah. She has written extensively about Utah's desert wilderness, and her book, *Red: Passion and Patience in the Desert,* is an extended meditation on this area. For Williams red rock country is endowed with a strong spirituality: "In the Colorado Plateau . . . I believe we are in the process of creating our own mythology, a mythology born out of this spare, raw, broken country, so frightfully true, complex and elegant in its searing simplicity of form. You cannot help but be undone by its sensibility and light, nothing extra. Before the stillness of sandstone cliffs, you stand still, equally bare." Not only does Williams ascribe a spiritual quality to this landscape, but she also seeks to uncover its erotic power as well: "I wanted to create a narrative that experimented with the question of what it might mean to make love to the land, not in an exploitative manner or a manner of self-indulgence but in a manner that honors our relationship to Earth, deep, primal, enduring."[43]

While Williams has gained a national reputation for her writings about this region, it is Edward Abbey who undoubtedly is the true poet laureate of red rock country. Abbey, too, had a passion for this area, starting with his work as a summer employee at what was then Arches National Monument in the 1950s. But Abbey's passion tended to express itself in a misanthropic vein. He extolled love of the land and expressed hatred for everyone who came to see it. Even in the 1950s, Abbey was already complaining about Arches being overrun with tourists, and he denounced the steps the federal government was taking to try and accommodate them.[44]

At one point, Abbey even celebrated the death of a tourist, a sixty-year-old who had wandered away from his car and ended up dying of thirst: "Looking out on this panorama of light, space, rock and silence I am inclined to congratulate the dead man on his choice of jumping-off place; he had good taste. He had good luck—I envy him the manner of his going: to die alone, on rock under sun at the brink of the unknown, like a wolf, like a great bird, seems to me a very good fortune indeed."As historian Patricia Nelson Limerick points out, however, Abbey did not display the same sort of joyful resignation when, several years later, he became trapped in a side canyon in Arizona. While "Abbey might admire the dead tourist's choice of death sites, he showed no particular enthusiasm for his own near luck in securing the beautiful Havasu Canyon."[45]

"A Great Place to Die" has yet to make it into the various promotional campaigns for red rock country, but, considering the steadily aging population of baby boomers, who seem to comprise the bulk of tourists to this area, perhaps the idea is not so far fetched. It would be simply yet another factor in the interwoven set of reasons why this area has gained popularity. Although a comprehensive list of these factors would be quite lengthy, there appear to be five elements that have had the greatest impact in the rise of tourism in the region: 1) improved transportation access, 2) diverse recreational opportunities, 3) growing environmental awareness, 4) regional literary advocates, and 5) promotional efforts that downplay the Mormon connection to the area. While the appearance of the railroads marked the first transportation breakthrough, it was the advent of paved highways throughout the area that really opened it up to tourists. The development of a diverse array of recreational options (hiking, biking, rafting, boating, climbing, and off-road riding, among others) gave people a reason to come. A growing sense of environmental responsibility, bolstered by the eloquent reflections of writers about the local landscape, led to a desire to preserve this region—an area that to a large extent has been consciously stripped of its Mormon identity. In light of Everett Ruess's desire to get away from it all, we have to wonder what he would think about this massive influx of visitors who seem to be consumers in the literal sense of the word.

Given Abbey's preoccupation with death and disappearing, it is perhaps not surprising that he wrote about the region's most famous missing person and the allure of the land:

> Even after years of intimate contact and search this quality of strangeness in the desert remains undiminished. Transparent and intangible as sunlight, yet always and everywhere present, it lures a man on and on, from the red-walled canyons to the smoke-blue ranges beyond, in a futile but fascinating quest for the great, unimaginable treasure which the desert seems to promise. One begins to understand why Everett Ruess kept going deeper and deeper into

the canyon country, until one day he lost the thread of the labyrinth. . . . And how could they hope to find this treasure which has no name and has never been seen? Hard to say—and yet, when they found it they could not fail to recognize it. Ask Everett Ruess.

It is this intangible quality of Utah's red rock country that fascinates so many people and continues to draw them to the area to visit, discover, or even disappear.[46]

NOTES

1.   *New York Times*, October 5, 2005; Jon Krakauer, *Into the Wild* (New York: Anchor Books, 1996).

2.   The most complete collections of Ruess's writings are contained in two books by W.L. Rusho: *Everett Ruess: A Vagabond for Beauty* (Salt Lake City: Gibbs Smith Publisher, 1983), and *Wilderness Journals of Everett Ruess* (Salt Lake City: Gibbs Smith Publisher, 1998). Rusho, *Vagabond for Beauty*, 160, 179; Wallace Stegner, *Mormon Country* (New York: Duell, Sloan & Pearce, 1942), 330; Leo W. Banks, "Wandering Soul," *Tucson Weekly* (May 8-May 14, 1997).

3.   N. Scott Momaday, "Everett Ruess," *American West* 24, no. 2 (April 1987): 69.

4.   Gibbs Smith, quoted in Rusho, *Wilderness Journals*, 8; Brock Vergakis, "Tourists Ignorant of Utah," *Deseret News*, April 27, 2006, A1.

5.   Angus M. Woodbury, *A History of Southern Utah and Its National Parks* (Salt Lake City: Utah State Historical Society, 1950), 155; Douglas D. Alder and Karl F. Brooks, *A History of Washington County: From Isolation to Destination* (Salt Lake City: Utah State Historical Society/Washington County Commission, 1996), 215.

6.   Alder and Brooks, *History of Washington County*, 215.

7.   Ibid., 219.

8.   Peter Blodgett, "Selling the Scenery: Advertising and the National Parks, 1916–1933" in *Seeing and Being Seen: Tourism in the American West*, ed. David M. Wrobel and Patrick T. Long (Lawrence: University Press of Kansas, 2001), 286, 297.

9.   Union Pacific Railroad, *They Say—Comments of Travelers on Zion National Park, Bryce Canyon, Cedar Breaks, Utah and Kaibab National Forest, North Rim, Grand Canyon National Park, Arizona* (Omaha: Acorn Press, 1926), 3, 7–8.

10.   Alder and Brooks, *History of Washington County*, 221. For the most prominent critique of the tourist economy, see Hal Rothman, *Devil's Bargains: Tourism in the Twentieth-Century American West* (Lawrence: University Press of Kansas, 1998).

11.   Blodgett, "Selling the Scenery," 280, 282.

12.   John Clark, "Utah's Original Tourfinder: News Motoring Pioneer Promoted State's Scenery," *Deseret News*, February 3, 2006.

13.   Ibid., C2. On the *Tribune's* Ruess search, see Rusho, *Vagabond for Beauty*, 203–4. Virginia Rishel, *Wheels to Adventure: Bill Rishel's Western Routes* (Salt Lake City: Howe Brothers, 1983).

14.   Arthur F. Bruhn, *Southern Utah's Land of Color!* (Bryce Canyon: Bryce Canyon Natural History Assn. and Zion Natural History Assn., 1962), 3, 29, 51–52.

15. *Utah Highways: The Crossroads of the West* 4, no. 1 (1996): 9 (photo caption).
16. Susan S. Rugh, "Branding Utah: Industrial Tourism in the Postwar American West," *Western Historical Quarterly* 37 (Winter 2006): 448–49. For a quick overview of Utah's attempt to create a brand image during the past sixty years, see also Brice Wallace, "Utah Tourism: Looking for a Pretty, Great Tag Line," *Deseret News,* February 12, 2006, M1.
17. Rugh, "Branding Utah," 449–51.
18. Ibid., 452.
19. Ibid., 459–62.
20. Wallace, "Utah Tourism," M9; Brice Wallace, "High Hopes Greet New Utah Brand," *Deseret News,* April 6, 2006.
21. Roy Webb, *Call of the Colorado* (Moscow: University of Idaho Press, 1994), 122–23. For further information on Nevills and the effect he had on others, see Roy Webb, ed., *High, Wide, and Handsome: The River Journals of Norman D. Nevills* (Logan: Utah State University Press, 2005).
22. Gary Topping, "Harry Aleson and the Place No One Knew," *Utah Historical Quarterly* 52, no. 2 (Spring 1984): 171–72.
23. Webb, *High, Wide, and Handsome,* 8
24. Ibid., 10.
25. Topping, "Harry Aleson," 173.
26. Mark W.T. Harvey, *A Symbol of Wilderness: Echo Park and the American Conservation Movement* (Albuquerque: University of New Mexico Press, 1994).
27. See Webb, *Call of the Colorado,* 123; David Brower, *For Earth's Sake: The Life and Times of David Brower* (Salt Lake City: Peregrine Smith Books, 1990), 342–43.
28. Eliot Porter, *The Place No One Knew: Glen Canyon on the Colorado* (San Francisco: Sierra Club, 1963).
29. Ibid., 13–14.
30. Ibid., 18.
31. Jared Farmer, *Glen Canyon Dammed: Inventing Lake Powell and the Canyon Country* (Tucson: University of Arizona Press, 1999), 184–89.
32. Grace Lichtenstein, "Hearing Draws Foes of Utah Power Plant That Would Be Near National Parks," *New York Times,* September 16, 1975; Charles Wilkinson, *Fire on the Plateau: Conflict and Endurance in the American Southwest* (Washington, DC: Island Press/Shearwater Books, 1999), 327.
33. Lichtenstein, "Hearing Draws Foes," 24; Liza Nicholas, Elaine M. Bapis, Thomas J. Harvey, eds., *Imagining the Big Open: Nature, Identity, and Play in the New West* (Salt Lake City: University of Utah Press, 2003), 274.
34. Nicholas, Bapis, Harvey, *Imagining the Big Open,* 275–76; "Redford Burned in Effigy for Opposing Power Plant," *New York Times,* April 19, 1976, 17.
35. Timothy Egan, "In Utah, a Pitched Battle over Public Lands," *New York Times,* November 13, 1995; Timothy Egan, "Clinton Enters Utah Battle over Fate of Wilderness Area," *New York Times,* September 17, 1996; James Brooke, "New Reserve Stirs Animosities in Utah," *New York Times,* October 13, 1996; Wilkinson, *Fire on the Plateau,* 328–31.

36. Brooke, "New Reserve Stirs Animosities," 26; Egan, "In Utah, a Pitched Battle," A14.

37. Brooke, "New Reserve Stirs Animosities," 26.

38. Michael A. Amundson, "Yellowcake to Singletrack: Culture, Community, and Identity in Moab, Utah," in Nicholas, Bapis, Harvey, *Imagining the Big Open,* 151–53.

39. Ibid., 157; "The Shrinking Majority," *Salt Lake Tribune,* July 24, 2005.

40. Farmer, *Glen Canyon Dammed,* 192–94; Jeff Hunter, "In the Land of Moab," *Cache Valley Magazine,* December 2005, 49.

41. Amundson, "Yellowcake to Singletrack," 159.

42. Porter, *The Place No One Knew,* 62.

43. Terry Tempest Williams, *Red: Passion and Patience in the Desert* (New York: Vintage Books, 2002), 4, 16. Williams, of course, is not the only advocate for the red rocks region who calls Utah home. Other home-grown advocates include Gibbs Smith, William Smart, Wayne Owens, Ted Wilson, and the environmentalist organization, the Southern Utah Wilderness Alliance. In terms of national name recognition and visibility, however, Williams occupies a unique niche.

44. Edward Abbey, *Desert Solitaire: A Season in the Wilderness* (New York: Ballantine Books, 1968).

45. Ibid., 240; Patricia Nelson Limerick, *Desert Passages: Encounters with the American Deserts* (Niwot: University Press of Colorado, 1989), 155.

46. Abbey, *Desert Solitaire,* 272–73. Postscript: As this book was going to press, David Roberts, in an article entitled "Finding Everett Ruess," in *National Geographic Adventure* (April/May 2009), announced that Ruess's remains had been discovered on Comb Ridge near Bluff, Utah. Forensic and DNA tests subsequently confirmed the identity of the remains.

2

"The Famous Blue Valley" and a Century of Hopes

Kristen Rogers-Iversen

Historians of nineteenth-century Utah frequently focus on the success-ful ranching and farming established by Mormon settlers. Historians of the twentieth century often describe mining, railroading, urban growth, and natural wonders. Kristen Rogers-Iversen looks beyond these success stories to tell the tale of a not-so-successful place in south-ern Utah. Blue Valley is a place that seemed so barren that Native Americans did not live there. Newcomers to Utah looked for open spaces in the late-nineteenth and especially the twentieth century. They believed promotional material and struggled to survive in an arid area. That attempt still continues in the twenty-first century as the few remaining residents of Blue Valley toil to remain or attempt to sell out. Rogers-Iversen masterfully interweaves her personal experi-ences with the residents' historical and contemporary stories. She draws on scholarly research by historians, archaeologists, environmentalists, and public-land policy makers and smoothly blends in her personal narratives and interviews. Her journalist/personal-essay style creates a delightful read about a place rarely written about in Utah history but one that is not all that unique.

The first time I remember seeing Blue Valley was in 1972. I was a college student and had just emerged from an astonishing backpack into the Maze sec-tion of Canyonlands, a paradise of creek and sandstone. Our group decided to spend the next night among the sandstone walls and apple blossoms of Capitol Reef. On the way there, we drove through Blue Valley, several miles or so of land along the Fremont River west of Hanksville, Utah.

It was without question the ugliest expanse of land I could ever imagine—only good "for holding the earth together," as people sometimes say about the

Remains of a roadhouse in Giles built by the Edward Abbott family. The photograph was taken in 1941.

arid West. Shining pale in the hot sun, the valley seemed only slightly less sterile than the moon. Stark mesas and dreary gray humps of Mancos shale lined the valley. In the few places with any vegetation, tamarisk and greasewood had taken over. A few cottonwoods clung to the sand along the river. A ruined stone building and a scattering of falling-down log structures implied that, incredibly, people had actually lived here once. But how could anyone have ever thought he or she could survive in this desert?

Thirty years later, this place has become beautiful to me—on its own terms, and also because of the stories it holds.

It started when I met, on paper, some of those people who had the temerity to think they *could* survive—and, in fact, build Zion—in Blue Valley. Niels J. and Minnie Nielsen came with their children to the valley in 1898. Later, the Nielsen boys wrote about Blue Valley and its people, and when I got a taste of those people's lives—how they lived by faith, gossiped, got sick, buried loved ones, built dams, danced, weeded, got stuck in quicksand, swatted millions of mosquitoes and killed snakes in their houses, drove schoolteachers crazy, fist-fought, made adobes, planted fruit trees, prayed—I could not rest until I got back to see the place—to see it again, with new eyes. Through their eyes. And through my own, standing a century apart from them.

The year is 2004. The ghost town of Giles—if you can call this lonesome stretch of ground a ghost town—lies on the gray clay flats south of the perennially coffee-colored Fremont River. To get there, you must cross the river—maybe on foot, because if the Fremont has been flooding, the river crossing will be a morass of "gumbo" mud for several yards before you can even get to the riverbank. Step in that mud, and you may sink to your thigh. So you must set out south from the rock ruin that was once the Abbott family's way station/hotel. You must cross land barren except for Russian thistle and a few other desiccated plants, then shoulder through thick tamarisk and slog through gumbo till the clay on your shoes adds a few inches to your height. Then you climb/slide down a steep bank to the river, roll up your pants, and work your way across—being careful not to leave a shoe in the quicksand—clamber up the clay bank on the other side, and start searching high and low for what remains of Giles.

When you find it, you will see the second law of thermodynamics writ large. You can find a few rock foundations of dugout houses, filled with greasewood and—after rain—standing water, as if these were the ruins of ancient Roman baths or pioneer swimming pools. You step over shards of purple, green, and blue glass. Pieces of white and brown earthenware. One chimney still standing. Old well holes yawning, eroding, in the blue clay. Red ant mounds. Coyote scat and cowpies. The last sad remains of an adobe church melting, melting, melting. The steeple still lies beside it, still pointing at the sky as if to keep the faith of the people who placed it atop their new church with satisfaction and relief. And then there are the peach pits: a pile of ancient, desiccated peach pits that lie there as testimony to the once-bright hopes of settlers.

This is a landscape of hope. Ruined hopes but also superhuman ones. Almost—not quite but almost—indomitable hopes. Through all the crazy twentieth century, people tried to make something here. Some were born here, but most arrived in the glow of those hopes, fully intending to do well, to live off the land, develop the land, herd on the land, mine the land—whatever they could do. Most of them gave up and left. Some, when they saw the place, never even tried but turned around and went back to where they came from.

The prelude to the twentieth century in Blue Valley began with the prehistoric groups who *didn't* choose to live here and then the late-nineteenth-century ones who did. Archaeologists simply can't find—or imagine finding—any conclusive evidence of prehistoric human habitation in Blue Valley. There are lithic scatters, a smattering of Fremont rock art, but nothing else, really, to show that the Fremont, Archaic, or even older peoples used this place much.[1] Probably they were just passing through on their way to better prospects.

When settlers arrived, small groups of Paiutes apparently lived at the base of the Henry Mountains, whose peaks rise up south of Blue Valley. The Paiutes grew corn there but by then had become almost destitute. For a while, they traded with the settlers and offered and received neighborly help, but then they faded from the historical record.

A mesa forms a dramatic backdrop to farms and homes in the young community of Caineville in Blue Valley. Floods repeatedly washed out homes and farms.

So, as far as we know, the first people to try to actually scratch a living out of the blue clay east of Capitol Reef came in 1883. Their hopes were pinned on the muddy Fremont River—they called it the Dirty Devil—which shrank alarmingly in the summer but brimmed full in wet or snowmelt times.[2] They tried to make the river a partner in their endeavor by damming it and running irrigation ditches to their farms. But the Dirty Devil, though it might placidly comply for a time, never failed to disappoint by tearing out the dams every few years. So, although hopeful families regularly arrived in Blue Valley to make a new start, discouraged families also regularly left—to make a new start somewhere else. In the early years, there *was* reason to hope, especially in the eyes of boosters. An 1886 notice in the *Deseret Evening News* bragged that the area had ten thousand acres of farmable land with plenty of water, and "animals on the range are looking fat."[3] In 1894 P. C. Christensen reported "heavy crops of grain," "fine orchards everywhere," and "alfalfa . . . about ready to cut for the second time" in Blue Valley. Therefore, for people "that need a home here is a good chance."[4]

The LDS Church had formed the Blue Valley Ward in 1885; in 1893 the Caineville Ward split off from the Blue Valley Ward.[5] The next year, huge floods destroyed the year's work and crops. So many people packed up and pulled out that the church dissolved the Blue Valley Ward. Another flood in 1896 washed out even more families.[6]

Despite the destruction, the boosters accentuated the positive. In 1898 F. H. Young urged people to "come see for yourself"—by making an easy trip.

Just take the train to Salina, then hire a buckboard or catch a ride with the mail wagon and travel 115 miles on rough roads to Blue Valley. If you were a "good farmer," Young wrote, the fantastic climate would enable you to grow grain, corn, cane, beans, potatoes, cabbage, onions, tomatoes, melons, apples, peaches, pears, plums, apricots, grapes, and hay. Oh, there was this one small thing: the current settlers really needed help repairing the dam and ditches "as they have been greatly damaged by floods the past two years." The residents wanted an infusion of new settlers and labor so badly that they had signed a contract with the LDS stake presidency promising to share their land and water rights with anybody who would come and join in their attempt to make something of this place.[7]

So on the cusp of the twentieth century, Blue Valley was still a landscape of "a good chance" and new beginnings, a wilderness that, with faith and communal work, could become a watered garden. Maybe. Hope continually clashed with discouragement. In fact, the Blue Valley settlers could not hide an undercurrent of something like desperation when they wrote to the outside world. On September 30, 1898, F. A. Young wrote that because the community had had to repair so many ditches and frost came earlier than usual, "we cannot boast of first-class crops." It was clear that "we need more people and like the inmates of a besieged fort, we have hoped and prayed and finally fancied that we could see in the distance the much-needed help." He finished his account with the best news he could muster—rather faint praise, actually: "We have not had any floods this season, and the health of the people is good."[8]

Apparently nobody actually expected a lot of people to take the bait voluntarily, because in 1897 or 1898 the LDS Church actually either issued a call for volunteers or officially "called" people to go to the aid of their flood-besieged brothers and sisters, according to family histories.[9] This is what brought Niels J. and Minnie Nielsen and their family to the valley. N. J., as he was known, came down first to prepare the way for his wife and children. He traveled with a group of others from Sanpete Valley who had been called to Blue Valley, and when they got there, they looked it over. One can only imagine how the Fremont River Valley looked in comparison to the cultivated, maturing towns of Sanpete Valley. The next morning everybody but N. J. Nielsen turned around and went back. N. J. felt "duty-bound to stay." He started planting corn and getting a drafty shack ready to house his family.[10]

So it was a group of determined, committed people who lived in Blue Valley at the turn of the century, people who were willing to live off the land great distances from the nearest railroad, flour mill, or doctor. James Nielsen, N. J. and Minnie's son, described them: the Whites, Abbotts, Mayhews, Youngs, Turners, Knights, Parkers, Busenbarks, Shirts, Lances, and Hunts—"a rugged and tough bunch of Mormons." He separated them into two groups: those on "the Lord's side" and the "bad influence"—those wayward folks who not only turned their grapes into wine but also started to make a hard liquor they called

The Blue Dugway near Caineville shows the dramatic scenery in the area. This primitive highway connected the remote settlements in Blue Valley to the outside world.

"white eye" out of the fermented skimmings of molasses. James described the town gossip, tightwads, dance musicians, and fighters (each dance ended in a drunken brawl; one time, so the story goes, a Hunt bit off the nose of a Burgess and swallowed it.)[11]

Whether on the Lord's side or the other, everybody pulled together to build a church, not just for devotions but also to hold those wild dances. N. J. was an adobe mason and a good organizer—a solid leader, in fact—so in 1901 he became the person to oversee the building of the church. He worked at it full time, contributing seven hundred dollars of his own labor and money. He found some good mud for making adobes, molded all the bricks, and did the masonry and carpenter work. Men worked with him when they could, and the families paid him in molasses, honey, and livestock. "How they ever done it I will never be able to explain," wrote James Nielsen. "They hauled in lumber from the Boulder Mountain, fifty miles away, and bought tongue and [groove] flooring in Richfield at seventy-five dollars per thousand feet and hauled it through what is called Wayne Wonderland now, we called it Capital Wash and . . . you can find nothing more rugged in Utah." [12] This is the building that now has almost all melted back into the clay.

It was a good thing the settlers had a symbol of their faith, a steeple pointing to heaven, a place to gain spiritual and communal strength, because anything could happen at any moment. The river could silt up the ditches, or the frosts could come. "The ditches were built . . . under the ledges and everytime it rained they were filled with mud. We were continually cleaning ditches or putting in a new dam with cottonwood, willows and rock and as hope springs eternal in the human breast, the men refused to quit," wrote James Nielsen. "I can still hear old Pappy Lance say, '[This dam] will never go out in Gods almighty world, no sir, it will never go out.' But it always did and the half developed crops died and the people lived on faith and hope and greasewood greens."[13]

But "we were never without food in our home, sometimes only bread and molasses and Brigham tea with a cottontail rabbit once in a while,"[14] James added. There were times when miracles helped them through. During one long stretch, the Nielsens' flour bin, like the Old Testament widow's barrel of meal, never failed, even though it always seemed as though there couldn't possibly be enough flour for another batch of biscuits.

Heartbreak outweighed miracles, though. You never knew when an accident or sickness would sweep away someone you loved. In 1892 a horse kicked Bishop Henry Giles and broke his leg. No doctor lived anywhere remotely close, so a "horse doctor" took the leg off with a crosscut saw. After a few days of ghastly pain, Henry died and became the first to lie in the cemetery. In 1919 his wife, Elizabeth, became the last person to be buried there.

Minnie Nielsen's German mother, Johanne Schiller, fell off the family's roof when she was up there laying out fruit to dry. She never recovered and, after some months of decline, was laid in her final bed in the Giles cemetery, up against the blue hills south of town. At the time, N. J. was in Carbon County trying to support his family by working for a mining company because floods had ruined the year's crops again. When he returned home, he marked his mother-in-law's grave by pounding nails in a board to spell out her name and death date.

In 1902 diphtheria went through the valley. It took sisters Jennie and Nell Turner at seventeen and thirteen; they reportedly went to bed with "colds" and were found dead in the morning. Jennie's death dramatically altered the life course of Fred Giles, son of the first bishop of the Blue Valley Ward. But then, Blue Valley altered the life of everybody who ever tried to live on that land. Fred and Jennie had planned to get married. He buried his hopes along with her body in the clay of the Giles cemetery and never did marry, though it is said that he made sure he was sealed to Jennie in a Mormon temple ceremony so he could be with her in the next life. Fred himself died in 1950 of a gastric disorder. By then Giles and all its inhabitants were long gone, so Fred was buried in Bicknell.[15]

Despite it all, the settlers got hundreds of acres under cultivation. They had orchards, fields of alfalfa and sorghum, big gardens, and animals. Giles had a post office, store, and blacksmith forge. True, some men had to leave for a while to earn money in places with steadier economies, but Blue Valley seemed to be coming along.[16]

When the Fremont River floods, you can smell it coming. You may never feel a drop of rain where you are, but the smell of water and mud churns the air ahead of the wave. And then you may hear it: boulders grinding along the river bottom, and then a huge wall of water comes for your land, speeding like a locomotive. It tosses trees like toothpicks. It carries cows, outbuildings, and great chunks of land. The river heaves up and over its banks and spreads across the land. So say those who have seen it, heard it, smelled it.[17]

According to a 1953 Geological Survey study, serious erosion on the Fremont drainage started with the 1897 flood. Before 1897 the river and its tributaries flowed gently through shallow channels lined with willows and brush. But after that, each flood scoured the channel deeper and wider until now, near the ghost town of Giles, the banks are fifteen feet high.[18]

No dam could ever hold back those floods. The water simply tore away the quicksand below the dam, and then it was all over. It is said that one dam builder went insane as he watched the flood carry off yet another "sturdy" dam that had taken the men months to build. "Other watchers rescued him from the crumbling bank on which he stood. . . . His sanity had collapsed. . . . As time went on, his condition improved; but he always was thereafter led about like a child, oblivious to all but childish things, amused at nothing."[19] The story may be apocryphal—but then again, it does make perfect sense.

The year 1909 was one that could easily drive a person mad. It started out looking quite fine, at least to some eyes. Lois Fulgate wrote a glowing report to the *Emery County Progress* that her home would soon no longer be known as "Old Blue Valley" but as one of the richest oil fields in the United States. This was in addition to its being a veritable agricultural paradise. Lois envisioned a hundred miles of the finest fruit orchards, watered by a massive reclamation scheme. Of course, given these features, a railroad through Blue Valley was in the not-so-distant future. "The people of the eastern Wayne county have come to a full realization of the value of their property and extend good wishes to all those wishing to locate near them," Fulgate wrote.[20]

And then, midsummer, the river began to flood. For two months, it flooded repeatedly, caving away the riverbanks. At times, kids could fish out melons and squash that had washed down from farms upstream. James Nielsen said, "We saw whole orchards with ripened fruit on the trees floating down the river along with the houses, barns…chickens and cattle and most everything we had. Father and mother were washed out completely, their whole farm was nothing but a river bed."[21]

The floods were not exactly "acts of God." During the Great Depression, writers working for the Federal Writers' Project documented the effects of over-grazing in Utah. Land that was covered with lush grasses when settlers arrived was, within a couple of decades, "et out" by thousands of cattle and sheep. Livestock ate and trampled lands on the Aquarius Plateau and Caineville Mesa and in the Fishlake Mountains, the Henry Mountains, and Rabbit Valley. As vegetation grew sparse, rainwater and snowmelt no longer soaked into the ground but gathered and raged down gullies, streambeds, and eventually the Fremont. Once-placid streams and rivers became embryo canyons, growing deeper and wider with each flood.[22]

Add to the sheep and cows the nature of the clay in Blue Valley, and you have a recipe for really big floods. "When that old clay gets wet, it seals itself off, and every drop runs down the drainage," Kelly Taylor told me. Kelly knows. He will come into this story, but much later. He is the bookend on the other side of the twentieth century.[23]

In September 1909, the Wayne LDS stake president, Gearson Bastian, and his counselor Joseph Eckersley traveled down from Loa to take a look at what the floods had done. They had done a great deal. The roiling river had decimated every bridge and dam between Fruita and Hanksville. Ditches and roads were silted up, washed out, and in general not usable. On Sunday, September 19, the little community of Giles gathered with its stake leader in the adobe church to worship God. I wonder how many were able to keep their minds on the sermon. They must have kept speculating on how the president would respond to what he had seen. After the service, the congregation walked with Bastian and Eckersley upstream to the dam site. The president looked over the gully that was now the river's course. Sixteen-year-old Joseph Nielsen was there with his family:

> I remember all those good people were standing up on a high bluff looking down on the dam site where they had labored so hard, standing there with the Stake President waiting for his verdict, almost holding their breath waiting to see what he was going to say, finely the President turned from looking down into the canyon, and spoke to the people, and he said this is a hard thing for me to say, but this thing has been tried out by you and others who have come and gone for the last 20 or 25 years, and you seem to be just about where you started, very little headway has been made, and my impression is that you had better give it up, some of the people cried and some of them shouted for joy.[24]

The stake president's authority was actual and final; the families who had been called to make this Mancos/bentonite desert blossom like a rose were released from their mission. Minnie Nielsen rejoiced and rejoiced and rejoiced, and the family hurried off to settle on the Provo Bench. (N. J. and Minnie would move to the Uintah Basin, Gunlock, and Manti before they died in 1939.) But some Giles citizens just couldn't throw in the towel, not after all they had gone through, and the president's decree bitterly disappointed them. After almost all their neighbors had packed up and left, two or three families stayed behind to throw good money (and sweat and tears) after bad. They just knew they could build a dam that would stay put. But the river knew differently.[25]

So ended Blue Valley's first historical wave—its largest wave, its most hopeful, most bitter wave.

Blue Valley is not an isolated story in Utah. After the first flush of settlement in the mid-nineteenth century focused on the land most suited for farming, later comers were forced to settle where the climate wasn't so ideal or water was a scarce commodity. For example, settlers made their way to northwestern Box Elder County late in the nineteenth century. The area supported some grazing, but farming was a tough go. Around 1912 the Promontory-Curlew Land Company tried to sell dry-farming parcels in the Curlew Valley, but the land was too arid even for the best dry-farming practices, and those who bought property went broke. Similarly, a group of a hundred Russian Molokons arrived in Park Valley in 1914 to create a farming-based colony. By 1918 the colony had failed. In Sanpete County, an intentional Jewish colony of two hundred in Gunnison Valley, settled in 1911, dried up within four or five years.

Failed towns dot the Utah experience, though not the collective memory. How many people have heard of the short-lived town of Osiris in Garfield County? Nearby Widstoe lasted longer, but in the end, the limiting factor was all too familiar: water. The few residents who remained in the 1930s were relocated by the Resettlement Administration. Each of these towns and many others has its own story, its own saga of hopefulness, labor, and disappointment.

In the 1930s, Zane Grey wrote about the last holdouts in Blue Valley in his book *Robbers Roost*.[26] Local newspapers ran the book in installments. In one chapter, the hero, Jim Wall, is trying to get the unconscious beauty Helen to safety during a rainy night. After a night of dealing with the "vicious Dirty Devil," mudslides, and a flash flood, he finally sees the dawn. The rain stops. Jim sees a purple butte and a "corrugated peak above yellow and brown hills." When he tops a divide, he is suddenly "confronted by an amazing and marvelous spectacle.

"'Blue Valley!' he ejaculated.

"The startling beauty of this lost valley struck Jim next. It resembled a winding jewel of emerald and amethyst, set down amid barren hills of jasper and porphyry, and variegated mosaics of foothills waving away on the left and golden racks of carved rocks, and mounds of brown clay and dunes of rusty earth."

It's a fine description, if by "emerald", he meant the cottonwoods or perhaps fields still under cultivation.

"'Blue Valley! . . . Helen, we're out of the brakes! . . . Safe! Men live here.'" But there is no sign of habitation. They pass deserted cabins along the river—not old, just deserted. They pass a dugout. They pass an abandoned church with "vacant eye-like windows" (N. J.'s church, perhaps?). Finally, they spot one cabin that has smoke drifting from the chimney. The rancher, "a typical pioneer, still-faced and bearded" (his name is Tasker), comes to the aid of Jim

Residents of Blue Valley posed after Sunday School in front of the Caineville School and meeting house, about 1900.

and Helen. Tasker is an individualist. He tells the couple, "I've stuck it out. But I'll be givin' up soon. No use tryin' to fight that Dirty Devil river. Five years ago there was eighty people livin' hyar. Blue valley has a story, friend—"

The book ends well, by the way, with Jim and Helen united in love.[27]

In 1900 the U.S. Bureau of the Census counted the folks in Giles (called the Burgess Precinct in the census). At that time, the total population stood at 134. There were sixteen farmers, one freighter, one day laborer, one cattle rancher, one silver miner, and thirty children "at school." Fifteen sons were "farm laborers." These people came from western states and eastern states but also from England, Denmark, and Germany. Almost all the adults could read and write. During the same census, Caineville, Giles's sister community mentioned earlier, had a population of 131.

In 1910 the population of Giles had shrunk to 89. Caineville was down to 38. In 1920 the Giles Precinct had disappeared from the census. The Caineville Precinct covered both areas, and the population had shrunk to 67. In 1930, 71 souls lived in the Caineville precinct. In 1940, 68 people were still hanging on. In the entire county, 97.2 percent of the population were "native white stock." Foreign-born whites represented 2.5 percent. All other residents totaled .3 percent. Agriculture by far outweighed every other means of livelihood.[28]

It seems there was always somebody willing to gamble on Blue Valley. After all, that big stretch of land is out there with nobody using it. It must be good for something, in a profitable sort of way—it just needs the right person to figure out what to do with it.

Although the 1909 floods put a damper on agriculture, people in 1910 were still expecting an oil boom in the valley. The *Eastern Utah Advocate* wrote that "eastern capital" had secured tens of thousands of acres in the area and was sending rigs to drill near Giles, where oil seeping into the river testified to what lay beneath the surface. The developer, a Mr. Levi, exulted that this was the most promising of any field in the state he had ever prospected. Levi was prepared to drill three thousand feet if he had to, but he was confident of striking oil at fifteen hundred feet.[29] Nothing came of it. Mr. Levi probably left the same way most people left Blue Valley—discouraged, poorer than when he had come.

In 1917 some outsiders thought they could do what the small farmers couldn't. With the goal of "reclaiming" thirty thousand acres, D. H. McMurtrey of Green River and Arthur Reeves of Denver were building a dam on the Fremont approved by two "well-known" engineers, complete with steel head-gates cemented in place. By May 1918 they planned to have water turned onto the "thirsty soil to increase the nation's production of foodstuffs for winning [World War I]." The *Grand Valley Times,* reporting on this scheme, hastened to mention that land in the "famous Blue valley" was available at forty dollars per acre, which included water rights. The developers were keeping the tracts small, at forty to eighty acres so that no one person could control the valley.[30]

In the meantime, Jabez (Ras) Durfey, then a resident of Salina, returned to the valley to finish a job he had started in the 1890s. He had figured that if he could simply tunnel through the Caineville Reef into Blue Valley, he could open up a thousand acres of land to cultivation. So he had started the tunnel but never finished it before the LDS Church called him to a mission in Mexico. Now, in 1918, he was ready to cash in, joining forces with a group that was building a dam with logs that looked as if they surely must be "strong enough to hold enough water for two valleys."[31]

The *Richfield Reaper* backed up Durfey and the dam builders with editorial enthusiasm (it just so happened that Richfield investors were heavily involved in this scheme). The paper played to people's hope that there had to be justice in the world, that all the years of disappointment must not be in vain: "This is another chance for those who did not get what they wanted in Blue Valley." The paper also encouraged a get-in-at-the-ground-level attitude: "Land seekers must not lose this opportunity as they have done the others. Don't let the war stop you from getting a good start in life. Now is the time to start a farm while prices are high." Finally, the paper trotted out the everybody's-doing-it argument: "Priesthood meetings [in the area] have been started and the first night brought out a large attendance."[32]

But nothing came of this project, even though Durfey finished his tunnel around 1921 and Erastus and Charles Durfey joined forces with Teancum Bean to build another tunnel upstream, 375 feet long. Their dreams ended the same way these dreams always seemed to end—in flooding and ruin.[33]

In 1931 the *Richfield Reaper* praised a dam and irrigation system being built by Arthur Chaffin, but a little more faintly: "If the project works as planned, Blue Valley will become a place for home builders." The next year, floods washed out those plans, too.[34]

As if history meant nothing at all, an investor thought he could get those lands under irrigation as late as 1955. Barbara Ekker, longtime Hanksville observer and recorder, wrote in her column for the *Green River Journal,*

> Mr. Bill Robertshaw stopped and visited with Mrs. Edna Philips on his way to the Shoot-the-Ring mine of Harold Ekkers. He stated that he had purchased Blue Valley (2500 acres west of Hanksville on the Fremont River). This property originally belonged to the late Harry Philips but was later purchased by Jack Rauer, Moab. This valley was once a very prosperous area which had a population of nearly two hundred residents. The valley was deserted because it was very difficult to irrigate. But Mr. Robertshaw plans to make it flourish as before. Good Luck Bill![35]

An October afternoon: the cottonwoods along the river are an explosion of sunlight. The sky is blue, wide, smiling. The sculpted shale slopes of Caineville Mesa are sharp with shadows. As we drive east, the country opens up, and we can look far to the south to the gray hills and see Steamboat Point standing grandly, pointing at Giles. We pass a couple of old buildings by the side of the road—make a stop, U turn, and go back to peer more closely at those buildings, then get out and walk over. One is a livestock shed; the other is a hewn log cabin with a doorway not much taller than I am. Inside sits an old green and white cookstove with a stovepipe hole above it, an ancient chair, a rusting iron, and a chest about to disintegrate back into dust. The walls were once covered with chicken wire, then plastered. What wallpaper remains has little hens and teapots on it. I'd swear the paper dates from the 1950s, but who on earth would have lived in a log cabin that late? Still, Laura Hunt, who grew up in Caineville in the first part of the century, did tell me that as a girl she knew a boy whose family actually lived in a dugout cut into a bank; they cooked squirrels and dug dandelions for food.[36]

A wooden box holds a pile of crumbling, yellow receipts, including a handwritten deposit slip: the Rainy Day Uranium Company making a deposit of $333.54 to the State Bank of Wayne. I want badly to take the receipts to put them in a repository; they seem incredibly valuable. Priceless, in fact. But taking them would make me a vandal, and I already feel badly enough being a trespasser.

On the door hangs a curling poster of a bathing beauty who looks like Ann Margret. Everything here is gently melting into the land. Someday it will be a dark spot of organic material for an archaeologist to investigate. Or, even farther down the road of time, a small pocket of coal.

Later, one of the locals explains that a family did live in this house during the 1950s, a large family who came during the summers to farm.[37] They were living here when the rest of the country was buying new automobiles and homes. New postwar suburbs were springing up at the margins of cities. People were getting their first TVs and listening to Buddy Holly and Perry Como. They were worrying about the Soviet Union and seeing Communists everywhere. In Utah the defense industry was beginning to grow and would mushroom into big-time business during the missile-building frenzy of the sixties.

Unlike Giles, Caineville, eleven miles away, never died completely, and a few people live there still. Laura Hunt grew up there and gave birth to her own children with the help of midwives. There was no electricity, of course. The family used coal oil lamps, a coal stove, and a boiler. They put lye in the water to settle and skim it. To prepare for washday, Laura put lye in ditch water to settle the dirt out. She washed the clothes twice using homemade soap and a scrub board, then she boiled them. People hauled water with a horse pulling a water lizard—a forked stick with boards across it onto which you could strap a water barrel. For a "refrigerator," they built a cooler with screens for sides. They put burlap over the screens and a leaky panful of water on top. Water dripping through holes in the pan kept the burlap wet and the food cool. Another strategy was to set a box into the side of the ditch, where mud and nearby water kept the food cool.[38]

In 1971 Vance and Kelly Taylor, father and son, bought the old Giles town site as an investment. For thirty years, the land sat as it always had, while the signs of human habitation gently melted back into the soil. In the meantime, Kelly Taylor and his father dug a well. ("It's good water," Taylor says. "I call it the blue flavor. I bottle it. Just as pure as can be.")[39] They mulled over various uses. Finally, they offered the land for sale as a feedlot. But even with the real estate sign up, something about those ruined homes and the stories they represented kept working in the back of Taylor's mind. Call it respect for the past. Call it hubris. Call it entrepreneurship of the sort that Blue Valley has inspired for a hundred years. Whatever it was, the two Taylors came up with an idea to resurrect the town, preserve its history, and make some money.

According to a 2004 press release that seems to echo some of the boosters' words from decades earlier,

> Kelly Taylor is practically giving away a historical Utah town.
> For $1 per member, families can purchase 1.1 acres of land to build a home or cabin. The only requirements are buyers must be descendants of one of the town's original settlers and agree to document their entire family history.
> "If there are 10,000 people in a family line, fine, each family member can each pay their $1 when they want to, there are no upfront requirements," explained Taylor. "But they have to trace their ancestry for us, starting with

the youngest newborn baby and going back to the original pioneer who lived in the town. Right now, we are working with one family who has traced their roots back to a settler who was a polygamist, and there are 1,000 descendants from him."[40]

Kelly Taylor is gray haired, energetic, tall and lean. He has collected boxes of manuscripts and photos on Blue Valley; he digs into archives, talks to family members. His vision is to create a town that looks like an 1800s town—not counting the cars and ATVs in the driveways, presumably. Presumably, also, there would be no burlap-covered coolers or washtubs in the yards. Only descendants of original residents can buy lots, and they must build homes "that are of the vintage and style and character of 1899. It might be a modular home brought in and the façade put on to make it look like adobe, rock, or stucco. You can build your own recreational getaway from the city . . . then come down and do ATVing. That's the main thing in the world that they do there."[41]

"Every week that goes by now, I've got people calling me that are just starting to hear that something is coming alive," Taylor told me. "The Abbott family just called me. They're wanting to come back and try and get a little piece of Blue Valley to help honor their heritage, and I'm encouraging them to prepare their family history. If I can just keep getting people to dig in their closet, . . ."[42]

Taylor has put up tall white stakes to mark the property. He has convinced the county to put a sign on Utah Highway 24 pointing to "Old Giles Townsite". (The sign points across a river crossing that is sometimes navigable and sometimes not.) He has got the BLM to agree to let him move a vintage 1896 house from Aldridge, another defunct town site upstream, and restore it as a "welcome center of sorts."

"I want to plant grapes and a whole bunch of pecan trees on every lot and block corner and put the roads in. I'd set them up on a drip irrigation system. . . . I'd like to have some green," he says.[43]

West of Giles, along the highway, Randy Ramsley has been working on having "some green" since the mid-1990s. His bakery/organic farm is neighbor to a cattle ranch, then the Luna Mesa Café—an establishment that hearkens back both literally and metaphorically to the 1970s, and, farther down the road, the lonely Caineville Motel. In autumn, Randy's Mesa Farm Market, which he runs with his wife, Debra, fronts two or three Quonset greenhouses, rows of tomatoes and peppers nearing the end of the season, an emerald green cover-crop field, and an outdoor wood-fired brick oven that he built himself.

Geographically, Ramsley lives in Giles's sister community, Caineville, but philosophically he has a lot in common with the Gilesians of a hundred years ago. For one thing, he's trying to make a go of agriculture in a tough place. For another thing, he has a vision, and it's not an unfamiliar one: to create an agriculture-based community of like-minded people. He even refers to Brigham

Young's thoughts on that subject. And finally, his motivation to try to farm the Mancos shale is largely spiritual.

When I went up the wooden stairs into his little bakery, Ramsley came in from outside wearing a tan baseball hat with the Mesa Farm logo on it—a rock art design that looks like something growing. Beneath the hat were straw-colored chin-length hair, pink skin, bright wide eyes, and horn-rim glasses.

He said that making a living out here is "a matter of pruning my needs and wants. I have pretty much eliminated my wants and pruned my needs way down." A hundred years earlier, the Nielsen family and all the other Gilesians had had to do the same thing. It didn't take much prodding to get him to expound on his worldview; in fact, he was eager to share it. "We are born into the world with a little spirit and a whole lot of physicality," he explained. "We have parents and teachers whose job it is to teach us how to build spirituality. But we've lost that in our culture today. It's not being addressed. And organized religions have slipped into the hands of people who have physical minds. It's physical spirituality—spirituality through the physical mind. The Bible says, 'Seek ye first the kingdom of God.'"[44] Ramsley quotes the Bible a lot.

Ramsley has chosen farming as his path to (or in) spirituality. He sees his work first as an opportunity for spiritual growth and second as a way to make a living. Nature is the teacher. Practicing the principles of sustainable agriculture—cover crops, rotation, organic soil amendments, and so on—he sells organic vegetables, bread, and cinnamon rolls both to local restaurants and to whomever, driving by, happens to see his sign and stops.

The "next door" neighbor is raising livestock. The two are friends. The neighbor supplies manure to help Ramsley improve his soil and is thinking about growing organic beef to complement the organic produce. Ramsley calls him "possibly the best man I've ever met. He has been the Mormon bishop in Hanksville. He tries to live his religion every day." And...when it comes to environmentalism, the two live on completely different planets. It's a weird divide between them. "We go to the BLM environmental study meetings and sit on different sides of the table. We yell at each other all night. Then we come back and act as if nothing happened," Ramsley says.[45]

About the time Kelly Taylor acquired the Giles town site, America—or certain segments of it, anyway—was in the beginning stages of a love affair with off-road vehicles. Before long, riders discovered a perfect Shangri-la—the smooth, rockless, plantless Mancos shale badlands north of the Fremont River. Blue Valley's reputation grew. By the end of the twentieth century, some three thousand to four thousand acres around Factory Butte had become a playground for ATVers and motocross riders from all over the country.

Attempts by the BLM to control or limit the riding have been stoutly and religiously resisted by the locals—those who like to ride, those who stand to make a living off those who like to ride, and those who don't ride at all but feel they have earned their promised land by the sweat of their brows and the brows of their ancestors. Nobody, they feel, especially not the government, can tell them what they can and can't do. "Dyed-in-the-wool ATVers are saying we will ride where we want to ride," explains Craig Harmon, the BLM archaeologist for the area. "The ATVers are joined by people who have lived in Wayne County for generations—and who feel their rights to the land are God given."[46]

Then there is the environmentalist view: ORVs erode the hills, pollute the rivers with runoff, churn up the soil so the wind can lift it off, grind vegetation into the ground, and scar the land with tracks that will remain for years. "We get a lot of letters from people who drive through here, out-of-staters," says Harmon. "They see the tracks and ask what the hell happened."[47]

The issue became the most controversial piece in a recent management plan the BLM created for the entire district. "More people have expressed an opinion about this area than they have about the other entire 2.1 million acres," explained BLM planner Frank Erickson in 2005.[48] In fact, comments on the Factory Butte unit date from the 1990s. Postcards and e-mail have poured into the office supporting area closures and strict control of ORVs. A subcommittee of the BLM's Resource Advisory Committee (RAC) spent several months studying, discussing, and arguing the issue. In March 2006 they made their report. They could not agree on a recommendation, so they presented three proposals. The entire RAC toured the area, heard the report, listened to public comment, and in the end could not make a decision, either.[49] In the final analysis, the BLM decided to try to restrict riding on most of the land by creating a network of designated routes. But it kept twenty-six hundred acres of badlands open for free and unrestricted riding.[50]

"The travel designations announced today will not only protect two endangered species of cacti from recreational impacts, but will also ensure that Factory Butte can remain open to OHV users in the years to come," the Richfield BLM field office said. BLM officials noted that those riding off-highway vehicles in Factory Butte will still be able to enjoy diverse activities over a wide area, from challenging terrain to easy-riding scenic loops to the twenty-six-hundred-acre "open play area" at Swing Arm City.[51]

So—after a century of hoping, striving, and for the most part failing, at this beginning of the next century, people are still pinning their hopes on Blue Valley: hopes for a revived "historic" town, hopes for the blooming of agriculture, hopes to stop the erosion, hopes for open ATV terrain, hopes for bodies to fill vacant rooms at the Caineville Motel . . . and on it goes. How this severe place became a Promised Land for anyone at all is somewhat puzzling. Nevertheless, people on the margins had to have *someplace* to locate their aspirations. Where else could they go? Other settlers took up the land in more-fertile valleys. Other investors with more money sewed up the more-promising deals. And other dreamers dreamed up the more-conventional schemes. Blue Valley, with its wide-open, undeveloped, unpaved, unbillboarded, unsubdivided, un-Wal-Marted spaces, must get people thinking, "somebody should *do* something with this land."

And somebody probably still will. Now that you can easily find Giles by the signs pointing to it, treasure hunters may strip it of its potsherds and old square-headed nails. Business-minded people may develop more amenities for ATV riders. Urban refugees looking for the "last, best, unspoiled place" may buy up land and build first or second homes. Will they find what they seek here? Will things pan out? Or will the dam wash out, metaphorically speaking? As the twenty-first century unfolds, the story of Blue Valley is still playing out.

NOTES

1. Craig Harmon, telephone interview by author, October 15, 2005.

2. Hyrum Burgess and Jonathon Hunt were the first to come. The next summer Henry Giles, E. C. Abbott, and J. C. White joined them; Charles B. Hunt, *Geology and Geography of the Henry Mountains Region, Utah,* Geological Survey Professional Paper 228 (Washington, DC: GPO, 1953), 216. Technically the river through Blue Valley is named the Fremont River. After its confluence with Muddy Creek near Hanksville, it becomes the Dirty Devil, so named by John Wesley Powell. But during this period, the settlers above the confluence called it the Dirty Devil.

3. "Local News," *Deseret Evening News,* March 3, 1886.

4. P. C. Christensen, "Visiting Wayne Stake," *Deseret Evening News,* October 28, 1894.

5. Miriam B. Murphy, *A History of Wayne County* (Salt Lake City: Utah State Historical Society and Wayne County Commission, 1999), 132, 134.

6. Esther Coombs Durfey, comp., "Notom—An Oasis in the Desert," 1984, MSS A 1161, State History Collections, Research Center of Utah State Archives and Utah State History, Salt Lake City (hereafter cited as RC).

7. F. H. Young, "Home Seekers," *Deseret Evening News,* July 9, 1898.

8. F. A. Young, "A Desirable Country," *Deseret Evening News,* October 15, 1898. F. A. Young may have been the same person as F. H. Young, but this is how the newspaper printed the names.

9. In response to the depression of the 1890s, the LDS church instituted a program of colonization between 1896 and 1904, sending groups to Wyoming, Canada, Nevada, Idaho, and parts of Utah. The settlers who were called to Blue Valley may have been part of this renewed church-colonization push. However, the details of the call are unclear, perhaps because it was not specifically prescriptive. For instance, in 1877 Brigham Young issued a general call: "There are numbers of brethren in Sanpete County . . . who would, no doubt, be happy to remove to a valley where the water is abundant and the soil good. We should like to have at least fifty families locate in Castle Valley this fall." Nancy Taniguchi, *Castle Valley, America: Hard Land, Hard-Won Home* (Logan: Utah State University Press, 2004), 35. See Leonard J. Arrington, "Utah and the Depression of the 1890s," *Utah Historical Quarterly* 29, no. 1 (January 1961): 3–20.

10. James Nielsen, "A History of Niels J. Nielsen and Minnie Schiller," circa 1965, The Niels Joseph Nielsen Family Papers, MSS B 1627, box 1, RC.

11. James W. Nielsen, letters to his sister, Pat Nielsen Davis, n.d., The Nielsen Family Papers, RC.

12. James Nielsen, "History of Niels J. Nielsen and Minnie Schiller."

13. Ibid.

14. Ibid.

15. Giles cemetery records, MS A206, RC; Nielsen, letters to Pat Davis; *Morgan County News,* obituary for Fred Giles, October 3, 1950.

16. Stephen L. Carr, *The Historical Guide to Utah Ghost Towns* (Salt Lake City: Western Epics, 1986), 120.

17. Esther Coombs Durfey, interview by author, January 2003; Durfey, "Notom—An Oasis."

18. Hunt, *Geology and Geography,* 19, 205–9.

19. Isaac Frank Nielsen, "I Can't Forget That River," excerpt from *Reminiscences* (publication data unavailable, n.d.), p. 24, MS B1627, RC.

20. Lois Fulgate, "Rambling Sounds from Wayne County," *Emery County Progress,* March 13, 1909.

21. Joseph August Nielsen, "Family History of Niels Joseph Nielsen and Minnie Schillar [sic] Nielsen", p. 7, RC; James Nielsen, "History of Niels J. Nielsen and Minnie Schiller," The Niels Joseph Nielsen Family Papers, RC. According to Charles B. Hunt, 1905–18 were wet years in the region; 1919–38 were dry. From 1895 to 1938, annual rainfall ranged from 2.24 inches to almost 12 inches; Hunt, *Geology and Geography,* 26.

22. Joseph J. Porter, c. 1935 statement to Works Progress Adminstration (WPA) writer about range conditions in Southern Utah, RC; Nethelia King Griffin, "Life in Boulder," WPA, typescript, 1938, MS A562, RC.

23. Kelly Taylor, telephone interview by author, October 15, 2005.

24. Joseph August Nielsen, "Family History," 13.

25. Ibid.; Murphy, *History of Wayne County,* 235–36.

26. Robbers Roost, the renowned hiding place of bandits like Butch Cassidy, lies in eastern Wayne County.

27. "Robbers' Roost," *Kane County Standard,* November 30, 1934; "Robbers' Roost," *Richfield Reaper,* February 14, 1935.

28. Allan Kent Powell, "Population," in *Utah History Encyclopedia,* ed. Allan Kent Powell (Salt Lake City: University of Utah, 1994), 434–35. Census information available on Ancestry.com for Wayne County; "Wayne County Basic Data of Economic Activities and Resources," Utah State Planning Board, 1940, RC.

29. "Another Field is Opening in Blue Valley, Wayne County," *Eastern Utah Advocate,* November 18, 1910.

30. "30,000 Acres to be Reclaimed," *Grand Valley Times,* December 14, 1917.

31. This may have been the Wonderland Irrigation Company. This company was formed by a group of men from Wayne County and a Salt Laker named Hickenlooper with investors from Richfield who bought land for back taxes. Their $25,000 dam washed out when it was almost completed. Murphy, *History of Wayne County,* 236.

32. "Cainesville," *Richfield Reaper,* January 26, 1918.

33. Murphy, *History of Wayne County,* 236. Another apparent attempt to put together a deal in Blue Valley is suggested by a public notice in the the *Richfield Reaper* on September 15, 1927, stating that a George W. Okerlund was suing many of the early settlers and some companies to obtain title to a thousand acres.

34. "Torrey," *Richfield Reaper,* January 8, 1931; July 21, 1932; Hunt, *Geology and Geography,* 216.

35. Barbara Ekker, "Hanksville News," *Green River Journal,* December 8, 1955.

36. Laura Hunt, interview by author, April 2002.

37. Randy Ramsley, interview by author, October 2004.

38. Laura Hunt interview.

39. Kelly Taylor interview.

40. Press release by Heritage Highway 89, October 23, 2004, www.utahheritage.com/press-releases/2004/pr-10–23–2004.htm.

41. Kelly Taylor interview.

42. Ibid.

43. Ibid.

44. Randy Ramsey interview.

45. Ibid.

46. Craig Harmon interview.

47. Ibid.

48. Frank Erickson, telephone interviews by author, October 15, 2005, and April 7, 2006.

49. BLM Resource Advisory Committee minutes, March 23–24, 2006, Bureau of Land Management website www.blm.gov/ut/st/en/res/resource_advisory.html.

50. See Notice of Off-Highway Vehicle (OHV) Travel Restriction for Factory Butte Area, Utah, dated September 20, 2006, available online at http://www.ut.blm.gov/factory-butte/federal_register.htm.

51. See news release dated September 20, 2006, "BLM Richfield Office Designates Motorized Routes at Factory Butte," available online at http://www.ut.blm.gov/factorybutte/federal_register.htm.

3

Selling Sleep

The Rise and Fall of Utah's Historic Motels

Susan Sessions Rugh

From the Progressive Era onward, boosters in Utah who belonged to organizations like the Salt Lake Commercial Club promoted convention and business travel to the Beehive State. Early promotional materials emphasized the Great Salt Lake and Mormon historic sites, but by the mid-1940s, the newly organized Utah Tourist and Publicity Council attempted to lure tourists by highlighting the state's national parks and mountains as well as water recreation and Temple Square. Susan Sessions Rugh describes the new lodging accommodations— motor courts and motels—that catered to automobile travelers during the 1940s and '50s in Salt Lake City, St. George, and near the state's national parks. Using promotional postcards, Rugh illuminates the amenities and facilities available to tourists, the ways motel owners highlighted local culture and scenery in their logos and neon signs, and the descriptions of their vacations that visitors chose to share with friends and relatives to whom they sent the cards. As the number of tourists rose and an interstate highway system funneled travelers more efficiently from one destination to another, national lodging chains superseded many of the smaller, locally owned motels. This was one of many ways in which the very success of tourism undercut local Utahns' ability to profit from it.

On August 18, 2005, thirty-year-old Darla Woundedhead was fatally shot through the doorway into room 26 at the Dream Inn Motel at 1865 West North Temple Street in Salt Lake City. Five persons were charged with murder in the drug deal gone bad, most prominently Kerri Armant of Elko, Nevada, who pulled the trigger. Woundedhead was seven months pregnant when she was killed, and upon her arrival at the hospital, a baby girl was delivered by emergency cesarean section. Baby "Janie" was found to have traces of cocaine, opiates, and barbiturates in her blood. After a few months' care, she was released into the custody of her father, Carlos Manuel Najera Godoy, who had visited her daily.[1]

How Woundedhead, a member of the Oglala Sioux Indian Tribe of Pine Ridge, South Dakota, who had lost custody of three older children due to prior convictions for use and sale of drugs, came to die at the Dream Inn is a story worthy of attention not only for the tragedy of her life but also for what it reveals about Utah's decaying motels. Utah's historic motels that eventually became havens for prostitutes, drug dealers, and domestic-violence victims were once beacons to weary travelers passing through Utah on Highways 40 or 89.[2] Many were on their way somewhere else: families headed for Yellowstone or Las Vegas or California, or African Americans migrating from the South to the West Coast. Some were Mormons who had moved out of Utah and were bringing their children back to visit historic sites like Temple Square in Salt Lake City. They all needed a place to sleep for the night, and they found it in Utah's motels.

The era after the end of World War II in 1945 was the golden age of motels. Maps, guides, and motel postcards are valuable sources of information about where tourists stayed and what they did while visiting Utah. The rise of motels in the era of industrial tourism represented local history and culture to travelers seeking an authentic experience. As chain motels and hotels drew travelers away from historic motels in the 1960s and 1970s, tourist lodgings became part of a homogenized national culture, and elements of the vernacular landscape disappeared. By studying the state's historic motels, we learn about not only those who visited the state but also the local business interests that built the tourism industry in Utah's postwar years. Motels help us understand the growth of automobile tourism and how tourism remade the West. After putting Utah's motels in the context of national lodging trends, this chapter focuses on Salt Lake City, St. George, and the red rock regions near the national parks to explore the rise and decline of motels in Utah.[3]

THE GOLDEN AGE OF MOTELS

The word *motel* was coined in San Luis Obispo, California, in 1926 but did not become a standard term for roadside lodging until the 1950s. The post–World War II boom in the automobile industry, new federal highways, and generous vacation benefits fueled the trend of the middle-class family summer vacation. Increased travel presented an opportunity for mom-and-pop motels across the nation to fill the demand for affordable lodging, both as destinations and stopping points along the way. Motels replaced campgrounds or tourist homes (private homes renting rooms to tourists) because travelers valued safety, comfort, and convenience and were willing to pay more for amenities. Historians of motels argue that motels were a "home away from home . . . an

The Towne House Motel in Moab. Swimming pools, generally located in the front of the property for visibility, were a key form of advertising for Utah motels.

interface with the private automobile, further cocooning and protecting the traveler away from home."[4]

Motels had their roots in the seasonal tourist cabins of the 1930s, primitive accommodations without plumbing or amenities, sparsely furnished but better than sleeping in a tent or the car. In the late 1940s and early 1950s, travelers abandoned tourist cabins for motels, which offered softer beds, better furnishings, and indoor plumbing. Consumers quickly converted to the commodified overnight experience offered by modern motels. In 1945 about half of American Automobile Association members preferred hotels with the rest staying in motor courts and tourist homes. In 1950 motorists could choose from among a half-million rooms in motels or tourist courts, a predecessor of the modern motel. A building magazine bragged in 1953 that there were fifty thousand highway hotels and two-thirds of all road travelers stopped at them. The number of motels peaked in the 1960s with sixty-one thousand in operation but began to decline by 1965.[5]

Motels were constructed with "appealing design and landscaping" to attract travelers who viewed them while moving along a road at forty miles an hour. Large signs added a vertical dimension to the low-slung motel architecture, but more importantly, their symbols promised an enjoyable experience. Motel aficionado Wayne Curtis notes, "In the era before online booking, motels were essentially billboards for themselves."[6] Thus, during the golden age of motel building, the way a motel appeared from the road was instrumental in attracting guests. Motel architecture and signage were key to profitable operation, so smart owners invested in their façades and signs.

In the golden age of motels, swimming pools were a form of advertising. Motel owners upgraded properties to retain their customer base, most notably

Colonial Village Auto Court. Motor courts like this one were the predecessors of motels.

by installing a swimming pool. In Utah adding a swimming pool "had the greatest effect on sales per motel and per room." In Salt Lake City, pools were located in front of the property, where tourists could readily see them. The Scenic Motel at 1345 Foothill Drive added a heated pool with diving board in 1965, two decades after it was built.[7]

To advertise their business, about half of all motel owners joined referral organizations like the American Automobile Association or Best Western. Utah's motel owners advertised in local and national directories. A discriminating guide was *Lodging for a Night* by Duncan Hines, which listed ten Salt Lake City establishments in its 1953 edition, from Hotel Utah and Hotel Temple Square to the New America Motor Court (later Little America). Several that have survived into the twenty-first century were listed in the Duncan Hines guide: the Alta Motor Lodge, Colonial Village, and Snyder's Covered Wagon.[8] Attractive motel architecture and distinctive signs were imperative to lure roadside tourists who did not plan ahead. Tourists who did plan ahead made reservations through referral organizations or wrote after consulting a guide. The proprietors of Utah's motels pursued both strategies—signs and referrals—to appeal to the weary traveler behind the wheel.

Finally, motels provided attractive picture postcards free to their guests, who sent them out as a type of word-of-mouth advertising. Motel postcards provide a rich source of information about historic motels and their visitors. The postcards had merit as a medium of advertising alone because they typically listed the features they hoped would attract visitors, thus documenting the way a night's stay was sold. Annotated postcards also contain information about visitors' experiences in the motels and the way they experienced the city.

Colonial Village Motel, a converted motor court modernized for the 1950s traveler.

SALT LAKE CITY

Local boosters claimed Salt Lake City was the "Center of Scenic America." Since the early part of the century, when the "See America First" movement was founded in the city, community leaders had promoted it as a tourist destination. It was not hard to find a place to stay in Salt Lake City since motels lined Highways 89 and 91, which ran north and south along the Wasatch Front. Motels sprang up along Second West and State and Main Streets because they were the major arteries through the city. Highway 40 continued its way east at Twenty-first South Street, and some motels did cater to travelers along that route.[9]

As Salt Lake City became a common tourist destination, the number of motels increased. In 1947 the Salt Lake City directory listed thirty-six hotels (some of them residential like the Belvedere) and sixty-two lodging houses, many of them small tourist homes akin to today's bed-and-breakfasts. None of them used the label motel; nearly all were listed as hotels. A decade later, the 1957 directory listed lodging under two headings: hotels, and motels and auto courts. The number of hotels had risen from thirty-six to eighty-six, and the number of motels and auto courts nearly doubled to a total of 109. Of these nearly all chose the name motel or motor lodge, which implied a larger motel with a coffee shop. Just a few years later, in 1960, the number of hotels had dropped from eighty-six to seventy-eight, and by 1963 there were only sixty-seven listed in the guide. As the number of hotels decreased, the number of motels was more consistent, with just ten fewer in operation in 1960 than in 1957.[10]

Courtesy of UPC.

The Spiking Tourist Lodge.

The Colonial Village, at 1532 South Main Street, exemplifies the transformation of motor courts to motels. The name capitalized on the image of New England hospitality and a sense of community in its design. Built in 1937, it promised "Delightful Accommodations for Visitors in Center of Scenic America" on its postcard. By the early fifties, it had been renamed the Colonial Village Motel and had expanded to an oxymoronic "36 modern colonial cottages." It offered visitors an environment that was "quiet & cool" with "lawns & trees." Visitors were attracted by "an Added Feature—The Doll House (next door) A good place to eat. Home Style Food and 'Homey' Atmosphere." It attracted a New York visitor in September 1953, who wrote on the back of the postcard, "Hi! Trip is wonderful. Staying here tonight. Off to Reno tomorrow—so far have seen some beautiful country." The addition of a swimming pool made the motel even more attractive. The new postcard advertised, "Swim, Refresh, Relax Aboard the USS Colonial (beautiful heated pool)."[11]

Enterprising local businessmen, many with no prior experience in the lodging industry, saw motels as a good way to invest their retirement savings. At the same time, they envisioned motels as a family business, one that could employ family members and thus keep labor costs down. Because the owners of the first motels were from the region, they drew upon the iconography of local culture and history to sell their services to travelers. Along Highway 89, leading into Salt Lake City from the south, a cluster of motels featured local symbols to advertise for customers.

A good example of such a motel was the Spiking Tourist Lodge, which cleverly featured both the name of the owner and the local history. Orvin

Closeup of the Spiking Tourist Lodge sign, 2008. Owners of many Utah motels celebrated the local landscape and culture in the names and signs for their businesses.

Spiking was a successful florist, who built a twenty-room tourist lodge on State Street just south of downtown Salt Lake City. Although he only held onto the motel for a few years before selling it in 1951, Spiking seemed typical of these early motel owners: a middle-aged family man with little experience in motel management but previous success in business. Spiking sought to promote the motel's high visibility and unique features to make it a stand-out attraction. His sign was a pun on his own name and a reference to local history, the driving of the golden spike in Utah that completed the nation's first transcontinental railway in 1869.[12]

A few blocks away were Bob's Zion Motel and the Temple City Motel, which hoped to benefit from a perceived local connection with the Mormon Church. Since many of the tourists to Utah were natives who had moved to other parts of the country in the postwar Mormon diaspora, they were familiar with local symbols. The Temple City Motel sign included a neon-outlined replica of the Mormon Temple that may have held a special appeal for Mormon travelers. Motels near Temple Square at the center of Salt Lake City, a prime destination for visiting Mormons, likewise capitalized on local themes. The Covered Wagon Motel was obviously meant to remind customers of the overland pioneer trek in 1847, perhaps not unlike the trek some had made in their cars on the highway! On its postcard, the Temple Square Motel made much of its location across the street from the city's number-one tourist attraction.[13] All these motels were located on the major highways entering the city, so their signs were designed to attract travelers looking for a place to stay. At night the neon signs were an even-more-dramatic inducement to weary travelers to choose that particular motel for a place to sleep.

Even the briefest note on a postcard tells us that Temple Square was the number-one attraction. A couple staying at the Tower Motor Lodge (1009 South State Street) wrote in July 1963 to Raleigh, North Carolina, "We enjoyed our visit to the Mormon Temple. We are enjoying everything. Love, Julie and Ovid." Their satisfaction may have been due to the fine accommodations at the Tower: "air conditioned, steam heated, unexcelled beds, tub and shower baths, attractive sun porch and roof garden affording magnificent view of mountains." During the summer, Temple Square was open in the evenings, and visitors could photograph the exterior and grounds of the Temple and tour the Tabernacle. A guest at the American Tourist Lodge sent one of its postcards in July 1952 to her friend in Stoughton, Wisconsin: "Dear Laura:—We arrived here yesterday, took in the Temple last night." Maybe the guide's remarks made an impression on her. Punning on Brigham Young's famous statement, she wrote, "This is the place we are staying, leaving for Yellowstone tomorrow noon."[14]

Some visitors combined business and pleasure, like a woman and her daughter from Omaha, who were along with Dad on a business trip in October 1947. They stayed at the Sorensen Western Motor Lodge, 323 West North Temple Street, and wrote home, "Haven't seen much of city yet except Rosie and I went to see 'Foxes of Horrors' last night while Dad went to bed. Dad is busy seeing guys so Rosie and I are soon starting out with the car to see what we can see and expect to go to the Temple at 12 to hear the organ." By staying at the Western Motor Lodge, they were within a few blocks of Temple Square and the downtown movie theaters. The Tabernacle was a favorite sightseeing spot because of its free organ concerts at noon. A 1954 sightseeing map featured the Tabernacle on its list of recommended attractions: "This mammoth oval auditorium with its great domed roof seats 8,000 people. Its unique design and construction, its huge pipe organ and the remarkable acoustics of its interior have made the Tabernacle world famous."[15]

Judging from the postcards, eating was an important part of the travel experience. Liz from Colorado wrote in August 1952, "Dear Montie: We made it to Vernal Utah for supper last night and to S.L. City for breakfast. We are having the car serviced now. We were rained on some but it was clear on the ridge trail it was a super trip the peaches were so good for lunch." She was writing on a postcard from Chick N'Box, a chain originating in 1950 in Salt Lake City. Guests at Covey's New America frequented its Hot Shoppes café and coffee shop. Pilot's Motel, near the airport on west North Temple, boasted the Pilot's Café that attracted young and old. China Village was a popular spot downtown, and Dee's hamburger restaurants offered great drive-in service at low prices.[16]

For those who could not afford to eat out, motels with kitchenettes helped keep expenses low. The postcard for Boulevard Tourist Lodges at 1457 South Main Street advertised, "All Electric Kitchens and Refrigeration" but

Courtesy of UPC.

This postcard for the Temple Square Motel depicts three elements of the 1950s family vacation: the nuclear family, the motel, and the family automobile.

not apparently for all units. One traveler complained in the card she wrote to Spokane on July 8, 1948, "This is where we stayed. We didn't have kitchen though Jerry & Arlene went Swimming at Saltair last night. Went thru Salt Manufacturing place." Saltair was a quick drive or train ride from the city. Swimmers enjoyed floating in the water despite the briny smell and lingering salt crust on their skin. In its heyday, Saltair featured an amusement park with a roller coaster and fast food stands like Tater-Dog. Evening visitors enjoyed the dance floor at Saltair. A fire destroyed the roller coaster in 1957, and Saltair closed in 1958.[17]

Not all travelers had their pick of motels. During the era of Jim Crow, African American travelers were refused service at most motels and restaurants throughout the country, not just in the legally segregated South. To avoid the humiliation of being turned away, blacks used specialized directories that catered to travelers of color in an era of de facto racial segregation. *The Negro Traveler's Green Book* (which began publication in 1936) and *Travelguide* (which dates from 1946) were both published in New York and had a nation-wide distribution.[18]

For Salt Lake City, the guide listed the St. Louis Hotel and Café at 242 West South Temple Street, the New Hotel J.H, and the YWCA as places open to black travelers. Mrs. Rutha Johnson took in guests (with meals) at 340 South Ramona Street, and in 1955 Sam Sneed opened the Sam Sneed Hotel at 250 West South Temple Street. A few more hotels were added in 1959: the Pacific Hotel and Jenkins Hotel near the Sam Sneed Hotel and the Hotel Harlem at 528 ½ West Second South Street. Located on the near west side, the hotels were

ROBERTS HOTEL, PROVO, UTAH   119877-N

African American travelers were welcome at only a few Utah hotels and motels prior to 1964, one of which was the stately Roberts Hotel in Provo.

not far from the city's notorious red-light district to the south. In 1962 the same five hotels served travelers of color in Salt Lake City: Harlem Hotel, Jenkins Hotel, Sam Sneed Hotel, St. Louis Hotel, and the YWCA. African Americans were often refused service at restaurants while traveling. In 1958 the guide listed only three restaurants for travelers of color in Salt Lake City: the Bamboo Restaurant at 755 South State Street, the Rotisserie Inn at 323 South Main Street, and the Harman Restaurant at 1270 East Twenty-first South Street.[19]

Although Salt Lake City was larger, Ogden was more open to African American travelers, probably because the railroad's Pullman porters made it their home. According to the travel guides, Bigler's Washington Motel, the Hotel Royal, and the Marriott Motel accommodated any guest regardless of color. Outside Ogden and Salt Lake City, black travelers were taking a chance on finding a place to stay. In 1953 travelers could stay reliably at the Roberts Hotel in Provo and the State Line Hotel in Wendover. Title II of the Civil Rights Act of 1964 made discrimination illegal in public places, although it persisted pervasively for some time. As a result of strong local lobbying by the NAACP and protests at local roller rinks and bowling alleys, Utah passed the Public Accommodations Act that allowed blacks access to the city's motels in 1965.[20]

Salt Lake City's motels provided travelers a place to stay with modern amenities like tiled baths, steam heat, carpeting, and air-conditioning. Because they were locally owned, motels drew upon symbols of local history like the Temple to create an authentic encounter with local culture. The motels that lined State and North Temple Streets provided affordable lodging for tourists who visited Temple Square and Saltair and went downtown to see movies or eat out. Until

1965 the golden age of motels applied only to white travelers, and black travelers were welcome at only a handful of motels in the city. Entrepreneurs like Orville Spiking and Sam Sneed were typical of local investors who went into the lodging business with capital earned from their major employment. Eager to make money while employing the family, they had little experience in the hospitality business, so they were unprepared to compete against the later corporate influx of motel chains.

St. George

In the postwar era, St. George emerged from its pioneer past to become a major stopping place on the route from Los Angeles to Utah's national parks and Yellowstone. Previously accessible by rail, Zion and Bryce National Parks were popular automobile tourist spots by the 1940s, and the Zion-Mount Carmel Highway provided access to automobiles and bus tours. With the creation of U.S. Highway 91 in 1930, tourist courts and motels sprung up in and around St George. They ranged from ten to thirty units each and were situated adjacent to diners and restaurants along Highway 91 or "the Boulevard," as it became known. In the 1950s, the Boulevard offered up to five hundred rooms to travelers.[21]

Early tourist courts offered a homelike atmosphere. The ten-unit Bennett Motor Court on U.S. Highway 91 was "a pleasant brick court on nicely shaded grounds. Comfortably furnished, air-cooled units have one or two rooms, electric heat and shower or tub baths. $5." The Motel St. George was where Ann from Paso Robles, California, stayed in 1948. She wrote, "Stayed overnight in one of these lovely cabins—$5 twin beds 85 cents for 2 lamb chops. Warm coming thro desert but it's perfect today."[22] Tourists found respite from the desert heat in the shaded motor courts of St. George.

Like their counterparts in Salt Lake City, St. George motel owners relied on creative signage to attract guests. The Paceo Lodge featured a southwestern style, with a man in a sombrero sleeping under a cactus. The postcard advertised, "Nice air-conditioned units with telephones, central heat and tiled shower or tub baths; some units have free radios; fireplaces. Restaurant near by." All this was available for $4.00 to $4.50 a night. Motel names, such as the Coral Hills and the Dixie Palm (formerly the Western Jayhawk, presumably built by a former Kansan), reflected the local environment.[23]

A good example of motel development in St. George is the Wittwer Travel Lodge, built in 1954. Moving to St. George from Las Vegas, where they had operated the Wittwer Motel with their brother, Lester and Vanola Wittwer built a twenty-seven-unit travel lodge. The Wittwer Travel Lodge included a heated swimming pool, refrigerator, and air conditioner, renovations that allowed the motel to satisfy the traveler's desire for the newest, most modern amenities available. Postcards for the Wittwer Travel Lodge boasted, "Fully tiled bathrooms and showers, heated swimming pool and oversized beds." Many of the

The Wittwer Travel Lodge in St. George, which opened in 1954.

travelers were known as "day sleepers," tourists who chose to avoid the heat by sleeping during the day and traveling at night on their way to Disneyland or Los Angeles.[24]

Places like the Motel St. George offered "kitchenettes" for travelers who wanted to prepare their own meals, but a number of restaurants also were available for the hungry traveler. The Sugar Loaf Café advertised itself as "one of Southern Utah's most popular eating places." The Big Hand Café was also conveniently located at the Greyhound bus depot in the heart of town and offered "steaks, chops, sea food, and fried chicken." Dick's Café, which was across from the Jayhawk Motel, grew from eight seats at a counter in 1935 to a capacity seating more than two hundred people in the 1960s. Dick's, owned by Dick Hammer, a rodeo announcer, was noted for its memorabilia collected from movie stars like John Wayne, who frequented the café while filming in places like Snow Canyon nearby.[25]

Like the first motel owners in Salt Lake City, the Wittwers were pioneers in the modern motel-building movement in Utah. They relied on family money and labor to create a prominent tourist landmark on the main highway through St. George. The Wittwer Travel Lodge was a bridge between the older tourist courts and the corporate franchises that began to dominate in the following decades. Dick's Café was similarly local, drawing upon western rodeo themes and locally made movie memorabilia to put St. George on the map for highway travelers in Utah.

Utah's Red Rock Regions

Utah's bit of Hollywood was left behind as tourists drove northeast into Utah's red rock region, home to three national parks: Zion, Bryce Canyon, and Arches. The parks were developed by the railroads, but in the postwar era, they welcomed more automobile travel. If they had the AAA *Western Tour Book* (1953) in the glovebox, tourists read that Zion National Park "features Zion canyon, spectacular multi-colored gorge in the heart of southern Utah's desert and canyon country." Points of interest included the East Temple, Court of the Patriarchs, Great White Throne, Great Organ, and Temple of Sinawava. Inside the park, the Zion Lodge offered 143 "attractive" units (117 with baths) at rates up to $6.50 from mid-June to early September. Cheaper accommodations could be found at the Zion Camp Center, open from mid-May to mid-October for $2.50 a night.[26]

More likely tourists stayed in the town of Springdale at the entrance to Zion. In Springdale (population 125), the AAA recommended the Zion Rest Motel on State Route 15: "A comfortable motel, ½ mile from west entrance to park. Air-cooled units have one or two rooms, shower baths and electric heat. Restaurant convenient." Postcards for the Zion Rest Motel boasted a heated swimming pool, bedside telephones, and air-conditioning. Its proprietors promised "true western hospitality," and the AAA rated it as "a comfortable motel." An alternative was the Driftwood Lodge, which had its own restaurant. Grandma's Kitchen was a popular place to eat in Springdale with its "old-fashioned hospitality and quaint surroundings." An adjacent gift shop made Grandma's a one-stop shopping experience for tourists.[27]

Tourists headed for Bryce Canyon left Zion National Park via the Mount Carmel Highway completed in 1930. Triple A's *Western Tour Book* explained that Bryce Canyon National Park covered "more than 36,000 acres and contains some of the most colorful rocks of the earth's crust, shaped by erosion into grotesque forms. . . . Domes, spires, and temples cover the floor and walls, decorated in all the colors of the spectrum, with reds, pinks and creams predominating." Bryce Canyon was open daily in the summer for only a one-dollar entrance fee. A California woman who arrived at Bryce in mid-May of 1955 wrote home about the scenery: "Well!!! We had the rare privilege of riding from Glendale Utah in a snow storm and seeing Bryce covered with snow and lovely soft flakes falling on us. I'm almost speechless and long ago ran out of oh's and ah's—lots to tell."[28] The California visitor discovered it was still winter in Utah's canyons.

Tourists could stay at Bryce Canyon Lodge from mid-June through September or at the Sleeping Lodges, which were individual cabins for guests. Camping began in May at the Bryce Canyon Camp Center for those on a budget. If a room was not available at the lodge, you could stay at Ruby's Inn, founded in 1923. Tourists also stayed in nearby Panguitch. The high end of lodging there was the Hi-Way Lodge with "a new idea in tourist accommodations—free inside parking." Guests at the Trail Lodge, at 500 North Main Street on U.S. Highway 89, paid a bit more for its "colonial design" and "well-kept rooms [with] radios, central heat and tiled shower baths." The Cameron Motel & Hotel offered forty "comfortable hotel rooms" but only thirty-five with baths. In 1953 rates were two to four dollars for a single room. The rooms "are attractively furnished and have vented heat and tiled shower or combination baths." Especially for tourists, "colored slides [were] shown each evening."[29]

In eastern Utah, Moab was the closest town to Arches National Monument, which came into its own in the 1950s. Charlie Steen put Moab on the national map with his Mi Vida uranium strike in 1952, briefly making the town the "uranium capital of the world." Civic leaders capitalized on the excitement to promote growth in the region. They established local events to bring publicity to the area. In July of 1956, Moab hosted an areawide competition for "Miss Atomic Energy of 1956 of the Colorado Plateau." A month later, Moab celebrated the first "Uranium Days," a two-day festival and gathering designed to bring publicity and tourism to Moab.[30]

The Moab Lions Club, a group of local businessmen and community leaders, made a concerted effort to capitalize on tourism through road-paving projects designed to enhance the accessibility of Arches. Sam Taylor took over the *Times-Independent* newspaper in 1956 and became an outspoken proponent of bringing visitors to Arches National Monument. Taylor and other civic leaders held informal slide shows weekly on Main Street with the hopes of encouraging people passing through to stay a day or two longer and see the sights. Later, Arches Superintendent Bates Wilson formalized the slide show and produced an informational video played on the local television station.[31]

Arches in the 1950s could prove a daunting experience for the average tourist. By 1959 Arches broke all previous records with 59,819 visitors during the calendar year. Wilson oversaw construction of new roads and bathroom facilities and met with VIP visitors to promote Arches. He was not, however, removed from the bizarre predicaments of the average tourist. In his monthly report of May 1957, Wilson wrote, "Most of our time in the past month has been spent in herding visitors out of the area before a rain and pulling those strays who got by us out of the mud after a rain."[32]

Tourists got lost, sometimes with dire results. In July 1959, Wilson expressed some exasperation after being up twenty-four hours straight assisting the Grand County Sheriff's office in rescuing a family of eight who had gone missing after they had set out from Moab to see Dead Horse Point. When they were finally located, it took five hours via jeep to reach them. They had spent the night outside, and since they had no food, they nibbled on prickly-pear cactus leaves and drank water from the broken radiator in their car. After their safe return, Wilson wrote, "It is unbelievable what poor judgment the average tourist has and there is no predicting what stupid things he will do."[33]

Encouraging tourism at Arches meant that Moab had to expand its lodging facilities. For a long time, the only motel in Moab was the eight-room Atomic Motel, named in honor of the uranium boom. Local businessmen built newer motels to lure tourists with comforts to insulate them from the environment. For example, the Towne House Motel featured room phones; air-conditioning; wall-to-wall carpets; Beautyrest beds; ultramodern, ceramic tile baths; thermostat-controlled heat; and piped music to each room. Visitors would find it convenient with its coffee shop and dining room, and heated pool. Travelers expected "ultra-modern" comforts to deal with the heat. Two tourists from New Jersey wrote home in 1956 from the Utah Motel on Highway 160, "This is a nice air conditioned motel and you need it here. Many interesting things around here but its desert country and hot as _____[hell]." The most creatively named local motel was the Apache, so named for the fact that John Wayne and other Hollywood celebrities had stayed there when they filmed *Fort Apache* in 1948 in Monument Valley.[34]

If they could not nab a spot in the park lodges or campgrounds, tourists to southern Utah's national parks found places to stay in the motels along the highways and small towns near the parks. In the wake of Moab's uranium boom, locals built motels with names like the Apache to provide accommodations for tourists to Arches, a park that did not have its own lodging. Thanks to local entrepreneurs, tourists found escape from the desert's horrid heat in air-conditioned motels with modern comforts.

END OF THE GOLDEN AGE

By the early 1960s, the golden age of motels was coming to an end. "The era of the small home builder who went into the motel business is over," declared the *Hotel/Motor Hotel Monthly* in its special research report in 1962. Rising bankruptcies and high turnover signaled the exit of small-scale owners from the motel business. The end of the "do-it-yourself" era led to the shrinkage in the number of motels in the face of the growth of motel chains. From their start in 1953 to 1962, Holiday Inns had grown to 300 motor hotels, Howard Johnson had 134, and TraveLodge had 216 motels.[35] The chains built their hotels close to the city center and aimed to attract not just the family vacationer but also the convention and business trade. They may have been locally franchised, but their architecture and amenities were standard throughout the nation with no hint of local color.

The national transition from mom-and-pop motels to corporate chains played out on the local stage in Utah. A study of Utah's motel industry in 1965 by James Swatsenbarg of the University of Utah noted the transition from small to large motels, similar to national trends in the lodging industry. Based on a survey of Utah's motel owners, it concluded that smaller motels were less profitable, in part because their owners were less experienced in business. Older motels could not compete because of an aging appearance.[36]

The professionalization of the motel industry occurred at the moment the interstates appeared, and rural motels on the old highways began to lose customers to urban motels that were accessible to interstates. Many city motels were dealt a blow by the construction of Interstate 15 that replaced U.S. 89 and 91, and Interstate 80 that replaced U.S. 40. In 1960 I-15 terminated at 500 North Street, but by 1967 it had been completed to 5300 South Street. By 1976 both I-15 and I-80 were complete, and I-215 was a spur to the airport northwest of Salt Lake City.[37] Changes in the road patterns routed tourists away from the highway motels that could no longer attract guests with a handsome appearance or a flashy neon sign.

The shift away from the automobile to air travel disadvantaged local motel owners at the same time that winter tourism boomed in the early 1960s with the expansion of sports like skiing. The successful slogan of "Ski Utah" helped create double-digit increases in ski visits in the 1960s, and the number of visits rose from 195,000 in 1960 to 649,000 in 1970. Many winter vacationers landed at the airport and drove or took shuttles to the newly popular ski resorts in the mountains, avoiding Salt Lake City entirely.[38] With the completion of Interstates 15 and 80 in the mid-1960s, visitors no longer traveled along the old highways and State Street looking for a place to stay. Instead, visitors to the city, many of them there on business, relied upon the reservation services of the major hotel chains like Holiday Inn, TraveLodge, and Marriott that ringed the downtown area.

The changing patterns of travel and tourism to Utah also affected the rural landscapes in the red rock regions. Travelers skirted the villages near the national parks because they could cover more miles on the new roads and stay in larger towns with more amenities or the expanded park-visitor facilities. Visits to Zion National Park almost doubled in the 1950s, crowding campgrounds. As automobile air-conditioning became standard, travelers between Utah and California no longer slept in St. George motels in the daytime to avoid the heat. Recreational enthusiasts who wanted to paddle the rivers or ride mountain bikes sought a wilderness that they threatened with their need for equipment rentals, food, and lodging. Towns like Moab experienced a visitor boom that taxed local resources, and without sufficient local capital to build enough motel rooms for a seasonal market, local owners bought franchises of national chains, resulting in a loss of local character and history.[39]

Despite the deterioration of locally owned motels, they remain historically important. These motels pioneered modern lodging for the tourist at a critical time, when the state was laying the groundwork for the strong tourist-based economy it enjoys today. The early motels marked out geographic areas of tourism in the state's towns and cities where travelers could find a bed and a meal for reasonable prices. The amenities these motels offered—from steam showers and tiled baths to Beautyrest mattresses and piped-in music—demonstrate that Utah's local motel owners were competing for guests in a regional and national travel industry.

The locally owned motels played a major role in the transformation of the western economy away from agriculture and industry toward the service economy of tourism. State officials created brands with slogans that evolved into the elaborate multimillion-dollar marketing campaigns of the early twenty-first century. By 1972 tourism was ranked as the second-largest industry in the state and generated an income of nearly $209 million per year. More than three decades later, the transformation of the Utah economy had brought millions

Courtesy of UPC

Romney's Motor Lodge in Salt Lake, complete with attractive pools and a Kiddies' Fairyland, catered to young families in its heyday in the 1960s.

of visitors and reordered the state's economic priorities. More than ten million visits were made to Utah's national parks, monuments, recreation areas, and historic sites in 2005. At the end of the twentieth century, tourism was valued at more than five billion dollars in Utah's economy, and what visitors want mattered a great deal to government officials and developers from Moab to Salt Lake City. The displacement of locally owned motels by national lodging chains can be viewed as a "devil's bargain" that compromised the local character of the landscape in the face of the tourism juggernaut.[40]

THE STORY OF THE SURVIVORS

A half century after they first beckoned to highway travelers, many of the state's historic motels were in severe decline or had adapted to a changed business environment. A brief look at a few of the surviving motels can tell us a second story about the global forces reshaping the environment in which we live.

The Continental Motor Lodge on North Temple Street was four decades old when it was renamed the Gateway Motel to link it with the nearby Gateway shopping development built for the 2002 Olympics. Construction of the eighty-eight units in 1962 was a corporate venture, a partnership between Dee Anderson, the owner of Dee's Drive-Ins, and Capson Investment Company, a real estate firm. A swimming pool and a nearby Dee's restaurant made it a good choice for visitors coming to the city. After the Olympics, the Gateway catered mostly to transients but attempted to keep them firmly under control with rules limiting guests to two visitors per room after 9:00 p.m.[41]

Across the street, the Sorenson Western Motor Lodge became Scotty's Romney Motor Lodge, the "world's most photographed motel." It featured

Lake Hills Motel, predecessor of the Dream Inn, in its heyday.

Room 26 of the Dream Inn
Motel, Salt Lake City, 2006,
where Darla Woundedhead
was murdered.

several swimming pools and Fairyland for children. Scotty's Fairyland survived
more than half a century, perhaps because it was located next to the popular Red Iguana Mexican restaurant. By the twenty-first century, it was known
as the All Star Motel, and Scotty's guests were transients who could not find
affordable housing in the city.[42]

Similarly, demand for affordable housing kept the Colonial Village Motel,
built in 1937, in business for more than three-quarters of a century. The adjacent restaurant, the Golden Dragon, replaced the once-classy Doll House. The
motel had fallen from its former days of glory, but with a coat of fresh paint, it
looked more presentable than many other motels of its era. Rooms could be had
for only twenty-nine dollars a night, similar to all the historic motels in town
and sign of a competitive market. The pool was long gone, a victim of rising
rates for property insurance.

The recyling and reuse of the city's historic motels by new owners displayed
an entrepreneurial spirit similar to the pioneers of the lodging business who built
the motels in the middle of the twentieth century. Independently owned motels
became tools for economic immigrants to enter American society, establish

themselves, and become upwardly mobile. For example, in 2008 the sign for the café at the Overniter Inn on west North Temple Street advertised both a Mexican restaurant and a Korean café. Many of Utah's motels were owned by Patels from India, whose families efficiently operated roadside inns.[43] Global flows of immigrants from foreign countries supplied the capital and labor to keep many of the old motels in business.

Some of the historic motels retained their original function into the twenty-first century, such as the Scenic Motel at 1345 Foothill Boulevard and the City Creek Inn at 230 West North Temple Street. Both motels modernized their facilities and retained their charm, and managed to attract guests who wanted a more-authentic road-trip experience at an affordable price. In 2008 their neon signs still glowed every night, welcoming travelers who made their reservations on the Internet or by telephone long before they arrived in the city. The success of these historic motels is evidence that location is a key determinant of how long a lodging business can survive in a changing urban landscape. But these motels are the exceptions that prove the rule of the deterioration of motels and displacement of tourists to national chains with their standardized amenities.

Let's go back to the Dream Inn, where Darla Woundedhead died. A few months after the shooting, a visitor wrote a rave review online: "My wife and I had a splendid second honeymoon at this fine motel. The price was very reasonable and the room we stayed in was very clean and tidy." Far from appearing to be a haven for drug lords, the reviewer wrote, "the people at this motel all seem to know each other. We were encouraged not to be a stranger and by the end of our stay we had exchanged addresses and telephone numbers." He gave it top billing: "EXCELLENT! EXCELLENT! EXCELLENT! Don't miss out on this great motel."[44]

In the early twenty-first century, while most travelers chose corporate-chain motels, some tourists found hospitality at Utah's historic motels at one-fourth the price. Historic motels offered cheap lodging for those who needed a place to stay for less money. By staying at the Dream Inn or the Colonial Village, they also got an authentic taste of the city's local culture. When guests at the Dream Inn realized the shooting of Woundedhead was not the noise of firecrackers, they found out a night at the motel was more than they had bargained for.[45]

We ought to pay attention to these motels not just because they have provided affordable housing but also because they remain an important feature of the urban landscape. It is important not to delay the investigation because motels that survived earlier urban-renewal campaigns began to disappear when they came under the eye of developers. In 2007 Bob's Zion Inn on State Street closed after a fire, and the next year, the magnificent neon sign for the Capitol Inn fell off the building and was discarded. The construction of new infrastructure such as a Trax public-transit line along North Temple

Street may raise real estate values and make it more attractive to developers, who will tear down the historic landmark motels of the 1940s and 1950s and replace them with strip malls.[46]

Relics of the historic motels can be seen along Utah's city streets and country highways, hints of a once-vibrant automobile tourist economy that was locally owned and expressed local character. These historic motels, with their distinctive names drawn from Utah's local culture, persist as a refreshing antidote to the sanitized sameness of the corporate lodging giants. Is there any hope for saving these historic motels? And their signs? Are they even worth saving? Some think so. Efforts are being made to restore motels on sections of U.S. Route 66 and in Miami, Florida, gambles that their owners hope will pay off.[47] In Utah so many have reached a state of disrepair that they should probably be demolished. But their signs, with their distinctive iconography drawn from local culture, remind us of a bygone era when our streets and highways were bustling with tourists who drove by and, if they liked what they saw, pulled in to sleep for the night.

Notes

1.   "Murder Charges Filed in Pregnant Woman's Death," *Salt Lake Tribune*, August 26, 2005; Kirsten Stewart, "Baby 'Janie' Could Leave Hospital Soon," *Salt Lake Tribune*, 7 October 7, 2005. I would like to thank Samuel Willis for his able help as a research assistant.

2.   "For the Record," *Salt Lake Tribune*, September 13, 2005.

3.   For the importance of studying the urban landscape, see Dolores Hayden, *The Power of Place: Urban Landscapes as Public History* (1995; repr., Cambridge, MA: MIT Press, 1997); and John Brinkerhoff Jackson, *Landscape in Sight: Looking at America*, ed. Helen Lefkowiz Horowitz (New Haven, CT: Yale University Press, 1997). For a valuable local study, see Martha Sonntag Bradley, "Colliding Interests: Mapping Salt Lake City's West Side," *Journal of Urban History* 31 (November 2004): 47–74. On the search for authenticity, see Dean MacCannell, *The Tourist: A New Theory of the Leisure Class* (Berkeley: University of California Press, 1999).

4.   John Jakle, Keith A. Sculle, and Jefferson S. Rogers, *The Motel in America* (Baltimore: Johns Hopkins University Press, 1996), 56; see also Warren James Belasco, *Americans on the Road: From Autocamp to Motel, 1910–1945* (Baltimore: Johns Hopkins University Press, 1979).

5.   American Automobile Association, *Post-War Travel Trends, Survey by the American Automobile Association*, 1945, p. 11, California State Automobile Association Archives, San Francisco; James V. Malone, "Motels—A Big Opportunity for Builders," *American Builder*, February 1950, 116; Jakle, Sculle, and Rogers, *Motel in America*, 18–20.

6.   Malone, "Motels"; Wayne Curtis, "Motel Paradiso," *Atlantic Monthly*, June 2007, available online at http://www.theatlantic.com/doc/prem/200706/motels

7.   "Hotel Pools Continue to be Popular," *The Hotel Monthly* 70 (April 1962): 18; James L. Swatsenbarg, "A Survey of Utah's Motel Industry in Comparison with the Nation's"

(MBA thesis, University of Utah, 1965), 21; Reappraisal card 9–4526, Salt Lake County Archives, Salt Lake City.

8. Swatsenbarg, "Survey of Utah's Motel Industry," 30; Duncan Hines, *Lodging for a Night: A Directory of Hotels, Motels, Motor Courts, Guest Houses, also Some Vacation Resorts* (Bowling Green, KY: Adventures in Good Eating, 1953), 218–21.

9. "Salt Lake City 'Center of Scenic America,'" *Hotel Greeters Official Guide* 32, no. 2 (July 4, 1958), Utah State Historical Society, Salt Lake City; Maguerite Shaffer, *See America First: Tourism and National Identity, 1880–1940* (Washington, DC: Smithsonian Institution, 2001), 27; Jakle, Sculle, and Rogers, *Motel in America*, 18.

10. *Polk's Salt Lake City Directory* (Salt Lake City: R.L. Polk & Co., 1947), 1507, 1519–20; *Polk's Salt Lake City Directory* (Salt Lake City: R.L. Polk & Co., 1957), 131–32, 151; *Polk's Salt Lake City Directory* (Salt Lake City: R.L. Polk & Co.,1960), 174–75, 196–97; *Polk's Salt Lake City Directory* (Salt Lake City: R.L. Polk & Co.,1963), 152, 175–76.

11. Reappraisal card 7–461, Salt Lake County Archives, Salt Lake City; Utah Postcard Collection, box 8, folder 16, nos. 18, 19, 23, Special Collections, J. Willard Marriott Library, University of Utah, Salt Lake City (hereafter cited as UPC).

12. Donna Spiking, interview by author, December 2, 2005; UPC, box 8, folder 19, no. 21.

13. UPC, box 8, folder 16, no. 9; box 8, folder 19, no. 17; box 8, folder 17, no. 3.

14. Ibid., box 8, folder 20, no. 2; box 8, folder 16, no. 6.

15. Ibid., box 8, folder 19, no. 18; *Salt Lake City and Ogden-Provo* (Chicago: Rand McNally & Co., 1954).

16. UPC, box 8, folder 34, no. 4; Classified Photograph Collection, Utah Historical Society, Salt Lake City.

17. UPC, box 8, folder 16, no. 10.

18. Cotton Seiler, "'So That We as a Race Might Have Something Authentic to Travel By': African American Automobility and Cold-War Liberalism," *American Quarterly* 58 (December 2006): 1091–1117.

19. Leslie Nash and Richard Diamond, eds., *Travelguide: Vacation & Recreation without Humiliation* (New York: Travelguide, 1953), 91–92; Leslie Nash, ed., *Travelguide* (New York: Travelguide, 1955), 104; Victor H. Green, ed., *The Negro Motorist Green Book* (New York: Victor H. Green and Co., 1949), 70; Victor H. Green, ed., *The Negro Travelers' Green Book* (New York: Victor H. Green and Co., 1953), 68; *The Negro Travelers' Green Book* (New York: Victor H. Green and Co., 1956), 63; *The Negro Travelers' Green Book* (New York: Victor H. Green and Co., 1958), 64–65; *The Negro Travelers' Green Book* (New York: Victor H. Green and Co.,1959), 67; *The Negro Travelers' Green Book* (New York: Victor H. Green and Co., 1960), 114–15; *The Negro Travelers' Green Book* (New York: Victor H. Green and Co., 1961), 106; *The Negro Traveler's Green Book* (New York: Victor H. Green and Co., 1962), 90.

20. *Negro Motorist Green Book* (1949), 70; *Negro Motorist Green Book* (1953), 68; John S. McCormick, *The Gathering Place: An Illustrated History of Salt Lake City* (Salt Lake City: Signature Books, 2000), 193–95; and F. Ross Peterson, "'Blindside': Utah

on the Eve of Brown v. Board of Education," *Utah Historical Quarterly* 73 (Winter 2005): 4–20.

21. Douglas D. Alder and Karl F. Brooks, *A History of Washington County: From Isolation to Destination* (Salt Lake City: Utah State Historical Society, 1996), 233.

22. UPC, box 10, folder 13, nos. 9, 19.

23. Ibid., box 10, folder 13, nos. 1, 2, 12; *Western Tour Book* (Washington, DC: American Automobile Association, 1953), 291.

24. Royden Wittwer, interview by Sam Willis, July 7, 2006; Wittwer postcard in author's possession.

25. UPC, box 10, folder 13, no. 7; *Western Tour Book,* 291; Alder and Brooks, *History of Washington County,* 309–12.

26. *Western Tour Book,* 292.

27. Ibid; UPC, box 10, folder 11, no. 3.

28. *Western Tour Book,* 292, UPC box 4, folder 1, no. 5.

29. *Western Tour Book,* 291; UPC, box 5, folder 23, no. 7; http://www.rubysinn.com/rubys-history.html

30. Richard A. Firmage, *A History of Grand County* (Salt Lake City: Utah State Historical Society, 1996), 312–13, 324, 326.

31. Ibid., 295, 307, 324–25, 346; Samuel Taylor, interview by Sam Willis, September 2006.

32. *Superintendent's Monthly Narrative Report, May 1957,* Record Group 79, box 169, National Park Service, National Archives, College Park, Maryland.

33. *Superintendent's Monthly Narrative Report, July 1959,* Record Group 79, box 123, National Park Service, National Archives, College Park, Maryland.

34. Dean Stephens, interview by author, September 2006; http://www.kokopellilodge.com/; UPC, box 3, folder 41, nos. 4, 1.

35. "Special Research Report on a Dynamic and Changing Industry," *Hotel/Motor Hotel Monthly* 70 (October 1962): 17–31.

36. Swatsenbarg, *Survey of Utah's Motel Industry,* 33–37.

37. Tom Lewis, *Divided Highways: Building the Interstate Highways, Transforming American Life* (New York: Penguin, 1997), 140–42. Maps tell the story of the highway construction; see Phillips Petroleum Co., *Salt Lake City Street and Vicinity Maps,* (Chicago: H.M. Gousha Company, 1956); American Oil Co., *Salt Lake City, Ogden and Provo* (Chicago: Rand McNally & Co., 1960); American Oil Co., *Salt Lake City, Ogden and Provo* (Chicago: Rand McNally & Co., 1963); Chevron Oil Co., *Salt Lake City in Scenicland U.S.A.* (Chicago: H.M. Gousha Co., 1967); Conoco Oil Co., *Salt Lake City, Ogden* (San Jose: H.M. Gousha Co., 1967); Conoco Oil Co., *Touraide City Map of Salt Lake City, Ogden, Provo* (Chicago: Rand McNally & Co., 1976); all of these are located in Map Collection, Harold B. Lee Library, Brigham Young University, Provo, Utah.

38. Susan Sessions Rugh, "Branding Utah: Industrial Tourism in the Postwar American West," *Western Historical Quarterly* 37 (Winter 2006): 464.

39. Ibid., 466–67.

40. Ibid., 469; Hal S. Rothman, *Devil's Bargains: Tourism in the Twentieth Century West* (Lawrence: University Press of Kansas, 2000).

41. *Salt Lake Tribune,* November 5, 1961.

42. UPC, box 8, folder 19, nos. 14, 15, 16; and author's visits to the sites.

43. Asian Americans of Indian descent own more than half of the economy motels in the country; see information on the Asian American Hotel Owners Association available online at http://www.aahoa.com/ For one such motel in Utah, see Kirk Johnson, "American Album: Torn from Parents, a Top Speller Vents His Anger, Letter by Letter," *New York Times*, May 6, 2007.

44. Review of Dream Inn at http://utah.citysearch.com/review/10390869

45. Nate Carlisle, "Suspect Held," *Salt Lake Tribune*, August 20, 2005.

46. Heidi Toth, "Provo Files Suit for Arts Center Land," *Provo Daily Herald,* April 11, 2006.

47. Lisa Chamberlin, "Square Feet: Checking In: New Kicks on Route 66 for Commercial Builders," *New York Times*, June 10, 2007, available online at http://www.nytimes.com; Curtis, "Motel Paradiso"; see also Wayne Curtis, "Motel Nostalgia," available online at http://www.theatlantic.com/slideshows/motels/. The National Trust for Historic Preservation named the Doo-Wop Motels of Wildwood, New Jersey, as one of the eleven most endangered places in the United States; see information available online at http://www.nationaltrust.org/11Most/list.asp?i=178

4

Bernard DeVoto's Utah

David Rich Lewis

Scholars have used dramatic words—including Americanization, assimilation, transformation, and transition—to describe the evolution of Utah and Mormonism that occurred between 1890 and the 1920s. Others have questioned the magnitude and uniqueness of the changes that coincided with the turn of the century. In the following chapter, David Rich Lewis revisits those changes as they were blisteringly chronicled by one of Utah's most famous native sons: Bernard DeVoto. Lewis urges Utahns to set aside their native pride and see beyond DeVoto's acerbic wit. As he cites and summarizes modern scholarship, Lewis invites readers to distinguish DeVoto's exaggeration from the essential "truth and vigor" of the cultural observations underlying his irreverent portrait of Utah in the 1910s and 1920s.

I had gone to a reception at the home of a Harvard professor. I was vouched for by a youth ancestrally near to the Cabots and Lowells. Later in the evening our hostess, on her rounds among the freshmen, casually asked me where I came from—and three centuries of Boston Kultur kept her face expressionless at my answer. Thereafter she was at pains to be kind to me, visibly shielding me from the severities of Brattle street, Cambridge. But as I left, amazement triumphed.

"So people really <u>live</u> in Utah!" she exclaimed.

I could see pity in her eyes—and, also, apprehension. And no wonder, for she heard a noise at the gates of Harvard, yes, at the Johnstone gate itself—the bridles and scabbards of the Goths.

"But how?" she asked.[1]

For Utahns who have lived outside the state for any length of time, this exchange probably seems familiar. For those who haven't, it may sound like Mark Twain poking fun at us again. But Twain was more urbane and playful in his parodies, and the unfolding explanation of how Utahns "really *live*" is as subtle as a skinning knife wielded by Alfred Packer.[2] Further into this narrative, the discomforted will discern that the combative tone and sarcasm could only have come from a Utahn, probably an Ogdenite, undoubtedly a non-Mormon, and at that point feel justified in dismissing both messenger and message as the product of disgruntled outsiders: Goths at the Seagull Gate. It's the same today as it was in 1926 when the essay first appeared. In turning away from the piercing gaze of the writer, twentieth-century Utahns missed a most coherent explanation of the cultural and religious transformation then sweeping their society, one that continues to resonate in the historiography of Utah and Mormon history. The writer was Bernard DeVoto, and the essay was titled simply "Utah."

Bernard Augustine DeVoto (1897–1955) was born an outsider in Mormon Utah in Ogden, a town that had not worn the saddle of Mormonism comfortably since the arrival of the railroad.[3] Bernard's father, Florian, was a Notre Dame–trained academic of sorts—an intellectual Jesuit and lapsed Catholic, a vocal Mormon critic and social curmudgeon—whose mundane office work offered his family a modest living but left him frustrated and unfulfilled. He read widely and argued bitterly, his cynicism and intellectual contempt for those around him making him an outcast in Ogden society. Bernard's mother, Rhonda Dye, was the daughter of a pioneer Mormon who farmed the Weber River floodplain outside Ogden. She left the farm, married badly, divorced, then married Florian. A Mormon backslider who matched her husband's lack of religious adherence (if not his contempt or intellectual bent), Rhonda was the quiet protector of her misanthropic husband and their son, Bernard. Theirs was a happy married and family life by Bernard's account, if one of limited financial means and less social status.

Bernard was baptized a Catholic at five by his Aunt Rose DeVoto Coffman, but his father's intellectual agnosticism was his only true faith. Florian taught Bernard to read at three and then sent him to Ogden's Sacred Heart Academy, where he was the only boy in a class of Catholic girls. By ten, having returned to Ogden's public schools, DeVoto was an odd child, well versed in the Latin, Greek, and Italian epics his father loved and sharing the same scorn for Catholicism, prejudice against Mormonism, and contempt for what passed as "culture" in Utah. As a boy, he found his escape in books and the nearby mountains. He prided himself on his expert marksmanship and outdoor skills. By the time he graduated from Ogden High School, DeVoto was a complete social outsider—according to Wallace Stegner, "precocious, alert, intelligent, brash, challenging, irreverent, literary, self-conscious, insecure, often ostentatiously crude, sometimes insufferable. To Ogden he looked like a cowbird in a robin's nest."[4] He was a suspect guest in the homes of Mormon friends, particularly girlfriends. That social oddity was compounded by his looks, in particular a broad flat nose (smashed in a childhood baseball accident) in a round face and piercing brown eyes, hidden behind glasses in later years. Young DeVoto grew a caustic outer shell to protect a fragile psyche.

Anxious to leave Ogden but too poor to attend college at his father's alma mater, DeVoto entered the University of Utah in 1914. But what he witnessed there reinforced all his intellectual and religious prejudices. In the spring of 1915, the university fired four "radical" professors, including Charles Wilbert Snow, who had taught DeVoto's freshman English class. Common wisdom held that the firings were the result of the LDS Church using its invisible hand to subvert academic freedom at the university. Fifteen faculty members resigned in protest, the American Association of University Professors investigated and blacklisted the university, and the university's president ultimately relinquished his job.[5] DeVoto, the student, resigned as well.

Pooling his resources, DeVoto left to study English at Harvard University. It was a fateful trip, for in Cambridge he discovered the intellectual culture he found so lacking in Utah as well as an eastern effeteness and provincialism that was every bit as troubling as the western parochialism he had fled. In New England, he *became* western by the same process of self-study that had made him look eastward for culture as a child. He made his way through Harvard's conservative curriculum of literature and writing classes, he read the primary accounts of those who explored the West, and he developed a continental and historical vision that marked the rest of his career. He became one of the young radicals presaging the literary temper of the 1920s.

After a stateside stint in the Army as a second lieutenant and marksmanship instructor during World War I, DeVoto returned to Harvard University and graduated Phi Beta Kappa in 1920. But instead of leaving for Europe to join his peers and the literary scene of expatriate artists gathering in Paris, DeVoto returned to live in Ogden one last time. He told his friends he was immersing himself in the subject matter of his first novel. In reality he was seeking a safe haven, a place to calm his manic depression and insecurity while helping Florian in the wake of Rhonda's death the previous year. In Ogden he read voraciously and wrote some; he took a job in a bookstore and later taught United States history to junior high schoolers; and between bouts of illness and despair, he fell in and out of love with unobtainable women. He remained the outsider, exiled in his own land.

In 1922 DeVoto accepted an instructorship in English at Northwestern University, arranged by one of his Harvard mentors. He boarded the train for Chicago and left Utah behind, but he never really left Utah or the West intellectually. After five years at Northwestern, with two novels and a marriage to Helen Avis MacVicar to his credit, DeVoto quit the safety of the academy to live as a writer in Boston and then New York City.

Over the next twenty-eight years, DeVoto pursued a distinguished career as essayist, novelist, historian, lecturer, editor, critic, and cultural commentator. During his life, he published ten novels, four books of literary criticism,

Bernard DeVoto at his desk in his study.

four works of collected essays, and a trilogy of prize-winning histories of the American West. *Across the Wide Missouri* (1947) earned him Pulitzer and Bancroft Prizes, and *The Course of Empire* (1952) won the National Book Award for history.[6] DeVoto edited more than two dozen works, including the journals of Lewis and Clark and Mark Twain's papers. He published more than eight hundred essays, some while an editor of the *Saturday Review of Literature* (1936–38) and many more within his monthly "Easy Chair" column as the powerful editor of *Harper's Magazine* (1935–55).[7] The National Institute of Arts and Letters and the American Academy of Arts and Sciences inducted him as a member. He sat on the National Parks Advisory Board and counseled Illinois governor Adlai Stevenson on the West and environmental issues during his 1952 presidential campaign. For twelve years, DeVoto participated at the prestigious Bread Loaf Writers' Conference in Vermont alongside the likes of Robert Frost, A.B. Guthrie, Fletcher Pratt, and Archibald MacLeish. There he mentored adopted Utahn Wallace Stegner, who was then gaining fame as a novelist. The two shared similar interests in the land and histories of the West (even if their attitudes toward Mormons and Utah were near-polar opposites), and they formed a friendship that shaped both their careers.[8]

DeVoto moved among the eastern literary and political elite; his home was a haven for ideas, debate, and the search for the perfect cocktail, the famed DeVoto martini.[9] He was irascible, petulant, opinionated, and blunt but also intellectually generous, able and willing to change his mind when necessary.[10] He was a defender of the public lands and the American West but a critic of the West's tendency to devour itself for the benefit of eastern capital.[11] DeVoto lived his life outside Utah and the West, loving the land and its history but loathing the society it had become.

Bernard DeVoto is arguably Utah's most distinguished writer, still acclaimed nationally by both historians and literary critics more than fifty years after his death. Yet he is virtually invisible in the state—and especially in the city—of his birth.[12] Why? Because of his writing—really just three pieces in particular—youthful parting shots at a society that already scorned him.[13] Few Utahns then or now have read these pieces, making it easier for them to ignore DeVoto's entire career from a position firmly rooted in ignorance. The last of these three pieces of writing tells us more about Utah and the nation in the 1910s and 1920s than many would like to admit. It is both emic and etic, the cultural, political, and economic observations of a (simultaneous) native son and outsider. Hidden in the pain of DeVoto's skinning-knife assault is the illumination of a fundamental transformation then in progress, of Utahns having forsaken their distinctive past and becoming something else: boring, normal, modern.

The first piece is a thinly veiled autobiographical novel, *The Crooked Mile* (1924). DeVoto tells the story of a bright Harvard graduate, Gordon Abbey, buried in Windsor, a provincial western town that has lost its frontier strength and romance, degenerated, and become sadly commonplace. Abbey falls into the small-town miasma but then rediscovers his frontier heritage, verbally destroys some prominent locals, and rises above the vulgarity of Windsor. The novel reflects DeVoto's mixed and complex feelings about Utah—his love of the land, his fascination with the history, his disdain for the society. National critics were cautiously enthusiastic, but Ogdenites saw themselves in the secondary characters of the novel and denounced DeVoto.[14]

The second DeVoto piece was titled "Ogden: The Underwriters of Salvation," commissioned by Duncan Aikman for his anthology *The Taming of the Frontier* (1925), a collection of ten essays intended to chronicle the fall of western towns from their frontier exuberance to "Rotary dullness."[15] The assignment fit DeVoto's mood perfectly, and paying jobs answered his financial needs. Abandoning the façade of fiction, he produced a furious attack on the provincialism of his hometown. He intended the essay to enlighten historically and wound contemporarily, and it succeeded admirably at doing both.

Washington Boulevard in downtown Ogden in about 1928, three years after Bernard DeVoto lampooned the city as a "small backwater American city, less immaculate than most, less energetic, less comfortable, but at one with its fellows in drowsiness, in safety."

Ogden, wrote DeVoto, began as a "cowpath settlement" of "pious Mormons who tilled their fields and obeyed the prophet, who looked at the mountains but saw the meadows of Jerusalem."[16] They brought forth bread out of alkali soil, while the world passed them by. Then the railroad came, bringing saloons, sin, and progress. Ogden became something. Miners, prostitutes, and the Irish battled Mormons for economic and political control of Utah until the federal government grabbed Mormons "where the hair was short," forcing them to abandon polygamy. "So vanished the last energy of Utah, of Salt Lake City and of Ogden," wrote DeVoto. It was the end of the frontier.[17] After that Mormon joined Gentile in the business of worshiping money, together becoming smug and insufferable in their self-appointed righteousness—the "underwriters of salvation." Boosters intent on cleaning up Ogden for commerce destroyed what little color remained, leaving the city to its "dirt and mediocrity," a "small backwater American city, less immaculate than most, less energetic, less comfortable, but at one with its fellows in drowsiness, in safety."[18] Culture clubs, conformity, and dullness descended on an already-artless people, who polluted this magnificent mountain home by their very existence. Not one to let bigger fish off the hook, DeVoto also lampooned Mormonism ("a religion of thrifty visions") and Brigham Young ("This frontier Moses . . . who held one hand beneath his flatulence and nodded as he fancied God would nod").[19]

"Injustice," wrote H. L. Mencken, "is relatively easy to bear; what stings is justice." This was justice dispensed DeVoto style—"Bald scorn and name-calling," according to Stegner, "with enough fact to make it uncomfortable."[20]

It took a while, but Ogdenites eventually discovered the essay and howled at the public ridicule heaped on them by one of their own.[21] The sting might have faded had DeVoto's writing not caught the attention of H. L. Mencken, America's most punishing social and literary critic, who was busy tweaking the noses of both middle-class guardians and commercial salesmen of American culture (the "booboisie") in his new magazine, *American Mercury*.[22] DeVoto's essay lived up to Mencken's standards of startling invective and irreverence, particularly toward the smugly self-righteous. At Mencken's suggestion, DeVoto distilled the core of his fictional and critical commentaries on Ogden into a new essay, lifting his sights from hometown to home state. In that process, he captured something larger—the pivotal moment and the essence of Utah's transformation.

"Utah," published in *American Mercury* in March 1926, was DeVoto's answer to his fictitious hostess's question about life in the state. Utahns lived well, wrote DeVoto, in a rude, frontier sort of way until 1906, when the U.S. Senate voted to seat LDS Apostle Reed Smoot and ended "one of history's most hilarious wars, the sixty years' strife between the Mormon and the Gentile." In that moment, Mormons were rehabilitated and vindicated, monotony descended, and "since then the State has never enjoyed itself."[23]

DeVoto backtracks to take readers on a whirlwind tour of Utah history: from Dominguez and Escalante ("One wishes that the Spaniards had lingered somewhere in that vast expanse of mountain and desert"), to the courageous and skilled fur trapper ("a nervous system only a little more sensitive than that of a goat"), to the Mormons ("Pious cowherds who believed themselves capable of summoning angels to converse with them"), who killed whatever frontier poetry the previous groups had bestowed on the landscape.[24] Seeking isolation, Mormons plunked themselves in the overland path of progress and fought it out with forty-niners, the railroad, miners, and anything resembling culture. "No poets lingered there, no musicians, philosophers, or scholars. The atmosphere was neither cultured nor urbane, but it was interesting" as a "first-rate religious war" arose amid "crescendoes of bitterness and farce." On one side were Mormons, "staid peasants whose only distinguishing characteristics were their servility to their leaders and their belief in a low-comedy God." On the other were Gentiles, "less fanatical than the Mormons and less ignorant" but also "less robust," the "unfit of the frontier," who had "given out at the first oasis—and then stayed there."[25]

"For sixty years," DeVoto continued, "their warfare made the State a matrix of living color," catching the attention of Christians and congressmen ("these prurient fools, the worst injustice the Mormon heresy has had to bear"), who titillated their constituents with tales of Mormon murders and polygamous sex. In came the army and federal officials ("all corrupt and stupid politicians") to ride herd on the Mormon rabble, but in opposing Brigham Young, "they were child-like and innocent." Young's words rained down on them like artillery from the Tabernacle. "The curses of God, most dreadful, and the wit of a giant joker, most obscene, took off their hide in patches. The Gentiles fumed and threatened, but Brigham ruled and ridiculed."[26]

"Then," wrote DeVoto, "Brigham died. Pygmies succeeded him, and the Gentiles entered a bull market." Congress investigated, and reformers wailed as they "stared with horror at these monsters of bigotry and licentiousness." Gentile Republican fought Mormon Democrat in Utah until the LDS Church declared polygamy "inexpedient," and chastened leaders sought presidential amnesty. Certain that the "Mormon question" had been settled, Congress granted Utah statehood in 1896, but polygamy and Mormon hegemony lingered beneath the surface. A decade later the Republican-controlled U.S. Senate forgot history and seated Reed Smoot. Without the stigma of polygamy, "its worst encumbrance," the LDS Church "progressed more in ten years than it had in the preceding sixty." It became mainstream. As the "old generation of inflexible haters and rigid doctrinaires, who had seen Joseph [Smith] in the flesh, began to die off," Mormons "set profit above principle." Freed from polygamy, the younger generation abandoned agrarian communalism, downplayed muscular millennialism, shifted its allegiance to the Republican Party, and joined Gentiles in an "era of Good Feeling for the Sake of Business," blazing a new path to dominance in the state.[27]

You might think DeVoto had already said enough to get him lynched, but his recitation of Utah's past was only prolegomena to his commentary on the present, *his* present: the 1910s and 1920s. From a state peopled by "ruddy, illiterate, herd-minded folk," a state where "the very process of survival demanded a rigorous suppression of individuality, impracticability, scepticism, and all other qualities of intelligence," Utah became something worse—BORING. "How am I to suggest the utter mediocrity of life in the new Utah?" asked DeVoto. "How can I suggest its poverty in everything that makes for civilization?" No art, music, sculpture, or architecture; no novelist, poet, or educator was noteworthy enough to be recognized outside Utah. "No artist ever lived there ten minutes after he had the railroad fare out. If the presence of one should become known, the Mormons would damn him as a loafer and the Gentiles would lynch him as a profligate." What "pictures" could be found in the state were "life-size portraits of Mormon apostles and blue-ribbon Holsteins."[28] An "accident of birth, not residence" might mark some individual a Utahn, but the best talents left to earn a living elsewhere or were driven out, like the University of Utah professors fired for "disseminating ideas." Safely mediocre intellects were hired to replace them. "Such," DeVoto wrote sarcastically, "are the adornments of Utah, the flowers of its art and learning."[29]

"But the people?" They, wrote DeVoto, are "normal": a "commonwealth of greengrocers who have lifted themselves from the peasantry"; a society of farmers no different from those in Indiana, Iowa, or Nebraska, except "a little absurd in their belief that Jesus was inferior to Joseph Smith"; a nouveaux-riches gentry "newly developed in the Babylons of Ogden and Salt Lake City" who "lead the most swinish life now discernible in the United States." Poverty was rare, morality high, and civic virtue even higher. "The state's roads, schools, per-capita ownership of Fords, patriotism, sewer system and modernity of office appliances are, in fact, well above average. Those who have no interest in social or intellectual or artistic life may live there as well as anywhere else in this best of all possible Republics." From watching their parents beget their siblings in front of them in one-room shacks, this new generation became conscious of its wealth, bought closed cars, learned about the existence of beverages other than straight whiskey, and "experimented with golf pants for men and riding pants for women." "In short," DeVoto observed, "they became civilized."

Yet really they weren't. They thought Hoover greater than Caesar, Coolidge greater than Mozart, and ignored Gaugin, Osler, and Huxley, when even the freshest Hollywood ingénue had a volume of Freud with her when arrested by the police for loitering. Even the leaders of the state's university and agricultural college—those erstwhile guardians of civilization—were illiterate buffoons, accomplices to church censorship of thought and art. "Civilized life," wrote DeVoto, "does not exist in Utah. It never has existed there. It never will exist there." Utahns had become civilized but only enough to talk about "the Prophet, hogs, and Fords."[30]

A lack of civilization was one thing, DeVoto lamented, but "Even the ancient color of the State is gone. Mormon and Gentile dwell together in amity and Rotary." "The State," wrote DeVoto, ". . . is whooping up the fellowship with its fingers crossed." Gentile churches look elsewhere for moral missions. The *Salt Lake Tribune,* "once the archfiend of Mormon persecution, is now the guardian angel of the followers of the Prophet," and Mormon legislators repeal Mormon-backed anticigarette laws to please Gentiles at the behest of a Mormon governor. Gentile merchants hire Mormon clerks and refuse to sell books that poke fun at the church, while Mormon merchants hire Gentile clerks and "uncouth Temple union-suits give way to officially sanctioned lingerie with lace and ribbons." While Mormon Utahns continue to profess that "We are a peculiar people," they also raise the plaintive cry, "We are no different from other people." And in that desire, DeVoto opined, they have become sadly, boringly, predictably NORMAL.[31]

"How do people live in Utah?" DeVoto concluded. "They join the business-men's calisthenics class at the gymnasium. Or they buy Fords on the five-dollar-a-week basis. Or they yawn. Or they die."[32]

As a freshman at the University of Utah in 1926, Wallace Stegner recalled walking past a history professor's door as a copy of the *American Mercury* containing DeVoto's essay came flying out and skidded down the hall. Stegner recognized the exaggeration of DeVoto's rhetoric but was swept up in its "happy vehemence." "If he got a few innocent bystanders," wrote Stegner, "I was willing to sacrifice them for the pleasure of looking at the more-deserving corpses."[33]

The essay exploded in Utah, then mushroomed through word of mouth as Utahns uncovered DeVoto's earlier and less-restrained rips on Ogden. DeVoto's essays marked him as "Utah Enemy Number One," wrote Stegner, "the contemporary avatar of all the Missouri Pukes and Illinois mobbers who had attained immortality in the Mormon memory for their persecution of the Saints."[34]

Bernard DeVoto publicly roasted Utah as only a native could, skewering his victims between fact and overstatement with a sense of humor and the perspective they lacked. The attack wounded so deeply, as Wallace Stegner noted, because "Mormonism's commentary upon itself had for so long been an instrument of solidarity. Because Mormon history was faith promotion and Mormon biography was hero worship and mythology, there existed in many Mormon minds a suspicion that in this chorus of self-praise there was a certain implausibility. Mormons wanted the praise of non-Mormons, if only as corroboration."[35] DeVoto's essay did anything but corroborate their insider narrative. In fact, equal-opportunity offender that he was, DeVoto lumped Mormons and non-Mormons together, universalizing preexisting national perceptions of Utah's oddity, deflating the way that Utahns as a whole wanted the world to see them.

From the safety of Evanston, Illinois, DeVoto reveled in the short-term attention this essay brought him, but in the long run, he never thought much of it, never reprinted it in any of his essay collections. Over the following years, DeVoto did publish a number of essays where he expressed open admiration for the power of Mormon communalism and experiences settling the West. He admitted privately to Utah historian Dale Morgan that "I was young, bumptious, intoxicated with print" and "full of resentment of an environment that had been unfriendly to me always and sometimes actually contemptuous or even hostile." In 1943 he offered a public apology of sorts, calling the tone of those early essays "ignorant, brash, prejudiced, malicious, and . . . irresponsible," a capitulation to the "*Mercury* mood," but he remained certain that what he had said was factually correct and legitimate, however stated.[36]

Being provocative, even confrontational, was DeVoto's rhetorical style. He was always more effective making a case when he had someone or something to argue against—the bigger, the better. "No point in putting a silencer on the gun when you shoot a sheriff," he advised Wallace Stegner.[37] As both friend and biographer, Stegner understood DeVoto's style. He suggested that if we look past DeVoto's rhetoric and "learn to discount him ten to twenty percent for showmanship, indignation, and the inevitable warping power of his gift for language, . . . there remained one of the sanest, most acute, most rooted-in-the-ground observers of American life that we have had."[38] Considering the intellectually playful, but deadly serious, way DeVoto wields the cultural skinning knife in "Utah" and how difficult it is to see the present becoming past and the past becoming history, the percentage of DeVoto's essay that remains is a piercing cultural description and prescient analysis of early-twentieth-century Utahns (and Mormons) in motion.

Bernard DeVoto with a .38 police special. This photograph, which illustrates both DeVoto's wit and his combative style, was originally published in the 25 April 1936 issue of *Saturday Review* in connection with DeVoto's harsh review of Thomas Wolfe, "Genius Is Not Enough."

That DeVoto chose an iconic event and individual as the crucible for his commentary is not surprising. History by synecdoche (focusing on a part that illuminates the whole) was a literary device he used to great effect in his most celebrated historical writings.[39] But that he chose the seating of LDS Apostle Reed Smoot as a U.S. Senator in 1907, instead of the 1890 Woodruff Manifesto, as the pivot point for his commentary indicates, as Stegner suggests, his acute powers of cultural observation. As Kathleen Flake persuasively demonstrates, the Smoot hearings were a transformative moment in Mormon and Utah history. They involved more than simply whether or not a Mormon apostle could be a senator but rather, whether Mormons in general could be good and loyal citizens, given their theological distance from mainstream Protestant Christianity, their history of conflict with the federal government, their practice of polygamy (especially postmanifesto), and the hegemonic power of the LDS Church.[40]

When Provo businessman and apostle Reed Smoot was selected as Utah's Republican senator in 1903, Protestant forces nationwide rallied to protest his seating. They argued that Smoot could not fulfill his constitutional obligations because he was an ecclesiastical leader of an institution that condoned polygamy, required oaths and secret rituals incompatible with national loyalty, enforced economic communalism, and continued to dominate the lives of its

"The Real Objection to Smoot," *Puck*, 27 April 1904. Those who opposed Reed Smoot's seating in the Senate argued that Smoot could not fulfill his constitutional obligations honorably because he was an apostle of a church that condoned polygamy, resisted federal authority, and allegedly condoned murder.

members. Between 1903 and 1906, the Senate Committee on Privileges and Elections held hearings into Smoot's (monogamous) marital status but more specifically into the beliefs and actions of Mormon leaders. Subpoenaed to testify, LDS President Joseph F. Smith (and other leaders) had to distance the church from institutional complicity in the persistence of polygamy and the domination of local politics and yet simultaneously demonstrate their ability to deliver a cohesive Mormon bloc vote to the Republican Party. In the process, Smith was forced to downplay both his revelatory power and the last and most iconic revelation of Mormon founder Joseph Smith Jr.—polygamy. Joseph F. Smith's Second Manifesto (1904), promising to excommunicate those conducting postmanifesto plural marriages, and the subsequent punishment of apostles Matthias F. Cowley and John W. Taylor in 1906 were a painful, but necessary, part of his larger strategy: first, to secure Smoot in a position of political power, where he could protect church interests; and second, to steer Mormonism out of its nineteenth-century parochialism and toward the theological and social mainstream as a modern and nationally acceptable institution.

However, as Flake points out, Smith's strategy was not without serious costs to his authority among the faithful. Mormon identity, so bound through persecution to polygamy and the theological timelessness of revelation, was undercut by the Senate testimonies of church leaders, forced to lie to protect the church and each other. To rebuild member confidence in an unchanging orthodoxy in the throes of orthopraxic change, Smith shifted Mormon theological attention from Joseph Smith's last revelation—polygamy—to his first—his vision of God in upstate New York. Emphasizing this first vision and subsequent events leading to the foundation of the church helped stabilize a sense of group identity and difference, of continuity and revelation, and reaffirmed a Mormon sense of "otherness" without the politically and morally explosive issue of polygamy. Over the next decade, Joseph F. Smith bridged other theological discontinuities that this "modern Mormonism" entailed, transitioning polygamy to eternal marriage, deification to perfection, gathering to international growth, vengeance to reconciliation, communalism and separatism to capitalism and nationalism. These theological compromises reassured Protestants and senators that Mormons could be loyal and patriotic citizens, that Mormonism could approach mainstream Christianity, and that Congress could effectively regulate the LDS Church as an institution. At the urging of Republican President Theodore Roosevelt, who saw the political benefits of Mormon bloc voting, the Senate voted to seat Smoot.[41]

"When God's ultimate histories are written," DeVoto observed, "1906 will stand out as the first vindication of the Saints." While the "Gentiles succeeded in barring a polygamist from the House of Representatives . . . they could not bar Reed Smoot from the Senate." The "old warfare was over," an older generation passed on, and "Leadership and public feeling among the Saints tended to soften, to set profit above principle, to accept Gentiles as good pay. And the Gentiles began to see the necessity of compromise." DeVoto juxtaposed Smoot's seating against the experience of B. H. Roberts—Mormon intellectual, member of the First Quorum of the Seventy, Democrat, and polygamist—elected to the House of Representatives in 1898 but denied his seat by a Republican majority uncomfortable with Mormons, Democrats, and polygamists. Smoot's success marked the crucial pivot point in the "Americanization" of Mormon Utah: from Mormon Democrats to Republicans, from polygamists to monogamous moralists.[42]

As DeVoto noted, this transformation was not a Mormon one alone—both sides saw "the necessity of compromise." Neither was it instantaneous nor narrowly theological but part of a broader regional and economic transformation that straddled the Smoot hearings by two decades on either side. Cultural geographer Ethan Yorgason explains that the conservative modern Mormonism that emerged as Mormons "moved in a nationally conformist direction" reflected the "need to find ways for Mormons to live peaceably with non-Mormons."[43] Between 1880 and 1920, Mormons made a series of incremental institutional and mental shifts that transformed them culturally into something acceptable to the nation: from challengers to defenders of Victorian morality and gender relations, from communitarians to capitalist individualists, from religious political dissidents to loyal citizens identifying with national purpose and power.

In the wake of the Smoot hearings that seemed to settle once and for all the nation's "Mormon problem," both Mormons and non-Mormons sought to minimize their differences, to forge a safe haven from the old conflicts, where new regional "coalitions of power in politics and business" could emerge. They understood, Yorgason suggests, that they could not afford to reopen the old wounds by attacking each other lest they undercut that new order.

Under Joseph F. Smith, and later Heber J. Grant, the palpable presence of LDS Church authority in daily life faded, even as those leaders exercised new sources of power and found ways to assure members that they were still a peculiar (but not too peculiar) people. Non-Mormons compromised as well, deemphasizing the past, forging a consensus with Mormons that stabilized their newfound political power and reinforced their existing economic self-interest. Class interests bridged religious fault lines. As this new class coalition emerged, more than ever before, Utah "began to look and feel more like the rest of the United States."[44]

That Bernard DeVoto made such a headlong attack on both partners in this tenuous cultural peace may help explain the gravity of his sin and the longevity of the grudge. It is this cultural transformation and compromise—evidence of changing orthopraxy, of the expediency of corporate class and political power whereby "Mormon and Gentile dwell together in amity and Rotary"—that was the essence of DeVoto's critique of modern Utah.

But the local specifics of DeVoto's critique—that there was no art, literature, music, or cultural or intellectual life in Utah—seemed to sting Utahns the most and continue to irk modern readers to the point of distraction. Although window dressing to his larger argument, those remarks were likewise perceptively on target.[45] Utah, in the 1910s and 1920s, was no cultural Mecca. As historian Thomas Alexander notes, the humanities in Utah experienced a "fallow" period stretching from 1880 to the 1930s, while the visual and theatrical arts "deteriorated under the onslaught of lowbrow, cheap, and increasingly accessible, nationally sponsored entertainment."[46] Aside from religious tracts, Utahns produced little imaginative prose or even history of note, and the popular Home Literature movement and women's literary clubs generated safe, formulaic works by forgettable authors.[47] Composers, symphony musicians, and vocal soloists disappeared in the collective voice and limited repertoire of the Mormon Tabernacle Choir.[48] Nationally renowned sculptors like Cyrus Dallin and Mahonri Young; painters like John Hafen, James Harwood, and Mary Teasdel; actresses like Maude Adams were, as DeVoto pointed out, the result of an "accident of birth, not residence." While some talented artists and intellectuals were able to live at home by securing teaching positions, Utah's greatest cultural talents worked outside the state, where their art and intellect were recognized and rewarded. DeVoto ultimately became one of them.[49]

While DeVoto's cultural critique was specifically local and personal—that Utahns had joined the rest of the nation in their conspicuous consumption and cultural conservatism, their praise of Republicans and big business; their small-town mediocrity, unabashed boosterism, Protestantism, and lack of culture—it reflected a broader reappraisal of what was then occurring in American society, voiced, in part, by one of our greatest generations of writers: Lewis, Fitzgerald, Dos Passos, Hemingway, Cowley, Masters, Dreiser, Anderson, and Mencken himself. This Lost Generation of "Young Intellectuals" criticized the crassness and anti-intellectualism of post–World War I American society, some from the cities and some from the safety of Europe.[50] In 1926, from the shelter of Northwestern University, DeVoto sided with the rebels in their attack on "Main Street," "Babbitt," and "dullness made God." In later years, he turned his opinionated wrath on the rebels themselves, arguing that they had gone too far, caricaturized too much, thrown the baby (the essence of democracy) out with the bathwater (the turbulence of the American experience).[51] But in 1926, he joined them, using Utah as a cultural synecdoche for the nation.

In the end, Bernard DeVoto was right—people really *do live* in Utah but with a past and present that often traps them in the ways they imagine and project themselves. In 1926 he pointed his cultural lens at his home and took a series of still images that, when arranged and fanned through sequentially, capture a kinetoscopic sense of the cultural transformations (in Utah, the LDS Church, and the nation) swirling around him. Blurred at points, jerky and incomplete at others, it is not the movie Utahns wanted to project, but it resonates, largely uncredited, in the current historiography of both church and state. It also resonates in Utahns' continued search for a religious and state identity beyond Mormonism and polygamy. When DeVoto observed that Utahns lost whatever exceptionalism they had claim to when they abandoned their colorful past and became sadly, boringly normal, he played on their basic human vanity and fears of being irrelevant at worst, the butt of a national joke at least. He put his finger on an institutional dissonance within Mormonism specifically as church leaders reworked theological memory and an identity grounded in peculiarity. The continuing insistence on peculiarity—even as Mormons insisted they were like everyone else—seemed more elusive in the twentieth century as their claims became more strident. In the transformation, this altered identity became a most difficult pill to swallow. It still is.[52]

The story of DeVoto's "Utah" also reminds us of the perils and prospects of writing and teaching state history. Too often cast in narratives that are triumphal, celebratory, parochial, and boosterish—a litany of firsts, biggests, highests, mosts in competition with the accomplishments of other states—state histories have the potential to become exceptionalist insider stories, sacrificing or suppressing voices and experiences that don't highlight state accomplishments, that don't affirm a positivist progressive narrative. In the process, they limit the more-complicated critical analysis needed to transcend state boundaries, to tell more-mature stories of multicultural, regional, and even national significance.[53]

DeVoto's is one of these dissonant voices and tells one of these stories, one that was (and is) hard for Utahns to embrace because it challenges our sense of self, our sense of humor, and the positive way we want others to see us and our very-human past and present. Like him or not, believe what he had to say or not, appreciate the way he said it or not, there is a truth and vigor in DeVoto's essay on life in Utah that transcends its reception, in 1926 or today, that presages and resonates in the analyses of modern scholars trying to explain *how* Utahns really lived in this most decisive of historical moments.

NOTES

1. Bernard DeVoto, "Utah," *The American Mercury* 7, no. 27 (March 1926): 317.
2. Mark Twain, *Roughing It* (1872; repr., New York: New American Library, 1962), 91–114. Fresh off a Provo chain gang, Alfred Packer ate five customers while guiding them from Utah to the Colorado goldfields during the winter of 1873–74. See Robert W. Fenwick, *Alfred Packer: The True Story of the Man-Eater* (Denver: Denver Post, 1964).
3. Biographical information comes from the following sources: Wallace Stegner, *The Uneasy Chair: A Biography of Bernard DeVoto* (Garden City, NY: Doubleday & Company, 1974); Catherine Drinker Bowen, Edith R. Mirrielees, Arthur M. Schlesinger Jr., and Wallace Stegner, *Four Portraits and One Subject: Bernard DeVoto* (Boston: Houghton Mifflin Company, 1963); Orlan Sawey, *Bernard DeVoto* (New York: Twayne Publishers, 1969); Russell Burrows, *Bernard DeVoto*, Western Writers Series 127 (Boise, ID: Boise State University, 1997); Bernard DeVoto, *The Letters of Bernard DeVoto*, ed. Wallace Stegner (Garden City, NY: Doubleday & Company, 1975); and Bernard DeVoto, "Fossil Remnants of the Frontier: Notes on a Utah Boyhood," *Harper's Magazine* 170 (April 1935): 590–600.
4. Stegner, *The Uneasy Chair,* 7.
5. Walter P. Metzger, "The First Investigation," *American Association of University Professors Bulletin* 47 (August 1961): 206; Jackson Newell and Takeyuki Ueyama, "Higher Education in Utah," in *Utah History Encyclopedia,* ed. Allan Kent Powell (Salt Lake City: University of Utah Press, 1994), 156.
6. Bernard DeVoto, *Across the Wide Missouri* (Boston: Houghton Mifflin Company, 1947); DeVoto, *The Course of Empire* (Boston: Houghton Mifflin, 1952); DeVoto, *The Year of Decision: 1846* (Boston: Little, Brown and Co., 1942). For DeVoto as historian, see Gary Topping, *Utah Historians and the Reconstruction of Western History* (Norman: University of Oklahoma Press, 2003), 44–109; Peter R. Hacker, "Shooting the Sheriff: A Look at Bernard DeVoto, Historian," *Utah Historical Quarterly* 58, no. 3 (Summer 1990): 232–43; Catherine Drinker Bowen, "The Historian," in *Four Portraits and One Subject,* 1–38; and James J. Rawls, "Bernard DeVoto and the Art of Popular History," *Pacific Historian* 25 (Spring 1981): 46–51.
7. For a list of DeVoto's writings, see Julius P. Barclay, "A Bibliography of the Writings of Bernard DeVoto," in *Four Portraits and One Subject,* 109–206.
8. See Jackson J. Benson, *Wallace Stegner: His Life and Work* (New York: Viking, 1996); Wallace Stegner and Richard W. Etulain, *Conversations with Wallace Stegner on*

Western History and Literature, rev. ed. (Salt Lake City: University of Utah Press, 1990); Topping, *Utah Historians,* 228–79; and John L. Thomas, *A Country in the Mind: Wallace Stegner, Bernard DeVoto, History, and the American Land* (New York: Routledge, 2000).

9. Bernard DeVoto, *The Hour* (Boston: Houghton Mifflin Company, 1951), 33–43.

10. Wallace Stegner, "The Personality," in *Four Portraits and One Subject,* 83–84.

11. Bernard DeVoto, "The West: A Plundered Province," *Harper's Magazine* 159 (August 1934): 355–64; DeVoto, "The West Against Itself," *Harper's Magazine* 194 (January 1947): 1–13. See also Bernard DeVoto, *The Western Paradox: A Conservation Reader,* ed. Douglas Brinkley and Patricia Nelson Limerick (New Haven, CT: Yale University Press, 2001); Edward K. Muller, ed., *DeVoto's West: History, Conservation, and the Public Good* (Athens: Swallow Press/Ohio University Press, 2005).

12. Darrell J. Greenwell, "Bernard A. DeVoto: Recollection and Appreciation," *Utah Historical Quarterly* 24, no. 1 (January 1956): 81–84, offered a brief eulogy after his death, and the Utah State Historical Society included him in its encyclopedia (Ann W. Engar, "Bernard DeVoto," in Powell, *Utah History Encyclopedia,* 140–41), but three local histories of Ogden and Weber County, coauthored by Richard C. Roberts and Richard W. Sadler, barely acknowledge him. Bob Sawatzki, ed., *The Word from Weber County: A Centennial Anthology of our Best Writers* (Salt Lake City: Publishers Press, for the Friends of the Weber County Library, 1996), 367–72, includes a selection from DeVoto's *Year of Decision* and a fine companion piece by Russell Burrows ("An Anger Once High and Righteous: The Writings of Bernard DeVoto") but doesn't explore this problematic relationship. The most telling comparison is the treatment DeVoto received at a 1994 conference at Weber State University in Ogden (full of defensiveness and open animosity) and a 1997 conference ("Devoted to the American West: The Century of Bernard DeVoto, 1897–1997"), organized by the Eisenhower Center for American Studies at the University of New Orleans, where a stellar cast of historians, writers, and editors celebrated his career and influence.

13. A fourth piece, "God-Litterateur," appeared in *The Guardian* 1 (March 1925): 188–97, but had limited circulation and impact in Utah. See Leland A. Fetzer, "Bernard DeVoto and the Mormon Tradition," *Dialogue: A Journal of Mormon Thought* 6, nos. 3 & 4 (Autumn–Winter 1971): 28.

14. DeVoto, *The Crooked Mile* (New York: Minton, Balch and Company, 1924); Stegner, *The Uneasy Chair,* 54–60.

15. Stegner, *The Uneasy Chair,* 61.

16. DeVoto, "Ogden: The Underwriters of Salvation," in *The Taming of the Frontier,* ed. Duncan Aikman (New York: Milton, Balch & Company, 1925), 41–42.

17. Ibid., 53, 55.

18. Ibid., 56, 29–30.

19. Ibid., 30–31, 34–35.

20. H. L. Mencken, "Footnote on Criticism," *Prejudices, Third Series* (New York: Alfred A. Knopf, 1922), 101; Stegner, *The Uneasy Chair,* 62.

21. Robert A. Wilkinson, review of *The Taming of the Frontier, Ogden Standard-Examiner,* April 10, 1927, 19.

22. Marion Elizabeth Rodgers, *Mencken: The American Iconoclast* (New York: Oxford University Press, 2005).

23. DeVoto, "Utah," 317. The Senate committee investigating Smoot concluded its hearings in 1906, but the full Senate vote to seat him didn't take place until February 20, 1907.

24. Ibid., 318.

25. Ibid., 319.

26. Ibid., 319.

27. Ibid., 320.

28. Ibid., 321. Displaying pictures of temples, church leaders, and Book of Mormon scenes in Mormon homes (what insiders call "Mocons," *The Mormonia Dictionary,* available online at http://www.salamandersociety.com/dictionary) continues today with the encouragement of church leaders. See Ronald S. Jackson, "We Would See Jesus: Visual Piety," 2002 David O. McKay Lecture, BYU-Hawaii, available online at http://w2.byuh.edu/academics/domckay/Lectures/Jackson2002.htm; Colleen McDannell, *Material Christianity: Religion and Popular Culture in America* (New Haven, CT: Yale University Press, 1995), 48; Jana K. Riess, "Stripling Warriors Choose the Right: Cultural Engagements of Contemporary Mormon Kitsch," *Sunstone* 22, no. 2 (June 1999): 36–47. For DeVoto's allusion to portraits of Holsteins as the epitome of passé artistic taste, see Elspeth Moncrieff, with Stephen Joseph and Iona Joseph, *Farm Animal Portraits* (Woodbridge, Suffolk: Antique Collectors' Club, 1996); and Michael S. Quinn, "Corpulent Cattle and Milk Machines: Nature, Art and the Ideal Type," *Society & Animals: Journal of Human-Animal Studies* 1, no. 2 (1993): 145–57.

29. DeVoto, "Utah," 322.

30. Ibid., 322–23.

31. Ibid., 323. See John S.H. Smith, "Cigarette Prohibition in Utah, 1921–23," *Utah Historical Quarterly* 41, no. 4 (Fall 1973): 358–72.

32. DeVoto, "Utah," 323.

33. Stegner, "The Personality," 83; Stegner, *The Uneasy Chair,* 396n9.

34. Stegner, *The Uneasy Chair,* 65. For the local response, see "'That's Enough' and Yarn Panning Utah Takes Rest Among Rubbish in Bucket," *Ogden Standard-Examiner,* April 18, 1926, 23; "Ogden High School Notes," *Ogden Standard-Examiner,* May 4, 1926, 8; and Wilkinson, review of *Taming of the Frontier,* 19.

35. Stegner, *The Uneasy Chair,* 66.

36. Bernard DeVoto to Dale Morgan, March 12, 1941, quoted in Topping, *Utah Historians,* 87; Bernard DeVoto, "A Revaluation," *Rocky Mountain Review* 10, no. 1 (Autumn 1945): 7–11, excerpted in *Improvement Era* 49 (March 1946): 154. See also Stegner, *The Uneasy Chair,* 66–67; and Fetzer, "Bernard DeVoto and the Mormon Tradition," 30–38. Gary Topping, *Utah Historians,* 86–87 and 349n9, rightly discounts the "apology" nature of DeVoto's response and highlights his continued disdain for Mormon theology.

37. Bernard DeVoto to Wallace Stegner, July 7, 1952, in *Letters of Bernard DeVoto,* 323.

38. Stegner, "The Personality," 83.

39. Stegner, *The Uneasy Chair,* 240, 245; Topping, *Utah Historians,* 60–63.

40. Kathleen Flake, *The Politics of American Religious Identity: The Seating of Senator Reed Smoot, Mormon Apostle* (Chapel Hill: University of North Carolina Press, 2004).

41. Ibid., see especially pp. 109–37 for Smith's conscious reworking of Mormon institutional memory.

42. DeVoto, "Utah," 320; Brigham H. Roberts, *The Autobiography of B. H. Roberts,* ed. Gary James Bergera (Salt Lake City: Signature Books, 1990).

43. Ethan R. Yorgason, *Transformation of the Mormon Culture Region* (Urbana: University of Illinois Press, 2003), ix.

44. Ibid., 172; see also 5, 7–11, 78–79, 127, 132, 163, 167–73. See also Thomas G. Alexander, *Mormonism in Transition: A History of the Latter-day Saints, 1890–1930* (Urbana: University of Illinois Press, 1986). For an analysis of Mormon reactions to their assimilation see Armand L. Mauss, *The Angel and the Beehive: The Mormon Struggle with Assimilation* (Urbana: University of Illinois Press, 1994).

45. "Some Aspects of Culture in Utah," *Ogden Standard-Examiner,* July 3, 1927, 14, attempts to rebut DeVoto as one "who lived with eyes closed in his native state," but in surveying Utah's cultural accomplishments, the writer acknowledges that DeVoto was the state's only "literary son" and that other native artists were "not familiar to all."

46. Thomas G. Alexander, *Utah, the Right Place: The Official Centennial History,* rev. ed. (Salt Lake City: Gibbs Smith, 2003), 265, see also his broader assessment on 256–75. James B. Allen offers a more pessimistic assessment in "Education and the Arts in Twentieth-Century Utah," in *Utah's History,* ed. Richard D. Poll, Thomas G. Alexander, Eugene E. Campbell, and David E. Miller (Logan: Utah State University Press, 1989), 587–608.

47. Eugene England, "Mormon Literature: Progress and Prospects," in *Mormon Americana: A Guide to Sources and Collections in the United States,* ed. David J. Whittaker (Provo: BYU Studies, 1995), 455–505, available online at http://humanities.byu.edu/mldb/progress.htm; Topping, *Utah Historians,* 12–42.

48. Roger L. Miller, "Mormon Tabernacle Choir," 378–80; and Cherie Willis, "The Utah Symphony," 605–6, in Powell, *Utah History Encyclopedia..*

49. Alexander, *Utah, the Right Place,* 265–75; Allen, "Education and the Arts," 596–605; Vern G. Swanson, Robert S. Olpin, and William C. Seifrit, *Utah Painting and Sculpture,* rev. ed. (Salt Lake City: Gibbs Smith Publisher, 1997), 85–180; Ann W. Engar, "Maude Adams," 1–2; and "Theatre in Utah," 551–54, in Powell, *Utah History Encyclopedia..*

50. Stegner, *The Uneasy Chair,* 54–55. See also Malcolm Cowley, *Exile's Return: A Literary Odyssey of the 1920s* (1934; repr., New York: Viking Press, 1951); Lynn Dumenil, *The Modern Temper: American Culture and Society in the 1920s* (New York: Hill & Wang, 1995); and Robert M. Crunden, *Body & Soul: The Making of American Modernism* (New York: Basic Books, 2000).

51. Stegner, *The Uneasy Chair,* 66–67; Topping, *Utah Historians,* 54–58.

52. Mauss, *Angel and the Beehive,* x–xi, 77–79. The insistence on simultaneous peculiarity and mainstream status that DeVoto noted has intensified at the turn of the twenty-first century with changes in the LDS Church's presentation of itself, both internally and in the media—what some refer to as the "Protestantization" of doctrinal teaching and image. Utah's 2002 Winter Olympics and recent state advertising campaigns offer interesting windows into these tensions. See Yorgason, *Transformation of the Mormon Culture Region,* 169, 212n22; Susan Sessions Rugh, "Branding Utah: Industrial Tourism in the Postwar American West," *Western Historical Quarterly* 37, no. 4 (Winter 2006): 445–72, especially 467–71; and Mark Dyreson, "Olympic Games and Historical Imagination: Notes from the Faultline of Tradition and Modernity," *Olympika: The International Journal of Olympic Studies* 7 (1998): 25–42, especially 31–33.

53. See Annette Atkins, "The State I'm In: Hubert Humphrey, Jesse Ventura, Bob Dylan, Garrison Keillor, and Me," *Western Historical Quarterly* 38, no. 4 (Winter 2007): 501–8.

Utah recruits stationed at Fort Lewis, Washington, for military training prior to shipping overseas during World War I.

II

Connecting to the Nation
Utah and the U.S.A.

Brigham Young's dream when he arrived in the Great Salt Lake Valley was that the Mormons could be self-sufficient. He established home industries and businesses and asked church members to patronize them. But as often happens, reality outpaced the dream. The California gold rush, the Utah War, the stagecoach, the telegraph line, the Pony Express, and finally the railroad in 1869 linked Utah more closely to the rest of the nation. Despite the ties established in the nineteenth century, in 1900 Utah retained a residue of insular characteristics that reflected its religious heritage, its earlier experiments with economic separatism and self-sufficiency, and its remoteness from the nation's economic, political, and cultural centers of power.

Throughout the twentieth century, Utah's connections to the rest of the nation continued to strengthen and multiply. In many ways, Utah's interactions with the country as a whole matched those of other states, but the presence of the Mormon Church created distinctive political, cultural, and economic twists. Some of the most profound links tying Utah to the nation during the twentieth century involved warfare and national defense. Economic and political trends also drew the state and its citizens more fully into the national community. The chapters in this section illustrate some of those connections, as do many other historical developments discussed briefly in this essay.

WAR

At the beginning of the twentieth century, Mormon Church President Lorenzo Snow issued his *Greetings to the World*, where he expressed his desire that in the new century, "war with its horrors should be but a memory."[1] Unfortunately, the century would be plagued with many conflicts. Hundreds of Utahns were already fighting in the 1899–1902 Philippine-American War, an outgrowth of the Spanish-American War. It was Utah's first chance on the battlefield to prove its loyalty to the United States.[2]

The next major conflict was World War I. A majority of Utahns initially deplored the war as the fruit of European corruption and hoped to remain aloof from the conflict. But after the United States entered the war in 1917, nearly twenty-five thousand Utahns served in the military, some as conscripts and others as volunteers. Greek immigrants feared the war's impact upon their homeland, and some complained that aliens should be exempt from the draft. But G.A. Papailion, the Greek consul, mobilized immigrants in prowar activities, and nearly one in five Greek Utahns served in the American military and received U.S. citizenship in return. Nearly 3 percent of Utah's soldiers died. In addition, Utahns donated $72,500 to the various bond drives in a show of exceptional patriotism. Many also reduced their consumption of beef, pork, and wheat to boost food supplies for America's soldiers. As Thomas Alexander has noted, "Utah's most significant contribution to the war effort" was likely the weaponry invented by John M. Browning of Ogden and produced by the Winchester Repeating Arms Company and the Belgian firm, Fabrique Nationale d'Armes de Guerre.[3]

While World War I led to deaths, it also affected the Utah economy in a positive way. There was an immediate need for Utah's agricultural and mining products from the state's two main industries at the time. Utah Senator Reed Smoot observed that as a result of the war, the "products of our state" were "highly prized" and "bring[ing] in dollars."[4] Among the most valued products were lead, copper, and sugar. In 1920 Utah mines produced roughly 14 percent of the nation's lead and 10 percent of its copper. By 1919 Utah ranked third in the nation in sugar beet production.[5]

LDS Church leaders in Salt Lake City vigorously sought to demonstrate their church's loyalty to the United States war effort, further cementing ties between Utah and the nation. A classic example was the sale of grain stored by the Relief Society, the church's women's organization. During World War I, the federal food administrator, Herbert Hoover, asked Presiding Bishop Charles W. Nibley for the grain. At first he said no because it belonged to the women. Eventually Nibley gave in to the pressure and agreed to the sale. However, he signed General Relief Society President Emmeline B. Wells's name to a letter authorizing the sale without her knowledge. Wells was unhappy with the way that the grain sale was handled and privately criticized Nibley for not telling her about it beforehand. It turned out that some of the grain had not been stored well, and the government encouraged Mormons not to continue the program after the war.

Despite such problems, the sale became an excellent public-relations plus for the LDS Church. Hoover visited Utah and thanked the women for their war efforts. Utah Representative Milton Welling read a letter of thanks into the *Congressional Record*. President Woodrow Wilson and his wife, Edith, personally visited Wells in her apartment to thank her.[6]

Rubber collected in a scrap drive at the Continental Oil Company in Salt Lake during World War II, June 19, 1942.

The nation's involvement in the Second World War had an even-more-sweeping impact on the state. Utahns believed strongly in the major objective of the war—defeating the enemy and its attendant evils. Residents volunteered (Utah's enlistment rate of 41 percent was exceptionally high) or accepted the draft. More than seventy-one thousand Utahns, nearly 2 percent of whom were women, served in the military during the war. More than thirty-six hundred of them died in the service. Residents responded to drives for bonds, fat, metal, and books and often exceeded their quota after friendly competition. During a national "kitchen fat" salvage campaign in 1943, Utah's monthly quota was 80,500 pounds. Utahns had only contributed half of that by May, so the *Salt Lake Tribune* asked residents "to forego pan gravy and smile." During the war, the federal government sponsored seven war-bond drives, and Utahns—especially churches and businesses—contributed. But there were always advertisements asking for more.[7]

Utah once again benefited economically as it competed with other states for federal funds. The U.S. War Department expanded two federal defense installations that predated the war, and the government constructed nine other major military installations. The most important of them, Hill Air Force Base, became the largest civilian employer in the state. In 1943 nearly fifteen thousand civilians and six thousand soldiers worked there. The federal government allocated $284 million in public funds to construct factories in the Beehive State between 1940 and 1945. Utah secured more than one-third of the government appropriations for industrial plants in the Rocky Mountain States and more than 2.8 times the national per-capita investment in new factories.[8]

Although federal funds paid for 91 percent of the factories built in Utah during the war, private capital also funded wartime production. The largest of the privately financed plants was the Parachute Company of Utah in Manti.[9] Amanda Midgley Borneman's chapter in this section explores the sweeping impact of defense industries on rural women workers and their families. She shows how economic modernization and increased federal involvement changed the lives of women in Utah during and after the war.

As Borneman suggests, the nationwide war effort helped to make lasting changes in Utah by encouraging women to work. In 1900 only 11 percent of Utah women over the age of fifteen were employed. Reflecting wartime demands and opportunities, the employment of women doubled during World War II as thousands of them, including many who were married with children, entered the workforce. Although women vacated a lot of industrial jobs after the war, many of them remained in the workforce, and others soon joined them. Like the situation in the Manti sewing factory, these women often did traditional women's work. By 1970, 41 percent of the state's women over the age of 15 were in the workforce, and that percentage rose to 61 percent by 2000. By contrast 69 percent of the state's entire population over the age of fifteen was employed in 2000. In 1979 women in Utah with bachelor's degrees earned on average $3,600 less than male workers who had never completed high school, however. That changed over the next decade. Wage differentials declined, and job choices increased during the 1980s and 1990s, reflecting new attitudes introduced by the women's movement. Nevertheless, by 2002 Utah women's wages were still only 70 percent of men's wages, the fifth-highest disparity in the nation. Near the end of the century, women owned about a quarter of the state's businesses, held about a third of the state's managerial and professional jobs, and comprised about half of the students enrolled in higher education.[10]

World War II was followed by the cold war where the United States and the Soviet Union struggled to control the world politically, economically, and militarily. Again, national policies and challenges affected the Beehive State. Utahns responded to President Harry S. Truman's Point Four program, and Utah State University, the University of Utah, and Brigham Young University sent more than fifty technicians to Iran to improve agriculture, health, and education between 1950 and 1964. By sharing technology and knowledge as the products of capitalism, Point Four was designed to prevent communism from gaining a foothold in Iran, which shared a long border with the Soviet Union. The Utah connection resulted from contact over the years between Iranian government officials and Utah universities. Those officials hoped that Utah's experience with irrigation in a desert environment could help the Iranians.[11]

Defense spending during the cold war generated significant income and employment; this included jobs at federal installations like Hill Air Force Base and defense industries such as Sperry Rand Corporation, Thiokol Chemical Corporation, and Hercules Powder Company, businesses that produced missiles and rocket engines and fuel. By 1963–64, when defense spending in Utah peaked, roughly one-third of Utahns' personal income was related to defense. Utah benefited again from generous cold war budgets during the Reagan years. Total defense spending in the state soared to $2.1 billion in 1987, and civilian employment at Hill Air Force Base topped fifteen thousand.[12]

The arms race with the Soviet Union during the cold war also ignited a mineral rush for uranium on the Colorado Plateau. In 1952 an unemployed petroleum geologist, Charlie Steen, discovered a glory hole of pitchblende uranium fourteen feet thick south of La Sal. That evening he and his mother celebrated with a quart of whiskey at a deserted hot dog stand in Moab. It was "the last time that Moab went to sleep at 10 o'clock for a long time," Steen later quipped: the discovery ignited a frenzy of prospecting. By 1954 at least fourteen hundred uranium miners were working the uranium-rich Four Corners region. Two years later, journalist Elizabeth Pope dubbed Moab "the richest town in the U.S.A.," claiming that nearly one in ten residents was a millionaire. Between 1946 and 1971, the Atomic Energy Commission purchased 348 million tons of ore and invested billions of dollars in roads, ore-processing mills, and uranium purchases.[13]

The cold war nearly produced another massive infusion of capital and technology for Utah with the MX missile system, which could have altered the state's environment, economy, and population. In his chapter in this section, Jacob W. Olmstead illustrates the relevance of the cold war for Utahns as he describes the proposed fifty-billion-dollar missile system, its anticipated effects, and the multipronged grassroots campaign to persuade Mormon Church leaders to publicly oppose the MX's placement in Utah.

When the cold war heated up, the United States sent troops to countries that seemed threatened by or vulnerable to the Soviet Union and China. The Korean War was a United Nations conflict, but the U.S. provided most of the troops, including 7,564 (436 of whom died) from Utah. To show its support of the federal government in the fight against communism, the Mormon Church modified its missionary program so that men could not avoid the draft by serving missions, a decision that affected thousands of young Utahns.[14]

In the following decade, another national conflict, the Vietnam War, also impacted Utahns. Many residents initially supported the war. Early in the war, a survey showed that 84 percent of the male students at Brigham Young University said they were willing to fight in Vietnam. In October of 1965, sixty-five hundred students in Provo held a rally where they carried signs with messages such as "I'm a War Monger—I Support the Troops." One participant told a reporter, "In these days of student protests, it is good to know that some colleges like BYU are not joining in."[15]

As the war deepened and hopes for a decisive victory dwindled, more Utahns protested. The state's largest war protest occurred on October 16, 1969, designated by national organizers as Moratorium Day. An estimated forty-two hundred people gathered at the corner of First South and State Street in Salt Lake City after marching down South Temple Street from Reservoir Park to

BYU students petition for support of the Vietnam War.

listen, chant, sing, and pray as Rev. G. Edward Howlett of St. Mark's Episcopal Church read the names of Utahns who had died in Vietnam. Carl Neering, a BYU student, implored the crowd to shout "peace! Loud enough for them to hear it in Provo." Smaller protests occurred at Utah State, Weber State, and Southern Utah State. By 1970, 27,910 Utahns had served in Vietnam—8.6 percent of those eligible for the draft.[16]

Utahns, like other Americans, celebrated the breakup of the Soviet Union, the removal of the Berlin Wall, and the end of the cold war. As tensions diminished, military spending declined, and the state's fortunes were affected. Fort Douglas, Defense Depot Ogden, and portions of the Tooele Army Depot closed. Hill Air Force Base survived a round of closures, but by 1996 only seven thousand civilians worked there. The following year total defense spending in the state amounted to $1.2 billion—little more than half of what it had been ten years earlier.[17]

Despite the collapse of the Soviet Union and cuts in military spending, wars arose elsewhere. Utahns supported Operations Desert Shield and Desert Storm in the Persian Gulf in 1990–91, and tens of thousands of Utahns were deployed in the region. The short-lived Persian Gulf War's direct impact upon the state's economy and military installations was minor, though, compared to the conflicts in Korea and Vietnam.

Students march from the University of Utah to demonstrate their opposition to the Vietnam War. Posters document the number of Americans killed 1961-1969.

Economics

In addition to warfare and national defense, national and global economic forces and trends tightly bound the fortunes of Utahns to the nation. After World War I, prices for Utah products dropped dramatically in national and international markets, and Utah entered what some historians call the Little Depression. Throughout the 1920s, Utah's major economic sector—agriculture—stagnated. Things went from bad to worse as the Great Depression engulfed the entire nation during the 1930s. The severity of Utah's distress demonstrated the state's dependence upon national markets. As a producer of raw materials such as coal, copper, beef, and wheat rather than finished goods, the state was particularly vulnerable to market fluctuations. Per capita income fell by 45 percent between 1929 and 1933, whereas the cost of living fell by only 25 percent. Nearly one-third of the state's banks closed between 1929 and 1933, and business failures rose by 82 percent. In 1933 nearly 36 percent of Utah's workforce was unemployed, compared to roughly one-fourth of the labor force nationwide.[18]

Economic problems swamped local and private relief efforts across the nation. Many called upon the federal government to mobilize its vast financial resources to address the problem. The Reconstruction Finance Corporation (RFC), chartered by Congress in 1932, turned the federal government into the primary source of relief funds for Utah. Between September 1932 and March 1933, Utah received the second-highest per-capita investment of RFC funds

WordPerfect grew from three employees in 1979 to nearly fifteen hundred in 1989. It moved into this modern campus carved out of orchards in North Orem in 1987.

in the nation. Beginning in 1933, Franklin D. Roosevelt's New Deal programs bequeathed additional relief. Utah ranked ninth in the nation in per capita expenditures by federal agencies between 1933 and 1939. At least five factors help to explain the state's success in attracting federal funds: the severity of Utah's economic plight; the federal government's ownership of land in the state suitable for public-works projects; well-organized Mormon congregations that worked with state and local officials to pinpoint financial need and unemployment quickly; the lobbying efforts in Washington of Utah's former governor, Secretary of War George Dern; and the readiness of Utah's legislature to raise the required matching funds for many federal programs through tax increases.[19]

Political conservatives nationwide cynically decried what they perceived as an avalanche of alphabet agencies buying votes with borrowed money and reducing state and local governments to vassals of a federal lord. Members of the LDS Church's First Presidency were Utah's most celebrated and controversial conservative opponents of the New Deal. The First Presidency's adverse perceptions of the New Deal led to the church's own welfare program, which today continues to relieve economic distress throughout the world.[20] Joseph F. Darowski's chapter explores the conflicts and sense of competition between representatives of the New Deal in Utah and advocates of the LDS Church Welfare Plan during the 1930s. Reliance upon federal spending persisted beyond the New Deal. In the decades following World War II, Utahns continued to benefit from federal investment in rocketry, national parks and forests, water storage projects, energy, and the interstate highway system.

In addition to federal investment, involvement in the high-tech revolution linked Utah to national economic trends and forces. Utah's entry into the world of high tech occurred in 1968 when David Evans and Ivan Sutherland, professors at the University of Utah, founded Evans and Sutherland, a firm that specialized in computer graphics and electronic simulations. A few years later, Alan Ashton, a University of Utah graduate and Brigham Young University professor, and his graduate student Bruce Bastian developed WordPerfect. The company's sales doubled almost yearly between 1982 and 1988. By 1988 WordPerfect had captured nearly one-third of the independent word-processing software market. Another Utah-based company, Novell Data Systems, incorporated in 1983 and had gained close to 70 percent of the market share for local-area networking by the late 1980s.[21]

During the heyday of the high-tech revolution, Utah seemed to outgrow its status as a state dependent upon external investment capital and federal spending. In his centennial history of the State of Utah, Thomas G. Alexander described the Beehive State from 1945 to the late 1970s as a colony because it was so dependent on the United States government, external investment capital in sectors such as transportation and steel production, and extractive industries like agriculture and mining. But between the late 1970s and 1992, Alexander argued, Utah became a "commonwealth," where locally owned businesses, including WordPerfect and Novell, were the dominant employers. During the 1990s, though, many of the most nationally visible, Utah-based companies moved on or were bought by out-of-state firms. Both WordPerfect and Novell fell on hard times in the 1990s as Seattle-based Microsoft made inroads into their markets. In 1996 a Canadian company, Corel, purchased the ailing WordPerfect, and the company closed its Utah offices in 1998. In a revised and updated version of his book published in 2003, Alexander noted that Utah's commonwealth economy had shrunk beginning in 1994.[22]

POLITICS

Along with economic forces and national defense, participation in national politics connected Utah to the rest of the nation during the twentieth century. Just as it is difficult to separate the twentieth-century war experience from the economy of Utah, politics and economics are equally closely tied. Once Utah became a state, its representatives and senators in Washington could wield influence to protect and promote its economic interests. Reed Smoot, who represented the state in the U.S. Senate for nearly a third of the twentieth century, became the most powerful Utahn in the nation's capitol. He secured significant appropriations for reclamation, conservation, and national parks in Utah. He firmly cemented his reputation as an old guard, reactionary defender of big business when he cosponsored the infamous Hawley-Smoot tariff in 1930, a measure that unintentionally exacerbated America's economic woes by discouraging international trade.[23] More to his credit, Smoot worked hard on tariff legislation to protect Utah's industries, especially sugar beets, because of their central role in the state's agricultural economy. Matthew C. Godfrey's chapter spells out Smoot's relationship to the sugar beet industry. It also demonstrates

In 1917 women in Glendale, Kane County, organized a parade in support of Prohibition.

the centrality of national economic policy for Utah by the 1910s.

During the Progressive Era, federal and state politics aimed to improve life for Americans and Utahns. Reformers focused on bettering life in the cities, eliminating corrupt governments, and humanizing health care. Many of them saw prohibition of alcohol as helping achieve these ends. They believed that alcohol caused many of the evils in the nation, state, and families. National organizations like the Anti-Saloon League enlisted support in Utah from Protestant clergy and Mormon Apostle Heber J. Grant. At the same time, Mormon Church leaders reinterpreted a Joseph Smith revelation known as the Word of Wisdom, which, among other things, advised against the consumption of alcohol, making it a precondition for entering the church's temples. Evangelical Protestants and Mormon leaders were both instrumental in having the state legislature pass laws to ban alcohol. Not all Mormon leaders agreed with the ban. Reed Smoot's Federal Bunch, a coalition of Mormons and non-Mormons working together for legislation, argued that the Latter-day Saints were too involved in Prohibition politics.[24]

Prohibition in Utah, as in the United States at large, reduced drinking but did so at a high price. A black market developed, making liquor easily available. Law-enforcement officials spent time and money trying to track the lawbreakers, but many eluded them. In the 1932 election, Franklin D. Roosevelt promised to repeal the Prohibition amendment to the Constitution. Most Americans agreed. However, Mormon Church President Heber J. Grant did not. He had supported Prohibition and appealed to Utahns not to change the law. His request fell on deaf ears: ironically Utah became the final state needed to overturn the amendment. That vote sent a message to the rest of the nation that Utahns did not always follow Mormon leaders' political advice.[25]

This did not stop church leaders from offering that advice. In 1936 the Church's First Presidency editorialized against Franklin D. Roosevelt's bid for reelection, and two years later, they enlisted Brigham Young University President Franklin S. Harris to run against Utah's pro-New Deal senator Elbert Thomas. In the second half of the twentieth century, individual church leaders occasionally endorsed candidates, but the institutional church increasingly withdrew from partisan politics and focused more upon moral issues, including civil rights, religious freedom, same-sex marriage, pornography, and abortion.[26]

Other significant national political movements and issues also shaped Utah's history during the twentieth century. The red scare of 1919–20 adversely affected Utah's labor movement and abetted anti-immigrant sentiment and race prejudice. McCarthyism, or the panicked pursuit of communists within the nation during the 1940s and '50s, contributed to the defeat of Utah's veteran Democratic Senator Elbert Thomas, who was viciously branded as a communist in the 1950 election. The environmental movement that gained strength in the latter decades of the century provided critical support for laws establishing Canyonlands National Park in 1964, the state's first wilderness areas in 1984, and emissions tests for automobiles in Weber, Davis, Salt Lake, and Utah Counties. Environmentalist politicking also provided critical opposition to plans for a Kaiparowits Power Plant, abandoned in the midseventies. The New Right of the 1980s fostered a political climate that encouraged the state legislature to joust with windmills and invite an expensive court challenge by enacting one of the toughest antiabortion statutes in the nation in 1991.[27]

SUMMARY

Utah became a state at the end of the nineteenth century, ending a half century of federal control. During the twentieth century, Utah's ties to the nation multiplied and gained strength, especially in the areas of war, economics, and politics. The chapters that follow provide case studies of Utah's involvement in World War II and the cold war. They also show the impact of tariff legislation and the Great Depression. Each of the chapters also reveals the economic, political, and cultural reach of Mormonism in twentieth-century Utah, a factor that made the state's history distinctive.

NOTES

1. Church of Jesus Christ of Latter-day Saints, *Church History in the Fullness of Times: The History of the Church of Jesus Christ of Latter-day Saints* (Salt Lake City: Church of Jesus Christ of Latter-day Saints, 2003), 458.

2. B. H. Roberts, *A Comprehensive History of the Church of Jesus Christ of Latter-day Saints* (Provo: Brigham Young University Press, 1965), 6: 457–58; Charles R. Mabey, *The Utah Batteries: A History* (Salt Lake City: Daily Reporter, 1900); A. Prentiss, *The History of the Utah Volunteers in the Spanish-American War and in the Philippine Islands* (Salt Lake City: Tribune Printing Co., 1900); D. Michael Quinn, "The Mormon

8

Church and the Spanish-American War: An End to Selective Pacifism," *Pacific Historical Review* 43 (August 1974):342–66.

3. Dean L. May, *Utah: A People's History* (Salt Lake City: University of Utah Press, 1987), 172; Thomas G. Alexander, *Utah, the Right Place: The Official Centennial History,* rev. ed. (Salt Lake City: Gibbs Smith, 2003), 279; John Browning and Curt Gentry, *John M. Browning, American Gunmaker: An Illustrated Biography of the Man and His Guns* (Garden City, NY: Doubleday, 1964); Helen Z. Papanikolas, "Toil and Rage in a New Land: The Greek Immigrants in Utah," *Utah Historical Quarterly* 38 (Spring 1970), 152–56; Charles S. Peterson, "'Crossing to Affluence': Utah from Statehood to World War II," chap. 6, pp. 89–90, unpublished manuscript in author's possession.

4. *Report of the 86th Semi-Annual Conference of the Church of Jesus Christ of Latter-day Saints* (Salt Lake City: Deseret News Publishing Co., 1915), 131–32.

5. Thomas G. Alexander, "Generating Wealth from the Earth, 1847–2000," in *From the Ground Up: The History of Mining in Utah,* ed. Colleen Whitley (Logan: Utah State University Press, 2006), 40; U. S. Bureau of the Census, *Fourteenth Census of the United States Taken in the Year 1920,* vol. 6, *Agriculture: Reports for States with Statistics for Counties* (Washington, DC: GPO, 1922).

6. Jessie L. Embry, "Grain Storage: The Balance of Power between Priesthood Authority and Relief Society Autonomy," *Dialogue: A Journal of Mormon Thought* 15 (Winter 1982), 59–66; Carol Cornwall Madsen, *An Advocate for Women: The Public Life of Emmeline B. Wells, 1870–1920* (Provo, UT: Brigham Young University, 2006), 28.

7. Jessie L. Embry, "'The Good War:' Utah and the World War II Homefront," *Utah Historical Quarterly* 63 (Summer 1995): 259, 261–265; Allan Kent Powell, *Utah Remembers World War II* (Logan: Utah State University Press, 1991), xi, xiii; Powell, "Utah and World War II," *Utah Historical Quarterly* 73 (Spring 2005):119; Alexander, *Utah, the Right Place,* 358; Leonard J. Arrington, "Utah's Ambiguous Reception: The Relocated Japanese Americans," in *Japanese Americans: From Relocation to Redress,* rev. ed., ed. Roger Daniels, Sandra Taylor, and Harry H.L. Kitano (Seattle: University of Washington Press, 1991), 94.

8. John E. Christensen, "The Impact of World War II," in *Utah's History,* ed. Richard D. Poll, Thomas G. Alexander, Eugene E. Campbell, and David E. Miller (Logan: Utah State University Press, 1989), 500–501; Leonard J. Arrington, Thomas G. Alexander, and Eugene A. Erb Jr., "Utah's Biggest Business: Ogden Air Material Area at Hill Air Force Base, 1938–1965," *Utah Historical Quarterly* 33 (Spring 1965):12–16.

9. Christensen, "Impact of World War II," 501; Albert C. T. Antrei and Allen D. Roberts, *A History of Sanpete County* (Salt Lake City: Utah State Historical Society and Sanpete County Commission, 1999), 267–68.

10. Maureen Ursenbach Beecher and Kathryn L. Mackay, "Women in Twentieth-Century Utah," in Poll et al., *Utah's History,* 577; *Deseret News,* June 4, 2002; Marie Cornwall, "Beyond Fertility: What We Don't Know about Utah Women," in *Utah in the 1990s: A Demographic Perspective,* ed. Tim B. Heaton, Thomas A. Hirschl, and Bruce A. Chadwick (Salt Lake City: Signature Books, 1996), 198–202,

206; Institute for Women's Policy Research, *The Status of Women in Utah 2004,* Publication R 288, November 2004, available online at http://www.iwpr.org/pdf/ UT_R288.pdf

11. Jessie L. Embry, "Point Four, Utah State University Technicians, and Rural Development in Iran, 1950–64," *Rural History* 14 (April 2003):100–113.

12. Gerald D. Nash, *The Federal Landscape: An Economic History of the Twentieth-Century West* (Tucson: University of Arizona Press, 1999), 95; James L. Clayton, "Contemporary Economic Development," in Poll et al., *Utah's History,* 535; *Deseret News,* June 9, 2001; Governor's Office of Planning and Budget, *2006 Economic Report to the Governor* (Salt Lake City: Utah State Government, 2006),142, available online at http://governor.utah.gov/dea/ERG/ERG2006/Chapters/19Defense.pdf

13. *Salt Lake Tribune,* September 19, 2005; Raye C. Ringholz, "Uranium Boom," in Whitley, *From the Ground Up,* 148–65; Ringholz, *Uranium Frenzy: Saga of the Nuclear West,* rev. ed. (Logan: Utah State University Press, 2002), 65–70, 152.

14. Benjamin Urrutia, "The Korean War and Utah," in *Utah History Encyclopedia,* ed. Allan Kent Powell (Salt Lake City: University of Utah Press, 1994), 307.

15. Gary James Bergera and Ronald Priddis, *Brigham Young University: A House of Faith* (Salt Lake City: Signature Books, 1985), 180–81.

16. *Salt Lake Tribune,* October 16, 1969, 1–2; Allan Kent Powell, "The Vietnam Conflict and Utah," in Powell, *Utah History Encyclopedia.*, 612–14.

17. Governor's Office, *2006 Economic Report,* 141–42; *Deseret News,* June 9, 2001; April 24, 2005.

18. Alexander, *Utah, the Right Place,* rev. ed., 276; "Measures of Economic Changes in Utah, 1847–1947," *Utah Economic and Business Review* 7 (December 1947): 23, 89; John F. Bluth and Wayne K. Hinton, "The Great Depression," in Poll et al., *Utah's History,* 483; Lester V. Chandler, *America's Greatest Depression, 1929–1941* (New York: Harper & Row, 1970), 7, 19; Garth Mangum and Bruce Blumell, *The Mormons' War on Poverty: A History of LDS Welfare, 1830–1990* (Salt Lake City: University of Utah Press, 1993), 112; Leonard J. Arrington, *Utah, the New Deal and the Depression of the 1930s* (Ogden, UT: Weber State College, 1983), 27; Arrington, "The New Deal in the West: A Preliminary Statistical Inquiry," *Pacific Historical Review* 38 (August 1969):313–14.

20. Brian Q. Cannon, "What a Power We Will Be in This Land": The LDS Church, the Church Security Program, and the New Deal," *Journal of the West* 43 (Fall 2004): 66–75.

21. Alexander, *Utah, the Right Place,* rev. ed., 409, 411–12; G. Wesley Johnson and Marian Ashby Johnson, *Centennial Utah: The Beehive State on the Eve of the Twenty-First Century* (Encino, CA: Cherbo Publishing Group, 1995), 162–65; W.E. Peterson, *Almost Perfect: How a Bunch of Regular Guys Built WordPerfect Corporation* (Rocklin, CA: Prima Publishing, 1994).

22. Thomas G. Alexander, *Utah, the Right Place: The Official Centennial History,* 1st ed. (Salt Lake City: Gibbs Smith Publisher, 1995), 408–13; Alexander, *Utah, the Right Place,* rev. ed., 408–13.

23. Milton R. Merrill, *Reed Smoot: Apostle in Politics* (Logan: Utah State University Press, 1999); Thomas G. Alexander, "Red Rock and Gray Stone: Senator Reed Smoot, the Establishment of Zion and Bryce Canyon National Parks, and the Rebuilding of Downtown Washington, D.C.," *Pacific Historical Review* 72 (February 2003):1–38; Michael E. Parrish, *Anxious Decades: America in Prosperity and Depression, 1920–1941* (New York: W.W. Norton, 1992), 247–48; Robert S. McElvaine, *The Great Depression: America, 1929–1941* (New York: Times Books, 1993), 32–33, 83–84.

24. Thomas G. Alexander, *Mormonism in Transition: A History of the Latter-day Saints* (Urbana: University of Illinois Press, 1986), 258–71.

25. Alexander, *Utah, the Right Place,* rev. ed., 323–24.

26. Brian Q. Cannon, "Mormons and the New Deal: The 1936 Presidential Election in Utah," *Utah Historical Quarterly* 67 (Winter 1999): 4–22; F. Ross Peterson, "Utah Politics Since 1945," in Poll et al., *Utah's History,* 516–18.

27. Steven Bligh McNutt, "Utah's Reaction to the 1919–1920 Red Scare" (master's thesis, Brigham Young University, 1995), 115; Peterson, "Utah Politics," 518; Charles S. Peterson, "Natural Resource Utilization," in Poll et al, *Utah's History,* 665; Alexander, *Utah, the Right Place,* rev. ed., 416, 424, 427.

5

"Proud to Send Those Parachutes Off"

Central Utah's Rosies during World War II

Amanda Midgley Borneman

In 1940 women held 28 percent of the jobs in the nation, compared to 18 percent in Utah. Four years later, women figured more prominently in the Utah workforce (37 percent) than in the nation at large (36 percent). Lucrative opportunities for work in the Beehive State's new and expanding defense installations and industries fueled the dramatic increase. Some women, like the legendary Rosie the Riveter, operated heavy equipment or machinery on the factory floor, challenging gender stereotypes by moving into jobs previously reserved for men. More women, like the parachute-factory workers in Manti that Amanda Midgley Borneman describes in this chapter, engaged in tasks such as sewing or secretarial work that corresponded more closely with traditional views of women's work. Although sewing in a factory might be regarded as "natural" work for women, it nonetheless altered social and economic relationships, particularly for married women, reducing their economic dependence upon husbands and broadening their involvement beyond the farm and household. Using survey data from the 1980s and interviews with former workers, Borneman investigates women's motives for working and some of the short-term and long-range implications of their wartime employment for themselves and their households.

World War II had a profound impact on Utah. At the outset of the war, several communities in the state were still feeling the pangs of the recent Depression, especially in the agricultural sector. For many Utahns, the World War II period marked the end of isolation and the beginning of a new era. Utah changed as the United States accelerated its preparations for combat through the establishment and expansion of wartime industries. New war-related businesses often meant

123

different and more-widespread opportunities for employment as well as exposure to people and influences from around the country and the world. Utah was
economically fortunate to receive some of these industries, helping its economy
out of lingering Depression conditions and increasing its access to federal funds.
Between 1940 and 1945, Utah obtained a large amount of federal money for
industrial plants, amounting to $534 per capita in comparison to the national
average of $188. Unemployment rates dropped, and in-migration rose.[1] Utah
was an ideal location for these war industries for a variety of reasons, including
its distance from West Coast ports—perfect for protection from foreign attack—
and its large amount of federally owned land—useful for setting up government
bases and operations. Utah's political leaders, including Governor Herbert B.
Maw, touted these advantages as they actively sought war industries.[2]

Yet a global war on multiple fronts meant a shortage of manpower for new
industry. Industry and government had to recruit new sources of labor because
the men were needed for military service. In Utah more than 10 percent of the
state's population served in the military, and war industries turned to women as
a new source of labor. The economic situation changed dramatically in the state
as total employment grew by eighty-two thousand and personal income rose
above the national average between 1940 and 1943. In 1944 women constituted
almost 20 percent more of the Utah labor force than they had in 1940. Long-
term trends for female employment also changed as older women and married
women joined the workforce in larger percentages than in previous decades.[3]

There were many industries around the state of Utah from which women
could choose. The popularized "Rosie" showed up for work not just as the
glamorized riveter; she took jobs in a variety of occupations around the state
and nation. In Utah facilities such as the Bushnell Military Hospital in Brigham
City employed the skills of a large number of nurses and other women. Military
installations such as the Ogden Arsenal, Hill Air Force Base, Clearfield Naval
Supply Depot, Wendover Air Force Base, Kearns Army Air Base, the Tooele
Army Depot, and the Deseret Chemical Depot employed hundreds of women
in a variety of tasks. Then there were private companies with government funding and/or contracts, such as the Eitel McCullough Radio Tube Plant, the
Remington Small Arms Munitions Plant, the Lehi Refractory, Geneva Steel,
and the Parachute Company of Utah.[4]

C. E. Fauntleroy's Parachute Company of Utah in Manti was situated in
the heart of Sanpete County, an agricultural area approximately 120 miles south
of Salt Lake City that had been the target of much economic distress. It was a
private enterprise with government contracts that manufactured parachutes for
the armed forces from April 1942 to July 1944, after which parachute production continued under the Reliance Manufacturing Company throughout the
duration of the war. Reliance, a large company with twenty-three sewing plants
across the nation, continued to produce textiles well after the war's conclusion. The local economy received a boost through such a large industry not

Workers sewing parachutes at
the Parachute Company of
Utah in Manti.

directly related to agriculture. The plant repaired and produced individual parachutes, cargo parachutes, and bomb parachutes over the course of its operation. Hundreds of workers from Sanpete and neighboring counties in central Utah and elsewhere were employed throughout the war in jobs ranging from sewing and inspection to supervising production. The plant was staffed and supervised primarily by women, who ranged from sixteen (though the advertised and legal age was eighteen) to forty years of age.[5]

Women more than forty and those with physical handicaps organized their own Independent Parachute Company of Utah, which was headquartered in the Church of Jesus Christ of Latter-day Saints' bishop's storehouse near the plant. According to Lila Keller, the leader of this independent company, Fauntleroy called her into his office and said that he could not hire the older women at the main plant, presumably because of insurance costs, but wanted them to be able to work.[6] With the help of an attorney and after several visits with Governor Maw, Keller handled the legalities and setup of the Independent Parachute Company, which operated as a subcontractor from the main plant. The women who worked at this independent company "did all the hand work on the packs including the cutting and waxing of the webbing."[7] This group was significant because it demonstrated that for some women, opportunity was limited by age, physical, or racial discrimination. Yet in this case, the women were proactive in creating their own opportunities.

The memories of central Utah's wartime workers share some general themes. Motivations for work varied, but the work itself had a significant impact on the women of Manti and their various situations in a rural community during World War II. In many ways, the lives of the parachute plant's workers illustrated the changes and experiences that many Utahns, especially women, felt during this time of war.

Of the twenty-nine workers about whom data was collected, twenty-seven were women. Twelve were married (one married after working for a year and then returned), eleven were single, two were widowed, and two were divorced (one divorced during her time at the plant). Eleven of the women had children, who ranged in age from infants to teenagers. These twenty-seven women said that they chose to work in Manti's parachute factory because the job presented opportunities for a patriotic contribution, offered alternatives to rural work, and provided desired economic necessities and benefits. Underlying the complexity of their motivations, however, was the common factor that economic incentives were paramount. Overall, then, these women primarily worked out of patriotic duty and for pay. Working in this wartime industry held a larger significance for these women as individuals because it empowered them by placing newfound economic resources at their disposal and gave them experiences outside of the traditional context of home and family.

Margaret LuRae Munk Greenwood, a worker in the parachute plant, remembered well the impact the war had on her central Utah community: "It was terrible for our community, because many of our fellows were in the navy, and many of the young men my age were in the National Guard. The casualties of the young men from Manti were great. Nearly all the young men from the small communities around Manti—Ephraim, Mayfield, Sterling, etc.—went, and a lot of them were lost."[8]

World War II influenced the lives of nearly every resident of Sanpete County in some way. A total of 1,803 residents, representing approximately 11 percent of the county population, served in the armed forces between October 1, 1940 and June 30, 1946; Sanpete ranked eighth of the twenty-nine Utah counties in the number of residents serving in the armed forces.[9] Accordingly a major motivation for women working in the parachute plant was the opportunity to contribute to the war effort. Because many of these workers had immediate family members in the service, personal ties spurred their desire to help win the war. As an alternative to joining a branch of the service themselves (such as the Women's Army Auxiliary Corps [WAAC][10] or the Nursing Corps), these women recognized working at the plant as an opportunity to contribute actively and escape the relative lack of power they felt on the home front to safeguard their loved ones or affect the course of the war.

Like Greenwood, many of the younger women who worked at the plant had connections to people in the service: friends, brothers, husbands, and other relatives. Luzon Sondrup Longaker had two brothers in the service, one a bombardier in the air force and the other in the navy on an aircraft carrier near Battaan. Zola Anderson Ruesch had a brother in the navy, and her boyfriend was a paratrooper. Wretha Peterson Nielsen had a nephew and six other school classmates killed in action. Doris S. Morley Hansen had two brothers in the service. Dora Price Fautin, who had brothers overseas as well, remembered that "we were also proud of working there. . . . We all had to do our part to win the war and get the men home to their families." Seventeen-year-old Marjorie Jenson Anderson had two older brothers in the service and felt that she "had to do something to help." Because her mother would not allow her to join the WAAC, Anderson helped "fight" through her efforts at the parachute plant instead. Alice Fredricksen Clark's younger brother was in the air force so she was "extra strict. . . . I went the extra mile on account of him. I didn't want him out in a parachute and have anything go wrong with it." The day he left, however, was such an emotional time that she could not bear to come to work. The war was a very difficult time for her personally because her brother was shot down over Germany and placed in a prison camp. He almost died of starvation and had to recover in a hospital in France for quite some time before coming back to the United States. She remembered that "the war was just hard, especially when you had relatives [in the service]."[11]

Several of these young women also married soldiers. Utah soldiers on furloughs were allowed to tour the parachute plant on several occasions. Through such meetings, Fautin and Georgia Torgerson Jolley met their future husbands. "The fellows were good lookin' in their uniforms," Jolley remembered. Greenwood married a soldier in August of 1943 and left the plant for a time while he was stationed in Chicago. She came back in November and worked as long as she could before pregnancy made it too difficult. In late 1944, Longaker also married a pilot in the air force. LuElla Peterson Thornton's husband was one of the first to be drafted from her hometown in Sevier County. They had a small daughter when he left to fight overseas for about three years, seeing action in Africa and Italy and receiving two wounds. His family allowance of forty dollars a month was not enough to live on, so Thornton took a job at the parachute plant. She moved to a house in Manti that she shared with her sisters, where they took turns on shifts, alternately caring for her child. She remembered that the job helped her both financially and emotionally to get through such a trying period in her life.[12]

The middle-aged women, including those at the Independent Parachute Company, often had sons in the service. Odessa Young Mower's oldest son was in the navy. Lillian Keller had a boy in the National Guard, and another was a gunner on an airplane that dropped bombs over Germany. Lila Keller remembered that one woman worker, Mary Peterson, had six sons and a son-in-law in the military at the same time. According to Keller, Peterson declared, "This is my contribution to the war. That job saved my sanity." Keller remembered that the women she knew "desired to be involved in the war effort."[13]

Employees stretching parachutes in the Manti parachute factory.

In general many women at the plant cited patriotic motivations for working there. Hansen "felt good, doing something for the War Effort." Greenwood remembered that "there were great patriotic feelings among the women workers" and "they were thrilled to be working in the plant." Zola Ann Jensen recalled that the women at the plant were held "in high regard" because of their patriotic contributions. Nielsen thought that the war brought people closer together. Vera Sorensen felt that she was doing her duty by helping in the war effort.[14]

Both supervisors and employees often funneled patriotism into precision and attention to detail. Fautin stated that "we took our responsibilities serious[ly]. We knew that it was a government project, and we respected that." Jolley, who inspected the parachute seams over a lighted table, remembered "watching real close for bad stitches, because if one didn't get picked up, it could ruin the chute. The soldier could get killed." Clark was "really strict with inspection" and recalled a "government inspector that would go over a lot of it, and check it to see if we'd done it right." She added that "the parachutes were safe. We inspected them until we about wore them out!"[15]

The women put notes to the soldiers in the parachutes, and sometimes they got replies of one kind or another. Greenwood remembered the women's notes, saying, "I'm so and so. I live in Manti, Utah. I'm making this parachute so that you can arrive safely on earth." Sorensen had letters from servicemen thanking the workers because the parachutes had saved their lives. Maurine Braithwaite Draper also recalled receiving such letters. Management used letters from soldiers whose lives had been saved by Manti's parachutes to build morale. One letter to Mrs. Betty K. Lowry, dated April 17, 1943, from Colonel Fauntleroy stated, "The Company has been advised that Sgt. W.R. Shaman of Hobbs Flying Field recently made a successful emergency jump in Standard parachute No. 42–193179 which was made here in the Manti plant. You will be especially glad to hear of his safe landing because you worked on this particular parachute. We are proud, as I am sure you will be, that your work has saved a man who is prepared to give his life in defending you and the rest of us on the home front."[16]

Another letter detailing the plant's duty to preserve soldiers' lives (and reinforcing work standards) was sent to Greenwood herself by John D. Mumma, Fauntleroy's right-hand man, on May 30, 1942. In a patriotic, yet slightly condescending, tone, it read, "It is our sincere hope that you will always work so carefully that you would not hesitate to ask your own brother to entrust his safety to your parachute, should he happen to be the American soldier, sailor or marine who will wear it."[17]

The plant workers' patriotic efforts were also celebrated in the local newspapers. In one instance, Reliance Manufacturing published a letter in the *Manti Messenger* from a soldier who was thankful for the chute that had saved his life. The accompanying article claimed "that letters arrive daily" of this sort and that the soldiers requested membership "in the famed Reliance Club, an exclusive organization for G.I.'s who have made successful emergency jumps."[18]

The tight security and inspection processes that the plant maintained were also reminders of the company's patriotic duty to the country's servicemen. Lois Tooth Kribs recalled, "The United States was at war, and we were building parachutes in Manti. We didn't want any aliens in the plant. There was a security guard at the door till the war ended, and the workers all wore a badge." The women were checked when entering and exiting the plant. Fautin said, "Everybody was checked at the door on the way out. Security was tight." Clark remembered that "we couldn't carry things in there [the plant building]; we had inspectors check us when we went in. They were very strict."[19]

Thus, their personal relationships to the war linked work for these women to patriotism as a duty. They had brothers, friends, husbands, sons, and other relatives in the service. Contacts with soldiers on leave and through letters and notes also made the war more of a reality for the women workers. Making a conscious effort in a war industry could at least partially alleviate the emotional trauma associated with wondering and waiting on the home front and therefore "save one's sanity." Longaker eloquently summed up the feelings of many women when she said that working at the plant "increased my patriotism and gave me greater love for my country and fellow men. Since then, I have had a greater desire to serve others. It gave me more appreciation for those who were serving their country and giving their lives that we might have peace."[20]

Since Manti was a rural community, many, if not most, of the women who came to work at the parachute plant had grown up in households whose focus was agricultural. Traditionally, in addition to housework (which included the time-consuming tasks of preparing and preserving food, providing and maintaining clothing, and cleaning house) and childbearing, farm wives often tended flocks, worked in a garden, and milked cows. They produced commodities such as eggs, vegetables, and butter on the farm to sell in the marketplace, thereby earning a small, independent income.[21] If women desired work for wages, however, options were limited due to the lack of industry in this rural area of the state.

In addition, the income derived from farms was often not enough to sustain families, especially because of the devastating effects of the Depression. Most of the fathers and husbands of the women who worked at the plant were small businessmen or farmers, like many others in the area. One former worker remembered that "it was hard making a living in this area, and everybody wanted to work hard," and another recalled that "the area was depressed at that time; we had nothing but our farms."[22]

Because opportunities to earn money were scarce for women and they often preferred work off the farm, the parachute plant's jobs were welcomed as a preferable alternative in a rural area. The advertisement of work in the parachute plant, with its relatively good wages and working conditions, enticed women.[23] Several of the parachute workers had been formerly employed in cafés or doing housework for others, and farm work was limited in the winter. Some women

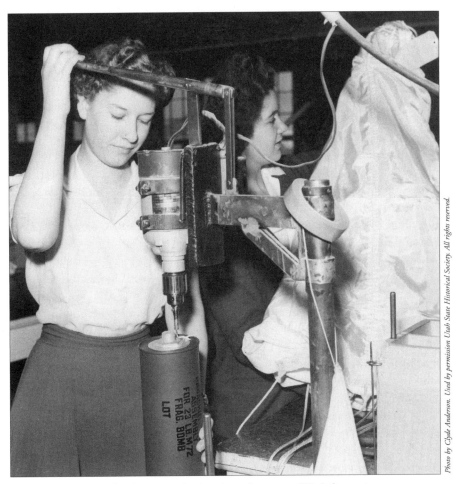

Wrapping a parachute for shipping at the Parachute Company of Utah factory.

disliked farm work altogether. One woman in particular was very relieved to escape unfeminine work clothes, the heat, and the unpleasant insects associated with her tasks on the farm.[24]

Work at the parachute plant also appealed to the women because of the social atmosphere. If they were lonely at home or on the farm or bored by other pursuits, such sociability provided a real attraction. The Independent Parachute Company workers also told stories and jokes, enjoyed refreshments, and shared a thought for the day. Greenwood remembered that the workers "were tired when we got through. But we had a lot of camaraderie. Even though the plant was noisy, with all the machines going, we visited a lot. We talked loud." A supervisor at the plant remarked, "The workers at Manti were basically all good workers. . . . They liked to talk a lot, but who doesn't?" (Objections, however, were raised against a woman singing opera while operating her sewing machine.)[25]

Another former worker thought that the women worked mostly harmoniously together because they had similar backgrounds. Women assumed different roles to help one another; one of the Independent Parachute Company workers became a self-appointed doctor, opening her black bag and prescribing old remedies whenever anyone had an ailment. Some workers made commuting more enjoyable by singing as they rode the bus to work. Workers gathered in the plant cafeteria to eat lunch and talk on their breaks. The women socialized outside the plant and storehouse as well, coming together for group dinners, ice cream, roller skating, movies, and a variety of other activities. Workers remembered and cherished these experiences and friendships, and even held reunions long after their war work ended. Prestige and social bonding were also important. Lila Keller, who had "a lot of connections, including all the leading women in Manti," said that the Independent Parachute Company workers were "elite," the most "prominent women in Manti." Social interaction was especially helpful to the women because their work was long, difficult, often tedious, and even painful at times. Visiting helped the minutes and hours go by faster.[26]

Yet of all the motivations for work in the parachute plant, economic necessity stands out as predominant.[27] The comparative value of the women's wages, individual circumstances, and the economic realities of the ongoing Depression made the situation for many people in Manti one of real need. For the women who worked there, as one worker put it, the plant "was a blessing to our area as most families had low incomes."[28]

Wages at the plant were generally considered good for the time and place. In comparison to other industries or occupations, the $25-to-$30-per-week paycheck at the parachute plant was considered a decent amount for a woman in rural Utah. Jensen remembered earning $.60 an hour, significantly more than her previous job as a waitress that had paid $.50 a day, later raised to $1.00. She also said that her pay at the parachute plant was "considered *big* wages" because men were getting about $1.00 or $2.00 a day for work then. Ruth Scow remembered that her husband only earned $1.00 a day at the time and exclaimed that "life was hard in the Depression!" At a local pea cannery, she had earned $.17 an hour, and during the 1930s, she had cooked and only earned $40 a month, less than what she could earn in only two weeks at the plant. One of Nielsen's paychecks is probably typical of what women earned at the plant. For the period between May 8 and May 14, 1943, she worked forty-eight hours, and, with an hourly rate of $.50 plus overtime, she made a total of $28.29 after taxes. Fautin remembered getting a bonus at Thanksgiving and Christmas. Her Christmas check stub recorded a $100 bonus, of which she received $79.00 after taxes. "It was a good bonus, a lot of money," she stated. In late 1943, she made $.55 an hour, and in 1944 it was $.60. Some women were paid more than others due to experience, rate of work, and job specificity, and Clark recalled making about $1.00 an hour.[29]

Though the wages were not as high as those in large cities, they were comparable or better than local options. In Salt Lake City at the Remington Arms Plant, workers earned about $22 a week, and a final inspector of small cartridges made about $30 a week. Women workers in Utah's department stores earned around $10.50 per week. In the United States at large, a waitress averaged $14 a week, whereas a woman shipyard worker averaged $37. In comparison a cleaning woman could earn as little as $2.00 a week. In addition, the women's memories about the differential between men's and women's wages are significant for what they do not say. Society seemed to accept without question the existence of a gap between men's and women's wages; women were not expected to earn as much as men did in a day's work at the time. With this newfound war work, however, women were able to make as much as or sometimes more than men did. In manufacturing in 1944, however, women in the United States at large averaged $31.21 per week, whereas men earned $54.65 on average.[30]

Individual circumstances dictated the value of the economic contributions of those wages for the women. Edith Buchanan Bown's statement is typical of their experience: "We had to make our own way through life; I know what a dollar means. To this day, a dollar means a lot to me." One of the women had been widowed at a young age and took the job to feed herself and her children. Two others were young divorcees in need of work to strike out successfully on their own; they greatly appreciated the parachute plant and its wages for their family survival. One divorcée's parents, with whom she was living, were very much in favor of her working because she had very little money. The other moved into an apartment with a friend and successfully made her own way, while relatives watched her children. Another woman was a twenty-six-year-old widow. She was happy to find work to support her family since she stated that "priar [*sic*] to the war it was a disgrace for women to work. If they were fortunate enough to find work–25 cents per hour was the wage." She called war work "a gold mine" in those "Depression days." Her comment about women's working being a disgrace likely reflects her attitude about men's inability to provide and a sense of propriety about female behavior: it was a "disgrace" if a man could not support his family and his wife had to work to do so.[31]

A dollar meant a lot to married women as well. One woman's husband did not want her to work, and neither did her parents, but she worked at the parachute plant to pay for their dry farm and a new home. Another woman and her husband were buying a store in their hometown of Fairview and needed the money to survive that transitional period. Others often either saved the money or used it for family necessities. Marjorie Anderson's mother, Mildred, had a separate checking account in which she kept her money. Her husband said of her, "I really have to hand it to Mildred. If we ever needed anything that I couldn't provide, she got out and she got a job and we got the money."[32]

Women did a variety of things with the money they earned because new resources were now at their disposal. According to Lila Keller, "When women make their own money, they're going to use it where they want and where they feel like they need it most." She remembered that many women saved and later used their money for indoor bathroom facilities and kitchen renovations. In Keller's own case, she bought an overstuffed chair and a bull for $250 because her livestock needed upgrading. "With money from work at the plant," Greenwood remembered, "families in the community got things in their home that they'd never had before—bathrooms, new kitchens. At that time, a lot of people didn't have refrigerators or bathrooms, and their kitchens were outmoded. We had been through a Depression era." Another worker mostly bought family necessities and living room furniture, including a prized overstuffed chair. She was also able to afford indoor plumbing for the first time and pay for her children to have music lessons. Yet another installed lights, water, and a bathroom in her home in Centerfield, upgrades that she had been wanting for some time. The young, single women were excited to have "money to spend" and mostly bought clothes and furniture; one even bought a 1941 Hudson coupe.[33]

New economic opportunities also played a major part in community support of women's working. Making a living in Sanpete County could be difficult at this time. In that context, one early parachute plant advertisement claiming that women could "work for national defense and *keep your earnings in your own home*" takes on greater significance. Likewise, one man's 1942 statement about the parachute plant coming to Manti revealed economic relief: "Now we can live here until we die." Another man thought that the parachute plant "looks like a golden opportunity. Our women have been holding on, now they [are going] to be OK with a good job."[34]

Retrospective comments also emphasized increased economic opportunity for the community. One young woman captured this feeling when she said, "We needed something here in town to help support because there just wasn't [*sic*] jobs here at the time" and added that she loved sewing and wanted "something to do" away from the farm.[35] One of the men who worked at the plant remembered that "community reaction to the factory was good," seemingly because of the opportunity for jobs. Ruesch recalled that "women were just happy to have a job." Her answers pinpointed the difficulty of supporting a family in a rural community. "I think it was a help" she said; "that was the way I looked at it. Every woman helped." Since she came from a family where her mother contributed significantly on the farm by doing chores like milking twenty-two cows, her experience verified that every woman helped. Even after women went out to work, that rural reality still held true.[36]

Overall, the motivations for going to work varied from woman to woman but they reveal a lot about women's personal lives during this period and what it meant for them to be able to work and earn money. Patriotic motives and rural alternatives appear to have shaped many women's decisions to take a job at the parachute plant. For many of the women, weekly paychecks provided a more stable income than did farming. Several used their wages to improve their standard of living, while other women, especially the young and unmarried, were able to enhance their purchasing ability and break away from more traditional types of rural work.[37] The work done by women at Manti's parachute plant and the wages they earned there increased their personal opportunities and impacted both their communities and their financial and personal independence.

Many women workers desired and continued to work after the war ended as public opinion polls suggested that they would. An article in the *Manti Messenger* in July 1944 reported that "women intend to stay at jobs." "Two out of every three women war workers," it stated, "will be in the postwar competition for peacetime jobs, according to preliminary returns in a survey by Northwestern National Life Insurance Company. . . . the survey finds that 71 per cent plan to seek postwar jobs, and only 17 per cent expect to go back to 'full-time' housekeeping, while 10 per cent are planning to be married at the end of the war, and 2 per cent expect to go back to school." The article discussed married women as well, who "like the experience of working and want to continue getting a pay check of their own."[38]

In all more than half of these parachute plant employees continued working after the war's conclusion (eighteen out of twenty-seven). They were typical. Nita Price Madsen recalled that "there was very little turnover at the plant" and "many women in the area have continued to work at the clothing manufacturing plant over the years." Betty Anderson did not "remember very many people quitting work at the Manti factory." Greenwood also remembered that "there wasn't much turnover at the plant. Once someone got a job there, they stayed."[39]

Historians have debated the short- or long-range impact of World War II on women's work opportunities and the importance of that period in shaping the women's movement of later decades. Some believe that the war significantly expanded women's economic opportunities, marking a watershed in the history of working women, while others argue that those benefits were mostly temporary.[40] Most studies focus primarily on urban areas such as Los Angeles or Baltimore and exclusively address women who worked in previously male-dominated industries such as shipbuilding or steel working. In these industries, most women lost their jobs to men at the conclusion of the war. In rural Sanpete County, though, women's work experiences during the war were central to their lives. Even if the work did not produce immediately discernible results for women's rights in the workplace, it had a long-term impact upon individuals. Personal, individual victories, often ignored or subverted in aggregate statistics on women's work during and immediately following the war, were a reality for these women in Manti and likely elsewhere in Utah and America.

If the influence on individual women was great, it was also significant for families and communities. In Utah industrial growth in places like Manti accelerated the state's shift from rural to urban, to a consumer society, and to increased reliance upon the federal government.[41] Manti, Utah's parachute factory, and its workers' experiences provide a case study for the economic modernization and increasing federal involvement that marked Utahns' lives in the war era.

Nonetheless, there are limitations to the evidence in this study. Oral interviews and questionnaires have their own problems, and not everyone who worked in the plant is represented. There is also reason to believe that some women came away from their wartime work with more negative than positive reactions. Unpleasant relationships with coworkers due to conflicting personalities or ideas could have made the workplace unpleasant. Sexual harassment, though likely less extensive in the plant because it was staffed primarily by women, was often a problem in war industries. Some women might have been fired for one reason or another. Others might have experienced marital disruption from unsupportive husbands and families. It is possible that women with negative experiences such as these would be unwilling to share their reminiscences and so are not represented here.[42] Yet one thing is clear. For the women in this sample, the long-range impact of their war experience was great and positive, and the story of the women of Manti who chose to work during a difficult and transitional period in American history is a compelling one that deserves to be told.

Even those who did not choose to continue working remember their experiences fondly. For example, Alice Johnson Anderson, who quit working after her brother was killed overseas and her mother's health declined rapidly, said that she enjoyed working at the plant. Eager to share her memories with the author, she commented that she had had good experiences with friends and felt proud of her war effort. She volunteered to show a variety of pictures and keepsakes relating to that period of her life. Anderson has pictures from the 1940s of the "parachute gang" that rode together in an old hearse to work every day. She also has pictures from a parachute plant reunion that she attended at the Nephi park in August of 1968 and copies of the obituaries of parachute company friends. She includes her time at the parachute plant in the narrative of her personal history. Zola Ruesch, who quit working at Safeway once she married, also took pleasure in her work at the plant: "I liked doing something at the time, and we enjoyed it." A portion of her personal history scrapbook is also dedicated to information and pictures of her experiences at the parachute plant, illustrating this period's importance among the events of her life.[43]

For many women, working at the parachute plant was a learning experience that promoted both their confidence and independence. These women proved to themselves that they could work outside the home, and it is evident that such experiences increased their self-esteem and gave them a broader concept of their capabilities. For nineteen-year-old Zola Jensen, working presented an opportunity for education: "My family could not afford to send me to college. If I had not had this job [at that time when I was college age] I probably would not have gone to college." She remarked that added education

Packaging parachutes for shipping at the Manti parachute factory.

helped her to get better jobs in the future as well. Kribs, in commenting on some work training in Los Angeles, said, "Imagine, I got on the train at Salt Lake City, hardly ever having been out of Manti, let alone the state of Utah," but she conquered her fears. She continued working for the government for many years, buoyed up by her newfound experiences. Mower was glad for the experience away from home while also doing something for her country. She knew that she could do housework, but she was unsure if she could work at a plant. She gained confidence, however, because she was able to do the work well. Betty Anderson said that she "learned discipline" and "learned to work with other people" at the parachute plant. Carol Beesley also remembered that working at the parachute plant in Manti taught her how to get along with others. She also said, "I learned how to run a machine and do what I had to do. So, it was a good education to start out there."[44]

The working women had additional resources at their disposal due to the money they were now able to earn and in some cases had the newfound ability to support themselves. Economic opportunity made Draper feel more independent, especially because she lived alone and had children. Recently divorced, she did not have to rely on her parents or move back in with them. She rented an apartment with a friend and moved on with her life, eventually remarrying. Two other women were also able to support themselves as young divorcées with children.[45]

Women's war work not only contributed financially to the economic prosperity of the family but influenced the way their children viewed working women. As historian Jessica Weiss has observed, the mothers of the baby boom balanced work, housework, and childrearing, and their daughters followed suit.[46] Accordingly there is a sense that central Utah's former parachute workers are proud of their children who work, including their daughters. One former parachute-plant worker spoke proudly of her daughter, an assistant manager at a local business, and a daughter-in-law who works at a local branch of Far West Bank. Clark mentioned her sons and daughters with equal pride: "They've all been real good–I'm proud of all of them." Her youngest daughter works for the IRS, and her oldest daughter is a schoolteacher.[47]

Altogether twenty-five of the twenty-seven women said that the experience of working at the parachute plant was significant for them in one way or another, especially providing new economic resources or new experiences.[48] As a result, a sense of pride emanates from talking to these women about their work, summarized deftly by Lila Keller: "My heart swells with pride when I think of the unity, love, and dedication they [the working women] displayed during those trying years." Another woman reflected, "I have spent a whole lifetime in that type of work [parachute and sewing production], and I haven't been sorry." Marjorie Anderson recounted, "When [my] mother was working at the plant, I was with her when her friend asked her if she wasn't afraid of the high-powered sewing machine, and as fast as she sewed wasn't she afraid of having the needle stick in her finger. Mother said, 'No, it's the only thing that goes as fast as I want it to.'"[49]

As LuRae Greenwood aptly stated, she was "proud to send those parachutes off."[50] *Proud* is an excellent word to describe these women as they attached meaning to their work experiences. Proud of their newly acquired economic resources; proud of a job done well; proud of finding a job that paid well and went "as fast" as they wanted it to—these were the experiences of central Utah's parachute plant Rosies. Manti's parachute plant and its workers provide a case study for the life-changing effects of work for women during World War II as they learned new skills, gained confidence in their abilities, chose various careers, and viewed themselves differently. As wartime industries took hold in Utah, wartime work shaped the rest of these women's lives.

NOTES

1. Gerald D. Nash, *The Federal Landscape: An Economic History of the Twentieth-Century West* (Tucson: University of Arizona Press, 1999), 42–54; Nash, *World War II and the West: Reshaping the Economy* (Lincoln: University of Nebraska Press, 1990); Carl Abbott, *The Metropolitan Frontier: Cities in the Modern American West* (Tucson: University of Arizona Press, 1993), 4; Thomas G. Alexander, *Utah, the Right Place: The Official Centennial History,* rev. ed. (Salt Lake City: Gibbs Smith, 2003), 344–45.

2. Allan Kent Powell, "Utah and World War II," *Utah Historical Quarterly* 73 (Spring 2005): 110–11; Herbert B. Maw, *Adventures with Life* (Salt Lake City: Privately printed, 1978), 164; Antonette Chambers Noble, "Utah's Defense Industries and Workers in World War II," *Utah Historical Quarterly* 59 (Fall 1991): 356–79.

3. Powell, "Utah and World War II," 119; Allan Kent Powell, *Utah Remembers World War II* (Logan: Utah State University Press, 1991), x–xiii; Antonette Chambers Noble, "Utah's Rosies: Women in the Utah War Industries during World War II," *Utah Historical Quarterly* 59 (Spring 1991): 126; Miriam B. Murphy, "Gainfully Employed Women: 1896–1950," in *Women in Utah History: Paradigm or Paradox?* ed. Patricia Lyn Scott and Linda Thatcher (Logan: Utah State University Press, 2005), 211, 213; Antonette Chambers, "Utah's Rosies: Women in the Utah War Industries during World War II" (master's thesis, University of Utah, 1987), 105–6.

4. Powell, "Utah and World War II," 111–12; Noble, "Utah's Defense Industries," 366–70; Alexander, *Utah, the Right Place,* 338–51.

5. "Parachute Plant Given to Manti," *Mt. Pleasant Pyramid,* April 10, 1942; "Ground Broken for New Parachute Building," *Manti Messenger,* June 26, 1942; "New Building for Chute Plant Started; Age Limit Raised," *Ephraim Enterprise,* June 26, 1942; Luzon Sondrup Longaker, "Memories of the Parachute Company of Utah and Reliance Manufacturing Company, World War II," January 1985, typescript, p. 1, copy in author's possession; Albert C. T. Antrei and Allen D. Roberts, *A History of Sanpete County* (Salt Lake City: Utah State Historical Society and Sanpete County Commission, 1999), 271; Betty Keller Anderson, interview by Don Norton, July 7, 1994, Manti, Utah, p. 2, copy of transcript of tape recording in author's possession.

"Local Plant Gets Maw's Help," *Manti Messenger,* May 5, 1944; "Governor Will Investigate Manti Plant," *Manti Messenger,* May 12, 1944; "Plant Workers Return to Their Home," *Manti Messenger,* May 5, 1944; "Manti Gets First Utah Post-War Plant," *Manti Messenger* and *Ephraim Enterprise,* June 30, 1944; Susie Fields Tatton, interview by Don Norton, March 25, 1997, Manti, Utah, pp. 4–5, copy of transcript of tape recording in author's possession; C.E. Fauntleroy to Herbert B. Maw, September 12, 1942, "Parachute Company of Utah," Governor Maw correspondence, 1942, Utah State Archives, Salt Lake City. Reports of the plant's total employment varied anywhere from 150 people at the outset to peak numbers around 450, although Fauntleroy had initially hoped for three shifts of 1,000 to 1,200 women.

Carlisle Manufacturing Company operated sewing plants in Ephraim and Gunnison for twenty years beginning in the 1950s. In 1961 the Manti Improvement Business Association and members of local women's clubs collected donations to help remodel and buy the building that had housed the parachute plant to lease it to a clothing manufacturer. Their efforts attracted Apparel Inc. of Seattle, makers of Pacific Trail Sportswear, which opened in 1961 with a force of 100 women and 5 men employees and expanded to more than 150 employees within the year. Another plant also opened in 1962 in nearby Richfield. The Manti plant was subsequently owned by other companies, including Pyke Manufacturing Company and River's West. Utah Sportswear opened a plant in Mt. Pleasant in 1980 as well. Katherine L. Lueck and John R. Evans, "From Overalls to Unmentionables," *Utah Economic and Business Review* 21 (April 1961), 4–5; Tatton interview, pp. 6, 8; Nita Price Madsen, interview by Don Norton, March 25, 1997, Manti, Utah, p. 4, copy of transcript of tape recording in author's possession; "Open House Scheduled by Factory at Manti," *Deseret News,* October 6, 1961; "Manti Enjoys New Unity, Hopefulness with 'Operation Bootstrap' Success," *Deseret News,* February 28, 1962; "Firm to Open New Plant at Richfield," *Salt Lake Tribune,* April 19, 1962; "New Business for Richfield," *Deseret News,* June 27, 1962; "Clothing Factory to Double Staff at Richfield," *Deseret News,* June 14, 1962; Antrei and Roberts, *History of Sanpete County,* 268; Albert C. T. Antrei and Ruth D. Scow, eds., *The Other Forty-Niners: A Topical History of Sanpete County, Utah 1849–1983* (Salt Lake City: Western Epics, 1982), 255–56.

6.   Lila Bartholomew Keller, interview by Don Norton, April 1, 1997, Manti, Utah, p. 1, copy of transcript of tape recording in author's possession.

7.   Lila Bartholomew Keller, "The Independent Parachute Company," n.d., typescript, pp. 2–4, 7, copy in author's possession; Keller interview, pp. 1–2.

8.   Margaret LuRae Munk Greenwood, interview by Don Norton, March 27, 1997, Orem, Utah, p. 1, copy of transcript of tape recording in author's possession.

9.   Powell, *Utah Remembers World War II,* xii; U.S. Bureau of the Census, *Sixteenth Census of the United States Taken in the Year 1940,* vol 2, *Characteristics of the Population,* pt. 7 (Washington, DC: GPO, 1943), 39, 61.

10. The Women's Army Auxiliary Corps, or WAAC, was established on May 15, 1942, after a bill authorizing it passed Congress and was signed by President Franklin D. Roosevelt. U.S. Representative Edith Nourse Rogers of Massachusetts had proposed

the idea of establishing a women's branch of the army in early 1941, but it was met initially with so much controversy and opposition in both Congress and the army that it was abandoned. The women of the WAAC were considered civilians serving with the army. Four other women's military branches followed in 1942 and 1943 for the United States Navy, Coast Guard, Marines and Air Force. Emily Yellin, *Our Mothers' War: American Women at Home and at the Front during World War II* (New York: Simon & Schuster Free Press, 2004), 113–16. By June 19, 1945, 1,343 Utah women were serving in uniform. Powell, *Utah Remembers World War II,* xi. Utah women also did countless hours of volunteer work in organizations like the Salt Lake City Minute Women. Katie Clark Blakesley, "'Save 'Em, Wash 'Em, Clean 'Em, Squash 'Em': The Story of the Salt Lake City Minute Women," *Utah Historical Quarterly* 71 (2003): 36–51.

11. Luzon Sondrup Longaker, questionnaire, January 9. 1985, p. 1, copy in author's possession; Zola Anderson Ruesch, interview by author, November 26, 2005, Mt. Pleasant, Utah, pp. 1–2, transcript of digital recording in author's possession; Wretha Peterson Nielsen, questionnaire, 1984, p. 1, copy in author's possession; Doris S. Morley Hansen, questionnaire, January 1985, p. 3, copy in author's possession; Dora Price Fautin, interview by Don Norton, March 27, 1997, Lindon, Utah, p. 4, copy of transcript of tape recording in author's possession; Marjorie Jenson Anderson, interview by author, September 17, 2005, Richfield, Utah, p. 4, transcript of digital recording in author's possession; Alice Fredricksen Clark, interview by author, September 17, 2005, Centerfield, Utah, pp. 3, 5, transcript of digital recording in author's possession. The author thanks Antonette Chambers Noble for the use of her questionnaires and Don Norton for the use of his oral interviews, which made a larger data pool possible.

12. Fautin interview, p. 4; Georgia Torgerson Jolley, interview by Don Norton, March 27, 1997, Lindon, Utah, p. 4, copy of transcript of tape recording in author's possession; Greenwood interview, pp. 2, 5; Longaker questionnaire, p. 1; LuElla Peterson Thornton, interview by author, October 17, 2005, American Fork, Utah, p. 1, transcript of digital recording in author's possession. Zola Ruesch and Carol Beesley also married soldiers, though after the war's conclusion; Ruesch interview, p. 1; Carol Ney Beesley, interview by author, November 26, 2005, Mt. Pleasant, Utah, p. 1, transcript of digital recording in author's possession.

13. Odessa Young Mower, questionnaire, August 4, 1984, p. 1, copy in author's possession; Lillian Keller, interview by Don Norton, April 1, 1997, Manti, Utah, p. 1, copy of transcript of tape recording in author's possession; Lila Keller interview, pp. 3–4.

14. Hansen questionnaire, p. 3; Greenwood interview, p. 2; Mower questionnaire, p. 2; Zola Ann Jensen, questionnaire, September 1984, p. 3, copy in author's possession; Nielsen questionnaire, p. 2; Vera Sorensen, questionnaire, August 4, 1984, p. 3, copy in author's possession.

15. Fautin interview, p. 3; Jolley interview, p. 3; Clark interview, pp. 3, 5.

16. Greenwood interview, p. 3; Sorensen questionnaire, p. 3; Maurine Braithwaite Draper, interview by author, September 17, 2005, Manti, Utah, p. 2, transcript of

digital recording in author's possession; C.E. Fauntleroy to Betty K. Lowry, April 17, 1943, copy in author's possession.

17. John D. Mumma to Miss LuRae Munk, May 30, 1942, copy in author's possession.

18. "Reliance Chutes Save Lives," *Manti Messenger,* March 16, 1945.

19. Lois Tooth Kribs, interview by Don Norton, April 1, 1997, Manti, Utah, p. 2, copy of transcript of tape recording in author's possession; Fautin interview, p. 3; Clark interview, pp. 3, 5.

20. Longaker questionnaire, p. 3.

21. Mary Neth, *Preserving the Family Farm: Women, Community, and the Foundation of Agribusiness in the Midwest, 1900–1940* (Baltimore: Johns Hopkins University Press, 1995), 250; Dean May, *Three Frontiers: Family, Land, and Society in the American West, 1850–1900* (New York: Cambridge University Press, 1994), 139; Susan Sessions Rugh, *Our Common Country: Family Farming, Culture, and Community in the Nineteenth-Century Midwest* (Bloomington: Indiana University Press, 2001), 65–67.

22. Kribs interview, pp. 3, 6–7; Greenwood interview, pp. 1–2; see also Longaker questionnaire, p. 1; Marjorie Anderson interview, p. 2; Hansen questionnaire, p. 3; Mower questionnaire, p. 3; Draper interview, pp. 4, 6; Fautin interview, p. 1; Ruesch interview, p. 3; Jolley interview, p. 2; and Jensen questionnaire, p. 3. According to the 1940 census, seventy-five men and two women in Sanpete County were employed in the manufacturing of food and associated products. Bureau of the Census, *Sixteenth Census, Characteristics of the Population,* 48.

23. Greenwood interview, pp. 1–2; Dortha Bagley Braithwaite, interview by Don Norton, March 25, 1997, Manti, Utah, p. 1, copy of transcript of tape recording in author's possession; Longaker questionnaire, p. 2; Clark interview, p. 2; Marjorie Anderson interview, p. 7.

24. Kribs interview, pp. 6–7; Fautin interview, p. 1; Ruesch interview, p. 3; Longaker, "Memories of the Parachute Company," p. 3; Clark interview, p. 3; Marjorie Anderson interview, p. 7; Draper interview, p. 7.

25. Lila Keller interview, pp. 4, 7; Greenwood interview, pp. 3, 6; Tatton interview, p. 6; Longaker questionnaire, p. 2; Clark interview, p. 7; Fautin interview, p. 3; Jensen interview, p. 2; Betty Anderson interview, p. 4.

26. Lila Keller interview, pp. 4, 6; and Keller, "Independent Parachute Company," pp. 3–5; Beesley interview, p. 1; Braithwaite interview, p. 3; Madsen interview, p. 3; Fautin interview, pp. 3–4; Longaker questionnaire, p. 2; Clark interview, pp. 6–7; Alice Johnson Anderson, autobiographical reminiscences, pictures, and sketches, April 2006, handwritten, in author's possession; Lila Keller interview, pp. 4, 7; and Keller, "Independent Parachute Company," p. 4; Betty Anderson interview, p. 2; Jolley interview, p. 4.

27. Of the twenty-seven women workers for whom information is available, seventeen strongly claimed patriotic motivations for war work (more than a simple yes), representing approximately 63 percent of the sample. Lack of rural alternatives was strongly cited by nineteen of the women, or roughly 70 percent. Economic factors

(working for reasons of economic survival) were identified strongly by twenty-one out of the twenty-seven, or about 78 percent, but one suspects that economic factors played a part for most, if not all, of the women even if they did not want to admit it. It is worth noting that patriotic factors, due to the passage of time and the popularity of World War II, may be overstated in these numbers. Also note that some women cited a combination of all three motivations, others identified a combination of two factors, and some mentioned only one.

28.   Longaker, "Memories of the Parachute Company," p. 4.

29.   Jensen interview, p. 3; Ruth Scow, questionnaire, July 29, 1984, p. 3, copy in author's possession; Nielsen questionnaire, p. 4 (copy of pay stub); Fautin interview, p. 3 (copy of check stubs in author's possession); Clark interview, p. 3. Dortha Braithwaite remembered getting a $100 bonus on one occasion; Braithwaite interview, p. 2. Bernitta Barney also remembered a $.50 per hour wage and that she earned $4.00 a day for four years. She thought that such a wage was "very good—[the] first work women had ever had"; Bernitta Barney, questionnaire, mid-1980s, p. 3, copy in author's possession. Apparently some personal incentive plans existed for the four-needle operators, four-needle tape operators, zigging operators, and two-needle operators as well. C.E. Fauntleroy to Herbert B. Maw, July 10, 1942, "Parachute Company of Utah," Governor Maw correspondence, 1942, Utah State Archives.

30.   Murphy, "Gainfully Employed Women," 209; Chambers, "Utah's Rosies" (thesis), 102; Yellin, *Our Mothers' War,* 41; D'Ann Campbell, *Women at War with America: Private Lives in a Patriotic Era* (Cambridge, MA: Harvard University Press, 1984), 136.

31.   Edith Buchanan Bown, interview by Don Norton, July 2, 1994, Manti, Utah, p. 1, copy of transcript of tape recording in author's possession; Hansen questionnaire, p. 3; Longaker questionnaire, p. 3; Draper interview, p. 6; Barney questionnaire, pp. 2–3.

32.   Nielsen questionnaire, p. 2; Mower questionnaire, p. 3; Marjorie Anderson interview, p. 5.

33.   Lila Keller interview, pp. 7–8; Greenwood interview, pp. 1–2; Sorensen questionnaire, p. 2; Draper interview, p. 5; Kribs interview, pp. 6–7; Clark interview, p. 2; Fautin interview, p. 3; Marjorie Anderson interview, p. 4; Braithwaite interview, p. 2.

34.   Advertisement in *Mt Pleasant Pyramid,* December 25, 1942 (italics added); Ralph Hougaard and Adolph Hope, quoted in "Parachute Plant to Employ Hundreds," *Manti Messenger,* April 10, 1942.

35.   Draper interview, pp. 4–6.

36.   Vertis Leroy Nielson, interview by Don Norton, February 21, 1997, Ephraim, Utah, p. 1, copy of transcript of tape recording in author's possession; Ruesch interview, pp. 2, 4.

37.   It is difficult to quantify definitely the number of women who used their money for necessities (defined as shelter, food, clothing) versus extra income because none of them can be considered wealthy by any means. Many of these women were not used to luxuries and came from humble backgrounds, especially compared to present-day standards. Of the twenty-seven women, at least eight (or about 30 percent) were working to put food on the table, though this number may be smaller than the actual

figure because this sample is biased toward women who were younger. The other nineteen used their income to buy other items, to improve their living standards, to obtain extra commodities and education, or for a combination of these goals.

38. "Survey Shows Women Intend to Stay at Jobs," *Manti Messenger,* July 7, 1944.

39. Madsen interview, pp. 3–4; Betty Anderson interview, p. 6; Greenwood interview, p. 6; Braithwaite interview, p. 4. See Amanda Sue Midgley Borneman, "'Proud to Send Those Parachutes Off': Central Utah's Rosies during World War II" (master's thesis, Brigham Young University, 2006) for a more detailed discussion of the jobs women took after the war as well as a description of some of their other war experiences.

40. Two studies that argue for the watershed theory include William H. Chafe, *The American Woman: Her Changing Social, Economic, and Political Roles, 1920–1970* (New York: Oxford University Press, 1972); and Gregory Chester, *Women in Defense Work during World War II: An Analysis of the Labor Problem and Women's Rights* (Jericho, NY: Exposition Press Inc., 1974). Examples of studies that argue for continuity rather than change include Leila Rupp, *Mobilizing Women for War: German and American Propaganda, 1939–1945* (Princeton, NJ: Princeton University Press, 1978); Karen Anderson, *Wartime Women: Sex Roles, Family Relations, and the Status of Women during World War II* (Westport, CT: Greenwood Press, 1981); and Campbell, *Women at War with America.* For examples of urban studies with emphases on male-dominated industries, see Anderson, *Wartime Women;* Alan Clive, "Women Workers in World War II: Michigan as a Test Case," *Labor History* (Winter 1979): 44–72; and Sherna Berger Gluck, *Rosie the Riveter Revisited: Women, the War, and Social Change* (Boston: Twayne Publishers, 1987).

The March 2006 issue of the *Journal of American History* featured articles arguing that World War II and its aftermath represent "a critical moment" and a "crucial decade." New scholarship continues to present new angles and discover different ways in which the war altered American life, especially the life of ordinary people in an era of burgeoning government. Gary Gerstle commented that this development in historiography shares "a conviction of the centrality of the 1940s" and a "belief that local and regional history archives contain untapped riches that, if properly mined, can yield answers to important questions." David Paul Nord, "A Critical Moment: World War II and Its Aftermath at Home," *Journal of American History* 92 (March 2006): 1211; Gary Gerstle, "The Crucial Decade: The 1940s and Beyond," *Journal of American History* 92 (March 2006): 1292–99. See also Lewis A. Erenberg and Susan E. Hirsch, eds., *The War in American Culture: Society and Consciousness during World War II* (Chicago: University of Chicago Press, 1996).

41. Historians have also debated the war's long-range impact upon Utah and the West at large. See, for example, Abbott, *The Metropolitan Frontier,* 4; Nash, *The Federal Landscape,* 42–54; and Nash, *World War II and the West;* and Roger W. Lotchin, "The Historian's War or the Home Front's War?: Some Thoughts for Western Historians," *Western Historical Quarterly* 26 (Summer 1995): 195–96.

42. For examples of the scenarios in this paragraph, see Murphy, "Gainfully Employed Women," 210–11; Campbell, *Women at War with America,* 125–26; Lila Keller,

"Independent Parachute Company," pp. 5–6. The author also talked with some former workers who did not wish to give an interview.

43. Alice Johnson Anderson, phone interview by author, March 18, 2006, pp. 1–2, notes from phone conversation in author's possession; also reminiscences, pictures, sketches, April 2006; Ruesch interview, p. 1.

44. Jensen questionnaire, p. 3; Kribs interview, pp. 5–7; Mower questionnaire, p. 2; Betty Anderson interview, p. 6; Beesley interview, p. 5.

45. Draper interview, p. 6; Longaker questionnaire, p. 3; Betty Anderson interview, p. 3.

46. Jessica Weiss, *To Have and To Hold: Marriage, the Baby Boom, and Social Change* (Chicago: University of Chicago Press, 2000), 49–81.

47. Beesley interview, p. 2; Clark interview, p. 6.

48. Twenty-five out of twenty-seven women represent approximately 92 percent of the sample. These twenty-five were more explicit about saying their experience was significant, though perhaps the other two women were affected in ways unknown to the author.

49. Lila Keller interview, p. 5; Tatton interview, p. 10; Marjorie Anderson interview, p. 1.

50. Greenwood interview, p. 5.

6

Educating the Mormon Hierarchy

The Grassroots Opposition to the MX in Utah

Jacob W. Olmstead

The federal government's ownership of more than half the land in the Great Basin invited conversion of vast tracts for bombing and missile ranges, weapons installations, and military bases during the twentieth century. One of the largest would have been the ninety-eight-thousand-acre MX missile base proposed by the Carter and Reagan administrations. The base would have brought fresh infusions of capital and jobs but potentially disrupted social and ecological relationships in Utah's sparsely populated west desert. In the following chapter, Jacob W. Olmstead draws upon a rich array of oral history interviews and the archival records of activists and politicians. He describes the multi-pronged lobbying efforts that helped persuade the LDS Church's First Presidency officially to oppose construction of the MX base in Utah and Nevada. In the process, Olmstead explores the relationship connecting denominational leaders within the state's religious community in the late 1970s and early 1980s and the communication between LDS leaders and elected officials. Whether or not the church's position definitively influenced the Reagan administration to abandon plans for an MX base in Utah, the decision was a triumph for liberals and the fledgling peace movement within the state.

In the late summer months of 1979, news that the deserts of Utah and Nevada had been targeted for the deployment of the MX (Missile Experimental) missile ignited a flurry of local activity bent on preventing the missiles and the proposed basing scheme from coming to these states.[1] A product of the nuclear arms race, the MX missile, containing ten nuclear warheads, was designed to inflict five times the destructive power of America's most deadly nuclear weapon.

146

It was proposed that the base would contain nine thousand miles of "racetrack" on which two hundred MX missiles would be constantly moving and forty-two hundred protective shelters from which the missiles could be launched. The goal of the MX missile and base was to discourage the Soviet Union from launching a first strike. With a conservative cost of fifty billion dollars, some estimated the basing scheme of multiple protective shelters (MPS) to be history's largest construction project.

As a significant expansion of the arms race, some found the enormous capacity for death and destruction contained in the MX morally objectionable. Still others felt the base's massive land and resource requirements and its potential to damage the desert environment were unsettling. Efforts opposing the project heightened in September after President Jimmy Carter officially announced the plans to the nation. Bound by common interest, the opposition movement brought together an unlikely consortium of citizens, special interest groups, and religious leaders spanning the political and ideological spectrum. Involved for various reasons, they worked together by pooling their resources, making strategies, organizing, and bringing in out-of-state help to form a grassroots opposition.

As scholars have grappled with the history of the MX/MPS in the West, the citizens movement has come to define the story.[2] Unfortunately, the cardinal effort of this movement in Utah, convincing the Church of Jesus Christ of Latter-day Saints to join the opposition, has received scant attention. In many ways, the story of the opposition in Utah *is* the story of obtaining the support of the church. Although the struggle to influence the LDS Church has not been written out of the history entirely, the activities of Edwin B. Firmage have dominated the prevailing narrative. Others whose efforts were also important have been left in obscurity. Moreover, no attempt has been made to outline the developments within the Mormon bureaucracy resulting from these efforts.[3]

Set within the larger context of the grassroots efforts in Utah, this chapter illuminates the strategies and attempts of key individuals in the movement to convince the LDS Church to oppose the MX/MPS. Through oral history interviews and the archived papers of persons involved, it also identifies several significant figures in the opposition, whose primary focus was the church. In the process, Firmage's die-hard contributions are placed within the context of a wider community of individuals who worked with LDS officials. The opposition movement is the central thrust of the narrative; however, to the extent possible with available sources, this essay also gives a limited view of the initial deliberations within the church's bureaucracy. These took place primarily within the Special Affairs Committee, whose members were the primary liaisons between the hierarchy and those attempting to influence the church. Ultimately this study illustrates the prevailing opinion held by those who orchestrated the grassroots opposition: they believed the church possessed potential political power over developments in Utah, even those relating

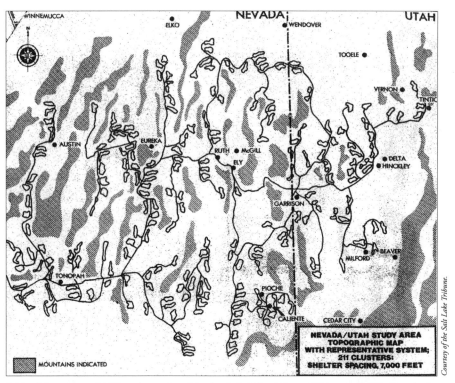

Map of the proposed MX system, printed in the *Salt Lake Tribune*, 28 January 1980. Hundreds of thermonuclear warheads would have moved from silo to silo along the proposed tracks outlined on this map.

to plans originating in Washington, through the church's relationship to the state's civic leaders and citizens.

Initially the United States Air Force garnered a great deal of support for its proposal to bring the MX to Utah and Nevada, particularly from Utah Governor Scott M. Matheson and other elected officials in both states. By the summer of 1979, it appeared as though the deployment of the MX in the Great Basin was a foregone conclusion. In Utah this situation changed on August 21, 1979, when Frances Farley, a non-Mormon Democrat in the state senate, learned the details of the air force's plans for the MX at a meeting of the Federal Research Committee. On this occasion, Farley and the other members of the committee were briefed by a retired air-force general employed by Hercules Inc., and Phil Dykstra, a senior scientist from Thiokol Corporation.[4] The group was told that each of the two hundred MX missiles that were to be housed at the base would need forty-six hundred launch sites, which had to be placed seven thousand feet apart. At the end of the presentation, Farley asked how much total land the base required. The general told her, "We don't like to talk about that." Farley quickly estimated that the base required at least seven thousand miles of road. Despite these awesome land demands, Farley seemed to be the only member of the committee dismayed or at least willing to vocalize any objections to the enormous specifications of the MX/MPS.[5]

Shortly after this meeting, Farley contacted Chad Dobson, a close Mormon friend who was the coordinator of research for the documentary unit of KUTV, a Salt Lake City television station, to see if he could help locate a military map documenting the MX plans. They hoped that these plans could then be made public.[6] Farley also contacted a Mormon state legislator and mutual friend Steve Holbrook, and together the trio discussed strategies for organizing opposition in Utah. In an effort to learn more about the basing system and what opposition was being mounted on the national level, they contacted the Committee for a Sane Nuclear Policy (SANE). Because of its concerns regarding national nuclear policy, SANE was keenly interested in opposing the development of the MX/MPS. SANE dispatched Michael Mawby and Marilyn McNabb, who had aided in squelching the air force's proposal for placing the MX in Nebraska under the Ford administration, to Utah in October to meet with Farley and the small band she had assembled.[7]

The opposition in Utah quickly gained supporters who opposed the MX/MPS for a variety of reasons, creating a network of friends and colleagues who began to combine their resources as they met to consider strategies. In mid-October, Farley and SANE contacted Dr. Herbert "Pete" Scoville Jr., an arms control specialist and former deputy director of research and technology in the Central Intelligence Agency, whose participation and support over the next two years proved significant. He was connected to a number of antinuclear activists and scientists who eventually came to Utah. At the behest of Farley and SANE, he also came to Salt Lake City to meet the growing number of individuals and citizen groups opposed to the MX.[8] Scoville urged those present to unite and challenge the air force.[9] This and subsequent meetings resulted in the organization of the MX Information Coalition (MXIC). Eventually the MXIC constituted more than a dozen special interest groups and many concerned individuals representing a wide spectrum of local interests with the aim of collecting and disseminating information about the MX/MPS.[10]

One of the individuals Farley contacted who attended these early meetings was Stanley Holmes, a recent graduate of the University of Utah and cofounder of an antinuclear organization based at the university known as the Brine Shrimp Alliance. In the following months, Holmes played a key role in setting up the headquarters of the MXIC and became its full-time coordinator, running its office out of the basement of the Campus Christian Center.

To many of the individuals involved, including Farley, Dobson, and Holmes, the opposition movement became a full-time commitment, and they continued to meet regularly to discuss and evaluate the way to implement its strategies. As part of their goal of amassing information on the MX/MPS, Holmes and other members of the MXIC immediately began meeting with members of Utah's congressional delegation, including Senators Orrin Hatch

Stan Holmes of the MXIC.   State Senator Francis Farley.

and Jake Garn, and Kenneth C. Olson, Governor Matheson's point man on MX issues, as well as networking with other anti-MX organizations in Nevada and Washington.[11] To dispense information, the MXIC initiated a number of rallies, letter-writing campaigns, and petitions to kindle public awareness and sought speaking engagements in a variety of venues, including schools and libraries. Representatives from the MXIC were also present at the many town meetings that were held at the behest of Governor Matheson and the air force to evaluate public concern about the MX/MPS.[12]

Many associated with the growing opposition believed Utah's religious community could play a vital role. Speeches given by members of the MXIC took place in the chapels of various Protestant denominations around the Salt Lake Valley. Soon a number of local churches and religious coalitions, including the Episcopal Diocese of Utah and Shared Ministry—a local coalition of Presbyterian, Disciples of Christ, and Methodist congregations—voiced their objections to the MX/MPS and its part in the expansion of the arms race.[13] Although courting the local clergy and their congregations was an important aspect of building support, the opposition had an ulterior motive. In August one of the first objectives which Dobson, Farley, and Holbrook had identified and viewed as paramount in successfully opposing the MX/MPS was obtaining the support of the LDS Church. In contrast to the efforts of many members of the MXIC, who were primarily interested in educating Utahns concerning the environmental issues, the initiatives of Farley, Dobson, Holbrook, and former congressman and Mormon Democrat Wayne Owens to bring the church into the dialogue stemmed from their familiarity with the power structure of the state. They knew of the potentially powerful impact the church could have upon the 70 percent of Utah's population who were LDS and the members of Utah's congressional delegation, who were also Mormon. It was hoped that if respected members of Utah's religious community came out in opposition, the LDS Church would take notice, and there would be an atmosphere where the church could comfortably enter the dialogue surrounding the MX/MPS.[14]

There were also some efforts to obtain the help of respected members, both within the Mormon leadership and the laity, whose politics leaned toward the Democratic Party. Because Farley and Dobson had become well acquainted with these individuals over the years, most of them were approached informally. They included Chase N. Peterson, vice president of the Health and Sciences Center at the University of Utah; Neal A. Maxwell, a member of the First Quorum of the Seventy, who had strong ties to the university; and Wayne Owens. Owens was a close friend of Apostle Gordon B. Hinckley's son, Richard G. Hinckley.[15v]

In addition, Dobson and Farley also hoped to create an awareness of the MX issue within the Mormon community by enlisting the help of a recognized theologian to question the reasoning for the construction of the base in the Mormon heartland. To this end, Dobson contacted Hugh W. Nibley—Mormon scholar and sage. Dobson and Nibley discussed whether bringing the MX to Utah, and thereby significantly increasing the military-industrial complex, was in the best interest of the church because Utah—as the home of the Saints and the center of God's kingdom upon the Earth—should not also be a center of war and destruction. After Dobson shared his ideas, Nibley agreed, believing the issue raised a fundamental question regarding "what Zion should look like." As a result, Nibley chided the Mormons in Utah for exchanging the state's beautiful landscapes for filthy lucre at a 1979 Brigham Young University conference.[16]

Although Farley and Dobson attempted to create an atmosphere of religiously based moral opposition, both within and outside of the Mormon Church, they also initiated a more direct campaign to bring the church on board. In September Farley contacted Richard P. Lindsay, the executive secretary of the church's Special Affairs Committee (SAC). This group, begun in 1974 as part of a bureaucratic reorganization known as "correlation," was assigned to monitor political issues of interest to the church both locally and nationally.[17] Since the mid-1950s, the church had abstained, for the most part, from getting directly involved in partisan politics. But, like many denominations, it maintained an interest in issues with consequences that it believed could weaken the moral fabric of Utah or the nation. Reporting directly to the First Presidency, this group was initially composed of four general authorities who had considerable political experience, including Chairman Gordon B. Hinckley; David B. Haight, an assistant to the Quorum of the Twelve Apostles; and Neal A. Maxwell and James E. Faust, both members of the First Quorum of the Seventy.[18] By 1979, while retaining their duties in this committee, both Haight and Faust had advanced to the Quorum of the Twelve. During the early years of the committee's existence, it dealt with a number of issues, perhaps the most notable and documented being management of the church's campaign to oppose the Equal Rights Amendment (ERA).[19]

Because of the expanding duties and travels of the members of the SAC, Lindsay, a political scientist who had served in a number of government positions in Utah, was hired as an executive secretary in 1977. His primary obligations were staff work and making the members of the committee aware of issues in which the church might have an interest. A short time later, William S. Evans, a colleague of Lindsay's with a background in public administration, joined him as an assistant. With the help of a secretary, Lindsay and Evans functioned as the Special Affairs Department to support the needs of the SAC.[20]

Beyond acting as political watchdogs, the members of the committee, particularly Lindsay and Hinckley, had also come to be recognized as touchstones when lobbyists and politicians sought to consult or inform the church on political matters.[21] Thus, it was not unusual for Farley, a Catholic, to approach Lindsay regarding a political topic. Prior to 1979, they had met many times to discuss political matters.[22] Inasmuch as the MX/MPS was becoming a topic of national interest during the spring and summer of 1979, by the time Farley approached Lindsay, it is likely that the SAC had already discussed the issue in its weekly meetings.[23] According to Dobson, Lindsay warmly agreed to transmit any data that Farley gave him regarding the MX/MPS to the other members of the SAC.[24]

Over the next two years, Dobson and Farley, with the aid of the MXIC, embarked on a campaign to educate Utahns by bringing in well-respected scientists, retired military personnel, and politicians with a variety of backgrounds and expertise to explain the hazards of the MX/MPS. They promoted alternate ways of thinking about the MX and brought credibility to the opposition movement in Utah.[25] Although these visitors often briefed Governor Matheson and other state officials, gave speeches in public forums, and consented to interviews with the local media, a primary purpose of their visits was to brief officials of the LDS Church. Typically those visiting spoke with Lindsay and Evans. The information presented was then reported at the committee's regular meetings. On some occasions, however, members of the SAC and others in the Quorum of the Twelve and First Presidency were briefed directly. Unfortunately, due to a lack of source material, the details of these meetings are not available.[26]

Herbert Scoville's visit to Salt Lake City in mid-October was part of this plan. During these initial visits, he met with members of the SAC and Bruce R. McConkie, a member of the Quorum of the Twelve. During these meetings with church officials, Scoville most likely argued that the construction of the MX/MPS would further destabilize Soviet/American relations, increasing the possibility of a nuclear conflict; that it would not render American ICBMs invulnerable; that it would open an unlimited expansion of the arms race; and that the costs to the national budget, the region's natural resources, and the environment were far too great. Scoville was also a proponent of basing the MX in submarines, which he believed would achieve the desired results.[27] During these meetings, the members of the SAC did not express their specific opinions to Farley and Scoville regarding the MX/MPS. However, in a letter to McConkie, Farley indicated that the members of the "church structure" demonstrated a "reassuring" concern over the possible impact the construction of the MX/MPS would have upon "the quality of life in Utah."[28]

In the months following Scoville's visit, Dobson brought in two more experts to meet with members of the SAC. First, in early December 1979, retired United States Navy Admiral Gene LaRocque, the director of the Center for Defense Information, an organization established by retired military officials dedicated to monitoring wasteful military spending, met with the SAC and described the budgetary extravagance the MX/MPS project represented.[29] Second, Dr. Richard Garwin—a professor at Harvard, former member of the president's Science Advisory Board, and member of the Federation of American Scientists—came to Salt Lake City at the end of February 1980.[30] Several other authoritative scientists were also brought before the SAC. These included Sydney Drell from Stanford University and Kosta Tsipis from the Massachusetts Institute of Technology (MIT). Drell argued that using a Shallow Underwater Mobile (SUM) system was much more economically feasible and effective for addressing fixed-silo vulnerability. Refuting the belief that fixed silos were vulnerable, Tsipis argued, among other things, that because of the numerous untestable factors, even precise Soviet ICBMs could not threaten the land-based portion of the American nuclear defense triad, making the MX/MPS superfluous.[31]

Beginning in the spring of 1980, opposition to the MX gained a significant ally who would eventually open an additional stream of information for the SAC. After more than a year of ardent support for bringing the MX to Utah, Governor Matheson began to speak out against the basing scheme. Initially Matheson had believed the MX/MPS was essential to American nuclear defense. Recognizing it as a potential economic boon, he had actively lobbied to bring the MX to Utah.[32] After Carter's October 1979 announcement, he continued to work closely with the air force to expedite possible deployment in the Great Basin.

However, Matheson recognized that the impact of the construction of the base would be immense.[33] He urged all citizens of the state to take an active role in assessing that impact so that all concerns would be addressed.[34] The governor also organized an MX Task Force and Coordination office to work in collaboration with a similar organization in Nevada. The creation of the task force was formally announced on November 5, 1979, in Cedar City before the Subcommittee on Military Construction of the House Committee on Appropriations. The task force, as explained by Matheson, was organized to evaluate and independently verify information provided by the air force. In addition, it would also assess the concerns of Utahns that would likely surface during the environmental impact study.[35] At the time of his announcement, 70 percent of Utahns, according to a recent poll, favored the deployment of the MX/MPS in the state. This support, Matheson believed, could be jeopardized by public perception of federal insensitivity or secrecy if the state was left out of the planning process.[36]

In early November, the MX Task Force began holding regular meetings. This large group included representatives from the Utah congressional delegation and officials from a number of state agencies. While Kent Briggs, Matheson's state planning coordinator and chief of staff, chaired the organization, Kenneth C. Olson, who had previously worked as a consultant for the governor, was appointed project manager. Olson ran the governor's MX office and coordinated the task force's probe into the MX/MPS.[37]

According to Olson, the task force was initially neutral about the MX/MPS. Within six months, however, the MX office had come to some troubling conclusions concerning the project's potentially large impact upon the environment and the small desert communities that would be at the mercy of a boom/bust economy resulting from the construction of the base.[38] Moreover, several scientists, including Garwin and Drell, also informed the MX office that the MX/MPS was not technologically feasible. These discoveries, in addition to the perceived indifference displayed by the air force for the concerns of the State of Utah, convinced Matheson to withdraw his support completely and actively oppose the missile base.[39]

Although there were many facets of the MX office's plan to assess and inform the public about the issues that ought to be considered about bringing the MX/MPS to the state, informing or working with the LDS Church was not among them.[40] Despite Matheson's good working relationship with church officials, it was not until after he and the MX office had formulated a negative opinion of the MX in April 1980 that the church was contacted. The initial approach was a rather informal one from Olson to his friend Lindsay—without a formal directive from the governor.[41] Olson offered to brief Lindsay or other members of the Mormon leadership. The primary motivation, according to Olson, was a belief that the church should know about some of the concerns uncovered by the task force. These were concerns and information that Matheson and Olson believed would be particularly helpful if the church was planning on taking a stance on the MX/MPS issue.[42]

Lindsay accepted the invitation and set up a meeting for Olson with both himself and Hinckley. In the following year, Olson recalled five or six briefings with Lindsay, Hinckley, and, on occasion, Faust. At these meetings, Olson presented an analysis of the information and research obtained by the MX office and answered questions. Although the members of the SAC did not indicate their position on the MX, Olson recalled that their questions and concerns were centered mostly on the potential impact to the small desert communities with high LDS populations that would be located nearest to the base. More specifically they appeared to be most interested in the quality of life and possible decline in moral fiber resulting from a staggering influx of population to cities near the project. Although the goal of these briefings was to inform rather than persuade, it is clear that Matheson believed the church had the potential to be the crucial factor in whether the MX/MPS would be deployed in Utah.[43]

In the spring of 1980, by the time the Matheson administration had shifted its position, the local religious opposition, cultivated by Dobson, the MXIC, and others, began to focus part of its efforts on convincing the LDS Church to join the religious community in opposing the MX. The burgeoning local religious opposition had received support from Catholic Bishop Joseph L. Federal, Unitarian Reverend Richard Henry, and Rabbi Eric Silver, and others had already formally announced their objections.[44] Perhaps the most important religious figure to join in terms of generating and organizing additional ecumenical support was United Methodist Minister Stephen J. Sidorak, who also helped convince Episcopal Bishop Otis Charles to join the campaign against the MX. This ad hoc religious opposition in Utah eventually donned the title Utah Clergy and Laity Concerned (UCALC).[45]

Sidorak was disheartened when he pressed the LDS Church for its position on the MX and was told by Jerry Cahill, a public-relations spokesman, that after weighing the various points of view, the church would not be making a statement—a conclusion likely reached early on by the SAC.[46] Finding this position "reprehensible," he began to "systematically t[ake] the LDS Church to task in the media."[47] Sidorak believed that LDS participation was essential to convince Utah's largely LDS political leadership, who still supported the MX, to change their position.

Sidorak's strategy was to isolate the Mormons publicly as the sole American religious institution not contributing to the anti-MX dialogue. He hoped that this would focus the attention of the nation's churches on the Mormons while showing them that they were outside the American religious mainstream—an image that the church had been trying to overcome for several decades. To spotlight the church's silence, Sidorak began speaking publicly about it and challenged its leaders to join the opposition with the local and national religious community.[48]

With the support of UCALC, Sidorak also contacted nationally recognized religious figures, including Henri J.M. Nouwen, renowned and prolific scholar and Catholic priest at Yale University, and Robert McAfee Brown, international civil-rights leader at the Pacific School of Religion at the University of California in Berkeley. He requested that they write LDS President Spencer W. Kimball, encouraging the church to join the national religious community in opposing the MX.[49] Many of those contacted responded by sending President Kimball short theological treatises questioning the ethics of the project.[50] With the help of UCALC, Sidorak also extended an invitation to several renowned national religious scholars and leaders to come to St. Mark's Episcopal Cathedral in Salt Lake City to speak at a series of ecumenical conferences. William Sloane Coffin, noted social activist and minister of the Riverside Church in New York City, came to Salt Lake as the featured speaker at the first conference in April 1980 and was followed by Dr. Harvey Cox from the Harvard Divinity School at the second conference in September.[51]

Although Sidorak's efforts succeeded in focusing the attention of the national religious community on the Mormon Church, they had yet to produce any tangible results. After the third interfaith conference held on November 5, which featured noted religious scholar John C. Bennett, former dean of Union Theological Seminary, and several other noted clerics, Sidorak's efforts were vindicated.[52] Unlike the experts brought out by Farley and Dobson, Coffin and Cox did not meet with members of the SAC. However, after Sidorak had built a relationship with Bill Evans and greased the wheels by providing a bibliography and samples of Bennett's writing and a short biography, Hinckley met with Bennett during his visit.

According to Sidorak, at this meeting, Bennett, who was noted for his commentary on the moral implications of the nuclear arms race, presented his views on the theoretical and moral problems of deterrence—the fundamental theoretical basis of the MX/MPS. It is likely Bennett argued that deterrence had a limited motivational effect, resulted in military buildup, did not solve the basic tension among nations, drained the earth of its natural resources, increased poverty, diverted funds from needed social programs, and eroded the national moral sympathy for death and destruction.[53] Bennett's remarks were apparently well received and prompted a number of questions from Hinckley. At the conclusion of the meeting, Sidorak believed, for the first time, that the SAC had finally gotten the message.[54]

This and other ecumenical meetings with the SAC were made possible with the aid of University of Utah law professor and political activist Edwin Firmage, who had worked closely with Sidorak and others. Moreover, Firmage had helped organize and had spoken at the interfaith conferences.[55] Firmage was a vocal opponent of the MX/MPS who had considerable background in international law and politics in Utah.[56] Back in December 1979, Firmage had authored an op-ed piece published in the *Salt Lake Tribune* arguing, among other things, that the mobile basing scheme was unnecessary, considering the strength of the American defense triad, and that Utah and Nevada would be destroyed in a nuclear exchange.[57]

Just after his article was published, Firmage began to work with the MXIC and offered to speak at some of its gatherings, though much of his effort was independent of any anti-MX organization.[58] In many ways, Firmage was an anti-MX army unto himself. Over the next year and a half, he regularly delivered speeches in a number of locations, presented workshops, hosted debates, testified at government hearings, and gave televised interviews. Between October 1979 and August 1980, he spoke on the MX or related topics on at least twenty occasions before groups, including the student body of the University of Utah,

Salt Lake Mayor Ted Wilson testifies at a 1981 hearing regarding the MX missile in Delta, Utah. Ed Firmage is seated behind Wilson (first row, second from the left).

the Senior Citizens of Utah, and at a rally at the Salt Palace in June. Since he was considered an expert on the subject, he also testified before the air force scoping hearings on the MX in January 1980 and before the House Subcommittee on Public Lands in February 1980.[59]

Firmage's first contact with LDS officials regarding the MX was in March 1980. Lindsay had contacted him and asked him to review some antiarms-race literature sent to the church by the Interfaith Center to Reverse the Arms Race in California.[60] Like Dobson, Sidorak, and others, Firmage believed official LDS support was paramount if the opposition was to succeed. He believed that because the church represented such a large population in Utah and Nevada, it would be nearly impossible for the air force to impose the MX/MPS on these states if the church opposed it directly.[61] After briefly commenting on the group that had sent the material, Firmage responded to Lindsay's request with an eleven-page memo where he cited lengthy quotes by J. Reuben Clark Jr., a former member of the First Presidency and a lawyer who had extensive experience in international diplomacy and strong and well-documented pacifist beliefs. Firmage included passages illustrating Clark's views on the place of the United States in the international community, as well as his view that war for almost any purpose or the accumulation of weapons was an affront to God. He suggested that a message from the church regarding the "evils of death and war," updating some of the opinions expressed by Clark, would be "refreshing."[62]

This memo led to a number of meetings between Firmage and Hinckley over the next year. On occasion these meetings also included Maxwell and Faust.

Although the SAC had given no indication of its position, except to say the church was not going to take a stand, Hinckley privately applauded Firmage's efforts, and he continued to provide the SAC with lengthy memoranda detailing past statements made by Mormon authorities.[63] Besides helping to arrange the meeting between Hinckley and Bennett, Firmage also directly initiated several meetings between Hinckley and members of Utah's religious community. On September 9, 1980, Episcopal Bishop Otis Charles met with Hinckley. Later, Hinckley met with the newly appointed Catholic bishop, William Weigand. Both encouraged the church to make a statement.[64]

Though the members of the SAC were willing to listen to the opinions of Firmage, religious leaders such as Weigand and Charles, and the other politicians, scientists, and retired military personnel, for the most part, this interaction was a "one way flow of information."[65] Those who met with the SAC received little indication of how or even if the information and opinions offered would be used. However, while not evident to those beseeching the church, from September 1979 to November 1980, the SAC was amassing data and discussing the issues encircling the construction of the MX/MPS, including information provided by the air force and entities supporting the MX, reports from the media, and legislative developments.[66] It appears that the issues concerning the location of the MX/MPS, specifically its proximity to the largely LDS communities and the headquarters of the church, were central to the SAC's initial deliberations.[67]

However, extrapolating from Cahill's comments to Sidorak, it appears that early in the discussions, the SAC was unpersuaded that it should bring this issue before the First Presidency. Although the SAC believed the church should be concerned over the location of the MX/MPS, the committee's members still believed the issues of the MX/MPS were largely political. The SAC was therefore not in a position to recommend further discussion. At some point, this position changed. As one individual close to the SAC described it, this was a period of "education," requiring perhaps more information and study than any other issue to come before the committee.[68] Beyond the insular issues regarding the base's location, the larger moral issues surrounding the MX/MPS, including the effects on the environment and arms race, were buried in the technicalities of the base, the MX missile itself, and American nuclear-defense theory. Moreover, the church's traditional position on the moral undertones of the MX/MPS was not as clear as the moral implications of other political issues such as the ERA and alcohol and pornography legislation.[69] Though the information provided through Farley, Dobson, and Olson provided technical details about the MX/MPS and illustrated why it presented a boondoggle for American nuclear defense, it was finally the persuasive moral arguments presented by both local and national religious leaders that convinced the SAC that the MX issues were moral at their core and, therefore, rightly within the realm of the church's purview.

Finally, on November 26, 1980, the SAC presented to the First Presidency a synthesis of the data it had accumulated on the MX/MPS.[70] Hinckley led this

Making The Desert Bloom

Mormons were well-known for making the desert bloom through irrigation. This cartoon by Tom Engelhardt was published 15 May 1981, shortly after the First Presidency announced its opposition to placing the MX missile system in the Great Basin.

presentation, with assistance from Lindsay, who had gathered most of the information.[71] The presentation played a significant role in persuading the members of the First Presidency that the MX/MPS issues warranted further discussion, including the possibility of issuing an encyclical in opposition.[72]

In the following months, as the First Presidency began to deliberate on MX/MPS issues, the SAC continued to gather information. It also continued to play an important role in the decision-making process. Hinckley, who acted as an informal counselor to the First Presidency on the MX/MPS and facilitated the flow of information between these leadership bodies, played a particularly important role.[73] On April 9, as the hierarchy was on the brink of making a final decision regarding the church's position on the MX/MPS, the SAC was again asked to brief the First Presidency, this time in a joint meeting with the Quorum of the Twelve Apostles. This meeting, led by Lindsay with assistance from Evans, played an important role in educating the members of the quorum.[74]

On May 5, 1981, the First Presidency finally issued a statement opposing the deployment of the MX/MPS in the Great Basin. "After assessing in great detail information recently available," the First Presidency warned that the massive construction of the MX/MPS would generate sociological and ecological problems, which would surely follow the large influx of construction workers and their families. Besides damage to the environment and the economy after the completion of the base, the message argued that the project would represent a substantial drain upon the inadequate water and power supply in the desert regions of Utah and Nevada. The statement also asserted that, should a nuclear war ensue, the MX base would be a primary target. Thus, "one segment of the population would bear a highly disproportionate share of the burden, in lives lost and property destroyed."[75]

Though they may not have recognized it, convincing the SAC to view the construction of the MX/MPS primarily in terms of its technical, environmental, and moral failings was a major victory for members of the opposition who had worked to get the church involved. Without this orientation, which developed as the SAC met with visitors and received technical and moral information concerning the MX/MPS, it is unlikely the discussion would have moved beyond the committee. Moreover, though the statement reflected the specific concerns of the First Presidency, its reference to published studies, strategic limitations, ecological issues—particularly the potential strain upon western water resources—and sociological and economic factors indicates that the information provided by the opposition movement played a significant role in shaping the First Presidency's position, a position some believe was essential to the end of the MX program in Utah and Nevada.[76] If this is the case, then the opposition movement in Utah played a crucial role in preventing massive alterations to Utah's demographic, social, and environmental landscapes as a result of this government project.

This episode also reveals something about the special relationship of the LDS Church to politics in Utah. The church's role in politics, in this instance, was exhibited through its relationship with government officials and Utah citizens. The interaction of government officials with the LDS leadership appears to have been benign. This contrasts with prevailing opinions that depict government officials operating out of the pockets of the Mormon hierarchy. In this instance, the Matheson administration sought out the LDS leadership. Though Matheson opposed the MX/MPS and believed the church had the power to squelch the project in Utah, the dialogue between the SAC and Matheson's office was noncoercive and initiated only to convey information.

Perhaps more importantly, this episode illuminates the church's relationship with Utah citizens. As a significant presence in the political dynamic of the state, the grassroots opposition mounted a substantial campaign to lobby LDS leaders into its corner. Its members believed, as did Governor Matheson, that the church possessed the political clout to quash the deployment of the MX in the Great Basin. Through providing an opportunity for politicians, scientists, and particularly local religious leaders to present their perspective, the church demonstrated a democratic quality in its pursuit of information. That Mormon officials listened to the opinions and concerns of local and national clergy on this issue is perhaps one of a kind in the history of the state. But, as this study also illustrates, it is possible for outsiders, using traditional lobbying tactics, to convince the LDS Church, often viewed as monolithic and unassailable, to use its political weight for partisan political issues.

NOTES

1.   The author wishes to thank Chad Dobson, Stan Holmes, and Steve Sidorak. Without their willingness to share their experiences, this study would not have been possible. He also thanks the Charles Redd Center for Western Studies and Vern O. Curtis for providing generous funding to support the research in this article.

2.   The major work on this episode in Utah and Nevada's history defines it as a citizens' movement, although its focus is slanted toward developments in Nevada. See Matthew Glass, *Citizens against the MX: Public Languages in the Nuclear Age* (Urbana and Chicago: University of Illinois Press, 1993). This perspective is also propounded in Lauren H. Holland and Robert A. Hoover, *The MX Decision: A New Direction in U.S. Weapons Procurement Policy?* (Boulder, CO: Westview Press, 1985), 95–119,187–208; and David Cortright, *Peace Works: The Citizen's Role in Ending the Cold War* (Boulder, CO: Westview Press, 1993), 133–58.

3.   In addition to several accounts published by Firmage describing his experiences with the church, the major histories which detail the opposition's efforts to influence the church are also based upon Firmage's experiences. See Glass, *Citizens against the MX,* 35; and Cortright, *Peace Works,*135–36, 139.

4.   Hercules Inc. and Thiokol Corporation were Utah corporations that developed aerospace technologies for the federal government and would receive lucrative government contracts to construct various portions of the MX missile. See Eric G. Swedin, "Thiokol in Utah," *Utah Historical Quarterly* 75 (Winter 2007): 75. The committee included Jack Dunlop, committee executive; Jack Gallivan; Barclay Gardner; Jim Hansen; and Frances Farley. Senator Farley did not identify the former air force general present at this meeting; Frances Farley, "The MX: A Case of Citizen Involvement," p. 2, unpublished manuscript, papers of David Cortright, folder MX sources, Swarthmore College Peace Collection, Swarthmore College, Swarthmore, Pennsylvania.

5.   Frances Farley, "A Women's Place Is in the House and the Senate," *Rendezvous* 24 (1988): 66. See also Farley, "The MX: A Case of Citizen Involvement," pp. 2–4.

6.   Chad Dobson, interview by author, December 23, 2004. A map documenting the proposed basing scheme was ultimately published in the *Salt Lake Tribune.* See "Map of Proposed MX System," *Salt Lake Tribune,* January 27, 1980, B1.

7.   Dobson interview; Cortright, *Peace Works,* 137–38. McNabb and Mawby also supported the opposition forming in Nevada. Milton S. Katz, *Ban the Bomb: A History of SANE, the Committee for a Sane Nuclear Policy, 1957–1985* (New York: Greenwood Press, 1986), 141. In addition to Nebraska, the air force had studied the possibility of placing the MX in Kansas, but these efforts were squelched by congressional and grassroots opposition. See Holland and Hoover, *The MX Decision,* 96; and Paul N. Stockton, "Arms Development and Arms Control: The Strange Case of the MX

Missile," in *American Politics and Public Policy: Seven Case Studies,* ed. Allan P. Sindler (Washington, DC: CQ Press, 1982), 246–47.

8.   Stanley Holmes, interview by author, February 26, 2005. Scoville also participated in the anti-MX movement burgeoning in Nevada. Glass, *Citizens against the MX,* 35–36.

9.   Holmes interview.

10. Ibid. Some of the organizations involved in the MXIC included the Sierra Club, the Utah Audubon Society, the Utah Senior Coalition, Utahns against Hunger, the Western Shoshone Sacred Lands Association, and the Women's International League for Peace and Freedom. See MX Information Coalition roster, January 31, 1980, Matheson Collection, series 1646, box 2, folder 6, Special Collections, J. Willard Marriott Library, University of Utah, Salt Lake City (hereafter cited as U of U Special Collections).

11. Some of these Nevada-based groups included Citizen's Alert, NOMX, and the Great Basin MX Alliance; Holmes interview.

12. Ibid.; Stanley Holmes, appointment calenders, 1979–81, copies in possession of the author. For a detailed discussion of both the scoping hearings and the public review of the environmental impact statement produced by the air force, see Glass, *Citizens against the MX,* 25–30, 54–64.

13. See the Episcopal clergy of the Diocese of Utah to Scott M. Matheson, October 13, 1979, Matheson Collection, series 1646, box 1, folder 3; Patricia A. Steiner, chairperson, Shared Ministry in Utah, to Scott M. Matheson, January 23, 1980, Matheson Collection, series 1646, box 1, folder 5; Scott M. Matheson to Steve Knowles, pastor of the Community Presbyterian Church, February 20, 1980, Matheson Collection, series 1646, box 1, folder 7; Scott M. Matheson to Otis Charles, Episcopal bishop of Utah, May 19, 1980, Matheson Collection, series 1646, box 1, folder 8; and Holladay United Church of Christ to Francis Farley, April 22, 1981, Frances Farley Collection, box 8, folder 4, U of U Special Collections.

14. Dobson interview. Glass argues that the primary reason for gaining the support of Utah's non-LDS religious community was to create a moral dialogue to which those outside of the West could relate. In the initial development of the opposition, this objective was secondary to convincing the LDS Church to join the protest. Glass, *Citizens against the MX,* 34.

15. The Quorum of the Twelve Apostles and the First Quorum of the Seventy constitute the second and third highest ecclesiastical and administrative authority in the LDS Church.

16. Dobson interview; see also Hugh W. Nibley, "How Firm a Foundation! What Makes It So?," *Dialogue: A Journal of Mormon Thought* 12 (Winter 1979): 37.

17. James B. Allen and Glen M. Leonard, *The Story of the Latter-day Saints* (Salt Lake City: Deseret Book Co., 1992), 659. Relatively little has been written regarding the origin and history of the Special Affairs Committee (SAC). See Q. Michael Croft, "Influence of the L.D.S. Church on Utah Politics, 1945–1985" (PhD diss., University of Utah, 1985), 108–9, 176–79; Robert Gottlieb and Peter Wiley, *America's Saints: The Rise of Mormon Power* (New York: G.P. Putnam's Sons, 1984), 81–82; and Thomas G.

Alexander, "The Emergence of a Republican Majority in Utah,1970–1992,"in *Politics in the Postwar American West,* ed Richard Lowitt (Norman: University of Oklahoma Press, 1995), 274. Moreover, the official biographies of the initial members of the SAC do not mention their contributions to this assignment; see Sheri L. Dew, *Go Forward with Faith: The Biography of Gordon B. Hinckley* (Salt Lake City: Deseret Book Co., 1996); Lucile C. Tate, *David B. Haight: The Life Story of a Disciple* (Salt Lake City: Bookcraft, 1987); and James P. Bell, *In the Strength of the Lord: The Life and Teachings of James E. Faust* (Salt Lake City: Deseret Book Co., 1999). The one exception is Bruce C. Hafen, *A Disciple's Life: The Biography of Neal A. Maxwell* (Salt Lake City: Deseret Book Co., 2002), 408–10. Due to the absence of source material documenting the history of the SAC, historians have offered speculative explanations regarding the committee's origins. D. Michael Quinn claims that "defeating the Equal Rights Amendment was apparently the specific reason for its [the SAC's] organization." D. Michael Quinn, *The Mormon Hierarchy: Extensions of Power* (Salt Lake City: Signature Books, 1997), 376. It has also been suggested that the creation of this committee represented the beginning of a more discreet and unified approach to the church's involvement in politics. Croft, "Influence of the L.D.S. Church," 108–9. Though the SAC did represent a more discreet and unified approach to politics, Robert Gottlieb and Peter Wiley offer the most convincing explanation. They argue that the formation of the SAC resulted from a larger movement in the LDS bureaucratic restructuring started under Harold B. Lee in 1961 known as "correlation." Gottlieb and Wiley, *America's Saints,* 81.

18. Richard P. Lindsay, interview by author, August 23, 2004. The First Presidency constitutes the highest ecclesiastical and administrative authority in the LDS Church. At the time, Spencer W. Kimball was president, with N. Eldon Tanner and Marion G. Romney serving as his counselors. Quinn, *The Mormon Hierarchy,* 636.

19. For a detailed discussion of the church's campaign against the ERA, see Quinn, *The Mormon Hierarchy,* 373–402.

20. Lindsay interview. Anonymous interview by author, September 10, 2004 (hereafter cited as anonymous interview 1). Because of the sensitivity of the information revealed by this individual, he has asked to remain unidentified.

21. Gottlieb and Wiley, *America's Saints,* 81–82; Dew, *Go Forward with Faith,* 291–94.

22. Dobson interview.

23. Richard Lindsay could not remember the exact date the MX/MPS became a topic of discussion but claimed it happened because of its growth as a national issue. Lindsay interview.

24. Dobson interview.

25. In a letter of recommendation from Frances Farley to Marilyn McNabb of SANE, she credits Dobson with bringing these individuals to Utah. Farley to McNabb, February 17, 1981, Farley Collection, box 7, folder 7.

26. The MX files compiled by Richard Lindsay as executive secretary of the SAC that contain the materials surrounding these meetings are in the possession of the First Presidency and are, at present, unavailable for research. Lindsay interview.

27. These were the points he made to Governor Matheson, and it is likely that Scoville shared similar information with the members of the SAC. Herbert Scoville Jr., "MX DEPLOYMENT: Summary of Remarks, Salt Lake City," October 17, 1979, Matheson Collection, series 1646, box 2, folder 16 (emphasis in original).

28. Frances Farley to Bruce R. McConkie, November 2, 1979, Farley Collection, box 5, folder 10.

29. Holmes, appointment calender, 1979. It is likely that LaRocque gave the SAC a copy of the Center for Defense Information's newsletter containing detailed information on the MX/MPS. Center for Defense Information, "MX: The Missile We Don't Need," *The Defense Monitor* 8 (October 1979).

30. Holmes, appointment calendar, 1980. Unfortunately, available sources offer little information concerning Garwin's visit with the SAC.

31. Dobson interview. See Sydney Drell, "SUM," *Arms Control Today* 9 (September 1979): 1–7; and Kosta Tsipis, "Precision and Accuracy," *Arms Control Today* 11 (May 1981): 3–4.

32. As early as November 30, 1978, Governor Matheson indicated support for the MX, noting the limited environmental and social impact while touting the economic benefits for Utah. Scott M. Matheson, *Out of Balance* (Salt Lake City: Gibbs M. Smith, 1986), 57–58.

33. "Statement of Governor Scott M. Matheson of Utah before the Subcommittee of Military Construction of the House Committee on Appropriations," November 5, 1979, Matheson Collection, series 4455, box 2, folder 12.

34. Douglas L. Parker, "Utahn's Views Urged on MX," *Salt Lake Tribune,* October 18, 1979, B1.

35. The 1969 passage of the National Environmental Policy Act (NEPA) provided that hearings should be held to evaluate the potential environmental and social implications of federal construction projects. For a detailed discussion of the influence of NEPA and other federal laws on the MX/MPS, see Holland and Hoover, *The MX Decision,* 109–19.

36. "Statement of Governor Scott M. Matheson," pp. 2–4.

37. Kenneth C. Olson, interview by author, February 4, 2005; Kent Briggs, interview by author, December 29, 2004.

38. Matheson, *Out of Balance,* 73.

39. While Matheson publicly challenged the MX project in April 1980, as early as November 1979 he began to be concerned with the air force's handling of the MX/MPS and believed the state of Utah was being intentionally left out of the decision-making process. Matheson, *Out of Balance,* 63–64. For a detailed discussion of Matheson's concerns, see Robert List and Scott Matheson to Jack H. Watson Jr., memorandum, January 3, 1980, Matheson Collection, series 1646, box 1, folder 10.

40. For a breakdown of the MX office's official task list, see "Utah MX Coordination Office Second Progress Report," Matheson Collection, series 1646, box 1, folder 22.

41. Croft, "Influence of the L.D.S. Church," 195; Olson interview. There are some disagreements between the recollections of Governor Matheson and Kenneth Olson

regarding the initial contact with the church. In his political biography, Matheson claimed the initial contact with the church was made at his directive after discussing it with his advisors. Matheson, *Out of Balance*, 83. Because Olson was Matheson's primary liaison with the church, his memory of the events is most likely more reliable.

42. Olson interview.

43. Steve Sidorak, [No Title], in *There's Hope: The Illustrated Record of an Evening of Peace, December 7, 1980, The Riverside Church,* ed. Cora Weiss (New York: Pilgrim Press, 1981), 55.

44. Dobson interview; Glass, *Citizens against the MX,* 34–35.

45. Stephen J. Sidorak, interview by author, March 28, 2005. See also Stan Holmes, "Critique of Ed Firmage's 'MX: A Personal Essay,'" p. 2, unpublished manuscript, in the possession of the author. In addition to the religious leaders mentioned, the UCALC was also supported by the Utah Commission for Ministry in Higher Education, the American Baptist Churches, the Christian Churches (Disciples), the United Church of Christ, and the Lutheran Campus Ministry. Jan Robert Bartlett to members and friends of U.C.A.L.C., May 12, 1981, Farley Collection, box 8, folder 4.

46. Sidorak interview.

47. Sidorak, [No Title], 54.

48. Sidorak interview; Stephen J. Sidorak, interview by author, April 15, 2005.

49. Stephen J. Sidorak, e-mail to author, May 6, 2005.

50. Sidorak [No Title], 54–55. Sidorak interviews, March 28 and April 15, 2005.

51. Holmes, appointment calendar, 1980; Glass, *Citizens against the MX,* 34–35.

52. Sidorak, [No Title], 56.

53. Although Sidorak could not remember the specific arguments Bennett made, he suggested they could be found in his work, *U.S. Foreign Policy and Christian Ethics.* Sidorak interview, April 15, 2005; see John C. Bennett and Harvey Seifert, *U.S. Foreign Policy and Christian Ethics* (Philadelphia: Westminister Press, 1977), 105–21.

54. Sidorak interview, March 28, 2005.

55. Ibid.; Edwin B. Firmage to Ulrich Albrecht, August 2, 1982, copy in possession of the author.

56. Firmage led an unsuccessful campaign in 1978 to unseat Republican Dan Marriott. Edwin B. Firmage, "MX: Democracy, Religion, and the Rule of Law—My Journey," *Utah Law Review,* no. 1 (2004): 28–29.

57. Edwin B. Firmage, "Common Carrier: Racetrack Basing of MX Missiles in Utah Misguided," *Salt Lake Tribune,* December 2, 1979, A17.

58. Ted Gurney to Edwin B. Firmage, December 21, 1979, Edwin B. Firmage Papers, box 9, folder 1, U of U Special Collections.

59. Edwin B. Firmage to Walter Oberer, annual report of activities, August 8, 1980, Firmage Papers, box 9, folder 2 .

60. Edwin B. Firmage, interview by Edward L. Kimball, May 23, 1986, copy in possession of the author. This information was most likely one of the responses to Sidorak's letter-writing campaign. Sidorak interview, April 15, 2005.

61. Edwin B. Firmage, "MX: A Personal Essay," *Beehive History* 28 (2002): 27.

62. Edwin B. Firmage to Richard P. Lindsay, March 17, 1980, Firmage Papers, box 9, folder 2.

63. Firmage interview. See also Firmage, "MX: Democracy, Religion, and the Rule of Law," 34.

64. Firmage interview, 23 May and 6 June 1986; see also Firmage, "MX: Democracy, Religion, and the Rule of Law," 34.

65. Dobson interview. Firmage claims the church "openly sought" many opinions. Firmage, "MX: Democracy, Religion, and the Rule of Law," 33. Although it is true the SAC was open to receive any information on the MX/MPS, it rarely sought input from organizations or individuals that did not first approach the church. Firmage may have been the only exception. See anonymous interview 1.

66. Richard Lindsay mentioned that air force officials and others advocating the MX met with the members of the SAC and provided information. However, he could not name any specifics. Lindsay interview.

67. Richard Lindsay recalled that the location of the MX/MPS was the initial concern of the SAC. Lindsay interview. Moreover, the questions and concerns Hinckley and others raised with Olson during his briefings of the SAC indicate the location of the base was the primary concern.

68. Anonymous interview 1.

69. Lindsay interview.

70. This date came from an interview with an individual who, because of the delicate information provided, wished to remain anonymous. Anonymous interview by author, April 30, 2004 (hereafter cited as anonymous interview 2).

71. Richard Lindsay, interview by author, August 27, 2004.

72. For a discussion of the impact of the SAC's presentation to the First Presidency, see Jacob W. Olmstead, "A Diabolical Disneyland in Zion: The Mormons and the MX" (master's thesis, Brigham Young University, 2005), 55–56.

73. Hinckley was present at a number of the First Presidency's meetings where the MX was discussed and was asked to perform a number of tasks in relation to the church's position on the MX/MPS. Anonymous interview 2.

74. Ibid.; Lindsay interview, August 27, 2004; anonymous interview 1.

75. Jerry P. Cahill, "First Presidency Statement on Basing of the MX Missile," May 5, 1981, Farley Papers, box 8, folder 4.

76. Matheson, *Out of Balance,* 84.

7

The WPA Versus the Utah Church

Joseph F. Darowski

The 1930s were an especially difficult time in Utah. Coming out of a recession in the 1920s that affected agriculture and mining, the state felt all the impact of the Great Depression. Other scholars have acknowledged that New Deal officials and the LDS Church leadership clashed over the role of the federal government and the church in meeting the needs of the state's residents. Both sides claimed that their own programs best met Utahns' needs. Joseph F. Darowski describes the way that New Deal administrators, especially a former Utahn and Mormon, Dean Brimhall, contracted with sociologist Louis Wirth to show that the church's welfare program was not meeting the needs of its members. Darowski's new evidence amplifies the disagreements between private, church-run programs and federal ones beyond what other researchers have previously discussed.

On September 21, 1937, the *New York Herald Tribune* carried an editorial on page eighteen, "The Mormons Show the Way." It extolled the Mormon people for tackling the economic and social chaos spawned by the Great Depression in their own way. The *Herald Tribune* reported that in early 1936, eighty thousand Mormons were on federal relief. Now, it suggested, only a handful remained on the "government payroll": those who preferred "to be supported in idleness." The wisdom and foresight of the Church of Jesus Christ of Latter-day Saints (LDS Church) was praised as its work and relief initiatives were reviewed. The *Tribune* concluded, "What the Mormons have done in Utah and Idaho other American communities could also do—if they had the will."

In stressing "Mormon" accomplishments, the *Tribune* was simultaneously criticizing federal relief efforts as a demoralizing dole. It was, in effect, a thinly veiled attack on President Franklin Delano Roosevelt (FDR) and one of the most visible federal relief agencies, the Works Progress Administration (WPA). The head of that organization, Harry L. Hopkins, quickly responded to the *Herald*

Tribune editorial by assigning one of his assistants, Utah native and estranged Mormon Dean R. Brimhall, the task of countering media reports of Mormon successes by documenting conditions in Utah. Over time, a behind-the-scenes battle was waged for control of the public's perception of both the WPA and the Mormon relief program. In the end, little proved to be what it seemed.

The Great Depression (1929–41) marked a fateful passage in the annals of American history. For the span of a decade, unemployment, poverty, disappointment, and despair came to dominate the daily existence of many people. Throughout that entire period, fidelity to principles of independence, self-reliance, and self-sufficiency was sorely tested.

At the Depression's onset, Utah and its Mountain West neighbors faced some exceptional challenges.[1] Still stagnating after a post–World War I recession, the region's narrow economy—concentrated in mining, agriculture, and manufacturing—experienced a devastating collapse.[2] In Utah mining fell a staggering 85 percent, agriculture declined by 66 percent, and manufacturing dropped by 65 percent. In 1929 these three sectors had represented 73.2 percent of the state's income.[3]

In 1930 the poverty line in the United States stood at about $2,000 for an average family, with the subsistence level estimated to be $1,200 for an urban family of four.[4] In 1929 Utah's per capita personal income hovered at $559. (For the Mountain West, the average was about $580, and for the nation, it was $703.) By 1932 Utahns' per capita income had declined to an average of $303. In 1940 that average had only risen to $487, still $72 below the 1929 mark. (That year the region averaged $509 and the nation $595.)[5]

In addition to the magnitude of its economic woes, Utah varied from regional and national norms in one unique respect—it was dominated by an ecclesiastical institution, the LDS Church. Thus, during a dispiriting decade, the people of Utah sought succor in two almost diametrically opposed responses to the situation—FDR's New Deal and the LDS Church's Church Security Plan.

Beginning in 1933, FDR proffered the country an innovative amalgam of programs and panaceas in an effort to deliver economic and social relief, recovery, and reform. Able to pour millions upon millions of federal dollars on troubled waters, the New Deal offered the struggling nation and the people of Utah a vision of personal security rooted in an expanded federal-state partnership.

In contrast, the Utah-based LDS Church inaugurated its own independent relief program among its members. Latter-day Saints were encouraged to organize themselves collectively to shoulder each other's burdens. The implications of the LDS Church's response reverberate down to the present day. They echo in a common adage that asserts that during the Great Depression, the Mormons "took care of their own." When it was announced in May 1936 that the LDS Church intended to remove all Mormons from government relief rolls, the church's initiative entered the realm of the political.[6] As noted, the national press subsequently portrayed the Church Security Plan not simply as an alternative but as a rival to the New Deal itself.

Thus, these two contending ideologies came emblematically to represent the larger choices facing Utah and the country. On the national stage, these programs became proxies in the debate over the proper roles of government, the private sector, and the individual in combating the crushing economic and social costs of the Depression. In an ironic twist of fate, two Utahns—both members of the LDS Church—came to epitomize the competing prescriptions. In Washington, D.C., Dean R. Brimhall spoke for supporters of the New Deal through his role as a federal WPA official. In Utah J. Reuben Clark Jr. helped envision the LDS Church's alternative response as a member of its First Presidency.

During the early stages of the Great Depression in Utah, state and county government, local charities, and LDS Church units coordinated relief efforts without significant federal involvement. However, resources were extremely limited, and as the crisis intensified, the inadequacy of state, county, and community efforts grew ever more apparent. No one had expected the Depression to linger as it did.

With substantial federal aid funds pouring into the region in 1933, many Utahns—Mormon and non-Mormon alike—enthusiastically embraced FDR and the New Deal. In March 1933, 36,151 families received federally sponsored public relief. The next year 20 percent of the state's population of about 500,000 was aided. In 1940 48,000 families were still receiving some form of federal assistance.[7] Over the course of the first six years of the New Deal (1933–39), Utah received 156.6 percent of the nationwide average per-capita aid on a statewide basis.[8]

As a presidential candidate, FDR fared extremely well in Utah. In the 1936 election, at the height of the New Deal, he received almost 70 percent of the state's popular vote despite the expressed objection of the leadership of the LDS Church to his candidacy.[9] He had received 58 percent of the popular vote in 1932. Moreover, FDR would draw 62 percent of Utah's popular vote in 1940 and 60 percent in 1944.[10]

However, as the crisis progressed, questions mounted in the minds of some LDS leaders concerning the long-term consequences of both the Depression and FDR's New Deal initiatives. In response to both concerns, the LDS Church inaugurated one of it most extensive and enduring fiscal and organizational programs. Marshalling all its energies and resources, the church chose to tackle the temporal devastation battering the Saints in its own way—as church leaders saw it, "in the Lord's way."

Leading this effort was J. Reuben Clark Jr., who began serving in the LDS Church's First Presidency in 1933. A career civil servant, he had successfully represented the United States domestically and internationally as assistant solicitor to the State Department, undersecretary of state in the Calvin Coolidge administration, and ambassador to Mexico. From the outset of his tenure in the church's presiding counsel, he brought his significant administrative and intellectual abilities to bear upon Depression-related issues. Something of his temperament became apparent in an October 1933 LDS Church General Conference address. He suggested that "if people shall shun idleness . . . and return to the old-time virtues—industry, thrift, honesty, self-reliance, independence of spirit, self-discipline, and mutual happiness—we shall be on our way to returned prosperity and worldly happiness."[11]

Clark sketched a plan anchored in these principles in a series of handwritten notes in June 1933. He envisioned a system of contiguous church units organized in regions for relief purposes. Regional efforts would be coordinated churchwide through the presiding bishopric's office at church headquarters in Salt Lake City. Members would also be counseled to turn to the church, rather than to government aid, when personal and family resources were exhausted.[12] Those notes were later developed into a set of detailed instructions for church-wide dissemination.[13]

Clark's program was initially approved by the First Presidency in 1933 and then, upon review, tabled. The presiding bishop of the LDS Church, Sylvester Q. Cannon, opposed it, failing to see any urgent need for change, given existing state and local cooperation. A survey conducted by his office supported the argument that the church's existing decentralized program was adequate to cope with prevailing conditions. Optimistic pronouncements emanating from the White House and the public's enthusiastic support of New Deal legislation had also raised expectations of an imminent economic recovery. In light of this combination of circumstances, LDS Church President Heber J. Grant decided the time was not yet right to move forward with the plan.[14]

Clark expressed his dismay in an intense exchange of correspondence with Bishop Cannon. He argued that the church's existing program fell far short of what was needed, that more "precision and direction" was required. Clark insisted that his plan, by centralizing the church's efforts, would compensate for such deficiencies. Referring to relief programs in general, Clark asserted that greed, graft, and corruption "characterized the use of relief funds among us during the last two years" and that this was "destroying morale [and] undermining moral and spiritual stamina."[15]

Clark again failed to prevail. President Grant and First Counselor Anthony W. Ivins concluded that "relief work throughout the Church was being carried out effectively" and Clark's approach might cause "confusion and misunderstanding."[16] Disappointed but undaunted, Clark continued to crusade for a more ambitious and concerted solution. As the New Deal morphed and expanded, he also became alarmed at the constitutional implications of recent legislation and the presumed enervating effect of direct relief. In response he began to speak openly and determinedly about the evils of the dole and the sacredness of the Constitution.[17]

The LDS Church's First Presidency, photographed here in 1942, envisioned a church welfare program that would remove Latter-day Saints from federal relief rolls. Left to right, J. Reuben Clark, Heber J. Grant, and David O. McKay.

By 1935 changing circumstances brought matters to a head once more. Church welfare surveys revealed that local unit resources were becoming overwhelmed. Even where there was coordination among local and regional units, things remained very tight. Members were drawing government-sponsored relief in growing numbers. To complicate matters, federal programs were in flux as FDR contemplated an end of direct relief payments by shifting that burden back to the states. Fearing events were outpacing the church's capacity to deal with them effectively, the First Presidency (which now consisted of President Grant and counselors Clark and David O. McKay, following the death of Anthony W. Ivins in September 1934) agreed that the time was now right to introduce a variation on Clark's original proposal that they named the Church Security Plan.[18]

The plan was announced on April 6, 1936. President Grant subsequently observed, "Our primary purpose in organizing the Church Security Plan was to set up . . . a system under which the curse of idleness would be done away with, the evils of the dole abolished, and independence, industry, thrift, and self-respect be once more established. . . . Work is to be re-enthroned as a ruling principle in the lives of our church membership."[19] The ultimate objective was to "set up within the Church an organization to make it possible for the Church to eventually take care of its people exclusive of government relief and to assist them in placing themselves on a financially independent basis."[20]

Subsequent reporting suggested that the security plan would not only alleviate the immediate distress of faithful members but also offer a "solution to grave national problems." Members were reminded that the church had a "great opportunity to attract the attention of the Depression-ridden world by showing them the way out with this new cooperative program."[21] Clusters of local units known as stakes were organized into regions presided over by executive councils. Regional storehouses were developed as well as more efficient employment committees. Storehouses were intended to (1) preserve surplus commodities; (2) eliminate waste; (3) collect, preserve, and distribute "relief materials"; (4) facilitate "economical marketing, equitable distribution, and efficient transportation of produce and other materials"; and (5) shunt the urban unemployed into farming, mining, and industrial activities.[22]

The security plan resulted in a statistical increase in relief-related activities. A church survey in late 1936 revealed significant progress as winter approached. Eighty-seven of 112 reporting stakes (out of a possible 117) anticipated meeting members' needs during the coming season. Tithing and other offerings rapidly increased. At the end of 1936, more than one thousand members had been placed in private employment again, and twenty-three thousand had been assisted in some way.[23] By June 1938, more than fifty-six thousand members had received some form of assistance, and sixty-seven storehouses were operating.[24]

Such success was achieved in large part because the program had clear, unambiguous, quantifiable goals. Production quotas were set for regions and stakes. These explicit assignments tested members' commitment and the church's ability to function effectively under severe stress. To the extent that members answered leadership's call to action, the church was measurably strengthened.[25]

The announcement of the plan garnered abundant national attention. The conservative media embraced it enthusiastically, interpreting it as anti-New Deal. The *Saturday Evening Post, Readers Digest,* and *The Nation,* among others, praised it. In contrast, liberals saw it as a backward step countering the

Mormon bishops and Relief Society presidents referred needy members to storehouses such as this one stocked with commodities produced by the Church Welfare Plan. Utah Writers' Project photo, 1941.

progressive programs of the New Deal, "an ultra-conservative gesture of withdrawal."[26] Clark contended that the Church Security Plan was not expressly politically motivated. Some of Clark's thinking, which was so influential in pressing the initiative forward, did predate the New Deal as realized by 1936. That is not to say that church leaders, especially members of the First Presidency, did not hold and express strong political opinions.[27]

Though the development and implementation of the security plan was remarkable, when viewed within the larger scope of the Great Depression, its achievements appear less dramatic. Certainly the security plan helped many church members, but many continued to draw upon the federal government's largesse for support. During the period from 1930 to 1935, prior to the rollout of the security plan, the LDS Church expended a total of $3.68 million on what it identified as "charity." During the plan's first full year of operation (1937), the church spent $1,835,000 for welfare and distributed an additional $115,000 worth of clothing, fuel, canned fruit, vegetables, and other produce. A total of $10.88 million in cash was disbursed churchwide over the entire period from 1930 to 1940.[28] However, the church's accomplishments were dwarfed, at least in monetary terms, by federal relief activities in Utah. Those efforts were valued at $48 million in 1936 alone and more than $300 million throughout the Depression.[29] The church was never fully able to realize its stated objectives during any phase of the Depression.

Regardless of that fact, media reports touting the presumed success of the Church Security Plan persisted throughout the 1930s. The exaggerated nature of such accolades, coupled with the perceived anti-New Deal tone of some prominent church leaders, drew the ire of influential New Dealers in and out of the church. Among the most determined critics of the Church Security Plan was, in fact, one of the LDS Church's own—Dean R. Brimhall.

Born in 1886, Dean was the son of George H. and Flora Robinson Brimhall. His father was president of Brigham Young University from 1903 until 1921. Dean served an LDS mission in Germany from 1907 to 1909. Graduating from BYU in 1913 with a BS in psychology, he went on to obtain a master's degree (1916) and a PhD (1922) from Columbia University. He subsequently taught at BYU and Columbia.[30]

During the early 1930s, his attention turned to some of the critical issues of that day. Reminiscing in a letter to Dale Morgan in 1945, Brimhall noted that "Greenwell, Bowman, Maurice Howe, and Bob Hinckley, together with a few doctors and lawyers, formed a liberal group in Ogden. . . .When the depression came on we, of course, became very interested in economics, and sociology. Marriner Eccles came to a few of our meetings. Then one by one we began to drift into government work."[31]

In 1933 Brimhall was appointed Utah director of aviation under the federal Civil Works Administration, helping develop municipal and other aircraft landing fields in Utah. He subsequently became the Utah planning director for the Federal Emergency Relief Administration (FERA). In January 1935, he was selected to serve as director of the Utah State Planning Board. Later that year he became an advisor on labor relations for the WPA in Washington, D.C., under its director and FDR confidant, Harry L. Hopkins.[32]

The WPA was the successor to the Civil Works Administration and FERA. As the most visible sponsor of work relief, it was one of the most high profile and controversial programs initiated during the New Deal. WPA "work relief" was federal aid disbursed and administered through state-sponsored public works projects. Though it did not offer any direct relief payments, it was erroneously, but inextricably, linked with what was pejoratively know as the "dole"—the distribution of relief funds to individuals simply on the basis of immediate need. Ultimately this misinterpretation became a critical point of contention between the LDS Church and the WPA.

Brimhall came to the WPA with serious reservations about the prospects for national recovery. In a 1935 letter, he expressed his doubts in writing, asking, "What now, is the matter of our democratic system that we cannot see the failure of our economics?" In another letter, he observed, "The Federal Government is committed to a policy of a works program that will take it out of the business of giving relief. It does not seem possible that it will succeed but it is certainly better for people to be producing schools, water-systems, sewage systems, roads and the like than to remain idle."[33]

To an extent, Brimhall took solace from the past as he confronted the challenges of the modern world. He collected a series of discourses delivered before the Temple School of Science in 1885 and 1886 by C.W. Nibley that questioned the morality of capitalism and the private ownership of land. He also retained transcripts of an 1873 address by Orson Pratt, which reviewed the successes and failures of the early Saints' efforts to live a communalistic "law of consecration."[34]

In an ironic coincidence, J. Reuben Clark had retained several copies of another Orson Pratt discourse on the law of consecration.[35] Though on opposite sides of a political and philosophical divide, both Brimhall and Clark drew inspiration from a common source, seeing in the cooperative efforts of the Mormon past a model for a better future. Brimhall endorsed the New Deal with its initial undercurrent of incipient national collectivism as a possible political/economic solution to the Depression crisis. Conversely, Clark rejected the New Deal in favor of the Church Security Plan, viewing FDR's approach as a form of dole destructive of self-reliance, independence, and that cooperative spirit he believed was the only sure foundation for a truly united or "collective" effort in a gospel sense.

During the Depression, Brimhall authored a paper entitled "Latter-day Saint New Dealers of 1879 to 1890," which revealed something of his antipathy toward the Utah LDS Church. It was written in response to LDS Church leaders' support of Supreme Court rulings that overturned key New Deal legislation. Brimhall's break with the church's leadership was both philosophical and personal. He wrote, "The Church has grown powerful and rich; its interests are with the corporate enterprise. . . . The Mormon leaders, with their new interest in banking, insurance, finance, and industry, declare those who want progressive legislation to be treasonable and disloyal." He noted that the church had once taken a very different stand on the authority of the Supreme Court to speak for the nation.[36]

As early as 1934, Brimhall had come to see church leadership as parochial and out of touch with the political and economic realities of the Depression. He was present when Lorena Hickok interviewed the LDS Church's First Presidency. Hickok roved the country as an unofficial agent for Harry Hopkins, at that time the FERA director. Hickok's report was rather unflattering in its depiction of Presidents Grant, Ivins, and Clark.[37] Thirty-some years later, Brimhall rehearsed his recollection of that visit for historian Leonard Arrington. He expressed his dismay at Clark's anti-Roosevelt and anti-New Deal posture. The First Presidency did not have a grasp of the fundamental purpose of FERA, especially the work-relief element. He noted that at the close of the interview, Hickok had asked them, "Can you take care of your own people?" Brimhall reported, "There was dead silence for fully a minute. She sat tight and finally Clark looked down at the table and slowly shook his head. Pres. Grant was looking at Clark and without a word shook his head. Then Ivins did the same. And that was that."[38]

Dean R. Brimhall, labor relations advisor for the Works Progress Administration and tireless defender of the New Deal. Official WPA portrait, Washington Press Photo Bureau, 1942.

When Brimhall was brought on board at the WPA in Washington, he poured himself into his work while keeping an eye on developments in his home state. Beginning in 1936, with the announcement of the Church Security Plan, he both commissioned and authored several studies probing the purpose and questioning the achievements of the program. At heart he believed the church leaders were motivated by their opposition to the New Deal and that they were bent on offering the nation an alternative of their own ill-considered devising.

Within two months of the announcement inaugurating the Church Security Plan, Darrell J. Greenwell, state administrator for the Utah WPA, sent Brimhall a report of Gordon Wirick's visit with Mark Austin, a member of the newly formed LDS Church's General Welfare Committee.[39] Wirick confirmed the number of LDS Church members on relief and described some planned initiatives. Austin suggested that 16,500 members currently on relief could and should return to farming. In the cities, microindustries were to be established. A barter system was also contemplated. In a curious turn that would be echoed in subsequent WPA reports, Wirick reached the conclusion that the security plan was, in part, an attempt to bail out the church-sponsored Utah-Idaho Sugar Company: "The Utah-Idaho Sugar company, as you know, is owned and controlled by the Mormon Church and I have been told that the best way to whip the growers into line was through the church officials."[40]

On July 8, 1936, Brimhall sent a wire to his personal friend, Robert Hinckley, then serving as a WPA regional field representative. Brimhall initiated a study "limited strictly to visiting actual projects in operation…[and] determination of the actual number of individuals in the Church program taken from eligibility rolls. Advised against visiting any church officials."[41]

A week later, Brimhall submitted a twenty-nine-page memorandum to Harry Hopkins concerning the security plan. He accurately recounted some of the First Presidency's deliberations, including information from the surveys they had conducted. Brimhall suggested that church officials were deliberately seeking to discredit the federal program. They were also reacting to the potentially adverse publicity reports that an "undue proportion of its [LDS Church] members were receiving assistance from government agencies" might generate. In his concluding analysis, Brimhall asserted, "The great value that will come to Utah and the Mormon people will be the enlightenment Church leaders will get. Their boasting has committed them, their capitalistic thinking will continue to restrain the formation of real cooperatives. Their members will refuse the conditions imposed on recipients of relief. Out will come an enlightened, though disillusioned leadership."[42]

Apparently Brimhall generated yet another report that year. It echoed much that had appeared in Wirick's earlier report and the memorandum to Hopkins. Once again Brimhall questioned the motivation behind the plan and directly challenged the church's ability to remove eighty-eight thousand members from relief rolls. The report's conclusions contended that "publicity surrounding any accomplishments, however slight, will serve to increase the prestige of the Church" and "LDS leaders, if they disregard the facts in the future as they have in the past will pronounce their program a howling success and project it to the public as vastly less expensive and more successful than the government's relief program."[43]

The suspicion that the church was actively hostile toward the New Deal and the WPA was reinforced over the ensuing two years. In October 1936, James H. Moyle, a Utah Mormon with connections to church leaders, contacted Brimhall seeking Utah relief statistics. Brimhall was willing to help but did not want his name used. As they discussed conditions back home, Moyle commented, "I am on excellent terms with Grant. I guess he even swears by me, but if they are wrong I will be the first one to take off my coat and get into the fight. … They want to kick the government anyway. I have been trying my best to keep politics out of the church but [it] is hard to do."[44]

A month later, Moyle wrote to Brimhall sharing part of a conversation he had had with President Grant concerning an editorial Grant had approved for the church-controlled *Deseret News* castigating the Roosevelt administration and challenging the constitutionality of New Deal programs. The editorial asserted that "Church members, who believe the revelations and words of the Prophet, must stand for the Constitution," leaving the impression that FDR and his New Deal did not.[45]

Moyle reported that he had had a long visit with President Grant. Though Grant had acknowledged he might have erred in approving the antiadministration editorial, he felt "people were entitled to his ideas on the subject." Grant still thought of himself as a Democrat and had voted for the party's candidate for governor but could not support FDR. Moyle felt that President Grant had "absorbed the views of the financiers and failed to appreciate the humanitarian purposes of the President. He really believes the policies of the New Deal are dangerous and that the President does not have the high regard for the Constitution that he thinks he should have." Moyle also reported that President Grant "merely said that he had followed the impressions which he had on the subject and did not claim he had received any inspiration concerning it."[46]

It was the *New York Herald Tribune* pro–Church Security Plan editorial, however, that prompted a concerted response to what was increasingly perceived as a mounting threat from the plan to the New Deal in general and the WPA in particular. Brimhall immediately composed an interoffice memo outlining a possible course of action for Harry Hopkins's approval. It involved a somewhat complicated, surreptitious plan to manipulate a congressional committee into investigating the *Herald Tribune's* claims regarding the LDS security plan.

Brimhall informed Hopkins that "Mr. Alan Johnstone, Counsel for the Byrns Committee, has offered to write a letter to the Herald Tribune expressing interest in the attached editorial *[Herald Tribune*, September 21, 1937] asking for the source of the data it reports. This, of course would be followed by letters to Mormon Church officials."[47] Hopkins replied to Brimhall almost two weeks later. Brimhall's original memo was returned with a penciled note in Hopkins's hand: "Brimhall, I think someone should explode this and your scheme is too slow, HLH."[48]

Although Brimhall's retaliatory "scheme" had been rebuffed by Hopkins as insufficiently aggressive, WPA personnel remained sensitive to any perceived criticism of their program, especially in comparison to the Church Security Plan. In October and November 1937, David Niles, a WPA assistant administrator, wrote to President Grant to explain WPA's work-relief approach, suggesting that any association of the agency's program by him with the dole was misinformed. After an exchange of several letters among Heber J. Grant, Harry Hopkins, and David Niles, President Grant terminated the dialogue asserting, "I made no specific reference to the Works Progress Administration and no indirect references to the Administration, except so far as it might be covered by my observation in regarding idlers receiving gratuities, that is a 'dole' from the Government. You know whether or not the Works Progress Administration could fall within that implied reference."[49]

Nevertheless, during the following year, articles continued to appear in the press associating President Grant with criticism of government relief efforts. On June 6, 1938, the *Chicago Tribune* published a piece by Howard Wood, "Lure of WPA Foils Mormon Self-Aid Aims." The *New York Times* picked up the story and ran it the same day with a page one headline that read, "Effort of Mormons to Avoid Relief Rolls Frustrated by Lure of Government Funds." The

WPA crew working on an underpass at Union School. New Deal relief laborers built roads, bridges, dams and schools across Utah during the Depression.

article reported that Mormon Church efforts to remove members from WPA rosters had thus far failed. President Grant was quoted as stating, "Because it has proved impossible to persuade many of the members to resist the temptation to lean on the government we now have to be content with urging those who go to work on WPA jobs to try to give an honest day's work for their money." He went on to observe, "I have watched men at work on these government jobs. I have counted slowly to four between their shovelfuls. In some cases I have counted as high as forty between shovelfuls—and they have been mighty skimpy shovelfuls at that."[50]

A number of overtly critical articles also began to appear questioning the accomplishments of the Church Security Plan.[51] Whether or not Brimhall personally promoted this shift of rhetoric has not been conclusively ascertained, though it is apparent that he stood ready to provide unflattering data whenever an opportunity occurred. In any case, by mid-1938 he was pursuing a new elaborate strategy to fully discredit the plan and, by association, the LDS Church's leadership. In August 1938, Brimhall and Nels Anderson (another estranged Mormon and a personal friend) were in contact with Professor Read Baine of Miami University in Oxford, Ohio. Brimhall indicated "We want somebody to organize a little project to determine just how much the Mormon Church Security Program has affected the relief situation." Baine declined the offer, recommending instead Utah sociologist Lowry Nelson. Brimhall countered that they needed someone more removed from the Utah church."[52]

Brimhall next contacted Professor Royden L. Dangerfield of the University of Oklahoma. He also declined.[53] Finally, in October he was able to interest Louis Wirth, a noted urban sociologist at the University of Chicago. Anderson was a former student of Wirth's and proved instrumental in obtaining his cooperation. Brimhall orchestrated arrangements at the WPA—personnel, statistics, and funding were assembled.

A lengthy memo from Brimhall to a Mr. Rauch (possibly Basil Rauch), assistant commissioner in the employment division, offered a detailed summary of the whole undertaking. Brimhall rehearsed the background for the study: "In April 1936 the Mormons announced they were going to take all their members off the State and Federal relief rolls. . . . The reactionary press of the country took up the report of the proposals with great gusto. Hundreds of newspaper and magazine articles were written extolling the virtues of the program and in many cases pointing out that Mr. Hopkins should learn from the Mormons how to handle relief."[54]

Brimhall recounted the reaction to the *New York Herald Tribune* editorial in 1937 and subsequent recruitment of Louis Wirth to supervise a study of conditions in Utah, focusing on Mormon relief achievements. Brimhall's superiors had endorsed the study before its launch. He noted that the WPA could have undertaken the study itself, but there was concern that "the value, however accurate the findings, would have been lessened by the fact that we are ex parte students of the problem." The advantage of having Louis Wirth conduct the study ensured that "when it is finished it will have the stamp of approval of one of the best departments, in one of the best universities in the world. It will be done much cheaper than we could have done it ourselves."[55]

He also considered the downside: "The only possible disadvantage I can see in the method we have used arises out of the fact that Professor Wirth may submerge the Mormon program in the study of other factors affecting relief requirements in the state of Utah. However, the only way we could obtain his services was by telling him that we would not control or direct his activities other than present the problem to him." Wirth felt he had his "professional standing at stake" and had to have a free hand to carry out the study as he felt appropriate.[56]

In July 1939, Brimhall sent another memo, in this instance to David K. Niles, summarizing the results of Wirth's study. Mormons represented approximately 60 percent of the population in Utah but 79.3 percent of the relief load in general. The total Mormon participation on WPA projects was even higher: 83.1 percent. Brimhall unhesitatingly asserted, "This gives the lie to the Mormon claim about taking care of their own."[57]

And so it did, for the truth of the matter had never varied—Utah Mormons were consistently overrepresented in relief statistics throughout the course of the Great Depression. Brimhall's extensive records, gleaned from sources in

Utah and at the WPA, consistently verified the fact that Mormons indeed did not take care of their own—for the most part, the state and federal government did. This did not detract from the exceptional accomplishments of the Church Security Plan, but media accounts of Mormon success in taking most of its members off relief rolls were exaggerations at best, if not outright distortions.

Despite obtaining the results he desired from Wirth's Utah study, Brimhall was never able to arrange for its publication. Draft copies were circulated among his friends and associates, and a manuscript was submitted to the University of Chicago Press. As late as January 1941, Brimhall was still corresponding with Wirth about salvaging the project and somehow getting it published. Eventually interest waned, and the University of Chicago Press returned Wirth's manuscript to him in 1942. The WPA also ceased operation in 1942 when the United States returned to full employment as a consequence of World War II.[58]

In later years, Brimhall either forgot or "misremembered" the details of the Wirth study. In correspondence with historian Leonard Arrington, Brimhall acknowledged arranging for Louis Wirth to direct a study of the "proportion of WPA reliefers" who were Mormon. Stating that Wirth had died during the study, Brimhall said he recalled that Wirth's assistant had reported that "LDS members numbered twenty percent more than non-members, proportionate to the population expectancy. . . . Shortly thereafter I left for work in the Dept. of Commerce and had no time or interest in trying to have the study completed."[59]

Contrary to Brimhall's recollection, Dr. Wirth died in 1952 and, as noted, he and Brimhall pursued publication of the Utah study for at least two years. After leaving the WPA in 1939, Brimhall served as director of research for the Civil Aeronautics Administration until 1951. He was also a noted expert on Native American rock art and an accomplished photographer. He died in 1972.

The Church Security Plan was rechristened the Church Welfare Plan in 1939 to avoid confusion with the federally sponsored Social Security program. It became, in many respects, one of the LDS Church's preeminent achievements, admired especially in terms of subsequent international humanitarian efforts. Contrary to the available evidence then and now, the impression that the Mormons "took care of their own" during the Great Depression persists.

NOTES

1. The Mountain West consists of Arizona, Colorado, Idaho, Montana, New Mexico, Utah, and Wyoming.

2. Thomas G. Alexander, "From War to Depression," in *Utah's History*, ed. Richard D. Poll, Thomas G. Alexander, Eugene E. Campbell, and David E. Miller, (Provo, UT: Brigham Young University Press, 1978), 464–69; Leonard J. Arrington, *The Changing Economic Structure of the Mountain West, 1850–1950* (Indianapolis: Bobbs-Merrill, 1963).

3. A. Smith Pond, "An Analysis of Effective Income Distribution in the State of Utah," *Proceedings: Utah Academy of Science* (November 1934), 121–22.

4. James T. Peterson, *America's Struggle against Poverty, 1900–1985* (Cambridge, MA: Harvard University Press, 1986), 16, 41.

5. Leonard J. Arrington, "Sagebrush Resurrection: New Deal Expenditures in the Western States, 1933–1939," *Pacific Historical Review* 52 (February 1983): 1–15; Arrington, "The New Deal in the West: A Preliminary Statistical Inquiry," *Pacific Historical Review* 8 (August 1969): 311–16; Don C. Reading, "New Deal Activities in the States, 1933 to 1939," *Journal of Economic History* 33, no. 4 (1973): 792–807; Leonard J. Arrington and George Jensen, "Comparison of Income Changes in the Western States, 1929–1960," *Western Economic Journal* 1 (Summer 1963): 205–17.

6. D. Michael Quinn, *Elder Statesman: A Biography of J. Reuben Clark* (Salt Lake City: Signature Books, 2002), 399; Garth Mangum and Bruce Blumell, *The Mormons' War on Poverty: A History of LDS Welfare* (Salt Lake City: University of Utah Press, 1993), 136–37.

7. John F. Bluth and Wayne K. Hinton, "The Great Depression," in Poll et al., *Utah's History*, 483.

8. Arrington, "Sagebrush Resurrection," 1–15; Arrington, "New Deal in the West," 311–16; Reading, "New Deal Activities," 792–810; Arrington and Jensen, "Comparison of Income Changes," 205–17.

9. Quinn, *Elder Statesman*, 79–84; Thomas G. Alexander, *Utah, the Right Place: The Official Centennial History*, 1st ed. (Salt Lake City: Gibbs Smith Publisher, 1995), 329–32.

10. Table K, in Poll et al., *Utah's History*, 700–701.

11. J. Reuben Clark Jr., in *104th Semi-Annual Conference of the Church of Jesus Christ of Latter-day Saints* (Salt Lake City: Church of Jesus Christ of Latter-day Saints, 1933), 100–104.

12. J. Reuben Clark Jr., "Suggested Directions for Church Relief Activities," July 15, 1933, J. Reuben Clark Jr. Papers, L. Tom Perry Special Collections, Harold B. Lee Library, Brigham Young University, Provo, Utah (hereafter cited as Clark Papers); J. Reuben Clark Jr., "Final Draft," October 23, 1933, Clark Papers; D. Michael Quinn, *J. Reuben Clark: The Church Years* (Provo, UT: Brigham Young University Press, 1983), 260; Mangum and Blumell, *Mormons' War on Poverty*, 124.

13. J. Reuben Clark Jr., "Course of Action," holographic notes, Clark Papers.

14. J. Reuben Clark Jr., "Tentative Notes for Group Meeting with Stake Presidents," October 1936, Clark Papers; "1932 Church Welfare Survey," Clark Papers; Quinn, *J. Reuben Clark*, 263.

15. J. Reuben Clark Jr. to Sylvester Q. Cannon, November 9, 1933, Clark Papers.

16. Minutes of First Presidency meeting, November 27, 1933, quoted in Quinn, *J. Reuben Clark*, 262–63.

17. J. Reuben Clark, "Remarks at Special Meeting of the Presidents of Stakes, Bishops, and Mission Presidents," April 6, 1936, Clark Papers; Leonard J. Arrington, Feramorz Y. Fox, and Dean L. May, *Building the City of God: Community and Cooperation among the Mormons* (Salt Lake City: Deseret Book Co., 1976), 349.

18. Draft statement by First Presidency announcing Church Security Plan, April 1935, unpublished document, Clark Papers; J. Reuben Clark Jr., "Remarks Presented at Special Priesthood Meeting," October 7, 1935, manuscript, Clark Papers; J. Reuben Clark Jr., note in file, November 1935, Clark Papers.

19. "The Presidency on Church Security," *Improvement Era,* January 1937, 131.

20. Henry A. Smith, "Church-Wide Security Plan Organized," *Improvement Era,* June 1936, 337; "The First Presidency Speaks on Church Security," *Improvement Era,* January 1937, 3; J. Reuben Clark Jr., "Tentative Program for Missions," typescript, Clark Papers; Mangum and Blumell, *Mormons' War on Poverty,* 147.

21. Smith, "Church-Wide Security Plan," 338; Clark, "Remarks Presented at Special Priesthood Meeting," Clark Papers.

22. Smith, "Church-Wide Security Plan," 334.

23. "1936 Church Welfare Survey," updates, Clark Papers.

24. J. Reuben Clark Jr., "Church Welfare Plan: A Discussion," June 30, 1939, Clark Papers.

25. Mangum and Blumell, *Mormons' War on Poverty,* 98.

26. "The Goal of Self-Support," *Saturday Evening Post,* March 6, 1937; Marc A. Rose, "The Mormons March Off Relief," *Readers Digest,* June 7, 1937; Martha Emery, "Mormon Security," *The Nation* 146 (February 12, 1938): 182–83.

27. Quinn, *Elder Statesman,* 57–106; Quinn succinctly chronicles Presidents Grant and Clark's opposition to the New Deal and Clark's continued involvement in Republican politics; Arrington, Fox, and May, *Building the City of God,* 348, 350; J. Reuben Clark Jr., in *115th Annual Conference of The Church of Jesus Christ of Latter-day Saints* (Salt Lake City: Church of Jesus Christ of Latter-day Saints, 1945), 25; J. Reuben Clark Jr., *Church Welfare Plan: A Discussion* (Salt Lake City: General Church Welfare Committee of the Church of Jesus Christ of Latter-day Saints, n.d.), 3.

28. See *Annual Conference Reports of the Church of Jesus Christ of Latter-day Saints* (Salt Lake City: Church of Jesus Christ of Latter-day Saints, 1930–1940); Fred Pasley, "Utah, Enemy of Dole, 12th in Federal Aid," *New York Daily News,* June 22, 1938.

29. U.S. Bureau of the Budget, *Report No. 10: Utah* (Washington, DC: Office of Government Reports, Statistical Section, 1939).

30. Biographical note, "Register," Dean R. Brimhall Papers, Special Collections, J. Willard Marriott Library, University of Utah, Salt Lake City (hereafter cited as Brimhall Papers).

31. Dean Brimhall to Dale Morgan, October 8, 1945, Brimhall Papers. Darrell Greenwell later served as Utah administrator of the WPA. Maurice Howe later directed the Federal Writers Project in Utah. Robert Hinckley later directed the State Emergency Relief Administration before being appointed assistant administrator of the FERA. Marriner Eccles chaired the Federal Resource Board for seventeen years beginning in 1935.

32. Biographical note, "Register," Brimhall Papers.

33. Dean Brimhall to Dorothy Nyswander, October 6, 1935, Brimhall Papers; Dean Brimhall to Mr. Strachey, June 24, 1935, Brimhall Papers.

34. C.W. Nibley, "Logan Temple Lectures," Brimhall Papers; Orson Pratt, 1873 address, Brimhall Papers.

35. Orson Pratt, "Stewardship and Consecration," June 14, 1874, Clark Papers.

36. Dean R. Brimhall, "Latter-day Saint New Dealers of 1879 to 1890," n.d., Brimhall Papers.

37. Lorena Hickok to Harry Hopkins, September 1934, copy in the Brimhall Papers.

38. Dean R. Brimhall to Leonard Arrington, July 14, 1966, Brimhall Papers. Hickok's letter to Hopkins does not directly corroborate Brimhall's recollections thirty years later.

39. The initial members of the General Welfare Committee were Elder Melvin J. Ballard, chairman; Harold B. Lee, managing director; Mark Austin, Campbell M. Brown, Stringham A. Stevens, and Henry D. Moyle. Glenn L. Rudd., *Pure Religion: The Story of Church Welfare Since 1930* (Salt Lake City: The Church of Jesus Christ of Latter-day Saints, 1995) 50.

40. Gordon Wirick, "Wirick Report," June 5, 1936, Brimhall Papers.

41. Dean R. Brimhall to Robert Hinckley, July 8, 1939, telegram, Brimhall Papers.

42. Dean R. Brimhall to Harry Hopkins, "The Mormon Relief Plan," memorandum, July 14, 1936, Brimhall Papers.

43. "Security Program of the Church of the Latter Day Saints," unattributed and undated report, Brimhall Papers. Circumstantial evidence within the collection suggests that Brimhall composed this report in mid-1936.

44. James H. Moyle and Dean R. Brimhall, notes of phone conversation, October 15, 1936, Brimhall Papers.

45. *Deseret News,* October 31, 1936.

46. James H. Moyle to Dean R. Brimhall, November 14, 1936, Brimhall Papers.

47. Dean R. Brimhall to Mrs. Goodwin (Hopkins's secretary), memorandum, September 22, 1937, Brimhall Papers.

48. Mrs. Goodwin to Dean R. Brimhall, memorandum, October 4, 1937, Brimhall Papers.

49. David K. Niles to Heber J. Grant (copy to Harry L. Hopkins), October 6, 1937; Heber J. Grant to David K. Niles, October 15, 1937; Heber J. Grant to Harry L. Hopkins, October 15, 1937; David K. Niles to Heber J. Grant, November 6, 1937; Heber J. Grant to David K. Niles, November 26, 1937, all in the Brimhall Papers.

50. Howard Wood, "Lure of WPA Foils Mormon Self-Aid Aims," *Chicago Tribune,* June 6, 1938; *New York Times,* June 6, 1938, 1.

51. Fred Pasley, "Mormon Church Failing to Wean Saints Off Dole," *New York Daily News,* June 20, 1938, 2; Pasley, "2,000 Salt Lake Mormons On WPA, Despite 'Dole' Fight," *New York Daily News,* June 21, 1938, 8.

52. Nels Anderson, Dean R. Brimhall, and Read Baine, transcript of telephone conversation, August 31, 1938, Brimhall Papers.

53. Dean R. Brimhall and Royden L. Dangerfield, transcript of telephone conversation, September 14, 1939, Brimhall Papers.

54. Dean R. Brimhall to Mr. Rauch, memorandum, March 28, 1938, Brimhall Papers.

55.   Ibid.

56.   Ibid.

57.   Dean R. Brimhall to David K. Niles, memorandum, July 31, 1939, Brimhall Papers. A portion of Louis Wirth's "Utah Study" is available in the Brimhall Papers. An outline of the proposed content, drafts of the first three chapters, and a portion of chapter seven are dispersed among several files.

58.   Louis Wirth Papers, boxes 12 and 38, Special Collections Research Center, University of Chicago Library, Chicago.

59.   Brimhall to Arrington, July 14, 1966.

8

The Battle over Tariff Reduction

The Utah-Idaho Sugar Company, Senator Reed Smoot, and the 1913 Underwood Act

Matthew C. Godfrey

Throughout the early twentieth century, Utah's economy was based on two major industries—agriculture and mining. The Mormon Church and the local sugar companies encouraged farmers to raise sugar beets as a cash crop. Utah representatives in Congress, especially Mormon Apostle and Senator Reed Smoot, supported a high tariff to protect the sugar beet industry in the state. Using newspapers, congressional records, and Smoot's diaries, Matthew C. Godfrey's essay documents the arguments to prevent the elimination of the sugar tariff in 1913. Because of a Democratic Congress, the Underwood Bill passed, reducing the tariff on imported sugar. Godfrey shows that the sugar beet industry was affected but not completely destroyed. Smoot remained convinced of the need for a high tariff and was an author of the 1930 Hawley-Smoot Act, which raised tariffs and isolated America at the beginning of the Great Depression.

In the 1910s, growing sugar beets was an important part of Utah's economy. Sugar had successfully been extracted from beets in 1889 by the Utah Sugar Company, a corporation supported both financially and verbally by the Church of Jesus Christ of Latter-day Saints. By 1920 more than eight thousand farmers in northern Utah, southern Idaho, and central Washington were planting more than ninety-three thousand acres in sugar beets and harvesting in excess of nine hundred thousand tons of the vegetable. The Utah-Idaho Sugar Company, one of two large sugar corporations headquartered in Utah (the other was the Amalgamated Sugar Company), generated approximately 2.3 million bags of beet sugar from these crops, producing twenty-eight-million-dollars worth of

The sugar beet plant.

beet sugar. In this time period, sugar beets were "the securest portion of the agricultural picture" for Utah farmers.[1]

As beet sugar became more and more important as an agricultural industry in Utah, the Utah-Idaho Sugar Company (first formed in 1907 from a merger of the Utah Sugar Company, the Idaho Sugar Company, and the Western Idaho Sugar Company) expanded its markets and began producing sugar for not only the Intermountain West but regions as far east as the Missouri River Valley. It also became entwined with the American Sugar Refining Company (which held 50 percent of Utah-Idaho's stock). These two factors integrated the Utah-Idaho Sugar Company into the national sugar industry and the economy. Because of this unification, national trends and politics began to affect Utah-Idaho Sugar and, by extension, Utah sugar beet farmers and the state's economy. To protect Utah interests from these impacts, state leaders, including U.S. Senator Reed Smoot, took up the fight against policies they perceived as detrimental to beet sugar.

A good example of such a fight—and a good way to explore how important the tariff was to the beet sugar industry in Utah—came in 1913 over a Democratic attempt to reduce the sugar tariff. Seen from the perspective of Reed Smoot and the Utah-Idaho Sugar Company, the debate over this national piece of legislation indicates the depth to which Utah's sugar industry—first proposed by Brigham Young as a way to make Utah Territory self-sufficient— had become subject to national trends and markets. According to leaders of the Utah-Idaho Sugar Company such as Joseph F. Smith (president of both the corporation and the LDS Church), Utah's beet sugar industry prospered only because of the tariff. First enacted by Congress in 1789, the duty added to the cost of cane sugar produced in Cuba and Indonesia (known then as Java), allowing domestic growers of sugar—including Louisiana cane growers and western beet sugar farmers—to compete with the cheaper imported product.[2] Although the sugar industry might have found the tariff beneficial, many American citizens, economists, and politicians believed that it amounted to an unfair tax on consumers. Because the price of tariff goods, whether imported or not, increased by the amount of the duty, the argument went, the consumer had to pay "an enhanced price, or tax, to the full extent of the duty."[3]

Arguing that the sugar tariff only benefited sugar producers at the expense of consumers, Democrats worked to rescind the duty, which amounted to nearly two cents a pound on raw and refined sugar. To worsen matters, the American Sugar Refining Company, which had purchased large amounts of stock in beet sugar, including Utah-Idaho Sugar, began selling off its stock because pending government investigations were threatening to break up its monopoly on U.S. sugar. American Sugar retained its investment in the Utah-Idaho Sugar Company, but, because it had few other holdings, the company regarded the beet sugar industry as a rival in need of destruction. Believing that domestic beet sugar would not be able to compete with cane sugar if the duty was removed on imports, the American Sugar directors agitated for tariff reform.[4]

As part of his 1912 presidential platform, Democratic nominee Woodrow Wilson pledged to lower tariffs on foreign products entering the United States to decrease prices for consumers.[5] After Wilson gained the presidency and the Democrats obtained a majority in the Senate (they already had a majority in the House), the stage was set for reform. President Wilson quickly called Congress into a special session on April 8, 1913, to fulfill his campaign promise, and the beet sugar industry, including Utah-Idaho Sugar Company, feared the worst.[6]

Representative Oscar Underwood, a Democrat from Alabama and chair of the House Ways and Means Committee, introduced the tariff revision bill (known as the Underwood Bill) in the House. It proposed an immediate 25 percent reduction of the sugar duty and its entire removal after three years.[7] The legislation shocked many Utahns, and the *Salt Lake Herald-Republican*, a Smoot-supported newspaper,[8] declared that sugar manufacturers such as the Utah-Idaho Sugar Company would have to "get out of business within three years" if the measure passed.[9] Leaders of Utah-Idaho Sugar agreed with the *Herald-Republican*'s assessment, claiming that if Congress removed the tariff, it "would absolutely cripple the [beet] sugar industry."[10]

Because Democrats had a large majority in the House of Representatives, Utah-Idaho leaders focused their attention on the Senate, hoping that that chamber would reject the bill. For one thing, the two Louisiana senators, both Democrats, opposed the plan, convinced that it would have the same effect on

Senator Reed Smoot.

their state's cane-sugar production as on the beet-sugar industry.[11] In addition, Smoot, a pronounced protectionist and member of the LDS Church's Quorum of the Twelve Apostles, resided in the Senate and, presumably, would protect the interests of the Utah-Idaho Sugar Company, whose stock his church owned.

At the time, many Utahns (and Americans as well) were convinced that Smoot was a Republican protectionist because Joseph F. Smith was forcing him to be one. Because Smith served as president of the LDS Church and Smoot was an apostle, some claimed that he could not go against Smith's desires. As president of Utah-Idaho Sugar, Smith clearly wanted the tariff maintained, so Smoot would have to do all he could to ensure its preservation.[12] Yet Smoot's personal beliefs were at least as influential on his tariff stance as any pressure from Smith or other Mormon leaders. Before becoming politically active, Smoot had studied the tariff issue and concluded that it was important enough to warrant his involvement with "the almost non-existent Utah Republicans."[13]

Smoot believed that protection was necessary for several reasons. For one he claimed that tariffs raised the wages of American workers by enhancing the profits of producers. "I have seen the poverty, the squalor, and suffering" experienced by laborers in other countries, Smoot once declared, "and I have made a vow that no act of mine shall ever place an American workman in the position of having to compete with such conditions." Smoot also supported the tariff because it helped to develop American industry: "I have been so proud of my country's development," he proclaimed, that "it is natural that I should be jealous of her every interest." With the protection that the tariff afforded, the United States could become more self-reliant and less dependent on other countries for its necessities. At the same time, it could retain the money it spent on foreign goods.[14] Because Smoot was "as fully convinced of the validity of protectionism as he was of the theology of Mormonism," the Utah-Idaho Sugar Company did indeed have a strong proponent in the Senate to work against Democratic tariff revisions.[15]

Another strong advocate was the U.S. Beet Sugar Association and its secretary, Truman G. Palmer. Palmer actively worked against reducing the tariff, reiterating the claim of others in the industry that U.S. beet sugar would die without protection.[16] His attempts to influence senators and congressmen led President Woodrow Wilson to proclaim that "extraordinary exertions [are] being made by the lobby in Washington to gain recognition for certain alterations of the tariff bill." Wilson continued,

> Washington has seldom seen so numerous, so industrious, or so insidious a lobby. The newspapers are being filled with paid advertisements calculated to mislead the judgment of public men not only but also the public opinion of the country itself. There is every evidence that money without limit is being spent to sustain this lobby and to create an appearance of a pressure of public opinion antagonistic to some of the chief items of the tariff bill. . . . The government in all its branches ought to be relieved from this intolerable burden and this constant interruption to the calm progress of debate.[17]

In response to Wilson's call for action, Senator Albert B. Cummins from Iowa introduced a resolution proposing a thorough investigation of interests lobbying against tariff reform. In addition to inquiring about individuals who had contacted senators, the probe would also examine "whether any Senator is financially or personally interested in the production, manufacture, or sale of any article or articles mentioned in [the] tariff bill," as well as whether congressmen were "connected, professionally or otherwise" with any corporation or individual "engaged in the manufacture, production, or sale" of tariff articles.[18] Because of his ties to the LDS Church and a nominal amount of stock he owned in the Utah-Idaho Sugar Company, Reed Smoot soon became embroiled in this investigation.

On June 5, 1913, Smoot appeared before a special Senate subcommittee charged with discovering senators' ties to those industries affected by the tariff. Smoot admitted that he owned 157 shares of stock in the Utah-Idaho Sugar Company worth $1,232.45 and that he was also interested in other items undergoing tariff revision, such as lead and wool. However, since his holdings in these industries were only nominal, he did not believe that they improperly influenced his actions as a senator. Smoot also testified that Palmer and other beet sugar men had contacted him about the sugar tariff on several occasions but that he did not regard them as lobbyists because that term described someone using "tricks, frauds, devices, or corruptions" to "misrepresent" themselves to legislators. Everyone had "a perfect right" to contact Smoot about legislation that they were interested in as long as they did not lie about their interests or positions. "If he confined himself strictly to the truth and never misrepresented the facts," Smoot declared, a lobbyist had "a perfect right to be here."[19]

Smoot did not say so, but it is probable that high-ranking Mormon Church leaders such as Joseph F. Smith and Charles Nibley (presiding bishop of the LDS Church) had also talked to him about the tariff. Nibley, who was a director in the Utah-Idaho Sugar Company and became its largest stockholder in 1914, frequently contacted Smoot (who was a good friend) about issues affecting beet sugar. In May 1913, for example, Smoot had outlined to Nibley in great detail the Democrats' tariff plan.[20] Whatever the case, because the LDS Church held extensive stock in the Utah-Idaho Sugar Company, Senator James Reed (a member of the subcommittee) made the accusation that Mormon leaders had influenced Smoot's tariff stance. Smoot hotly denied the charge, declaring that "in Washington I represent all the people of Utah. I do not represent the Mormon or Jew or Gentile, or black or white, or Methodist or Presbyterian, as such. I am equally interested in every person in Utah, whether they belong to the church or whether they do not."[21]

Smoot later confided that he regarded Reed as "a contemptable [*sic*] cuss as ever lived" because "he undertook to investigate the church and not me" in the lobbying hearing.[22] The *Salt Lake Tribune*, which exhibited little love for the LDS Church at this time, disagreed with Smoot, declaring that Senator Reed "was fairly justified" in intimating that the church was behind "Smoot's mission in Washington." Indeed, the *Tribune* argued, Smoot did not really represent all of the people because there were "many" in Utah "who do not in the least consider him as representing them."[23] Although the *Tribune* referred to non-Mormons, the paper could have been speaking about church members as well. According to political scientist Milton R. Merrill, Smoot probably received a minority of the Mormon vote in 1902, 1914, and 1932, and even in other years, he never received an overwhelming majority of LDS votes. Even some of his fellow apostles (largely Democrats) refused to support him. As Merrill concluded, "It could not be said at any time that Smoot was the senator of the Mormon Church, in the sense that he got the Church vote."[24]

The furor over lobbying soon subsided with no firm conclusions reached. As debate over the Underwood Bill heated up, Smoot expanded his efforts to protect duties on Utah products. However, he soon received word of a Democratic plan that would allow Louisiana Democrats to support tariff reductions and still save face with their constituents (who were against such revisions). According to this plan, the Senate would amend certain aspects of the tariff, including the sugar schedule, in favor of domestic production. Some Democrats would vote for the amendments with the understanding that after the bill went into conference, the Senate would "yield to the House provision[s] as indorsed [*sic*] by President Wilson" (meaning restoring provisions in the bill calling for an immediate 25 percent reduction in the duty and the entire removal of the tariff within three years). Thus, no real changes to the bill would occur as it came out of the House, and the sugar schedule would stand.[25]

Such machinations disheartened Smoot, convincing him that he was virtually helpless to amend the bill and save the sugar duty. Yet he still put much time and energy into excoriating tariff reductions, becoming one of the Republicans' main forces against decreases and leading the *Salt Lake Herald-Republican* to anoint him "the leading champion of American commerce and industry" in the Senate because of "his intimate knowledge of the tariff." Ever since Smoot had entered the Senate, the *Herald-Republican* editorialized, he had constantly studied tariff issues. Thus, "the Republican party has no fear that the Utah senator will prove unequal to the task" of leading the tariff fight.[26] Although the *Herald-Republican* was a biased source, its assessment of Smoot was not greatly exaggerated because Republicans, acknowledging his knowledge, asked the senator to prepare "a lengthy analysis" of the bill to highlight its "serious defects."[27]

In addition to preparing this report, Smoot attacked tariff reductions on the floor of the Senate. Throughout the debates, he frequently questioned Democratic senators, proposed amendments to the Underwood Bill, inserted newspaper editorials supporting the tariff into the *Congressional Record,* and issued diatribes against reductions. On two occasions, Smoot read prepared speeches. He tried to transcend the interests of Utah's beet sugar industry by focusing on national reasons why the tariff was necessary. On July 21 and 22, for example, Smoot analyzed every schedule of the tariff and offered his objections to the proposed Underwood Bill as a whole. "I shall not attempt to make an extended argument on any particular schedule of the bill," he began, "but simply call the Senate's attention to many of the inadequate, excessive, and inconsistent rates provided for in the bill." By the conclusion of his speech, Smoot declared, he hoped to show the Senate "that our marvelous industrial growth for the last 40 years can not be maintained nor will it continue to increase under this Democratic tariff bill."[28]

In this address, Smoot used many of the same arguments that he had employed in the past against tariff reduction: that it would harm American industry and workers, that it would destroy the economic prosperity of the United States, and that it would eradicate the nation's self-sufficiency. But Smoot also focused on some of the unfair measures that he believed the Underwood Bill specifically contained. One of his biggest complaints was that the legislation seemed to favor the eastern and southern United States at the expense of the West, including Utah. For example, although "wheat, flour, corn and corn meal, meats, potatoes, swine, cattle, sheep, and various other farm products" were placed on the free list, rice retained a duty. Smoot could see no reason for this except that it was an attempt to favor the rice-producing South, a strongly Democratic region. "When other products are put on the free list with the pretense of reducing the cost of living," Smoot declared, "there is not a shadow of reason why rice should not be treated in the same way." Smoot also could not understand why there was a duty on bananas, a crop grown to some extent in the South. He asserted that it was "a most extraordinary proceeding" for bananas to retain a duty when "sugar, wheat, flour, [and] potatoes" did not.[29]

Although Smoot's arguments about sectional favoritism had some validity, his assertions also contained inconsistencies. For one thing, placing sugar on the free list would harm not only beet sugar producers in Utah but Louisiana cane growers as well. For another, the bill proposed "a sweeping reduction in duties" on cotton, one of the most important southern crops.[30] Because the tariff reductions affected both cotton and Louisiana cane sugar, it is difficult to believe that the Democratic Congress was deliberately hurting western agriculture while refusing to touch southern industries.

Smoot justified the cotton provision in the bill by claiming that "the manu-facturers of heavy-weight cotton and coarse cotton," most of whom were in the South, "are not seriously threatened by the rates of this bill." However, numerous cotton growers who would be adversely affected by the tariff *were* in the South. Why would Democrats aid cotton manufacturers but not growers? According to Smoot, it was because the tariff reductions were aimed at hurt-ing farmers at the expense of industry. "With free trade in farm products," the senator declared, "the farmers in the West will suffer without any redeeming features." If other countries could export agricultural products at cheaper prices than American farmers could raise them, the United States would naturally rely more and more on foreign imports at the expense of American agriculture.

Because of this, Smoot argued, the Underwood Bill worked against the "back-to-the-farm" movement, which counseled farmers to forsake cities and remain in agriculture to preserve the virtue of American democracy. If tariff reductions occurred, Smoot continued, it would push people from rural to urban areas by destroying agriculture. This eradication of agriculture would hurt commerce, Smoot insisted, because "railroads will employ fewer men" (since they would not have as many agricultural products to transport), "the demand for home products will diminish, and there will be surplus help in many lines." Indeed, Smoot claimed, "it will cause a further increase in the ranks of the unemployed in cities, lower wages, strikes, disorder, and discon-tent generally."[31]

Perhaps worst of all, Smoot declared, was the effect that reduced duties would have on the beet sugar industry. He stated that Democrats influenced by cane sugar refiners had designed the tariff "to annihilate the production of sugar in this country." He cautioned against such action, in part because he did not

Beets loaded on a train for transportation to the factory.

want to see money "sent abroad to pay for sugar raised by half-civilized labor in Java and other foreign countries."[32] It is interesting that Smoot focused more on nativist reasons why foreign production of sugar was undesirable rather than emphasizing how the Utah farmers and economy would specifically be hurt by reducing the sugar duty. In doing so, Smoot was trying to avoid another sectional argument by tapping into ideas that many Americans held at the time.

Throughout the late-nineteenth and early-twentieth centuries, ethnocentric and racist ideas permeated American society. Drawing on the ideas of Herbert Spencer, who had applied Darwinian evolution to the human race, many Americans (as well as Britons) exhibited intense nationalism and declared that Anglo-Saxons were the most advanced and therefore the best race in the world. Those who came from a different background were inferior politically, economically, and socially.[33] Some proponents of beet sugar, including Smoot, thus concluded that it was better for Americans, rather than workers from other countries such as Cuba and Indonesia, to produce the nation's sugar. Because these laborers were not Anglo-Saxons, it was abhorrent for Americans to give them money to produce something that could easily be grown within the United States. At the same time, the beet sugar industry protested that laborers in foreign nations received a mere pittance for their work, while American sugar producers paid good wages to their farm workers. As a result, beet sugar could not compete with foreign-produced sugar.[34]

Those who supported tariff reductions, however, declared that the beet sugar industry's arguments were inconsistent because farmers employed laborers from Japan, India, and Mexico to harvest their crops. Indeed, these tariff reformers argued, these corporations lied when they declared that they could not produce sugar as cheaply as foreign countries did. By using "Mexicans, Syrians, Chinese, Japanese, Austrians, Germans," and other nationalities, farmers and corporations spent very little on labor because "the wages are as cheap as those of any labor on this continent."[35]

Leaders of the Utah-Idaho Sugar Company, as well as Smoot, vehemently rejected these assertions. In hearings before a House of Representatives committee investigating the American Sugar Refining Company in 1911, for example, Joseph F. Smith declared that farmers working for Utah-Idaho Sugar did not employ "Japanese or Hindus" on their farms; instead, "white men and boys and girls" did the labor.[36] In the 1913 tariff debates, Smoot supported Smith's statements: "I know it has been charged that the labor in American sugar beet fields is labor of an inferior grade," Smoot declared, "and that it is not entitled to the consideration due to genuine Americans." But in Utah, Smoot continued, this assertion was false because "the beets grown in Utah are grown by native American farmers on their own little farms and the labor devoted to the task is their own labor and the labor of their sons." When hired help was contracted, he said, it was "mostly of American stock."[37]

At the same time, Smoot argued, it would not matter if the labor *was* from foreign countries because whenever anyone came to America "seeking here a better living and a better opportunity," the United States had an obligation to "give them an opportunity to earn good wages." Otherwise their condition would be no different than in their homeland, where they were "half-naked and half barbarous, . . . wearing but a single garment, living in miserable huts without fire and without light, subsisting upon . . . uncooked food." Smoot finished by declaring that he would never ask workers in this country "to descend to the level of the blacks in Cuba or the brown men of Java, . . . or the yellow men of Formosa, who labor under conditions forced upon them by their cruel masters of Nippon."[38] By using these arguments, Smoot was clearly trying to appeal to the prejudiced and racist beliefs held by many Americans at the time.

A month after Smoot laid out his general ideas about the tariff, the Senate began debating the sugar schedule, leading the senator to make another three-hour discourse on the floor. "I put into the speech all the energy I was capable of doing," Smoot wrote in his diary that night. "I was completely tired out at the close of the speech and even my shirt was wet with perspiration."[39] Smoot expended all his energy to explain his views on why Congress should leave the sugar tariff untouched. To combat the arguments of tariff revisionists that beet sugar was a "hothouse industry" that could never exist without federal support, Smoot explained the involvement of the LDS Church and the people of Utah in the industry's establishment.

The senator admitted that in the early 1890s, the Utah Sugar Company had gone through a period of "desperate struggle to keep alive," but, he declared, this merely showed a bright "record of persistence in the face of overwhelming

The Utah Sugar Company factory in Lehi, Utah, 1895.

discouragement" unmatched by any other industry in the United States. With the help of the 1897 Dingley Tariff, beet-sugar production had expanded in Utah because duties had enabled farmers to receive "a price for their beets sufficient to make the cultivation of the crop attractive." Because of the tariff and the diligence and perseverance of beet companies and farmers, "the 6 struggling factories of 1897 have increased to 73." This tremendous growth in just a few years proved that with the maintenance of tariff protection, the beet sugar industry would soon be able to produce enough sugar for every American, thereby making it worthy of government support.[40]

Smoot also condemned the constant battle that Congress had been waging since 1897 over the sugar tariff. He especially criticized Cuban reciprocity, which enabled Cuban cane sugar to enter American markets with a 20 percent tariff reduction. Because Cuban sugar could be produced more cheaply than beet sugar, Smoot claimed that it had "served to thwart the growth of the domestic industry and . . . checked the building of many new beet sugar factories in this country." No matter how harmful Cuban reciprocity was, however, its destructive effects were equaled "by the prospect or the actual application of a reduction in the tariff duty upon sugar." Fearing that Congress would remove the sugar tariff and beet sugar would be unable to compete with free trade, entrepreneurs were refusing to create additional sugar companies, and existing corporations were scaling back on costs to survive the ensuing battle. Uncertainty in the tariff, Smoot claimed, was the reason why beet sugar was still unable to produce the entire nation's sugar supply, not some inherent defect in the industry. Yet even with all of these setbacks, Smoot declared, beet sugar continued to thrive, vindicating "the policy and efforts of those who placed the present protective sugar tariff upon the statute books."[41]

Smoot also stated that the production of beet sugar lowered the price of cane sugar, a common argument of beet advocates. Smoot used the year 1911 as support. In that year, crop failures had generated a worldwide shortage of sugar, and American refiners had taken advantage of the situation by raising the price from five cents to seven-and-a-half cents a pound. One of the leading proponents of the increase, Smoot claimed, was Claus A. Spreckels, president of the Federal Sugar Refining Company and a supporter of tariff reduction. Only when beet sugar finally came on the market in October had sugar prices finally fallen. "The beet sugar was sold at prices ranging from 5 ¼ to 5 ¾ cents," Smoot explained, "and it forced the refiners down to the same level for their product." The industry was therefore a friend to the American people since it had saved consumers "millions of dollars on their sugar bills." If Congress reduced the tariff, Smoot warned, nothing would stop cane sugar refiners from elevating prices again. Although sugar rates might temporarily drop, he argued, they would rise again after refiners had driven beet sugar from the market and obtained a monopoly.[42]

Smoot also believed that tariff reduction would not even cause a temporary drop in prices, although theoretically it should. Smoot claimed that cane refiners would merely maintain the product at current prices and pocket the difference themselves. Thus, Smoot stated, the Underwood Bill should really be called "a bill for the destruction of the domestic sugar industry and for the enrichment of the refiners beyond the dreams of avarice."[43] Because almost all beet sugar companies lay west of the Mississippi River, while the majority of cane refineries were east, the battle over the tariff, in Smoot's opinion, was really a war between eastern and western businessmen and not a measure to lower consumer prices.

Finally, Smoot countered the arguments of those who contended that the removal of the tariff would have few, if any, harmful effects on the beet sugar industry. Although tariff-reduction proponents insisted that only wasteful and inefficient companies would go under, Smoot disagreed. The cost of producing beet sugar, he declared, was roughly three to four cents a pound. Some foreign nations, including Cuba and Indonesia, produced sugar for only two cents a pound. Without the tariff, beet sugar producers could not compete with these nations and still maintain a profit. Some Americans declared that beet companies must therefore find a way to lower the price of production, but, declared Smoot emphatically, "how in the name of common sense are you going to reduce cost in an industry in which the one great item of cost is labor unless you reduce the reward of labor itself?" As Smoot had already stated, he did not believe it was morally right to pay American workers the paltry sums that foreign laborers received; therefore, the tariff must be maintained. The senator stated that his arguments were both reasonable and true, and he concluded his remarks by appealing to Democratic senators to "vote according to your honest convictions and sincere beliefs" rather than party policy. If they did so, Smoot was convinced that a reduction in the sugar tariff would either be rejected or not be as extensive as the Democrats proposed.[44] His plea was ultimately unsuccessful: several senators later told Smoot that "their sympathy conscience [*sic*] and heart was with [him]," but they still planned to vote for the revisions.[45]

Although Smoot continued to fight against tariff reductions on the Senate floor, he did not give any other extensive speeches on the subject. However, he did enlist the help of George Sutherland, Utah's junior senator. Sutherland, who also held a nominal amount of stock in the Utah-Idaho Sugar Company, addressed the Senate regarding the tariff in September and expounded many of the same arguments as Smoot, such as the inability of beet sugar producers to pay their laborers properly without a tariff on imported sugar. He concluded by denouncing Democrats for blindly obeying the will of President Wilson and refusing to vote according to their own beliefs. This situation, Sutherland claimed, showed that "the separation of the executive and legislative departments of the Government, . . . has been set aside as though it were a meaningless platitude worthy of no man's respect."[46]

In addition to Smoot's and Sutherland's arguments against tariff reductions in the Senate, the Smoot-sponsored *Salt Lake Herald-Republican* fought against revisions. In April Utah-Idaho Sugar placed an advertisement in the newspaper, stating that "even the finest imported sugar" did not surpass the quality of the corporation's beet sugar, which sold "for less money than the imported sugar, too."[47] Later, the company took out another advertisement, explaining that protection was the best path to take. "Is it not to the Direct Interest of every citizen to have Sugar Beet Growing and Beet Sugar Making as Triumphantly Successful as Possible in Utah and Idaho?" the blurb asked. "These Mountain States Should Make All the Sugar They Consume and a Surplus for Other States."[48]

Throughout 1913, the *Herald-Republican* also ran numerous editorials criticizing free trade and extolling the virtues of protection. It called for unity in Utah among the sugar, wool, and lead interests in fighting against the proposed reductions and especially requested that the *Salt Lake Tribune* cease its attacks on Smoot until the tariff fight was over.[49] Although the *Tribune* continued to condemn Smoot and the *Herald-Republican* on other matters, its editors—perhaps believing that tariff reduction was not in the best interest of the state—followed the Republican newspaper's advice and made little criticism of Smoot's tariff stance throughout 1913.[50] In addition, the *Tribune*, which had frequently denounced the Utah-Idaho Sugar Company for gouging Utah consumers, declared that although it did not believe that tariff reduction would destroy beet sugar corporations, it supported Utah-Idaho's fight to maintain duties.[51]

This newspaper campaign seemingly had some success in influencing opinion in Utah because some prominent Democrats in the state declared themselves against tariff revision. William H. King, a Democratic judge, for example, claimed that he was in favor of "a slight duty on sugar," while W.H. Browning, an Ogden Democrat, asserted that reductions would discriminate "against the western industries." For the most part, however, Utah Democrats maintained the party's position on the tariff.[52]

Despite the best efforts of the Utah-Idaho Sugar Company, Smoot, and the *Salt Lake Herald-Republican*, the Underwood Bill passed the Senate in roughly the same form as it had when it came out of the House of Representatives, with Louisiana senators as the only Democrats who rejected it. The duty on sugar would thus be reduced by 25 percent and completely eliminated within three years. Pleased with Congress's passage of the Underwood Bill, President Wilson signed it into law on October 3, 1913.[53] Beet sugar supporters resigned themselves to the new act, hoping "that business will enjoy the stimulation the measure's sponsors have predicted" but certain that "disastrous effects" would follow. "As to Utah," the *Herald-Republican* declared, "this tariff legislation is the only fly in the ointment. . . . Every other circumstance points to an unusually active and prosperous fall and winter."[54]

Despite all the forecasts of doom for beet sugar, however, the Utah-Idaho Sugar Company remained afloat, although some difficulties occurred. Because of fears that the industry might go under, the company's stock dropped from ten dollars to five dollars per share, while "salaries of many staff officers and employees were reduced 10 percent." Yet production still continued, and the company was even able to maintain a profit. In 1914, for example, the corporation manufactured more bags of sugar than any previous year, and the increases continued through 1915. In 1914 the corporation harvested 565,977 tons of beets and produced 1,551,348 bags of sugar, while in 1915, it harvested 631,141 tons of beets and made 1,749,298 bags of sugar. This was a sizable increase from the production of 1,119,907 bags of sugar in 1912, and an even greater expansion from only 709,658 bags of sugar in 1910.

One of the major reasons for the increase was the 1914 outbreak of the First World War in Europe. As Germany and France became embroiled in the conflict, they could no longer produce as much beet sugar. Aware of this situation, Nibley and other Utah-Idaho leaders expanded the corporation's factories and beet production.[55] Because of this growth, the company paid out $566,984 in dividends in 1914. In addition, Utah-Idaho Sugar continued to pay the same price to farmers for their sugar beets. Other companies were not so lucky, and by September 1914, ten beet sugar factories had been forced to shut down because of falling profits.[56]

Perhaps more alarming for Utah-Idaho Sugar was that the passage of the Underwood Bill convinced the American Sugar Refining Company, which owned 50 percent of Utah-Idaho's stock, that it was time to extricate itself from the corporation. The withdrawal of American Sugar's financial power would have been devastating to Utah-Idaho Sugar, and it also presented the possibility that interests adverse to the LDS Church (the other sizable stockholder) could obtain control. Therefore, the First Presidency of the church authorized Nibley, as presiding bishop, to purchase American Sugar's holdings in May 1914—some in the church's name and some in his own. This purchase secured the financial solvency of Utah-Idaho, both because Nibley was a wealthy business-man and because the church had money it could pump into the business. The long-standing interests of the LDS Church in the corporation were protected as well, allowing church leaders to maintain and even increase their influence over the direction that the company would take.[57]

Throughout the 1910s, Republicans continued to denounce the sugar revi-sions with Smoot leading the way. In September 1914, Smoot gave another speech on the floor of the Senate about the effects of the 1913 tariff revisions on the sugar industry. According to Smoot, the consumer had not seen any reduc-tion in the price of sugar because of the decreased duty; instead, "the retail price of sugar was from one-fifth to one-third of a cent per pound higher than it was for eight weeks before the 25 per cent reduction became effective." Although Smoot did not elaborate on why the beet sugar industry maintained that the tariff was hurtful if sugar prices remained high, he did assert that "the profits of the sugar refineries had increased about the same amount that the duty was decreased." Thus, Smoot argued, the full tariff on sugar should be restored since the consumer had received no benefit.[58]

Smoot also declared that Congress should prevent sugar from going on the free list in 1916 because of the outbreak of the First World War. Since the fighting had begun in August 1914, the senator claimed, "the wholesale price of sugar in the world ha[d] increased at least 3 cents per pound." If the United States could produce its own sugar supply, the American consumer would not have to pay such high prices. The key was to stimulate the beet sugar industry by keeping the duty. "If those interested in the beet sugar industry could now be assured of a stable tariff policy as regards sugar for a sufficient length of time," Smoot argued, "the time would come in the not distant future when we would produce enough sugar at home for our entire needs." Once independent of the world's markets, the United States would never see sugar rise above five cents per pound, even in times of war. But for this to happen, Smoot maintained, sugar must never go on the free trade list.[59]

Some politicians, worried about sugar prices and possible worldwide short-ages because of the First World War, listened to the reasoning of Smoot, other Republicans, and the beet-sugar industry. As the war continued and Democrats lost some of their legislative power in the 1914 elections, the prospect of free sugar became less appealing. In 1916 the Underwood Act was amended to state that the current duty on sugar (about 1.25 cents) would be maintained indefi-nitely.[60] Not until the early 1920s did the beet sugar industry have to deal again with tariff reform. Unfortunately, at that time, the end of the First World War caused a disastrous drop in sugar prices, forcing numerous beet sugar compa-nies to go under, although Utah-Idaho remained solvent by obtaining large federal loans. The corporation continued to manufacture beet sugar well into the 1970s (with a continued LDS Church presence—both financially and in terms of leadership). In 1979 the corporation decided to get out of the sugar business and focus instead on potato production. The LDS Church sold the company in the mid-1980s, and it subsequently changed its name to AgraWest, relocating its headquarters from Salt Lake City to Kennewick, Washington.[61]

In many ways, the tariff battle was national in scope. Smoot's arguments against reductions focused on their impact on America as a whole rather than Utah in particular. Likewise those in favor of the revisions wanted them to help American consumers, not just those in Utah. But the prominence of Smoot in fighting tariff revisions—including several extensive speeches on the floor of the Senate—and the depth to which newspapers such as the *Salt Lake Herald-Republican* editorialized against reductions, especially to the sugar duty, indicate that at least some Utahns saw the legislation as directly impacting the state. Indeed, any revisions to the tariff would have an effect because Utah's beet sugar industry had become more national than regional in scope. By 1911, for example, Utah-Idaho was selling the majority of its sugar in Nebraska, Iowa, and along a line extending from St. Paul, Minnesota, to Oklahoma. Only 20 percent of its sugar production was marketed in Utah, Idaho, Oregon, Wyoming, and Nevada. Because of that, the company had to follow national price trends, meaning that any reduction in the tariff would impact it.[62] As we have seen, such impacts were not as dire as Utah-Idaho leaders or Smoot had predicted, but, arguably, that was because of the outbreak of the First World War.

In any case, the battle over the Underwood Bill in 1913 showed Reed Smoot's staunch support of the tariff and some of the reasons for it. Although Smoot never said so on the floor of the Senate, a major reason for his support of the sugar duty was due to the LDS Church's involvement with the Utah-Idaho Sugar Company. Indeed, some muckrakers in the early 1900s felt that the church's influence in the beet-sugar industry was so strong that Joseph F. Smith could set prices and force western senators to vote for tariffs that benefited Utah-Idaho Sugar. Such claims were clearly overstated: Smith did not have the kind of political clout to convince politicians to support tariffs solely for the sake of the LDS Church, but, whether directly or indirectly, his position that the sugar duty was crucial to the survival of the beet sugar industry had some influence on Smoot, who continued to be a strong pro-tariff supporter throughout his political career.[63]

One of the most important outcomes of the tariff revisions—at least in terms of Utah's beet sugar industry—was strengthening the LDS Church's involvement in the beet sugar industry through Nibley's purchase of the American Sugar Refining Company's holdings in Utah-Idaho Sugar. With this church support, Utah-Idaho weathered the vicissitudes of reduction, yet there were also negative consequences. Critics had already charged the church with continually manipulating Utah's economy, and the increased holdings of Nibley and the church in Utah-Idaho Sugar after 1914 only provided detractors with further proof of church control. By 1920 Utah-Idaho Sugar found itself in the midst of a Federal Trade Commission trial charging that its officers used Mormon influence to further the company's interests. Had Congress not lowered the tariff in 1913, such problems might have been avoided because there would have been no need for the church to increase its holdings in the corporation. The tariff battle, then, had significant effects on Utah's economy, some of which were not apparent until several years later.

Notes

1.   Thomas G. Alexander, "The Burgeoning of Utah's Economy: 1910–18," in *A Dependent Commonwealth: Utah's Economy from Statehood to the Great Depression*, ed. Dean L. May, Charles Redd Monographs in Western History 4 (Provo, UT: Brigham Young University Press, 1974), 37–39; see also Leonard J. Arrington, *Beet Sugar in the West: A History of the Utah-Idaho Sugar Company, 1891–1966* (Seattle: University of Washington Press, 1966), 201.

2.   John E. Dalton, *Sugar: A Case Study of Government Control* (New York: Macmillan Co., 1937), 20–23; F.W. Taussig, *Some Aspects of the Tariff Question: An Examination of the Development of American Industries under Protection*, 2d ed. (Cambridge, MA: Harvard University Press, 1915), 53–56; F.W. Taussig, *The Tariff History of the United States*, 5th ed. (New York: G.P. Putnam's Sons [The Knickerbocker Press], 1910), 14–15.

3.   Taussig, *Some Aspects of the Tariff Question*, 8–9.

4.   Ibid., 108, 112–13.

5.   "Should Stick to Promises," *Salt Lake Tribune*, April 20, 1913.

6.   "Will Meet the Developments as They Arise," *Salt Lake Tribune*, March 13, 1913; "Democratic Tariff Plans," *Salt Lake Tribune*, March 19, 1913; Robert H. Wiebe, *Businessmen and Reform: A Study of the Progressive Movement* (Cambridge, MA: Harvard University Press, 1962), 128.

7.   "Radical Tariff Changes Proposed by Democrats," *Salt Lake Herald-Republican*, April 8, 1913. This was not the first time that Representative Underwood had introduced a resolution to drastically revise the tariff. In March 1912, he initiated a measure that would have removed the entire sugar duty immediately. It apparently ran into problems among Republicans and thus never became a law. See 62nd Cong., 2nd sess., *Congressional Record*, 48 (1912), pt. 4: 3307, 3457.

8.   The *Herald-Republican* was formed because "Smoot was always anxious to have a friendly Republican newspaper" in Utah. E.H. Callister, a friend and fellow Republican, served as the manager, and Republican federal officeholders who had obtained their positions through Smoot's support bought stock in the newspaper. In 1913 the LDS Church bought twenty thousand *Herald-Republican* bonds to help the newspaper pay off some of its debts. Milton R. Merrill, *Reed Smoot: Apostle in Politics* (Logan: Utah State University Press, 1990), 137–38.

9.   "Senator Smoot Believes Senate May Retain Protection on Sugar and Wool," *Salt Lake Herald-Republican*, April 8, 1913.

10. "Tariff Only Cloud on Sugar Industry Prospects—Cutler," *Salt Lake Herald-Republican,* April 5, 1913.

11. "Senate May Upset President's Tariff Revision Program," *Salt Lake Herald-Republican,* April 8, 1913; "Senate Will Amend," *Salt Lake Tribune,* May 9, 1913.

12. For an example of this argument, see Judson C. Welliver, "The Mormon Church and the Sugar Trust," *Hampton's Magazine* 24 (January 1910): 85–86. See also Merrill, *Reed Smoot,* 146–49.

13. Merrill, *Reed Smoot,* 287.

14. 63rd Cong., 1st sess., *Congressional Record,* 50 (1913), pt. 3: 2611, 2583.

15. James B. Allen, "The Great Protectionist: Sen. Reed Smoot of Utah," *Utah Historical Quarterly* 45 (Fall 1977): 326, 340.

16. "Testimony of Truman G. Palmer," June 12, 1913, in Senate Subcommittee of the Committee on the Judiciary, *Maintenance of a Lobby to Influence Legislation: Hearings before a Subcommittee of the Committee on the Judiciary Pursuant to S. Res. 92, 63rd* Cong., 1st sess. (1913): 985–98, 1062 (hereafter cited as Lobby Hearings).

17. Lobby Hearings, 3; "Attack Made by Wilson on Lobby," *Salt Lake Herald-Republican,* May 27, 1913.

18. Lobby Hearings, 4.

19. "Testimony of Sen. Reed Smoot," June 5, 1913, 432–47, Lobby Hearings.

20. Reed Smoot to Hon. C.W. Nibley, May 26, 1913, Reed Smoot Papers, MS 1187, box 41, folder 1, L. Tom Perry Special Collections, Harold B. Lee Library, Brigham Young University, Provo, Utah (hereafter cited as Smoot Papers).

21. "Testimony of Sen. Reed Smoot," 451–52.

22. Reed Smoot, *In the World: The Diaries of Reed Smoot,* ed. Harvard S. Heath (Salt Lake City: Signature Books, 1997), 187.

23. "The Apostle's Claim," *Salt Lake Tribune,* June 7, 1913.

24. Merrill, *Reed Smoot,* 171.

25. Smoot to Nibley, May 26, 1913.

26. "Industry's Champion," *Salt Lake Herald-Republican,* July 8, 1913.

27. "Smoot Taken in by Neat Trick in the Senate," *Salt Lake Tribune,* July 9, 1913; see also "Wisdom by Larceny," *Salt Lake Herald-Republican,* July 10, 1913.

28. 63rd Cong., 1st sess., *Congressional Record,* 50 (1913), pt. 3: 2576.

29. Ibid., 2579, 2604.

30. Ibid., 2605.

31. Ibid., 2606, 2582–83. See also "Senator Smoot Brands Democratic Tariff Bill as Sectional Measure," *Salt Lake Herald-Republican,* July 22, 1913.

32. 63rd Cong., 1st sess., *Congressional Record,* 50 (1913), pt. 3: 2583.

33. Robert H. Wiebe, *The Search for Order, 1877–1920* (New York: Hill and Wang, 1967), 136, 156–57.

34. See, for example, 63rd Cong., 1st sess., *Congressional Record,* 50 (1913), pt. 4: 3505.

35. Ibid., pt. 2: 1398.

36. "Testimony of Mr. Joseph F. Smith," June 27, 1911, House Special Committee on the Investigation of the American Sugar Refining Co. and Others, *Hearings Held before the*

Special Committee on the Investigation of the American Sugar Refining Co. and Others, 62nd Cong., 1st sess. (1911), 1065 (hereafter cited as American Sugar Hearings).

37.   63rd Cong., 1st sess., *Congressional Record,* 50 (1913), pt. 4: 3505.

38.   Ibid.

39.   Smoot, *In the World,* 190–91.

40.   63rd Cong., 1st sess., *Congressional Record,* 50 (1913), pt. 4: 3496–3500.

41.   Ibid., 3498–99.

42.   Ibid., 3500–3503.

43.   Ibid.

44.   Ibid., 3504–5, 3507.

45.   Smoot, *In the World,* 190–91.

46.   63rd Cong., 1st sess., *Congressional Record,* 50 (1913), pt. 4: 4296–98.

47.   "The Quality Sugar," *Salt Lake Herald-Republican,* April 14, 1913.

48.   "Beet Sugar Competition Cuts Price," *Salt Lake Herald-Republican,* October 4, 1913.

49.   "Utah and the Tariff," *Salt Lake Herald-Republican,* March 27, 1913; "Harmony Seems Restored," *Salt Lake Herald-Republican,* March 31, 1913; "Let Us Have Peace!" *Salt Lake Herald-Republican,* April 1, 1913.

50.   "Smoot on the Tariff Bill," *Salt Lake Tribune,* July 23, 1913; "An Organ's Harsh Grind," *Salt Lake Tribune,* July 25, 1913; "Comment on the Debate," *Salt Lake Tribune,* July 28, 1913; "Sugar Schedule Debate," *Salt Lake Tribune,* August 20, 1913.

51.   "The Free Sugar Threat," *Salt Lake Tribune,* March 25, 1913; "Sugar Producers Resentful," *Salt Lake Tribune,* June 13, 1913. However, the *Tribune* did not cease its general attacks on Utah-Idaho Sugar. For example, in July 1913, it ran an article asserting that the corporation, in concert with the LDS Church, dominated Utah politics, a statement that it frequently reiterated; "Charges Sugar Trust Directs Utah Politics," *Salt Lake Tribune,* July 16, 1913.

52.   "Utah Democrats Discuss Underwood Bill," *Salt Lake Herald-Republican,* May 18, 1913.

53.   Act of October 3, 1913 (38 Stat. 114); "Tariff Bill Signed; Revised Rates Go into Effect Today," *Salt Lake Herald-Republican,* October 4, 1913.

54.   "A Business Basis," *Salt Lake Herald-Republican,* September 15, 1913. See also "Honest but Mistaken," *Salt Lake Herald-Republican,* October 5, 1913.

55.   Arrington, *Beet Sugar in the West,* 80–82, 201.

56.   Leonard J. Arrington, "Minutes of Utah-Idaho Sugar Company Jan. 12, 1915 to Dec. 27, 1916," Leonard J. Arrington Papers, MS 1, Leonard J. Arrington Historical Archives, Special Collections and Archives, Merrill-Cazier Library, Utah State University, Logan; *Speech of Hon. Reed Smoot, of Utah, in the Senate of the United States, Friday, September 25, 1914* (Washington, DC: GPO, 1914), 1 (copy in box 78, folder 4, Smoot Papers).

57.   Charles W. Nibley, "Facts Are Given about the Sugar Industry," *Salt Lake Tribune,* June 25, 1916; Nibley, *Reminiscences* (Salt Lake City: Utah Family Society, 1934), 128; Arrington, *Beet Sugar in the West,* 80–81.

58. *Speech of Hon. Reed Smoot,* 1.

59. Ibid., 2–4.

60. Taussig, *Aspects of the Tariff Question,* 54; Dalton, *Sugar,* 33; Arrington, *Beet Sugar in the West,* 82; Merrill, *Reed Smoot,* 310.

61. Rowland M. Cannon to Matthew C. Godfrey, June 22, 1999, letter in possession of the author. Rowland Cannon was president of Utah-Idaho Sugar from 1969 to 1981.

62. See "Testimony of Mr. Thomas R. Cutler," June 23, 1911, American Sugar Hearings, 788, 791–93, 800, 830, 842.

63. For an example of Smith's views on the tariff, see "Testimony of Mr. Joseph F. Smith,"American Sugar Hearings, 1076–77. For an example of the charge that Smith forced western senators to support the sugar tariff, see Welliver, "The Mormon Church and the Sugar Trust," 86. For more information on Smoot's tariff stance throughout his senatorial career, see Allen, "The Great Protectionist," 325–45. See also Thomas G. Alexander, *Mormonism in Transition: A History of the Latter-day Saints, 1890–1930* (Urbana: University of Illinois Press, 1986), 80.

Ute Indians posed in ceremonial dress for this publicity photo with Governor Herbert Maw. Maw's assistant attorney general, Grover Giles, upheld the voting rights of reservation Utes in 1940. (See page 248.)

III

Voicing Government
Politics and Participation

When members of the Church of Jesus Christ of Latter-day Saints arrived in the Great Basin, their leaders formed a theocracy called the State of Deseret, whose proposed boundaries included all of Nevada and extended to the Pacific Coast. Those ambitious arrangements did not last. Instead, Congress took control, made Utah a territory, and progressively trimmed its size. Countering Congress's assumption of sovereignty, Mormons in Utah Territory asserted their right to control the moral climate and discourse of their communities; in the process, they violated the constitutional rights to life, liberty, and property of some outsiders and apostates whom they regarded as their enemies. In turn federal officials, Congress, and the U.S. Supreme Court whittled away at some Latter-day Saints' rights to practice their religion, vote, and serve in public office. Distrust ran rampant. Utah did not become a state until 1896—only after the Mormons had agreed to a constitution that prohibited polygamy and strongly separated church and state.

With statehood Utahns acquired full representation in Congress and the right to elect their own state officials. They shared equally with the citizens of other states the guarantees vouchsafed under the Bill of Rights. Utah's Constitution reiterated these rights, including "the right to enjoy and defend their lives and liberties; to acquire, possess and protect property; [and] to worship according to the dictates of their consciences." It further enumerated their right "to assemble peaceably, protest against wrongs, and petition for redress of grievances; [and] to communicate openly their thoughts and opinions, being responsible for the abuse of that right." Citizens were also guaranteed the right to vote and bear arms, the right to trial by jury, and protection from unreasonable searches and seizures.[1]

The chapters in this section examine Utahns' participation in politics and government, their quest for legal equality, and their campaign for constitutional rights. Like other Americans, most Utahns supported the mainline Republican and Democratic Parties, but others backed Socialists and independents. Local elections—supposedly nonpartisan—were often hotly contested. Utah women were among the first to receive the right to vote, although they continued to face obstacles to economic parity and social equality, issues that were discussed and debated in the landmark Utah International Women's Year meeting of 1977. Utahns were slow to grant voting rights to Native Americans. Many citizens—including radicals, racial minorities, women, immigrants, polygamists, union members, and gays and lesbians—fought for recognition of their constitutional rights over the course of the twentieth century. Utah citizens also sought to make state government more democratic through a host of reforms. In sync with national trends, they also experimented with various forms of local government—mayor, commission, or city manager. In addition to changing their organization, local governments also increased their responsibilities. Some changes resulted from new federal regulations. Others were ways to make government more efficient and responsive to citizens' needs.

PARTISAN POLITICS

While Utah was a territory, federal appointees and Mormon Church leaders often clashed. Neither group completely trusted the other. Most non-Mormon residents sided with the federal officials, as did some Mormons who had become alienated from church leaders through political and economic disagreements. The territory's two political parties reflected these divisions. The People's Party represented faithful Mormons, while the Liberal Party encompassed nearly everyone else. In 1891, in a pragmatic gesture of reconciliation and compromise, Mormons disbanded the People's Party. Church leaders instructed members to "divide about equally on national party lines" so they could "receive favors from whichever party was in power." According to some accounts, local church leaders assigned everyone seated on one side of the chapel to become Republicans and everyone on the other side to vote for the Democrats. As Mormons gravitated toward the national parties, members of the Liberal Party did, too.[2]

A classic election that showed Utahns' embrace of the national political system occurred in 1896. Ten candidates ran at large for five seats in the state senate: Martha Hughes Cannon, a plural wife, ran as a Democrat. Her husband, Angus Cannon, ran as a Republican. On the coat tails of Democrat William Jenning Bryan, the Democrats swept the election. Martha Hughes Cannon was elected and became the first woman state senator. Her husband was defeated.[3]

Mormons embraced their new parties ardently, often disagreeing with fellow church members. Emmeline B. Wells, for example, edited the *Woman's Exponent,* a Mormon independent women's journal that supported women's rights. She was a strong Republican and a leader in the Utah women's suffrage movement who ran unsuccessfully for political office but maintained a strong editorial voice in the community. Emily S. Richards, the wife of Mormon

Church attorney Franklin S. Richards, was a Democrat. She turned down invitations to run for office but spoke out strongly against the Republicans. Wells and Richards argued vigorously over politics, but they tried to confine that disagreement to the political level. They supported each other in national and international women's organizations and the Mormon Church's women's organization, the Relief Society.[4]

While most Utahns embraced the Republican and Democratic Parties, others joined alternative political parties, including, in the early twentieth century, the Socialists. Organized in the United States in 1901, the Socialist Party eventually enrolled 120,000 members. Five-time Socialist presidential candidate Eugene V. Debs polled nearly one million votes in 1912, including about 10 percent of the Utah vote. He polled almost as many in 1920, when he ran for president from a federal prison cell. Socialists also ran in state and local elections. The labor and union movement in the state intermittently supported the Socialist Party, and in turn the Socialists supported labor. Utahns elected a hundred members of the Socialist Party to offices in nineteen communities between 1901 and 1923. Eureka, a mining town in central Utah, elected a Socialist mayor four times and a complete Socialist administration twice in the early twentieth century.[5]

Utahns who joined the Socialist Party came from many religious traditions, including Mormonism. At a time when more than six in ten Utahns were Mormons, 40 percent of the Socialists were Latter-day Saints. In Eureka Mormons made up only 25 percent of the population, but 40 percent of the Socialists were Mormons. Historian John S. McCormick suggests that some Utahns who had been Populists turned to Socialism. Members of the Socialist Party were "radicals in theory" and "gas and water" party members in practice. In other words, they supported radical reforms in theory but then proposed more practical measures related to local government once they were in office. Historian John R. Sillito explains that the Socialists were successful among Mormons because of the church's communal tradition. The party lost favor as the church moved to a more capitalist system. The Socialists also struggled in Utah because of religious divisions.[6]

Tens of thousands of Utahns also voted for other third parties and their candidates. In 1912, after Theodore Roosevelt bolted from the Republican Party and became the newly christened Progressive Party's nominee for president, nearly one-fourth of Utah's voters opted for him. In 1920 colorful Salt Lake lawyer Parley P. Christensen, who ran for president on the Farmer-Labor ticket, outpolled Debs in the Beehive State. In 1924, when Wisconsin Senator Robert Lafollette ran for President on the Progressive ticket, more than one in five voters in the state chose him.[7]

Independent candidates also attracted significant attention and support. After losing the Republican nomination to George Dewey Clyde, Utah Governor J. Bracken Lee ran for reelection as an independent in 1956 and secured more than 28 percent of the vote. Two years later, Lee again ran as an independent candidate, this time for Senator Arthur V. Watkins's seat. Lee won 26 percent of the vote, splitting the Republican vote in the process and paving the way for Democrat Frank E. Moss's victory. Multimillionaire businessman Merrill Cook ran as an independent for Utah governor in 1988 and 1992, winning 21 percent of the vote in 1988 and 34 percent in 1992. Cook ran unsuccessfully as an independent for the second-congressional-district seat in 1994 and then won in 1996 and 1998 on the Republican ticket. In 1992 Democrat Bill Clinton (25 percent) finished third in Utah, behind Republican George Bush (43 percent) and independent H. Ross Perot (27 percent). Nationally Perot secured only 19 percent of the vote.[8]

The 1992 election results were indicative of a broader trend in the late twentieth century: Utahns overwhelmingly voted conservative and Republican. In their chapter in this section, Wayne K. Hinton and Stephen Roberds use data from 1980 to 2002 to burrow more deeply into the dimensions and roots of Republicanism in Utah late in the twentieth century. Moving beyond party lines, they also investigate Utahns' conservative political orientation.

The following list of Utah's governors and members of the United States Congress provides a broader historical backdrop for power shifts that Hinton and Roberds describe. Note that Republicans were governors from 1896 to 1917. Simon Bamberger broke that trend for four years. Then Democrat George Dern bested Charles Mabey in 1924, running with the memorable slogan, "Utah Needs a Dern Good Governor and I Don't Mean Mabey."[9] After Dern's victory, Democrats held the position until the 1949 inauguration of Republican J. Bracken Lee. Utah had a Republican governor for the next sixteen years, followed by Democratic governors for the next two decades. Republicans dominated the governorship from 1985 through the end of the century.

Most of Utah's U.S. senators belonged to the GOP in the twentieth century, although Utahns often voted for the man as much as the party. Of course, a six-year term helped the incumbent stay in office. For example, Frank Moss served almost twenty years because Utahns thought he was doing a good job, but also because they became accustomed to having him there. When Orrin Hatch sought to unseat him, he argued that Moss had held his position too long, but Hatch went on to serve much longer than Moss had. Republican Wallace Bennett was a popular senator and was replaced by fellow Republican Jake Garn, a well-liked Salt Lake City mayor. Robert Bennett, Wallace's son, replaced Garn when he retired.

With only a two-year term, members of the House of Representative from Utah experienced a higher turnover. Again, though, personality played an important part. In the first district, Laurence Burton and Gunn McKay were popular representatives even though they sat on different sides of the aisle. The second district saw a change from Republican to Democratic as Salt Lake City grew and became more liberal and non-Mormon. Personality—for good or ill—was also significant. Wayne Owens, a popular Mormon representative, lost his bid for the Senate but was elected again in the second district. Allen Howe faced problems with the law and lost his bid for reelection.

Utah did not receive a third district until 1983. Some Democrats complained of gerrymandering in the setting of district boundaries. They accurately charged that the third district was very conservative. Democrat William Orton's exceptional election in that district in 1990 was a surprise, but he may have won because of indiscreet negative campaigning by his opponent. But even Orton's party affiliation was somewhat misleading: a Utah Democrat is often far more conservative than one from elsewhere in the country.

Governors
> Heber M. Wells (R) (1896–1905)
> John C. Cutler (R) (1905–1909)
> William Spry (R) (1909–1917)
> Simon Bamberger (D) (1917–1921)
> Charles R. Mabey (R) (1921–1925)
> George H. Dern (D) (1925–1933)
> Henry H. Blood (D) (1933–1941)
> Herbert B. Maw (D) (1941–1949)
> J. Bracken Lee (R) (1949–1957)
> George D. Clyde (R) (1957–1965)
> Calvin L. Rampton (D) (1965–1977)
> Scott M. Matheson (D) (1977–1985)
> Norman H. Bangerter (R) (1985–1993)
> Michael O. Leavitt (R) (1993–2003)

Senators

> *Seat 1*
> Frank J. Cannon (R) (1896–1899)
> Vacant (1899–1901)
> Thomas Kearns (R) (1901–1905)
> George Sutherland (R) (1905–1917)
> William H. King (D) (1917–1940)
> Orris Abram Murdock, Jr. (D) (1941–1946)
> Arthur V. Watkins (R) (1947–1958)
> Frank E. Moss (D) (1959–1976)
> Orrin Hatch (R) (1977–

> *Seat 2*
> Arthur Brown (R) (1896–1897)
> Joseph L. Rawlins (D) (1897–1903)
> Reed Smoot (R) (1903–1933)

Elbert D. Thomas (D) (1933–1950)
Wallace F. Bennett (R) (1951–1974)
E.J. (Jake) Garn (R) (1975–1992)
Bob Bennett (R) (1993–

Representatives

First District
William H. King (D) (1897–1901)
George Sutherland (R) (1901–1903)
Joseph Howell (R) (1903–1917)
Milton H. Welling (D) (1917–1921)
Don B. Colton (R) (1921–1933)
Abe Murdock (D) (1933–1940)
Walter K. Granger (D) (1941–1952)
Douglas R. Stringfellow (R) (1953–1954)
Henry A. Dixon (R) (1955–1960)
M. Blaine Peterson (D) (1961–1962)
Laurence J. Burton (R) (1963–1970)
K. Gunn McKay (D) (1971–1980)
James Hansen (R) (1981–2002)

Second District
Jacob Johnson (R) (1913–1915)
James H. Mays (D) (1915–1921)
E.O. Leatherwood (R) (1921–1930)
Frederic C. Loofbourow (R) (1930–1933)
J. Will Robinson (D) (1933–1946)
William A. Dawson (R) (1947–1948, 1953–1958)
Reva B. Bosone (D) (1949–1952)
David S. King (D) (1959–1962, 1965–1966)
Sherman P. Lloyd (R) (1963–1964, 1967–1972)
Wayne Owens (D) (1973–1974, 1987–1992)
Allen T. Howe (D) (1975–1976)
Dan Marriott (R) (1977–1984)
David S. Monson (R) (1985–1986)
Karen Shepherd (D) (1993–1994)
Enid Greene (R) (1995–1996)
Merrill Cook (R) (1997–2000)

Third District
Howard C. Nielson (R) (1983–1990)
William Orton (D) (1991–1996)
Chris Cannon (R) (1997–2008)

VOTING RIGHTS

The Mormon Church's practice of polygamy shaped voting rights in Utah Territory. One way that Congress and national women's groups felt they could destroy polygamy was by letting women vote. The territorial legislature beat them to the punch, granting women suffrage in 1869. Utah women did not oust Mormon lawmakers or vote to end polygamy, and the U.S. Congress rescinded the vote: the 1882 Edmunds Act prevented plural wives from voting; the 1886 Edmunds-Tucker Act completely eliminated woman suffrage. Mormon and non-Mormon women worked to regain the vote—but generally not together. They presented a divided front at suffrage meetings and argued in national publications.[10]

One of the most highly debated issues at the 1895 Utah Constitutional Convention was whether women should be allowed to vote. Leaders were split on the subject, but eventually woman's suffrage was included in the constitution. Women filed for office and prepared to vote, but the territorial Supreme Court blocked them. Even without their vote, the constitution passed, and then women could vote and run for office.[11]

Utah's Constitution enfranchised all U.S. citizens, male and female, ages twenty-one and older, who were residents of the state, except for convicted criminals and the mentally incompetent. It forbade property qualifications except in bond elections. But it left Native Americans in legal limbo. Until 1887 the United States regarded Indians as citizens of separate nations, and Indian leaders therefore negotiated with the federal government rather than with the individual states. The federal government tried to change this relationship and provide for Indian citizenship through the Dawes Act of 1887 and the Indian Citizenship Act of 1924. These laws did not immediately guarantee Native Americans the right to vote in Utah, though. As Brian Cannon explains in his chapter, the threat of a U.S. Supreme Court case in 1957 finally induced the state legislature to repeal an 1898 statute that prohibited Indians on reservations from voting. Then in 1984, the 1965 Voting Rights Act, subsequent amendments, and a lawsuit finally resulted in the restructuring of voting districts in San Juan County. That redistricting at last enabled Navajos, who comprised a majority of the county's residents, to run successfully for the county commission.[12]

CIVIL RIGHTS

Unlike Indians on reservations, other minorities in the state could vote throughout the twentieth century, but many were denied other liberties, including the rights of free speech and assembly. In response they protested legally, defied the law, went on strike, and pressured powerful organizations and lawmakers. In their chapter, John R. Sillito and John S. McCormick discuss the campaign of the much-maligned Wobblies, or members of the Industrial Workers of the World, for the rights to assemble and speak freely in the Beehive State early in the twentieth century.

The Salt Lake Theater debuted the film *The Birth of a Nation*, which celebrated the Ku Klux Klan.

The Wobblies were especially feared because of their radical views, but workers and organizers of other unions also suffered repression. Prior to 1933, state officials used force to undermine strikes, and company officials often required employees to sign nonunion pledges as a precondition for employment. Miners, smelter workers, and other laborers at last won the right to join unions and bargain collectively in 1933, when Congress passed the National Industrial Recovery Act. Under federal protection, union membership soared.

One reason that unions attracted such intense hostility was that many of their members were immigrants. Thousands of eastern and southern European and Asian immigrants moved to the state between 1900 and 1920. They faced widespread prejudice because of old-timers' fears of racial inferiority and labor radicalism and concerns that the immigrants would never assimilate.[13]

The Ku Klux Klan focused anti-immigrant sentiment. Following the 1915 release of *The Birth of a Nation*, a film which praised the Klan for protecting white Americans, the organization grew in Utah, as it did throughout the nation. Its recruiters played to local prejudices as a means of selling memberships. Recruiters in some states focused on African Americans, but in Utah they chose to emphasize the larger population of recent immigrants and the threat they allegedly posed to racial purity and white womanhood. Historian Larry Gerlach estimates that 5,000 Utahns joined the Klan, including 2,500 in Salt Lake County, 750 in Ogden, and 500 in Carbon County, sometimes called

Utah's Ellis Island, where many Greek Orthodox and Catholic immigrants had settled. The Klan conducted rallies and intimidated and threatened immigrants who fraternized freely with "whites." Immigrants fought back through their churches and lodges. In Helper, after the Klan burned a huge cross on the mountain overlooking town, the Knights of Columbus defiantly lit a large zero on the same peak, implying that the Klan and its agitation would come to naught. Membership in the Klan plummeted in Utah and nationwide after a well-publicized scandal in 1924, stemming from investigations of a rape and murder in Indiana, that revealed the hypocrisy and corruption of some prominent Klan leaders.[14]

Minorities continued to face problems in the state after the Klan's demise. Particularly egregious was the treatment of people with Japanese ancestry during World War II. President Franklin Roosevelt's Executive Order 9066, permitting mass relocation of civilian populations, only applied to West Coast Japanese. But members of Utah's substantial Japanese community, numbering more than two thousand when Pearl Harbor was bombed, still had to endure racial epithets, threats, surveillance, and occasional physical attacks. "Yukus" Inouye, a young farmer, was cleaning the ditch in front of his home in Utah County when he waved hello to three boys who were out hunting. They retorted, "Don't you wave at us, you yellow bastard! We'll shoot you!" Law-enforcement officials confiscated belongings of Japanese residents, including radios, cameras, large knives, and other weapons. Many were summarily fired or refused housing. Administrators at the State Agricultural College in Logan expelled all students of Japanese ancestry using the rationale that their presence jeopardized national security because of military activities and facilities on the campus.[15]

Although the war against Japan focused racist hostility in Utah upon the Japanese, African Americans and Latinos experienced continued discrimination after the war, whereas the treatment of the Japanese moderated rapidly. In the middle decades of the century, black entertainers were turned away from most downtown hotels, and those who were admitted were forced to ride the freight elevators. In 1955 Marion Mills, an African American student in Utah, reported that "Negroes are required to occupy balcony seats in many local theaters. Negroes are not served in many cafes or other eating establishments. Many types of employment are closed to Negroes. Most night clubs, bars, etc., do not admit Negroes as customers." Latinos, northern Utah's largest minority in those years, were unable to buy homes in many neighborhoods because of restrictive covenants and informal local agreements.[16]

In the 1960s, minorities in Utah secured more rights through persistent lobbying and organization. Entities including the National Association for the Advancement of Colored People (NAACP), the American GI Forum, the National Congress of American Indians, the Spanish Speaking Organization for Community Integrity and Opportunity (SOCIO), and the American Civil Liberties Union fought discrimination aggressively. From 1947 onward, the state legislature had rejected civil-rights bills. By 1964 Utah, Arizona, and Nevada were the only states outside the South that did not positively prohibit discrimination in employment or public accommodations. In 1965 the state legislature resoundingly passed three civil-rights-related laws, although they rejected a fair-housing bill. One law validated all existing interracial marriages. Another, stipulating equal treatment in public accommodations, aside from private clubs, churches, and small boardinghouses, was patterned after the U.S. Civil Rights Act of 1964. Unlike the federal law, it also covered taverns, bars, beauty salons, barbershops, and medical and dental offices. The third act prohibited discrimination in the workplace and unions on the basis of race, color, sex, religion, ancestry, or national origin. As originally introduced, the bill would have banned discrimination in any business; wanting to concede no more than federal law mandated, however, legislators amended it to apply only to businesses with at least twenty-five employees—the same number the U.S. Congress had adopted in the Civil Rights Act. Eager to preserve the LDS Church's autonomy in hiring, lawmakers also amended the original bill to exempt church-owned businesses.[17]

The threat of federal intervention under the Civil Rights Act motivated some legislators to enact matching state legislation, but others spoke eloquently for racial equality. For instance, M. Phyl Poulson told his colleagues in the House that it was time to make it illegal for a person to "massacre another person's pride, and murder his self-esteem." Pressure from the NAACP may have also influenced lawmakers. In 1964 Hugh B. Brown, acting on behalf of the LDS Church's First Presidency, had read a generic statement supporting civil rights at the church's General Conference, thereby persuading the NAACP to cancel plans to picket Temple Square. As legislators debated the bill guaranteeing equal treatment in the workplace in 1965, fifty members of the NAACP, led by state director John Driver, picketed the LDS Church Administration Building in a nationally publicized protest. Recognizing the church's influence on Capitol Hill, Driver called for "positive steps . . . to make unmistakably clear the position of the LDS Church with regard to the right to equal employment opportunity and the right of a person of any race to rent or buy a home where he chooses." The church took no public action, but one of the picketers, Charles "Chuck" Nabors, credited the bill's passage partly to the protest. He also noted the role of a "very productive" meeting between the NAACP and Utah's governor and legislative leaders.[18]

During the heyday of the civil rights movement in the 1960s, people of color comprised less than 3 percent of Utah's population. When Representative W. Malin Cox stated in 1965 that he had "never seen a colored person or an Indian discriminated against in St. George," he reflected the sentiments of many white Utahns who had seldom interacted with minorities and were thus largely oblivious to their struggles. The passage of civil rights laws did little to change this lack of concern, and de-facto discrimination persisted. Determined to increase minority hiring, SOCIO's leaders worked with the NAACP and other minority organizations to establish a Minority Advisory Board in 1968 within the Utah State Department of Employment Security. They also worked with local governments and appealed to the conscience of employers in the private sector to boost minority hires. When minority jobs remained disproportionately low, Salt Lake County, Weber County, and Salt Lake City adopted minority hiring plans and quotas in 1971–72. These measures, along with the appointment of minorities to administrative bodies like the State Merit Council, helped to raise nonwhite employment in the public workforce to nearly 5 percent by June 1974.[19]

On a separate front, a dramatic shift in LDS Church policy strongly encouraged more-progressive attitudes toward minorities in the state. Many Utahns had used the church's exclusion of African American males from its priesthood as proof of their moral inferiority. In 1977 Church President Spencer W. Kimball announced a revelation ending the priesthood ban. The announcement not only permitted the ordination of African American men but also helped discredit racist folk doctrines, although they continued to circulate in some circles.[20]

Late in the century, dramatic increases in the Latino population of Utah elicited new expressions of distrust and suspicion. Some Utahns feared change in general, while others blamed increasing rates of crime and gang violence on recent immigrants. As late as 1980, nonwhites still comprised only 3 percent of the population, although Hispanics made up an additional 4.1 percent. During the 1990s, though, the Hispanic population grew by 138 percent. By 2000 the U.S. Bureau of the Census reported that 9 percent of the state's population was Hispanic, up from 4.9 percent in 1990, but discrimination persisted. At the end of the century, Latino representation in city, county, and state government remained pitifully small, and only 3 percent of the University of Utah's student body was Hispanic. Theresa Martinez, associate professor of sociology at the University of Utah, was the first Hispanic woman to receive tenure there, in 1996. During an ultimately successful citizens' initiative campaign in 2000 to designate English as the state's official language, she told a reporter, "The silent majority is uncomfortable with people who are different. They will not say it, but they can in the voting booth."[21]

As racial minorities sought the American dream, other minorities within the state battled those who would deny them constitutional rights, too. Gays fought for equal treatment in the workplace, protection from hate crimes, and the right to marry and adopt children. In 1969 gay men and women in Utah formed the Utah Gay Liberation Front, patterned after a similar organization established in New York City after the Stonewall riot. Gays and lesbians organized a community council in Salt Lake in 1989. After the Nebo School District imposed a gag order on Spanish Fork High School teacher Wendy Weaver and replaced her as volleyball coach because she was a lesbian, Weaver and the American Civil Liberties Union successfully sued the district. In 1998 a

U.S. District Court judge ordered the district to restore Weaver's coaching job and lift the gag order.[22]

Polygamists, most of whom described themselves as Fundamentalist Mormons, also struggled, as had their nineteenth-century Utah predecessors, for their constitutional rights. In 1944 federal and state officials in Utah, Idaho, and Arizona raided the homes of prominent polygamists. Forty-six men and women were subsequently brought to trial on a variety of charges, including abducting and marrying a minor, violating the Mann Act by transporting women across state lines for immoral purposes, unlawful cohabitation, and criminal conspiracy. Fifteen men were convicted of cohabitation and sent to the Utah State Prison. In 1953 Arizona law-enforcement officials conducted a new raid, this time on the Fundamentalist refuge of Short Creek, straddling the Utah/Arizona line. They carried warrants for the arrest of thirty-nine Utahns and eighty-three Arizonans. Subsequently Arizona authorities took custody of 153 children on that side of town. Then in 1954, the Utah Department of Public Welfare seized and placed in foster care the seven children of Leonard Black and his plural wife Vera from Short Creek. Vera Black protested the treatment by reminding the state, "Ours is a nation of equal rights before the law." The Utah Supreme Court upheld the seizure, and the children remained in foster homes until their mother perjured herself by signing an oath renouncing her belief in polygamy. For the rest of the twentieth century, historian Martha Bradley has written, "Partly in reaction to negative opinion about the Black case and the raid itself, the Utah Attorney General's office assumed a position of ignoring rather than actively prosecuting polygamists." However, several polygamists were brought to trial in Davis County in 1960, and the city of Murray fired a polygamous policeman in 1982.[23]

Utah's Constitution mandated that "both male and female citizens of this state shall enjoy equally all civil, political, and religious rights and privileges." This provision was expanded when inequitable treatment of women in public accommodations and the workplace was specifically outlawed under civil rights acts passed by Utah's legislature in 1965. Unequal treatment persisted in the workplace, though, as measured by lower wages than men received for the same work, underrepresentation in managerial and executive positions, and difficulty in obtaining credit. Utah women organized local chapters of the National Organization of Women in 1966 and the National Women's Political Caucus in 1971 to expand their opportunities and rights. These organizations vigorously championed passage of the proposed Equal Rights Amendment (ERA). The amendment, which Congress sent to the states for ratification in 1972, prohibited the United States or any state from denying or abridging equal rights "on account of sex." Utah legislators rejected the amendment in 1973. Mormon Church leaders said they supported equal rights, and they did not speak out against the amendment in the beginning, but from late in 1974 on, they publicly objected to it, arguing that it was "unnecessary, uncertain, undesirable";

took away women's protections; and threatened the family through its sweeping abrogation of gender distinctions. The church's opposition sounded the death knell for the ERA in the state legislature when lawmakers reconsidered the amendment in 1975 and 1977.[24]

In 1977 thousands of Utah women gathered in Salt Lake for a congressionally funded Utah International Women's Year meeting. After LDS Church leaders asked ward and stake leaders to encourage women from every congregation in Utah to attend the meeting, more than twelve thousand showed up. Determined to represent local values, rather than what they regarded as an externally imposed feminist agenda, the attendees rejected every resolution proposed by a national coordinating committee on women's rights, including those endorsing the ERA and a woman's right to choose abortion. The event became one of the most significant and polarizing events in Utah women's history, widening rifts between conservatives and liberals. Many Mormon women supported some of the national resolutions, but the majority's voting pattern abetted stereotypes of Mormon women as backward and manipulated or insensitive and naïve. Reflecting the attitudes of most Utahns, Utah lawmakers delivered another blow to the women's movement in 1991, when they enacted a statute permitting abortion only in instances of incest, rape, severe fetal deformity, or life-threatening pregnancies.[25]

LOCAL GOVERNMENT STRUCTURE AND FUNCTIONS

The United States is—as the name implies—a union of separate states. At the beginning of the twentieth century, state and local governments played a more-pronounced role in the lives of their citizens during peacetime than did the federal government. Beginning with Franklin D. Roosevelt's New Deal of the 1930s, the federal government funded many programs that states and local governments had formerly controlled. By holding the purse strings, the federal government acquired a voice in local issues.

Despite the expansion of federal power, states, counties, and municipalities continued to influence many aspects of Utahns' daily lives. The Tenth Amendment gives the states and the people all powers not spelled out in the Constitution. In turn Utah's Constitution vests legislative power in a Senate and House of Representatives; executive power in the hands of a governor, secretary of state, state auditor, state treasurer, attorney general, and superintendent of public instruction; and judicial power in a system of courts and justices of the peace.

Over the course of the twentieth century, Utahns modified this structure to make it more democratic. Some of the most significant reforms were achieved early in the century as part of the nationwide Progressive movement. In 1918 Utah's legislature approved laws establishing the initiative and referendum. The initiative enabled citizens to propose and enact a law independent of the legislature by using petition drives and the voting booth.

The referendum provided citizens with the means to reconsider and repeal a recently enacted law. These measures created a check on the power of the legislature. Utah's lawmakers rejected another proposal of the Progressives—the recall—which would have permitted citizens to oust an official from office before his or her term expired.[26]

Some Utahns also lobbied to make state government reflect the population more closely through a process known as reapportionment. The state constitution granted each county at least one representative in the Utah House but instructed the legislature to reapportion the allocation of representatives based upon regular censuses. Between 1931 and 1950, the state legislature repeatedly refused to reapportion representation, thereby favoring sparsely populated rural counties. Other states resembled Utah in this respect. Citizens of states, including Utah, challenged these inequities in the courts. Finally, in 1964 the U.S. Supreme Court ruled in a case that originated in Alabama that "legislators represent people, not trees or acres. Legislators are elected by voters, not farms or cities or economic interests." This decision forced Utah lawmakers to redraw the boundaries of legislative districts in 1965.[27]

Voters and officials worked to make local as well as state government more responsive, democratic, and efficient. Sometimes efficiency took a back seat to democracy; in other cases, the reverse was true as the type and functions of local government were altered.

The state's constitution directed the legislature to "establish a system of County government" and "provide for the incorporation, organization, and classification of cities and towns." When Utah became a state in 1896, there were twenty-seven counties. As populations grew, the state legislature created two more, Duchesne in 1914 and Daggett in 1917. The county offices include land records and courts, sheriffs, and health services, among others. County responsibilities decreased over the twentieth century as more municipalities incorporated and expanded their services to include regulating education, health, transportation, water, police, and land use.[28]

Two examples, the cities in Salt Lake County and the small town/city of North Logan, illustrate the changing roles of municipalities as they took over responsibilities and shifted their focus to change government form and functions. Salt Lake City and the surrounding communities represent the large metropolitan area; North Logan illustrates the rural areas of the state. Together they show that no one escaped the lengthening arm of the federal government and the changing responsibilities of communities in the twentieth century.

Thomas G. Alexander and James B. Allen explain in their history of Salt Lake City, *Mormons and Gentiles,* how these changes took place. Up until 1911, city elections still reflected the Mormon/Gentile division that characterized Utah politics in the nineteenth century. From 1905 to 1912, the American Party, a group of anti-Mormon ministers and business leaders, controlled city elections. While some saw the city's adoption of a commission form of government in

1911 as an attempt by the Mormon Church to destroy the American Party, the move actually reflected the nationwide introduction of a more businesslike government, where elected commissioners who answered to the people controlled city departments.[29]

Reformers' hopes that commission government would be more professional because it was nonpartisan were blasted, however. While commission elections were technically nonpartisan, political parties were interested in the outcomes. In 1957 reformers attempted to replace the commission form of government with a more efficient system featuring a strong mayor and city council or a manager. They blamed commission government for problems with civil service, police protection, and a lack of capital improvements. Their proposal was defeated at the polls, but in 1979, voters overwhelmingly scrapped the commission government. In 1980 the city adopted a strong mayoral system, where the mayor assumed responsibility for the daily operation of the city.[30]

But Salt Lake City officials did more than change their government's organization. The city joined municipalities elsewhere in the nation in the City Beautiful movement and progressivism by establishing parks, improving water supplies and waste removal, developing transportation, cleaning up crime, and protecting individual property. In 1925 the state legislature passed laws that allowed cities to control land use, and zoning became a new concept to regulate lifestyles in sections of the city.[31]

The issues city government faced varied over the years. During the 1930s, a major concern was securing enough water for a growing urban area. Salt Lake City and other urban areas formed the Metropolitan Water District as a prerequisite for the Bureau of Reclamation's construction of Deer Creek Reservoir. After World War II, more Utahns moved from the city into the surrounding suburbs. Salt Lake City needed to deal with urban blight and provide transportation for suburban dwellers who continued to work in the city. City officials worked to improve downtown. As one of the major landholders, the LDS Church joined the efforts, leasing land for a convention center—the Salt Palace—and building malls, businesses, libraries, and museums.[32]

As Salt Lake City's population moved into the county, the county and city often furnished overlapping services. During the 1970s, Commissioners Jake Garn and Ted Wilson wanted to combine city and county government because of this duplication. Garn's efforts failed, so he combined city and county services when possible and cooperated with the Council of Government of Salt Lake County. Garn was especially concerned that Salt Lake residents should not be double taxed for services provided by both the city and county. Wilson again tried to combine city and county government for the same reasons: to avoid double taxation and special-service units that were too independent. However, many county residents opposed the consolidation because they were afraid it would result in a large central government and higher taxes for the unincorporated areas. Those in the city feared lost revenue for water that the county purchased

Aerial view of North Logan showing expansion that eliminated open space, 2008.

from the city. Although the media, most city officials, and political-science professors at the University of Utah favored the change, county residents had the final say. The consolidation measure lost by 61 to 39 percent. In the years following, unincorporated areas of Salt Lake County created their own communities so the residents could have greater control. In 1980, for example, three towns formed West Valley City, creating the third largest city in the state overnight.[33]

Salt Lake City and the surrounding county (which by 2000 formed a single sprawling metropolis) was the most populated area. But the concerns that faced local governments were replicated throughout the state in small towns and larger cities. Almost any town in the state reflected the increased role of the federal government and the need to provide more services.

North Logan, a small village just north of Logan city, illustrates many of the concerns that small towns faced. Up until the 1930s, the area was unincorporated. Farmers lived on their land, and North Logan existed as a Mormon ward. The area did not incorporate until the Works Progress Administration required that a town be organized as a precondition for receiving federal grants. Residents voted to incorporate to obtain federal funding for a water system.

State government also forced changes in North Logan. The state legislature stopped a practice of dividing sales taxes with communities and required the money to stay in the town where goods were purchased in the 1970s. In response North Logan annexed land adjacent to the highway and encouraged businesses to build there. For example, the city gave community-development funds to K-Mart. Hyde Park also annexed land, and soon a business strip developed on the road from Logan to Smithfield.

North Logan, like many other small rural areas in Utah, is no longer a farming village. As Utah State University expanded and Logan grew, people moved to the open spaces. By 1970 North Logan had grown enough to become a third-class city. It continued to grow, and problems developed. These included decisions on the types of houses, businesses, and apartments that would be permitted; the size of lots they could occupy; and the best way to provide roads and water to new subdivisions, many on land once devoted to dry farming.[34]

All of these issues—type of government, impact of state and federal regulations, role of the dominant religion, and ways to deal with growth while maintaining established lifestyles—represent some unique concerns in each town but also follow national patterns. As Jessie L. Embry, a native of North Logan and a resident of Provo, explains in her article, these two factors—local determination and city government trends—determined how Provo elected its officials.

Summary

In their quest for good government, Utahns supported major and minor parties and independent candidates. They experimented with new forms of government and new modes of enacting and repealing laws. In their partisan leanings, Utahns often reflected national trends, including the strength of the Democratic Party in the Franklin D. Roosevelt years and the appeal of Republicans in the Reagan years. Conservatives dominated the political landscape in Utah from the 1970s onward, though, to a greater extent than in the nation at large. Utah legislators were progressive in their stance on women's suffrage but repeatedly rejected the ERA. Radicals, racial and ethnic minorities, and gays and lesbians struggled to achieve basic civil rights in Utah, as they did in the rest of the nation. The articles that follow explain Utah's recent conservative Republican leanings. They explore the denial of voting and civil rights to radicals and Native Americans. And they examine the impact of local government structure and role changes on Utahns' lives.

Notes

1. Utah Constitution, art. 1, available online at http://www.onlineutah.com/constitution.shtml

2. Edward Leo Lyman, *Political Deliverance: The Mormon Quest for Utah Statehood* (Urbana: University of Illinois Press, 1986), 166.

3. Thomas G. Alexander, *Utah, the Right Place: The Official Centennial History,* rev. ed. (Salt Lake City: Gibbs Smith, 2003), 257.

4. Carol Cornwall Madsen, *An Advocate for Women: The Public Life of Emmeline B. Wells* (Provo, UT: Brigham Young University Press, 2006), 324–25.

5. John S. McCormick, "Hornets in the Hive: Socialists in Early Twentieth Century Utah," *Utah Historical Quarterly* 50 (Summer 1982): 225–40; John S. McCormick and John R. Sillito, "Respectable Reformers: Utah Socialists in Power, 1910–1925,"

in *A World We Thought We Knew: Readings in Utah History,* ed. John S. McCormick and John R. Sillito (Salt Lake City: University of Utah Press, 1995), 115–29.

6. Ibid.; John R. Sillito and John S. McCormick, "Socialist Saints: Mormons and the Socialist Party in Utah, 1900–20," *Dialogue: A Journal of Mormon Thought* 18 (Spring 1985):123, 127.

7. Richard D. Poll, Thomas G. Alexander, Eugene E. Campbell, and David E. Miller, eds., *Utah's History* (Logan: Utah State University Press, 1989), 700.

8. Ibid., 703, 705; Alexander, *Utah, the Right Place,* 405; James A. Henretta, David Brody, and Lynn Dumenil, eds., *America: A Concise History,* 3d ed. (Boston: Bedford St. Martins, 2006), 967.

9. Alexander, *Utah, the Right Place,* 298.

10. Madsen, *Advocate for Women,* 114–34.

11. Ibid., 280–88.

12. Daniel McCool, Susan M. Olson, and Jennifer L. Robinson, *Native Vote: American Indians, the Voting Rights Act, and the Right to Vote* (Cambridge: Cambridge University Press, 2007), 90–110.

13. Alexander, *Utah, the Right Place,* 389; Katharine E. Groebli, "On the Housing Problem in Salt Lake City" (master's thesis, University of Utah, 1914–15).

14. Larry Gerlach, *Blazing Crosses in Zion: The Ku Klux Klan in Utah* (Logan: Utah State University Press, 1982).

15. Leslie G. Kelen and Eileen Hallet Stone, eds., *Missing Stories: An Oral History of Ethnic and Minority Groups in Utah* (Logan: Utah State University Press, 2000), 323, 339, 346; R. Todd Welker, "Utah Schools and the Japanese American Student Relocation Program," *Utah Historical Quarterly* 70 (Winter 2002):16–17.

16. F. Ross Peterson, "'Blindside': Utah on the Eve of Brown v. Board of Education," *Utah Historical Quarterly* 73 (Winter 2005):10; Jorge Iber, *Hispanics in the Mormon Zion, 1912–1999* (College Station: Texas A&M University Press, 2000), 77.

17. *Salt Lake Tribune,* March 3, 1961; July 13, 1964; *Deseret News,* February 19, 1964; February 5, 1965; March 13, 1965; Alexander, *Utah, the Right Place,* 391; *Laws of the State of Utah, 1965 Passed by Regular Session of the Thirty-Sixth Legislature* (Kaysville, UT: Inland Printing Co., 1965), 634–35; James B. Allen, "Utah's Ethnic Minorities and the Quest for a Pluralistic Society," unpublished manuscript in editors' possession, 4–5.

18. *Deseret News,* February 5, 1965; *Salt Lake Tribune,* March 13, 1965; *New York Times,* March 10, 1965, 24; March 11, 1965, 19; Kelen and Stone, *Missing Stories,* 115–16.

19. *Deseret* News, February 5, 1965; Iber, *Hispanics in the Mormon Zion,* 93–96.

20. Jessie L. Embry, *Black Saints in a White Church: Contemporary African American Mormons* (Salt Lake City: Signature Books, 1994), 70–78; Armand L. Mauss, *All Abraham's Children: Changing Mormon Conceptions of Race and Lineage* (Urbana: University of Illinois Press, 2003), 223–26, 241, 248–50, 253–55, 261–62.

21. *Deseret News,* July 25, 2000; Cardell K. Jacobsen, "Racial and Ethnic Groups," in *Utah in the 1990s: A Demographic Perspective,* ed. Tim B. Heaton, Thomas A. Hirschl, and Bruce A. Chadwick (Salt Lake City: Signature Books, 1996), 73.

22. Ben Williams, Utah Stonewall Historical Society, "This Week in Lambda History," available online at http://qsaltlake.com/2005/21/lambdalore.shtml; Alexandra L. Woodruff, "Being Gay in Utah: For Men and Women Practicing an 'Alternative Lifestyle,' Utah is a Pretty Intolerant Place," available online at http://www.canyoncountryzephyr.com/archives/gayinutah.html; *Weaver v. Nebo School District,* "Memorandum Opinion and Order" 2:97-CV-819, (U.S. District Court, Utah, Central Division, November 25,1998) available online at http://www.acluutah.org/weaverdecision.htm

23. Martha Sonntag Bradley, *Kidnapped from That Land: The Government Raids on the Short Creek Polygamists* (Salt Lake City: University of Utah Press, 1993), 68–90, 127–47, 176, 182; Alexander, *Utah, the Right Place,* 392.

24. Utah Constitution, art. 4, sec. 1; Miriam B. Murphy, "Gainfully Employed Women, 1896–1950," in *Women in Utah History: Paradigm or Paradox?,* ed. Patricia Lyn Scott and Linda Thatcher (Logan: Utah State University Press, 2005), 214–15; Kathryn L. Mackay, "Women in Politics: Power in the Public Sphere," in Scott and Thatcher, *Women in Utah History,* 384; "Equal Rights Amendment," *Church News,* January 12, 1975; D. Michael Quinn, "The LDS Church's Campaign against the Equal Rights Amendment," *Journal of Mormon History* 20 (Fall 1994): 85–155; Martha Sonntag Bradley, *Pedestals and Podiums: Utah Women, Religious Authority and Equal Rights* (Salt Lake City: Signature Books, 2005), 93–111.

25. Jenny Harris, "The Silent Majority: Conservative Perception, Mobilization, and Rhetoric at the Utah State International Women's Year Conference" (master's thesis, Brigham Young University, 2004); Bradley, *Pedestals and Podiums,* 155–222; Alexander, *Utah, the Right Place,* 416. In some exceptional cases, the Utah women's meeting facilitated bridge building across religious and cultural lines. One example involved the Task Force on Women in Utah History that planned and conducted a workshop at the Utah International Women's Year meeting. Two task-force members, Patricia Scott and Linda Thatcher, have written, "The workshop was so successful and the relationships formed so rewarding that several of the women decided to continue their association with the formation of the Women's History Association." The association was "a combination of support group and network—a place where women in history could share common concerns, network with each other, exchange ideas, and report successful methodologies." See Scott and Thatcher, *Women in Utah History,* xv.

26. Alexander, *Utah, the Right Place,* 262.

27. Ibid., 390–91; *Salt Lake Tribune,* March 9, 1965; *Reynolds v. Sims,* 377 U.S. 533 U.S. Supreme Court (June 15, 1964), available online at http://supreme.justia.com/us/377/533/case.html

28. Utah Constitution, art. 11.

29. Thomas G. Alexander and James B. Allen, *Mormons and Gentiles: A History of Salt Lake City* (Boulder, CO: Pruett Publishing Company, 1984), 142–46.

30. Ibid., 268–71, 290.

31. Ibid., 151–57, 163–69.

32.   Ibid, 221–23, 273, 278–80, 286, 292–93; Linda Sillitoe, *A History of Salt Lake County* (Salt Lake City: Utah State Historical Society, 1996), 241, 274.

33.   Sillitoe, *History of Salt Lake County,* 274.

34.   Jessie L. Embry, *North Logan Town* (North Logan, UT: North Logan City, 2000), 26, 39–57, 79–81.

9

Public Opinion, Culture, and Religion in Utah

Wayne K. Hinton and Stephen Roberds

Although Utah had a liberal tradition, that is not the image that most people have when they consider Utah politics. In this essay, Wayne K. Hinton and Stephen Roberds use 2002 Brigham Young University exit-poll data to support the opposite point of view. They show that Utahns are very conservative and Mormon. But what is a conservative? Hinton and Roberds carefully define the beliefs of several types of conservatives and liberals. Readers will find these definitions helpful in understanding not only this essay but others in the volume. In addition, the authors make excellent use of tables that compare Utahns to each other and with the rest of the nation. They then attempt to answer the question of how Utahns became so conservative and Republican by looking at Utah history in the nineteenth century and decade by decade in the twentieth. The essay concludes that Utah public opinion and culture are a mixture of Mormon and western American values.

INTRODUCTION

This chapter examines (1) public opinion as well as (2) political culture and (3) religion in Utah. Through statistical analysis, it compares Utah to other states in these three areas. An historical perspective then shows the ways that the cultural and religious dominance of the Church of Jesus Christ of Latter-day Saints affects Utahns' public opinions.

PARTISANSHIP AND IDEOLOGY IN UTAH

Two key terms with regard to public opinion are partisanship and ideology. Partisanship means the ways citizens align themselves with political parties. Ideology reflects the way they align themselves along a conservative/liberal spectrum. There are various ways to measure partisanship and ideology. One method, survey data, asks respondents to describe themselves. Another approach involves examining behavior. Partisanship and ideology near the turn of the twentieth-first century were measured through an analysis of survey data gathered by the KBYU/Utah Colleges Exit Poll, administered at randomly selected voting places throughout the state of Utah on the day of the 2002 general election.[1]

Table 1 reports the findings about where Utah voters placed themselves on the questions pertaining to partisanship and ideology. The data are striking and show that Utahns are overwhelmingly Republican and conservative. In 2002 Republican identifiers outnumbered Democrats 61 percent to 26 percent. More than a third of GOP identifiers claimed to be strong Republicans. Of those identifying themselves as Democrats, most described themselves as independent but leaning toward Democratic policies.

Table 1. Self-placement on Partisan and Ideology Scales

Strong Democrat	7%
Not-so-strong Democrat	4%
Independent, leaning Democrat	15%
Independent	8%
Independent, leaning Republican	15%
Not-so-strong Republican	18%
Strong Republican	28%
Other/don't know	5%
	100%
	N = 1,018
Strong liberal	4%
Moderate liberal	12%
Neither	19%
Moderate conservative	46%
Strong conservative	15%
Don't know	5%
	100%
	N = 1,003

Data: Kelly D. Patterson, "KBYU/Utah College Exit Poll" (Provo, UT: Brigham Young University, 2002).

Table 1 also shows that Utah is a conservative state. In 2002 conservatives outnumbered liberals in Utah 60 to 16 percent. The terms *conservative* and *liberal* are slippery and lack precision so they need definitions. Most political scientists agree that basic attributes go with the terms. Conservatives tend to favor state and local governments as best suited to deal with social problems. They are likely to be suspicious of the federal government and Washington, D.C. They stress "family values" of heterosexual marriage, oppose pornography and alternative lifestyles, and believe that government should support and promote traditional values. Conservatives tend to stress individualism in relation to property rights. In Utah the term conservative also entails a belief in the individual's right to own firearms, state control over natural resources and land, and government support of basic religious values found in the LDS Church.

The term liberal tends to be associated with a belief in equality over individualism, but liberals do stress individual freedom in the realms of press, speech, and privacy. Liberals usually have more faith in government as a legitimate agent of positive social change and a higher tolerance for those with alternative lifestyles and views. Liberals generally believe that religion and politics should be separate and that traditional values, while important, should not be imposed on those who favor less traditional values.

While the data from Table 1 are quite revealing, they are just a start in understanding the opinions of Utahns. To understand public opinion, politics, and government in Utah, you must comprehend the pervasive role that religion plays in the state. Table 2 reports that 66 percent of voters in the 2002 survey identified themselves as LDS.

Table 2. Religious Affiliation of Utah Voters

LDS	66%
Protestant	5%
Catholic	6%
Jewish	1%
Other	6%
No preference	12%
Prefer not to say	4%
	100%
	N = 1,032

Data: Kelly D. Patterson, "KBYU/Utah College Exit Poll" (Provo, UT: Brigham Young University, 2002).

Table 3 indicates just how overwhelmingly Republican and conservative Mormons are in their political attitudes. More than three-quarters of all LDS respondents in the survey identified themselves as Republican and conservative. In terms of ideology, 64 percent of Protestants and 59 percent of Catholics identified themselves as liberal or moderate. A mere 23 percent of Mormons claimed to be moderate or liberal. In relation to partisanship, 30 percent of Protestants, 37 percent of Catholics, and a whopping 79 percent of Mormons identified themselves as Republicans. With roughly two-thirds of the voters being LDS, and three-fourths of Mormons tending to favor the Republican Party and conservatism, Utah appeared quite heavily one-sided in ideology and partisanship.

Table 3. Partisanship and Ideology by Religious Affiliation

	Protestant	Catholic	LDS
Democrat	56%	63%	13%
Independent	14%	0%	8%
Republican	30%	37%	79%

Number of Respondents	43	59	653	(755)

Jewish, Other, No preference, and *Prefer not to say* are omitted.

	Protestant	Catholic	LDS	
Liberal	32%	19%	5%	
Moderate	32%	40%	18%	
Conservative	37%	41%	77%	
Number of Respondents	41	58	619	(718)

Jewish, Other, No preference, and *Prefer not to say* are omitted.
Data: Kelly D. Patterson, "KBYU/Utah College Exit Poll" (Provo, UT: Brigham Young University, 2002).

Table 4. The Role Religion Plays in Determining Voting Choices

	Protestant	Catholic	LDS
Very Important	28%	38%	47%
Somewhat Important	19%	7%	27%
Not Important	53%	55%	26%
Number of Respondents	47	55	662

Total (764)
Data: Kelly D. Patterson, "KBYU/Utah College Exit Poll" (Provo, UT: Brigham Young University, 2002).

One final measure of the relationship linking religion to partisanship is presented in Table 4. Voters were asked, "How important were your own personal religious beliefs in deciding your vote for representative today?" Among Protestants, 47 percent said religion played a very or somewhat important role in their voting choice, while 45 percent of Catholics responded that religion was important or somewhat important. Among Mormons, 74 percent said that religion had some impact on their voting choice. Conversely, more than 50 percent of Protestants and Catholics said religion played no part in their voting decisions compared to 26 percent of Mormons. It seems evident that Mormons place considerable emphasis on their religious beliefs in determining how to vote in elections, and apparently those beliefs lead them to vote overwhelmingly Republican and hold a conservative ideology.

Utah Compared with Other States

Compared to the nation at the turn of the twentieth century, Utah was very conservative and Republican. Recall that 16 percent of Utahns identified themselves as liberal and 60 percent as conservative in 2002. During the 1990s, 20 percent of all Americans described themselves as liberal and 30 percent as conservative.[2] Thus, Utah was twice as conservative according to voters' descriptions. Similarly, whereas only 26 percent of Utahns identified themselves as Democrats, 51 percent of all Americans called themselves Democrats.[3] Around 37 percent of Americans, but 61 percent of Utahns, described themselves as Republicans.

Utah's exceptional conservatism extended across the final quarter of the twentieth century. In one of the most thorough analyses of public opinion across the fifty states, three social scientists pooled 122 CBS News/*New York Times* surveys from 1976 to 1988 to measure ideology and partisanship by state.[4] Based on these data, it is possible to rank the states according to two different scales: liberal/conservative and Democratic/Republican.

Table 5 charts the state scores for ideology. The first three columns represent the percentage of respondents in each state identifying themselves as conservative, moderate, and liberal. The fourth column reports the mean state ideology score.[5] Positive numbers represent liberal states, and negative numbers are conservative states. The further the score is from zero (the perfect moderate point) in either direction, the more liberal or conservative the state is.

Utah, with a mean ideology score of -28.0, was the most conservative state in the nation, and its northern neighbor, Idaho, was the next most conservative with a score of -27.9. Generally the Deep South and the rural West were the most conservative sections of the country, and the Northeast and Pacific Coast states were the most liberal.

Table 5. Ideology by States

State	Conservative	Moderate	Liberal	Mean	N
Alabama	40.5%	42.0%	17.5%	-23.1	2,142
Arizona	37.4	43.4	19.2	-18.2	1,578
Arkansas	36.8	44.6	18.6	-18.3	1,528
California	31.6	43.1	25.4	-6.2	13,369
Colorado	31.3	46.1	22.6	-8.6	1,724
Connecticut	29.4	45.6	25.0	-4.4	2,095
Delaware	32.0	48.2	19.8	-12.2	409
District of Columbia	24.6	44.4	31.0	6.3	504
Florida	37.1	42.9	20.0	-17.1	6,735
Georgia	36.6	44.6	18.8	-17.7	3,443
Idaho	42.5	42.9	14.6	-27.9	666

Illinois	32.5	45.1	22.4	-10.1	6,456
Indiana	36.0	44.7	19.3	-16.7	3,510
Iowa	33.0	47.5	19.5	-13.5	1,980
Kansas	36.5	42.9	20.6	-15.9	1,810
Kentucky	33.7	45.8	20.5	-13.2	2,103
Louisiana	40.0	43.0	17.0	-23.0	2,119
Maine	36.1	42.6	21.3	-14.7	685
Maryland	30.4	44.8	24.8	-5.7	2,723
Massachusetts	28.2	44.5	27.3	-0.8	3,704
Michigan	31.6	45.6	22.8	-8.8	6,135
Minnesota	33.2	46.5	20.4	-12.8	2,942
Mississippi	41.2	43.0	15.8	-25.4	1,223
Missouri	34.4	46.7	18.9	-15.5	3,167
Montana	34.3	42.5	23.2	-11.1	551
Nebraska	37.5	43.7	18.8	-18.7	1,128
Nevada	29.6	41.0	29.4	-0.2	446
New Hampshire	34.2	44.5	21.3	-12.8	685
New Jersey	30.1	43.2	26.7	-3.4	4,833
New Mexico	36.2	43.6	20.2	-16.0	746
New York	30.4	42.4	27.3	-3.1	10,619
North Carolina	37.8	45.1	17.1	-20.7	3,326
North Dakota	40.5	45.6	13.9	-26.6	447
Ohio	32.4	45.2	22.3	-10.0	7,013
Oklahoma	42.0	43.4	14.7	-27.3	1,866
Oregon	32.8	42.3	24.9	-7.9	1,890
Pennsylvania	33.0	44.5	22.4	-10.6	7,783
Rhode Island	29.0	44.1	26.9	-2.1	562
South Carolina	39.8	41.8	18.4	-21.4	2,128
South Dakota	38.4	47.2	14.4	-24.1	627
Tennessee	36.6	43.3	20.1	-16.6	2,764
Texas	40.6	42.0	17.4	-23.2	8,745
Utah	**44.1**	**39.7**	**16.1**	**-28.0**	**868**
Vermont	34.8	41.7	23.5	-11.4	405
Virginia	37.0	43.9	19.1	-17.9	3,948
Washington	29.2	47.5	23.3	-5.9	2,915
West Virginia	32.2	44.8	23.0	-9.2	1,348
Wisconsin	32.6	45.4	22.1	-10.5	3,113
Wyoming	39.7	38.4	21.9	-17.8	292

Reprinted with permission from Robert S. Erikson, Gerald C. Wright, and John P. McIver, *Statehouse Democracy* (New York: Cambridge University Press, 1993).

Table 6 provides state scores on partisanship with a similar interpretation to ideology. On this scale, each Republican is scored as -100, each Democrat as 100, and each Independent as zero. Again, Utah and Idaho ranked as the most Republican states with scores of -17.4 and -13.5, respectively.

Table 6. Partisanship by State

State	Republican	Independent	Democrat	Mean	N
Alabama	23.4%	32.2%	44.4%	21.1	2,419
Arizona	34.7	29.9	35.4	0.6	1,767
Arkansas	20.3	32.8	46.8	26.5	1,727
California	33.3	27.3	39.4	6.2	14,773
Colorado	32.6	38.8	28.6	-4.0	1,863
Connecticut	24.5	43.2	32.3	7.8	2,269
Delaware	28.7	40.6	30.7	2.0	443
District of Columbia	18.8	28.8	52.4	33.6	565
Florida	32.7	27.9	39.3	6.6	7,466
Georgia	21.0	31.0	48.0	27.0	3,814
Idaho	37.3	39.0	23.8	-13.5	724
Illinois	28.7	36.5	34.8	6.1	7,096
Indiana	32.9	36.0	31.2	-1.7	3,964
Iowa	32.4	38.1	29.6	-2.8	2,230
Kansas	38.3	32.7	29.0	-9.3	2,037
Kentucky	25.5	24.8	49.8	24.3	2,458
Louisiana	20.0	24.7	55.3	35.3	2,405
Maine	27.0	43.5	29.5	2.4	777
Maryland	24.2	29.4	46.4	22.2	2,996
Massachusetts	15.8	50.0	34.2	18.3	4,158
Michigan	29.8	38.3	31.9	2.1	6,806
Minnesota	27.3	35.8	36.8	9.5	3,181
Mississippi	27.0	29.2	43.8	16.7	1,416
Missouri	26.8	38.6	34.6	7.8	3,583
Montana	27.4	40.4	32.2	4.7	594
Nebraska	40.2	28.9	30.9	-9.3	1,252
Nevada	31.8	31.2	37.0	5.1	487
New Hampshire	31.8	46.3	21.8	-10.0	760
New Jersey	27.5	39.9	32.6	5.1	5,252
New Mexico	26.3	31.7	42.0	15.7	843
New York	29.7	32.6	37.7	8.0	11,599
North Carolina	27.6	25.8	46.6	19.0	3,885

North Dakota	36.2	36.6	27.3	-8.9	495
Ohio	31.0	33.6	35.4	4.4	7,778
Oklahoma	29.9	19.2	50.8	20.9	2,115
Oregon	31.2	30.2	38.6	7.4	2,063
Pennsylvania	34.8	26.8	38.4	3.7	8,710
Rhode Island	15.5	56.4	28.2	12.7	614
South Carolina	27.5	33.2	39.2	11.7	2,304
South Dakota	38.4	21.3	40.3	2.0	717
Tennessee	26.5	34.2	39.3	12.9	3,149
Texas	26.1	34.5	39.4	13.4	9,696
Utah	**41.9**	**33.5**	**24.5**	**-17.4**	**966**
Vermont	28.6	48.0	23.4	-5.1	448
Virginia	29.4	37.9	32.7	3.3	4,245
Washington	24.0	44.1	31.9	7.8	3,179
West Virginia	28.6	22.7	48.7	20.1	1,559
Wisconsin	27.1	38.7	34.2	7.1	3,413
Wyoming	34.5	35.1	30.3	-4.2	333

Reprinted with permission from Robert S. Erikson, Gerald C. Wright, and John P. McIver, *Statehouse Democracy* (New York: Cambridge University Press, 1993).

While survey data offer a good measure, social scientists also frequently look at actual voting results to determine partisan leanings. If voting data tend to support survey answers regarding state partisanship and ideology, then categorizing Utah as one of the more conservative and Republican states will be on firmer ground.

Political scientist Austin Ranney developed a measurement called interparty competition, which standardizes scores for states based on (1) the competitiveness of the two major parties, and (2) the degree to which one of the parties controls state elective offices.[6] Ranney combined the following variables into a single index: (1) percentage of votes won by each party in gubernatorial elections; (2) percentage of seats won by each party in state house and senate elections; (3) length of time each party controlled the governorship; and (4) the proportion of time the legislature and governorship were divided between the two parties. Scores for party control range from 0 for the most Republican to 1.0 for the most Democratic. Scores for party competition range from 1.000 for the most competitive to .500 for the least competitive. Table 7 provides the scores for each of the fifty states for the years 1980–98.

Table 7. Party Competition by State 1980–98

State	Party Control [a]	Party Competition [b]
Maryland	.810	.690
Arkansas	.803	.697
Hawaii	.791	.709
Georgia	.786	.714
Louisiana	.772	.728
Mississippi	.762	.738
West Virginia	.753	.747
Rhode Island	.750	.750
Kentucky	.742	.758
Massachusetts	.740	.760
Alabama	.727	.773
North Carolina	.674	.826
Oklahoma	.674	.826
Virginia	.648	.852
South Carolina	.639	.861
Missouri	.624	.876
New Mexico	.624	.876
Texas	.623	.877
Tennessee	.621	.879
Florida	.603	.987
Minnesota	.601	.899
Nevada	.593	.907
Washington	.591	.909
California	.591	.909
Connecticut	.577	.923
Maine	.568	.932
Oregon	.544	.956
Vermont	.540	.960
New York	.530	.970
Wisconsin	.526	.974
Delaware	.508	.992
Michigan	.495	.995
Illinois	.488	.988
Alaska	.477	.977
Iowa	.475	.975
New Jersey	.470	.970
Montana	.463	.963
Ohio	.455	.955

Pennsylvania	.436	.936
Indiana	.432	.932
Colorado	.412	.912
North Dakota	.391	.891
Wyoming	.358	.858
Arizona	.350	.850
Kansas	.334	.834
New Hampshire	.327	.827
Idaho	.321	.821
South Dakota	.275	.775
Utah	**.240**	**.740**

[a] The scores range from 1.0 for the most Democratic to 0 for the most Republican.
[b] The scores range from 1.000 for the most competitive to .500 for the least competitive.
Source: Austin Ranney, "Parties in State Politics," in *Politics in the American States: A Comparative Analysis,* 3rd ed., ed. Herbert Jacob and Kenneth Vines (Boston: Little Brown, 1976). Reprinted with permission from Malcolm E. Jewell and Sarah M. Morehouse, *Political Parties and Elections in American States.* (Washington, DC: CQ Press, 2001).

In terms of party control, Maryland and Arkansas were the most heavily Democratic and Utah and South Dakota the most heavily Republican states in the 1980s and 1990s. Rural western states made up six of the eight most Republican states, with Utah ranking first. In terms of party competition, Utah was one of the least competitive states with a score of .740. A perfectly competitive state would have a score of .500. Only six southern Democratic states were less competitive than Utah. Thus, the Ranney index of voting behavior reveals that Utah was the most Republican state in America during the 1980s and 1990s.

Public Opinion on Social Issues

Utah conservatism is a mix of two distinct types. Some conservatives tend toward libertarianism and others toward social conservatism. Libertarians value the individual and personal freedom above all other social values. They believe that government should not interfere with the choices made by individuals except when it is necessary to keep the peace and enforce contracts and the few laws that they believe should be on the books. Libertarians do not believe that the individual should be subservient to the group, whether that group is the national government, a state government, or a local community. Social conservatives also respect individual freedom, but they also honor certain community, traditional, and family values. They believe that government should promote morality and community values and that individuals must temper their individual desires in favor of the welfare of the larger social group. Both of these strains of conservativism run through Utah's political culture.

Several questions on the 2002 KBYU/Utah Colleges Exit Poll tapped into these conflicting conservative ideological strands. Respondents were asked whether Utah should allow same-sex marriages and relax state liquor laws. On both issues, Utahns overwhelmingly adopted the social conservative view. Only 35 percent favored easing Utah's rather stringent liquor laws. This issue clearly pits individual freedom against moral/religious values, and 64 percent wanted to impose moral values.

It is difficult to see opposition to same-sex marriages as anything but the preference of societal moral/religious values over individual liberty. Support for individual choice was lowest on this question. A mere 19 percent of the respondents favored legalizing same-sex marriages. More than 80 percent of Utahns opposed redefining marriage to include homosexual couples. On the surface, there is a certain irony in this response; it appears odd that citizens of a state with a history of polygamy and a general policy of turning a blind eye toward existing polygamy should be so closed to another novel kind of union. But when you consider that some feel there is a religious justification for polygamy, and others see polygamy as an historical past for their church and ancestors, the apparent contradiction is not so difficult to explain. Mormons are opposed to same-sex marriages. Church doctrine holds that marriage should only exist between a man and a woman, and sexual relations outside the bonds of marriage are immoral.[7]

One issue where Utahns appeared to be somewhat libertarian involved concealed weapons. When asked whether concealed weapons should be banned from Utah churches and schools, only 19 percent were in favor. More than 80 percent of the respondents supported the right of individuals to carry concealed weapons into churches and schools, despite the fact that the LDS Church favors a ban on concealed weapons in churches. This view appears to represent a type of western frontier libertarianism, where individuals have rights that trump other values. This attitude is diametrically opposed to the view on liquor laws. After all, the frontier libertarian value system supported not only carrying guns but also saloons and easy access to alcohol.

RELIGION AS A FACTOR IN UTAH POLITICAL BEHAVIOR

Every state has a distinctive political culture or personality arising from a blend of economic and social ingredients and its history. Additionally new ingredients such as demographic changes and a new age of middle-class suburbanism have emerged to cause states, including Utah, to shed some inherited traits.

In nineteenth-century Utah, high-ranking church officials often filled political offices. They supplied the political, industrial, and financial leadership. The overlap between religious and secular affairs became all pervasive. This unity of church and state seemed to be essential to building the Kingdom of God and overcoming the opposition that had uprooted Mormons from three previous states in the union. Mormons based their system on a claim to divine authority and First-Amendment constitutional protection.[8]

The federal government and Utah Mormons carried on arguments for more than forty years about local rights, ecclesiastical domination, constitutional protections, and liberty that have continued to color Mormon political attitudes today. Religious beliefs and practices have profoundly influenced the politics of many individual Mormons, and some people in key leadership roles have continued to advocate states' rights and resist expansion of federal power in their quest for autonomy. Mormons developed an unusual respect for authority exercised by leaders within the church hierarchical priesthood structure. This willingness to follow trusted authority made the Mormons an orderly, unified people who valued consensus politics.[9]

Not until the 1890s were national political parties organized in Utah. In an attempt to win statehood, church leaders urged members to affiliate politically with the national parties, hoping the Republican Party might look more favorably upon statehood for Utah. One result was uncertainty and instability in political loyalties. Working behind the scenes, Church President Joseph F. Smith favored the Republican Party, hoping to ensure that Utah politics followed national trends. His closest associate in Americanizing and Republicanizing Utah politics was Mormon Apostle Reed Smoot, who was elected to the United States Senate in 1903. Together Smith and Smoot successfully launched a stable Republican Party in Utah that adhered to a stand-pat, big-business-oriented conservatism.[10]

Smith endorsed Republican incumbent William H. Taft's bid for reelection in 1912, a factor which contributed to Taft's narrow margin of victory in the three-way presidential race that year. However, other prominent Mormon leaders, including Heber J. Grant and Charles W. Penrose, were Democrats. General Authority B.H. Roberts went so far as to publicly question the political authority of the church president at the church's October 1912 General Conference. Republicans embraced moderate progressive reforms such as conservation, the eight-hour day, and minimum wage legislation, and those stands contributed to their appeal. More importantly, Utah prospered during most of the Progressive Era, and as the party in power, the Republicans took credit for the strong economy.[11]

Utah moved briefly into the Democratic fold beginning in 1916, partly because Democratic President Woodrow Wilson's moral rectitude and crusading progressivism resonated with Utah voters and partly because the state's economy was riding at high tide with Wilson in the White House. Conservative Republicans had also stymied popular proposals for reform in Utah, including the initiative, the referendum, utility and railroad regulation, and Prohibition. Under Democratic governor Simon Bamberger, a Democratic legislature enacted a sweeping series of reforms, including workmen's compensation, business regulation, and Prohibition.[12]

Republicans again swept the state in 1920 as the economy fell into a tailspin and Wilson's popularity plummeted. They enacted some of the more coercive elements of the Progressive agenda, including cigarette prohibition and bans on property ownership by Asian immigrants. Although Utah elected Democrat William King to the Senate and Democrat George Dern as governor during the 1920s, Republicans won most of the elections between 1920 and 1932.[13]

The Great Depression and the New Deal further reoriented Utah politics to change. The Depression, along with World War II, marked the heyday of the Democratic Party in the Beehive State. After three decades in the Senate, Reed Smoot was ousted in 1932 by Democrat Elbert Thomas, a University of Utah political science professor who became a staunch advocate of the New Deal. A coalition of miners; urbanities; traditional Democrats; a small, but organized, labor movement; and farm bloc support began to form, creating a New Deal alliance in Utah.[14]

National planning under the New Deal opposed the laissez-faire economy that had prevailed under Republican administrators of the 1920s. The approach was similar to Mormon economic practices of the nineteenth century, but that had caused much turmoil and been a factor in bringing down the wrath of the federal government upon the Mormons. Once they had been weaned away from a planned economic approach, the church hierarchy was not anxious to return to it; instead, states' rights and constitutionalism became major issues in the minds of many in the church hierarchy. The Mormon Church renewed political activism based on the philosophy that when great moral issues are involved or principles of church belief or doctrine are in peril, the church must inform the people.[15] Notwithstanding repeated attempts by the LDS Church's First Presidency to discredit the New Deal, Roosevelt, Thomas, and the Democratic Party remained popular with most Utahns through the end of World War II.[16]

Between 1947 and 1977, the two parties were fairly evenly matched, although Republicans enjoyed an overall edge. Over these three decades, more than any other time in the twentieth century, the two-party system thrived. In the state capitol building, Republicans dominated 53 percent of the legislative sessions in the Senate, while Democrats held the majority in the other 47 percent. In the House, the two parties were evenly matched in 1951–52. Democrats outnumbered Republicans in 40 percent of the other sessions, and Republicans dominated in the remaining 60 percent. Power oscillated repeatedly over the three decades. Republican candidates for governor prevailed in 1948, 1952, 1956, and 1960, while probusiness Democrats won in 1964, 1968, 1972, and 1976.[17]

Still, during this time period, state politics began moving markedly toward a preference for conservatism. This shift to the right stemmed in part from the cold war with communist Russia as well as unrest with government controls. Utah followed a national postwar trend and partook of the anticommunist frenzy known as McCarthyism with its Red hunts and loyalty oaths. Despite the church's official political neutrality adopted in 1954, bedrock conservatism, patriotic fervor, and conformist tendencies had become the prevailing political sentiment among the majority of Mormons.[18]

The 1964 election saw a brief departure from the political slide toward the Right. Utah, and all the western states except Arizona, voted for Lyndon B. Johnson of Texas. During the Johnson administration, another wave of liberal reform expanded federal power. Reforms included federal support for education and Medicare for the elderly and a rising environmental consciousness preached by Mormon Secretary of the Interior Stewart Udall and implemented by a series of laws.[19]

Soon the Vietnam War resulted in many protests and brought with it the greatest resurgence of political activism since the 1930s, which included demands for women's rights, gay rights, and civil rights. The upsurge of protest and militancy fueled a conservative reaction. In 1968 Republican Richard Nixon captured the presidency, and he won a landslide reelection in 1972 over outspoken liberal Senator George McGovern of South Dakota. Nixon's popularity in Utah and the West generally outpaced his national support. Watergate blunted the move Right for a time, but a long-term conservative phase emerged again in the late 1970s. The liberal elements in Utah's Republican Party had long since atrophied, leaving the conservatives firmly in control. Progressives and family farmers who had voted Democratic had dwindled in number and influence. Democratic governors such as Calvin L. Rampton and Scott Matheson did win elections by keeping down taxes, being probusiness, and successfully seeking to garner federal dollars for favored Utah projects, but larger economic interests linked to wealth, business, and Republicanism had redefined political loyalties.[20] A large influx of retirees into areas such as Washington County and enormous growth in high-tech employment along the Wasatch Front added to the conservatism of Utah politics.

In the 1990s, more than 90 percent of Utah legislators and state officeholders were Mormons, even though the state population was only about 70 percent Mormon. These factors added to the moralizing nature of the state's politics.[21] After 1950, when the church-owned *Deseret News* endorsed Wallace F. Bennett's bid for the Senate, the Mormon Church no longer publicly supported candidates, but it continued to take stands on what its leaders considered to be moral issues, including gay marriage.[22] The Word of Wisdom, issued in 1833, counsels against the use of tea, coffee, tobacco, and liquor for members of the Mormon Church, accounting for Utah's strict moral attitudes on liquor and its restrictive liquor-control laws.[23] Liquor-by-the-drink laws fall into the realm of morality and righteousness, but the conservative attitudes about this issue mellowed over the years as Utah sought to cash in on tourism.[24]

Abortion is prohibited in Mormon teachings except in cases of rape, incest, threat to a mother's life, or severe deformity of the fetus.[25] Members understand these teachings, and faithful Mormons usually uphold them. In fact, some Mormons are even more restrictive and rigid in their attitudes on abortion than church teachings dictate, a case of members perhaps "being more

Many Utahns always have enjoyed the yearly deer hunt. School children often got out of school the day before the hunt started, and it was almost a holiday in the state. With this focus on hunting, many state citizens believed strongly in the right to bear arms.

Catholic than the pope." The Mormon Church also opposes gambling and gaming.[26] Mormonism is a remarkably homogeneous faith, and members are deeply influenced in their thoughts and actions by what they perceive to be church positions on these moral issues.

Even so, some elements of conservatism in Utah are not easily explained by the Mormon religious domination. Conservative attitudes opposing gun control probably originate from the western tradition of gun-toting cowboys, who have been romanticized into self-reliant individuals, full of energy and action, and who are regarded in much of today's West as totally masculine. Some opposition to gun control probably comes from antigovernment sentiment, and some comes from the broadly accepted hunter culture in the state. In Utah hunting is often associated in the popular mind with family outings, and that kind of activity is highly prized among Mormon people. Until the 1980s, Utah schools dismissed elementary and secondary students for the deer hunt. Even those who never hunted knew families who made hunting a regular family outing. The *Deseret News* estimated that two hundred thousand hunters took part in the first day of the Utah deer hunt in October 1989.[27] Perhaps many Utahns have rationalized the importance of the family aspect of the hunting tradition to overcome statements by at least two Latter-day Saint church presidents, Joseph F. Smith and Spencer W. Kimball, not to kill birds and animals unless you actually need the food.[28] Some church leaders have also questioned the need for owners to tote concealed guns to church and school with little effect on changing behavior and attitudes.[29]

Californian Ronald Reagan's presidency was another factor that helped the growth of the Utah Republican Party. His defiance of taunting students, slashing of welfare budgets, call for balanced budgets, and announcement that he was on board as a "sagebrush rebel" made him popular in Utah. (See Jedediah Rogers's chapter in this volume, "Quarreling Communities.")

In the twentieth century, Utahns generally reflected conservative attitudes on racial and ethnic-minority issues. Member misunderstanding of church positions explains some of these attitudes. Many orthodox Mormons are convinced that other religions and cultures are in error and have consequently developed an extreme ethnocentrism that has blinded many to diversity, ethnicity, and racial pluralism. This outlook persists despite many talks by church general authorities admonishing members to be more tolerant and accepting of multiculturalism.[30] Many Mormons feel that diversity is embraced only through conversion.

The church practice of denying the priesthood to people of African racial descent until June 1978 was justified by a number of doctrinal speculators, most of whom cited God's placing a "curse" on dark-skinned people as a consequence of their sinfulness. One result of this attitude is that many Mormons, along with conservatives, tend toward a neoconservative interpretation of racial equality, which stresses the supremacy of individual rights over the prerogative of groups, especially racial minorities. Neoconservatives (a political term developed in the 1950s to describe those who rejected liberal social attitudes) generally voice abhorrence of prejudice and discrimination while opposing government initiatives based on race or ethnicity such as hate crimes legislation or affirmative action. In three consecutive sessions, the state legislature rejected a moderate hate crimes bill, despite the fact that in 2003 officials of the Mormon Church announced they had no objections to it.[31] Neoconservatives promote a society where individuals may rise as high as their talents and ambitions will carry them. This stance effectively protects the status quo because members of racial minorities usually start with significant socioeconomic disadvantages. For many Mormons, neoconservative racial ideology also coincides with an emphasis on individual salvation based on good works and righteous living.[32]

Historically Utah has been a conservative, moralizing state. The 2002 exit poll data support that conclusion. As this chapter has shown, one of the major factors is the dominant religion, the Church of Jesus Christ of Latter-day Saints.[33] Throughout the twentieth century, the LDS Church's policies toward what its leaders considered moral issues strengthened the state's conservative nature. Utah is changing; Salt Lake County, for example, is now more Democratic than Republican and more liberal than the rest of the state. But Utah still is not a diverse state, and in most rural areas, the Mormon Church still dominates and determines political attitudes.

NOTES

1. Kelly D. Patterson, "KBYU/Utah College Exit Poll" (Provo, UT: Brigham Young University, 2002).

2. Center for Political Studies, University of Michigan, *The NES Guide to Public Opinion and Electoral Behavior* (Ann Arbor: Center for Political Studies, University of Michigan, 1995–2000), available online at http://www.umich.edu/~nes/nesguide.htm

3. Ibid.

4. Robert S. Erikson, Gerald C. Wright, and John P. McIver, *Statehouse Democracy: Public Opinion and Policy in the American States* (New York: Cambridge University Press, 1993). The 122 surveys yielded 157,393 usable responses for partisanship and 141,798 for ideology. The mean sample size per state was about 3,500 with state samples ranging from more than 14,000 to just fewer than 300.

5. Means are calculated by assigning a score of 100 for each liberal, 0 for each moderate, and -100 for each conservative. Thus, the mean is a relative point difference between liberals and conservatives. Hawaii and Alaska were not included in this study due to a lack of surveys and too few respondents.

6. Austin Ranney, "Parties in State Politics, in *Politics in the American States: A Comparative Analysis,* 2nd ed., ed. Herbert Jacob and Kenneth Vines (Boston: Little and Brown, 1971, 82–121.

7. *Ensign,* November 1995, 102.

8. Nels Anderson, *Desert Saints: The Mormon Frontier in Utah* (Chicago: University of Chicago Press, 1966), 300.

9. Dean L. May, *Utah: A People's History* (Salt Lake City: University of Utah Press, 1987), 93.

10. Ibid., 160–61; Thomas G. Alexander, *Utah, the Right Place: The Official Centennial History,* rev. ed. (Salt Lake City: Gibbs Smith, 2003), 201–2.

11. Thomas G. Alexander, "Political Patterns of Early Statehood, 1896–1919," in *Utah's History,* ed. Richard D. Poll, Thomas G. Alexander, Eugene E. Campbell, and David E. Miller (Provo, UT: Brigham Young University Press, 1978), 417–18; Brian Q. Cannon, "'Taft Has Made a Good President': Mormons and Politics in the Election of 1912," in *Times of Transition: Proceedings of the 2000 Symposium at the Joseph Fielding Smith Institute for Latter-day Saint History at Brigham Young University,* ed. Thomas G. Alexander (Provo, UT: Joseph Fielding Smith Institute, 2003), 55–66.

12. Alexander, "Political Patterns," 423–24.

13. Thomas G. Alexander, "From War to Depression, in Poll et al., *Utah's History,* 472–75.

14. Wayne K. Hinton, "The New Deal Years in Utah: A Political History of Utah (1932–1940)" (master's thesis, Utah State University, 1963), 96.

15. Wayne K. Hinton, *Utah: Unusual Beginning to Unique Present* (Sun Valley, CA: American Historical Press, 2000), 142.

16. John F. Bluth and Wayne K. Hinton, "The Great Depression," in Poll et al., *Utah's History,* 485; Brian Q. Cannon, "'What a Power We Will Be in This Land': The LDS

Church, the Church Security Program and the New Deal," *Journal of the West* 43 (Fall 2004):66–75.

17.   Table O, in Poll et al., *Utah's History,* 711–12.

18.   Daniel Jay Combs, "Official LDS Anticommunism, 1901–1972: The Articulation of an LDS Conservative Ideology" (master's thesis, Brigham Young University, 2005), see especially chap. 2.

19.   Michael P. Malone and Richard W. Etulain, *The American West: A Twentieth Century History* (Lincoln: University of Nebraska Press, 1989), 276, 286–87.

20.   Hinton, *Utah: Unusual Beginning*, 143.

21.   Alexander, *Utah, the Right Place,* 419.

22.   *Ensign,* November 1995, 102.

23.   Doctrine and Covenants (Salt Lake City: Church of Jesus Christ of Latter-day Saints, 1979), 89.

24.   Hinton, *Utah: Unusual Beginning,* 144–45.

25.   *Leadership Hand Book of Instruction* (Salt Lake City: Church of Jesus Christ of Latter-day Saints, 1992), 112.

26.   Gordon B. Hinckley, "Gambling," *Ensign,* May 2005, 58–61.

27.   *Deseret News,* October 20, 1989.

28.   Spencer W. Kimball, "Strengthening the Family—The Basic Unit of the Church," Priesthood Session, 148th Annual Conference of the Church of Jesus Christ of Latter-day Saints, April 1978. *Ensign,* May 1978, 45–48.

29.   *Salt Lake Tribune,* November 11, 2001, *Ensign,* November 2001, 35–38.

30.   M. Russell Ballard, "The Doctrine of Inclusion," Semi-Annual Conference of the Church of Jesus Christ of Latter-day Saints, October 2002.

31.   *Deseret News,* February 23, 2003.

32.   Doctrine and Covenants (Salt Lake City: Church of Jesus Christ of Latter-day Saints, 1979), 6.

33.   Alexander, *Utah, the Right Place,* 414–16. Other factors also contributed to Utah's conservatism. Utah is less industrialized than many more-liberal states; it is also more middle class and less diverse. Certainly a closeness of life, especially in small towns and LDS neighborhood wards, makes it difficult to dissent and go your own way, thus producing a greater consensus in politics.

10

Utah's Denial of the Vote to Reservation Indians, 1956–57

Brian Q. Cannon

Following World War II, the denial of voting rights to racial minorities galvanized activists across the nation to fight for civil rights. In Utah voting rights for racial minorities were a particularly volatile issue in San Juan, Uintah, and Duchesne Counties, where large numbers of Ute and Navajo residents created potentially significant political blocs. Many Anglos and Native Americans in these counties eyed one another with apprehension. In the following chapter, Brian Q. Cannon discusses Utah's decision in 1956 to uphold a nineteenth-century statute by denying Indians on the Uintah-Ouray Reservation the right to vote. The legal battle that ensued reveals the indifference of Utah's governor and general populace to racial injustice, the conservatism of Utah's Supreme Court and attorney general, and the importance of old-stock legal talent and nationally based Pan-Indian organizations in the campaign for Indian voting rights in Utah. Although voting rights were restored, interracial suspicion and misunderstanding persisted and resurfaced many times during the rest of the century.

In 1956 Utah's attorney general barred Indians living on reservations from voting. Utah's enforcement of this prohibition developed relatively late, but it grew out of legal strategies and reasoning that many states had used to disfranchise Native Americans. As political scientist Glenn Phelps has observed, "Indian reservations and the Indians who live on them introduce unique ingredients into the political mix surrounding voting rights." State and federal officials employed four main arguments rooted in constitutional or legal requirements to deny Indians the right to vote. Some argued that unassimilated Indians were unqualified to vote. Using this rationale, the state constitutions of North Dakota, South Dakota, Minnesota, and Idaho originally barred Indians who

245

did not speak English from voting. Similarly Arizona's constitution stipulated that citizens must be able to read the United States Constitution to exercise their franchise. States also disfranchised Indians because they were wards of the federal government. In *Porter v. Hall* (1928), for instance, the Arizona Supreme Court embraced this reasoning.[1]

Indians were also denied the right to vote because the U.S. Constitution, the Fourteenth Amendment, and many state constitutions exclude "Indians not taxed" from consideration in determining legislative representation. As late as 1940, Idaho, Maine, Mississippi, New Mexico, and Washington all used this rationale to bar Indians from voting. Over the next seven years, all of these states, except for New Mexico, retreated from that stance. In 1948 Miguel Trujillo, a resident of Isleta Pueblo, New Mexico, sued in federal court after he tried unsuccessfully to vote. A panel of three judges ruled in Trujillo's favor, overturning New Mexico's ban on Indian voting. More than two decades later, a group of New Mexicans attempted unsuccessfully to prevent nontaxpaying Indians from voting in a school-bond election. Similarly Arizonans in 1973 contested an Indian's right to run for office because he did not pay property taxes.

One final legal rationale for denying Indians the right to vote derived from the Supreme Court's finding in the 1886 case *United States v. Kagama* that Indians were subject to federal law, but "Indians owe no allegiance to a state within which their reservation may be established, and the state gives them no protection." In the 1920s, New York and Arizona cited this rationale, pointing out that some state laws did not apply on Indian reservations. In 1948 New Mexico officials attempted to block Indians from voting on the same grounds.[2]

Although many states prohibited Indians from voting early in the twentieth century, Utah has "the distinction of being the last state in the Union to permit Indians to vote," as political scientist Daniel McCool has observed. The state's ban on voting by reservation Indians drew upon each of the legal arguments already cited. Utah thus provides historians with a model, albeit a regressive one, of American Indian policy.[3]

Despite the importance of voting rights, Utah's denial of the vote to Indians has received only fleeting scholarly attention. The state's dubious distinction is mentioned by Jere Franco (Utah was "the last state to grant the franchise to Native Americans") and Vine Deloria Jr. and Cliff Lytle ("Utah was the last state to permit Indians to exercise their voting franchise"). Thomas Alexander notes in his centennial history of the state that "Utah repealed the restriction on Native American voting" in the mid-1950s but offers no further information. Other prominent state histories do not mention it at all.[4]

Likewise published histories of Utah's Indians mention the denial in passing, if at all. Nancy Maryboy and David Begay note that "Utah was the last state to allow Indians to vote. The ruling did not come until after a lawsuit in 1957." Although the state statute did not apply to the Southern Paiutes, whose tribal status had been terminated under Public Law 83–762 in 1954, Martha Knack indicates that "the Utah state legislature blocked native voting until 1956, arguing that reservations, as federal trust lands, were not part of the state." Anthropologist Joseph Jorgensen offers only a bit more information on the legislation and Utah Supreme Court ruling, devoting portions of three paragraphs to the matter.[5]

This chapter fleshes out the story of Utah's restriction on Native American voting. Governmental officials on the state level claimed they believed Indians should be able to vote, but the executive branch must enforce laws on the books, however objectionable they might appear, while the courts must uphold any law that appeared reasonable. This strict constructionist approach contrasted with the activist view the U.S. Supreme Court had taken in 1954 and 1955 in the landmark case *Brown v. Board of Education* regarding school desegregation. More than a sense of constitutional propriety undergirded Utah's denial of the vote to reservation Indians, though. Officials were willing to sacrifice civil rights upon the procedural altar because they did not view Indians as equal citizens. Resentment over the exemption of reservation Indians from property taxes, a sense that Indians benefitted unjustly from governmental paternalism, a conviction that Indians were ill prepared to vote, and disappointment that the full-blooded Utes had rejected the federal program of termination all influenced Utah's decision to deny voting rights to Indians in 1956.

In Utah Indians residing on or near reservations likely first voted in the Uinta Basin. Under the provisions of the Dawes Severalty Act of 1887, unallotted lands on the Uintah Reservation in eastern Utah were opened to homesteading in 1905 by presidential proclamation. As settlers flocked to the region, voting districts were established within the boundaries of the original reservation, and residents, including Indians who had obtained citizenship, were permitted to vote. Under the terms of the Dawes Act and the Burke Act of 1906, the Utes were awarded U.S. citizenship after going through the allotment process and receiving a final patent to their land. Regardless of whether or not they had received a land patent, though, all Indians became citizens of the United States under the Indian Citizenship Act of 1924.[6]

Not all Indians welcomed citizenship and voting rights. In western Utah and eastern Nevada during World War I, some Gosiutes had resisted the draft, arguing that they were not citizens of the United States and should therefore not be bound by those obligations. When all Indians became citizens by law in 1924, most Shoshones opposed their new status, fearing that it might undercut the governmental benefits they received as tribal members. According to historian Steven J. Crum, "most Shoshones—at least those in northern Nevada— refused to register to vote in local, state, and national elections" until the New Deal ushered in "socioeconomic reforms that Shoshones favored." Even by 1953, only thirteen of the sixty-three adult Gosiutes residing on reservations in Utah were registered to vote.[7]

Four years after Congress approved the Indian Citizenship Act, non-Indian residents of the Uinta Basin challenged the Utes' right to vote, based upon a long-ignored statute the state legislature had enacted in 1898. The law denied voting rights to "any person living upon any Indian or military reservation" who had not previously established residency elsewhere in the state, judging he or she to be "not . . . a resident of Utah." From 1928 on, county officials in the basin used the law to deny reservation Indians the right to vote despite the Fifteenth Amendment's prohibition against excluding voters based upon race or color. Meanwhile, they continued to permit non-Indians living within the original reservation boundaries to vote even though the 1898 statute theoretically applied to them as well. Throughout the 1930s, as Indians across the West became more active politically, each year at election time the policy became "a serious bone of contention among the people in Uintah County," but county officials stood firm. Finally, Sterling John Talbot, a fifty-four-year-old Episcopal minister in Whiterocks, raised the matter with Assistant Attorney General Grover Giles in 1940. The Episcopal Church had the largest number of adherents of any religious organization on the reservation. At the time, Giles was the Democratic Party's candidate for attorney general.[8]

On October 25, 1940, Giles issued a legal opinion in which he argued that the statute did not apply to the Uintah Indian Reservation. Giles asserted that state lawmakers had "contemplated a closed reservation" and allotment had geographically splintered the area to the extent that the statute was no longer relevant. He observed that the state now exercised jurisdiction over and taxed lands lying within the original reservation boundaries that had since been opened to homesteading. He further noted changes in the legal status of Indians under the federal government in light of the Citizenship Act of 1924. He concluded, "I am of the opinion that the Indians themselves residing upon the Uintah Reservation who are of the age of twenty-one years, and who are otherwise eligible under Utah law, are eligible to vote within the precinct within which they are residing though such precinct may be within the territorial boundaries of the Uintah Reservation." Acknowledging that the law on the books suggested otherwise, Giles recommended that the legislature "earnest[ly] consider" repealing the statute. The editor of the *Vernal Express* reported Giles's ruling straightforwardly, and that article was reprinted without commentary in the *Salt Lake Tribune* and the *Roosevelt Standard*.[9]

Giles's ruling was unambiguous with regard to Indians residing on a reservation that had been opened to allotment, but it implied that Indians residing on closed reservations, where allotment had not been implemented, might be ineligible to vote. Despite Giles's admonition, however, the legislature did not clarify the matter. It seems unlikely that the ruling even crossed most legislators' radar screens.

Indian voting rights again became an issue in the Uinta Basin in the altered climate of the 1950s. Some taxpayers resented the fact that Utes on the reservation were largely exempt from local taxation. Similar resentment of the benefits and restrictions Indians faced as tribal citizens festered across the nation. Partly in reaction to that resentment, Congress approved House Resolution 109 in 1953, which committed that body to terminate the federal government's trust relationship with tribes at the earliest feasible date. Utah Senator Arthur Watkins, "the leading congressional proponent of termination," prioritized termination of the Ute Indians' tribal status. Watkins was convinced that Indians "have innate ability just the same as other people," but they needed to be "stimulated with a little ambition and necessity." He believed termination would provide that stimulus. Under termination the Uintah-Ouray Reservation could be liquidated or managed by a trust, the Utes would have the same relationship to government as non-Indians, and they would be subject to taxation. Watkins minimized the fact that the Indian trust relationship entailed permanent obligations the federal government had assumed in return for Indian concessions of land, independence, and sovereignty.[10]

In March of 1954, about four hundred members of the Ute Tribe (roughly 22 percent of the population) met in a General Council and voted to exclude any Ute whose blood quantum was less than 50 percent Indian from membership in the tribe. This arrangement, the brainchild of Robert Bennett, an Oneida employee of the Bureau of Indian Affairs, was presented to the Utes by Ernest Wilkinson, the attorney who had successfully represented them in their monetary claims for lands they had once controlled. At the time, some mixed bloods supported Bennett's plan. Historian Warren Metcalf has argued that the full-blooded Utes sacrificed the Métis from the tribe to "protect the full-bloods from termination" and secure a greater share of the $31.9 million that the Indian Claims Commission had recently awarded to the Utes. But many mixed bloods saw the same arrangements as a means of gaining access to their share of the settlement.

Subsequent to the General Council's vote, Congress passed the Ute Partitioning Act, which launched the termination of the mixed-bloods' tribal status and rights. Instead of ending the tribal citizenship of only those who possessed less than 50 percent Ute ancestry, the act provided for the termination of all Indians with less than 51 percent Ute ancestry. On April 5, 1956, the tribal rolls were redrawn to exclude 490 mixed-blood Utes, lowering the tribal population to 1,314. The following month the mixed-blood Utes formed the Affiliated Ute Citizens of the State of Utah (AUC).[11]

In the context of proposals for Ute termination, the full-blooded Utes' rejection of termination, and the renewed focus upon tribal members' distinctive legal status, local and state officials once again raised questions regarding the propriety of voting by Indians who were exempt from local taxes. Should taxpayers be required to provide voting facilities for Indians under these circumstances? Secretary of State Lamont Toronto requested a legal opinion on the matter from Attorney General E.R. "Dick" Callister in 1956. Callister assigned his newly appointed assistant, K. Roger Bean, a recent graduate of George Washington University's law school, to study the issue. Bean was familiar with the debates surrounding termination and the provision of government services to Indians since he had worked for Senator Watkins on Capitol Hill while he was a law student. Bean concluded that the residency statute was unambiguous: "Indians who live on the reservations are not entitled to vote in Utah," Bean stated, "and a Board of County Commissioners has no duty to provide them with voting facilities. Indians living off the reservation may, of course, register and vote in the voting district in which they reside, the same as any other citizen."[12]

Callister validated Bean's report, informing county clerks of the statute and instructing them to enforce it. The *Deseret News* reported that Callister's order was not malicious; he merely intended to test the constitutionality of the statute. Callister may have had more interest in the matter than the *News* implied, though. After all he could have relied upon the opinion Giles had issued in 1940. The mere request for a new opinion suggests that the former one dissatisfied him, unless he knew nothing about it. Perhaps he was predisposed to disregard the earlier opinion because its author had announced his candidacy to unseat Callister that year. Or perhaps he wanted to make a political statement about the legal status of Indians vis-à-vis county and state government at a time when that issue was a concern to many Utahns.[13]

Although Callister's order applied to Indians on all reservations in the state, only the press in the Uinta Basin reported it, and only the Utes challenged it in the courts. Symbolically the order was momentous in the context of the growing civil-rights movement since it challenged the civil rights of a racial minority on the basis of their residency. But in practice, it would scarcely affect the outcome of elections: of the 591 full-blooded and mixed-blood Utes of voting age, only about 50 were registered to vote in 1953.[14]

An editorial in the *Deseret News* laid bare many Utahns' criticism of Indians' status, a criticism that Callister's order and the termination movement reflected: Indians had been confined to reservations and treated as "ward[s] of the government" who were "unable to cope with the normal pattern of 20th Century life." It was unwise to "hold them indefinitely as a people apart." Instead, they should "establish their rightful place as full-fledged American citizens, mingling with the rest of the community."[15]

The Ute Tribal Committee quickly mobilized a court challenge, joining forces with the National Congress of American Indians (NCAI) and the American Heritage Foundation. Formed in 1944, the NCAI was a natural ally, for one of its key objectives was protecting Indian legal rights. Some lawmakers had assured Francis McKinley, director of community services for the Ute Tribe, that they intended to amend the law if the courts upheld it, but the Utes were taking no chances. Besides, the legislature would not reconvene until after the next election, and the only hope the Utes had of voting in 1956 was to challenge the law immediately.[16]

Students at the Intermountain Indian School, a federal boarding school in Brigham City, pledge allegiance to the United States, n.d. Utah officials denied the full benefits of U.S. citizenship to American Indians residing on reservations.

McKinley and the Ute Tribal Committee sought the most auspicious test case possible; their case would be strengthened if a mixed-blood Indian who had recently been excluded from the tribal roll—someone who had already embarked on the legal road toward assimilation—challenged the 1898 law. Preston Allen, a forty-one-year-old mixed-blood (one-eighth Indian) Uintah Ute rancher and farmer residing in a log cabin in Altonah, fit the criteria to a tee. Born in 1913 and educated in Indian boarding schools, Allen had risen to the rank of sergeant during World War II in Burma, where he served as a cook in a quartermaster detachment. After he returned from Asia in 1948, Allen leased 120 acres of pinyon and juniper forest from the tribe near the base of the Uinta Mountains in Altonah, where he built a log home and raised beef cattle. He had been drawn into politics through the termination process. He had served on the Altonah planning board and as a delegate to the tribal planning board. In April 1956, Allen campaigned for a seat on the board of directors of the AUC, the organization that would manage and distribute the mixed bloods' share of tribal assets following termination. Allen told voters that the mixed bloods needed articulate and savvy men like him, "men who can understand and plan for these things, qualified representatives who can deal with the full-blood group, government and state officials." After Allen was elected to the board, the other four members designated him as the president.[17]

On September 8, the foundation for the test case was laid when Allen requested an absentee ballot for the upcoming primary election. Duchesne County Clerk Porter Merrill, refused his request, citing the attorney general's instructions. A native of the Uintah Basin and descendant of some of the first

The wedding of Antone Apparoo and Leah Root, Ute Indians, in Whiterocks, September 10, 1951, reflects the blend of old and new, traditional and contemporary, that characterized reservation life in the 1950s.

Mormon settlers there, Merrill was in his midfifties at the time. He apparently bore no personal malice toward Allen but felt bound to uphold the law. In a deposition, he explained that he could not legally give Allen a ballot "because he has stated to me that he lives on an Indian Reservation and did not establish a residence in any other precinct in the State of Utah prior to this time." Vernon Wash, a Ute, complained to the governor, though, that officials like Merrill did bear the Indians ill will. Wash alleged the Utes had been "intimidated and kept from registering [to vote] under the threat of prosecution."[18]

On September 21, attorneys sued the State of Utah on behalf of Allen "and other American Indians similarly situated" and asked the court to order election officials to permit Indians to vote. Salt Lake attorney John Boyden represented Allen and the Utes. Boyden was a Latter-day Saint bishop who considered himself a friend of the Indians and had cultivated business relations with several tribes. According to an article published in the *Deseret News* in 1951, learning about Indians and collecting their artifacts was "perhaps [Boyden's] most engrossing hobby." A prominent Democrat, Boyden had unsuccessfully sought the party's nomination for governor in 1956. From 1933 to 1946, he served as an assistant U.S. district attorney in Utah and became acquainted with tribal leaders. During that time, he also spent six weeks on the Navajo Reservation observing tribal courts and compiling a report on the court system for the Department of the Interior. For a decade, Boyden had represented the Utes in legal matters ranging from reservation boundaries and grazing rights to land claims (in conjunction with Ernest Wilkinson) and termination. At the time, "most" mixed bloods, including Allen, "thought well of him." Boyden arranged for the court to hear the case on October 8, well in advance of the election, so that plaintiffs would be able to vote if the law was overturned.[19]

Three days after Boyden filed suit on behalf of Allen, the NCAI's annual convention opened in Salt Lake City. In honor of that event and at the request of the Indian rights organization, Governor J. Bracken Lee proclaimed September 24–28 American Indian Week. Despite the governor's attempt to make the delegates feel welcome, in her opening address to the convention, Executive Director Helen L. Peterson, an Oglala Sioux, called attention to the underside of Utah politics, noting that Utah was the "only state where Indians are going to court for the right to vote." Later that day Boyden spoke to the delegates on the upcoming test case and charged that Utah's restriction on reservation Indians violated the Fifteenth Amendment.[20]

The complaint and class action lawsuit drafted and filed by Boyden on behalf of Allen and "others similarly situated" charged that Duchesne County's refusal to permit Allen to vote boiled down to "an arbitrary and discriminatory denial" of his constitutional rights. Under the terms of the Dawes Severalty Act of 1887, lands that had originally been part of the Uintah Reservation had been opened to white settlers, resulting in a checkerboard pattern of occupancy. Rather than applying the law to "certain white persons who reside on patented land and other land within the original Uintah Indian Reservation," Duchesne County had only barred Indians from voting. In the event that the Utah Supreme Court upheld Utah's residency qualifications for voting, Boyden asked that the law be applied evenly to prevent "any white person residing on non-Indian land within the former Uintah Indian Reservation from voting."[21]

On October 8, the Utah Supreme Court heard arguments from attorneys on both sides. Two assistant attorneys general, Walter Budge and K. Roger Bean, defended the statute. As the author of the state's brief, Bean contended that the law did not violate the Fifteenth Amendment because "the basis of the exclusion is federal control and not race or color." The law applied to anyone living on the reservation who had not previously lived elsewhere in the state. Reflecting concerns in the wake of the *Brown v. Board of Education* rulings of 1954 and 1955 that an activist U.S. Supreme Court was overturning discriminatory legislation and policies and usurping the authority of state legislators, Bean said he believed that "strong reasons impel us toward granting the vote to those who reside on Indian reservations" but insisted that the law should be modified by the legislature, not the courts.[22]

Arguing on behalf of the plaintiff, Boyden showed that the statute in question had been interpreted inconsistently by the state: one attorney general had ruled that the law did not apply to the Utes, while the current attorney general had contradicted that conclusion. The current interpretation betrayed the spirit of Utah's Constitution, which guaranteed voting rights to virtually all citizens. Boyden was joined by Robert W. Barker, a native of Ogden, a graduate of Georgetown University's Law Center, and a partner in Wilkinson's Washington, D.C., law firm. Responding to the argument that Indians did not deserve the benefits of state citizenship because they did not share the obligations of other citizens, Barker and Boyden pointed out that reservation Indians were "not exempt from state jurisdiction exercised within constitutional limits." They were subject to the draft the same as other citizens, paid estate taxes, paid taxes to the state on royalties they received for oil or gas exploration or mining, and were in some cases subject to state court jurisdiction. They were citizens of Utah and were directly affected by state law. The law violated the provisions of the Fifteenth Amendment by denying Indians the right to vote "on the sole ground that they have not resided elsewhere in the state." Theoretically the law might be color blind, but in practice it had been applied exclusively to Indians. If the court found the law valid, "equal protection and application of the law requires that white persons residing within the former reservation also be excluded from voting."[23]

The supreme court unanimously upheld Utah's law on October 25 and rejected the notion that the law was racially discriminatory. The court's rationale resembled that of white citizens' councils and state officials in the South, who used criteria other than race to purge thousands of blacks from voter-registration rolls. Justice J. Allan Crockett, a relative rookie with only five years' experience on the court, outlined the justices' rationale, first in a preliminary ruling and later in the court's final decision in mid-December. While Indians were citizens of the United States, the court noted that the right to vote was not an "absolute" right of citizens. State legislatures had long exercised their authority to impose "reasonable qualifications" upon prospective voters. Out of respect for the balance of powers between branches of government, Crockett and his peers preferred to "proceed with the utmost caution in reviewing legislative acts" and not overturn laws for which there "appear[ed] to be any reasonable basis for the requirements imposed by the statute."[24]

Boyden and Barker had argued that Indians were full-fledged citizens, but the Utah justices concluded that Indians differed significantly from other citizens. Indian tribes "retain[ed] a substantial degree of autonomy." They could draft and adopt constitutions; enact their own laws; tax their members; prohibit land sales; and negotiate with officials at the local, state and federal levels. They did not support government services to the same extent as property owners outside the reservation because they did not pay taxes on reservation lands or any personal property received from the federal government. Thus, they were not subject to the state to the same extent as other citizens, nor did they hold the same financial stake in state or local government as other citizens.[25]

By virtue of treaty obligations and entitlements, the court found, Indians also were wards of the federal government in ways that others were not. The Department of the Interior supervised their real estate and business transactions

ONE GOD   ONE NATION
ONE BROTHERHOOD

This entry by the Uinta Basin LDS Mission, Whiterocks and Randlett Branches, in the Vernal Pioneer Day Parade, expressed assimilationist ideals of unity under "one nation," ideals that broke down in the face of cultural prejudice, treaty rights, and tribal citizenship in the 1950s.

on reservations and endowed them with "paternalistic favors," including health care and education. Consequently, county and state regulations regarding sanitation, business licensing, education, and law enforcement "would not . . . concern" the Indians to the extent that they impacted other citizens. In short Indians "sustain a different relationship to the federal government than do other citizens." If federal officials desired to do so, they might use their relationship to leverage Indian voting.[26]

Indians on reservations were also isolated and poorly educated and therefore presumably had "much less interest in or concern with it [voting]" than others, the justices hypothesized. Most of them lived in isolated rural locations where they had "practically no access" to the news media or telephones. "A very high percentage" could not read or write, and many could not communicate in English. How could they exercise the franchise responsibly under such conditions?[27]

Reservation Indians in some counties comprised a sizable proportion of the population, and if they were permitted to vote, they might exercise "substantial control" over local government. This would be inappropriate, the justices thought, because Indians "had an extremely limited interest in" local government and "very little responsibility in providing financial support for it."[28]

The justices applauded and underscored the stance taken by the Utah legislature in 1955 calling for "an orderly termination of federal supervision over the persons and property of Indians to the end that Indians may become self-sustaining." Indians who desired to vote should move from the reservation and jettison the "paternalistic favors" of reservation life. As a property owner or renter off the reservation, the Indian would directly or indirectly pay taxes and become a full stakeholder in local and state government. Unless Indians were willing to take these steps, the state had no obligation to extend voting privileges to them.[29]

In adopting this position, the court placed the state of Utah within a long American tradition of eliciting desired behavior by making suffrage contingent upon reform. In Utah the Utah Commission had pursued the same policy in the nineteenth century when it had required prospective voters to swear that they were not polygamists. Commenting on the Utah court's ruling, Helen Peterson of the NCAI observed that the court had essentially required "Indians to break up their communities" by moving from the reservation to vote. Despite the justices' distinction between citizenship and suffrage, their ruling was "in direct contravention of the principle of self-government and the right to full political participation by a citizen." The ruling had deprived Indians of "a fundamental method of deciding group opinion in matters of common interest and concern."[30]

Newspapers in the Uinta Basin and Salt Lake City reported the court's ruling without any editorial comment. It failed to elicit any letters to the editor, either. Joseph Jorgensen, a college senior in Utah at the time who had developed an interest in Indian-white relations, later found it remarkable that the issue "did not cause a statewide furor." The apparent disinterest of most Utahns suggested that the civil-rights movement as applied to Indians had not yet made much headway in the state. This fact was particularly evident in the Uinta Basin with its large Indian population: in Duchesne County in 1953, a list of qualifications for Miss Duchesne County included the stipulation that all contestants must be "members of the white race."[31]

Ironically, the plaintiff, Preston Allen, was part of the mixed-blood community on the reservation undergoing the type of "termination of federal supervision" that the court advocated, yet he was still disenfranchised. Allen's attorney in Washington, Robert Barker, immediately prepared to appeal the state ruling to the U.S. Supreme Court. Barker charged that, while the law appeared to be color blind, its application was racist because "non-Indians residing within the exterior boundary of the reservation . . . are not being denied the right to vote." Barker argued that the ruling was "in conflict" with other recent U.S. Supreme Court decisions— specifically *Smith v. Allwright,* which had invalidated all-white primary elections—and that it also violated principles the Supreme Court had established in *Korematsu v. United States.* In that case, the Court had upheld Japanese relocation as a military necessity but had cautioned that "all legal restrictions which curtail the civil rights of a single racial group are immediately suspect." Barker also noted that the Utah court's ruling clashed with that of the federal district court in *Trujillo v. Garley*, the legal decision that had overturned New Mexico's ban on Indian voting.[32]

With the election fast approaching, Barker asked the justices in Washington to order Duchesne County officials to permit Indians to register and vote. If this could not be done, "the ballots cast by all persons, Indian and non-Indian, who do not meet the eligibility requirements" with regard to residency would be held in reserve, along with a final announcement of election results, until the appeal had been heard and a decision rendered. On Monday, November 5, the day before the election, the U.S. Supreme Court agreed to hear the case but refused to impound election returns or dictate to local officials. Indian voters on reservations in the state, estimated by Barker to be between seven hundred and a thousand, had lost their voice in the 1956 election.[33]

Rather than celebrating the high court's agreement to hear the case, Barker appealed to the state to settle the matter outside of court. Back in September, after learning of Preston Allen's lawsuit, Frederick M. Haverland, area director of the Bureau of Indian Affairs in Phoenix, had written to Utah's governor, J. Bracken Lee, requesting information on "any plans your office has that are designed to adjust this situation." Haverland and his assimilationist associates in the BIA were "most anxious to have our Indians assume the responsibilities that devolve upon non-Indians," including "the duty to vote." Lee had informed Haverland that his term as governor was ending shortly, but he said he was "sure" the law would be "taken care of" when the legislature reconvened in January. Having seen a copy of the governor's letter, Barker quoted from it in a letter of his own addressed to Utah Attorney General E.R. Callister on November 21: "It seems to me that from the point of view of judicial and public administration that it may be desirable to solve this matter by eradicating the discrimination against Indians residing on Indian reservations by appropriate legislation," Barker advised. As a result, both parties could avoid the labor and expense of "further briefs, arguments and opinions before the courts." If Utah was interested in settling the matter out of court, Barker recommended, it might be best for the Utah Supreme Court to save face and delay issuing a final opinion in Allen's case until after the next legislative session.[34]

The court chose not to wait; a month before the legislature convened, the justices reiterated the position they had taken in their preliminary opinion by issuing a final decision. But in January, the legislature proceeded as Barker had advised and quietly amended the statute in question—so quietly and quickly that the Utah press did not even report the action. The amendment rendered the case moot, so Barker petitioned the U.S. Supreme Court to remove the case from its docket on April 4. The Court acquiesced later that month.[35]

Utah's most blatant discrimination against Indians at the polls had quietly vanished, but as civil rights activists discovered in the nation at large, it was simpler to change laws than alter attitudes. The underlying perception that reservation Indians are not full-fledged stakeholders in local government endured.

Acting upon that perception, politicos in counties with large Indian populations devised other means to circumscribe the Indian electorate. Nationally
"one of the most pervasive techniques" for negating the Indian vote was gerrymandering—and Utah was no exception. This practice persisted in some counties for decades. Although Navajos comprised more than half of the population
of San Juan County, for instance, election districts were drawn in such a way
that a Navajo was never elected to the county commission until 1984, when the
Department of Justice forced county officials to redraw election-district boundaries. Even then the boundaries were redrawn so that only one election district
had a Navajo majority. Disputes over county-level funding arising from reservation Indians' exemption from property taxes led to proposals in the 1990s to
divide San Juan County into a primarily Navajo southern county and a mainly
Anglo northern one.[36]

It was no accident that Utahns dusted off an outmoded statute in 1956,
an era when their elected representative in the U.S. Senate, Arthur Watkins,
was the most visible advocate of termination on Capitol Hill. Support for termination fed upon many Americans' resentment of the separation of Indians
from the rest of America, a separation that many attributed to Indians' tribal
citizenship, trust relationship with the federal government, and immunity
from taxation on reservation lands. Utah officials withheld voting privileges
in 1956 as a means of making a statement about the separateness of Indians
and indirectly advocating termination. The Utah Supreme Court's final decision withheld suffrage as a bargaining chip that might make termination more
attractive to the Utes.

Outside of Duchesne, Uintah, and San Juan Counties, reservation Indians'
exemption from taxes or dual citizenship mattered little to most Utahns. But
neither did their voting rights. The failure of the issue of Indian voting rights
to engage Utahns and galvanize demands for civil rights is silent evidence of
the complacency of most Utah residents in the 1950s in racial justice matters. As one reader of the *Deseret News* noted in a letter to the editor in 1956,
Germany and Japan were being rebuilt with American tax dollars, while
America was neglecting its own underclass: "When we conquered the Indians
what did we get? We took their lands. We killed the game, thereby eliminating their way of making a living." Americans had prospered on Indian lands.
But in their "modern enlightenment" and concern for fairness and economic
recovery around the world, they had conveniently forgotten the economic and
legal plight of the Indians.[37]

NOTES

1.   Glenn A. Phelps, "Mr. Gerry Goes to Arizona: Electoral Geography and Voting Rights
       in Navajo Country," *American Indian Culture and Research Journal* 15 (1991): 66;
       Daniel McCool, "Indian Voting," in *American Indian Policy in the Twentieth Century*,
       ed. Vine Deloria Jr. (Norman: University of Oklahoma Press, 1985), 105–16; Phelps,

"Representation without Taxation: Citizenship and Suffrage in Indian Country," *American Indian Quarterly* (Spring 1985): 136.

2.   McCool, "Indian Voting," 105–16.

3.   Ibid., 108.

4.   Jere Franco, "Empowering the World War II Native American Veteran: Postwar Civil Rights," *Wicazo Sa Review* 9 (Spring 1993): 33; Vine Deloria Jr. and Cliff Lytle, *American Indians, American Justice* (Austin: University of Texas Press, 1983), 224–25; Thomas G. Alexander, *Utah, the Right Place: The Official Centennial History,* rev. ed. (Salt Lake City: Gibbs Smith, 2003), 390; Richard D. Poll, Thomas G. Alexander, Eugene E. Campbell, and David E. Miller, eds., *Utah's History* (Provo, UT: Brigham Young University Press, 1978); Dean L. May, *Utah: A People's History* (Salt Lake City: University of Utah Press, 1987); Charles S. Peterson, *Utah: A History* (New York: W.W. Norton, 1984).

5.   Nancy Maryboy and David Begay, "The Navajos," in *A History of Utah's American Indians,* ed. Forrest S. Cuch (Salt Lake City: Utah Division of Indian Affairs, 2000), 296; Martha C. Knack, *Boundaries Between: The Southern Paiutes, 1775–1995* (Lincoln: University of Nebraska Press, 2001), 211; Joseph G. Jorgensen, *The Sun Dance Religion: Power for the Powerless* (Chicago: University of Chicago Press, 1972), 3, 135. A contemporary discussion of the constitutional ramifications of Utah's law is John H. Allen, "Denial of Voting Rights to Reservation Indians," *Utah Law Review* 5 (1956–57):247–56. Valuable histories of the Utes, including Fred A. Conetah, *A History of the Northern Ute People* (Salt Lake City: Uintah-Ouray Ute Tribe, 1982); Virginia McConnell Simmons, *The Ute Indians of Utah, Colorado, and New Mexico* (Boulder: University Press of Colorado, 2000); Parker M. Nielson, *The Dispossessed: Cultural Genocide of the Mixed-Blood Utes, An Advocate's Chronicle* (Norman: University of Oklahoma Press, 1998); and R. Warren Metcalf, *Termination's Legacy: The Discarded Indians of Utah* (Lincoln: University of Nebraska Press, 2002), do not mention the matter. Neither does Robert W. McPherson, *Navajo Land, Navajo Culture: The Utah Experience in the Twentieth Century* (Norman: University of Oklahoma Press, 2001); nor Peter Iverson, *The Navajo Nation* (Westport, CT: Greenwood Press, 1981). The law likely prevented few Navajos who otherwise would have voted from doing so. Iverson notes that it was not until the 1970s that Navajo voter registration rose rapidly. Navajos began to register in greater numbers at that time because they desired to influence local school boards. Ibid., 172. John Bluth, "Confrontation with an Arid Land: The Incursion of Gosiutes and Whites into Utah's Central West Desert, 1800–1978" (PhD diss., Brigham Young University, 1978); and Steven J. Crum, *The Road on Which We Came: A History of the Western Shoshone* (Salt Lake City: University of Utah Press, 1994), 69, do not discuss the Utah law, either. The Northern Shoshoni had no reservation in Utah, so the law did not apply to them. Thus, not surprisingly, the statute is not mentioned in Brigham D. Madsen, *The Northern Shoshoni* (Caldwell, ID: Caxton Printers, 1980).

6.   Simmons, *The Ute Indians of Utah,* 221–39; David Rich Lewis, *Neither Wolf Nor Dog: American Indians, Environment and Agrarian Change* (New York: Oxford

University Press, 1994), 53–59; Francis Paul Prucha, *The Great Father: The United States Government and the American Indians,* abridged edition (Lincoln: University of Nebraska Press, 1986), 226, 272–73.

7.   Crum, *The Road on Which We Came,* 69; David L. Wood, "Gosiute-Shoshone Draft Resistance, 1917–18," *Utah Historical Quarterly* 49 (1981): 173–88; Richard N. Ellis, "'Indians at Ibapah in Revolt': Goshutes, the Draft and the Indian Bureau, 1917–1919," *Nevada Historical Society Quarterly* 19 (Fall 1976):163–70; *Report with Respect to the House Resolution Authorizing the Committee on Interior and Insular Affairs to Conduct an Investigation of the Bureau of Indian Affairs Pursuant to H.R. 89,* House Report 2680, 83rd Cong., 2d sess. (Washington, DC: GPO, 1954), 211.

8.   *Biennial Report of the Attorney General to the Governor of the State of Utah for the Biennial Period Ending June 30, 1942* ([Salt Lake City]: n.p., [1942]), 272–74; *Salt Lake Tribune,* October 26, 27, 1940; September 1, 1946; *Provo Daily Herald,* November 29, 1974; *Report with Respect to the House Resolution,* 149.

9.   *Biennial Report,* 273, 274; *Vernal Express,* October 24, 1940; *Salt Lake Tribune,* October 27, 1940; *Roosevelt Standard,* October 31, 1940.

10.   Deloria and Lytle, *American Indians, American Justice,* 18; Nielson, *The Dispossessed,* 60.

11.   Metcalf, *Termination's Legacy,* 58, 126, 146, 149, 154–56, 168, 180, 204.

12.   E.R. Callister and K. Roger Bean to Lamont F. Toronto, March 23, 1956, box 17, folder 3, Parker Nielson Papers, Special Collections, J. Willard Marriott Library, University of Utah, Salt Lake City; K. Roger Bean, interview by author, April 10, 2006.

13.   *Uintah Basin Record,* April 5, 1956; October 25, 1956; *Deseret News,* September 11, 1956.

14.   *Report with Respect to the House Resolution,* 229. Neither Callister's order nor Indian voting rights are mentioned in the fall of 1956 in newspapers printed in Tooele or San Juan Counties. On the entire Navajo Reservation in 1953, there were an estimated 25,550 Navajos of voting age of whom an estimated 3,000 were registered to vote. Ibid., 211. Most of the reservation population resided outside of Utah, though. According to the 1950 census, there were only 1,807 Navajos in San Juan County, including children. U.S. Bureau of the Census, *Census of Population Taken in the Year 1950,* vol. 2., *Characteristics of the Population,* pt. 44, "Utah" (Washington, DC: GPO, 1952), 61. With no more than 1,000 Navajos of voting age residing in Utah, it is unlikely that many more than 100 were registered to vote. The order did not apply to the Paiutes, who were undergoing termination, or to the Northern Shoshoni, who had no government reservation in Utah. For a discussion of some of the reasons for low voter-registration rates on Indian reservations, see Jorgensen, *The Sun Dance Religion,* 135–41.

15.   *Deseret News,* September 26, 1956.

16.   Thomas W. Cowger, *The National Congress of American Indians: The Founding Years* (Lincoln: University of Nebraska Press, 1999); Peter Iverson, "Building toward Self-Determination: Plains and Southwestern Indians in the 1940s and 1950s," *Western*

Historical Quarterly* 16 (April 1985): 165–66; *Deseret News,* September 24, 1956; *Uintah Basin Record,* September 20, 1956.

17. Nielson, *The Dispossessed,* 45, 48, 51, 65, 76; *Allen v. Merrell,* "Brief of Plaintiff," (1956), case no. 8589, 2–3, Utah Supreme Court Library, Salt Lake City; *Allen v. Merrell,* "Complaint for Mandatory Order," 2–3, AUC 650a, box 17, folder 3, Nielson Papers; "Final Role [*sic*]— Mixed Blood," n.d., box 7, folder 20, Nielson Papers.

18. *Allen v. Merrell,* "Complaint for Mandatory Order," 4–5; *Deseret News,* September 11, 24 1956; Vernon Wash to J. Bracken Lee, October 31, 1956, box 44, folder 9, reel 36, J. Bracken Lee Papers, Utah State Archives, Salt Lake City.

19. *Allen v. Merrell,* "Complaint for Mandatory Order," 1; John S. Boyden, Orpha Amanda Sweeten Boyden, John Sterling Boyden, Jr., Stephen George Boyden, Carmen Sweeten Boyden Pingree, Paul Walter Boyden, *Three Score and Ten in Retrospect* (Cedar City: Southern Utah State College Press, 1986), 1–2, 22–26, 31, 34–36, 46–49, 52–53, 115, 136–38, 162, 164–75; Metcalf, *Termination's Legacy,* 169; *Uintah Basin Record,* September 20, 1956; *Salt Lake Tribune,* September 22, 1956. Many of the mixed-blood Utes, including Allen, later came to resent Boyden for his role in divesting them of much of their land. See Nielson, *The Dispossessed,* 133–39.

20. J. Bracken Lee to Rex O. Curry, September 6, 1956, box 44, folder 9, reel 36, series 211, Lee Papers; "Court Agrees to Hear Vote Case on Indians," *Deseret News,* September 24, 1956; "Delegates Told Indians May Hold Vote Key," *Deseret News,* September 25, 1956.

21. *Allen v. Merrell,* "Complaint for Mandatory Order," 2, 5, 7–8, 10.

22. *Allen v. Merrell,* "Brief of Defendant," 8, 11.

23. *Allen v. Merrell,* "Brief of Plaintiff" 4, 7, 30; W. Dee Halverson and Micah J. Halverson, *The Life and Times of Robert W. Barker* (Salt Lake City: Heritage Associates, n.d.), 165–79.

24. *Vernal Express,* November 1, 1956; *Deseret News,* October 25, 1956; December 9, 1956; November 10, 1994; *Salt Lake Tribune,* December 16, 1956; *Allen v. Merrell, Pacific Reporter* (Supreme Court of Utah, December 15, 1956), Pacific Reporter, vol. 305, 2d series, (St. Paul, MN: West Publishing Co., 1957), 490–95.

25. *Allen v. Merrell,* (Supreme Court of Utah).

26. Ibid.

27. Ibid.

28. Ibid.

29. Ibid.

30. Poll et al., *Utah's History,* 259–61; Helen L. Peterson, "American Indian Political Participation," *Annals of the American Academy of Political and Social Science* 311 (1957):122.

31. *Vernal Express,* December 20, 1956; *Deseret News,* December 9, 1956; *Salt Lake Tribune,* December 16, 1956; Jorgensen, *The Sun Dance Religion,* 3; *Report with Respect to the House Resolution,* 434.

32. *Allen v. Merrell,* (Supreme Court of Utah), 493; *Korematsu v. United States,* December 18, 1944, available online at http://www.tourolaw.edu/patch/Korematsu/; *Allen v. Merrell,* "Petitioner's Motion for Immediate Consideration," box 17, folder 3, Nielson Papers.

33. *Deseret News,* October 26, 1956; *Salt Lake Tribune,* November 6, 1956.

34. F.M. Haverland to J. Bracken Lee, September 13, 1956, box 44, folder 9, reel 36, Lee Papers; Robert W. Barker to E.R. Callister, November 21, 1956, box 17, folder 9, Nielson Papers.

35. *Laws of the State of Utah, 1957, Passed at the Regular Session of the Thirty-Second Legislature* (Salt Lake City: State of Utah, 1957), 89–90; *Allen V. Merrell,* "Petitioner's Motion to Vacate Judgment," box 17, folder 3, Nielson Papers; Walter Wyatt, *Cases Adjudged in the Supreme Court at October Term, 1956,* United States Reports, vol. 353 (Washington, DC: GPO, 1957), 932.

36. McCool, "Indian Voting," 115–16; *Deseret News,* July 28, 1996. Many of the same debates regarding political participation and provision of governmental services to Indians who are exempt from county property taxes continue to reverberate in San Juan County. See McPherson, *Navajo Land, Navajo Culture,* 226–29.

37. *Deseret News,* September 7, 1956.

11

"We are not seeking trouble and so will just go along quietly just now"

The IWW's 1913 Free-Speech Fight in Salt Lake City

John S. McCormick and John R. Sillito

In the late-twentieth and early twenty-first centuries, Utah was one of the most Republican and conservative states in the country. As John S. McCormick and John R. Sillito, historians of socialism in Utah, note, however, Utah also has a rich radical tradition. It was not just a place where Joe Hill, the Industrial Workers of the World (IWW), or Wobbly, organizer, was executed in 1915. It was also a place where the Socialist Party thrived, and where in the early twentieth century, the IWW led both strikes and free speech fights. As this chapter makes clear, responses in 1913 to the IWW's demand for the right to hold public rallies in Salt Lake City included the contention that the public expression of radical ideas and beliefs should be suppressed and thereby the right of free speech should be abridged. McCormick and Sillito carefully detail the events and conflicts between the IWW and Salt Lake City police, governmental authorities, and even private citizens. Their study raises the question whether it is ever acceptable for a minority message to be silenced by majority violence and intolerance.

On the evening of August 12, 1913, a dozen men broke up an Industrial Workers of the World (IWW) street meeting in downtown Salt Lake City. It was not a spontaneous act but one they had planned in advance. "Wobblies" were radical critics of the existing economic and political system who indicted capitalism for its exploitation of workers and called for its replacement with a fundamentally different system. The preamble of their constitution clearly expressed their point of view: that it was the "historic mission of the working class to do away with capitalism." "The working class and the employing class

263

have nothing in common," it said. "Between these two classes a struggle must go on until the workers of the world organize as a class, take possession of the means of production, and abolish the wage system. . . ."[1]

In the view of the men who disrupted the meeting, people who held such views had no right to speak in public and should be suppressed when they tried. For Axel H. Steele, the leader of the group, Wobblies were a "horde of traitorous un-American foreigners" whose beliefs "highly" offended him, and he and the others had a perfect right to disrupt their meeting, "tear down their banner and place the Stars and Stripes on the stand" in its place. Indeed, he said, no one "with an ounce of manhood" could have tolerated their speeches.[2] Salt Lake City police arrested eight Wobblies, but neither Steele nor any of the others who had planned and carried out the attack were taken into custody. City authorities then prohibited all future IWW street meetings; proclaimed that anyone who tried to organize, speak at, or attend such meetings would be subject to arrest; and said that any Wobbly who came to Salt Lake in the future would either be forced to leave or arrested and confined to jail for six months on a diet of "salt water."[3]

The disruption of the IWW street meeting that summer was not an isolated incident but just one of a series of "free-speech fights" in Salt Lake City between 1909 and 1913 involving socialists, Wobblies, labor-union members, and others. Though most were peaceful, some triggered violence. Such events were, in turn, common throughout the United States at the time, part of the emergence of a significant radical movement and its commitment to an ongoing struggle over the meaning of the U.S. Constitution's First Amendment right of free speech and assembly in public places. What restrictions might legitimately be placed on it, including which individuals and groups were entitled to speak, what conditions limited them, and who had the right to decide?[4] The question at issue was not merely what *words,* but what *radical words,* if any, would be allowed.

By the early twentieth century, as historian and playwright Barrie Stavis says, "The open-air street meeting . . . was an important part of life in the United States. In towns and cities, large and small, religious, social and political organizations used the street-corner soapbox to attract and propagandize the passerby."[5] This was as true of Utah cities as any in the country. According to the *Salt Lake Tribune,* for example, Salt Lake had its "full quota" of "street singers, street preachers, and street corner orators," with the "festive socialist" usually following the "religious enthusiasts."[6]

Indeed, political radicals of all stripes regularly used outdoor public spaces in Salt Lake, including street corners and city parks, for speeches, discussions, and meetings, typically attracting hundreds and, on occasion, thousands of people. They felt it was crucial that they did so. They relied on street speaking—though not on it alone—to spread their message, and they felt their success depended to a considerable extent on not only their right to speak but their ability to do it where they could reach people who might not otherwise hear them. More to the point, they thought it essential to gather in the most visible locations in the center of downtown, where they could not only reach poor people, ordinary workers, and disenfranchised groups, hoping to build both solidarity and political power, but also confront "respectable" citizens, both those of modest circumstances and the more privileged, about the fact and cause of poverty and deprivation in a way that would transform the poor, ordinary worker from a symbol of irresponsibility or moral deprivation into an indictment of the capitalist economy and its exploitation of workers.

Open-air speakers were always subject to regulation, but in the early twentieth century, Salt Lake City officials, in common with those throughout the United States, decided to control not merely public speech, but especially radical public speech, more thoroughly than they had in the past. While they had always been more sympathetic to the claims of certain groups, like the Salvation Army, to free speech and the unrestricted use of public spaces than to the rights of radicals, they had already begun to attempt to discourage radical speech by selectively enforcing existing ordinances; arresting speakers on a variety of misdemeanor charges, including vagrancy, disturbing the peace, blocking the sidewalks and entrances to buildings, obstructing traffic, or "loafing;" or scheduling band concerts at the same time as, and adjacent to, socialist meetings in the hope that speakers and their audience would find the music too distracting.

As radical movements grew, however, and radical speakers became increasingly common, city officials adopted a new approach. They now decided that radical speech demanded regulation or prohibition in advance rather than waiting until meetings were under way and then gauging whether or not to step in. In Salt Lake City, new ordinances were enacted that required speaking permits from police and/or city officials, and they were then implemented in a way that disadvantaged radical speech. One required any individual or group that wanted to speak in public parks to obtain a permit from the city park commission. Another required permission from either the chief of police or the city commission for meetings on streets, sidewalks, or alleyways; allowed the city to set the time and place of these meetings; and stipulated penalties for those who either spoke at or attended meetings with no permit. After these regulations went into effect, Salt Lake radicals were typically allowed to speak only at locations outside the central business district, most often in the city's main—though not only—red light district, while other groups could speak on Main Street in the middle of the central business district, and religious groups were exempt altogether from the permit process.

These approaches were common throughout the United States at the time. Public officials argued that prohibiting certain kinds of speech—dangerous, libelous, offensive, vulgar, unpatriotic, too critical of government, or merely unpopular—was legitimate, and, they said, those were all characteristics of radical speech. Radicals responded that the First Amendment guaranteed them the right to assemble and speak and people had long used public space to gather, speak, petition various levels of government, publicize grievances, and protest. The courts should protect those activities, they argued; regulation and outright prohibition of speech were dangerous deviations from both the meaning of the First Amendment and basic American traditions; and a meaningful right to free speech required access to public space. Moreover, since government at all levels, in their view, was designed to protect private property and the interest of the capitalist class, local officials, judges, and police who sought to limit or prohibit street speaking were simply doing the bidding of business interests, for whom First Amendment protection essentially meant speech that did not offend capitalists or the government that supported them. In this debate, the argument that ultimately prevailed was the one for restriction. This led to a redefinition of public space that helped lay the groundwork for the well-known, and much-studied, restrictive legislation of World War I.

The August 12 street meeting in Salt Lake City was a direct result of a strike two months earlier by several thousand railroad workers, who were laying track over a distance of about twelve miles between the central Utah town of Tucker and Soldier Summit in Spanish Fork Canyon. Members of Salt Lake City's IWW Local 69 had successfully led the strike against the Utah Construction Company (UCC). Founded in 1900, the UCC was one of the state's most significant companies, and building rail lines throughout the western United States and Mexico was one of its major activities.[7] Strikers made a number of demands: a twenty-five-cent-per-day increase in pay to $2.75; a shorter working day of nine, rather than ten, hours; abolition of the company practice of paying workers with checks and then assigning a company agent to cash them at a discount; improved bathing and laundry facilities; free bunks and bedding; and, since UCC had no hospital at Tucker, abolition of monthly hospital fees.

UCC President William H. Wattis maintained that working conditions for company workers were not as bad as strikers claimed; blamed the strike on Wobbly "agitators," asserting that "until this IWW agitation" most workers had had no complaints; and threatened to fire all workers unless they returned to work. Wattis felt that not only were the strikers' demands unreasonable, but an important principle was at stake: the right of owners to control their property and operate their company without interference from workers. He particularly did not want to give in to demands from a radical group, feeling it would set a dangerous precedent and only encourage further radicalism and union activity.[8]

Thus, A.H. Christensen, the UCC official in charge of the Tucker project, refused to meet with strikers, accept their written demands, or even acknowledge their right to present them.[9] However, after the strike had gone on for two weeks with no end in sight, the company agreed to raise pay by the demanded amount and improve sanitary conditions, including providing beds and blankets for the workers. They did not meet the strikers' other demands, and the

Utah Construction Company President William H. Wattis defended working conditions at Tucker, and blamed IWW "agitators" for the strike. He not only believed the strikers demands were unreasonable, but thought they challenged the right of owners to control their property and operate their company without interference from workers.

work day continued to be ten hours. The main reason UCC officials agreed to the strikers' demands was because Denver and Rio Grande Western Railroad trainmen refused to allow workers to ride the line unless they either had IWW cards or could produce a pass from the strike committee. On June 24, with some of their demands met, the workers ended the strike and returned to work.

In the July 3, 1913 issue of its national publication, *Solidarity,* the IWW declared the Tucker strike a clear victory for the union and proof of the value of "direct action" in the war against capitalism. According to Ed Rowan, secretary of Local 69, it was "plain to see what organization can do when carried on with up-to-date methods as expressed in the principles of industrial unionism." He pledged the IWW would continue its organizing work in spite of the "avowed intention" of the company to oppose it; predicted the workers would prevail no matter what the UCC did; and said the union "proposes to keep on wringing concessions right along with the final abolition of the peonage system as our goal."[10]

Rowan and E. A. Smith—who constituted the local's press committee—further asserted that the IWW's victory at Tucker had "torn the mask off their lying countenances. The moment the workers organize for material benefits on the job, not a stone is left unturned to use any means violent or otherwise to thwart them . . . profit is a serious proposition to tamper with. The masters never forgive or forget any action tending to reduce their bank rolls."[11]

According to historian Philip Foner, years later a member of the strike committee recalled that after the strikers' victory, a company official had said, "You
IWWs caught us with our pants down this time, but I can assure you that
before the end of a year every damn single IWW will be run out of the state of
Utah." Indeed, Foner says, a "well-organized assault" against the union followed
the victory at Tucker.[12]

Before the strike was settled, however, and in an ultimately unsuccessful
effort to break it, the UCC sent fifty men to its construction camps under the
direction of a well-known strikebreaker, Axel H. Steele. A Salt Lake City police
officer since 1893, Steele had also worked previously as a strikebreaker for a
number of Utah companies. The *Salt Lake Tribune* described him as a "prominent figure" in many Utah strikes as a sworn deputy sheriff of five Utah counties that had experienced labor troubles during recent years.[13] Most recently
Steele had led the Utah Copper Company's private police force during a strike
led by the Western Federation of Miners (WFM) at Bingham in September
1912. The strike had lasted for several weeks before the company had broken
it, "not merely with superior financial resources," as historian Gunther Peck
says, but by successfully pitting workers against each other, both native born
against immigrant and immigrant against immigrant.[14] Several months before
that, in May 1912, Steele had successfully led the American Smelting and
Refining Company's (ASARCO) private police force against striking workers
at its Murray smelter.

Steele elicited strong responses from the opposition, both at the time and
later. Wobbly leaders called him a "notorious scabherder."[15] Similarly Franklin
Rosemont, a historian of the IWW, characterized him as a "gunman, thug,
union-buster, and a prime example of what passed for 'law enforcement' in
Utah in the 1910s." In Rosemont's view, Steele was a highly paid "hoodlum,"
valued by "the mine-owners and other corporations for his strikebreaking and
violence against union organizers," who was allowed to "commit the most nau-
seating crimes not only with impunity, but with the warm encouragement and
support of the 'better classes' and the State."[16] For his part, Steele said of himself, "I have lived just as near right as I knew how. I never wronged a man that I
know of, and I have no fear as to what is coming to me on the other side."[17]

Steele's orders from the UCC were to remove the strike leaders from the
job site. According to historian Allan Kent Powell, company officials were anxious to do that for two reasons. First, they feared sabotage against company
property. Second, with the "agitators" and their sympathizers gone, it would be
much easier to bring in new men willing to work under the conditions that had
existed before the strike. Thus, as Powell reports, on June 11, three days after
the strike began, Utah County Sheriff Henry East, his deputies, and Steele and
the men working for him as special agents of the company began forcing workers to leave the camps. They "rounded up 128 men at Tucker, loaded them into
railroad passenger coaches, and started for Provo. As the train approached other

construction camps, it stopped, and the deputy sheriffs invited other strikers to board the train." If they refused, deputies fired warning shots over their heads.[18] Over the next few days, East and Steele removed nearly three hundred strikers from the camps. Most were taken by train to Salt Lake City and released on the outskirts of town.

In addition to those men forced to leave the camps and others who were harassed, Sheriff East arrested sixteen men, those the company regarded as the principal agitators and troublemakers, including James F. Morgan, whom the *Provo Herald* described as an IWW "spellbinder," Ed Rowan, L. Weaver, A.C. Ridgeway, A.J. Rice, George McCue, Frank Duffy, Frank Eubanks, and Frank Rice. Charged with disturbing the peace, inciting a riot, threatening men who wanted to continue to work, and destroying property belonging to the UCC, they pleaded not guilty and asked for separate jury trials—a common IWW tactic designed to clog the justice system. Ultimately they were found guilty and given sentences ranging from sixty to seventy-five days in the Utah County jail in Provo.[19]

Two of the most interesting cases involved Ridgeway and Morgan. When Ridgeway was brought before the judge, he admitted that he had tried to convince workers to go on strike and declared that "some day there would be enough of his way of thinking in the country so that he might be sitting in the prosecuting attorney's chair."[20] On the other hand, at his trial Morgan said the IWW had sent him to Tucker to recruit members, not to organize a strike, and workers had initiated the walkout on their own. Originally a mining engineer, he had been "blackballed," he said, and now sought to make his living as an "ordinary worker." Morgan also denied that, as a Wobbly, he counseled violence; on the contrary, he said that he supported peaceful means of effecting change.[21]

While the men were serving their time in jail, rumors circulated that hundreds of Wobblies were on their way to Provo to hold protest meetings and rallies and demand their release. The local organizer was said to be Jacob Gease. He and his brother, Henry, were both active socialists and small businessmen, owning and operating a Provo cigar factory and selling their cigars, among them the "Provo Girl" and the "Little Socialist," throughout the state. After Morgan and the others were released from the county jail in August, they traveled to Salt Lake City and organized the August 12 meeting, where they planned to denounce the role of Steele and his company deputies in the Tucker strike and recruit new members into the union. In organizing the meeting, they deliberately violated a recently adopted city ordinance by refusing to apply for a permit from the city commission. Wobblies typically began their meetings with a song, and they opened this one with Joe Hill's new song, "Mr. Block." It had been published several months earlier in the IWW's *Little Red Songbook*. The *Salt Lake Tribune* printed the chorus of "Mr. Block," sung to the tune of "It Looks to Me Like a Big Time Tonight": "Oh, Mister Block, you were born by mistake, you take the cake, you make me ache. Tie a rock on your block and then jump in the lake. Kindly do that for Liberty's sake."[22]

As Hill portrayed him in the song, Mr. Block was a worker not ready either to accept or act upon his class position, and as a result, his life was one error after another. The song expressed the IWW's humor, its passionate opposition to the capitalistic system, and, as Barrie Stavis says, its vision of a future society "without exploitation, bosses, policemen, or jails."[23] Some IWW songs, Stavis points out, were written to meet the needs of a specific situation, often by a direct participant. In contrast, "Mr. Block" was a "teaching" song, "designed to strip away false and romantic notions of the way the world operated and set in their place more real understanding" and offer the IWW's solution to the ills of the world.[24]

Following the singing of "Mr. Block," Morgan mounted the platform, from which the IWW banner hung, and began to speak, denouncing, according to the *Salt Lake Tribune,* "the American government, the Stars and Stripes," and the "guards of corporate interests." In doing so, he later said, he was "speaking for the working man." After he had been holding forth for only a few minutes, Steele and more than a dozen of the men who had been with him at Tucker, including A.C. Coray, whose job it had been to recruit strikebreakers; Thomas D. Price, "one of the nerviest men in Utah;" and a bartender named Fred J. Clifford, charged the platform, tore down the IWW banner, unfurled an American flag, dragged Morgan from the speaker's stand, and began beating him.[25] Later, Steele said that, after learning of the planned meeting, he and his men had decided to disrupt it by attacking speakers and audience members alike. Gathering in the Du Nord Saloon across the street from the meeting site, they had drawn lots "for the privilege of striking Morgan first and decided on a signal—the waving of the American flag by Steele—to begin the attack."[26]

According to Morgan, "I started my speech by saying that I had no apology to make to Axel Steele or any of his thugs, but that if I thought it possible to convert Steele to the right cause, I would walk up and embrace him with every touch of fraternity, friendship, and love." Waving an American flag, Steele then approached; shouted, "Get him"; struck Morgan with a club; and directed some of those who were with him to shoot "now or never." One of them pulled Morgan from the soapbox, wrestled him to the sidewalk, and kicked him in the face. As soon as he could, Morgan remounted the soapbox and resumed speaking—pausing every few minutes to wipe the blood from his face—and saying that "if Axel Steele and any of his crowd hope to still my voice they would have to spatter my heart's blood on every inch of the street."[27]

At this point, fighting broke out between Steele and his men and members of the audience. Wobbly Thomas Murphy drew a gun and fired—in self-defense, he said—at four of his assailants, slightly wounding one of Steele's men, Fred J. Clifford, in the leg. Murphy was later prosecuted and convicted on a charge of assault with intent to commit murder. When the police arrived,

Deseret News, August 13, 1913.

The IWW Logo. After Wobbly James Morgan denounced the defenders of "corporate interests," Axel Steele and a dozen others tore down Local 69's banner and replaced it with the American flag.

Steele again pulled Morgan from the platform and forced him into a squad car. Another Wobbly, Harry "Haywire Mac" McClintock,[28] then climbed onto the platform and tried to continue the meeting, but police forced him to stop and arrested him and other Wobblies, including Tom Murphy, Jack Gillon, Otto A. Tresen, Roy Cotton, Frank Jerome, and Fred Grof.

After police had taken them away, Steele led the crowd, which by this time had grown to perhaps two thousand people, in "three cheers for the American flag." Shouting over the din of the crowd, he asked, "Where are some of those people who do not stand for the American flag? Show them to me. Let some of them speak up. I'll show them. They . . . can't trample on the American flag while I am here."[29] He also announced his intention, "with the aid of my friends, to disrupt every public meeting the IWWs start in this city" and said breaking up the meeting was "entirely within my power, as an officer of the law."[30] After Steele's speech, police sought unsuccessfully to disperse the crowd. Only after the fire department arrived and turned fire hoses on them did they leave. In the view of the *Salt Lake Tribune,* that method of breaking up crowds was entirely justified. "The right of the citizens to use the streets is absolute under ordinary conditions," the paper said, "but this right is subject to the public interest," and at times a fire hose was the "best, quickest, and least harmful way to disperse a crowd."[31]

McClintock was charged with violating the Salt Lake City ordinance requiring permission to speak at a street meeting. According to the ordinance, it was "unlawful" for any person to hold meetings, deliver any kind of speech, or take part in any debate in public without permission in writing from the board of commissioners.[32] The penalty was a fine of ten dollars or a day in the city jail "at labor" for every dollar of the fine unpaid. On August 18, McClintock entered a plea of not guilty before city Judge N.H. Tanner. William S. Dalton, former editor of the socialist newspaper, *The Crisis,* as well as a former assistant city attorney under the American Party administration and the IWW's attorney, represented McClintock and argued that the ordinance violated the constitutional right to free speech.[33] In response assistant city attorney William Folland contended that the ordinance was valid because its purpose was to prevent riots. McClintock's trial was set for September 2.

Morgan and Murphy were arraigned before Judge Tanner on August 14 and charged with assault with intent to commit murder and assault with a deadly weapon. At the arraignment, Police Chief Brigham F. Grant said he was fearful "a gang of IWWs" would pack the courtroom, and he stationed policemen outside it to prevent "any one who looks or acts like a Bohunk" from entering. According to the *Salt Lake Tribune,* a number of witnesses were ready to testify against Morgan and Murphy and would say Morgan's remarks about the United States government and the American flag were "repugnant."[34] Dalton represented Morgan and Murphy as he had McClintock. The men pleaded not guilty, and bail was set at a thousand dollars each. Lacking the money, they were held in the Salt Lake County jail. Morgan was released on August 18 after Mrs. Celia Florence and Mrs. W.H. Emms put up the bail.[35]

Charges were never filed against Steele or his companions. A committee, consisting of Wobblies Sam "Scottie" Scarlett and R.J. Horton, and George Meyers, who had been at the street meeting but was not a Wobbly, asked County Attorney I.E. Willey to issue a complaint against Steele, saying, "We want to see if there is any justice in the land and if there is any law that will give us protection from a man who deliberately incited and forced a riot." Meyers said he was only a bystander but had felt his life was jeopardized during the confrontation. He simply "wanted to have the law enforced against a person who was responsible for instigating such affairs," and he identified Steele as "the instigator of the trouble."[36] Willey refused to issue the complaint, saying he "would not require the arrest of a man for defending the American flag and for putting a stop to such abuses as were charged against Morgan, the IWW orator."[37]

County Sheriff Andrew Smith agreed with Willey, saying it was "preposterous" to presume that he or anyone else in authority would arrest Steele for his actions "when IWW speakers insulted the flag and used obscene language." Moreover, Sheriff Smith asserted, since Steele was "properly deputized," he "acted with full authority" when he sought to arrest someone who was "defaming the flag." Morgan was clearly "disobeying the law," and, in stopping him, Steele was simply "doing his duty."[38] Scarlett, Horton, and Meyers then met with Folland, who also refused to charge Steele, saying he saw no evidence Steele had violated any state or local law but was simply performing his official duty as a police officer.[39] At the same time, Mayor Samuel Park said future requests of the IWW, or "similar organizations," to hold street meetings would be denied, and he instructed Police Chief Grant to enforce the new speaking ordinance "to the letter" and "break up" meetings held without permission. In Grant's view, such a policy was entirely justified because "unpatriotic oratory" should not be allowed.[40]

For the next few nights, every member of the Salt Lake City Police Department was on "IWW duty." Under the direction of Inspector of Police Carl A. Carlson, "the streets were carefully guarded," gatherings were quickly broken up, and no person was allowed to stop long in one spot. Carlson assigned one squad to remain at police headquarters and stand ready for reported trouble, while another constantly patrolled downtown city streets. In addition, half a dozen deputy sheriffs "in plain clothes operated in the area." All that would continue, the *Salt Lake Tribune* said, "until the police are convinced that the IWW will make no further attempts to hold street meetings."[41]

Rumors began to spread that hundreds, or even thousands, of Wobblies were on their way to Salt Lake to hold street meetings in violation of city ordinances and conduct the kind of "free-speech fight" for which the IWW had become well known, but Chief Grant said he and his men were prepared. Not only had he instructed them to disperse the crowd if Wobblies tried to hold a street meeting and to arrest the speakers, but, in addition, any incoming Wobblies would be required to leave the city and arrested if they did not comply. According to the *Salt Lake Tribune,* Grant, "in a determined and emphatic manner," made it plain that police would regard incoming IWWs as "undesirables," saying that "if they attempt to come here as they did recently in Denver and other cities for the purpose of creating trouble and strife," prompt action would be taken, and "there will be many more 'industrious workers' on the chain gang which is building roads in City Creek Canyon."[42]

A mass meeting held Sunday, August 17 in Unity Hall protested the actions of police and city officials.[43] Five people spoke: Wobblies R.J. Horton, President of Local 69; Sam Scarlett, the local's secretary; and Franklin Riter; along with William S. Dalton, the local's attorney; and William Knerr, a Socialist Party candidate for the Salt Lake City Commission.[44] According to the *Salt Lake Tribune,* the speakers all "disclaimed violence as an object of the IWW, refuted any purported attack upon the American flag, and assailed . . . Steele as being the originator of the trouble at last Tuesday evening's street scene." Horton said the meeting was one of ordinary workers protesting "against violence and the high-handed methods employed by gunmen to break up peaceable street speaking." They simply wished to present their side of the story and called for "fair play" in being allowed to do so. He and other Wobblies had no fight with the American flag but were fighting for "bread and butter." Rather, it was Steele who "had dragged the flag in the dust to a greater extent than it had ever been dragged before."[45]

Knerr was the main speaker. A prominent socialist and labor-union leader, he told those in attendance that, while he had been introduced as a socialist, he was there as a "free thinker" to speak "in the name of freedom and liberty." Though he did not entirely agree with the IWW's point of view, he believed that no one had the right to organize a band of citizens and "use violence to break up their meetings. The law of these free United States gives us the right to believe and speak what we think is right. No law compels anyone to listen. Who gave Steele the right to take the law into his own hands and club Morgan?"[46]

Moreover, Knerr asserted, the police were clearly biased. If Steele had "gone to Chief Grant and sworn out a complaint," he said, "the latter would have been only too willing to arrest Morgan." Though Steele was a "lawbreaker," he was still at large and even honored, while Morgan, whom he had clubbed and kicked, was to be "railroaded" to the state prison.[47] "Are you going to make men love and respect the flag in that fashion?" Knerr asked the crowd. "My understanding of the flag is that it is an emblem of liberty. It stands as a warning to all that their rights will be protected and held sacred. When Steele used the flag as a signal to assault Morgan, as he said was his intention, he disgraced it worse than any IWW dared to do. His flag should be black with a skull and crossbones emblem, so people would know what to expect."[48]

Following Knerr's speech, audience members passed a resolution "condemning" Steele's actions in "breaking up the IWW meeting" and calling upon city authorities to hold a "fair and impartial investigation in order to fix the blame for the trouble"; they also took up a collection to help defend Morgan and the others as their cases came to trial.[49] At its annual convention a month later on September 23, 1913, the Utah State Federation of Labor—while noting its lack of sympathy with the IWW—passed a similar resolution supporting "free speech and individual liberty" and the "sacred right of the people to assemble peaceably at all times.[50] Asserting that Steele, "without cause and in disregard of all law, interrupted a peaceful meeting of workingmen at Salt Lake City, and conspired with other criminals for the purpose of starting a riot," the delegates demanded that he be prosecuted for "inciting a riot" and denounced him and all those who supported "his disregard of law and applaud his criminal conduct as an enemy of the working class."[51] On the other side of the issue, the E.A. Wedgwood Camp of the United Spanish War Veterans unanimously passed a resolution "deploring the action of the authorities in permitting the IWW agitators to use the streets for unpatriotic addresses" and promised at their next meeting to consider "the matter of public recognition of the actions of Axel Steele and others in resenting insults to the American flag."[52]

Salt Lake City's major newspapers all supported city officials and the police and uniformly condemned the IWW, both in general and for what happened at the meeting, arguing that the right to free speech was limited and IWW speakers could legitimately be prohibited on a number of grounds: they were seditious, unpatriotic, immoral, and, in addition, threatening to business interests. A *Deseret News* editorial asked the question, "Who is to blame for the riot at the IWW street meeting in this City?" Strictly speaking, it answered, Steele and the others had had no right to break up the meeting, but it was "understandable" why they had, and they should not be criticized or punished since the IWW was a "dangerous organization" and should not be allowed to say what it did. Furthermore, the paper editorialized,

> The IWWs are making trouble wherever they go. That is their very mission. They are revolutionists. They preach contempt for the flag, for property rights, for moral standards, and they consider organized government as tyranny, and their language is often coarse and vile. They should not be given the freedom of the streets of American cities for such doctrines. There is good reason for permitting the preachers of pure morals to address the people in the streets, but not for tolerating the appeals to the passions, in which the IWW speakers always revel.[53]

The *News* went on to say that, while "any illegal measure" against the IWW strengthened their cause, creating a "sympathy which they do not deserve, but which they are quick to turn to advantage," at the same time, the honor of Salt Lake City "demands that the law be upheld, and that every demonstration that partakes of the character of mob violence be put down." Regardless of the action other cities in the country took, "We must make it clear that here law reigns supreme."[54]

The *Salt Lake Herald-Republican* agreed with the *Deseret News* that the IWW was a dangerous organization whose members were irresponsible, lazy lawbreakers, and that, while Steele and others may have acted inappropriately, ultimately the IWW—a "ragbag army of discontent" composed of "migrant malcontents" who "mistakenly assume the world owes them a living and are determined to collect it with the maximum of disturbance and the minimum of effort"—was at fault. More seriously, the paper commented, "Riot, disorder, and contempt for law follow the entrance of their leaders into any community. Discord covers their operations like a cloud of evil; every decent citizen regards them as his own and his country's enemy." The IWW goal in holding the August 12 meeting was to "resist lawful processes" and incite a riot. When they did so, "Liberty had degenerated into license." Though free speech was an important right, it was limited. City authorities had taken the "proper stand;" the IWW should be prosecuted and prohibited from conducting future meetings; any Wobblies who came to Salt Lake City "should either be forced to leave or be jailed and made to labor on public works projects;" and Steele and the others should be commended for recognizing the danger the IWW posed and dealing with it, and in the future, similar actions by private citizens might be necessary.[55]

In the aftermath of the August 12 incident, the *Salt Lake Tribune* editorialized on three separate occasions, echoing the argument of the other papers that, while in the abstract Steele and his men had had no right to act as they had, ultimately the IWW was to blame for the disturbance because its rhetoric, in "provoking condemnation from loyal citizens," had "incited the riot." Under the First Amendment, people had wide latitude in what they said but only within the bounds of "decency and order," and the IWW had clearly gone too far. It was a dangerous, even a "treasonous," organization and was fast getting to be a universal menace to the public peace, a standing threat against the good order of the community everywhere. Thus, the city's decision to refuse to let the Wobblies meet was not only perfectly appropriate but necessary, and in the future, when any group applied for a speaking permit, it should be required to make clear not only where and when it wanted to speak but on what subject, and city officials would be within their rights to deny permits for speeches on certain topics.[56]

The IWW initially considered challenging the constitutionality of Salt Lake's street-speaking ordinance and filing lawsuits for damages against both Steele and the others who had attacked them and the city for failing to protect them. In Sam Scarlett's view, police had no right to prohibit IWW meetings; he noted that

> so long as any person or sect, say, take the Salvation Army, has the right to expound their religion on the streets, we have the right to discuss the present economic discontent that exists throughout the country. Last night's affair was deplorable, but it is something that was not altogether unexpected. Before we get through with this thing we expect to show some of these deputy sheriffs up in their true light. It was a premeditated attack.... The Constitution of the United States allows peaceful assemblages on the streets, and we, as citizens, propose to uphold the Constitution.[57]

Attorney Dalton said that, while the IWW "deeply regretted the riot of Tuesday night caused bloodshed" and had taken his advice to hold no more street meetings until the cases of Morgan and Murphy were settled, it intended to challenge the constitutionality of the city's ordinance,[58] and on August 18, he "filed a demurrer in the police court attacking the validity of the ordinance under which Harry McClintock was arrested." In Dalton's opinion, the city ordinance was in "direct conflict" with the Utah Constitution as well as the Constitution of the United States, neither of which gave cities the right to "enact such an ordinance."[59] As Dalton feared, however, the IWW's legal argument did not prevail, and the constitutionality of the ordinance was upheld.

Local 69 also thought seriously about bringing in Wobblies from other parts of the United States—hundreds and perhaps thousands—and staging a free-speech fight, as the IWW did throughout the country in at least thirty instances between 1907 and 1916, to challenge Salt Lake's prohibition of IWW speech making on the streets,[60] and Salt Lake City newspapers regularly reported that they were on their way. According to Sam Scarlett, Salt Lake was one of the "centers of power" for the IWW in such a demonstration because of its location. "It is a pivotal center of railroads and within a day or two we could bring thousands here from every direction. We can command, too, an unusually large number of men because of our proximity to the coast and northwestern states, where the organization is strong and where the right of free speech is demanded. I think there will be at least several thousand members of the IWW who will come if necessary to Salt Lake City."[61]

According to the *Salt Lake Tribune,* Wobblies were working to mobilize a "moving audience" that would be "calculated to put the police at sea. Every available member of the IWW will be used. Each will be provided with a box upon which to stand, and will address a crowd if one can be attracted." Scattered over a radius of two city blocks, the paper asserted, a given Wobbly would "speak until the police remove him," and then another would "mount his box and preach the IWW gospel, and so on," while to inconvenience the authorities further, every Wobbly arrested would give the "same name, age, occupation, and nativity when booked at police headquarters. All are to demand a jury trial."[62]

Ultimately, though, Local 69 decided not to stage a free-speech fight but instead to comply with what they hoped would be a short-lived ban on their street speaking and after that to apply for permits and speak only when such permission was granted and only at the locations the city designated.[63] On the one hand, Salt Lake Wobblies realized, as Joyce Kornbluh, a noted historian of the IWW, stated, that free-speech fights elsewhere had sometimes been such a formidable weapon—creating crowded jails, congested courts, and the high costs of paying extra police and feeding prisoners—that some cities had repealed their speaking ordinances, showing the power that demonstrations and passive resistance could wield.[64] The IWW also knew, though, that the outcome of free-speech fights was often very different. They could be bloody and costly as in San Diego, for example, where a nine-month-long fight broke out in 1911–12 after the city council had prohibited street speaking, and Salt Lake Wobblies feared that, while in the short run, they might be successful, in the long run, a free-speech fight might be counterproductive because the IWW would be painted as an essentially violent and lawless organization, making it difficult to recruit new members.[65]

Finally, then, the position of Salt Lake's IWW, as Sam Scarlett expressed it, became, "We are not seeking trouble and so will just go along quietly just now."[66] Thus, at the September 22 meeting of the city commission, the union requested a "permanent permit" to "hold and conduct propaganda meetings in this city at the corner of 2nd South and Commercial Street." Commercial Street had been the city's main red-light district since the early 1870s, and the location the IWW asked for was at its edge. The next day the commission answered the IWW's request. It granted the organization permission to hold outdoor meetings, not permanently, but only "during the current year." It also changed the location from the one requested to a "strictly confined" site in the center of the red light district, rather than at its edge. The commission approved that location on the recommendation of Mayor Samuel Park and Police Chief Grant after Park said he was nervous about allowing meetings at the corner the IWW had requested because "respectable" people, including theatregoers, would be

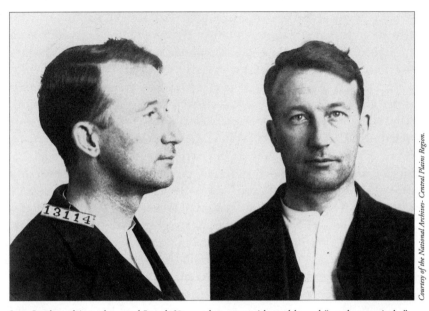

Courtesy of the National Archives- Central Plains Region.

Sam Scarlett ultimately urged Local 69 members to avoid trouble and "go along quietly." After leaving Utah he continued his radical activities, and was arrested by the Federal government in a roundup of IWW members in 1917. Convicted in 1918, Scarlett was sentenced to twenty years, fined $20,000, and imprisoned at Leavenworth as convict #13114. His sentence was commuted in 1923.

"passing the location about the time the meetings are in progress." The IWW protested, asserting that neither the issuing of permits for the current year only, nor the changed location, was acceptable and, to demonstrate its resolve, held a meeting that very night without a permit. According to the *Deseret News,* it was "the first street meeting to be held by the IWW in Salt Lake City since they were denied the privileges of the streets for bursts of oratory following the riot in August," and, the paper assured its readers, "the crowd was very quiet and orderly."[67]

The quiet and order would not last long. Wobblies, and members of other radical political groups as well, continued to be criticized in the most extreme terms and faced opposition and repression. A month after the IWW's "orderly" meeting, the *Salt Lake Tribune* announced that law enforcement officials throughout the state were stepping up their efforts to "repress IWW activities in Utah" and had removed twenty-one men from a Oregon Short Line railroad car, alleged that they were Wobblies on their way to attend an IWW meeting in Salt Lake City, and charged them with trespassing.[68] Three months later, two masked men killed a Salt Lake grocer, J.G. Morrison, and his teenage son, Arling. A few days later, when IWW songwriter and organizer Joe Hill—whose "Mr. Block" had been sung at the August 12 meeting—was charged with the crime, all of the vituperation toward the IWW reemerged in the local press, creating an odor of hostility that hung in the Utah air throughout the series

Courtesy of Special Collections, J. Willard Marriott Library, University of Utah.

University of Utah faculty member Virginia Snow Stephen (pictured seated at center) was a strong supporter of the IWW which led to her dismissal in 1916. She is shown with an unknown group, possibly IWW members and supporters. Note the photo of Joe Hill contained in what appears to be a copy of an IWW songbook held in the young man's hand to her front and left.

of events that resulted in his conviction for murder on circumstantial evidence and his execution on November 19, 1915, and afterward. While it is impossible to know for sure, some historians believe Hill had come to Utah in 1913 in response to the free-speech issue. At a meeting held at the IWW's office in Salt Lake on August 13, those in attendance "voted that public meetings be suspended until reinforcements should arrive from the west and east."[69]

In April 1915, while Hill was in jail awaiting trial, the Salt Lake City Commission refused to give a parade permit to the IWW, the Socialist Party, and University of Utah students protesting the university's firing of several individuals over the teaching of evolution.[70] That fall, on October 30, 1915, Salt Lake police officer H. P. Myton shot and killed the head of Local 69, Roy J. Horton, who was unarmed, on a downtown street while the two were arguing. Myton was originally charged with first-degree murder, then with voluntary manslaughter, and finally with a reduced charge of involuntary manslaughter and, at his February 16, 1916, trial, was found innocent.[71] A faculty member at the University of Utah, Virginia Snow Stephen, a defender of Joe Hill and a daughter of former Mormon Church President Lorenzo Snow, sang at Horton's funeral, accompanied the IWW songs used as funeral hymns, and, in her eulogy, called his death "industrial murder." Several months later, the University of Utah fired her.[72]

After the United States entered World War I in April 1917, the IWW came under fierce attack throughout the country, both from government at the local, state, and national levels and private citizens. For example, in a June 15, 1917, editorial, the local newspaper in Eureka, a mining town in central Utah, expressed concern that the IWW had begun a membership drive and was attracting new members. Because the group's goal was to create "unrest and strife" and undermine law and order, its members were enemies of the country "which has given so much to them." In the next week's issue, June 22, an article called for the arrest of Wobblies simply because they belonged to the group and not for any actions they had undertaken, just as, it said, one did not wait for a rattlesnake to strike.[73]

On September 5, 1917, more than three dozen federal and local officials, as well as civilian members of the Committee on Public Safety, an organization connected to the State Council of Defense, raided the IWW's Radical Book Store in downtown Salt Lake City, confiscated its stock of books, and closed it down. They acted under the provisions of the federal Espionage Act, passed in June 1917, which gave federal authorities wide powers to suppress dissent. They also raided the Wobblies' Salt Lake headquarters, where Charles McKinnon, the brother-in-law of Big Bill Haywood, a founder of the IWW, was in charge; the offices of the metal-workers' union; and five private residences. The complaints that formed the basis of the search warrants stated that at both the bookstore and IWW headquarters, "treasonable" literature was being sold, and agents confiscated more than five tons of material, including books, pamphlets, pictures, "seditious letters," insignia, stickers, typewriters, and "lists of members."[74] According to the *Salt Lake Tribune,* in addition to literature from national headquarters, a series of papers focusing on "local situations" was found, including "poems penned by IWW members." Some of the material "was of such a licentious type," the paper said, "that it shocked even the deputy marshals and police officers when it was opened." McKinnon objected to the raids, saying that the government would not prosecute the rich in a similar fashion, and told officers that if they read all the literature they were carrying away, he was sure they would return and apply for an IWW card.[75] Similar raids took place that month on every IWW office in the country. Within a few months, two thousand Wobblies were in jail. Most of them were eventually sentenced to long terms, and some of them were deported.

Unlike their counterparts elsewhere, Wobblies in Utah accepted all of this with little protest.[76] Thus, according to the Salt Lake Police Department's *Annual Report,* published in 1916, "During the agitation of the Hillstrom case we had no serious trouble with the Industrial Workers of the World or any other class, and during the past four years we have had very little trouble with street meetings by different organizations."[77]

In studying the past, Cary Nelson has suggested the importance of "putting the left at the center," rather than treating it as marginal to the main story.[78]

When we do, a different picture emerges, not only in its details but its essentials, requiring us to think differently about the past and also, then, about the present and future. In this instance, what becomes clear is the extent to which Utah was a contested site in the early twentieth century, neither self-contained, homogeneous, nor one-dimensional, a place where public space was defined, or redefined, to disadvantage certain groups, making it difficult for them to be heard, both at the time and in the future.

Clearly important questions were at issue in early-twentieth-century Utah: Who belongs? Who has the right to appropriate space and participate in decision making? Who will be acknowledged and heard, and who will not? Whose interests will be served, and who will pay the price? The answers were often narrow and exclusionary, and they have continued to be that way to the present. In the end, those questions have emerged from the historical record. They are fundamental questions Utahns, and people throughout the United States, have always faced, and they remain crucial questions today.

NOTES

1. The origin of the nickname Wobbly is unclear. It may refer to a tool known as a wobble saw; derive from an immigrant's mispronunciation of IWW as "eye-wobble-you-wobble you;" or be a pejorative term San Francisco socialists used and IWWs adopted as a badge of honor. The wording of the preamble itself changed over time. For the original language, see Industrial Workers of the World, *Proceedings of the First Convention of the Industrial Workers of the World* (New York: New York Labor News Company, 1905), 247–48. For the more familiar version, see "Proceedings of the 1908 Convention of the I.W.W.," *Industrial Union Bulletin* 2 (November 7, 1908).

2. "Dispute Over American Flag is Cause of Downtown Riot; Four are Shot; I.W.W. is Held as Gunman," *Salt Lake Herald-Republican*, August 13, 1913.

3. "Seven Hurt in Rioting," *Deseret News*, August 13, 1913.

4. For an in-depth discussion, see David M. Rabban, *Free Speech in Its Forgotten Years, 1870–1920* (New York: Cambridge University Press, 1997).

5. Barrie Stavis, *The Man Who Never Died; A Play about Joe Hill, with Notes on Joe Hill and His Times* (New York: Haven Press, 1951), 11–12.

6. "Songs and Sermons on Zion's Corners," *Salt Lake Tribune*, September 30, 1907.

7. A definitive history of the Utah Construction Company—especially in that period—remains to be written. For the time being, see Stewart Library, Weber State University, *Preserving the Memories* (Ogden, UT: Stewart Library, Weber State University, 2001); and Gene A. Sessions and Sterling D. Sessions, *Utah International: Biography of a Business* (Ogden, UT: Stewart Library, Weber State University, 2002).

8. "End Strike in Tucker; 160 Deported," *Salt Lake Tribune*, June 12, 1913.

9. Ibid.

10. *Solidarity*, July 3, 1913.

11. Ibid.

12. Philip S. Foner, *The Case of Joe Hill* (New York: International Publishers, 1965), 17.

13. "Deputy Steele Has Record of Long Service in Strikes," *Salt Lake Herald-Republican*, August 13, 1913. For additional biographical information, see *Ogden Standard*, "Salt Lake Notes," January15, 1903; "Makes Big Haul," February 13, 1907; "Sheriff Warned Criminal," April 22, 1908; and "Religious Battle Fought," August 8, 1908.

14. Gunther Peck, "Padrones and Protest: 'Old' Radicals and 'New' Immigrants in Bingham, Utah, 1905–1912," *Western Historical Quarterly* 24 (May 1993): 157–78.

15. *Solidarity*, January 3, 1914.

16. Franklin Rosemont, *Joe Hill: The IWW and the Making of a Revolutionary Working Class Counterculture* (Chicago: Charles H. Kerr Publishing Co., 2002), 357.

17. "Death Summons City Detectives," *Salt Lake Tribune*, October 27, 1919. The paper said that although Steele had been born in Sweden, he was "intensely American" as his anti-IWW activity had shown.

18. Allan Kent Powell, *The Next Time We Strike: Labor in Utah's Coal Fields, 1900–1933* (Logan: Utah State University Press, 1985), 98–99.

19. "Sheriff East Routs I.W.W.," *Provo Herald*, June 12, 1913; "End Strike in Tucker, 160 Deported," *Salt Lake Tribune*, June 12, 1913.

20. *Salt Lake Herald-Republican*, June 14, 1913.

21. Ibid. Interestingly William Jarman, chief clerk of Ogden's United Cigar Store, identifies Morgan as "the same fellow who spoke in Ogden about two months ago." See "Witnessed the Rioting in Salt Lake," *Ogden Standard*, August 13, 1913.

22. "Six Shot in Riot at I.W.W. Meeting," *Salt Lake Tribune*, August 13, 1913. The paper mistakenly used the phrase "Mr. Blockhead," instead of the proper wording.

23. Barrie Stavis, *The Songs of Joe Hill* (New York: Oak Publications, Inc., 1955), 4.

24. Ibid., 4–5.

25. "Six Shot in Riot at I.W.W. Meeting," *Salt Lake Tribune*, August 13, 1913.

26. Ibid.; see also *Carbon County News*, August 14, 1913.

27. "Morgan Says He Was Pulled From Box and Given Kicks in Face," *Salt Lake Herald-Republican*, August 13, 1913.

28. A migrant worker and songwriter, McClintock was active in the IWW from about 1909 to 1916. He remains best known for his poem, "Hymn of Hate." Joyce Kornbluh characterized it as "a relentless indictment of Capital and the State" in *Rebel Voices: An IWW Anthology* (Ann Arbor: University of Michigan Press, 1964), 29–30.

29. "Steele Leads Crowd in Wild Cheer for 'Stars and Stripes,'" *Salt Lake Herald-Republican*, August13, 1913.

30. "I.W.W. Meeting Broken Up By Mob," *Salt Lake Tribune*, August 15, 1913.

31. "Citizens in the Streets," *Salt Lake Tribune*, August 16, 1913.

32. "Speech Making on Streets Prohibited; Exceptions," Salt Lake City Laws, section 1205; "Six Men Shot in Attack on I.W.W. Rally," *Salt Lake Tribune*, August 13, 1913.

33. Salt Lake City Court, Criminal Case Minutes Books, August 18, 1913; *Salt Lake Tribune*, August 19, 1913.

34. Salt Lake City Court, Criminal Case Minutes Books, August 14, 1913; "Seven Hurt in Rioting," *Deseret News*, August 13, 1913.

35. "Mrs. Celia Florence and Mrs. W. H. Emms Give Bail for J. F. Morgan," *Salt Lake Tribune,* August 19, 1913.

36. "Ask for Complaint," *Salt Lake Herald Republican,* August 14, 1913.

37. "Ample Precautions Taken," *Deseret Evening News,* August 15, 1913; "I.W.W. Threatens to Meet Again," *Salt Lake Herald-Republican,* August 15, 1913. Scarlett was an important figure in the IWW. For more information see Donald H. Avery, "British-born 'Radicals' in North America, 1900–1941: The Case of Sam Scarlett," *Canadian Ethnic Studies* 10, no. 2 (1978): 65–85.

38. "No Intention of Arresting Steele," *Salt Lake Herald-Republican,* August 15, 1913.

39. Ibid.

40. "I.W.W. Meeting Broken Up by Mob," *Salt Lake Tribune,* August 15, 1913.

41. Ibid.

42. Ibid

43. Located on Second East between First and Second South, Unity Hall served as an important gathering place, providing both office space for many radical and labor groups and space for public meetings and lectures.

44. He had also been a Socialist Party candidate for the Salt Lake City Commission in 1911.

45. "Speakers Condemn Action of Steele," *Salt Lake Tribune,* August 17, 1913; *Deseret Evening News,* August 1, 1913.

46. Ibid.

47. Ibid.

48. "Speakers Condemn Actions of Steele," *Salt Lake Tribune,* August 18, 1913. According to the *Tribune,* Knerr also said, "We are engaged in a great battle where arguments are swords and facts are bullets," and "the only dynamite laboring men should use is intellectual dynamite."

49. Ibid.

50. "To Designate Place for I.W.W. Meetings," *Deseret Evening News,* September 23, 1913.

51. Ibid.

52. "In County Jail," *Salt Lake Herald-Republican,* August 14, 1913.

53. "An Unfortunate Occurrence," *Deseret Evening News,* August 13, 1913. In addition to the Salt Lake newspapers, it is valuable to examine the attitude of the Ogden papers, the city where Utah Construction Company had its headquarters. The *Ogden Standard* observed that two "elements of lawlessness met in Salt Lake City . . . and, as a result, innocent bystanders were shot." The paper further stated that "the I.W.W. should be held in check, but not by I.W.W. methods. One offense against good government does not justify another and Axel Steele and his rioters should be made to understand that very thing." See "The Rioting in Salt Lake," *Ogden Standard,* August 13, 1913.

54. "An Unfortunate Occurrence," *Deseret Evening News,* August 13, 1913.

55. "The I. W(on't) W(ork)," *Salt Lake Herald-Republican,* August 14, 1913

56. "Personally Conducted Riot," *Salt Lake Tribune,* August 14, 1913.

57. "I.W.W. Meeting Broken up by Mob," *Salt Lake Tribune,* August 15, 1913.

58. "In County Jail" *Salt Lake Tribune,* August 15, 1913.

59. "Fight for Free Speech," *Salt Lake Tribune*, August 19, 1913.

60. See Kornbluth, *Rebel Voices*, 94–126.

61. "Seven Hurt in Rioting," *Deseret Evening News*, August 13, 1913.

62. "I.W.W. Leader Has New Plans for Meetings," *Salt Lake Tribune*, August 17, 1913.

63. "Workers Hold Meeting," and "To Designate Place for I.W.W Meetings," *Deseret Evening News*, September 23, 1913; Salt Lake City Commission, Meeting Minutes, September 22, 1913.

64. Kornbluth, *Rebel Voices*, 98.

65. Ibid.

66. "Workers Hold Meeting," *Deseret Evening News*, September 23, 1913.

67. Ibid.

68. "IWW Leaders Are Released by Police," *Salt Lake Tribune*, October 24, 1913.

69. See "Threat Made to Kill Axel Steele," *Ogden Standard*, August 14, 1913. The literature on Hill is voluminous. In addition to the works previously cited, an essential starting point is Gibbs Smith, *Joe Hill* (Salt Lake City: Peregrine Smith, 1984).

70. "Police Stop University of Utah Parade, Students Linked to Rioters," *Salt Lake Telegram*, April 26, 1915; "University Students Insulted," *Goodwin's Weekly* 27 (May 1, 1915).

71. "Myton is Acquitted of Murder Charge for Shooting Horton," *Deseret Evening News*, February 21, 1916.

72. For information on Virginia Snow Stephen, see John R. Sillito, "Women and the Socialist Party in Utah, 1900–20," *Utah Historical Quarterly* 49 (Summer 1981): 220–38; and Rosemont, 130–31.

73. *Eureka Reporter*, June 15, 22, 1917.

74. For a fuller account of the raid, considered within the context of the "red scare" that took place in the United States during and after World War I, see Andrew Hunt, "Beyond the Spotlight: The Red Scare in Utah," *Utah Historical Quarterly* 61 (Fall 1993): 357–80.

75. *Eureka Reporter*, June 15, 22, 1917.

76. A number of scholars have examined this important period. A contemporary account is Theodore Schroeder, *Free Speech for Radicals* (New York: Free Speech League, 1916). Other standard accounts include Philip S. Foner, *Fellow Workers and Friends: IWW Free Speech Fights as Told by Participants* (Westport, CT: Greenwood Press, 1981); Robert K. Murray, *The Great Red Scare: A Study in National Hysteria* (Minneapolis: University of Minnesota Press, 1955); and William Preston Jr., *Aliens and Dissenters: Federal Suppression of Radicals, 1903–33* (Cambridge, MA: Harvard University Press, 1963). Another interesting overview appears in Patrick Renshaw, "The IWW and the Red Scare, 1917–24," *Journal of Contemporary History* 3 (October 1968): 63–72.

77. Salt Lake City Corporation, *Municipal Record* (Salt Lake City: Salt Lake City Corporation, 1915–16).

78. Cary Nelson, "What Happens When We Put the Left at the Center?" *American Literature* 66 (December 1994): 771.

12

What Is the Best Way to Govern a City?

Jessie L. Embry

During the twentieth century, especially after the New Deal, the federal government played an increasingly important role in Americans' lives. As a result, many Americans look to Washington, D.C., for relief from natural disasters and policies that affect education, the environment, and just about everything else. But the local government still maintains city streets and highways, provides water and garbage and sewage removal, protects residents, and determines zoning and building requirements. Unlike the federal government, there is no set way that a town or city meets these needs. Using Provo as an example, Jessie L. Embry explains the way that city government has changed throughout the United States following the popular concepts of the time. Provo went through mayor, commission, and council-manager types of government like many other Utah cities and towns. The city adopted new forms of government used by other U.S. cities as it connected to the rest of the nation; it also adapted to local concerns. Newspapers and oral histories provide the framework for this chapter, which shows the importance of local government in everyday life.

In the 1970s, Cindy Orton and A. LeGrand (Buddy) Richards purchased a home near the Franklin Elementary School in downtown Provo, Utah. The area had always been a blue-collar, working-class neighborhood; many residents had worked as laborers, on the railroad, or in the steel industry. By the time that the Richardses moved to the area, most of these residents had retired. Over the years, the older people had passed away, and their homes had been torn down and replaced by businesses or apartments. Often the historic homes that remained became rental properties.

As the Richards family grew, they elected to stay in this pioneer neighborhood despite its low-income housing, the small number of children, a drive-by shooting, and drug busts. They made a commitment to improve the place where they lived. Cindy Richards, a former sociology high school teacher and stay-at-home mom, went to a "meet-the-mayor" night and described the neighborhood problems. Then she and some neighbors started with small projects. Their first plan for obtaining a crossing guard to help their children cross Fifth West (U.S. Highway 89) at Fourth South to attend Franklin Elementary was a success.

Based on that initial effort, Richards helped form Townhall Neighbors Together (TNT). They carefully selected the name to remind officials that their neighborhood included the city center. TNT successfully used city funds and volunteer labor to plant trees, paint homes, and clean up yards and vacant lots. With a better neighborhood and city financial help, newcomers purchased rental properties and became home owners. Richards also convinced a national nonprofit organization that works with cities, residents, and banks—Neighborhood Housing Services (NHS)—to set up a program in Provo and start in the Franklin neighborhood. NHS has built new houses, offered loans for first-time buyers, and assisted residents in upgrading their older homes.

After working with these committees and getting to know city officials, Richards decided to run for Provo's City Council in 1997. Her outgoing, caring style convinced friends and strangers in southwestern Provo to vote for her. In 2001 she was reelected.

Initially Richards planned a short political career. But after being in office for two terms, she recognized that seniority and knowledge were important. So with the support of her family and friends, she ran again in 2005. By then Richards had become the establishment. With money from a group of businessmen who felt the status quo had mistreated them, Richards's opponent mailed out flyers that complained about current city government and promised change. The flyers focused on the negative and did not include the candidate's qualifications or what changes he proposed. Richards feared she might lose the election because her district was larger than her neighborhood, but she got out the vote and won easily.

Richards's experiences are typical of government on any level, but sometimes the results are reversed. When a government seems to be ineffective, citizens vote for a change. United States President Herbert Hoover lost because his methods to deal with the Great Depression failed. Franklin D. Roosevelt promised change and won. In Utah, as throughout the rest of the nation, the Republicans lost to the Democrats. Reed Smoot, who had served as a senator since 1904, lost to Elbert D. Thomas. As historian Thomas G. Alexander explains, "The Republicans had claimed the credit for the nation's prosperity during the early 1900s. . . . Now the Republican Party held power during the nation's worst economic collapse." This pattern is also repeated on a local level. After a scandal in the Salt Lake City government in 1979, the *Salt Lake Tribune* blamed the problems on its commission form of government. The newspaper suggested that the city should change its governmental organization.[1]

The Taylor Building, formerly a furniture store, was one of the anchor businesses on the west side of Provo. These photographs show some of the changes that have taken place on the front over the years. Since Center Street is a local historic district, any changes to the front must be reviewed by the Provo City Landmarks Committee and approved by the city council.

City governments are different, though, from federal and state ones. First, local governments control more aspects of Americans' lives than do state and federal ones. But most Americans do not recognize that impact. As a result, fewer people vote in municipal elections than in national ones. As long as the police arrest criminals, the streets have only a few potholes, the water comes out of the pipes, the waste goes away, and the library has books, most residents barely recognize the government. Those who care are neighborhood activists like Richards; business owners who do not want to be controlled by city regulations; home owners who do not like dogs, noise, and drugs in their area; and people who want to promote their "pet projects," such as private or city-owned utilities.

Yet city services do not come automatically. While federal and state governments make up the corpus that people notice, local entitles are the necessary tissues of the body politic.[2] A *Deseret News* editorial in 1931 agreed: "City government is very close to the lives of urban citizens. It touches us daily. The streets and sidewalks that we use, the lighting, the parks, the water that we drink, the fire department, the protection against violence, theft or the criminal lore of youth, the assessment, licenses, taxes all affect us intimately every hour of the twenty-four whether we wake or sleep."[3]

A historic preservation example demonstrates this point. In 1966 the national government created a National Register of Historic Places to encourage Americans to preserve buildings. States created preservation offices to nominate structures and help residents recognize historical value. But only city governments could pass and enforce a law that forced their citizens to save old buildings through zoning laws, city preservation districts, and a review process.

Provo's Center Street Historic District demonstrates the difference in the way the state, federal government, and city control buildings. In 1980 Provo's Center Street became a National Register Historic District, but this did not change the way owners remodeled their properties. In the 1990s, Provo adopted a Landmarks Preservation Ordinance and created a Landmarks Commission. After that the commission had to review all changes to buildings on the city register. For example, in 1995 the owners of the Taylor Building, a significant structure in the district, asked to restore a canopy that had been there in the 1900s to the front of the building. The canopy did enhance the building's looks, but it also provided a place to mount lighting. The change fit the historic character of the downtown district, and the commission approved the addition.[4]

A second major difference among federal, state, and local governments is that cities have organizational options. Federal and state constitutions require a legislative, executive, and judicial system. But cities, with the support of the state legislature and governor, can change their governmental form. The traditional city government was a mayor and council. During the twentieth century, two other forms of government—council-manager and commission—became popular. Utah cities followed the national trend. Those in favor of making a change argued that the new systems were better forms of government. But

Provo City Arts Council has added paintings and sculptures to the downtown area. The council asked permission to have this mural of Provo City history painted on the side of a contributory building to the Center Street Historic District. The Landmarks Commission approved the mural since historically some buildings had paintings or advertisements on them and because the majority of commission members agreed that art makes Center Street more attractive and enjoyable for residents who shop downtown.

when there were problems, some citizens blamed the type of government, not just the officials.

It takes a special group to care enough to fight for a change in government. Who are these people? And why do they care so much? This chapter describes the mayor and city council, commissioner, and council-manager forms of government, explains how Utah has adapted them, and then uses Provo as a case study to show the way all three forms work. While many residents saw the conflicts as tempests in a teapot, those who fought for changes felt very strongly that the type of government does make a difference. In the end, though, Provo's example shows that personalities and local issues are the reasons why city governments change.

Forms of Government

The United States Constitution did not mention cities and towns because the Founding Fathers struggled over states' rights and federal control. They allowed the states to create cities and counties and set their forms of government. State constitutions spelled out the requirements for different classes of cities and types of government. Since many constitutions copied each other, the provisions were very similar. Usually the requirements were uniform for all

Mayor-Council

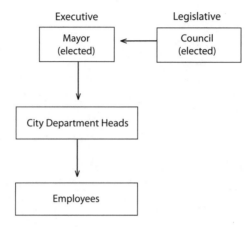

Council-Manager

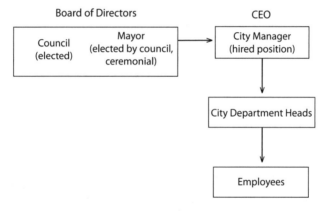

Commission

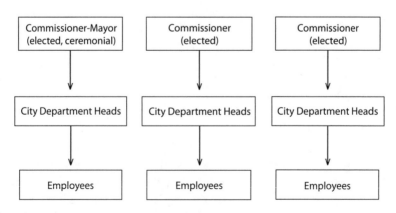

The three types of city governments that were popular in the United States during the twentieth century.

cities, although state legislatures could change those rules for individual cases. In the late nineteenth and early twentieth centuries, states amended their constitutions to allow "home-rule charters" so that a city could adopt its own form of government without special permission from the state legislature.[5]

Types of government went in and out of style just like fashion. The three forms favored in the twentieth century were the mayor and council, council-manager, and commission. In 1981 the mayor-council form was the most popular in American cities. But according to *U.S. News and World Report,* the council-manager format was the fastest growing for cities between five thousand and five hundred thousand. Only 5 percent of the cities still used a commissioner form.[6]

MAYOR-COUNCIL

The mayor-council governmental form started during the colonial period and continues to be used. In practice it assumes various configurations: the strong mayor, the strong mayor with a chief administrative officer, and the weak mayor. A strong mayor serves as the executive branch for his or her city. A weak mayor works with the city council and is a figurehead. Over the years, some very powerful mayors completely controlled city hall. They won votes by promising positions in city government to supporters. Many voters saw them as corrupt and wanted better checks and balances.

Those favoring the mayor-council form of government argued that it matched the federal and state constitutions. A mayor and council were the executive and legislative branches. Citizens selected the officers and could vote them out of office if they did not agree with the decisions. However, a heavy-handed mayor still controlled the government. In addition, the position was full time, and many qualified people were not willing to give up their regular employment to serve. In the twentieth century, state, federal, and local regulations made city life more complex. Many people felt it took a professional to keep track of all the requirements and finances. To address those concerns, many cities with strong mayors added an administrative officer in the late twentieth century who is similar to a city manager and takes care of day-to-day activities.

COUNCIL-MANAGER

In the early 1900s, New Yorker Richard S. Childs especially disliked the corruption in his city and proposed a council-manager structure to eliminate shady mayors and politicians. He was inspired by the Progressive Era's devotion to efficiency and streamlined operations. Childs envisioned a city running like a company with a CEO—the manager—and a board—the council. He favored an elected, part-time council that passed ordinances and an appointed, full-time manager who handled all administrative decisions. Dayton, Ohio, became the first city to adopt the change officially in 1914.[7]

This form of government flourished during the urban and industrial growth in the first decade of the twentieth century and then slowed during World War I. It experienced its greatest growth after World War II as suburbs developed, cities annexed them, and residents demanded services. It popularity spread rapidly, and by 1957, only three states—Arkansas, Indiana, and Louisiana—did not allow managers. Council-managers were especially popular during growth periods because city governments had to deal with new issues, including annexation and extension of services.

In 1965 Childs published *The First 50 Years of the Council-Manager Plan of Municipal Government* and bragged that hundreds had adopted the plan, and only eighty-six had voted it out. He explained that this form of government succeeded because a trained city manager worked with the departments. Elected council members set the laws and could fire the manager. The few cities that eliminated the council-manager form of government usually did so because of personality conflicts where elected city officials felt managers had too much control. Some cities complained that managers often were not even city residents but frequently job-hopped to a bigger city with a higher salary.[8]

COMMISSION

About the same time that some cities changed to a council and manager, others adopted a commission form of government. The idea started in Galveston, Texas, following a hurricane in 1900. Five years before the hurricane, Galveston businesses had pushed for citywide elections to avoid control by politicians who only had to answer to part of the city. These same businessmen favored the commission form as the island city struggled to rebuild. Some leaders suggested that problems resulted from elected officials who could not respond fast enough; they wanted appointed commissioners. This proposal was undemocratic, but the residents liked a plan where elected officials headed the city departments and got results faster than they would working through a council that had to make rulings and then wait for city employees to carry them out.[9]

Commissioners were so successful in restoring Galveston that cities and counties throughout the United States believed that form was a magic fix. Houston, Texas, and Des Moines, Iowa, changed their governments in 1905, and other cities followed. Political scientist Martin J. Shiesll saw the same benefits from commissioners that Richard Childs had envisioned with the council-manager government—eliminating "bossism."[10]

Those who favored commissioners also saw a balance. The elected officials had to answer to the people. But as in Galveston, they could complete an assignment more quickly because they passed the information directly to city departments. However, the system has weaknesses. Like a mayor, being a commissioner is a full-time job, so many people are not willing to give up regular employment to serve. Councils in the council-manager or council-mayor form of government are usually part time and can come from all walks of life.

Another problem is that commissioners may not be trained for the job and may bumble through their assignments as a result.

UTAH STATE LAW

Until 1888 Utah's territorial legislature required the three largest cities— Provo, Ogden, and Salt Lake City—to have a mayor, four aldermen (a British term for an appointed official one step below the mayor), and nine councilmen. During that year, the legislature eliminated the aldermen and only required a council. City size determined the number of council members. When Utah became a state in 1896, the new constitution spelled out the requirements for a city government. The new state government was "a patchwork of bits and pieces borrowed from other state constitutions." Like the Illinois model that the Utah Constitution followed, the state required a first-class city of more than thirty thousand to have a fifteen-member council from five wards and a mayor and a second-class city to have a ten-member city council and a mayor.[11]

During the Progressive Era, some Utah cities looked at other forms of government and supported the Galveston commission format. In 1907 a Salt Lake City civic improvement league asked the state legislature to allow a similar change, but the bill failed that year. The 1909 legislature passed a bill that would allow commissioners, but Governor William Spry pocket-vetoed it because he felt it was unconstitutional. He especially opposed the recall of public officials. Spry signed a bill which allowed commissioners in 1911 after the referendum, recall, and initiative provisions had been removed.[12]

But commissions were not the most popular form of government at the time. Many states permitted council-manager governments. Often these were tied to "home rule" charters that allowed cities to control more of their activities without going to the state legislature. While a charter worked with any form of government, it was usually tied closely to the council-manager type. Cities in Utah could not adopt a charter without an amendment to the state constitution since it dictated the type of city government and did not allow cities to choose their own form. In 1931 the state legislature agreed to put the question of home rule charters on the ballot.[13] In the November 1932, hotly debated election, where the dominant issues were who would become president of the United States and what party would control Congress, Utah voters also had a small item at the bottom of their ballots: "Constitutional Amendment—a joint resolution proposing an amendment to Section 5 of Article XI of the Utah Constitution—Municipal Corporations. Yes/No."[14]

The proposed amendment changed the Utah Constitution so an "incorporated city or town [could] frame and adopt a charter for its own government." The process was a lengthy, three-step procedure. First, two-thirds of a city's governing body—commissioners or council—or 15 percent of the voters in the last mayoral election could call for an election to appoint a committee to draft a charter. Second, the city held an election. At the time of that vote, the electors also voted for a fifteen-member committee. If the question to have a committee failed, the elected members had no responsibilities. If it passed, however, the committee wrote a charter. Finally, residents voted for or against the charter.[15]

Utah newspapers disagreed about whether the change was good. The *Salt Lake Tribune* carried a neutral article. The reporter surveyed eighteen mayors; six did not support the amendment, nine agreed with it, and three had no comment.[16] The *Provo Herald* opposed the amendment. A November 7 editorial worried that there was not a lot of interest in the amendment since it was not about liquor or taxes. But the editor disagreed with changing the type of government without the state legislature making the decision. He feared "damage" to the city because the change allowed "sweeping powers" for taxation. If a city really wanted the change, the elected officials could go to the state legislature.[17] The *Deseret News*, however, came out strongly in favor of the change. When the paper announced a series of articles about the amendment, the first one stated that the pros and cons would be discussed. But all the articles were in favor of the amendment.[18]

The amendment barely passed: 22,856 to 17,999. In Utah County, 4,651 voted for it, while 2,985 voted against. Its passage was barely mentioned in the newspapers, which focused on the Democratic victors on the state and federal level.[19] Utah cities did not attempt to adopt charters after the referendum because of the Depression and World War II. In 1945 Spanish Fork was the first to put the issue on the ballot. The voters approved a commission form of government, but two years later, they did not pass the charter.[20] In 1948 Ogden became the first Utah city to adopt a charter and a council-manager government.[21]

Provo

Provo provides a good example of the way a Utah city used these forms of government. It followed the territorial model of a mayor, four aldermen, and nine council members until 1888. Then the law changed, and governments were determined by city size. Provo had fewer than five thousand residents and was a third-class city. A mayor and seven-member council presided. Two years later, Provo became a second-class city with a mayor and a ten-member council.

In 1909 the Provo Commercial Club first discussed the full-time commission form of government. Some believed that Salt Lake City should try it first, but actually no city could adopt it until the 1911 law. At that time, the state allowed commission government, and Provo made the change. The new government had mixed results in Provo. Looking back in 1953, Jacob Coleman, Provo City attorney for seventeen years, said that government option was ineffective because "some [commissioners] learned fast. Others, elected to office after failing at every previous job or business, knew no more at the end of their four years than when they went in. You can fire a city manager for incompetence but you can't fire a commissioner."[22]

A 1955 *Provo Herald* editorial also cited commissioner problems: "Lacking both experience and numbers, the city commission has come up with such dud legislation as the Sunday closing law, which had to be hurriedly repealed and the too-stringent zoning of a few years back which was rushed through without adequate public notice and later revamped." Aura Hatch, who was the last mayor before the council-manager charter went into effect, said that small grocers requested the Sunday closing act. The commissioners adopted the change without a wide survey of the community because they felt the grocers spoke for the majority. After the ordinance passed, many residents called to complain. In response to this opposition, the commissioners repealed the ordinance. The editorial implied that the commissioners did not gather enough information and a city council with members from all areas of the city would have recognized the Sunday closing act was not what the residents wanted. "Seven men and women, representing all parts of the city, undoubtedly would have found better solutions," the *Herald* stated.[23]

After the 1932 amendment to the Utah Constitution, Provo residents voted on a council-manager form of government twice. It failed in 1945 by a vote of 1,283 to 2,939. While the election for mayor was highly contested that year, very few residents voted. The *Provo Herald* lamented that only a hundred people showed up at a public hearing before the election to hear about the issues.[24]

The charter idea disappeared until 1953. Then a Brigham Young University (BYU) journalism class attended a commission meeting and asked for a change. The local newspaper brought the issue back by carrying a series of fifteen articles on the council-manager form of government. Some Provo residents formed the Citizens Committee for Good Government and convinced the city commissioners to put the charter question on the ballot. While the charter did not require a council-manager form of government, those supporting the charter also favored that option.

While the *Herald* had complained that too few residents came to the public hearing in 1945, the paper proudly announced that they "packed" a mass meeting to hear the pros and cons of the new government structure. The newspaper editorials clearly supported the charter. Its coverage was so one sided that some citizens bought advertisements in the paper to oppose the change. The election was very close. Some charter supporters worried that citizens might not know what they were voting for since there were 630 more ballots cast for mayor than for the creation of a committee to write a charter. Still, the vote was 3,082 for forming the committee and 3,015 against.[25]

The elected committee spent two years writing a Provo city charter. When it was completed in July 1955, city officials asked the residents if they wanted to adopt it. The *Herald* supported the charter and carried a front page article and editorial stating their approval the day before the election. The article implied that there had been a lot of interest: "Campaigning between charter advocates and opponents has been quite brisk with a last minute flurry of newspaper and radio ads, distribution of handbills and some personal contact." The editorial asked everyone to go to the polls. "If the vote is heavy—if the big majority of the citizens express themselves—then whatever the decision is will be the people's choice." However, a majority did not vote. Only 30 percent of the residents approved the charter that created a council-manager form of government. What was a greater concern was that the charter and new form of government won by only twenty-five votes (2,400 to 2,375).[26]

Those who had opposed the council-manager form of government watched very closely to see if the business approach to government was what they wanted. In January 1959, Mark Anderson, a former mayor, wrote to the *Provo Herald* that after three years, it was a good time to grade the new government. Anderson complained that there had not been much progress and the council and manager were dealing with immediate needs and did not have a long-term plan. While the manager claimed he had improved power, zoning, and water, Anderson insisted all of those elements had been in place before the new government took over.[27]

Anderson was not alone. On August 17, 1959, some citizens asked for an amendment to the charter that would give the manager less control. Specifically they did not want the manager to control the city-owned utilities and be able to fire city-department heads. The *Herald* disagreed, saying that it did not support reopening these hotly debated issues. The council was more willing to listen and voted four to three to ask the citizens to put their requests in writing. Neither side acted, however.[28]

In 1960 the first manager, Earl Udall, left for a higher-paying job in California. The council hired Edward J. "Bud" Connell, a thirty-nine-year-old Tooele native with degrees in business administration. Connell had applied in 1955 but had not been considered the top candidate then. In 1960, though, the council hired him. After he had been in office for only a year, some Provo residents felt that he was a poor manager. The question of doing away with the charter and the council-manager form of government came up again. Forty citizens worked with two hundred volunteers and collected three thousand signatures to put the issue to repeal the charter and replace the government format on the ballot.[29] The city council, the federated women's club, and the Provo adult education program (headed by city council member Stella Oaks) held a town meeting on the subject.

The city council and manager published a nine-month report from January to October 1961 to document their achievements. The opposition poked fun at the report. Why would the city publish a nine-month instead of an annual report except that the council wanted to speak out against the repeal at city expense? Those against the charter started their own newsletter to express their views because they felt the *Herald* was not objective. An election was held, and 57 percent voted to repeal the charter. Provo returned to a mayor-council form of government.[30]

Provo residents for and against the council-manager form of government used the same arguments in 1945, 1953, 1955, and 1961. Most matched those circulating on the national level. Those who favored this form of government used a business model. They compared a manager to a CEO, the city council to a board of directors, and the citizens to stockholders. This arrangement, they said, led to "far greater efficiency and economy." An expanded part-time city council allowed more men and women from all walks of life to serve. While the manager was not elected, the council was and could fire the manager. While some feared "autocratic government," the *Herald* insisted, "Democracy consists of controlling public officers, not necessarily of electing them." Those who opposed the council-manager approach felt that it took local government out of the hands of the voters.[31]

In the end, the council-manager government created by the charter was removed but not because of the national arguments. There were two major local issues—municipal power and a senior citizen center—that forced the change. These concerns, along with a strong-willed city manager, who took more control than some residents liked, prompted the change.

Electric Power Company

The most important long-term issue that initiated the government change was who owned and kept the profits from the electric-power company. The issue had been highly debated since the 1930s, and a few citizens believed strongly that the city should own the electric company, while others felt a private business should own and operate it. Provo made the change to a public power plant in the 1930s at the same time when other cities throughout the United States became interested in municipal power as a public utility. Local governments reasoned that they could provide the same service for less and make money for the city. During the 1930s, Hotel Roberts owner Mark Anderson supported municipal power. When he ran for mayor in 1935, it was the only issue on his platform. With his support, city officials put municipal power on the ballot. After a highly debated campaign, more voters turned out than for any previous election. By a narrow margin—only 119 votes—residents agreed to city-owned power.[32]

After several elections and court decisions, the city power plant was finally contracted in 1939 and started providing electricity in 1940. The power company became a separate part of city government that controlled its own budget and kept all its profits. Those on the power board believed that the company's profits should be used to improve the system and not go into the city's general funds. Others felt that the city provided many free services to the utility and its money should come from and go back into the general funds, or else the company should pay taxes. Power was the central issue in the 1945 mayoral election. Anderson, who was no longer mayor, decided to run again because his opponent, George Collard, wanted to move the power profits to the city. While not as many people voted in this election as when power was initially approved, Anderson won, and he saw his election as a clear mandate not to change the power company. In the same election, the residents voted down a plan for a city charter.[33]

When the charter issue returned in 1953, Anderson spoke out against it because he feared a manager would request changes to the power plant. He was right. The first city manager, Earl Udall, tried to shift power profits to the city. Many city leaders disagreed with this decision and got an opinion from an attorney, who said the conditions for the power plant's bonds required a separate board that controlled the finances. As a result, Udall backed off.[34] In 1959 Anderson again spoke against the new government. Other citizens agreed and asked for amendments to the charter to clarify the concerns. But the bottom issue was always power. The newspaper recognized that and argued, "Why amend the Charter? Why a re-enactment of the old power fight?"[35]

Udall did not force his hand, but Edward J. "Bub" Connell did. Mayor Harold Van Wagenen explained years later that Connell "was very hard-headed and lots of time I think not well trained . . . because of his poor public relations and his lack of appeal to the public."[36] For example, in 1961 Connell bulldozed changes to Provo Power that allowed up to 16 percent of the profits from the company to be transferred to the city's general funds.[37]

So that year Anderson again called for the repeal of the charter because it represented the council-manager form of government. According to newspaper reporter Theron Luke, Anderson's public meeting "took an unexpected moderate turn (from the standpoint of the system's foe)."[38] Those attending voted to amend the charter rather than repeal it. They wanted self-rule; they also liked a council-manager form of government. They felt that there should be ways to limit the manager's control. In response to the public meeting, the city council attempted to put both issues—eliminating the charter and amending it—on the ballot. The Utah Supreme Court said that was too confusing. There could only be one question on the ballot, and the repeal issue was already there. Provo's citizens voted to eliminate the charter.[35] When the charter was repealed, Verl Grant Dixon was elected mayor and served from 1962 to 1973. Dixon was familiar to Provo residents. He had served as a county commissioner for eight years and resigned his job as Provo Metropolitan Water District manager to oppose the charter.[40]

Senior Citizens Center

Anderson's pet project, Provo Power, might not have been enough to overturn the charter and eliminate the council-manager form of government. Another important issue that brought voters out was the sale of the senior citizens center, the Eldred Center. Even before the federal government passed laws requiring cities to help older Americans in the 1960s, Provo had started a center. In 1951 Provo resident William McCord noticed some residents playing cards in Pioneer Park and wanted a better place for them to go for recreation. He and ten men formed a recreation group. At first they met in the basement of the Provo library. By December 1952, they had moved their club to the Utahna Gardens, a dance hall at the corner of First West and First South. Business owners Mr. and Mrs. L.J. Eldred donated the Utahna Gardens to the city as a senior citizens' center.[41]

In 1961 the federal government decided to relocate the downtown post office and looked for a suitable site. The postal service selected the corner where the Utahna was located, and the city agreed. Provo senior citizens felt betrayed by the loss of their center. Some were not aware that the council had promised the Eldreds that the city would use the sale funds to build another center. Many senior citizens only knew their building was gone and felt that the manager and council did not care about them. As a result, senior citizens, who traditionally voted in the largest numbers, supported a governmental change.[42]

The Manager

In 1962 BYU political-science student Neil K. Coleman wrote a thesis on the repeal of the charter and the elimination of the city manager. He mentioned Provo Power and the senior citizens center as the major issues prompting the change. He also explained that many city employees and residents disliked the manager's heavy-handed techniques. His comments about the managers were echoed when some of the 1960 city leaders—George Ballif, an attorney who worked for the city of Provo; J. Earl Lewis, a Provo commissioner who was on the charter commission; Aura C. Hatch, Provo mayor from 1953 to 1955; and Harold Van Wagenen and Lloyd L. Cullimore, both mayors under the council-manager charter—were interviewed in 1974. Looking back, they put all the responsibility on Connell's management style. Van Wagenen especially felt Connell should have been fired and the city should have kept the charter.[43]

Other Changes

Provo eventually returned to the commission form of government, which many felt was very successful. Some leaders and citizens bragged that the commissioners built new fire stations, dug deep water wells, and improved city parks. They saw the new Eldred Center, which the commissioners completed, as one of the best senior citizens facilities in the West and maybe the entire United States.[44]

But the commission form of government was completely out of style by 1981. A group of citizens asked for change. In response Verl Dixon organized another committee, Citizens Opposed to the Change. In a letter to the editor of the *Provo Herald,* he wrote, "This is the finest city in America because of the citizens, the good leaders, the dedicated personnel, and the best educational facilities." Mark Anderson also wrote letters to the editor of the *Herald* opposing the change, arguing that the departments worked and responded well to questions. The issue was not as heated as before; very few letters questioned Dixon and Anderson's view that the city government was not broken and there was no reason to change. Even the *Provo Herald* was quiet until just before the election. Then the newspaper published an editorial supporting a mayor-council form because the government would be "more efficient, more responsive, more broadly representative." Since commissioners were so closely connected to individual departments, they could not see the impact of their decisions on the rest of city government, according to the paper. With this support, the change in government passed. Joe Ferguson, mayor under the commission form of government, decided to run for mayor under the new system and won.[45]

Summary

In 2005 some Provo residents favored changing from the strong mayoral government to a council-manager one. Outgoing Provo city-council member Dave Knecht conducted a straw poll about Provo's government. His e-mail to neighbors and friends showed he favored a manager. He explained that he and others were disappointed with the outcome of the elections that had just taken place: "Some felt they were choosing between the lesser of two evils in the mayor's race." He felt that Provo had a full-time city manager in the administrative officer and a full-time mayor who was in charge of a hundred employees. The council, which only had six employees, he explained, was "at a real disadvantage of trying to provide a check and a balance to the mayor's administration." Of those who responded, 67 percent wanted to change to a council-manager form of government. One person was opposed, though, because he remembered the earlier time when Provo had attempted a council-manager government.[46]

During the 2006 Utah legislative session, Peggy Wallace, a House representative from West Jordan, tried to force the change on Provo. She introduced a bill requiring all cities larger than sixty thousand to adopt the council-manager form of government. She explained that her legislation "is recognizing the city as a corporation, and a lot of it is a service business. We're making sure that the business is extremely well-run because it's taxpayers' money." The bill was not popular, though. Lincoln Shurtz studied legislation for the Utah League of Cities and Towns and explained, "Cities have real heartburn about this bill. The voters have told us how they want their cities to be governed." Shurtz saw advantages to the manager option because the mayor's office could not "politicize" the issues that the council passed. But Salt Lake City council members Jill Remington Love and Dave Buhler disapproved of the state forcing a specific government form on cities.[47]

Provo's history shows some of the pros and cons of all three forms of government. The city followed national trends when it adopted the commission and the council-manager forms of government. The arguments in favor matched those used throughout the United States that business was more effective than government. But in the end, all politics are local, and residents who felt passionate about local issues were able to change the government. Most residents did not care; few voted, and the elections were always very close. The story shows that, while Utah followed national trends for local governments during the latter half of the twentieth century, its cities, including Provo, were not always willing to give up their peculiar views about who should control city government to become like other Americans.

NOTES

1. Alexander, *Utah, the Right Place: The Official Centennial History*, rev. ed. (Salt Lake City: Gibbs Smith, 2003), 316; *Salt Lake Tribune*, February 14, 1979.

2. George S. Blair, *American Local Government* (New York: Harper and Row, 1964), 9.

3. Editorial, *Deseret News*, October 15, 1931.

4. Provo City Landmarks files, Community Development Office, Provo, Utah.

5. Blair, *American Local Government*, 38, 63–65.

6. "The ABCs of How We Are Governed," *U.S. News and World Report*, May 11, 1981, 56–57.

7. Charles M. Kneier, *City Government in the United States*, 3rd ed. (New York: Harper and Row, 1957), 263.

8. Ibid.; Richard S. Childs, *The First 50 Years of the Council-Manager Plan of Municipal Government* (New York: National Municipal League, 1965).

9. Gary Cartwright, *Galveston: A History of the Island* (Fort Worth: TCU Press, 1991), 184–86; David G. McComb, *Galveston: A History and a Guide* (Austin: University of Texas Press, 1986), 134–37; Martin J. Shiesll, *The Politics of Efficiency: Municipal Administration and Reform in America, 1800–1920* (Berkeley: University of California Press, 1977), 142.

10. Kneier, *City Government in the United States*, 244–46; Shiesll, *The Politics of Efficiency*, 142.

11. J.D. Williams *The Defeat of Home Rule in Salt Lake City*, Case Studies in Practical Politics, Eagleton Institute Cases in Practical Politics (New York: Holt, Rinehart and Winston, 1960), 2; F. Ross Peterson and Robert E. Parson, *Ogden City: Its Governmental Legacy: A Sesquicentennial History* (Ogden, UT: Chapelle Limited, 2001), 206; John J. Flynn, "Federalism and Viable State Government," *Utah Law Review* (September 1966): 323, 325; Martin Hickman, *The Utah Constitution: Retrospect and Prospect* (Salt Lake City: Utah Constitutional Revision Commission, 1969), 2, 17.

12. Thomas G. Alexander and James B. Allen, *Mormons and Gentiles: A History of Salt Lake City* (Boulder, CO: Pruett Publishing Company, 1984), 145–46; Utah Legislature, House, *Journal*, (Salt Lake City, 1911), 156, 493, 568–69; Utah Legislature, Senate, *Journal*, (Salt Lake City, 1911), 471–75; *Salt Lake Tribune*, March 4, 9, 1911.

13. Senate Joint Resolution 5 was introduced on February 19 and sent to the committee for revision. It was introduced in the House on March 9. It passed and was signed into law on March 12. There is very little additional information. See Utah Legislature, House, *Journal* (Salt Lake City, 1931) and Utah Legislature, Senate, *Journal* (Salt Lake City, 1931), and Utah Legislature, *Laws of Utah* (Salt Lake City, 1930), 290–92. The only mention in the newspapers at the time was a January 7, 1927, editorial in the *Deseret News* that said cities should have the right to choose.

14. *Salt Lake Tribune,* November 3, 1932.

15. F. Robert Paulsen, *Utah Experience with Constitutional Home Rule* (Salt Lake City: University of Utah Institute of Government, 1948) looked at the Spanish Fork example and then examined the constitution changes and the possibility of home rule in Utah.

16. *Salt Lake Tribune,* November 4, 1932.

17. *Provo Herald,* November 7, 1932.

18. *Deseret News,* November 2, 3, 4, 1932.

19. *Salt Lake Tribune,* November 10, 1932; *Provo Herald,* November 11, 1932.

20. Paulsen, *Utah Experience.*

21. Peterson and Parson, *Ogden City,* 208. Peterson and Parson also outline the successes and failures of the council-manger form of government in Ogden as this chapter does for Provo.

22. *Provo Herald,* July 8, 1953.

23. Ibid., August 1, 1955. Aura Hatch, who was the last mayor before the council-manager charter went into effect, said that small grocers had requested the Sunday closing act, and the commissioners thought they had support. After the ordinance passed, they had a lot of complaints, mostly phone calls, so they repealed it. Still, Hatch insisted few businesses were open on Sundays. Aura Hatch, interview by Kay Alta Haynes, 1974, p. 22, Provo Oral History Project, Charles Redd Center for Western Studies, L. Tom Perry Special Collections, Harold B. Lee Library, Brigham Young University, Provo, Utah.

24. *Provo Herald,* September 11, 1945; October 9, 1945; November 7, 1945.

25. Ibid., November 4, 8, 1953.

26. Ibid., November 15, 1955.

27. Ibid., January 15, 1959.

28. Neil K. Coleman, "A Study of the Campaign for the Repeal of the Provo City Charter in 1961" (master's thesis, Brigham Young University, 1962), 45.

29. *Provo Herald,* January 15, 1959; August 17, 1959; February 26, 1961; February 27, 1961; November 19, 1961; Coleman, "A Study of the Campaign," 42–45.

30. *Provo Herald,* June 18, 1961.

31. Ibid., January 15, 1959.

32. Coleman, "A Study of the Campaign," 42–45.

33. *Provo Herald,* September 11, 1945; October 9, 1945; November 7, 1945.

34. Terry J. Oldroyd Papers, box 2, folder 15, L. Tom Perry Special Collections, Harold B. Lee Library, Brigham Young University, Provo, Utah.

35. *Provo Herald,* January 15, 1959; Coleman, "A Study of the Campaign," 42–45.

36. Harold Van Wagenen, interview by Kay Alta Haynes, 1974, pp. 4–5, 19–22, Provo Oral History Project.

37. *Provo Herald,* February 7, 21, 1961.

38. Ibid., February 26, 1961.

39. Ibid., October 25, 28, 1961; November 6, 1961.

40. Ibid., February 26, 1961

41. Coleman, "A Study of the Campaign," 56–79.

42. Ibid.

43. George Ballif, interview by Kay Alta Haynes, 1974, pp. 25, 32; J. Earl Lewis , interview by Kay Alta Haynes, 1974, pp. 2, 28–29; Aura C. Hatch, interview by Kay Alta Haynes, 1974, pp. 21, 25; Harold Van Wagenen, interview by Kay Alta Haynes, 1974, pp. 4–5, 19–22; Lloyd L. Cullimore, interview by Kay Alta Haynes, 1974, pp. 25, 27–35, Provo Oral History Project.

44. *Salt Lake Tribune,* March 18, 20, 1981.

45. *Provo Herald,* March 5, 6, 19, 23, 1981; May 20, 1981; June 1, 7, 12, 18, 22, 24, 25, 1981.

46. E-mail from Dave Knecht to neighbors and friends, 2005.

47. *Deseret News,* November 21, 2005.

Glen Canyon Dam under construction. Water backed up behind the dam, flooding historical, archaeological, and scenic landmarks.

IV

Growing Challenges
People and Resources

Over the course of the twentieth century, Utah's population multiplied eight-fold, rising from 276,749 in 1900 to 2,233,169 in 2000. The number of residents swelled every decade, due partly to high birthrates. The most dramatic gains occurred from 1900 to 1910 (31.3 percent) and during the 1940s (25.2 percent), 1950s (29.3 percent), 1970s (37.9 percent), and 1990s (29.6 percent). People moved to the state to take advantage of expanding economic opportunities during the first decade of the century (dryland farming, irrigation, mining, and smelting) and the 1940s and 1950s (defense industries and installations associated with World War II and the cold war). During the 1970s, especially after 1975, new coal mines, oil and gas exploration, residential and commercial construction, and continued defense contracts lured job seekers to the state. Economic hard times led to out-migration in the 1980s. But that reversed in the 1990s, when Utah's strong economy and low unemployment rates lured thousands of move-ins—71 percent from California between 1991 and 1993. The newcomers included large numbers of Latinos, primarily from the American Southwest and Mexico.[1]

Population growth stretched Utah's resources and raised questions such as how can the state meet the needs of its growing population, what should the state do about the number of young people who need to be educated, and what resources are required by an aging generation—especially those who move to Utah's Dixie to enjoy a warm retirement? Who should have the rights to limited resources such as water? Should traditional industries—especially agriculture and mining—enjoy preferential rights on public lands? Or should the aesthetic and recreational interests of rapidly expanding metropolitan populations take precedence?

Educating a Young Population

Throughout the twentieth century, Utah had one of the youngest populations in the United States. At the beginning of the century, for instance, when slightly less than 24 percent of the nation's population was under ten years of age, four in ten Utahns were children. Between 1976 and 1979, Utah experienced a "baby boom" with a birthrate roughly 50 percent higher than the national average. The baby boom possibly evidenced a resurgence of "family values" in Utah in reaction to abortion, family planning, and the Equal Rights Amendment. Although Utah's birthrate fell by nearly one-third between 1979 and the mid-1990s, the proportion of children in the state's population remained exceptionally high—35 percent in 1990. One reason for that anomaly was religion: Mormons traditionally have large families because of the centrality of family and reproduction in the church's doctrines. The influx of Spanish-speaking Catholics, who also traditionally have large families, partly because of their religion's stance on birth control, also helped boost the birthrate slightly at the end of the century.[2]

A large young population created heavy demands for education, always a highly debated issue. The nineteenth century witnessed a conflict revolving around religious education—Mormons and Catholics providing education for members of their own religion and Protestant groups creating schools like Wasatch Academy in Mt. Pleasant to educate and convert Mormons. The primary-school landscape changed after 1890, when the territorial legislature passed the Utah Free School Act, which provided for tax-supported public schools throughout Utah.[3]

Most schools at the time only offered education through the eighth grade, so secondary education continued to be a hotly debated topic. Not until 1911 did voters amend the state constitution to require cities and counties to finance high schools. In that year, lawmakers also earmarked funds from the state property tax for high schools. By 1916 high schools had been established in all but four counties.[4]

As public education improved and the taxes to support public schools increased, religious organizations closed most of their schools. By the mid-1920s, only five non-Mormon elementary and secondary schools, serving 525 students, remained, and the LDS Church had closed or turned over to the government twenty-five of its thirty-three academies. By 1934 all of the LDS high schools/academies had closed or been given to the state except for Brigham Young High School, a teaching-laboratory school for education majors associated with Brigham Young University.[5]

Over the course of the century, the number of religious colleges also dropped, while the number of public institutions grew. Early in the twentieth century, the Catholic Church sponsored the College and Academy of St. Mary's of the Wasatch, and the Presbyterians bankrolled Westminster College, while the LDS

Church operated Dixie, Snow, and Weber Junior Colleges and Brigham Young University. Meanwhile, the state financed the University of Utah, Utah State Agricultural College (which later became Utah State University), and a branch agricultural college (which evolved into Southern Utah University) in Cedar City. In 1930 the LDS Church decided to transfer its three junior colleges in Utah to the state. In 1954 Governor J. Bracken Lee attempted to return them to the Mormon Church with the support of the church, but citizens defeated the plan. In 1959 the Catholic Church phased out collegiate work at St. Mary's, although it continued to operate a high school on the campus. The Presbyterians ended their ownership of Westminster in 1974.[6]

In the 1930s, the state founded the College of Eastern Utah, and during the 1940s, it created Salt Lake and Utah Technical Colleges. As the needs and interests of students changed, these two schools became community colleges. Other junior colleges—the College of Southern Utah and Weber State College—became universities. State universities also opened satellite campuses in communities that included Blanding, Roosevelt, Brigham City, and Richfield. Recognizing a need for technical skills, the state created the Utah College of Applied Technology in 2001 with nine campuses.[7]

Although public education improved, money was always a concern. Because of the large proportion of school-age children in the population, Utah spent less per student than most other states in the Union. At the same time, a large part of the state's budget went to pay for schools. In his chapter in this section, James B. Allen discusses the perennial challenges of educating Utah's growing population from 1945 to 2000—the years when the state's population grew most rapidly.

Water Development

Population growth necessitated not only new schools and education dollars but new water supplies. Utah's average annual precipitation (thirteen inches) is the second lowest in the nation behind Nevada. But while Utah is often perceived as a desert, there are water resources if they can be transported. Two of the West's great rivers—the Green and Colorado—drain the eastern third of the state, and the average annual precipitation in Utah's high mountains exceeds forty inches of water. The Bear and Weber Rivers flow through northern Utah and then into the Great Salt Lake. Early settlers tapped the water from these rivers and their tributaries to irrigate farms and generate electricity.[8]

The first canals moved water within the same valley. In the nineteenth century, for example, Cache Valley residents built four canals that transported water from the Logan River, a tributary of the Bear. In the first decade of the twentieth century, Wasatch County residents developed lakes in the Uinta Mountains at the headwaters of the Provo River. The Provo Reservoir and Irrigation Company worked with representatives from Summit, Wasatch, and Utah Counties to build dams and canals to transport the water. The Wasatch

County example was an exception, though. For the most part, a huge canal project that could move water from one valley to another was something that Utah residents living in individual communities could not afford. Enter the state and federal governments.[9]

Early in the twentieth century, the state used proceeds from the sale of federal lands to partner with private companies and develop irrigation projects. Two of the most ambitious projects, Piute and Delta, reclaimed a total of eighty thousand acres. The Piute Project entailed a ninety-five-foot-high dam on the Sevier River near Junction and a sixty-mile canal running along the western side of the Sevier River Valley between Joseph and Fayette. The project provided water for some lands already in private ownership and thousands of acres between Richfield and Fayette that the state land board offered for sale to would-be farmers. A group of Jewish immigrants purchased six thousand acres from the project and established a colony at Clarion, west of Centerfield.[10]

The Newlands Act of 1902 that created the U.S. Reclamation Service (later renamed the Bureau of Reclamation) provided the basis for even more elaborate projects to divert water through mountains from one river system serving a sparse population to another with a longer growing season and greater population. The earliest federal reclamation project was Strawberry Reservoir on the edge of Wasatch County. Other reservoirs followed, including Deer Creek in the 1930s and Jordanelle in the 1990s. These projects were a boon for those who received the water—but they came at others' expense. For example, Strawberry furnished a large, dependable water supply to the farmers in southern Utah County but reduced the water available to the Utes and the people of Wasatch County. In his chapter, Adam Eastman describes this and subsequent federal projects designed to furnish supplemental water along with the complicated negotiations that preceded water-storage projects.[11]

The construction of large projects that withdrew water from the Colorado River and its tributaries necessitated interstate negotiations and agreements. In 1922 representatives from Utah and other states in the Colorado River drainage agreed to partition the river's water between the upper- and lower-basin states. Building upon that agreement, the upper-basin states, including Utah, divided their share in 1949, and Utah received rights to 23 percent of the upper-basin's allotment.[12]

Throughout the twentieth century, most Utahns applauded new water projects, viewing them as an essential response to growth. As Eastman illustrates, though, by the 1970s and 1980s, Utah branches of the Sierra Club of Utah, the Utah Wildlife Federation, and the Utah Wilderness Association questioned the desirability and need for additional water projects. They argued that dams were inefficient, environmentally destructive, and unsafe. This included not only elements of the Central Utah Project described by Eastman but also the Glen Canyon Dam and Lake Powell and proposals for damming the Bear River. In a debate at the University of Utah in 1995, David Brower, former executive

Construction of the Piute Reservoir Dam, 1892.

director of the Sierra Club, proposed draining Lake Powell. Two weeks later, the Sierra Club accommodated Brower by passing a motion requesting the government to drain the reservoir. The club argued that Lake Powell was inefficient and doomed: 8 percent of the water stored in the lake each year was lost to evaporation, and the reservoir was gradually filling up with river silt. In 1996 activists led by Richard Ingebretsen, a University of Utah professor of medicine and physics, organized the Glen Canyon Institute in Salt Lake to promote the restoration of the canyon.[13]

While some Utahns late in the twentieth century opposed dams on the grounds that they were inefficient, they also questioned their safety after the catastrophic failure of the Teton Dam in neighboring Idaho in 1976. In 1988 the *Deseret News* identified eighty-nine dam failures historically in Utah and cautioned that only 7 percent of the dams in the state where failure would be disastrous met minimum safety standards. The adverse impact of many reclamation projects upon fish and wildlife also gave some Utahns pause. The fact that few Utahns depended upon agriculture for their income but agriculture consumed nearly five times as much water as municipal and industrial uses led some urban Utahns to conclude that they could continue to enjoy lush lawns and green space without new projects if farmers would use water more efficiently. Farmers and their defenders retorted that their critics' comfortable lifestyles depended upon a foundation of cheap, abundant food.[14]

Farmers also pointed out that they *were* using water more efficiently. For example, in 1959, North Logan residents recognized the need to save water by piping it to fields and lawns. With a federal grant, engineer Bertis L. Embry installed a gravity-piped system down Seventeenth North. Other piped systems followed. Those changes came to Wasatch County later in the 1990s, when Jordanelle Dam forced water users to measure their consumption. Bob Mathis, the county planner, saw positive benefits with "an opportunity now to modernize the irrigation systems so that we can water more land with less water and be more efficient."[15]

Public Lands

Growth fostered competition for land as well as water. Federal ownership of more than two-thirds of the state's land constrained economic development during the twentieth century. Arable lands in the public domain were already in short supply by 1905, when the federal government opened portions of the Uintah-Ouray Indian Reservation to homesteaders; applicants for homesteads outnumbered available farms by seven to one. Later in the twentieth century, as the state's urban, nonagricultural population mushroomed, competition for control over its rural lands intensified. Traditional users such as ranchers and miners competed with those who valued the land for aesthetic and recreational reasons. For example, after preservationists scored a victory in establishing the Mt. Nebo Wilderness Area, closing that area to vehicular traffic, the Forest Service denied Robert Steele, the owner of a gypsum mine in the wilderness area, permission to haul his gypsum in trucks. In 1996 Steele won a lawsuit against the Forest Service, arguing that a dirt road leading to the mine should never have been closed to vehicular access because it had been regularly used and maintained by local residents and governments prior to the creation of the wilderness area.[16]

Until 1934 private citizens could purchase or homestead public lands outside of the national forests, parks, monuments, and reservations. During the Great Depression, though, Americans who believed that unregulated grazing and homesteading did not serve the interests of a rapidly growing, urbanizing nation gained the ascendancy. Some called for an end to homesteading and advocated tougher restrictions on the use of public lands to prevent overgrazing and erosion. Don Colton, who represented Utah in Congress from 1920 to 1932, played a leading role in campaigning for tougher federal controls. In 1934 Congress passed the Taylor Grazing Act, with support from most Utah residents, including ranchers, which removed the remaining twenty-four million acres of unreserved public lands in Utah from homesteading and cultivation. In 1946 a new federal agency, the Bureau of Land Management (BLM), was created to regulate and manage use of this land.[17]

By the 1960s, many Americans were convinced that the regulations imposed by the Forest Service and BLM were insufficient to safeguard and preserve the pristine beauty of public lands. They were concerned that activities, including logging and mining, were jeopardizing these lands. In 1964 Congress provided for tighter regulation on the use of primitive lands in the Forest Service system through the Wilderness Act. The act applied to pristine portions of the 15 percent of Utah's total land managed by the Forest Service. The act required the Forest Service to review all roadless areas under its jurisdiction in Utah and elsewhere to determine which ones were suitable for designation as wilderness. After an area was set aside as wilderness, motor vehicles would be barred, making mining or logging virtually impossible and eliminating off-road recreational vehicles as well.[18]

Twelve years later, Congress passed the Federal Land Policy and Management Act of 1976 (FLPMA), requiring the BLM to survey its vast holdings in Utah (nearly 42 percent of the state's total land area) and elsewhere for possible wilderness designation. The FLPMA also required the BLM to manage its lands "under principles of multiple use and sustained yield" and imposed safeguards designed to "protect the quality of scientific, scenic, historical, ecological, environmental, air and atmospheric, water resource, and archaeological values." The BLM outlined three characteristics that must be met for an area to qualify as wilderness: it must contain at least five thousand acres, it must lack a noticeable human imprint, and it must offer an outstanding opportunity for solitude or primitive recreation. Preservationist laws such as the Wilderness Act and the FLPMA sparked angry reactions from some Utahns, who questioned the right of Congress and federal bureaucrats to regulate or entirely prevent development of so much of the state's land.[19] Their unrest galvanized the Sagebrush Rebellion, which Jedediah S. Rogers describes in his chapter.

While the Sagebrush Rebellion soon fizzled, the debates surrounding it persisted. Remarkably, Utahns on both sides of the wilderness controversy compromised under the leadership of Senator Jake Garn and Utah Wilderness Association founder Dick Carter and agreed to set aside 750,000 acres as wilderness in 1984—the first state-level wilderness act in the nation. But subsequent efforts by the Utah Wilderness Coalition to designate between 5 and 9 million additional acres as wilderness foundered. In 1986, for instance, Congressman Wayne Owens advocated adding 5 million acres as wilderness, while Congressman Jim Hansen claimed that "mainstream Utah" wanted fewer than 2 million. Opinion polls showed that most Utahns desired to protect desert and mountain landscapes but disagreed on the means of doing so. An Emery County resident who opposed setting aside vast tracts as wilderness in the San Rafael Swell—the BLM had designated 262,435 acres there as potential wilderness—still desired to protect the environment: "My personal wish is for clean air and water and unpopulated land." Those who depended upon mining and ranching for their livelihood generally wanted smaller wilderness areas than environmentalists, who hoped to preserve as much land as possible from possible degradation.[20]

Changing Communities

Growth, along with economic and technological changes, also altered the orientation and livelihood of communities. Brigham Young envisioned

Park City was a booming silver mining town in 1891. Note the houses built on the hills and the mining mills.

small agricultural communities, where the Mormons could be self-sufficient. Following Joseph Smith's plan, he laid the towns out on a grid system with a center, square blocks with gardens, and farms outside of the town limits. In the 1860s, Colonel Patrick Connor helped to bring mining to the state, and typical mining towns sprang up on the hillsides. When mining towns boomed, nearby Mormon towns also prospered: the mines provided temporary employment for the Mormons and a market for their agricultural produce.

Over the twentieth century—especially in the years after World War II—the need for agricultural workers dropped as machinery appropriated many of the tasks formerly performed by people. As ore supplies played out, some of the state's most productive mines also closed. After 1925 the state's importance as a producer of silver and lead declined, although Utah remained a significant producer of copper and coal. Between 1960 and 2000, though, the number of Utahns employed in mining fell, except for a temporary rise in the number of coal miners during the 1970s' energy crisis. By 2000 the number of Utahns employed in mining was 8,001, down from 18,128 in 1980. Communities that had depended on these two major industries began to lose population, even though the state's metropolitan areas were booming. Whereas the population of Cache, Weber, Davis, Salt Lake, and Utah Counties in northern Utah grew every decade of the twentieth century, Beaver, Emery, Juab, Piute, Rich, Summit, and Wayne Counties suffered net

After the Park City mines closed in the 1960s, the companies converted the area into the Treasure Mountain Ski Resort (later Park City Mountain Resort). This photograph shows the lower part of the resort including base lodge, parking lot, and ski runs.

losses of population in at least half of the century's decades. In 1990 fewer people resided in Beaver, Garfield, Juab, Piute, Rich, and Sanpete Counties than had lived there in 1920. For instance, Juab County's population dropped every decade between 1910, when it had 10,702 residents, and 1970, when only 4,575 remained.[21]

Declining counties needed new sources of income, but the possibilities were limited. Capitalizing upon climate and recreational possibilities, some communities shifted gears beginning in the 1960s and assumed new identities. For example, Park City, once one of Utah's most successful silver and lead mining areas, was dying by the 1960s as the ore played out. But the mine owners cultivated new opportunities. In 1961 they floated plans to develop a ski resort. After it opened in 1963, Treasure Mountain Resort converted the Spiro Tunnel that had been built to drain the mine into a subway for skiers. The winter sports haven did not develop all at once; there were failures and sellouts.

But eventually the area became a place where the rich live; in 1998 Summit County ranked within the top 1 percent of counties in the nation in terms of its residents' income. Many who worked in Park City could no longer afford to live there.[22]

An even-more-dramatic transformation occurred in St. George and the surrounding communities in Washington County. Brigham Young sent the first Mormons there to grow cotton. While that effort produced little money, Young appreciated the warm climate and built a winter home there. St. George always struggled with the heat and the mercurial Virgin River. But with the invention of air conditioning and some success in controlling the river, more people began moving to Dixie. In his chapter, Douglas D. Alder describes how abundant sunshine, warm winter temperatures, recreation amenities, an increasing number of senior citizens, nearby scenic attractions, and the presence of religious and educational institutions helped St. George remake itself from an agricultural town with small farms and limited irrigation to a booming retirement community. By the end of the century, Washington County ranked sixth in the state in population, up from thirteenth in 1960.

Growth in places like St. George and Park City produced new cultural and commercial opportunities, but it also taxed local water supplies and infrastructure and fostered inflation and pollution. Leisure-based growth produced what historian Hal Rothman calls a "devil's bargain." Communities such as Park City or Moab that catered to tourists or communities such as St. George that lured retirees had to become what the tourists and the move-ins wanted them to be. Old-timers had to "act and believe differently" to "market their place." As the cost of living rose and powerful and wealthy newcomers moved in, original residents found themselves squeezed out of their own communities economically, politically, and socially.[23]

Other agricultural or mining communities managed to reverse the tide of population loss by accepting businesses that others saw as less than desirable and welcoming the jobs they created. Examples include large, coal-fired power plants in Uintah, Emery, and Millard Counties constructed in the 1970s and 1980s; a prison in Gunnison; nuclear waste facilities and a weapons incinerator in Tooele County; and a large landfill near East Carbon City. Despite their negative impact, these businesses generated jobs and income, and some donated funds for educational materials and scholarships. As Carbon County Commissioner Emma Kuykendall said in response to critics of the proposed landfill, "If Utah can accommodate the need [for landfill sites] without damage to the environment, then bring on the garbage."[24]

Not all residents of these communities believed that the economic benefits of these installations outweighed the social and environmental liabilities, though. Chip Ward, who worked for many years as a librarian in Grantsville, emphasized the negative in his characterization of Tooele County's economic profile in 2000: "Utah's western desert is burdened with the largest toxic air polluter in the U.S., two chemical-weapons incinerators, two hazardous-waste incinerators, a massive radioactive waste landfill, a hazardous waste landfill, the largest stockpile of chemical weapons in the world, a proving ground for biological and chemical warfare (much of it contaminated with unexploded ordinance and anthrax spores), a massive bombing range, and an Army depot with a large underground plume of carcinogenic water."[25]

Summary

Utah changed a great deal during the twentieth century. Growth was a major factor and impetus for change, especially from the 1940s to the end of the century. A high birthrate stretched limited education dollars. Taxpayers and government agencies coped with growth by funding new water projects, but opponents argued that conservation was preferable to water development. As urban sprawl engulfed the Wasatch Front, preservationist sentiment rose, and some Utahns argued for new restrictions on public-land use. Capitalizing upon climate and scenery, some rural communities reinvented themselves as tourist centers or retirement communities. Others assumed responsibility for managing the detritus of metropolitan growth from waste to prisons.

NOTES

1.   Table D, in *Utah's History*, ed. Richard D. Poll, Thomas G. Alexander, Eugene E. Campbell, and David E. Miller (Logan: Utah State University Press, 1989), 688; Cathleen D. Zick and Ken R. Smith, *Utah at the Beginning of the New Millennium: A Demographic Perspective* (Salt Lake City: University of Utah Press, 2006), 4–5; Marie Cornwall, "Beyond Fertility: What We Don't Know about Utah Women," in *Utah in the 1990s: A Demographic Perspective,* ed. Tim B. Heaton, Thomas A. Hirschl, and Bruce A. Chadwick (Salt Lake City: Signature Books, 1996), 196; Kristen Sturgill and Tim B. Heaton, "High Utah Fertility: Implications for Quality of Life," in Zick and Smith, *Utah at the Beginning,* 20; Utah Office of Vital Records and Statistics, *Utah's Vital Statistics: Births and Deaths, 2005,* Technical Report 246 (Salt Lake City: Utah Department of Health, 2006), S-5, available online at http://health.utah.gov/vitalrecords/pub_vs/ia05/05bx.pdf; Pam Perlich, "Population Growth, 1970–1995," in Heaton, Hirschl, and Chadwick, *Utah in the 1990s,* 3–8; *Deseret News,* September 12, 1995, A8.

2.   Tim B. Heaton, "Birth Capitol of the Nation," in Heaton, Hirschl, and Chadwick, *Utah in the 1990s,* 20–23.

3.   Arnold K. Garr, Donald Q. Cannon, and Richard O. Cowan, eds., *Encyclopedia of Latter-day Saint History* (Salt Lake City: Deseret Book Co., 2000), 4–5.

4.   James B. Allen, "Education and the Arts in Twentieth-Century Utah," in Poll et al., *Utah's History,* 587–89; Thomas G. Alexander, *Utah, the Right Place: The Official Centennial History,* rev. ed. (Salt Lake City: Gibbs Smith, 2003), 282.

5.   Allen, "Education and the Arts," 587, 594; James B. Allen, "Religion in Twentieth-Century Utah," in Poll et al., *Utah's History,* 616.

6.   Lynn M. Hilton and Hope A. Hilton, "Westminster College," in *Utah History Encyclopedia*, ed. Allan Kent Powell (Salt Lake City: University of Utah Press, 1994), 633–34; Alexander, *Utah, the Right Place,* 375; Allen, "Education and the Arts," 592–95; Allen, "Religion in Twentieth-Century Utah," 616.

7.   Allen, "Education and the Arts," 594; Frederick S. Buchanan, "Education," in Powell, ed., *Utah History Encyclopedia*, 153–55; "Utah College of Applied Technology," available online at http://www.ucats.org/abouthistory.html

8.   Utah Division of Water Resources, *Utah's Water Resources: Planning for the Future* (Salt Lake City: Utah Division of Water Resources, 2001), 5, 12–15, available online at http://www.water.utah.gove/waterplan/

9.   Jessie L. Embry, *A History of Wasatch County* (Salt Lake City: Utah Historical Society and Wasatch County Commission, 1996), 83–85.

10.   State of Utah, *Second Report of the State Bureau of Immigration, Labor and Statistics, for the years 1913–1914* (Salt Lake City: Arrow Press, 1915), 27–28; and Robert Alan Goldberg, *Back to the Soil: The Jewish Farmers of Clarion, Utah, and Their World* (Salt Lake City: University of Utah Press, 1986).

11.   Embry, *History of Wasatch County,* 85–89; Kathryn L. MacKay, "The Strawberry Valley Reclamation Project and the Opening of the Uintah Indian Reservation," *Utah Historical Quarterly* 50 (Winter 1982): 71; Thomas G. Alexander, "An Investment in Progress: Utah's First Federal Reclamation Project, The Strawberry Valley Project," *Utah Historical Quarterly* 39 (Summer 1971): 286–304.

12.   Norris Hundley, *Water and the West: The Colorado River Compact and the Politics of Water in the American West* (Berkeley: University of California Press, 1975); Adam Eastman, "From Cadillac to Chevy: Environmental Concern, Compromise, and the Central Utah Project Completion Act" (master's thesis, Brigham Young University, 2006), 28.

13.   Jared Farmer, *Glen Canyon Dammed: Inventing Lake Powell and the Canyon Country* (Tucson: University of Arizona Press, 1999), 182–83, 185; Glen Canyon Institute Web site, available online at http://www.glencanyon.org/index.php

14.   *Deseret News,* April 24, 1988; March 20, 2005; Utah Division of Water Resources, *Utah's Water Resources,* 14–15, 19–21; "Slow the H20 Flow, Farmers," editorial, *Signpost* (Weber State University), August 4, 2004; M. Holmes, "Comment," *Signpost,* August 26, 2004, available online at http://www.wsusignpost.com

15.   Jessie L. Embry, *North Logan Town* (North Logan, UT: North Logan City, 2000), 34; Embry, *History of Wasatch County,* 285; Bob Mathis, interview by Jessie Embry, August 4, 1994, 21, Wasatch County Oral History Project, Charles Redd Center for Western Studies, L. Tom Perry Special Collections, Harold B. Lee Library, Brigham Young University, Provo, Utah.

16.   Alexander, *Utah, the Right Place,* 421; Craig Woods Fuller, "Land Rush in Zion: Opening the Uncompahgre and Uintah Indian Reservations" (PhD diss., Brigham Young University, 1990); *Deseret News,* June 25, 1995.

17.   Charles S. Peterson, "Natural Resource Utilization," in Poll et al., *Utah's History,* 662–63. See also E. Louise Peffer, *The Closing of the Public Domain: Disposal and Reservation Policies, 1900–1950* (New York: Arno Press, 1972).

28. Alexander, *Utah, the Right Place,* 424; Paul W. Hirt, *A Conspiracy of Optimism: Management of the National Forests since World War II* (Lincoln: University of Nebraska Press, 1994), 229–33, 254.

19. Federal Land Policy and Management Act, available online at http://www.blm.gov/flpma/FLPMA.pdf; Alexander, *Utah, the Right Place,* 424–25; Jeffrey O. Durrant, *Struggle over Utah's San Rafael Swell: Wilderness, National Conservation Areas, and National Monuments* (Tucson: University of Arizona Press, 2007), 44. For a tabular breakdown of the number of acres in Utah managed by the Forest Service, the BLM, and other government agencies, see Renee A. O'Brien, *Comprehensive Inventory of Utah's Forest Resources* (Ogden, UT: U.S. Department of Agriculture, Forest Service, Rocky Mountain Region Research Station, 1999), 27.

20. Alexander, *Utah, the Right Place,* 426; *Emery County Progress,* May 21, 1986; October 31, 1989; *Deseret News,* September 19, 1996; December 26, 1996; Durrant, *Struggle over San Rafael,* 44.

21. Real Estate Center, Texas A&M University, County Population Data by Decade: Utah, available online at http://recenter.tamu.edu/data/popcd/popcs49.html; Thomas G. Alexander, "Generating Wealth from the Earth, 1847–2000," in *From the Ground Up: The History of Mining in Utah,* ed. Colleen Whitley (Logan: Utah State University Press, 2006), 40, 47.

22. David Hampshire, Martha S. Bradley, Allen Roberts, *A History of Summit County* (Salt Lake City: Utah State Historical Society and Summit County Commission, 1998), 321–23; Kristen Smart Rogers, "'We Didn't Think He Was Gonna Build It': Skiing Hits a Mining Town," *Utah Historical Quarterly* 69 (Fall 2001):310–25; *Deseret News,* April 12, 1999; Hal Compton and David Hampshire, "Park City," in Whitley, *From the Ground Up,* 318–41.

23. Hal K. Rothman, *Devil's Bargains: Tourism in the Twentieth-Century American West* (Lawrence: University Press of Kansas, 1998), 12, 27; Rogers, "We Didn't Think," 321, 323.

24. Richard H. Jackson and Matthew Shumway, "Transforming the 'Old West' to the 'New West': The Origin and Persistence of Locally Unwanted Land Uses in Utah," unpublished paper presented at Charles Redd Center Symposium on Utah in the Twentieth Century, May 2006, copy in authors' possession; *Deseret News,* March 9, 1991.

28. *Deseret News,* June 26, 2000. See also Chip Ward, *Canaries on the Rim: Living Downwind in the West* (New York: Verso, 1999).

13

Utah's Public Schools

Problems, Controversies, and Achievements, 1945–2000

James B. Allen

*Education has always been a concern in a state with a high birthrate.
Throughout the twentieth century and into the twentieth-first, Utah
rated among the lowest states in money spent per pupil. Yet at the end
of the twentieth century, nearly half of the state revenues went to education. In 2007 former Governor Olene Walker told a Brigham Young
University audience that in the past, Utahns had justified spending
less because the students' test scores were high and state incomes were
low. But conditions had changed; state incomes were higher, and test
scores were lower. James B. Allen examines the reasons why Utah
schools ended up, as Walker put it, on life support. Using newspapers,
Utah Foundation and State Board of Education reports, and national
magazines, Allen explores the crisis Utah schools faced from World
War II to the end of the twentieth century. Each governor from J.
Bracken Lee to Michael O. Leavitt tried different programs to fund
education while still meeting other obligations. Their efforts encountered resistance and were complicated by demands from parents and
the federal government. Allen carefully details the way each governor
tried to solve the education dilemmas.*

As the people of Utah know well, public education costs. At the end of the
twentieth century, in fact, it accounted for about 42 percent of all state and local
expenditures. Little wonder that eyebrows are raised, tempers occasionally flare,
and major, sometimes acrimonious, debates occur each time someone makes a
new proposal for more school funding. This chapter attempts to summarize the
major challenges, controversies, and accomplishments relating to public education in Utah from 1945 to the end of the century. The emphasis is twofold: the
perennial problem of school finance and the dilemmas of educational reform.

Funding public schools has been a perpetual challenge in the Beehive State. On October 30, 1930, twelve months after the Wall Street crash, opponents of new tax proposals for education unfurled this banner outside Temple Square in Salt Lake City.

Public School Finance: A Brief Summary

Funding for public education comes from three different sources: the state, local school districts, and the federal government.[1] The Uniform School Fund (USF), which provides the largest share, relies mostly on state income and corporate franchise taxes. In addition, a restricted account within that fund comes largely from the federal government in the form of grants for special purposes. The bulk of the local school district revenue is raised from local property taxes, but some additional funds come through investment interest, tuition payments, and student fees. The most significant tax is a state-mandated school levy, but the state also authorizes several other taxes.

Utah's basic state-supported school program recognizes a significant disparity among school districts as to the amount of money they can raise through property taxes. In districts where the mandated levy does not provide enough to meet minimum standards, the state makes up the difference from the USF. At the same time, the state recaptures excess funds from the more wealthy districts and places them in the USF.

In 1973 the legislature adopted the weighted pupil unit (WPU) as another way to help promote equalization. In general one WPU represents a pupil, but the formula is "weighted" to take into account other factors, such as small schools, education for the handicapped, vocational and technical training, and career ladder programs. Such considerations increase the number of WPUs allocated to a district, depending upon its need or involvement in these programs. Each year the legislature assigns a financial value to the WPU and then distributes funds to each school district according the number of its WPUs. In the year 2000, there was a total of 669,408 WPUs, each worth $1,901, thus providing more than $1.27 billion in funding.

Utah's Minimum School Program (MSP) incorporates the basic program but also provides for certain additional programs not funded through WPUs. These include various benefits and incentives as well as class size reduction. Certain leeway programs also allow school boards to impose taxes for other state-approved purposes. The state guarantees that a *board leeway* (voted by the State Board of Education) and a *voted leeway* (imposed locally if a majority of voters in a district approve) will each produce a certain level of funding per WPU. Any shortage is made up by the state, but if a district exceeds the level, it keeps the money. For this reason, complete equity among districts still does not exist.

Governor Lee Versus the Schools

In 1945 the war-weary people of Utah were anxious to get back to peacetime pursuits, but the job would not be easy. Not the least of their challenges was public education, where wartime scrimping had created a multitude of problems. There was a shortage of qualified teachers (nearly fifteen hundred did not have the required certification); schools were seriously overcrowded, with some holding classes in churches or other improvised facilities; and there was a serious need for more-adequate vocational education. Only a major infusion of funds could solve most of these problems. Nevertheless, Utahns took comfort in the fact that, despite wartime problems, their level of educational attainment was consistently better than the national average.[2]

At first things seemed to bode well for public education, for in 1947 the legislature increased the state education budget to $23 million, a remarkable 48 percent jump over the previous school year. However, Utah's rapid population growth, which was well above the national average, foreshadowed serious challenges. E. Allen Bateman, state superintendent of public instruction, pointed out in 1950 that there would be fifty thousand more children attending school in 1956–57, creating a need for fifteen hundred more classrooms and that many more teachers.[3] His message was clear: Utah was facing a school crisis, and Governor J. Bracken Lee's economy drive could only make it worse.

It seemed that Lee, who assumed office on January 3, 1949, had picked a fight with the legislature and educators over school appropriations. His passionate economic and political conservatism, his uncompromising tactics, and his crusade for economy at every level of state government made him perhaps the most controversial governor in Utah history. His tug-of-war with teachers

A *Salt Lake Tribune* photographer captured J. Bracken Lee's combative mood in this photograph of a press conference in 1960. Governor Lee aroused the ire of educators with his massive cutbacks in education budgets.

began almost immediately as both higher and public education came under his axe at his first opportunity to deal with the state budget. Though he cut the requests of nearly every department of government, the most massive cutbacks were reserved for education. He slashed the Department of Public Instruction's request by more than half.

Wrestling with what seemed to be impossible recommendations, the legislature passed several bills that Lee promptly vetoed as too expensive. Trying again, lawmakers trimmed another $29 million from the proposed budget. Still dissatisfied, the governor wielded the axe again, vetoing, among other things, an appropriation for the Extension Division of Utah State Agricultural College and a $20,000 appropriation for the Research Division of the Department of Public Instruction. The Extension Division veto was soon declared unconstitutional, for the funds were part of a larger budget item; then the state attorney general issued an opinion that the veto of the Research Division funds was likewise unconstitutional. Superintendent Bateman quickly applied for release of that money, but Lee stubbornly refused. Even after the Utah Supreme Court upheld the lower court's ruling on the Extension Division, Lee would not honor the attorney general's opinion and release the public school money. Much of his criticism was focused directly on Bateman, with whom he had a running battle all through his administration, but he also attacked the "school lobby" frequently and disparagingly.[4]

However, Utah's lawmakers saw things differently. In 1951 they passed Senate Bill 75, which increased the minimum school program, boosted transportation allotments, made changes in leeway tax provisions, and allowed local districts to set their own limits on school taxes. Lee quickly launched another public attack upon educators, arguing, among other things, that many teachers were merely mediocre and not worth a raise in salary; that their average salaries were already above the national average; and that the new expenditures demanded by "special interests" and "greedy minorities" would lead to socialism. True to form, he vetoed Senate Bill 75 as well as a subsequent compromise bill.

The 1951 legislature was not finished, however, and in its biennial budget made another effort to provide more funds for education. Again Lee wielded the veto liberally, disapproving, among other things, the entire recommended appropriation for higher education. This made it necessary to call a special legislative session in June. The result, for Lee, was a disaster. The legislature restored all the items he had line-vetoed and passed a compromise measure relating to Senate Bill 75. In the end, the total appropriation for education in the special session amounted to $3,300,000, more than the one in the regular session. Lee exercised no more vetoes, contenting himself with taking verbal swipes at the politicians responsible for "excessive appropriations."[5]

The war between Lee and Utah's educators only heated up during his 1952 campaign for reelection. In response to his opponent's charge that his "retrenchment in education" was "hollow economy," Lee listed eleven ways that he had advanced education, asserting that public-school expenditures had increased 42 percent during his first term. The Utah Education Association (UEA) issued a sharp rejoinder, pointing out that most of this was expense for building programs and actual operating funds had increased only 17 percent, which was more than offset by the 12 percent increase in number of students and 7 percent increase in cost of living. The UEA also noted that when Lee had taken office, the average teacher's salary was $277 higher than the national average and four years later, it was $40 below that average. To the dismay of educators, Lee was reelected, and the impasse went on. Meanwhile, the shortage of well-trained teachers only grew worse, for higher salaries in other states induced some of them, especially younger ones, to move elsewhere.[6]

In 1951, after his veto of Senate Bill 75 and its successor, Lee had persuaded the legislature to fund a sixty-member school survey commission, promising to honor its findings and, if necessary, call a special session to implement them. The commission issued its report in February 1953, but its recommendations, which included raising teachers' salaries, could cost the state $3 million or more. Despite his promise, Lee stubbornly resisted convening a special legislative session. The result was a summer-long standoff, with the UEA advising teachers not to sign contracts for the coming school year unless Lee relented. At the end of August, however, the UEA urged them to sign, fearing that failure to do so would simply play into the governor's hands. Finally, after the legislative council worked out a compromise proposal, the governor called the special session to meet in December. At that time, the legislature adopted a school finance program that included $340 more per classroom unit than Lee had recommended, so the governor exercised his veto once again. Another compromise measure finally became law without his signature, and his veto of an improved teacher-retirement program was overridden. Education still remained underfinanced, but Governor Lee had suffered another major defeat.[7]

Lee was also stubbornly opposed to federal aid for education. He even refused, in 1954, to send a Utah representative to Washington to participate in hearings on federal funding for public school construction. Educators, as well as many other people in districts that badly needed new buildings, were irate, for Lee also wanted to eliminate state funding of local school construction. In 1955 he vetoed a bill extending the mill levy for that purpose but was overwhelmingly overridden by the legislature. However, he successfully vetoed a bill that would have permitted Utah to qualify for federal aid for school construction and maintenance.

Actually, by the 1950s federal aid was becoming increasingly important in Utah public-school financing, having grown from half of 1 percent of all school revenue in 1930–31 to 6 percent in 1950–54. Most of these funds went to four school districts heavily affected by federal installations: Davis, Tooele, Weber, and Ogden. In addition, most Utah schools participated in the federal school lunch program, while some also profited from other miscellaneous programs.

How much Lee permanently damaged or set back public education is a matter of conjecture, though it is clear that his administration saw a definite decline in the relative amount spent per child, when compared with the nation or nearby states,[8] and that critical building needs were not met. At the same time, Utah education faced a continuing anomaly that threatened to become endless. Even though the state devoted a larger share of its individual income to education than any other state, it spent less money per student than the national average and had larger classrooms.[9] "Utah's education paradox," as it was dubbed later by the Utah Foundation, lasted throughout the rest of the century. Even so, Utah continued to rank unusually high in educational achievement.

Fresh Air, a New Crisis, and Sanctions

Lee's successor, George D. Clyde, seemed like a breath of fresh air to teachers as he worked with a sympathetic legislature to improve funding for education. In 1957, with Clyde's support, the legislature increased the basic school-finance program by raising both state and local property taxes. It also raised teachers' salaries, actually putting them above both regional and national averages. In

Pupils in Miss Clawson's kindergarten class at Madison School, March 25, 1957. Note the student-teacher ratio of 23 to 1. The vast majority of Utah's children were educated in Utah's public schools.

addition, it financed a badly needed driver education program, provided funds for educational television, accelerated curriculum revision, and strengthened requirements for teachers.

Lawmakers also tried to address the school building crisis inherited from Governor Lee. In 1959 they guaranteed seven hundred dollars per "building unit" to each local district for long-term capital improvements. However, the results were disappointing, partly because local levies were often spent on immediate, rather than long-range, capital needs. In 1961, therefore, the legislature increased local bonding power and adopted further measures to try to provide additional construction funds.[10]

Congress helped a little with school finance when it passed the National Defense Education Act of 1958 that provided funds for states to enhance their science, math, and modern foreign language curricula. The Utah legislature had to come up with $94,000 in matching funds, but that was quickly forthcoming. A total of $700,000 from the federal government helped local school districts provide laboratory equipment, textbooks, and remodeling.[11]

However, all this stepped-up funding was only a stop-gap solution. Financial needs continued to spiral as costs associated with teacher improvement and curriculum enhancement grew, the school-age population soared, overcrowding continued, and the number of required days in the school year jumped from 172 in the mid-1950s to180 in 1960, bringing Utah close to the national average. In some districts, students went to school only half a day because of the need to double up on classrooms. In addition, salaries once more fell behind regional and national averages. Partly for this reason, an estimated 12 percent of the state's teachers left its classrooms in 1960. Only about half the trained teachers graduating from Utah institutions remained in the state to teach, so nearly half the available positions had to be filled with people trained elsewhere or uncertified teachers given emergency authorization.[12]

Almost inevitably another school crisis hit the state. It began with a UEA-sponsored bill called CAPS (Cooperating Agencies for Public Schools), presented to the 1963 legislature. The ensuing debate was sometimes identified by the public as a salary dispute, but, in fact, the bill called for increases in everything but salaries. Governor Clyde, who considered himself a friend of education, was aghast at the financial implications of CAPS, which would cost a minimum of $24.5 million. Raising such an amount was "totally unrealistic," he said, for it would require the state to "double the state income tax, or add nearly 2 percent to the sales tax, or substantially boost the property tax."[13] The UEA responded that it was asking only for a minimum program at least equal to that of surrounding states.

The bill that finally passed did not provide anything near the amounts CAPS called for, whereupon the UEA voted in March to halt all contract negotiations until the impasse was resolved. Even after school boards throughout the state increased salaries by four hundred dollars in some districts and as much as a thousand dollars in the highest, the teachers refused to sign, demonstrating their resolve to stay out of the classroom until they were satisfied that minimum classroom standards would be met. They pointed to outmoded and unsafe buildings, leaky roofs, makeshift cafeterias, small and overcrowded classrooms, inadequate materials, and rocky playgrounds as some of the continuing problems that must be dealt with. They demanded that the governor call a special session of the legislature to address these issues, but he refused.[14]

The confrontation seemed all too reminiscent of the Lee era. In May 1963, the governor agreed to appoint an impartial citizens committee to study school needs and the capacity to finance them, promising to be guided by the findings of that committee and call a special legislative session if their conclusions made it seem advisable. The *Salt Lake Tribune* heartily approved, reflecting what must have been the sentiment of most Utahns: "There has been far too much emotion, even vindictiveness, in this school dispute. The time has come to set things straight."[15]

In August teachers voted to sign contracts for the coming school year, pending the committee report and the implementation of the CAPS program. However, the situation blew up again after the committee issued an interim report recommending an emergency session of the legislature to increase school finances by $6 million for 1964–65. The governor refused again to call a special session, whereupon the teachers voted for a two-day "recess" on May 18 and

19, 1964. Most districts continued classes during the walkout by hiring substitutes, but others simply closed school. In addition, the National Education Association (NEA) invoked sanctions against Utah—the first time in its history that it had sanctioned an entire state.

Not even Lee had suffered that kind of national humiliation, but among the people of Utah, there was severe public criticism of the teachers. Even Clyde's political opponents had some sympathy for him in this impasse. As reported nationally in *Time* magazine, one father of four observed, "It isn't easy to be stupider than Clyde, but the teachers managed it."[16]

Clyde suffered harsh censure from the educational establishment and others; he even received threats of violence.[17] Teachers refused to sign contracts until late in the summer. In December the governor's committee submitted its final report, which called for about $11.5 million additional state school support annually. But Clyde's term of office was over, and what to do about the problems became the challenge of the next administration and legislature. Nevertheless, NEA sanctions aside, Clyde could point with pride at progress in equalizing educational opportunities and nearly doubling teacher salaries, as well as the state's overall financial support for public education. He also left a state building program in place (something Lee had not dealt with) that showed promise of solving the problem of ailing physical facilities within the next six years.[18]

Improvement and Relative Calm: 1965-Early 1980s

Calvin L. Rampton, the first Democratic governor since 1949, had a remarkable ability to get along with both sides of the legislative aisle as well as special interest groups such as the UEA. In his first "state of the state" address, he outlined the most extensive program of governmental reform and educational and economic development that any governor had presented since statehood. When he went before the legislature in January 1965, he commended the UEA for its efforts and called for huge increases in educational spending. On March 9, he signed an education finance bill that provided $24.6 million in additional state and local funds. Six days later, the NEA lifted its sanctions. Fall contracts were signed in most districts, though it took Rampton's direct intervention to resolve a continuing impasse in Box Elder County.[19]

However, Utah was still not out of the woods, for by almost every standard of comparison, the state's ability to pay remained low. In addition, the school system was frequently criticized for failing to prepare students for current and future job opportunities, particularly in the areas of vocational and technical training needed by a society that was rapidly become more dependent upon technology. Nevertheless, the next twelve years saw substantial improvement in many aspects of public education. An infusion of federal funds allowed Utah to spend $1,135,000 during the 1964–66 biennium for badly needed equipment and instructional materials as well as minor remodeling. Schools also spent some $2,857,000 on special programs to help more than 16,500 elementary and secondary school children who came from economically deprived homes or were otherwise disadvantaged in their ability to achieve educational success. Though driver education had been part of various high-school programs for several years, the 1967 legislature passed a mandatory driver education law, which produced a major expansion of driver education programs in all of Utah's school districts.[20]

During the 1969–70 school year, federal funds allowed the development of several bilingual programs to meet the special needs of children who had limited ability to speak English. A number of elementary schools in the San Juan District, for example, where a major portion of the students were Navajo, adopted two-teacher teams in first- and second-grade classrooms. One teacher spoke English, and the other was bilingual. Federal funds further allowed the implementation of various professional-development programs for teachers, particularly those from minorities. Utah also expanded its emphasis on, and funding for, special education, though some students remained unserved or served inappropriately.[21]

The state also began to place emphasis on a Limited English Proficiency (LEP) Program. The problems faced by non-English speaking students became especially apparent in 1975, when the first group of refugees from Southeast Asia arrived in the state. In 1977 the legislature authorized an initial $317,100 for a bilingual program in school districts to serve students with language needs. This was only a beginning, however, for in the early 1980s, the State Office of Education pointed out that LEP students needed considerable more help.[22]

The state also paid attention to migrant children. Initially established in 1968, the migrant education program was an attempt to provide well-rounded academic instruction as well as recreational, vocational, and cultural activities. Most of the children involved were Hispanic, but there were also Asians, Native Americans, and some Anglos. By the 1980s the state was making a commendable effort to meet the needs of this distinctive group of students.[23]

Utah schools also stepped up their efforts to deal with drug abuse, which, in the late 1960s, literally exploded among adolescents and young adults throughout the nation and dramatically changed the nature of the challenges faced in the schools. As explained by the Utah Department of Human Services some years later, "The top discipline problems in the public schools in 1940 were talking, chewing gum, making noise, running in the halls, getting out of turn in line, and not putting paper in wastebaskets! By the early 1980's, when Utah started focusing on substance abuse prevention the top problems in schools included the following: drug abuse, alcohol abuse, pregnancy, suicide, rape, robbery, assault, burglary, arson, bombings, murder, absenteeism, extortion, gang warfare, abortion and venereal disease. Times have changed!"[24]

In fall 1969 school districts were given new guidelines for teaching about the effects of drug abuse. A decade earlier there had been little reference to drugs in the schools, partly because police officers had asked educators to "tread lightly" on the issue. However, as drug abuse spread from college campuses to students in public schools, the need for drug education became all too clear.[25] In summer 1970 a one-week, "live-in," drug-abuse-prevention program was held for more than 180 educators, students, parents, and community leaders. It was followed by twenty-one regional workshops throughout the state. From 1972 through 1975, supported by federal funding, Utah's drug-abuse team promoted other special projects, including teacher in-service training on preventing drug abuse, programs for parent-student-teacher involvement and interaction, development of interpersonal-relationship skills, and education on values.[26]

At the same time, parents were becoming increasingly concerned in the face of this national social disaster. In 1980, responding to a statewide PTA survey that demonstrated this concern, the legislature charged the State Office of Education with working out a collaborative program with the Utah Department of Health, the State Division of Substance Abuse, the PTA, and others to improve education on substance abuse in the schools. The legislature appropriated an initial $145,000 to begin the program. Now known as Dimensions Preventions, the program was permanently funded in 1983 by increasing the tax on beer. It was designed to implement alcohol and drug prevention programs in the schools as well as communities at large by employing specialists, providing more in-service training for teachers, and producing and distributing curriculum materials. Evaluations in the 1980s and later showed that students had a better knowledge of the effects of drugs and alcohol, used them less, and improved in their decision-making skills (one of the goals of the program).[27] The problem certainly was not solved, but at least by the end of the century, this cooperative program between the schools and other state agencies was helping.

Evaluations of Utah's progress in education showed mixed results by the early 1980s. One discouraging report revealed that between 1972 and 1982, the performance of Utah students slipped from fourteenth to seventeenth place among the twenty-eight states administering the American College Test. In some areas, however, Utah's educators did a remarkable job. In 1983, for example, President Ronald Reagan commended 6 Utah schools as among the most effective 144 high schools in the country. Utah schools also made some noteworthy accomplishments in various kinds of specialized education. In 1983 about thirty-two hundred out of nearly twenty thousand graduating seniors had taken advanced-placement classes—a higher proportion than in any other state.[28]

A Nation and a State at Risk: Challenges and Reforms of the 1980s and 1990s

Utahns seemed generally comfortable with the achievements of public education, but in 1983 they were stunned, along with Americans everywhere, by a grim report from the National Commission on Excellence in Education. Entitled *A Nation at Risk: The Imperative for Educational Reform*, the report amounted to a scathing indictment of the public-school system and a dire warning that national security was threatened by a "rising tide of mediocrity." American students were behind those of other nations on nineteen academic tests and last on seven; twenty-three million American adults and 13 percent of all seventeen-year-olds were functionally illiterate, and among minority youth, the rate was as high as 40 percent; the average achievement of high school students on most standardized tests was lower than twenty-six years earlier, when Sputnik had been launched; Scholastic Aptitude Tests (SATs) demonstrated a virtually unbroken decline from 1963 to 1980; nearly 40 percent of American seventeen-year-olds could not draw inferences from written material, only one-fifth could write a persuasive essay, and only one-third could solve a mathematics problem requiring several steps; there had been a steady decline in science and mathematics skills; and business and military leaders were spending millions of dollars on remedial education and training programs in such basic skills as reading, writing, spelling, and computation. At the same time, the demand for highly skilled workers trained in complex technological fields was rapidly expanding, yet the nation's youth was not being prepared to meet that crucial need. The rising generation was "scientifically and technologically illiterate."[29]

As might be expected, *A Nation at Risk* sparked a spate of reforms around the nation. They focused on curriculum, new approaches to learning techniques, establishment of national standards and ways to meet them, local initiatives, and many other things, and they all demanded better financing.

Utah educators and political leaders also took *A Nation at Risk* seriously. The state must act immediately, Governor Scott Matheson declared, and he outlined six key areas it must work on: revising sources of funding for education; guaranteeing a strong basic education program in every school; making the teaching profession more attractive financially, including some kind of merit pay; making equity adjustments in higher education; advancing the use of technology in the classroom; and improving vocational-educational programs.[30] The State Board of Education quickly appointed a blue-ribbon Commission on Education Excellence and soon implemented the commission's recommendations by establishing five goals, not too different from those of the governor: "(1) curriculum reform; (2) enhancing teaching as a profession; (3) improved planning for vocational-technical education; (4) utilization of physical resources; and (5) public and parental involvement in decision-making." Meanwhile, Governor Matheson formed a Utah Education Reform Steering Committee, which, in November, published *Education in Utah: A Call to Action*. It urged the people of the state to support efforts to raise more funds for education. Various educational-support groups, such as the PTA, also launched intensive campaigns aimed at generating legislative support for needed reforms and the money to implement them. The 1984 legislature considered a package calling for a $109 million boost in appropriations for the public schools. It eventually approved only $69.4 million, but this was still a remarkable 10.4 percent increase over the previous spending level.[31]

Among the improvements many teachers wanted was a career ladder program that provided financial incentives to improve their effectiveness. In 1984 the legislature appropriated an initial $15.2 million for inaugurating such a program, and permanent funding came the following year. [32] Periodic reviews revealed a variety of problems, but after nine years of operation, teachers and administrators gave the program generally favorable ratings. Interestingly, however, a legislative audit in 1998 showed that the merit pay component was difficult to administer and highly unpopular with teachers, so much so that in just one year, its use had fallen from 23 percent of total career ladder funds to 12 percent. The most beneficial aspect of the program for students and teachers alike was teacher compensation for taking extra training, performing extra duties, and working extra preparation days. [33]

The 1984 legislature also increased support for scholarships to outstanding high school graduates, as well as some students already in college, to recruit them into teaching careers; more than tripled the amount available to school districts for productivity incentives; and allowed the Utah State School Board to press for curriculum reform. In addition, it hiked the budget for vocational training from $300,000 to $1 million, but this was actually only a fraction of what most people agreed was needed. [34]

Among the ways of increasing school efficiency and productivity was the controversial year-round school program. The first program in Utah began at Westridge Elementary School in Provo in the fall of 1984, and by the 1990–91 school year, sixty-five Utah schools, with 12.4 percent of the state's total enrollment, were conducting year-round classes. An evaluation by the State Board of Education showed that 83 percent of the parents with children involved in year-round schools and 84 percent of the teachers were happy with the program. [35] Over the next several years, various districts tried it with varying degrees of success and satisfaction, but by the end of the century, there was still no general consensus among school districts.

A much-maligned effort at educational reform that began to sweep the nation in the 1980s was Outcome-Based Education (OBE), sometimes called standards-based education. Complex to explain and difficult to implement, this program focused more on individual "outcomes" related to the personal abilities and goals of each student in contrast to specific, content-based instruction correlated to grade levels. By 1990 it had been adopted in one form or another by sixteen states, including Utah. The 1985 legislature appropriated $500,000 toward OBE, and within five years, that annual amount had more than doubled. By 1987–88 all forty school districts had adopted OBE "to some degree," and the program was credited with sparking curriculum modifications in such subjects as world geography, ancient world studies, and the sciences and giving educators "a deeper conviction that all students are capable of achieving high level learning." [36] Some districts implemented only selected parts of the program, but by 1990 more than half of them had adopted a widely accepted model that

Educators and staff at Rose Park Elementary School, ca 1970s. Administrators struggled to retain teachers on meager salaries.

had been approved by the U.S. Department of Education. The heaviest focus was in the elementary schools, where nearly all the teachers were positive about OBE. However, teachers in secondary schools were not as convinced.[37]

OBE remained, and still remains, controversial. Among other things, critics decried the de-emphasis on specific subject matter (such as traditional history classes) in favor of so-called broader outcomes along with less emphasis on teaching basic mathematical and literary skills in traditional ways. Some complained, too, that by assuming that all students could eventually achieve whatever standards or goals were set, the schools were really "dumbing down" educational standards. In 1991, however, the state superintendent of public instruction claimed that OBE continued to exert "a positive impact on student learning, teacher satisfaction, and the support of administrators, board members, and parents to a varying degree."[38]

In 1988 the Utah State Office of Education implemented a complementary, but less controversial, reform known as "A Shift in Focus" (SIF), which, like OBE, emphasized individual student education goals and innovative teaching methods.[39] Unlike OBE, however, it did not necessarily involve inaugurating new programs but, for the most part, enhancing and improving those already in place. A case in point was the volunteer program, whereby volunteers provided one-on-one help to individual students who needed tutoring or academic enrichment. During the 1988–89 school year, approximately twelve hundred teachers and parents around the state were trained in setting up local volunteer programs. Volunteers came from diverse segments of the community, including senior citizens, businesses, and service organizations.[40] The results were often outstanding.

The world was changing rapidly at the end of the twentieth century, and one of the forces driving the changes was technology—especially computer and Internet technology. At the beginnings of a massive technological reform, some 35 percent of the public schools in the United States had Internet connections in 1994, but by the year 2000, that figure had grown to 98 percent.[41] The cost was high, but Utah could not avoid the inevitable, and the legislature took the matter seriously during the 1990s. Many schools had already begun to acquire computers for instructional purposes, but in 1990 the state allocated an initial $15 million, to be matched by contributions from local districts and the private sector, to help schools purchase computers for classroom instruction and train faculty and staff in their use. Under this Educational Technology Initiative (ETI), all school districts benefitted in one way or another. As the program grew, the state also completed a statewide telecommunications network (EDNET) that gave students access to many instructional programs not otherwise available. This was especially helpful in remote and rural areas. Between 1991 and 2001, the legislature appropriated a total of $188 million to ETI.[42]

So versatile was the new technology that in 1994, Utah established an Electronic High School, which served students who needed to make up credit, homeschoolers, students who wanted to graduate early, or those who wanted to take classes not offered at their high schools.

By the end of the century, classes could be taken on television via KUED and KULC (Utah's Learning Channel, now known as UEN-TV), over the EDNET system (which served sixty-five sites), or on the Internet. During the 1998–99 school year, students from every Utah school district, as well as many other states and several foreign countries, earned more than thirty-one thousand credits in the Electronic High School. Fully accredited by the Northwest Association of Accredited Schools, the high school even offered diplomas to homeschoolers, students who had previously dropped out of school and whose classes had graduated, and others who had been specially referred by their districts.[43]

In September 1989 President George Bush and the nation's governors met in a remarkable educational summit, where they agreed to establish a set of six national education goals: (1) preparing all children to start school ready to learn; (2) increasing the high school graduation rate to at least 90 percent; (3) improving student achievement and citizenship; (4) making the United States first in the world in science and mathematics; (5) emphasizing adult literacy and lifelong learning, and (6) ridding America's schools of drugs and violence. Over the next few years, the State Office of Education prepared a series of reports in an effort to inform citizens of Utah's progress toward those goals. The record was mixed, for even though Utah seemed to be doing fairly well on most of the goals, and exceptionally well on goal two, it fell short on goals four and six. Utah's performance was lower than average in mathematics, partly because only 32 percent of the teachers whose primary assignment was math had majored in the subject in college, as opposed to 47 percent in the nation. With respect to drugs and violence, the reports cited a 1989 survey that showed that, even though drug use among high school juniors and seniors had declined in recent years, "one in three of these students had consumed alcohol in the past month, one in five had used tobacco, one in ten had used marijuana, one in twenty had taken amphetamines, and one in fifty had used cocaine." Another survey three years later confirmed that information. In addition, a 1991 survey showed that 20.8 percent of all male students and 2.3 percent of the female students reported carrying weapons more than five days during the past thirty.[44] Despite the state's vigorous program aimed at drugs and violence in the schools, clearly there was more to do.

With reform piling upon reform in almost-confusing cadence, the legislature attempted even more reform in 1992 by passing the Utah Strategic Planning Act. By the end of 1993, however, the extremely high goals—such as having 100 percent of all Utah students achieve the goals of individual education plans—simply were not being met at the hoped-for rate. One unfortunate reason was that more than a third of Utah's forty district superintendents had never even heard of the plan.[45]

In a way, this was not surprising, for the rapid barrage of attempted reforms in the previous few years might have simply overwhelmed administrators and teachers alike. The authors of a 1994 study of reform in the previous decade noted that

> The mission statement included in the Utah Strategic Planning Act for Educational Excellence passed in 1992 makes explicit the lofty ideal for Utah education to be "the world class standard." Yet . . . the number of individual reform programs and initiatives and the conflicting demands of . . . reform programs of the last decade may result in Utah school-based educators being the "busiest educators in the world." No clear path has been identified for reform activities to have the desired impact on the educational experience of all Utah students or on their progress toward becoming the "best citizenry in the world."[46]

As far as administrators were concerned, the authors noted that "because there are so many innovations and policy groups involved, school-based administrators are struggling to find the central focus of the myriad of directions and guidelines." Further, they reported, the Education Commission of the States said in 1990 that "at best principals receive mixed signals on what state policymakers want for them," and this was as true in Utah as elsewhere.[47]

Still, however, the efforts at reform piled up, and in 1993 the Clinton administration got into the act by proposing another plan: Goals 2000. This one established eight national objectives, six of which were the same as those detailed by Bush. Over the next several years, Utah received millions of dollars in federal funding to implement the program, but, again, the results fell short of national goals. Goals 2000 funding was phased out at the end of the century.

One of Governor Michael O. Leavitt's reform plans was a restructuring process to involve parents and teachers, as well as school principals, in more-innovative and effective administration of local schools. In 1993 the legislature appropriated $2.6 million to inaugurate the Centennial School Program, whereby schools could apply for money to institute special programs, including self-governing ones. Schools designated as centennial schools could reapply and receive financing, in diminishing amounts, for up to three years, after which they were expected to continue their programs within their regular budgets. During the first year of operation, 97 schools were designated as centennial schools. After two years, there were nearly 200 centennial schools in the state. They received mixed reviews, however. In some cases, school district offices did not look enthusiastically upon giving up some aspects of curriculum control. Some principals, too, were reluctant to share authority. In addition, except for the neighborhoods where the centennial schools were located, they were not well known to a majority of citizens in the state. In all, however, some 395 schools in thirty-five of Utah's forty school districts participated in the Centennial Schools Program, which was phased out in the year 2000.[48]

There were questions as to whether the Centennial School Program accomplished all the governor had hoped. An audit in 1996, for example, revealed that some of the money went toward questionable programs—even, in one case, toward forming a bowling league. In other cases, there were warmly satisfying results. At Snowcrest Junior High in Weber County, for example, centennial school funds were used, in part, to help students whose average grades were below a C. They received special tutoring after school and in the summertime. Before the program began, 34 percent of the school's students received grades below C, but at the height of the program, that figure dropped to 10 percent.[49]

As the Centennial School Program phased out, the legislature showed support for the charter-school movement that was gaining popularity throughout the nation. Charter schools were public schools that, after receiving a charter from the state, were freed from some regulations under the assumption that they would produce superior results. Lawmakers authorized the program in 1998, requiring schools wanting to convert to show evidence that two-thirds of their parents and students supported the change. Charter schools received 75 percent of public-schools' per-pupil funding. Some school boards disliked charter schools, however, for they drew not only students but funding from traditional public schools. The Utah School Boards Association immediately challenged the charter school law as unconstitutional, asserting that the Utah Constitution authorized the State Board of Education to control only one uniform system. In January 2001, however, the Utah Supreme Court upheld the constitutionality of the law, for the constitution granted the board authority over "such other schools and programs that the legislature may designate." Initially, after four rounds of applications, the state board authorized eight charter schools. By the year 2005, some twelve thousand of around five hundred thousand Utah school children were registered in thirty-six charter schools.[50]

In another response to *A Nation at Risk,* lawmakers and educators throughout the country worked to find better ways to make schools accountable. In 1999 the Utah legislature created a Task Force on Learning Standards and Accountability in Public Education. That task force immediately proposed a system known as UPASS (Utah Performance Assessment System for Students) to set up clear criteria for evaluating how well Utah's schools were doing. Then, in 2001, with the support of President George W. Bush, the federal government passed the highly controversial No Child Left Behind Act (NCLB), which established national criteria for evaluating schools and threatened to withhold certain federal funds if those criteria were not met. Thus began a long battle between Utah and the federal government, with Utah educators as well as legislators believing that UPASS provided better and more-accurate assessment.[51]

ALTERNATIVES TO PUBLIC EDUCATION?

While this chapter has focused on public education, it should be noted that some Utah students attended private schools, though the comparative number was not great. At the turn of the century, 2.8 percent of Utah students were in private schools, as compared with 10 percent nationally. Private schools were only minimally regulated by the state, and evaluating comparable achievements was complicated. Based on standardized tests, such as the Scholastic Achievement Test, it was clear that private school students consistently scored higher than those in public schools. Also students in private schools took advanced-placement classes more frequently. However, the Utah Foundation pointed out that various demographic factors, not just the nature of instruction, could account for these differences. Studies demonstrated, for example, that family income was often correlated with educational achievement and students in private schools generally came from wealthier families. Race, too, was an important factor, and minority enrollment in private schools was only 10.27 percent as compared with 15.15 percent in the public schools. (And if the schools in San Juan County operated by the Bureau of Indian Affairs with 100 percent minority students were excluded, then minority enrollment in private schools was only 8.59 percent.)[52]

Another educational phenomenon spreading across the nation in the 1980s was homeschooling. As more parents became dissatisfied with public education and demanded the right to teach their children at home, many state legislatures passed laws allowing them to do so. Utah had allowed home education since 1953, but exact figures on the number of students in home schools were elusive. One study estimated that there were approximately thirty-five hundred in 1992. However, home schools grew rapidly (possibly by as much as 25 percent per year), and by 1999, the Sutherland Institute noted that there were seventy-five hundred families in the database of the Utah Home Education Association, which raised the possibility of around twenty-five thousand students in home schools. The institute also found that, with a combination of good materials and one-on-one parental tutoring, homeschooled students generally did well in national achievement tests, usually above national norms.[53]

CENTURY'S END: A CONTINUING CHALLENGE

As the twentieth century drew to a close, the story of public education in Utah maintained a familiar ring: generally high achievement in the face of serious underfunding. Utah students continued to earn above-average scores on most national tests, and the number of high school students taking and passing college-level advanced-placement courses remained high. Utah also stood among the best states in the nation in terms of high school graduation rates. In 1998 it was tenth highest, with 81 percent of the senior class graduating.[54]

However, Utahns knew well the continuing cost of public education. During the 1998–89 fiscal year, total public-school revenue came to $2.8 billion. The largest portion ($1.5 billion, or 53.1 percent) came from the state, mostly from the Uniform School Fund. The next-largest amount (40.8 percent) came from local school districts. Other funding (6.2 percent of total state expenditures) came from the federal government, mostly in the form of grants for such things as school lunches, instruction for children with disabilities, and other programs for the disabled.[55]

Meanwhile, the extent of Utah's continuing commitment was illustrated by the fact that about 42 percent of all state and local expenditures went for education (both public and higher), as compared with a national average of 34 percent. Education took about ninety-two out of every thousand dollars of personal income, compared with a national average of sixty-four dollars. The largest portion (fifty-two of the ninety-two dollars) went to public education (grades K–12).[56]

At the same time, Utah's education paradox continued: even though it ranked third in the nation in terms of education as a percentage of all state and local government spending and second in terms of spending as a percentage of personal income, Utah still spent less per student than any other state, and the average class size was larger than in any other state. The Utah Foundation explained this paradox in terms of demographics: Utah had the highest birthrate in the country, the youngest population, and 483 school-age children for every 1,000 adults in the labor force, compared with the national average of 402, which meant that Utah's labor force had to support a student population that was 20 percent larger than the national average. However, by the year 2000, the education paradox was beginning to unravel, for Utah's spending on public education as a percent of state and local revenue fell, and continued to fall, below the national average.[57]

The Utah Foundation also noted another uncomfortable anomaly related to demographics. One of the main reasons Utah students achieved above average results on national tests was that the state had a higher percentage of white students than other states. Since historically white students performed better, the state's average test scores were higher. However, when this racial difference was adjusted, Utah students did not do so well.[58] The uncomfortable reality was that as these demographics continued to change, and if the percentage of revenue spent on public education continued to decline in comparison with other states, then the overall achievement of Utah's students as compared with other states would drop. In 1999 the state superintendent of public instruction seemed to recognize this as he noted, with a mixture of pride and concern, "For many years, Utah has been the preeminent model of education efficiency, producing consistently high results with a modest per student investment. Unfortunately, our comparative excellence is slipping as other states have more aggressively addressed the needs of their students and invested in the personnel, programs, services, materials, and facilities necessary to meet those needs. While we will continue to be competitive, we must reconsider the needs of our increasingly diverse student body and increase our commitment to provide adequate educational experiences for all students."[59]

That, of course, was the challenge all along and would continue to be for the twenty-first century. Would vast new sums of money help? Would Utah continue to rank high in educational achievement, and would its comparative standing with respect to per-pupil spending change or remain low? Would either NCLB or UPASS succeed in their goals? The period from 1945 to 2000 began with high expectations but quickly turned to a time of bitter confrontation between the governor and educators over funding. As the century progressed, some of the problems were smoothed out, but Utah never came up to national norms in terms of per-pupil spending on public education. However, it maintained remarkably high educational achievements when compared with the rest of the nation. The end of the century saw a number of major reforms, both in financing and school programs, as Utah and the nation recognized that the United States suddenly faced serious educational shortcomings that, some believe, even threaten national security.

NOTES

1.   Utah Foundation, "Utah Public School Finances: FY 1998–99," Research Report 634 (Salt Lake City: Utah Foundation, June/July 2000); Patrick F. Galvin and Hal B. Robbins, "Utah," 2. This remarkable and very useful article may be found in *Public School Finance Programs in the United States and Canada, 1998–99,* a publication

of the National Center for Education Statistics, which may be accessed only on the Web or a CD-ROM. The Web site includes a link to an article about each state. It is available online at http://nces.ed.gov/edfin/; click on "education finance data publications," then, under "reports," the title of this report, then "online availability," then "Utah." *Public Education Data Book* (Salt Lake City: Office of the Legislative Fiscal Analyst, February 2001), available online at http://le.utah.gov/lfa/reports/Data2001Book.pdf

2. *Deseret News,* March 15, 1947; State Superintendent of Public Instruction, *Utah School Report, 1948–49* (Salt Lake City: Utah State Department of Public Instruction, 1950). The average number of school years completed by persons over twenty was the highest in the nation. The state was second only to Oregon in the percent of youth finishing eighth grade, highest in the percent enrolled in high school, second only to Washington in percent graduating from high school, second in the nation in the percent of its college-age youth enrolled in colleges, and highest in the percent of its youth graduating from college. *1969 Statistical Abstract of Utah* (Salt Lake City: Bureau of Business and Economic Research, University of Utah, January 1969), 44.

3. *Deseret News,* July 26, 1945; E. Allen Bateman, "What Lies Ahead for Education in Utah," *Utah Educational Review* 38 (1945): 261–64; James O. McKinney, "Readin' Ritin', and Remodeling," *Utah Magazine* 8 (1946): 16–17, 38–39. Bateman's estimates were not far off the mark. In 1956 there were 39,032 more children enrolled in the public schools than in 1950, but this jumped to 45,603 more in 1957 and 53,941 more in 1958. *Deseret News,* August 8, 1945; Raymond Hughes and William Lancelot, *Education: America's Magic* (Ames: Iowa State College Press, 1946); John T. Wahlquist, "Education in Utah, 1947," *Utah Educational Review* 40 (September–October 1947):11–13, 38; John T. Wahlquist, "Utah Schools Rank High," *Utah Educational Review* 41 (December 1947): 20–21, 30; Wahlquist, "Status of Education in Utah," *Utah Academy of Sciences, Arts and Letters* 24 (1947): 109–31.

4. For a full discussion of the ongoing battle between Lee and Bateman, see Edwin Lee Reynolds, "J. Bracken Lee and Utah Public Education" (master's thesis, Brigham Young University, 1973): 15–27, with the correspondence between Lee and Bateman reproduced in App. A; Dennis L. Lythgoe, *Let 'Em Holler: A Political Biography of J. Bracken Lee* (Salt Lake City: Utah State Historical Society, 1982): 109–15.

5. For details on the fight over Senate Bill 75, see Reynolds, "J. Bracken Lee and Utah Public Education," 38–64, and App. B, which reproduces radio addresses by Lee, Bernhard, and West; Lythgoe, *Let 'Em Holler,* 117–22.

6. The problem is illustrated by the fact that 82 percent of the 773 teachers trained in Utah in 1947–48 remained in the state, but only 37 percent of the 802 Utah-trained teachers in 1954 took jobs in Utah's schools. Lythgoe, *Let 'Em Holler,* 127.

7. He also received bad national press, exemplified by a *Time* magazine article in January 1954, criticizing him for his "passion for economy" that, it said, had inflicted "definite signs of malnutrition" on Utah's schools. "The Governor and the Schools," *Time,* January 11, 1954, available online at www.time.com/time/magazine/article/0,9171,819343,00.html

8.   In 1945–46 the average expenditure per child in Utah was $129.30, compared with $136.41 in the nation, $153.33 in other mountain states, and $158.38 in other western states. Utah ranked thirtieth among all the states. By 1957–58 it had dropped to thirty-fifth place, spending $261.40 per student as compared with $341.14 in the nation, $359.54 in the mountain states, and $369.27 in the western states. Floyd Samuel Wilcox, "The Major Financial Policies of Governor J. Bracken Lee of Utah, 1949–1957" (master's thesis, University of Utah, 1967), 79. To put it another way, before Lee took office Utah's expenditure per child was 94.8 percent of the national average, 84.3 percent of the mountain states' average, and 81.17 percent of the western states' average. When he left office, the respective averages were 76.7, 72.7, and 70.8, a decline of more than 10 percent in each instance.

9.   Utah had a more severe funding problem than most other states. Its birthrate was 30 percent higher than the national average. It also had a significantly higher proportion of its students enrolled in public schools, yet the average individual income in the state was only 88.4 percent of the national average. Utah Foundation, "Public School Finance in Utah—1955," Research Report 119 (Salt Lake City: Utah Foundation, March 1955). See also the editorial in *Utah Educational Review* 50 (November 1956): 8–9.

10. Utah Foundation, "Utah's Public School Building Program—1961," Research Report 188 (Salt Lake City: Utah Foundation, September 1961).

11. State Superintendent of Public Instruction, *Utah School Report, 1958–60* (Salt Lake City: Utah State Department of Public Education, 1960).

12. State Superintendent of Public Instruction, *Utah School Report, 1956–58* (Salt Lake City: Utah State Department of Public Instruction, 1958); Utah Foundation, "1962–63 Teacher Salary Survey," (Salt Lake City: Utah Foundation, 1964); Jefferson N. Eastmond, "Why Teachers Leave Utah Classes," *Utah Educational Review* 54 (January 1961): 22–23; State Superintendent of Public Instruction, *Utah School Report, 1962–64* (Salt Lake City: Utah State Department of Public Instruction, 1964).

13. Clyde quoted in "Showdown in Utah," *Time* 81 (May 24, 1963): 62–63, available online at www.time.com/time/magazine/article/0,9171,830441,00.html

14. At this point, he explained, he saw the issue as more than just the schools themselves. It was "whether the state shall remain sovereign or be dictated to by an organized group." It was, he said, "like having a pistol at my head." *Salt Lake Tribune,* June 6, 1962.

15. *Salt Lake Tribune,* editorial, May 28, 1963.

16. "Utah Off Limits," *Time* (May 14, 1964), available online at http://www.time.com/time/magazine/article/0,9171,940454,00.html

17. Ora P. Clyde, interview by Keith Melville, November 23, 1979, 9, Utah Politics Oral History Project, Charles Redd Center for Western Studies, L. Tom Perry Special Collections, Harold B. Lee Library, Brigham Young University, Provo, Utah.

18. *Salt Lake Tribune,* December 30, 1964.

19. See Calvin L. Rampton, *As I Recall,* ed. Floyd A. O'Neil and Gregory C. Thompson (Salt Lake City: University of Utah Press, 1989), 157–58.

20.   State Superintendent of Public Instruction, *Utah School Report, 1964–65* (Salt Lake City: Utah State Department of Public Instruction, 1966).

21.   State Superintendent of Public Instruction, *Utah School Report, 1969–70* (Salt Lake City: Utah State Department of Public Instruction, 1970). In 1973 the legislature provided pupil weightings for each recognized disability, thus increasing the funds available to special-education programs. By 1977 the amount of money available for those with disabilities from federal, state, and local funds was more than 10 percent more, per student, than that for regular students. Utah Legislature, Handicapped Children's Research Team, "Utah Schools Special Education Study: A Report to the Education Study Committee of the Utah State Legislature" (Salt Lake City: n.p., [1977?]), 1–2, 27.

22.   *Survival Communication Instruction for Classroom Teachers of Students with Limited English Proficiency (LEP)* (Salt Lake City: Utah State Office of Education, Division of Program Administration, 1981), iv.

23.   See annual reports (variously titled) of the migrant education program, published by the Utah State Office of Education; *Migrant Education in Utah: Portraits of Success* (Salt Lake City: Migrant Education Section, Curriculum and Instruction, Utah State Office of Education, 1985), 3. The latter publication is devoted mostly to portraits and personal sketches of migrant students who have graduated from high school in recent years.

24.   From the "Preventions Dimensions" page on the Web site of the Utah Department of Human Services, available online at http://www.dhs.utah.gov/ Click on A–Z index, then "Prevention Dimensions."

25.   *Salt Lake Tribune,* February 5, 1970, citing statement by State Board of Education health specialist Robert L. Leake.

26.   For a full discussion, see *A Review of the Federal and State Funded Utah Drug Abuse Education Project, 1970–1976* (Salt Lake City: State Board of Education, 1976).

27.   "Preventions Dimensions" page on the Web site of the Utah Department of Human Services.

28.   *Deseret News,* June 10, 1981; May 30, 1983; January 22, 1984; July 1, 1983. The schools so honored were Bingham High School, Butler Middle School, and Highland High School in Salt Lake City; Wasatch Middle School in Heber City; Logan High School in Logan; and Bountiful High School in Bountiful; *Deseret News,* May 22, 1983.

29.   National Commission on Excellence in Education, *A Nation at Risk: The Imperative for Educational Reform* (Washington, D.C., April 1983), 7, 11.

30.   *Deseret News,* July 1, 1983.

31.   *Twelfth Annual Report of the Superintendent of Public Instruction of the State of Utah, for the Period Ending June 30, 1984,* (Salt Lake City: Utah State Office of Education, 1984) 4.

32.   According to one study, this could add as much as a thousand dollars per year to the average salary. *Deseret News,* May 20, 1984; December 3, 1984.

33.   "Survey of the Utah Public Education Career Ladder Program," November 12, 1998, by President R. Lane Beattie and Speaker Melvin R. Brown, cochairmen and members

of the Audit Subcommittee. This report may be found online at http://www.le.state. ut.us/audit/98_09rpt.pdf See also Carolyn B. Horan and Vicki Lambert, *Evaluation of Utah Career Ladder Programs,* prepared by the Beyrl Buck Institute for Education, San Rafael, CA, for the Utah State Office of Education, Salt Lake City, 1994, available online from Education Resources Information Center at http://www.eric.gov

34. As early as 1980, a commission appointed by Governor Matheson had made a number of recommendations for improvement, but it was estimated that their full implementation would require sixteen million dollars over the next five years. Utah Foundation, "Vocational Education in Utah," Research Report 400 (Salt Lake City: Utah Foundation, February 1980).

35. For a summary of the arguments for and against year-round schools, as well as the survey, see Utah Foundation, "Evaluation of Year-Round Schools in Utah," Research Report 530 (Salt Lake City: Utah Foundation, December, 1990).

36. *Annual Report of the State Superintendent of Public Instruction 1987–88,* (Salt Lake City: Utah State Office of Education, 1988), 22.

37. See Utah State Office of Education, *OBE in Utah: A Study of Outcome Based Education in Utah,* prepared by Research and Development Consultants, Salt Lake City, Utah, 1991. Available at Utah State Office of Education, Salt Lake City, and online through Educational Resources Information Center (ERIC) at http://www.eric.ed.gov

38. *Annual Report of the Utah State Superintendent of Public Instruction 1990–91,* (Salt Lake City: Utah State Office of Education, 1991), 7.

39. For discussion of the origins of "A Shift in Focus," see *Annual Report of the State Superintendent of Public Instruction 1988–89,* (Salt Lake City: Utah State Office of Education, 1989),1–4. For pros and cons of the new program, see Utah Foundation, "A New Focus for Utah Public Schools?,"Research Report 527 (Salt Lake City: Utah Foundation, September, 1990).

40. *Report of the State Superintendent 1988–89,* 13–14.

41. "Internet Access in U.S. Public Schools and Classrooms: 1994–2002," report by National Center for Education Statistics, U.S. Department of Education, Institute of Education Sciences (2005), available online at http://nces.ed.gov/pubsearch/pubsinfo.asp?pubid=2005015

42. "Report to the Utah Legislature Number 2005–04, Best Practices in Using Technoloy in Public Education" (February 2005), available online at http://media.centerdigitaled.com/K12_Blueprint/Utah_Legislative_Audit.pdf

43. See the Web site of Utah's Electronic High School at http://ehs.uen.org; *Annual Report of the State Superintendent of Public Instruction, 1998–99.*

44. Utah State Office of Education, *A Utah Perspective on the National Education Goals* (Salt Lake City: Utah State Office of Education, 1993), 29.

45. *Provo Daily Herald,* December 15, 1993.

46. Carolyn M. Shields and Karen V. Berner, "Surviving the Waves of Curriculum Reform in Utah," chap. 2 of *Education Reform in Utah: Years of Promise,* ed. Patrick F. Galvin and David J. Sperry (Salt Lake City: Utah Education Policy Center, Graduate School of Education, University of Utah, March 1994), 46–47.

47. Ibid.

48. *Report of the State Superintendent, 1998–99,* available online at http://www.usoe.k12.
ut.us/board/docs/rpt.htm

49. "Leavitt and Schools: He Stuck to His Goals but How Much Did They Help?" *Deseret
News,* November 9, 2003.

50. The Heritage Foundation, "Utah," available online at http://www.heritage.org/
Research/Education/Schools/utah.cfm; *Report of the State Superintendent, 1998–99*;
"Charter Schools Blossom," *Deseret News,* August 23, 2005. For a general report on
funding and other challenges of charter schools, see Utah Foundation, "Challenges
Facing Utah Charter Schools," Research Report 672 (Salt Lake City: Utah Foundation,
October 2005).

51. "Measure on School Testing is Approved," *Desert News,* March 2, 2000; "Testing to
Get Reality Check," *Desert News,* February 3, 2001; "President Bush's Address to a
Joint Session of Congress," *Desert News,* February 28, 2001.

52. Utah Foundation, "The Status of Private Schools in Utah," Research Report 651 (Salt
Lake City: Utah Foundation, May 2002).

53. Stacey Elizabeth Marlow, "Home Schools, Public Schools, Policies, and Practice:
Superintendents Implementing Home Education Policy in Four Western States"
(EdD thesis, University of Michigan, 1992); Sutherland Institute, "Utah Schools: An
In-Depth Look: An Analysis of Spending and Achievement in Utah Schools" (Salt
Lake City: Sutherland Institute, August 1999), 35–36; 47–48.

54. Jay P. Greene, "High School Graduation Rates in the United States," *Civic Report*
(New York: Manhattan Institute for Policy Research, November 2001, rev. April
2002), table 2.

55. "Utah Public School Finances: 1998–99"; see also Utah State Office of Education,
"School Finance and Statistics, Taxation," available online at http://www.usoe.k12.
ut.us/FINANCE/tax; "Utah Public Education Financing." For details, see "Utah
Public School Finances 1998–99"; Utah Foundation, "Utah Foundation Research
Report and the State School Trust Fund," Research Report 632 (Salt Lake City: Utah
Foundation, March/April 2000).

56. "Utah Public School Finances 1998–99," 2.

57. Utah Foundation, "Utah's Education Paradox," Research Brief (Salt Lake City: Utah
Foundation, October 7, 2004). This report refers to a similar report with the same
title, issued in November 1999. See also Utah Foundation, "Paradox Lost: Utah
Public Education Funding Effort No Longer Surpasses the Nation," Research Report
674 (Salt Lake City: Utah Foundation, April 2006).

58. As explained in the report: "When this racial difference is adjusted for, Utah students
do not perform as well. White students in Utah perform lower than the U.S. average
for white students. Utah Hispanic students generally perform lower than the U.S.
average for Hispanic students, but better than the U.S. average in 8th grade reading,
and 4th and 8th grade science. Also, Utah's Asian and American Indian students score
lower than their U.S. counterparts." Utah Foundation, "Paradox Lost."

59. *Report of the State Superintendent, 1998–99.*

14

From Cadillac to Chevy

Environmental Concern, Compromise, and the Central Utah Project Completion Act

Adam Eastman

In a region with scant precipitation, Utahns, like most residents of the American West, consume prodigious amounts of water to maintain lush lawns and productive farms. In 1986 journalist Marc Reisner completed his muckraking exposé of water usage and reclamation in the West, aptly entitled Cadillac Desert. Reisner argued that the immense cost of federally funded dams and canals designed to support the water-rich lifestyles of westerners defrauded American taxpayers. In 1987, one year after Reisner's exposé appeared, leaders of the U.S. House and Senate, who likewise viewed western water projects as boondoggles, refused to approve increased expenditures for the "Cadillac" of Utah water projects: the Central Utah Project (CUP). In the following essay, Adam Eastman uses the reports and records of federal and local agencies, articles from newspapers, and interviews with key participants to describe the history of federal water projects in the Beehive State, culminating in the battle for passage of the Central Utah Project Completion Act. Eastman shows that in that battle, municipal water users, farmers, Native Americans, politicians, and environmentalists divided and coalesced in patterns that confound traditional binaries: urban versus rural, East versus West, or federal versus local. The end product was a less-ambitious water project that Utah Representative Wayne Owens named "a Chevy instead of a Cadillac." Despite Owens's metaphor, as Eastman indicates, the CUP delivers some of the West's most expensive water to the Wasatch Front and Uinta Basin.

Water development has been a key to Utah's history and the success of its desert communities. During the twentieth century, the state's farmers, municipal water providers, and politicians lobbied the federal government for larger water projects. These projects provided needed water but also came with consequences. As Utah interests pushed for the "Cadillac" of Utah water projects—the Central Utah Project [CUP]—the high economic and environmental costs of large-scale water development heightened existing concerns and anxieties. As a result, the CUP faced numerous legal and political challenges that delayed its completion and altered its design, scope, and beneficiaries. The fight over the CUP climaxed in a five-year congressional battle to rescue and reauthorize the project. The resulting compromise legislation converted the Cadillac into what Utah Congressman Wayne Owens called a Chevy.[1]

The events surrounding the political battle provide an interesting case study of the changing environmental attitudes of the public, politicians, and water officials. Further, these attitudes dynamically interacted with other local and national concerns. Different groups and individuals expressed fears about property rights, economic development, farm subsidies, fiscal responsibility and the national debt, public power, and the government's commitment to keep promises, contracts, and treaties. The battle lines surrounding individual issues were clearly drawn. The fight for and against the reauthorization legislation—titled the Central Utah Project Completion Act or CUPCA—reinforces the images of a divided West. But the divisions did not fall neatly along the common lines of natural resource battles in the West that pit East versus West, urban versus rural, federal versus local, or New West versus Old West.[2] Instead, the size and complexity of the project, combined with the varied interests, caused lines between these groups to overlap and appear fuzzy and faint. The resultant political fight challenges historical models and perceptions of conflict in Utah and the West.

Cadillac Unveiled

During the early years of pioneer settlement, farmers constructed simple weirs and diversions on the numerous mountain streams and rivers flowing out of the western flank of the Wasatch Mountains. The most fertile soils and best climate for agriculture exist in the valley of the Bonneville Basin, largely due to its lower elevation. The settlement and development of the Wasatch Front was driven by these geographical and environmental factors.[3]

Another environmental factor—precipitation patterns—hampered the development of irrigation communities in the state. During many years, streams swollen by melting snow in early summer slowed to a trickle later as crops matured. Winters of light snowfall compounded the problem, while heavy snows led to spring flooding. The eventual solution to the threefold problem of inadequate late-summer supplies, floods, and drought was the construction of storage reservoirs, coupled with connections to more-distant supplies. These new large-scale projects required large sums of capital beyond the means of communal irrigation companies. To secure the requisite capital, westerners turned to the federal government.[4]

With the support of President Theodore Roosevelt, Senator Francis G. Newlands of Nevada led the battle to secure passage of the Reclamation Act on June 17, 1902. The act established the Reclamation Service, the predecessor of the Bureau of Reclamation, to build projects funded by the sale of public lands. The water users then repaid the projects' costs, making funds available for additional projects.[5]

Seeking to build political favor, the Reclamation Service chose to spread its projects as broadly as possible in its early years. In Utah Reclamation Service engineers worked with Utah's state engineer, Abraham Fairbanks Doremus, to select a suitable project. Motivated by a drought that had begun in 1896, Doremus had prepared an ambitious plan for future water development by 1902. His proposal served as a blueprint for much of the water development during the twentieth century. Included in the plan was the Strawberry Valley Project, first proposed by Utah state senator Henry Gardner of Spanish Fork. It called for a reservoir on the Strawberry River and a diversion tunnel through the Great Basin divide to the Spanish Fork River drainage. Doremus expanded Gardner's idea by proposing canals to intercept and transport the water of the Duchesne River and its tributaries to the Strawberry Reservoir, and irrigation canals to divert Strawberry water from Spanish Fork Canyon to Salt Lake County.[6]

After conducting additional investigations based on Doremus's idea, the Reclamation Service chose to build the Strawberry Valley Project as its first in Utah. Because of the technical difficulty and expense of the additional diversion canals, Reclamation Service engineers scaled down the plans. However, in subsequent decades, Reclamation utilized Doremus's original ideas to expand the Strawberry Valley Project into the CUP.[7]

The Reclamation Service began construction of the Strawberry Valley Project on March 6, 1906. After the project began delivering water to southern Utah County, farmers in eastern Juab County petitioned Reclamation to be included. They paid for the Reclamation Service to conduct investigations in 1919 and 1920. A board of engineers reported on June 11, 1920, that water delivery to Juab County by gravity required a long and expensive canal beginning four miles up Diamond Fork Canyon. The engineers determined that such a canal was not economically practical.[8]

As the Strawberry Valley Project neared completion, the Utah Water Storage Commission entered into a contract in 1922 to fund cooperative investigations into the next reclamation project in Utah. As a result of this inquiry, the Bureau of Reclamation selected the Weber River Project in 1924 as its second in Utah. Crews began construction on the project's primary feature, Echo Dam, in 1927. A secondary element included the Weber-Provo Canal in the Kamas Valley to divert water from the Weber to the Provo River.[9]

In response to the Great Depression and a severe drought that devastated Utah agriculture and threatened municipal water supplies, President Franklin D. Roosevelt authorized additional "emergency" reclamation projects. These projects included the Hyrum Project near Logan, the Ogden River Project, the Provo River Project, the Moon Lake Project on the Lake Fork River in the Uintah Basin and the Sanpete Project.[10]

The Provo River Project consisted of a new reservoir at Deer Creek on the Provo River. Water to fill the reservoir would be imported from the Weber River through an enlarged Weber/Provo River Canal and the North Fork of the Duchesne River through what was then Reclamation's second-longest tunnel. Water would be delivered to irrigators in northern Utah and Salt Lake Counties through the enlarged Provo Reservoir Canal—renamed the Murdock Canal—and the Salt Lake Aqueduct. The project's final element incorporated an idea outlined by Doremus in 1902: the construction of dikes to close off the shallow Provo and Goshen Bays on Utah Lake to reduce water loss from evaporation. Funding and political roadblocks delayed construction of the dikes. Eventually the Bureau rolled plans for the proposed dikes and additional transbasin diversions into the CUP.[11]

The Bureau's evolving plans for the CUP were ambitious. In the 1940s, the agency proposed storing the water saved by diking Utah Lake in a new reservoir above Heber City. A water-rights exchange would store additional water. Rights to Provo River water in Utah Lake held by Salt Lake County irrigators would be fulfilled by importing water from an expanded Strawberry Reservoir, allowing the original Provo River water to be held upstream for diversion to other users. To make additional water available from Strawberry Reservoir, engineers envisioned a massive dam on the Green River at either Flaming Gorge or Echo Park. Using gravity and a long tunnel from Flaming Gorge, or the hydroelectricity generated at Echo Park to power pumps, they planned to divert water directly from the Green River to an expanded network of reservoirs, canals, and pipelines to supply the cities and farms of the Uinta Basin. A series of pipelines could then direct the existing water from virtually every stream and river along the southern slope of the Uinta Mountains into an enlarged Strawberry Reservoir, and then to the farms and cities of the Bonneville Basin.[12]

But the complicated and expensive project, first proposed to Congress by Utah Senator Abe Murdock in 1946, quickly met with opposition. This resistance came first on economic grounds, to which later was added the opposition of downstream users of the Colorado River and environmentalists concerned about a proposed dam at Echo Park inside Dinosaur National Monument. Despite the protests, a coalition of western senators and congressmen secured passage of the Colorado River Storage Project (CRSP) in 1956. The CRSP authorized the construction of "main stem" dams along the Colorado and its significant tributaries in the upper basin states. The power stations at these dams would develop hydroelectricity to generate revenue that offset the cost of irrigation projects, and the water stored in the reservoirs would guarantee deliveries to the lower basin. Additionally the CRSP authorized thirteen participating irrigation projects, including the CUP, the largest of them all.[13]

To win approval, CRSP proponents, led by Congressman Wayne Aspinall, amended the legislation to remove the controversial Echo Park Dam. In exchange the Sierra Club agreed to drop its opposition to the CRSP. Utah politicians and water officials preferred the Echo Park alternative because it would have been cheaper to construct and would have produced more hydropower and impounded more water of a higher quality than the Flaming Gorge alternative. However, as a result of the compromise, Reclamation altered plans for the ultimate phase of the CUP to include a diversion from Flaming Gorge to the Uinta Basin through a long tunnel.[14]

After the passage of the CRSP, work progressed quickly on the large mainstem storage reservoirs—Flaming Gorge and Glen Canyon—but lagged on the CUP as the bureau completed its detailed planning. Because of the size and scope of the CUP, Reclamation divided it into six units. Congress authorized the four initial ones—Bonneville, Vernal, Jensen, Upalco—in 1956 in the CRSP Act. In 1968 Congress authorized the Uintah Unit, and advance planning for the Ute Indian Unit—also known as the ultimate phase. Because planning for the Vernal Unit had been completed as an independent project, it was the first one started. In June 1958, the newly created Uintah County Water Conservancy District entered into a repayment contract with Reclamation for the Vernal Unit. Construction on Steinaker Dam—the unit's primary feature—began on May 14, 1959.[15]

By the early 1960s, planning for the Bonneville Unit had progressed to the point where construction could begin. However, the bureau first needed a repayment contract with a sponsoring local agency. After two years of negotiation, the Utah Fourth District Court formally organized the seven-county Central Utah Water Conservancy District (CUWCD) in 1964. Forming the CUWCD had become another political challenge that required a compromise. The district court had to balance the interests of the Uintah Basin, which would provide much of the water, with those of the urban areas, which would pay for most of the project, and the irrigators in central Utah, who would receive the majority of the water. Maintaining a balance among these interests later proved to be part of the challenge of crafting the CUPCA.

While scaled back from the ultimate-phase plan, the Bonneville Unit was still large and ambitious. In 1965 voters within the CUWCD approved a repayment contract for it. Construction began in 1967 with the Starvation Dam on the Duchesne River to store surplus flows and allow later diversion of Duchesne water into the Strawberry system. The Strawberry Aqueduct and collection system would accomplish the diversion. Reaching from the Strawberry Reservoir to Rock Creek, the thirty-seven miles of tunnel and pipeline would intercept the flows of twenty-three streams and rivers and redirect a large portion of

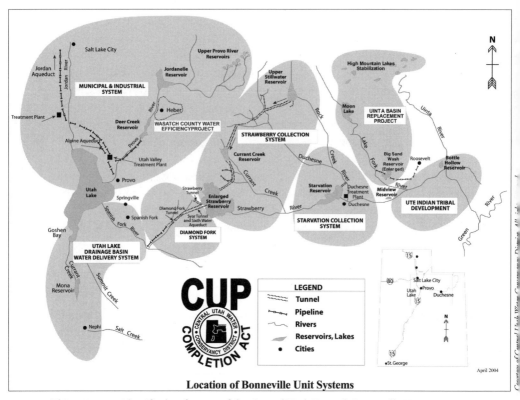

This 2008 map identifies key features of the Central Utah Project's Bonneville Unit.

them. The collection system also included two small diversion dams and two larger dams. The reservoirs behind the two larger dams—Currant Creek Dam in the middle and Upper Stillwater Dam on Rock Creek at the upper end—would regulate the system.[16]

The water diverted through the Strawberry Collection System would be stored in the enlarged Strawberry Reservoir behind the new Soldier Creek Dam. A new tunnel and pass through a series of reservoirs and power plants in Diamond Fork Canyon would direct water from Strawberry to the Wasatch Front and generate hydropower. The Wasatch Aqueduct would conduct Strawberry water from Diamond Fork Canyon eighty-three miles to Sevier Bridge Reservoir, passing through three tunnels totaling 5.6 miles along the way. Reclamation also retained plans to dike Utah Lake and construct Jordanelle Dam and Reservoir to develop a large municipal water supply for northern Utah and Salt Lake Counties.[17]

But almost as soon as construction began on the Bonneville Unit, the project encountered fiscal challenges. Due to budgetary pressures created by the ongoing Vietnam War and President Lyndon B. Johnson's War on Poverty, Congress significantly reduced appropriations for the project. Additionally new environmental concerns began to surface nationally. Worsening air and water pollution, fears of chemical contamination, and the loss of wildlife led to a greater environmental consciousness. As a result, Congress passed a series of significant new environmental laws with bipartisan support. Of them the Wilderness Act (1964), the National Environmental Policy Act (NEPA) (1969), and the Endangered Species Act (1973) had the greatest impact on the CUP.[18]

Following the passage of NEPA, work on the Starvation Reservoir complex, Soldier Creek Dam, and the first sections of the Strawberry Aqueduct under existing contracts could continue. But the law required the bureau to complete an environmental impact statement (EIS) before it could issue any new construction contracts. The EIS took two years to complete. However, unsatisfied with the conclusions of the bureau's EIS, a coalition of environmental groups, led by the Sierra Club, filed a lawsuit in 1973 in federal Utah District Court. They claimed that Reclamation had only analyzed a portion of the Strawberry Aqueduct and Collection System and had not considered the cumulative impacts of the entire CUP. The district court ruled in favor of the bureau. The Sierra Club filed an appeal heard by the Tenth Circuit Court of Appeals, which upheld the lower court's ruling. Work on the project could continue but was now several years behind schedule.[19]

If water officials celebrated their court victory, those celebrations were short lived. In 1977, citing environmental and budgetary concerns, newly elected President Jimmy Carter deleted funding for a list of water projects, including the CUP. Through the efforts of Utah's congressional delegation and many local politicians, the CUP won a stay of execution. With the project off the "hit list," Congress began to increase appropriations to the CUP. However, progress still proceeded at a snail's pace during Carter's term due to construction problems. The Teton Dam failure in 1976 also prompted seismic studies and the subsequent redesign of dams.[20]

The project soon faced another challenge. With costs escalating due to these construction problems and delays, it became apparent that the bureau could not finish the project within either the budget authorized by the CRSP or the amount authorized by the 1965 repayment contract approved by voters in the CUWCD. Both limits needed to be raised. The bureau began negotiating a new repayment contract with the CUWCD. To keep construction moving forward, the CUWCD brainstormed ways to work around the limit. While it came up with some solutions to keep the project alive in the short term, the measures were not enough. Ultimately economic realities forced it to take the issue to the district's voters to increase the authorized spending limit and the repayment obligations. Voters overwhelmingly approved the increase in the special election in November 1985. With this support, Utah's congressional delegation began working to pass legislation to increase the congressionally authorized funding.[21]

Reclamation and Utah's congressional delegation thought they could quickly obtain congressional approval. Senator Jake Garn introduced legislation to increase the total authorized project cost by $750,000,000. But, when Democratic leaders Senator Bill Bradley (D-NJ) and Congressman George Miller (D-CA), who controlled the key House and Senate subcommittees, refused to move the bill forward without addressing the lingering environmental and economic concerns, it quickly became apparent that the CUP now faced its largest hurdle.[22]

Bradley and Miller had not singled out the CUP for scrutiny. Rather, they were focusing on Reclamation as an antiquated agency in desperate need of reform. Neither of them would allow any reclamation bill that did not address their environmental and economic concerns out of their subcommittees. Thus, blocking Garn's reauthorization bill was not a partisan move. In fact, both Bradley and Miller worked openly with Utah's Republican-dominated congressional delegation to draft reauthorization legislation because it provided an opportunity to reform the bureau in the process.[23]

FROM LUXURIOUS TO UTILITARIAN

Determined to keep the project alive, the entire Utah delegation continued to work on reauthorizing the CUP. Congressman Wayne Owens, a Democrat representing the Salt Lake City area, served as a majority member of the House Subcommittee on Water and Power Resources. Because of his assignment and the fact that he was the only Utah Democrat serving in Congress, Owens took the lead in the effort to draft new legislation that met the demands of Chairman Miller.

In February 1988, Owens began spending a great deal of time developing a plan to address the fiscal and environmental concerns. It was a daunting task but one Owens accepted with enthusiasm. If he succeeded, he could earn a great deal of political capital in Utah. But more importantly, Owens felt strongly about the environmental damage the project had caused in Utah. In response to his efforts, the Sierra Club of Utah, Utah Wildlife Federation, Utah Wilderness Association, and sixty additional environmental, conservation, and sportsman's groups organized the Utah Roundtable of Sportsmen and Conservationists.

The Utah Roundtable quickly identified problems they had fought for many years. First, the Strawberry Aqueduct and Collection System diverted the entire flows of twenty-three streams and rivers in the Uintah Basin, dewatering a total of 245 miles. Wildlife specialists estimated that 78 percent of the fish in the streams would be lost. In 1979 the Utah Division of Wildlife Resources requested an increase in the minimum flows below the Strawberry Aqueduct. At the same time, the Army Corps of Engineers threatened to block construction of the Vat Diversion Dam by refusing to issue a 404 permit if stream flows did not increase. Governor Scott Matheson helped broker a deal with the CUWCD in 1980 to increase the minimum stream flows from 6,500 to 22,300 acre-feet (af). They further agreed that until the Strawberry Aqueduct was completed, 44,000 af would be released. But wildlife biologists felt that the

Representative Wayne Owens.

full 44,000 af was necessary to maintain 50 percent of the fish population and should become permanent.[24]

But the loss of water did not just impact fish; it threatened the entire river ecosystem. In addition to the habitat lost by diverted streams, the dams and reservoirs built by the project jeopardized additional riparian and wetlands habitat. Reduced habitat would impact both game animals and endangered species. Diverting water from Utah Lake also posed a threat of increasing the salinity level to amounts beyond the toleration of its native plants and animals. Specifically environmentalists and wildlife advocates worried about the impact on the endangered June sucker in Utah Lake.[25]

While environmental groups lobbied to increase minimum stream flows on some rivers, they also sought to set maximum flows on others. Several streams experienced increased flows because of project diversions. For example, the Strawberry Tunnel emptied directly into Sixth Water and Diamond Fork Creeks. During the peak irrigation season, the flows in these creeks were ten times the normal amount. A large quantity of water in a narrow streambed caused erosion of the banks, scouring of the bed, and destruction of the cottonwood saplings on the riverbanks. Because the saplings did not survive the irrigation season, the trees did not replenish themselves, and much of the cottonwood forests along these creeks had died. Owens, along with environmental groups, also expressed concern over a similar situation in the Provo River, particularly between Deer Creek Dam and the Olmstead Diversion near Upper Falls.[26]

Owens needed to find solutions to three additional issues. Little had been done to mitigate the damage caused by the project. He discovered that of the

$1.2 billion that had been spent on the project, only $10 million had been expended to repair the environmental, fish, and wildlife damages. Additionally Owens had to come to terms with the cost of the Bonneville Unit's irrigation component. The bureau's studies showed that the project's benefits slightly exceeded its costs, but, using different formulas, some economists found that the costs actually exceeded the benefits. Finally, the legislation needed to address the water-rights claims of the Uintah and Ouray Ute Tribes. In 1965 they had been promised water development in exchange for a forty-year deferral of their water rights. Because their projects had not been constructed, it appeared that the Bonneville Unit could not legally divert any water after 2005.[27]

As he searched for solutions to these problems, Owens found help readily available. He asked the CUWCD to prepare alternative plans for the irrigation project, including cutting some components and possibly using private financing. The district proposed streamlining the project by dropping several features that had questionable cost-benefit ratios. Congressman Owens also turned to the Utah Roundtable of Sportsmen and Conservationists to determine priorities and propose solutions to mitigate the project's adverse effects on the environment. He worked with the organization's member groups through March and into April of 1988 as they prepared a draft of a new reauthorization bill. Chairman Miller scheduled a hearing in Salt Lake City to promote and gather comments on the draft from all interested parties. Owens continued to work on the draft, making changes right up to the day prior to the hearing. The process led him to comment at the hearing that "the Central Utah Project is now a Chevy instead of a Cadillac."[28]

Chairman Miller opened the hearing on the rainy Monday morning of April 18, 1988, in the auditorium of the Utah State Capitol. Owens's new draft contained seventeen sections and stretched to twenty-six pages. The proposal contained two provisions that quickly divided the group in the auditorium. The first proposal was the mandated permanent increase to 44,000 af of in-stream flows in the rivers, creeks, and streams intercepted by the Strawberry Aqueduct. The second was a proposal for an independent federal commission to oversee the fish and wildlife mitigation that the bureau had neglected. Although these proposals generated controversy amongst the groups at the hearing, the divisions did not entirely fall along expected battle lines.[29]

The proposal to increase the in-stream flow on the tributaries of the Duchesne River and Rock Creek produced interesting splits. Senator Orrin Hatch and Governor Norm Bangerter supported the increased in-stream flows; however, Third District Congressman Howard Nielson expressed skepticism. He worried that the increase would cut the amount of water promised to Juab County and Sevier River Basin farmers. He also believed that if left undiverted, the water "would make its way into the Colorado River and be lost to Utah." While Congressman Nielson seemingly represented the rural, Old West interests of farmers in central Utah, a similar group of farmers and politicians in the

Uintah Basin supported the proposal. These basin proponents saw the increased water as an economic benefit because they could capture it lower in the river system and store it in Starvation Reservoir for irrigation. Additionally protecting the fisheries on the streams and rivers would not only provide local recreation but attract tourist dollars. The split is understandable since the Uintah Basin stood to benefit while Bonneville irrigators would lose.[30]

Although Nielson worried about the Bonneville irrigators, the CUWCD board and staff believed they could still deliver enough water to them and supported the in-stream flow agreement as "fundamentally fair and environmentally sound." The district also supported the creation of a new, independent commission to oversee environmental mitigation. They felt that the commission represented "a truly innovative method of mitigating for water project construction." The district believed that an independent commission would be more efficient than the bureau and would also prevent the transfer of appropriations away from the intended project. The commission board would also provide a voice for sportsmen and environmental groups. Thus, the CUWCD, traditionally classified as representing Old West and rural interests, enthusiastically supported both proposals and thus sided with environmental interests representing the New West. To a certain extent, some may see the district's position as making a willing sacrifice to ensure survival of their primary interests. But in many ways, they demonstrated genuine concern for their environmental stewardship.[31]

In contrast to the CUWCD, Garn, Hatch, Nielsen, and Bangerter all opposed the formation of the commission. While they all agreed that Reclamation had done a horrendous job and suffered from huge inefficiencies, they felt that an existing state or federal agency could supervise environmental mitigation. Another group opposing the commission was public power users. Owens proposed using revenues from the sale of CRSP hydropower to fund the mitigation commission. Power officials reacted with concern because the proposal would increase rates.[32]

In fact, public power interests opposed Owens's bill almost universally. Power revenues would largely subsidize the irrigation project. Furthermore, diverting water out of the Colorado River Basin decreased the capacity of hydroelectric plants downstream. Thus, the one provision that they could support was increased stream flows in the Uinta Basin. But Owens's bill contained an even more threatening proposal for them: a National Academy of Sciences study of hydroelectric plants throughout the CRSP to determine if their operational practices caused environmental damage. If the study concluded that the practices did cause damage, it would cut the capacity and revenues of the plants significantly.[33]

Despite the major environmental concessions in the bill, serious objections still remained over unresolved environmental issues and fiscal questions about the irrigation unit. Unsatisfied with the bill, Miller again refused to let it out of committee. Undaunted, the Utah delegation and CUWCD General Manager Don Christiansen moved forward with more negotiations to resolve the concerns. National environmental and wildlife groups represented by Ed Osann, director of the National Wildlife Federation's water-resources program, and David Conrad, a Friends of the Earth water-resource specialist, also became involved in the negotiations. Their concerns over the environmental issues surrounding Jordanelle, the irrigation projects, and the water rights of the Ute Indians prompted Chairmen Miller and Bradley to scuttle another attempt to move the bill forward in the spring of 1990.[34]

Getting the Chevy off the Lot

Failing again, the Utah delegation, CUWCD, and the national environmental groups met for another round of negotiations. Miller imposed a unanimous-vote rule. Owens, trusted by all parties, acted as a mediator. In addition, all parties agreed not to run to the press to influence the negotiations. Frustrated by continued delays and unwillingness to compromise, Miller left the bureau completely out of the negotiations. After several long weeks, a revised bill that met the concerns of Miller, Bradley, and the environmental groups began to emerge.[35]

However, when Don Christiansen called to relay the details of the compromise to water officials in the Salt Lake area, they reacted with alarm. They felt that Christiansen had given away too much to the environmental groups. Christiansen hurriedly arranged a meeting between the water managers and the environmental groups. Six water managers from the Salt Lake Valley flew to Washington.[36] Meeting in Owens's office, the water managers; Don Christiansen; Marcus Faust, the CUWCD's Washington counsel; and Ed Osann and David Conrad, representing national environmental organizations, negotiated into the night. Osann and Conrad's interests centered on mandated water conservation. They both emphasized that the water districts that used CUP water should do more to promote conservation. Finally, just after two o'clock in the morning, the group came to an agreement.[37]

The compromise provided that the CUWCD had to use cost-effective and environmentally sound means to make "prudent and efficient use of currently available water prior to the importation of Bear River water into Salt Lake County."[38] This language challenged the old concepts of water development that had focused on increasing supply rather than decreasing demand. The issue seemingly pitted the New West against the Old—the environmentalists against the old "water buffalos." The water districts balked at the proposal because conservation posed the threat of decreased revenues and potential difficulty repaying bonds. But in the end, the districts were able to compromise, proving that they were not too entrenched in traditional views to give politically expedient concessions to New West environmentalists.[39]

The conservation compromise cleared the way for a version of the legislation Miller and Bradley let out of their respective committees following hearings in February and September 1990, respectively. The new version, officially called the Central Utah Project Completion Act, contained four main sections.

The crown jewel of the Bonneville Unit of the Central Utah Project was Jordanelle Dam and Reservoir. Jordanelle, like other parts of the Bonneville Unit, transferred water from high mountain valleys like those of Wasatch County to the heavily populated Wasatch Front, especially Salt Lake Valley. CUPCA jettisoned features of the Central Utah Project but preserved funding for Jordanelle. The reservoir was filled in 1996.

CUPCA raised the authorized costs by $924,206,000. But it also implemented a local cost-sharing agreement that mandated the CUWCD to pay 35 percent of the reimbursable project costs. The legislation deauthorized several features of the original CUP plan, including the diking of Utah Lake, irrigation projects in the Mosida area southwest of Utah Lake and the Leland Bench in the Uinta Basin, and the Ute Indian Unit, which proposed the diversion of water directly from the Green River. Additionally the legislation scaled back plans for the Uintah and Upalco Units.

The CUPCA took further steps which changed long-standing reclamation policy. It allowed counties that had not received project water to withdraw from the CUWCD and receive a rebate of property taxes paid toward the project. It took oversight of the project from the bureau and gave control to the CUWCD. Furthermore, the legislation addressed environmental criticisms by stipulating that mitigation must proceed concurrently with construction. The act created a new federal agency to oversee environmental mitigation and established a fund to complete these efforts. The act mandated that the CUWCD and its customer agencies meet goals for water conservation and that the District fund those efforts. Finally, it provided a monetary payment to the Northern Ute Tribe to settle their environmental justice claims and satisfy their water rights.[40]

Utah's congressional delegation again had a difficult time moving the bill out of committee. But this time it was not Miller or Bradley applying the brakes; rather, it was the bureau and the Bush administration. Reclamation unilaterally opposed the bill. It objected to the district taking over oversight and construction. It opposed the formation of the mitigation commission and compensation to the Ute Tribe. It was against the legislation because it simply had been left out of the negotiations. However, exerting his influence, Garn pressured the administration and pushed the bill onto the floor. As it moved forward, the legislation became an omnibus bill that attracted funding provisions for twenty-two other projects and provisions that further reformed reclamation policy. After an additional two years of debate, Congress passed the bill in October 1992. Despite veto threats, President George H.W. Bush signed it into law on October 30, 1992.[41]

THE AFFORDABLE, DEPENDABLE, AND RELIABLE CAR

After the passage of the CUPCA, the project moved forward. However, President Bush's signature did not end criticism or political controversy over the CUP. Individual groups still pushed their interests, and some battles continued to be fought.

One of the first challenges facing the CUWCD was the withdrawal of Millard and Sevier Counties under CUPCA's provision allowing counties that had not received any benefit from the project to leave the district. Farmers in Millard and Sevier Counties felt that the provisions of the CUPCA were too costly. Thorpe Waddingham, a water rights attorney representing the farmers, said, "We are big supporters of the CUP. But the CUP has steadily deteriorated from the 1970s to the 1980s until now in the 1990s it's gone completely to hell."[42]

Waddingham cited concerns that the project had been modified to meet the demands of cities and environmental groups; as a result, the amount of water available to the two counties had decreased, the local cost share had risen, and accepting the water under the new law would bring unwanted federal regulation. While the move by the two counties initially caused some concern within the district's board, it had little long-term impact. Because those counties withdrew, the original irrigation project was scaled back to serve Juab and southern Utah County.[43]

In 1999 the Strawberry Water Users Association withdrew its support of the CUWCD's EIS for the proposed Spanish Fork/Nephi Pipeline. The association felt it could get more CUP water if the pipeline remained unbuilt. With the Strawberry users no longer supporting the EIS, the Department of the Interior would not approve the project. As a result, the project was scaled back further so that Juab County water would be split between Salt Lake County and southern Utah County. However, Juab County received assistance through water conservation programs to offset the loss of project water.[44]

Both of these cases demonstrate that interest groups' behavior does not fit within an expected model. Waddingham's comments suggest both a federal versus local and urban versus rural split. But this assessment is not completely accurate because the farmers in central Utah supported the project when the federal Bureau of Reclamation controlled it, but they left because they feared increased costs and more environmental regulation. The urban versus rural contention also seems to break down when we remember that the two counties' withdrawal meant less water for neighboring, rural Juab County.

The completion of the Diamond Fork System provides another case study of the way interests have responded to the CUPCA. During the negotiations surrounding the CUPCA, the CUWCD and environmental groups cooperated with each other in negotiating a compromise. Both environmental groups and the Democrats pushing for reform of the bureau supported the transfer of project construction to the district. But these alliances seemed to shift as the district moved forward with construction.

Reclamation's original plan for the Diamond Fork System had called for three reservoirs in that drainage. As the district proceeded with its planning of the project, it deleted two of the reservoirs. However, local environmental groups still criticized the decision to build a dam at Monk's Hollow. Demonstrating the benefit of local control over the project, the CUWCD responded by reengineering the project to use the completed features without the need for the dam. As a result, the water flows through a series of pipelines and tunnels. This adjustment produced the environmental benefit of reducing the flows in Diamond Fork Creek and, as a result, extended the mitigation plans outlined in the CUPCA to a larger area of the river.[45]

Despite this decision, some people continued to criticize the project and the district. For example, political scientist Dan McCool chastised the district for wasting millions of dollars planning for the Monk's Hollow Dam, which it then canceled. He also railed against the district for continuing to plan for the Spanish Fork/Nephi irrigation project "at a time when such projects were considered wasteful boondoggles." McCool's complaints seem to represent an urban versus rural or, more correctly, a New West versus Old West debate. They assume the water would be better used by the urban residents of Salt Lake County than the rural farmers. However, the derision of the rural irrigation project as a "wasteful boondoggle" may simply reflect McCool's discontent that the irrigation project was not removed during the crafting of the CUPCA. More significantly, this example seems to demonstrate that local conflicts have replaced a local versus federal quarrel. It seems that having control in the hands of a local agency that responds to the petitions of the local environmental community should be a good thing.[46]

Although many rural or Old West critics doubted the need for an independent mitigation commission, after the passage of the CUPCA, the Utah Reclamation Mitigation and Conservation Commission was extremely successful in completing a wide array of mitigation and conservation projects and winning over its critics. The commission worked with the district to develop mitigation plans for ongoing construction such as Diamond Fork. Other projects focused on mitigating impacts of completed projects. For example, in

A site in Wasatch County where ponds and wetlands were slated to be artificially created to provide suitable habitat for wildlife under the terms of the Central Utah Project Completion Act.

conjunction with the construction of Jordanelle Dam, the Provo River is being restored to its original course between Jordanelle and Deer Creek. Section 308 of the CUPCA also required the restoration of twelve lakes in the drainage of the Upper Provo River in the Uinta Mountains. Local water companies had converted the lakes into reservoirs in the early 1900s. The storage capacity of these high-mountain reservoirs was transferred to Jordanelle, and the lakes were stabilized at their original levels.[47] The district and mitigation commission also plan to stabilize thirteen lakes on the Yellowstone and Lake Fork Rivers as they enlarge the Big Sand Wash Reservoir in the Uintah Basin.[48] The commission also undertook other projects to protect native species, protect and preserve wetland habitat, and enhance riparian habitat throughout the CUP area.[49]

Similarly, as already discussed, managers of several of the local municipal water agencies expressed an Old West concern over the conservation programs included in the CUPCA. Their reluctance, however, largely evaporated. The districts adopted progressive conservation campaigns that alleviated the need to institute water rationing during a six-year drought. Additionally the CUWCD created the Water Conservation Credit Program to meet the mandate of Section 207(b) of the CUPCA. The program provides 65 percent of the funding for selected conservation projects. As of 2004, the program had funded thirty-three projects, saving 94,969 af of water. Thus, many with Old West objections to conservation changed their position to support the very New West concept of conservation.[50]

The same site as in facing photograph after ponds and wetlands became established.

Therefore, after the passage of the CUPCA, the district experienced mixed success. In some cases, the alliances between irrigators in central Utah and environmentalists frayed or completely broke down. However, the highly controversial mitigation commission and conservation requirements of the CUPCA proved highly successful as the district resolved conflicts between traditionally oppositional groups. While the commission was successful in meeting its goals, many CUPCA critics remained skeptical. Congressman Howard Neilson maintained that Utah's delegation gave too many concessions to the environmental community, which increased the cost of the project and reduced the amount of water it delivered. Some opponents of the CUP, including McCool, argued that the compromise amounted to "green pork." To some extent, both criticisms seem valid. Due to changes resulting from the passage of CUPCA, the amount of water delivered by the Bonneville Unit was cut, and the price increased. As a result, CUP water ranks among the most expensive ever developed by the Bureau of Reclamation. [51]

In the end, recognition that both sides in the debate felt CUPCA fell short does not discount the very real benefits for the environment and water users. Tangible environmental advantages produced by the legislation include the restoration of Uinta lakes and the middle Provo River, mandated stream flows, deauthorization of plans to dike Utah Lake, other mitigation efforts, and water conservation programs. Municipal water users, primarily in Salt Lake and Utah Counties, benefit from an additional 60,000 af of water. As already explained, controversy over the proposed Spanish Fork/Nephi Pipeline resulted in the reformulation of the project to provide municipal water. In October 2007, the CUWCD began construction of the first pipeline segments of the revised scheme, now called the Utah Lake System. When completed, one new pipeline will supply cities in southern Utah County, while another will run from Spanish Fork Canyon to Provo Canyon to link with existing CUP delivery systems to Salt Lake County.[52]

The end results of the battle over the CUP are vital to Utah. The benefits of the project, and reclamation throughout Utah for that matter, are not arcane figures on a ledger sheet. By making additional water available to Utah's cities and increasing environmental mitigation, the passage of the CUPCA impacts contemporary life in Utah, including the quality of the environment, the taxes Utahns pay, and the ability to lead "water-rich" lifestyles in an arid environment. Additionally the battle over the CUP and the passage of the CUPCA are significant in terms of the lessons they offer. While twenty-first-century environmental attitudes make it unlikely new large-scale reclamation projects will be attempted, the negotiations and compromise involved in drafting the legislation do serve as a potential example for other natural-resource controversies in the West. For instance, former Wayne Owens congressional aide and lawyer Thomas Melling used CUPCA as a case study, concluding that using a trusted mediator and unanimous vote rule to produce favorable results may serve as a model for resolving other natural resource conflicts in the west.[53]

For historians the fight over CUPCA demonstrates the difficulty of fitting an array of interest groups into a preconceived model. More than eight different interest groups lobbied the Utah congressional delegation during the drafting of the CUP compromise. The varied interests did not act according to their stereotypes in all cases. Traditional allies split, while traditional foes joined. Irrigators did not band together to help each other keep their water supply. Water districts took differing stands on conservation. The Bureau of Reclamation and the Bush administration fought to maintain their turf. The CUWCD abandoned the bureau, its former ally, to save money and speed the project. It supported environmental measures that it would have likely opposed in the past, allying with its critics and foes. It remained committed to those alliances, even when faced with more-expensive design choices. All these examples, along with the other details surrounding the political conflict to draft the CUPCA, thus remind historians of the difficulty of reducing complex events into an oversimplified caricature that misses the detail and nuance the interpretation deserves.

NOTES

1.   Remarks of Congressman Wayne Owens in *Proposals to Raise the Authorized Cost Ceiling for the Colorado River Storage Project: Hearings before the Subcommittee on Water and Power Resources of the Committee on Interior and Insular Affairs,* 100th Cong., 2[d] sess., April 18, May 4, 1988, 40, 422–26.

2. Depictions of the divided West are most clearly visible in polemical histories from the late 1970s and early 1980s. For an example of an East versus West/federal versus local argument, see Richard D. Lamb and Michael McCarthy, *The Angry West: A Vulnerable Land and Its Future* (Boston: Houghton Mifflin Company, 1982), especially 5–18, and 186–207. Philip L. Fradkin saw the controversy over the Carter hit list as a fight between what could be called Old West water interests and the New West environmental concerns that influenced President Carter; see *A River No More: The Colorado River and the West* (New York, Alfred A Knopf, 1981), 3–14. Fradkin also presents a rural versus urban argument for water use; see 31–33 and 74–77 in that volume. While most historians have not depicted the natural resource controversies as a battle between the Old West and New West, historical actors who subscribe to a particular interpretation are often at odds over land use and natural resources. For the changing meaning of New West within the historical profession over time, including its current use, see Joseph E. Taylor III, "The Many Lives of the New West," *Western Historical Quarterly* 35 (Summer 2004): 141–66.

3. On early efforts at irrigation in Utah, see Thomas G. Alexander, "Irrigating the Mormon Heartland: The Operation of the Irrigation Companies in Wasatch Oasis Communities, 1847–1880," *Agricultural History* 76 (Spring 2002): 172–87; Leonard J.Arrington and Dean May,"'A Different Mode of Life:' Irrigation and Society in Nineteenth-Century Utah," *Agricultural History* 49 (January 1975): 3–20; and George D. Clyde, "History of Irrigation in Utah," *Utah Historical Quarterly* 27 (January 1959): 27–36.

4. On the effects of modernization and the evolution of water development, see Thomas G. Alexander, "Interdependence and Change: Mutual Irrigation Companies in Utah's Wasatch Oasis in an Age of Modernization, 1870–1930," *Utah Historical Quarterly* 71 (Fall 2003): 292–314. For more on the shifts in water institutions and development of the state's role, see John Swenson Harvey, "A Historical Overview of the Evolution of Institutions Dealing with Water Resource Use, and Water Resource Development in Utah—1847 through 1947" (master's thesis, Utah State University, 1989).

5. On the passage of the Newlands or Reclamation Act, see Donald Pisani, *To Reclaim a Divided West* (Albuquerque: University of New Mexico Press, 1992), 298–319.

6. Abraham Fairbanks Doremus, *Third Biennial Report of the State Engineer to the Governor of Utah 1901–1902* (Salt Lake City: Star Printing Company, 1903), 9–14; U.S. Department of the Interior, Reclamation Service, *Third Annual Report of the Reclamation Service 1903–1904* (Washington, DC: GPO, 1905), 509. (Hereafter these annual reports are cited with just the title of the volume and the page numbers.

7. Doremus had presented detailed plans of his grand scheme to the Utah gongressional delegation in an all-day meeting on January 28, 1904. On these meetings, see *Eastern Utah Advocate,* February 4, 1904. In addition to the development of the Strawberry Valley Project, his plans called for the regulation of Utah Lake and Bear Lake as storage reservoirs; a second transbasin diversion of water from the Blackfoot River, a tributary of the Snake River, into the Bear River; and a series of canals to make the water from Strawberry and the Bear River available to the Salt Lake Valley. Reports

of this plan, "Millions for Utah, Irrigation Scheme Which Will Benefit Three Great Valleys," appeared in several Utah weekly newspapers, including the *Davis County Clipper, Eureka Reporter,* and *Tooele Transcript,* February 19, 1904. On the feasibility of diverting the Duchesne and its tributaries, see *Third Annual Report of the Reclamation Service,* 510–14.

8.   On the Strawberry Valley Project, see Thomas G. Alexander, "An Investment in Progress: Utah's First Federal Reclamation Project, the Strawberry Valley Project," *Utah Historical Quarterly* 39 (1971): 286–304; Kathryn MacKay, "The Strawberry Valley Reclamation Project and the Opening of the Uintah Indian Reservation," *Utah Historical Quarterly* 50 (1982): 68–89; and Jessie Embry, "From Self Sufficiency to Colony: The Bureau of Reclamation and Wasatch County, Utah," in *Reclamation: Managing Water in the West,* ed. Brit Allan Storey (Washington, D.C.: GPO, 2008), 429–45. On the expansion of the project to Juab County, see *Nineteenth Annual Report of the Reclamation Service 1919–1920,* 429–30; and *Twentieth Annual Report of the Reclamation Service 1920–1921,* 437.

9.   Interior Secretary Hubert Work reorganized and renamed the Reclamation Service on June 20, 1923. For funding and investigation of the Salt Lake Basin/Weber River Project, see William D. Rowley, *The Bureau of Reclamation: Origins and Growth to 1945* (Denver: U.S. Department of Interior, Bureau of Reclamation, 2006), 218–20. On the investigations, see *Bureau of Reclamation Annual Report,* 1922, 131; *Bureau of Reclamation Annual Report,* 1923, 133. For project specifications and construction history, see Water and Power Resources Service, *Project Data* (Denver: GPO, 1981), 1325–28; and Stephen A Merrill, "Reclamation and the Economic Development of Northern Utah: The Weber River Project," *Utah Historical Quarterly* 39 (Summer 1971): 254–64.

10.   On the drought, see Leonard J. Arrington, "Utah's Great Drought of 1934," *Utah Historical Quarterly* 54 (Summer 1986): 245–64. For a history of the Bureau of Reclamation during the Depression, see Rowley, *The Bureau of Reclamation,* 307–74; for a list of Utah projects, see particularly 325–26. For a history of the Newton Project, see Leonard J. Arrington and Thomas C. Anderson, "The First Irrigation Reservoir in the United States: The Newton, Utah, Project," *Utah Historical Quarterly* 39 (Summer 1971): 207–23.

11.   Leonard J. Arrington and Thomas G. Alexander, *Water for Utah Reclamation: The Provo River Project,* Utah Resources Series 29 (Logan: Utah State University Press, 1966), 4; Fisher Sanford Harris, *One Hundred Years of Water Development* (Salt Lake City: Metropolitan Water District of Salt Lake City, 1942), 11, 95, 110–11. For an early description of the Central Utah Project see U.S. Department of the Interior, *The Colorado River, "A Natural Menace Becomes a National Resource: A Comprehensive Report on the Development of the Water Resources of the Colorado River Basin for Irrigation, Power Production, and Other Beneficial Uses in Arizona, California, Colorado, Nevada, New Mexico, Utah, and Wyoming"* (Washington, DC: GPO, 1946), 117–18.

12.   U.S. Department of the Interior, Bureau of Reclamation, *Colorado River Storage Project and Participating Projects, Upper Colorado River Basin* (Salt Lake City: USBR Region 4, December 1950), particularly 13–14.

13. For Murdock's proposals, see S. 2313, 79th Cong., 2nd sess., *Congressional Record* 92, pt. 5 (June 7, 1946): 6438; and "Echo Park Project Goes to Senate for Approval," *Vernal Express,* June 13, 1946. For the Colorado River Storage Project Act, see Department of the Interior, Bureau of Reclamation, *Federal Reclamation and Related Laws Annotated,* vol. 2 (Denver: GPO, 1972), 1248–59.

14. On the compromise, see Mark W.T. Harvey, *A Symbol of Wilderness: Echo Park and the American Conservation Movement* (Seattle: University of Washington Press, 2000), 223–27; Stephen C. Sturgeon, *The Politics of Western Water: The Congressional Career of Wayne Aspinall* (Tucson: University of Arizona Press, 2002), 47–50; Marc Reisner, *Cadillac Desert* (New York: Penguin Books, 1987), 283–88; and John Upton Terrell, *War for the Colorado,* vol. 2 (Glendale, CA: Arthur H. Clark Company, 1965), 237–38. On the preference for the Echo Park alternative, see Harvey, *Symbol of Wilderness,* 38–42.

15. On the construction of and subsequent controversy over the Glen Canyon Dam, see Russell Martin, *A Story That Stands Like a Dam: Glen Canyon and the Struggle for the Soul of the West* (New York: Henry Holt & Co., 1989); and Jared Farmer, *Glen Canyon Dammed: Inventing Lake Powell and the Canyon Country* (Tucson: University of Arizona Press, 1999). On the Vernal unit, see "Vernal Project Contract Signed in Washington," *Vernal Express,* June 12, 1958; "Vernal Project Groundbreaking Planned Today," *Vernal Express,* May 14, 1958; "Massive Bulldozers Plough Earth in Vernal Project Opening Rites," *Vernal Express,* May 21, 1958. In 1956 the Bureau of Reclamation also began construction on its second-largest project in Utah, the Weber Basin Project, which Congress authorized in 1949. See Richard W. Sadler and Richard C. Roberts, *The Weber River Basin: Grass Roots Democracy and Water Development* (Logan: Utah State University Press, 1994).

16. For an early description of the CUP, see Bureau of Reclamation, *The Colorado River, "A Natural Menace Becomes a National Resource,"* 117–18. For a complete description of the CUP, see U.S. Department of the Interior, Bureau of Reclamation, *Central Utah Project, A Supplement to the Colorado River Storage Project Report* (Salt Lake City: USBR Region 4, February 1951), synopsis 1–4; and Bureau of Reclamation, Region 4, *Central Utah Project Initial Phase Bonneville Unit, Definite Plan Report* (Salt Lake City: August 1965), summary sheets 1–3; Bureau of Reclamation, Region 4, *Final Environmental Statement, Authorized Bonneville Unit, Central Utah Project, Utah,* (Salt Lake City: USBR, Upper Colorado Basin Region, 1973), 19.

17. *Final Environmental Statement,* 19.

18. On the growth of the environmental movement and passage of federal legislation, see Charles A. Reich, *The Greening of America* (New York: Random House, 1970).

19. *Sierra Club, et al. v. Gilbert Stamm, Commissioner, U.S. Bureau of Reclamation, et. al.,* 507 F. 2nd 788 (Tenth Cir. 1974), No. 74–1425. Bob Hilbert, interview by author, May 20, 2004.

20. Reisner, *Cadillac Desert,* 313–22; Jake Garn, interview by author, March 25, 2004.

21. Carrie L. Ulrich and R. Terry Holzworth, "Opening the Water Bureaucracy," in *Waters of Zion,* ed. Daniel McCool (Salt Lake City: University of Utah Press, 1995), 56–58. Lisa Mote, "Voters Approve CUP Repayment by 3-to-1," and "Provo Voters Fail to

Support Council Stand," *Provo Daily Herald,* November 20, 1985. Don Christiansen, interview by author, March 24, 2004.

22. Two key individuals engaged in the hit list fight later used the data they gathered to attack the Bureau of Reclamation and the CUP. Journalist Marc Reisner, who served as communications director for the Natural Resources Defense Council during that time, wrote a best-selling book, *Cadillac Desert,* which helped reshape opinion. Additionally Dan Beard, who served as deputy assistant secretary of the interior for land and water for President Carter, later was the chief legislative aide to California Congressman George Miller, who was seeking major reforms for the Bureau of Reclamation. Later, as Bureau of Reclamation commissioner during the Clinton administration, Beard led the charge to divert its mission away from large-scale construction projects toward environmentally and economically sound water management.

23. Christiansen interview; Garn interview; Thomas Melling, "Dispute Resolution within Legislative Institutions," *Stanford Law Review* 46 (1993): 1693.

24. On the dewatering of streams, see Tom Melling, "The CUP Holds the Solution: Utah's Hybrid Alternative to Water Markets," *Journal of Energy, Natural Resources, and Environmental Law* 13 (1993): 186. On the 404 permit, see Rod Collett, "CUP Officials Question 404 Dam Permit Delay," *Provo Daily Herald,* October 12, 1979. For the 1980 stream flow agreement, see Central Utah Water Conservancy District [CUWCD], "Minutes of the Special Meeting of the Board of Directors" January 30, 1980, Orem, Utah, 2–14; and CUWCD, "Minutes of the Regular Meeting of the Board of Directors" April 10, 1980, 2, Bureau of Reclamation Office, Orem, Utah.

25. "Water Official Warns Salinity Will Increase in Utah Lake," *Salt Lake Tribune,* November 1, 1989.

26. Michael Weland, interview by author, May 14, 2004; "River Proposals Upsets Officials," *Provo Daily Herald,* October 31, 1989.

27. *Proposals to Raise the Authorized Cost Ceiling,* 40, 422–26. For a critical analysis of the economics of the Bonneville Irrigation Unit, see Jon R. Miller, "The Political Economy of Western Water Finance: Cost Allocation and the Bonneville Unit of the Central Utah Project," *American Journal of Agricultural Economics* 69 (May 1987): 303–10.

28. Remarks of Congressman Wayne Owens in *Proposals to Raise the Authorized Cost Ceiling,* 40; also see Owens's comments on 422–26.

29. Ibid., 4–29.

30. Ibid., 56, 59, 69, 371.

31. Ibid., 91–92, 96.

32. Ibid., 334–44, 407–12.

33. This proposal arose from environmentalists' concern over the practice of increasing power generation during peak demand, which caused significant fluctuations in the river downstream from the dams. Of particular concern was damage within the Grand Canyon below Glen Canyon Dam. Congress addressed these issues by including the Grand Canyon Protection Act in the same omnibus bill that included CUPCA, Public Law 102–575. Title XVIII of the law restricts the generation of

peaking power at Glen Canyon Dam. Further it mandated an EIS on the long-term operation of the dam. *U.S. Statutes at Large* 106 (1992): 4669–73. The Colorado River Energy Distributors Association (CREDA), the public power agency that markets the power from Glen Canyon, estimates that the legislative restrictions reduced the capacity of the plant by one-third while the EIS has cost power users $104 million. "Glen Canyon Dam," http://www.creda.org/Pages/Glen.html

34. "Wildlife Foundation Wants CUP Funds Stopped," *Provo Daily Herald,* April 10, 1990; "Clock Ticks Away on Controversial CUP Funding," *Provo Daily Herald,* April 14, 1990.

35. Christiansen interview; Thomas Melling, "Dispute Resolution," 1695.

36. The six water officials were Dave Ovard, Jerry Maloney, and Dale Gardiner from the Salt Lake County Water Conservancy District, and Nick Sefakis, LeRoy Hooton, and Joe Novak from the Metropolitan Water District of Salt Lake and Sandy. Dave Ovard, interview by author, June 30, 2004.

37. Christiansen interview; Ovard interview; Marcus Faust, interview by author, August 10, 2005. *Central Utah Project Completion Act,* Public Law 102–575, titles II–III, *U.S. Statutes at Large* 106 (1992): 4605–55.

38. This wording remained in the legislation as a stated purpose of the conservation or "water management improvement" provisions of the CUPCA. Ibid. 4617.

39. Ovard interview; Gerald Maloney, interview by author, August 10, 2004.

40. *H.R. 3960, Central Utah Project Completion Act: Hearings before the Subcommittee on Water, Power, and Offshore Energy Resources of the Committee on Interior and Insular Affairs,* 101st Cong., 2d sess., February 6, 1990, 2–116.

41. The bill became Public Law 102–575; Titles II through V comprise the CUPCA.

42. Steve Hinchman and Larry Warren, "Two Utah Counties Flee Water Project," *High Country News,* September 20, 1993.

43. Ibid.

44. Ibid; Roscoe Garrett, interview by author, April 16, 2004; Christiansen interview.

45. Christiansen interview; Weland interview.

46. Daniel McCool, "The CUP: A Project in Search of a Purpose" in *Water in the West: A High Country News Reader,* ed. Char Miller (Corvallis: Oregon State University Press, 2000). For other examples of McCool's criticism of the CUP, see Daniel McCool, *Waters of Zion: The Politics of Water in Utah* (Salt Lake City: University of Utah Press, 1995); and McCool, "Water Welfare, Green Pork, and the 'New' Politics of Water," *Halcyon* 14 (1992): 85–102.

47. Three lakes (Trial, Lost, and Washington) have been maintained to supply irrigation water to farmers in the Kamas area above Jordanelle Reservoir. The Bureau of Reclamation and the CUWCD rebuilt the dam at Trial Lake in 1989 and the ones at Lost Lake and Washington Lake in 1994–95. The CUWCD and the Mitigation Commission partnered on the stabilization of twelve lakes stipulated in the CUPCA's section 308 of the CUPCA law—Big Elk, Crystal, Duck, Fire, Island, Long, Wall, Marjorie, Pot, Star, Teapot and Weir—to their natural water levels. *U.S. Statutes at Large* 106 (1992): 4638.

48. Stabilization of thirteen high mountain lakes will provide constant levels year-round. Nine of these lakes (Bluebell, Drift, Five Point, Superior, Milk, Farmers, East Timothy, White Miller, and Deer) are located in the Upper Yellowstone River watershed, and four (Brown Duck, Island, Kidney, and Clements) are in the upper Lake Fork watershed.

49. Weland interview. Extensive information on the projects of the Utah Reclamation Mitigation and Conservation Commission is available on its Web site at http://www.mitigationcommission.gov/index.html

50. Lee Wimmer, interview by author, March 24, 2004; Central Utah Water Conservancy District, *Annual Report 2004* (Orem, UT: CUWCD, 2004), 7.

51. Howard Neilson, interview by author, June 29, 2006; the first use of the term "green pork" is attributed to Daniel McCool, "The New Politics of the Environment and the Rise of 'Green Pork,'" *Free Perspectives* IV (December 1990): 5–7. McCool specifically offers the CUP as an example of green pork in "Water Welfare, Green Pork, and the 'New' Politics of Water," 98.

52. "Construction Begins on Spanish Fork Pipeline," *Provo Daily Herald*, June 19, 2008; Central Utah Water Conservancy District, *Annual Report 2007* (Orem, UT: CUWCD, 2007), 17–19.

53. Thomas Melling, "Dispute Resolution," 1677–1714.

15

The Volatile Sagebrush Rebellion

Jedediah S. Rogers

Utahns' icy relationship with the federal government in the nineteenth century thawed considerably after the state's admission to the Union. Federal investment during the New Deal, World War II, and the cold war enhanced Utahns' income and prosperity, while federal investment in highways, national parks, and water projects facilitated transportation, recreation, agricultural productivity, and verdant landscaping. Responding to their constituents' expectations, Utah representatives and senators lobbied assiduously for federal dollars. In the minds of some Utahns, though, the benefits of federal subsidies were partly offset by government control and management of more than half of the state's land. In the following chapter, Jedediah S. Rogers traces Utah's participation in one of the most significant manifestations of opposition to federal control in the West during the twentieth century: the Sagebrush Rebellion of 1979–81. Drawing upon newspapers pieces, other articles, public-opinion polls, and the manuscript collections of politicians and activists, Rogers argues that the Sagebrush Rebellion reflected serious concerns about the federal/state relationship and galvanized substantial organization and opposition by environmentalists but failed to resolve the underlying concerns.

When President Bill Clinton stood on the south rim of the Grand Canyon and created Grand Staircase-Escalante National Monument in September 1996, after informing Utah's congressional delegation and governor only twenty-four hours earlier, local and state reaction to the announcement nearly reached a breaking point. Certainly aware that some people in the local communities would not be pleased with the designation, the president could not fully have anticipated the maelstrom that followed and the controversy that the establishment of the monument continues to provoke. State officials and local residents of the sleepy communities in southern Utah balked at the move, angry that the onument had been created in secret and that it would close off 1.7 million acres of multiple-use federal lands to economic "development" and phase out Old West activities such as grazing, hard-rock mining, and gas and oil extraction within a massive section of southern Utah's backcountry. Utah Senator Orrin Hatch called it "the mother of all land grabs."

Hatch's words echoed back to a long history of conflict over ownership and management of public lands. During the 1940s, the renowned writer Bernard DeVoto, a Utah native, had used the language "land grab" in response to proposals by western congressmen to give ranchers a "vested right" to the title of the public domain.[2] Environmentalists resurrected the language in the 1970s in response to the Sagebrush Rebellion, a western movement that aimed to transfer ownership of public lands to the western states—and, presumably, to private hands. The first salvo in the Sagebrush Rebellion came in 1979, when the Nevada legislature passed Assembly Bill 413 and laid claim to Nevada's right to own and manage forty-nine million acres of the public lands within its borders. It was a meaningless act since the federal government had no intention of ceding ownership of the land and Nevada had no authority to seize it, but it symbolically represented the anger many westerners felt toward what they saw as an overbearing federal presence in the West. Utah's own Orrin Hatch termed the rebellion a "second American Revolution" and described environmentalists as "selfish," "radical," "dandelion pickers," and "a cult of toadstool worshippers."[3]In response Utah's environmental community joined opponents nationwide in dubbing the movement nothing more than a traditional western land grab, attacking the rebels' "greedy" motives, and attaching pejorative appellations to the rebellion such as the "sagebrush ripoff."[4]

Such rhetoric reflects the division, anger, and polarization over public-land issues in Utah. This chapter seeks to make sense of these debates, using the Sagebrush Rebellion as an example of the way public-land issues were serious business, yet addressed in a way that made it impossible to find solutions to enduring problems in Utah and the rest of the West. Although the rebellion is usually viewed from a regional perspective, it was on the local and state levels where most of the politicking and debate took place.[5] Another key point is that Utah was (and is) hardly monolithic; rather, the issue of public lands was a heated and multilayered controversy. State officials, rural cattlemen and county commissioners, and environmentalists all participated in the conflict yet understood it from varying angles. The purpose here is to explore the ideologies that shaped the movement, the determination that drove local environmental opposition, and the complex forces and contradictions that made the Sagebrush Rebellion a nonissue by 1981.

THE SAGEBRUSH REBELLION

The idea to transfer the public lands from governmental to private or state control was an ongoing, if inconsistent, issue in the West long before "sagebrush rebels" came onto the scene. However, it was an issue that never garnered much support nationwide. Various attempts at a large-scale transfer failed in the 1920s and 1940s, thanks in part to Bernard DeVoto's scathing criticisms of the proposals in articles published in *Harper's Magazine*. Later, in the early 1970s, few took seriously a similar attempt by Calvin Black, a one-term member of the Utah state legislature from San Juan County, who believed that although the country was not ready for a large-scale land transfer, his legislation would "serve as an educational tool."[6] So when the Nevada State legislature passed a bill and Republican Senator Orrin Hatch introduced a national bill in the Senate in August 1979, salvoes in the burgeoning Sagebrush Rebellion, the idea of a transfer was not new. What was different about the events of 1979 was that they captured media attention and signaled the beginning of a broad-based movement designed to "return" the federal lands to their rightful owners.

Many westerners spoke of the West being on "unequal footing" with the East since only in the West did the federal government own and manage large sections of public lands. Such was the sentiment throughout the West, and from Nevada it quickly spread to neighboring states. Congressional delegates, state legislatures, and urban and rural westerners claimed allegiance to it. Polls taken in the Rocky Mountain states showed that support for the movement increased from one-third of those surveyed in 1979 to a slight majority in 1981.[7] Congressional delegates from all eleven western states in the continental United States actively promoted themselves as sagebrush rebels. Over a period of about two years, western politicians attempted to push through several pieces of legislation on the national and state level patterned after the Nevada bill. Orrin Hatch was joined by Utah's other senator, Jake Garn; Dennis DeConcini and Barry Goldwater of Arizona; Alan Simpson and Malcolm Wallop of Wyoming; and Paul Laxalt and Howard Cannon of Nevada when he introduced Senate Bill 1680 on August 3 and called for the "return" of "rightful title" to public lands and national forestlands in the West. Many Utah legislators also expressed anti-government sentiment, for example, during a special session, when some wore insignias that read, "Welcome to the West: Property, U.S. Government."[8]

But if it was clear where the West's congressional delegates stood on the issue, less clear was the response of western governors. Utah Governor Scott M. Matheson was an early supporter, but, like most other governors, he approached the issue with considerable caution. In 1976 he toyed with the idea of making public lands a foremost campaign issue for the governorship, but he decided against it, not wanting to make any major changes in his platform. A lawyer, Matheson had family roots in the rural community of Parowan. He recognized the problems of state ownership of public lands—inadequate resources, lack of environmental safeguards, agencies incapable of managing the land—but he was also an ardent proponent of greater state control of land and resources within its boundaries. So as governor of Utah, he took a keen interest in the developments of the Sagebrush Rebellion, taking it upon himself to evaluate the validity of a legal claim to public lands and decide how involved Utah should be.[9]

In the summer of 1979, Matheson commissioned the Utah Agricultural Experiment Station personnel at Utah State University to conduct a study of state management capabilities to determine the economic impact of state ownership of public lands. The governor publicly stated that he would not take a position until the report was released. In Colorado, New Mexico, and Wyoming, too, governors requested a similar report from their land-grant colleges.[10]

With so many uncertainties about a state takeover and early legal warnings that the "equal footing" doctrine would not prevail in the courts, the governor understandably took a cautious approach to Utah's own sagebrush bill, prefiled in December 1979 by Ivan M. Matheson (no relation), a Republican state senator from Cedar City and chairman of the Public Lands Committee. The Public Lands Reclamation Act of 1980, or Senate Bill 5, was essentially the same as Nevada's bill passed in February 1979. It asserted state ownership of all Bureau of Land Management (BLM) lands, which would be turned over to the Utah Division of State Lands and a public-land committee by July 1, 1980. According to Ivan Matheson, the state would adhere to the multiple-use concept of land management and take all necessary environmental precautions in place under the current system. Permission from the state legislature would be required before any of this land could be sold to private individuals or corporations. One of the bill's more controversial provisions would make public enemies of the more than four hundred federal employees: BLM officials could be jailed for up to fifteen years on a second-degree felony charge for attempting "to assert jurisdiction over public lands."[11]

Early on, the bill enjoyed wide support in the legislature and seemed certain to pass. The legislature's interim Agricultural Committee endorsed the bill, and two-thirds of the Senate and the House decided to permit it to be debated during the budget session in January. One of fifty-one bills that passed the Utah Senate during the budget session, Senate Bill 5 sailed through the House, fifty-seven to eleven, and the Senate, twenty to seven, and was signed by the president of the Senate on January 22, 1980. Ten days later, the House passed a Federal Lands Bill Resolution that gave formal support to the legislation Senator Orrin Hatch had introduced in the U.S. Senate.[12]

Still, even with solid backing in the state legislature, it was not a foregone conclusion that the governor would sign Senate Bill 5. In December 1979, Jim Butler, a member of Governor Matheson's staff, sent a memo to Kent Briggs, the state planning coordinator, suggesting that more information was needed regarding the public support for the bill before the governor could take an official position. Later, Butler called together a few members of his staff for a brainstorming meeting to discuss Senate Bill 5 and ascertain the general sentiment on the issue. In a memo to the governor, he expressed the fear that the bill "will raise as many questions as it answers" and stated that there remained a "pressing need for a good analysis of public opinion on this issue."[13] On January 16,

"SIR, THERE'S A GENTLEMAN WAITING TO see YOU WHO CLAIMS TO KNOW A THING OR TWO ABOUT REBELLIONS AGAINST FEDERAL INTERFERENCE."

Governor Scott Matheson cautiously approached Senate Bill 5, which asserted state ownership of all BLM lands. Cartoonist Pat Bagley alluded to the bill's strong assertion of states rights, reminiscent of the South's secession from the Union, in this *Salt Lake Tribune* cartoon, printed 7 February 1980. After legislators amended the bill at his request, Matheson agreed to sign it.

the governor's staff concluded that he could sign the bill if certain amendments were made—i.e., legislators needed to delete the criminal penalties for federal land managers and the restrictions placed on the governor regarding creation of the state public-lands committee. Matheson also wanted to ensure that the transfer applied only to BLM lands, as opposed to all federally owned lands, and that the state would manage the land according to the environmental constraints already in place. If these changes were made, he and other Democrats in the legislature vowed to endorse the bill. In addition, since 1980 was an election year, he feared a drubbing at the polls if he did not sign it. So he pledged to sympathetic county officials on February 6, "I will sign it this week or next, and Utah will officially become part of the Sagebrush Rebellion." After the Judiciary Committee inserted the amendments, Matheson kept his word and signed Senate Bill 5 on February 14.[14]

The governor's decision to sign the bill was influenced by several interim updates and a final report by agricultural economists at Utah State University. The report gave high-, mid, and low-cost estimates in its comparison of management expenses by the BLM and Forest Service as opposed to state land agencies. The range was tremendous. The high-cost estimate assessed the expense of current management by the BLM and Forest Service, while the low-cost estimate was based on current state-management expenses. The report concluded that a state takeover of federal lands would be economically feasible and potentially practical.

Although some research analysts in state agencies claimed the report was seriously flawed in its analysis and suppositions—for instance, a state document criticized the report for not factoring in the potential loss of payments by the federal government to counties in lieu of property taxes—Governor Matheson used the report to help justify his decision to support the controversial legislation.[15]

In other western states, governors also had to decide how much they would support the rebel cause, if at all. Between 1979 and 1981, legislatures in Wyoming, New Mexico, and Arizona (over the veto of Governor Bruce Babbitt) passed legislation; bills in Montana and Colorado never materialized, in Colorado due, in part, to the opposition of Governor Richard Lamm.[16] Indeed, the level of activity of rebels and their opponents varied from state to state, with the Sagebrush Rebellion taking different turns in Utah than in neighboring states.

Yet in the months following passage of Senate Bill 5, Matheson became increasingly wary of turning over lands to state ownership. All along he believed that the bill was mostly a symbolic gesture of Utah's frustration with federal management of public lands and a means to force the government to be more responsive to state and local needs. In this sense, he believed that the Sagebrush Rebellion "did some good." In his autobiography, he wrote, "It dramatically increased public involvement in the public land planning process at the state level. We had a significant turnaround in the way we dealt with federal land managers, and the attitudes of those land managers also changed."[17] What he did not state was that his initial support for Senate Bill 5—for the "symbolic" gestures of the Sagebrush Rebellion—encouraged the rebels but enflamed the opposition and, if he's right, extorted the federal government. In this sense, then, it did little to ease tensions. The legislation probably only inspired more-violent displays of protest that began to occur in some rural areas of the state.[18]

THE RURAL REACTION

That the more-aggressive manifestations of the rebellion occurred in Utah's backwater communities, where the concentration of public lands was highest, is no surprise. As the issue swept like brushfire through the West in 1979, embattled ranchers, miners, and other rural people, who felt that the federal government was an insensitive landlord and environmental legislation did not serve local interests, fanned its flames.

In the 1970s, particularly under the Carter administration, rural Utahns felt strapped by increased regulations embodied in the Federal Land Policy and Management Act of 1976 (sometimes known as the BLM Organic Act). In a nutshell, the act established guidelines and policy for managing public lands. Notably it stated that the federal government would manage public lands in perpetuity unless "it is determined that disposal of a particular parcel will serve the national interest." Management was to be based on principles of sustained yield, multiple use, and conservation "in a manner that will protect the quality of scientific, scenic, historical, ecological, environmental, air and atmospheric, water resource, and archeological values."[19] Many rural Utahns objected to the act on several grounds. It reversed the long-standing policy of disposal of public lands in favor of their perpetual retention. It led to tightened restrictions on grazing, mining, and access. And it put in motion an intensive inventory of BLM lands for possible designation as wilderness.

Many rural citizens in southeastern Utah felt they had been dealt a particularly tough hand. In Grand County, the United States owned and managed about 90 percent of the land. Residents had what they perceived to be an insensitive and authoritarian BLM district manager in S. Gene Day. Moreover, the BLM's first wilderness study inventory, completed in April 1979, designated the Moab district of the BLM with the highest percentage of land earmarked for wilderness study in the state.[20]

The wilderness inventory in particular produced a ripple effect in southern Utah. One story frequently told concerns staunch rebel Calvin Black, a hard-nosed commissioner from San Juan County, who, on April 12, 1979, after receiving word of the wilderness inventory, stormed into a BLM meeting and threatened the federal employees in attendance: "We've had enough of you guys telling us what to do. I'm not a violent man, but I'm getting to the point where I'll blow up bridges, [Indian] ruins and vehicles. We're going to start a revolution. We're going to get back our lands. We're going to sabotage your vehicles. You had better start going out in twos and threes, because we're going to take care of you BLMers." The response was, "Mr. Black, I hope you are not threatening me?"; Black replied, "I'm not threatening you, I'm promising you."[21]

Black never made good on his promise, but the sentiment he so pointedly expressed erupted in a specific pitched battle over one particular wilderness study area (WSA)—Negro Bill Canyon, a scenic and popular side canyon off Highway 128 about three miles northeast of Moab. When the BLM began the process of screening potential wilderness areas, Negro Bill made the initial cut, despite the fact that the canyon had seen human activity for a long time. The name of the canyon comes from William Granstaff (known as "Nigger Bill" well into the twentieth century and still called that by some Moabites today), an African American man who built a cabin and grazed cattle up the canyon in the first years of Moab's settlement. The old road extended up the canyon a short distance and was used in the subsequent century, along with other seismograph trails directly above the canyon, to stake mining claims. Mike Shumway and D. H. Shields had two hundred mining claims in the canyon at the time of the wilderness inventory. Nevertheless, the BLM determined that the area exhibited wilderness characteristics. It closed access to an old mining road on December 4, 1978, conducted the inventory of the area, and, based on the recommendation of a staffer that the canyon possessed "outstanding opportunities for both solitude and primitive recreation" and "little evidence of human activity," designated it as a WSA.[22]

On July 4, 1980, the symbolic climax of the Sagebrush Rebellion in Utah took place. About eighty vehicles snaked behind a Grand County highway department bulldozer from a park in Moab to the boundary of a wilderness study area where the dozer's blade was lowered to "up-grade" a road. During the protest, sagebrush rebels celebrated the American revolutionary tradition, hoisting Old Glory and singing "The Star Spangled Banner."

After learning that their July 4 protest had mistakenly never crossed the wilderness study area boundary, Grand County commissioners called out a bulldozer plastered with "Sagebrush Rebel" bumper stickers a second time to finish the task on July 7, 1980.

On July 7, in direct defiance of federal regulations, Mike Shumway removed the boulders from the road and drove his bulldozer partway up the canyon. The BLM responded by replacing the barrier. Then it happened again—Shumway, with the apparent blessing of the Grand County commissioners, removed the boulders, and the BLM once again replaced them. The federal government quickly filed suit in response, demanding a court order to prevent the county from removing future barricades and demanding an assessment of damages. Meanwhile, in an apparent act of appeasement, Gene Day recommended whittling down the size of the WSA from the original 26,800 acres to 8,406 in "a fairly natural condition."[23]

A year after Shumway's defiant gestures, Grand County commissioners organized what may be considered the symbolic climax of the Sagebrush Rebellion in Utah. In a meeting on June 26, 1980, the Grand County Commission and other local officials publicly declared their intentions to "upgrade" the road up Negro Bill Canyon. They assured the public that the action would be "peaceful in nature" and would only set the county back about two hundred dollars to operate the road equipment. They did warn that additional expenses could accrue if the county was sued, and the commission set aside ten thousand dollars for this possibility, but private interests had also offered to help cover any legal expenses.[24] As for the timing of the protest, the date of July 4 was deliberately selected, an emblematic gesture linking their cause to the venerated Declaration of Independence.

An estimated 250 to 300 citizens turned out for the event, congregating as planned in the Moab City Park on a Friday morning. The protesters and several environmentalists who decided to observe the proceedings caravanned in eighty four-wheel-drive vehicles and a few cars over rickety dirt roads, not to the mouth of the canyon but about seven miles east of Moab up Mill Creek Canyon. The place, known as the Sand Flats, was partly situated within the boundaries of the Negro Bill Canyon WSA, UT-060–138. Brief speeches, mostly from the commissioners, welcomed the crowd. Harvey Merrell criticized "the cancerous growth of the [federal] bureaucracy" and promised to "take control of our destiny in Southeastern Utah." Larry Jacobs, also a commissioner, reportedly proclaimed in religious syntax, "We have prayed we are doing the right thing, and at this point I think we are doing the right thing." Following the speeches, a bulldozer displaying a U.S. flag and flashing a sticker that read "I'm a Sagebrush Rebel" blazed a dirt trail into federal land. Almost. A few days later, Gene Day announced that the bulldozer had failed to enter the WSA boundary. So on July 7, the county called out a grader to finish the job.[25]

In his speech on that "Independence" day, commissioner Ray Tibbetts indicated the action was not illegal; all roads within the county were in the control of the commission, and the purpose of the bulldozing was to let the BLM know that the road existed. But Tibbetts and others certainly were not ignorant of the real legal challenges. In a letter to protest organizer Ron Steele postmarked more than a week before the scheduled event, Utah's assistant attorney general, Richard Dewsnup, plainly stated the attorney general's office would not in any way become involved in the protest, nor would it legally defend those who did if the United States decided to file a lawsuit. Though personally sympathetic to the proposed aims of the rebellion, he felt that the protest was nothing more than "a local reaction to local frustrations."[26] The BLM's official response to the incident was to demand that the county commission restore the area, within ten days, to the condition it was in "pre-July 4, 1980." If the commission failed to comply, then the restoration would occur anyway, and Grand County would be charged with the bill, or the expenses would be deducted from federal funds coming into the county. Understandably the commission caved in to the threat of a lawsuit and agreed to restore the area, but their members were never charged or prosecuted for their participation in the illegal act.[27]

July 1980 by no means marked the end of the Negro Bill Canyon saga. In November the BLM announced that it had cut the Negro Bill Canyon WSA and more than half of the other units in the Moab area from the intensive wilderness review.[28] In an additional gesture of truce, it transferred Gene Day—"the most hated man in southern Utah," according to the *Washington Post*—from his assignment in Moab.[29] The Utah Chapter of the Sierra Club fought the decision to drop Negro Bill from the list of WSAs in court. The court ruled in its favor, and the BLM restored Negro Bill Canyon as a WSA, though most of the 1.25 million acres dropped from the inventory stayed off the list.[30]

THE OPPOSITION

On the same day that bulldozers revved on the Sand Flats above Negro Bill Canyon—July 4—another group of a different sort had its own patriotic celebration nearby. Dave Foreman, environmental activist and founder of Earth First!, and two hundred of his comrades gathered for the first annual Round River Rendezvous near Moab, where they "drank lots of beer, sang to Johnny Sagebrush ([Jack] Koehler's stage name) songs, and complained about RARE II." (Roadless area review and evaluation—phase two completed in 1979—was the Forest Service's program to recommend wilderness areas on forestland.) The next day Foreman's newly organized Earth First! held a rally protesting the commissioners' bulldozing display.[31] On one level, these activists represented environmentalists nationwide who opposed the stated aims of the sagebrush rebels and their most recent manifestation. But these folks also reflected the sizable local opposition. Moab was an eclectic community: ranchers and miners represented the roots of its settlement, but federal employees and recreational enthusiasts also comprised a significant portion of the county's nearly ten thousand residents. Whatever the rhetoric, Grand County commissioners did not represent a clear majority. Indeed, it was not clear which side had either the demographic majority or the loudest voice.

Statewide, however, reaction to the bulldozing was overwhelmingly negative. For nearly a month after the fact, letters to the editor in the *Deseret News* and the *Salt Lake Tribune* mocked the public demonstration; one writer called it "a sad point of violence and lawlessness," and another said it was a "childish" act of a "small group of Utah red-necks." One letter expressed dismay over the new level to which proponents were willing to stoop to make their voices heard. Another lamented that tax dollars had been used in the protest and both the Grand County Democratic and Republican chairpersons had endorsed the activity. Yet another writer, referring to the rebels' sagebrush bill, found it "ironic," given the rebels' anathema to centralized direction, that Senate Bill 5 required "written permission from the Division of State Lands before any person can use, manage or dispose of public land." The letters printed in the newspapers generally reflected the opinion that the Sagebrush Rebellion was an illegitimate solution to western problems. If sagebrush rebels violated federal law and employed what one reader called "bulldozer diplomacy," then the movement as a whole could not be trusted.[32]

In a sense, it would be misleading to judge the Sagebrush Rebellion by the local incident in Grand County. It is unlikely that the decision to proceed with the protest was made by more than a handful of people or supported by a majority of Grand County residents, or even all sagebrush rebels.[33] But from the beginning, environmental organizations nationwide determined to tarnish the rebellion's image. In 1979 leaders of the Wilderness Society also directly confronted the movement by launching an offensive campaign of their own. Brant Calkin of the Sierra Club proposed covering it "with disrepute," while Dave Foreman suggested dropping the "romantic" term Sagebrush Rebellion for a more negative one such as "Public Lands Rip-Off," a moniker picked by the Sierra Club for its antirebellion newsletter.[34]

Utah environmental organizations and key individuals actively took part in the efforts to mobilize grassroots opposition. The Utah chapter of the Sierra Club responded in kind by forming the Sagebrush Rebellion Committee, which met regularly, set up booths at various conferences, delivered speeches, and put out an antirebellion newsletter. One was published in the spring of 1981, a tabloid edited by Michael Budig.[35] More active was the Utah Wilderness Association (UWA), established in 1979 and headed by Dick Carter, who on a tight budget and with a small staff took the lead on several fronts. UWA did newspaper editorials, brochures, big displays, and radio and television appearances. The association put together three separate television shows. Carter appeared on a program called *Crossfire* before a public audience opposite Calvin Black, where "[seventy-five] of our folks showed up, only 4 of Cal's." Efforts like these convinced national environmentalists like Foreman that the Utah branch under Carter was way ahead of other western states in organizing an opposition movement to the threat of a transfer. Foreman was particularly impressed with the steps the UWA took to distribute material through the media, and he suggested

Carter head that department at a meeting being held in Denver "to talk, brain-storm, strategize, and come to grips with the Sagebrush Rebellion."[36]

Early on, opponents seemed to make some real gains. Dick Carter reported in September 1979 that his organization had made "converts" of the governor, the state planning-coordinator's office, and the Utah Department of Agriculture and had "been able to keep [Dan] Marriott, [Gunn] McKay and [Jake] Garn from screaming about the 'Sagebrush Rebellion.'"[37] The silence did not last, however, as Utah's congressional delegation and state legislators joined the campaign to pass Senate Bill 5, Utah's own rebellion bill.

In response Carter lambasted the bill and encouraged citizens to write their representatives in opposition. To a gathering at the Salt Lake Kiwanis Club, as in his other public appearances, Carter characterized the rebels' rhetoric as little more than a smokescreen. He assured the audience that a transfer would do little to meet "the mandates of an ethical, moral and equitable multiple-use philosophy." On another occasion, this time in a UWA newsletter, he noted that the bill was not so much a benign attempt to change land ownership from the feds to the states or facilitate greater multiple use on the public lands but a malignant scheme "to allow rampant unrestricted development on BLM lands." Even if the state did succeed in a takeover, Utah had few resources to manage the land. The two best land agencies were probably the Utah Division of Wildlife Resources and State Parks and Recreation. Neither could guarantee to protect the land because there was no state-imposed Wilderness Act, Antiquities Act, Multiple-Use and Sustained-Yield Act, Endangered Species Act, or Natural Areas Act.[38]

The strength of the opposition was not enough to prevent the state legislature from passing the bill and the governor from signing it. A year later, with several prefiled bills pending in the state House of Representatives, Carter once more spearheaded efforts to shut them down. This time he was even more prepared for the brawl. By early January 1981, when the Utah Senate convened in session, UWA had predetermined the stance of each senator and distributed materials to several key senators and representatives. Desperate for community supporters to step up participation in the antirebellion efforts because "we simply are dealing with too many issues," Carter wrote to twenty activists and invited them to a strategy meeting on January 13. He hoped to make specific assignments for people to "know exactly what is happening to any SBR legislation" and "work the phones and organize . . . key friends and neighbors."[39]

Raymond Wheeler has argued that before 1981, Utah's environmental community, specifically the UWA, was rather "moderate" in its approach to environmental issues. His opinion is that only after Ronald Reagan and James Watt took office did more confrontational organizations, like the Southern Utah Wilderness Alliance, form and succeed in challenging the BLM's wilderness inventory in Utah.[40] There is no doubt that the Reagan administration did much to mobilize the environmental community and raise membership in environmental organizations. Nevertheless, the UWA's strategy in response to the Sagebrush Rebellion was quite aggressive. In the year and a half preceding Reagan's election, Dick Carter and his grassroots offensive was successful in keeping rebels on their toes and diminishing much of the legitimacy of the rebel rhetoric.

THE DEMISE

The response in Utah to the Sagebrush Rebellion underscored the complex feelings that people harbored about the question of public lands. Even among Utahns who felt frustrated by the federal government's management of public lands, there was not a clear sense of what should be done to redress the grievances. Some attempts were made to bring the varied interests together, for example, when in November 1980 five hundred politicians, academics, ranchers, and other westerners met at the Little America Hotel in Salt Lake City for a conference sponsored by the League for the Advancement of States' Equal Rights (LASER). But these rebels were strange bedfellows with diverse viewpoints. For some the rebellion was mainly a state's rights issue; for others it was a question of extracting the most economic benefit from the land. Some hoped to make a living off the land, but others sought to profit mightily from it. Moreover, many were mainly concerned with local or state issues and less interested in fighting on the regional or national levels, and thus had problems building cross-state coalitions.[41] The conference was simply a reflection of the movement as a whole, which "had been damaged by its confusion," as Colorado Governor Richard Lamm and writer Michael McCarthy observed in *The Angry West.*[42]

In addition to these complex factors, the Sagebrush Rebellion as a movement to transfer public lands to the states ironically languished under the leadership of one of its seemingly most ardent spokesmen: Reagan's new interior secretary, James Watt. Watt, the savior of economic development and darling of the Sagebrush Rebellion, apparently had little intention of pursuing a land transfer. Instead, he introduced the so-called good neighbor policy, a four-pronged strategy that emphasized multiple use, reduced dependence on foreign energy, formulated a minerals policy, and promoted restoration of national parks and monuments.[43] The national sagebrush legislation introduced by Hatch in 1979 and again in 1981 never had a real chance of passage, but it met its final demise when Watt and several key senators withdrew their support. The rebellion had outlived its usefulness with a man like Watt at the helm.

THE REBELLION'S SIGNIFICANCE

Although the movement itself disappeared rather quickly, its issues and problems are more enduring. Indeed, these speak to the broader western experience. In two classic studies, historians Patricia Limerick and Donald Worster suggest that the Sagebrush Rebellion hearkens back to the Old West. Limerick calls it another example of westerners' tendency to assume the role of "innocent

Pat Bagley

In this cartoon printed in *High Country News* on 20 March 1995 Pat Bagley memorably highlighted the tension between developers and environmentalists in his caricature of extremists on both sides.

victims"—in this case, from government abuse and unyielding authority. Worster argues that the movement drew upon a prominent notion—at least since the 1890s—of the West as a colony of the East—a "plundered province," in the words of Bernard DeVoto.[44] As these two historians have suggested, the Sagebrush Rebellion reflected issues and sentiments that have always been a part of the West.[45]

These themes of westerners as innocent victims of governmental authority and the West as a plundered province certainly resonated in Utah. In a state long accustomed to perceived abuse at the hands of the federal government, stemming back to the so-called Utah War in the 1850s and stepped-up anti-polygamy legislation in the 1880s, antigovernment sentiment is hardly unprecedented. Staunch rebels like the commissioners of Grand County proactively resisted the government's presence in Utah, believing that state or private ownership of federal land would loose the West from the shackles of colonialism and at last place it on "equal footing" with the East. These notions resonated with Utahns, not only in rural areas but urban centers as well. The bulldozing incident, the state and national legislation, the large media events, the newspaper and magazine attention—all these indicate that the Sagebrush Rebellion was serious business to many Utahns. Opponents took the rebellion seriously, too, determining from the start to smear the movement with disrepute. They felt real anxiety over the prospect of state or private ownership of the nation's public lands and did not hesitate to defend the current system of federal ownership and management.

No doubt the grievances were real, but the way each side addressed those grievances did not even begin to work toward a lasting and common solution. Each side postured, protested, and spewed out offensive rhetoric that only heightened the tension over Utah's public lands. One problem was that what rebels and opponents said was, in some ways, contradictory and inconsistent. For instance, opponents argued that the federal government safeguarded the land from ruin, yet during the same period the government pushed for large-scale, potentially environmentally devastating federal projects, ranging from MX missiles to toxic waste repositories. On the other hand, rebels spoke of a government that "locked up" the land and its resources from the public, yet that is exactly what would likely have happened if the states had gained ownership of the land and put it into private hands. Critics also like to point out that while rebels complained bitterly of the federal presence, many enjoyed subsidies and additional support from Uncle Sam. In the end, the rhetoric, the violent protests, and the contradictions did not solve the problem of ownership and management of public lands. The rebellion may have thrust public lands issues to the fore and prompted land managers to be more responsive to local concerns, but its primary legacy was that it served to polarize, alienate, and entrench, not bring together.

Notes

1. Paul Larmerstaff, "The Mother of All Land Grabs," *High Country News,* September 30, 1996, available online at www.hcn.org.

2. Bernard DeVoto, "The West Against Itself," in *The Western Paradox: A Conservation Reader,* ed. Douglas Brinkley and Patricia Nelson Limerick (New Haven: Yale University Press, 2001), 45–73.

3. Utah's Republican Senator Orrin Hatch made these remarks at a three-day conference of the Western Coalition on Public Lands in Reno in September 1979. See LaVar Webb, "Sagebrush Rebels Prepare for Battle," *Deseret News,* September 5, 1979; Webb, "'Sagebrush Rebels' Wind up Summit, Pledge to Push Fight on all Fronts," *Deseret News,* September 7, 1979.

4. "The Sagebrush Ripoff," summer 1981, box 3A: 15, folder 14, MS 148, Papers of the Utah chapter of the Sierra Club, Special Collections and Archives, Merrill-Cazier Library, Utah State University, Logan (hereafter cited as PUCSC).

5. The best source on the topic is R. McGreggor Cawley, *Federal Land, Western Anger: The Sagebrush Rebellion and Environmental Politics* (Lawrence: University Press of Kansas, 1993). General histories of the American West may mention the movement in a paragraph or two. See Michael P. Malone and F. Ross Peterson's essay, "Politics and Protests," in *The Oxford History of the American West,* eds. Clyde A. Milner II, Carol A. O'Connor, and Martha A. Sandweiss (New York: Oxford University Press, 1994), 529–30; Richard White, *"It's Your Misfortune and None of My Own": A History of the New American West* (Norman: University of Oklahoma Press, 1991), 567–68; Carl Abbott, *The Metropolitan Frontier: Cities in the Modern American West*

(Tucson: University of Arizona Press, 1993), 167–68; Robert Gottlieb and Peter Wiley, *Empires in the Sun: The Rise of the New American West* (New York: Putnam, 1982), 300–301, 307; Gerald D. Nash, *The Federal Landscape: An Economic History of the Twentieth Century West* (Tucson: University of Arizona Press, 1999), 136–37. For a Utah state or county perspective, see Thomas G. Alexander, *Utah, the Right Place: The Official Centennial History,* rev. ed. (Salt Lake City: Gibbs Smith, 2003), 424–25; Scott M. Matheson and James Edwin Kee, *Out of Balance* (Salt Lake City: Gibbs Smith, 1986); and Richard A. Firmage, *A History of Grand County* (Salt Lake City: Utah State Historical Society and Grand County Commission, 1996). Political scientists tend to focus on the constitutional and legal aspects, a perspective I do not address here.

6. William L. Graf, *Wilderness Preservation and the Sagebrush Rebellions* (Savage, MD: Rowman & Littlefield Publishers, Inc., 1990), 146, 147, 167–68; Jerry Ford, "Sagebrush: 'It Is Important We Control Our Destiny,'" *Logan Herald Journal,* October 26, 1980.

7. Rocky Mountain poll, Behavior Research Center, November 1981, box 15, folder 15, series 19161, Scott M. Matheson Papers, Utah State Archives, Salt Lake City.

8. "How about Cutting Back Utah's Biggest Landlord?" *Deseret News,* June 16, 1978.

9. His was a somewhat contradictory role: he signed Utah's own Sagebrush Rebellion bill but also searched out other methods of addressing the issues; he agreed with the movement philosophically but was wary of its tactics. For Matheson's political philosophy, see his autobiography, *Out of Balance.*

10. Douglas L. Parker, "Coloradoan Hesitates to Take a Stand on Sage Rebellion," *Salt Lake Tribune,* September 16, 1979; "Governors Wary of Sagebrush Rebellion," *Salt Lake Tribune,* October 28, 1979.

11. "'Sagebrush Rebel' Drafts Bill," *Salt Lake Tribune,* September 15, 1979; Peter Gillins, "Sagebrush Rebellion Bill Prefiled," *Deseret News,* December 11, 1979; "Land Takeover Bill Likely to Pass," *Deseret News,* December 16, 1979.

12. State of Utah, Senate Journal, *Budget Session of the Forty-Third Legislature, Commencing Monday, January 14, 1980, Adjourning February 2, 1980,* 510.

13. Jim Butler to Kent Briggs, December 12, 1979; Butler to Gov. Scott Matheson, January 4, 1980; Butler, memo, January 9, 1980; Butler to Gov. Scott Matheson, January 16, 1980, all in box 15, folder 10, Matheson Papers.

14. The meeting with the governor is reported in LaVarr Webb and Joe Costanzo, "'Sagebrush' Bill Sailing Along," *Deseret News,* January 17, 1980; Bill Heaton, "Matheson Tells Counties' Officials He'll OK Sagebrush Rebellion Bill," *Salt Lake Tribune,* February 7, 1980. See also Matheson and Kee, *Out of Balance,* 126–27.

15. Utah Agricultural Experiment Station, "An Economic Evaluation of the Transfer of Federal Lands in Utah to State Ownership" (Logan: Utah State University, Utah Agricultural Experiment Station, May 1980). For critical comments on the report, see "State Comments on Utah State University's Report," box 15, folder 12, Matheson Papers.

16. Richard D. Lamm and Michael McCarthy, *The Angry West: A Vulnerable Land and Its Future* (Boston: Houghton Mifflin, 1982), 276–77.

17. Gov. Scott Matheson to Joelle Reece, Febuary 5, 1980, box 15, folder 11, Matheson Papers; Matheson and Kee, *Out of Balance,* 128.

18. See Matheson and Kee, *Out of Balance,* 129–34.

19. U.S. Department of the Interior, Bureau of Land Management and Office of the Solicitor, *The Federal Land Policy and Management Act, as Amended* (Washington, DC: GPO, 2001), 1–2.

20. See Joe Bauman, "BLM Proposes Utah Wilds Review," *Deseret News,* April 2, 1979. Wilderness study areas contain public lands that are roadless and have other wilderness characteristics but have not yet been officially designated by Congress.

21. Jim Pissot, "Cal Black's Threats," *Deseret News,* January 18, 1980; also quoted in Margot Hornblower, "BLM Manager on Front Lines of Sagebrush Rebellion in Utah," *Los Angeles Times,* December 16, 1979, 19. The quote comes from the staff report on file at the BLM office in Moab. In a letter to the *High Country News* after that publication made reference to the April 12 meeting, Black wrote that "those were the things the people were saying in their anger and frustration at what Gene Day and others were doing." See Raymond Wheeler, "Boom! Boom! Boom! War on the Colorado Plateau," in *Reopening the Western Frontier,* ed. Ed Marston (Washington, DC: Island Press, 1989), 22, 298–99.

22. "Wilderness Inventory, Situation Evaluation, Negro Bill Canyon, UT-060–138," unpublished report on file in the BLM office in Moab, Utah.

23. See "Few Protesters Turn Out for Canyon Camp-Out," *Deseret News,* September 10, 1979; *Moab Times Independent,* July 5, August 9, 1979; "Utah Files Wilderness Road Suit," *Salt Lake Tribune,* August 5, 1979; Lee Holley, "U.S. Suing Grand County for Road," *Salt Lake Tribune,* August 16, 1979; Helen Lacko, "The Good Ol' Boys vs. the BLM in Negro Bill Canyon," *Utah Holiday* 8, no. 11 (August 1979): 10, 12, 14; Firmage, *History of Grand County,* 369.

24. "County to Open Road into Study Area as 'Symbolic Gesture,'" *Moab Times–Independent,* July 3, 1980, 1.

25. Joe Bauman, "250 Watch 'Rebellion' Dozer Cut BLM Land," *Deseret News,* July 5, 1980; Bill Davis, "County Action Aims to Challenge 'Organic Act,'" *Moab Times–Independent,* July 10, 1980. The event was widely covered in state and local newspapers and is replayed in Firmage, *History of Grand County,* 369–74; Cawley, *Federal Land, Western Anger,* 5–8; and Wheeler, "Boom! Boom! Boom!," 20.

26. Richard L. Dewsnup to Ron Steele, June 27, 1980, box 15, folder 12, Matheson Papers.

27. See Cawley, *Federal Land, Western Anger,* 6–7.

28. *Moab Times-Independent,* November 20, 1980.

29. Wheeler, "Boom! Boom! Boom!," 20.

30. Wallace Stegner, *Wilderness at the Edge* (Salt Lake City: Utah Wilderness Coalition, 1990), 3–8. Also see extensive court documents in BLM files in Moab, Utah.

31. James M. Cahalan, *Edward Abbey: A Life* (Tucson: University of Arizona Press, 2001), 192.

32. Margaret Pettis, "Untrustworthy Rebellion," *Salt Lake Tribune,* August 2, 1980; Jack T. Spence, "Doubly Useful," *Salt Lake Tribune,* July 12, 1980; Dick Carter, "The Rebels, the Road, and the Law," *Deseret News,* July 10, 1980.

33. Bauman, "250 Watch 'Rebellion' Dozer."

34. Debbie Sease to et al., August 26, 1979, box 3C: 36, folder 11; Brant Calkin to Mike et al., memo, August 13, 1979, box 3C: 36, folder 5, PUCSC; Dave Foreman and Bob Langsenkamp to western public land leaders, August 10, 1979; and Dave Foreman to conservation leaders, August 22, 1979, box 2, folder 7, MS 200, Archives of the Utah Wilderness Association, Special Collections and Archives, Merrill-Cazier Library, Utah State University, Logan (hereafter cited as AUWA).

35. "Sagebrush Rebellion Committee Resolution," April 9, 1981, box 3A: 15, folder 16, PUCSC.

36. Dick Carter to Dave Foreman, September 22, 1979; Dave Foreman to Dick Carter, September 28, 1979, box 2, folder 7, AUWA.

37. Dick Carter to Dave Foreman, September 22, 1979, box 2, folder 7, AUWA.

38. Speech to Salt Lake Kiwanis Club, February 14, 1980, box 1, folder 1, AUWA; "Senate Bill 5 and the Sagebrush Rebellion," January 1980, newsletter, box 2, folder 15, AUWA; Margaret Pettis, "'Rebellion' Anti-Conservation," *Deseret News,* September 20, 1979; Pettis, "Familiar Rhetoric," *Salt Lake Tribune,* October 6, 1979. Judging by the number of letters written in opposition to Senate Bill 5, Carter must have reached an audience. The governor's correspondence files contain numerous letters with protests ranging from outrage that a nonbudget bill was being considered during a budget session to complaints that no public hearings or debates had been held regarding the matter. See box 15, folders 10 and 11, Matheson Papers.

39. Dick Carter to Sagebrush Rebellion activists, January 5, 1981, box 2, folder 6, AUWA.

40. Raymond Wheeler, "Stroke and Counterstroke," in Marston, *Reopening the Western Frontier,* 144–46.

41. *Agenda for the '80s: A New Federal Land Policy. Proceedings of the National Conference on States' Rights, The Sagebrush Rebellion, and Federal Land Policy* (Salt Lake City: League for the Advancement of States' Equal Rights, prepared by Political Economy Research Group, 1981).

42. Lamm and McCarthy, *The Angry West,* 283.

43. Ron Arnold, *The Eye of the Storm: James Watt and the Environmentalists* (Chicago: Regnery Gateway, 1982), 55, 69, 227–28.

44. Patricia Limerick, *The Legacy of Conquest: The Unbroken Past of the American West* (New York: W.W. Norton, 1987), 46–47; Donald Worster, *Rivers of Empire: Water, Aridity and the Growth of the American West* (New York: Pantheon, 1985), 14; DeVoto, "The West: A Plundered Province," 3–21.

45. For more, see Char Miller, "Tapping the Rockies: Resource Exploitation and Conservation in the Intermountain West," in *Reopening the American West,* ed. Hal K. Rothman (Tucson: University of Arizona Press, 1998), 168–82.

16

Utah's Recent Growth

The St. George/Washington County Example

Douglas D. Alder

According to most Salt Lake City television stations, there are two types of weather in Utah: the Wasatch Front (basically Salt Lake City) and Utah's Dixie (St. George). One of the fastest-growing areas in the United States because of its mild winters, St. George played an increasingly important role in Utah during the twentieth century (although Brigham Young's winter home may have forecast the area's future). While other authors use St. George to illustrate their conclusions, Douglas D. Alder focuses on the way that Utah's Dixie changed from a provincial religious community to a retirement one and how it differs from Cache Valley, another rapidly growing area in northern Utah. Using local development records and personal experience, he carefully spells out the reasons why people come to St. George and why they stay. He also points out the challenges and advantages the increased population has brought to the area. His essay provides a model to help us understand other changing areas in the state. Alder's experience as a professor at Utah State University and president of Dixie College makes him the ideal person to put the St. George story in a larger Utah context.

Utah's population increased by 1 million people between 1980 and 2006. Of the 2.5 million people in Utah in 2006, nearly 2 million lived on the well-watered Wasatch Front, the narrow stretch of land on the foothills of the mountains from Brigham City on the north, through Ogden, Salt Lake City, and Provo, to Santaquin on the southern boundary of Utah County. It was not surprising that the outlying twenty-four counties of the state, with only 500,000 people altogether, did not command a lot of attention.

In the late twentieth century, however, two of those distant "colonies," Cache Valley on the northern border and Utah's Dixie on the southern state

385

Aerial photographs clearly show how the St. George area has expanded. The first photograph was used in the *Utah Historical Quarterly* in July 1961.

This photograph was taken around 2008.

Utah State University's Innovation Campus and Research Park became, in the 1990s, home to high-technology industries that helped spur economic development in Cache Valley.

line, developed well beyond their agricultural roots and scenic attractions to become population centers, each containing more than 100,000 people, as well as industries, shopping malls, and higher-education centers.

The story in Cache Valley was one where agriculture gave rise to agricultural industries—Cache Valley Cheese, Gossner's Cheese, E.A. Miller Inc., Pepperidge Farms, and Lundahl Farm Equipment. In the 1990s and 2000s, high-technology industries such as Hyclone Laboratories, Campbell Scientific, and several firms connected to the Utah State University Research Park, as well as the university's Center for Atmospheric and Space Studies and its Space Dynamics Laboratory, stimulated economic development. Highly skilled employees were drawn to the valley. The growth of Utah State University (USU) also attracted students, faculty, and staff. The increase was steady and substantial.

How could even more growth occur in the aridity of distant Washington County, which was twice as far from the state's capital city? Until the 1960s, Dixie was limited to tourism and self-sustaining agriculture—but farming was less productive than in Cache Valley because arable land was in short supply. The scarcity of water limited many farms to five acres; ranchers had to range their cattle in the desert. The Dixie pioneers doggedly labored at their vision of family farms to make the "desert blossom as a rose." The early settlers of Cache Valley, in contrast, had to endure some harsh winters, but for about seven months of the year, they farmed with ample water and acreage. The Dixie folks had to battle a cycle of floods and droughts, but they stayed at it. After a century of such efforts, these southern Utahns had achieved moderate stability but accumulated little capital. By 1965 only 10,600 people lived in Washington County as compared to 40,900 in Cache County.

Beginning that year, steady growth started in Washington County. Forty years later, the population had increased to 127,000 (as compared to 105,500 in Cache Valley). In 2006 St. George was listed as the fastest-growing metropolitan community in the United States, and home price appreciation was cited as number one in the nation. A year later, St. George had the number-one growth rate.[1] These two counties were not the only growing areas in the state. Salt Lake County, Davis County, and Utah County were expanding rapidly, too, but Washington County grew faster than them all percentage wise.

There was a transformation in St. George. The pioneer past was still visible—the LDS Temple, the St. George town square—but the original straight streets were limited to the inner city. A score of California-like suburbs surrounded that core and spread beyond it, peopled largely by move-ins who chose the amenities—curving streets, palm trees, tile-roofed luxury homes, golf courses—all enhancing their enjoyment of the southwestern weather.

In contrast to the economic booms in both Cache Valley and Washington County, another place was growing in Utah's Dixie, but not mainly due to economics. Hildale, Utah, and adjacent Colorado City, Arizona, are in the remote southeastern corner of Dixie, but they eschew consumerism. At the turn of the century, together they had an estimated population of ten thousand people, who practiced plural marriage and were members of the FLDS Church (Fundamentalist Latter-day Saints). Their goal was to perpetuate pioneer principles of frugality and preanifesto Mormonism. They dressed like pioneers and worked like them at farming and trades. Their per-family income was less than half of that of the rest of the county because they divided salaries among several families. They were intent on isolation in contrast to the destination mentality of the St. George area.

From their founding in 1930 to 2006, Hildale and Colorado City tried to remain as unnoticed as possible. An attempt by the state of Arizona to prosecute the polygamists of Colorado City in 1953 attracted national attention and thereby backfired. After that the situation remained fairly low key, and the movement spread well beyond Washington County with affiliated groups located in northern Utah, Montana, Texas, South Dakota, and Colorado, as well as Alberta and British Columbia in Canada. The Dixie headquarters was just more visible.

In 2006 the states of Utah and Arizona nipped at the edges of the issue by prosecuting some of the polygamists for marrying underage plural wives. The sustained litigation escalated to the point that the state of Utah appointed a team of outside individuals to take over the management of the hundred-million-dollar FLDS trust fund, which controlled land ownership in Hildale and Colorado City.

Warren Jeffs, the head of the FLDS Church, lashed out at fellow polygamist leaders who attempted some accommodation with the rest of Washington County. This group, led by the Barlows, worked with the school districts and the state governments in Utah and Arizona for two decades. Jeffs ejected them from the community along with several others supporting their position. He also threw out many young men, called the "lost boys," whom he claimed were becoming secular by watching the wrong television shows and adopting teenage fads. Jeffs urged parents in the communities to take their children from the public schools and homeschool them. The whole confrontation created tension and furthered divisions. This was a case where once remote Washington County was involved directly in an issue that was central to the state of Utah. Jeffs's trial began in November 2006 and attracted news media from the entire nation, including network television broadcasters who captured the testimony of a Jane Doe witness, who stated that Jeffs had performed her marriage to a nineteen-year-old cousin when she was fourteen and instructed her to have sex with her husband.[2]

Here were three communities on the northern and southern borders of the state, each drawing the Wasatch Front population from the center to the borders. This chapter focuses on Utah's booming Dixie, but the other two communities provide perspective.

Why did so many people come to Utah's Dixie, nearly doubling the population during the recent decade (from 72,900 in 1996 to 130,000 in 2006)? The general movement of Americans into the U.S. Southwest offers one important explanation. The growth of Palm Springs, California, and Sun City and Scottsdale, Arizona, illustrates the desirability of the southwestern climate and its ability to attract retirees and others. Even more important has been the growth of Las Vegas, Nevada, and Phoenix, Arizona. These are major urban centers that are attracting people and businesses and industries to the Southwest.

St. George's location offered a desirable alternative with southwestern climate, scenery, and a smaller community. St. George was Utah's version of the Southwest, sort of a small combination of Las Vegas and Palm Springs, including both retirement and business opportunities. The aging of America created an increasing retirement cohort, some of whom selected St. George, while the thriving economy drew others.

The existence of national parks and monuments was another draw, bringing millions of people each year to see Dixie's scenery. Three other features of St. George impressed people: Dixie State College, the LDS Temple, and the new Intermountain Health Care hospital. Many people were attracted to the idea of living in a college town, and another set wanted to live near an LDS Temple. Some came to utilize advanced health care. Recreation amenities like golf, trails, and Lake Powell were another enticement. The resulting growth created employment that draws workers to the service industries—construction, merchandising, education, medicine, government, and business. The cycle of growth and expansion has fueled more growth.

What were the specific elements and challenges of the growth in Washington County in 2006? The most visible was construction. In addition to major commercial, government, and road projects, housing developments sprang up throughout the county. The construction industry made up 13 percent of the county's employment as compared to 5 percent in Cache Valley and 6 percent statewide.[3] Building permits doubled in a decade to four thousand a year, and home sales trebled to twelve thousand in 2005.[4] Whole new communities were added as suburbs or expansions—Entrada, Kayenta, Crystal Lakes, Sun River, The Ledges, Coral Canyon, Sky Mountain. Existing towns experienced major expansion, such as the Santa Clara Heights, the new neighborhoods on the east side of Ivins, the many new projects in Sunset and adjacent Green Valley, Hurricane's expansion to the south, and a new project near Sand Hollow Reservoir, as well as Sky Mountain, and St. George's growth in Washington Fields (Washington City is also there) and nearby Bloomington Hills. Most of these projects were developer initiated, designer constructed, and agent sold. In addition, there were scores of new condominium projects, bringing the total to some fifteen thousand units.[5]

Another indication of growth was the multiplication of merchandising options in this decade. This was the case particularly along Red Cliffs Drive (parallel to I-15) and its southern extension, the new River Road. Box stores were built along these two roads, adding to the three malls already there. The new outlets included Wal-Mart, Costco, Home Depot, Albertson's mall, Sportsman's Warehouse, Kohl's, Bed Bath & Beyond, Best Buy, Big 5 Sporting Goods, Pineview Stadium 10, Ashley Furniture, Boulevard Home Furnishings, Target, and Lowe's. At the south end of River Road were the SkyWest corporate offices, the new Dixie Regional Medical Center, and Harmons.

This was the county's new main street, not for pedestrians but for automobiles to park in the huge parking lots adjacent to each facility. The three-mile-long collection of outlets had no Dixie character. Most were national chain stores, similar to new commercial centers all over the country. Certainly they demonstrated the arrival of capital investment in the county and the dominance of national merchandising.

Other smaller developments of a similar nature included the business park at the Bloomington freeway exit, which hosted another Wal-Mart and a hotel as well as banks and stores. Sunset Corner was a new mall with a movie megaplex at Sunset Boulevard and Bluff Street. Stores extended along Sunset Boulevard to Dixie Drive, where Lin's Market and the Albertson's mall were located. Hurricane saw large new stores built on Highway 9 west of the city center, such as Stout Home Furnishings, Lin's Market, and yet-another movie megaplex. Thus, the new mode of merchandising—the big parking-lot complexes—extended to serve the bulk of the county residents. All of this resulted in the continuing growth of sales. Washington County had 7 percent of the state's taxable sales, whereas Cache County had slightly less than 4 percent, even though it also had new box stores.

Tourism expanded during the first decade of the twenty-first century. Six new hotels, a score of motels, and about one hundred restaurants and drive-ins, most of them national chains, welcomed visitors in St. George. In addition, there were fifteen food outlets in Springdale and a dozen motels. Hurricane had five motels and a dozen dining facilities. Several bed-and-breakfasts were established, both in the Springdale/Rockville area and St. George. By 2006 there were more than four thousand beds available in the county's tourist accommodations (compared to eight hundred in Cache Valley).

Many of the occupants of these motels and hotels were not just passing through as tourists. The Dixie Center convention facility, located near the freeway at Exit 6, attracted sixty conventions in 2005. In addition to these meetings, people came for sponsored events, such as golf tournaments, the St. George Marathon, the Huntsman World Senior Games, the St. George Arts Festival each spring, and the continuing softball/baseball tournaments for youth teams all through the winter. Tourism had come a long way since Wylie Camp, the first campground near Zion National Park in 1917. For example, two and a half million visitors came to the site of the Great White Throne every year. Dixie tourism was enticing national and international visitors in a sophisticated manner as well as becoming a major employer.

One concern about the growth in Washington County was how to spread the economic base beyond merchandising, where the profits were soft. As agricultural production declined after the 1970s, community leaders tried to replace it with industry. Two industrial parks were built, one near Middleton in 1961 and the Millcreek Industrial Park in 1980. A decade later, the Gateway Industrial Park was created in Hurricane near I-15. Then in 2000 the Fort Pierce Industrial Park began, hosting fifty businesses by 2006. That year a new high-tech industrial park sprang up in Tonaquint with a new Utah Interlinx fiber-optic line. These five industrial parks created a more-stable economy and higher-paying jobs. In addition, a score of high-tech firms were established, some spin-offs from Dixie College.[6] This helped transform the situation where the younger generation found it necessary to leave the county to find careers and employment.

Washington County was not as successful as some counties in this effort. An examination of Utah Workforce Services data shows that Washington County was still behind its "seniors" because Salt Lake County had 10.7 percent of its workforce in industry. Weber County had 14 percent, Davis County had 12 percent, and Utah County had 12.9 percent. Cache County had 18 percent, while Washington County had only 7 percent.[7]

A consequence of the growth in the county was a demand for improved medical services. A highly visible result was the building of the hundred-million-dollar Intermountain Healthcare hospital. It was the fifth in a series of hospitals, the first constructed in 1917. In 1976 Intermountain assumed the ownership of the county hospital. The corporation constructed five additions

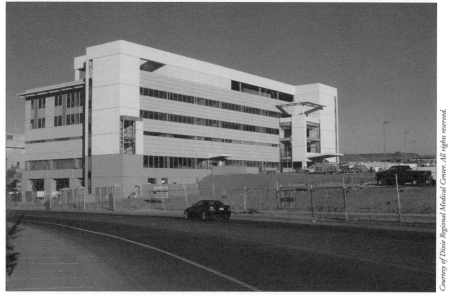

St. George is one of the fastest growing cities in the United States because of its mild winter weather and its attractiveness to senior citizens. To meet the growing demands for medical services, Intermountain Healthcare has constructed Dixie Regional Medical Center, a state-of-the-art hospital.

but finally ran out of space on its 400 East site. After much planning, Intermountain acquired a new sixty-acre site on River Road. The community responded by raising ten million dollars in private donations. In the new hospital, medical services were expanded, including open heart surgery. The old hospital was retained and remodeled again to house the cancer services, the Women and Children's Center, and psychological services, completely occupying the old building. The hospital in St. George was a magnet for the many retirees moving to the area.[8]

People in Cache Valley were outspoken in their desire for both a cancer center and the heart facilities that St. George enjoyed. In the last year, some cancer services have begun in Cache Valley, where chemotherapy is now available. Patients still had to travel to Ogden for radiation treatments, but there were plans to add them in Logan.

Some thought that Dixie was for retirees. Actually the upswing in the economy drew many young families to the community. Only 17 percent of the county were older than sixty-five (in contrast to 9 percent statewide), and those younger than nineteen made up 31 percent (in comparison to 33 percent statewide).[9] The remaining 52 percent were the middle-age cohort, many of them parents and employed. By comparison Cache Valley had 7.2 percent older than sixty-five and 31.3 percent younger than nineteen, leaving 61.6 percent in middle age.

The influx of people into Washington County, especially in the last decade, put major demands on the school system. In the 1990s, there were twenty-four public schools in Washington County to serve 17,915 students, and in 2006 there were thirty-seven schools serving 23,160 students. County residents approved a $150-million bond for more buildings and services in 2006. In higher education, the county also experienced an increase. In 1996 Dixie College had 5,318 students (3,218 full-time equivalent). By 2008 the fall enrollment was 6,443 (4,421 full-time equivalent).[10] A branch campus in Hurricane served 331 students. Courses were also taught in Kanab. Several four-year degrees were added to the curriculum, including computer and information systems, business, English, elementary education, medical radiography, nursing, communication and new media, and biology. These baccalaureate degrees led to a change of the college's name in December 1999 to indicate its new four-year status: from Dixie College to Dixie State College of Utah.

There was only one new elementary school in this decade in the Logan City School District because the population of Logan was not growing as fast as the county, where the Cache County School District had three new elementary schools and two new middle schools. In contrast, the number of students at USU was 23,107, far above the enrollment in Washington County. USU's budget was $250 million per year in contrast to Dixie's $25 million. Much of USU's funding came from research grants; that significant budget had a great deal to do with the thriving economy of Cache Valley, whereas the Dixie College budget had much less impact.

Another specific element of the growth in Washington County was an increase in cultural offerings. Some of these were a direct result of education efforts; others were linked to the tastes that newcomers brought with them. As a result, two art museums now existed in St. George. One was at the Pioneer Center for the Performing Arts, sponsored by the city. The other was in the new Eccles Fine Arts Center at Dixie State College. Several commercial art galleries also opened during the 1990s. Three theaters were also active—one at the college, the St. George Musical Theater, and Tuacahn Theatre in Ivins. The Celebrity Concert Series at Dixie State College started in the 1960s but doubled its offerings in 2006 because of the growing audience. That year the series presented concerts in the twelve-hundred-seat Cox Auditorium two nights each, including such performing groups as the Russian National Ballet Theatre of Moscow, the King's Singers, the Prague Opera Company, and even some shows from Branson, Missouri. The local Southwest Symphony Orchestra and Chorale also presented their concerts two nights each. There were also a dozen choirs, particularly the two-hundred-voice Heritage Choir.

During the same period, Cache Valley became well known for its Utah Festival Opera, which features two months of major productions in the Ellen Eccles Theatre (the old Capitol Theatre) in downtown Logan each summer; the Festival Opera drew people to the valley in large numbers. Other major cultural offerings in Cache Valley were comparable to Washington County: the plays at the Lyric Theatre in downtown Logan as well as USU productions in the Morgan Theatre on campus, the USU Concert Series, concerts by the Cache Chamber Orchestra, musical performances at the new, award-winning Manon Caine Russell Kathryn Caine Wanlass Performance Hall on the USU campus, the many Music Department recitals, and concerts sponsored by the Cache Valley Center for the Arts in the Ellen Eccles Theatre.

In the first decade of the twenty-first century, Washington County built seven new libraries in its countywide system—Santa Clara, Springdale, New Harmony, St. George, and Hurricane, Enterprise, and Washington City. These were the result of a bond election for twenty-three million dollars that passed in 1998. Washington County enjoyed the benefit of having a countywide library system. That did not exist in Cache Valley, but North Logan built a library, and Hyrum planned a new building. These all demonstrated the community vitality in both counties.

Washington County has long been known for its many recreational opportunities. The 1990s and 2000s saw a major increase in such amenities. St. George built many parks and trails. In 2006 there were thirty-eight parks plus eighteen trails and twenty other facilities, such as swimming pools, a recreation center, and tennis courts. Many of these were built with funds from a parks bond that was passed in 1995. It was fascinating to see that a community known for retirees was able to pass such bonds. It is questionable that this would have happened without the growth.

Golf was another popular recreation activity. In 2006 there were ten golf courses in Washington County with three more being constructed or planned. They were located in Hurricane, Washington City, and St. George, and five of them were owned by city governments. Golf was almost a religion with some retirees, but it was also popular with working adults and youth. In contrast, Cache Valley had only three golf courses. Perhaps the difference in number was another testimony that retirees preferred the warm winters of Dixie.

St. George promoted many recreational programs, including swimming, tennis, golf, softball, and baseball, even horseshoes, as well as the St. George Marathon. The city's Leisure Services Department actively promoted recreational events aimed at all ages and particularly wanted to draw people to the city to occupy the hotels and motels. The county sponsored the Washington County Tourist and Publicity Bureau, receiving funds from the 1 percent sales tax on motels, hotels, and restaurants and allocating them to projects to promote tourism.

Another consequence of growth was the diversity of people coming to live in the county. For the first century, Anglo-Americans largely occupied the Dixie region; nearly all the people were one ethnicity and members of one religious congregation. Since the inflow of people, this uniformity has changed. The Mormon population grew rapidly, but so did other groups. One noticeable influx was the arrival of about six thousand Spanish-speaking people in the 1990s and 2000s. Another, but smaller group, included several hundred Polynesians. Native Americans and black Americans also lived in the county, but they numbered fewer than the Polynesians. Still, Cache Valley's proportion of Spanish-speaking people was higher than Washington County's. Cache County had 7.9 percent in 2004 in contrast to Washington County's rate of about 5 percent. Why? Because Cache Valley has more industrial employers, such as the E.A. Miller/Swift meatpacking company, and agricultural businesses, which hired Hispanic workers who helped establish a community that then grew through other connections. Washington County had more service-related jobs, such as lodging and food-related businesses, than Cache Valley, but those jobs attracted Latinos in both counties.

Religious diversity was an increasing change. In 1950 virtually everyone in Dixie was Mormon. By 2005 there were thirty-seven other congregations, most with new church buildings. The Latter-day Saints had 180 regular congregations plus twenty branches and seventeen student wards. The Mormons constituted about 65 percent of the population. This compared to 172 regular congregations and twenty branches in Cache Valley, plus sixty college wards and ten young single-adult wards. The large number of student wards reflected the size of the student body at USU and its residential nature. The LDS component of the Cache County population was 72 percent. There were twenty-one religious congregations other than Latter-day Saints in Cache Valley. The FLDS people in Hildale and Colorado City were another group with distinctly different religious practices. Almost everyone in those communities was or had been an FLDS member. A vibrant new diversity came to Dixie by virtue of the growth, but not as much as along the Wasatch Front, where the LDS membership was below 60 percent and Spanish speakers represented more than 10 percent of the population.

One of the interesting aspects of life in Washington County was the high level of volunteerism in the society. What was the cause? Maybe it was the large numbers of retirees. Perhaps it was the high degree of religiosity. Whatever motivated these members of the community, many people found volunteering a way to make their life meaningful. They served as greeters and helpers in the hospitals. The Doctor's Free Clinic was another volunteer activity. There were volunteers in the public schools, in the historic St. George LIVE tours, in the Dove House, and Dixie Care and Share, and the St. George Detention Center. They shelved books at the libraries and served as members of Friends of the Library to raise funds; forty-five volunteers worked each week at the St. George Area Chamber of Commerce. Nursing homes depended on volunteers. The St. George Marathon required seventeen hundred volunteers to make the event possible. The Huntsman Senior Games used hundreds. Others ushered at concerts and served as guides at museums. The LDS Temple required fifteen hundred volunteers. Many served in the LDS Welfare Cannery and the orchard that supplies it. All denominations utilized volunteers to teach classes and sing in choirs and visit families. All city and town communities depended on volunteers to serve on committees; they promoted and staffed scores of fund-raising efforts. The county was driven by this citizen effort and thrived because of it.

These are some of the aspects of growth in Washington County in the first decade of the twenty-first century. What were the challenges these growth factors caused?

The number-one crucial issue raised by the growth was water. Where was the water going to come from if such growth continued? This was the continuation of the same concern that had begun in the 1850s. After the creation of five reservoirs and twenty wells, all of the growth and development in Washington County hinged on the same central issue—water. Several ambitious water projects enabled growth as the new century began. The flood of 2005 was the most severe one since 1862; it showed that water management was far from mastered.[11]

The Washington County Water Conservancy District built the Quail Creek Reservoir with a capacity of forty thousand acre-feet in 1985. In 2003 it added Sand Hollow Reservoir that also diverts water from the Virgin River, producing fifty-thousand additional acre-feet. Another project was the district's effort to link all of the water sources in the county so that supplies shifted easily. The long-range plan was to build a pipeline from Lake Powell to provide another seventy-thousand acre-feet of water. That plan was signed by Governor Jon Huntsman in 2006, and a funding proposal and land route are being negotiated.[12]

Critics argued that conservation should be tried first and limiting growth was urgent. Some opposed the pipeline, hoping to halt the expansion. Statistics were on their side when it came to water consumption per person. People in Las Vegas and Phoenix have learned to consume much less water than those in Utah's Dixie. Washington County citizens used far too much water to keep their lawns green. Xeriscaping as an option was beginning to be accepted, but not many were willing to do it voluntarily. Concerned citizens cited recent studies that showed a warming trend throughout the Intermountain Region, possibly linked to global warming. They also saw problems with a pipeline, such as terrorism, but mostly they opposed the pipeline because it would facilitate bringing 300,000 more people to Washington County. The crowding, the sprawl, the pollution, the damage to the fragile landscape and wildlife would be devastating, according to environmental spokespersons.

In the summer of 2006, the water issue focused on the Washington County Growth and Conservation Act, proposed by Senator Robert Bennett and Representative Jim Matheson with the backing of the Washington County Commission. It was based on legislation passed for Clark County in Nevada, sponsored by Senator Harry Reid. This Utah bill would determine whether existing wilderness study areas were wilderness or not, doing away with interim status and freeing some of the land for development. It would expand wilderness areas but also establish corridors for pipelines, roads, and utilities and designate access for off-road vehicles.

The debate was quite polarized. The environmentalists knew that St. George citizens had rejected a proposal to limit growth in 1993. That was not a great concern to them in 2006; a new set of leaders was on the scene. Their biggest worry was that passage of this bill for Washington County would set a precedent for the rest of the state, where the federal government owns 62 percent of the land and there was support, both in the government and the citizenry, to transfer a considerable portion of that ownership to the private sector. It was a major controversy with widespread implications. In late 2006, the Washington County Commisson invited Envision Utah to come to the county and involve the citizens in a planning process. That group had previously implemented its engaging sessions in Salt Lake and Utah Counties. It adopted the name Vision Dixie and received wide attention in all of the county's communities. The opponents of the Bennett bill argued vigorously that it should be delayed until the results of the Vision Dixie process produced revisions. In January 2009 a more limited lands bill was passed by the U.S. Congress.

Growth also caused other problems. The airport was too small. Waste was expanding exponentially, wages were too low, real-estate inflation was rampant, infrastructure was behind schedule—especially roads—pollution was increasing, open land was disappearing, sprawl was growing, workforce housing was too limited, planning needed updating. There was plenty for community leaders to work on.

The airport issue had been under consideration all during the 1990s because of the limited length of the runway. After a long environmental debate about flights approaching over Zion National Park, plans to build a new airport south of Washington Fields were nearing completion in 2006, and approval by federal agencies resulted in a recent favorable decision by the FAA. With a much longer runway, larger airplanes could service the area. This situation contrasted with Cache Valley, where air service was rather limited, mainly because the Salt Lake International Airport is only an hour and a half away. The fact that SkyWest Airlines had its national headquarters in St. George prioritized the drive for the new airport. In addition to increased air service, plans were under way to build another large industrial park near the airport. This effort was another evidence that the community is adopting the Wasatch Front mentality.

In 2006 the Washington County Solid Waste District implemented a modern landfill technique at the dump near Coral Canyon. It involved compressing layers of waste in rubber-based troughs, preventing the sewage from leaking into the ground. The volume of garbage increased, but so did the technology of compacting. The district intended to expand the present site to last several more decades. It contracted with private firms to collect waste based on a competitive bid.

Building roads and sewers and providing electrical services were continuing problems. Financing these utilities posed a challenge. The increase in revenue from building permits did not take inflation into account, so St. George boosted impact fees from $5,700 in 1996 to $10,000 in 2006. Hook-up and building-permit fees also went toward raising funds. The resurfacing and redesign of St. George Boulevard caused much discussion and concern, but in 2006 it was completed, creating a slower, more-decorative road in the city center. The extension of Skyline Drive and its resurfacing in the fall of 2006 diverted some of the traffic from the boulevard. Constructing Riverside Drive facilitated traffic flow from the River Road area to the I-15 access. A major plan called for a circle road that went completely around the main urban area, extending from Exit 2 of I-15 east past the new airport, then onto Highway 9 near Hurricane to the new Exit 13 at Washington City. Planners also wanted to build a highway west through the Desert Tortoise Preserve to join Snow Canyon Parkway to Santa Clara and Ivins, although the preserve does not now allow such a road.

Pollution became an increasing problem as the growth continued. If you stood at the current airport and looked over the city toward the Zion Canyon mountains, it was easy to see that there was already air pollution. The county did not have a limited-exhaust regulation like Salt Lake County and Utah Valley. Dixieites often watched the television reports about serious inversions there and especially in Cache Valley. Such inversions were rare in Washington County, but pollution levels were rising despite the decline in wood-burning stoves. It was obvious that city and county administrations would have to tackle the pollution caused by motor-vehicle exhaust.

Economic changes precipitated by growth also caused serious difficulties. The biggest one was housing inflation. The *Salt Lake Tribune* announced in June 2006 that St. George led the entire nation in home-price boom, with a 38.4 percent increase in one year. Homes that had sold for $125,000 two years earlier were selling in 2006 for $225,000. Land prices increased at least as much. Some of the newer developments were selling lots for more than $100,000 and still finding buyers. Homes constructed in these areas generally cost $500,000 or higher. As a result, workforce housing had nearly disappeared. This made it very difficult for middle-level workers such as teachers, policemen, and nurses to find any housing to purchase. The result was that many who had accepted jobs were forced to give them up and chose to go elsewhere. St. George established a Workforce Housing Task Force and proposed the construction of new housing complexes with regulations to accommodate these people.

Wages were another serious problem. For a long time, Washington County wages were 78 percent of the state average.[13] A similar situation existed in Cache Valley. What caused this? The availability of nine thousand college students in Washington County might have been a factor in depressing wages, and Cache Valley had more than two times as many. The distance from the Wasatch Front or Las Vegas, where wages were much higher, likely lowered the pay scale. The fact that most jobs were in the service sector—restaurants and merchandising—clearly had an influence. Obviously market forces were in charge on this issue, and they were not responding to the need for higher wages, despite the creation of higher-paying jobs in the industrial sector. Nonetheless, unemployment was only 2.8 percent in Washington County, with Cache Valley at 2.9 percent; both were below the state average at 3.5 percent.

As more and more people came to Utah's Dixie, housing developments moved farther and farther out onto the open land. The space between Washington City and St. George was completely filled, and Washington Fields was a place where upscale homes were quickly replacing agriculture. The area between St. George and Santa Clara was occupied, and most of the land between Santa Clara and Ivins filled up, also. The land from Kayenta on the west to Coral Canyon on the east became one metropolitan area. Hurricane experienced the same spreading; expectations were that it would extend from Coral Canyon east to the city center. Expansion south from the city center was already well under way, but plans already existed to develop large tracts on the way to Colorado City. There was talk of Hurricane incorporating 40,000 people by 2016 in contrast to its 2006 population of 11,376.

Where was the open land going to be? In a fragile desert landscape, such sprawl threatened the nature of the county—the scenic red desert that tourists came from around the world to see. Of particular concern was the Virgin River parkway—the highway going toward Zion National Park and passing through Virgin, Rockville, and Springdale. This road is a scenic treasure. If it started to look like Dixie Downs or Bloomington Hills, much of the mystique of the desert scenery would disappear. Should this be prevented and how? That will result in a hefty debate.

What did all this mean, all this growth, vitality, space expansion, water consumption, opulence, waste, traffic, industry, infrastructure, culture, and population? Was it breathtaking or a matter of concern? Was it evidence of the vitality of the American economy or a bubble about to burst? Had the growth come to a point where it was no longer sustainable?

Clearly the growth was a continuation of a forty-year steady trend. The same occurred in Cache Valley and all along the Wasatch Front. Dixie's growth was linked to the aging of America, a definite trend. It was defined by desert beauty. The mix of people who lived in the county was very desirable—youth, young parents, and grandparents, most of them well-educated. Unemployment was well below the state and national average. People felt safe.

There were also factors that caused concern—the heavy dependence on motor vehicles and gasoline, the resulting pollution in a desert landscape as population increased, the link to retirement incomes that might not be as stable in coming generations, the reliance on national economic prosperity because so much of the local economy was in service industries, the ever-spreading occupation of open spaces, the volatile situation in Hildale and Colorado City, and above all, the increasing necessity to import water.

As you walked around the county communities and the trails and the parks in 2006, you marveled—at the scenic vistas, the beautiful sky, the stunning red hills, the orderly society. Then immediately followed the hope that this could be preserved in the face of so much change tumbling in.

NOTES

1. *St. George Spectrum,* September 22, 2005; *Salt Lake Tribune,* August 22, 2006. A more specific statement is that in the decade from 1990 to 2000, the St. George metropolitan area was the fastest growing in the nation, measured as a percentage of growth—86.1 percent. Scott Hirschi, Washington County Economic Development Office, interview by author, October 2005. See also Nora and Pat Flannery, "Desert Playground," *The AARP Magazine,* July–August 2006.

2. *St. George Spectrum,* February 19, 2005; March 25, 2005; May 28, 2005; June 23, 2005; November 8, 2005; *Salt Lake Tribune,* March 14, 2004; August 1, 2004; August 4, 2004; August 21, 2005. *St George Spectrum,* November 21, 2006; November 22, 2006; *Salt Lake Tribune,* November 22, 2006; *St. George Spectrum,* December 14, 2006; December 15, 2006.

3. Utah Department of Workforce Services, *Washington County Demographic and Economic Profiles* (Salt Lake City: Utah Department of Workforce Services, August 2005), 9, 10, 27, 31.

4. John Willie, Washington County Planning Office, interview by author, October 2005.

5. Garry Bedingfield and Gary Campbell, officers of the Association of Private Unit Development and Condominiums, interview by author, October 2005.

6. Eric Pederson, interview by author, November, 2005.

7. *Demographic and Economic Profiles*, 9, 10, 27, 31.

8. Terri Draper and Steve Wilson, Dixie Regional Medical Center, interview by author, September 2002; Douglas D. Alder, *History of Health Care in Utah's Dixie* (St. George, UT: Dixie Regional Medical Center, 2003).

9. *Demographic and Economic Profiles,* 9, 10, 27, 31.

10. David Roos, Dixie State College registrar, interview by author, January 2009; Washington County school superintendent's office staff, interview by author, October 2005.

11. Lyman Hafen, *Portraits of Loss, Story of Hope* (St. George, UT: St. George Stories of Hope Volunteer Committee, 2005).

12. Julie Breckenridge, Washington County Water Conservancy District, interview by author, November 2005; also Washington County Water Conservancy District reports available at WCWCD offices, St. George, UT. See also *St. George Spectrum,* November 7, 2005.

13. *Demographic and Economic Profiles*, 9, 10, 27, 31.

Contributors

Douglas D. Alder is professor emeritus at Dixie State College where he served as president from 1986 to 1993. Previously he was professor of history at Utah State University. He and Karl Brooks wrote the *History of Washington County: From Isolation to Destination* (1996, 2006). He holds a PhD from the University of Oregon with doctoral research at the University of Vienna in Austria.

James B. Allen taught at Brigham Young University from 1963 until his retirement in 1992. He also served, half-time, as assistant church historian, from 1972 to 1979. He was chair of the History Department at BYU from 1980 to 1986. From 1986 to 1992 he held the Lemuel H. Redd Chair in Western American History. He has authored, co-authored, or co-edited a dozen books and numerous articles, including the award-winning book *Trials of Discipleship: The Story of William Clayton, A Mormon* (1987).

Amanda Midgley Borneman was born and raised in Utah. She graduated magna cum laude with a bachelor of science and received a master of arts degree in history from Brigham Young University. She has worked at the LDS Family and Church History Department and as an adjunct professor at Utah Valley University. A version of her chapter received the Helen Z. Papanikolas Award from the Utah State Historical Society in 2006.

Brian Q. Cannon is director of the Charles Redd Center for Western Studies and associate professor of history at Brigham Young University, where he has taught since 1992. He is the author of over two dozen publications in Utah, western, Mormon, and rural history including *Reopening the Frontier: Homesteading in the Modern West* (2009).

Joseph F. Darowski received a bachelor of science from Cornell University and a master of arts in history from Brigham Young University. He has done additional graduate work at the College of William and Mary and earned a diploma from the Institute for the Editing of Historical Documents at the University of Wisconsin-Madison. He is currently a volume editor for the Joseph Smith Papers Project of the Church of Jesus Christ of Latter-day Saints History Department.

A<small>DAM</small> E<small>ASTMAN</small>, a native of Orem, Utah, is currently a PhD candidate at the University of Oklahoma. He received his bachelor of arts degree. from Utah Valley University in 2003 and his master of arts from Brigham Young University in 2006. He has authored a history of the Jordan Valley Water Conservancy District published in 2006 and a forthcoming history of the Central Utah Water Conservancy District.

J<small>ESSIE</small> L. E<small>MBRY</small> is the associate director of the Charles Redd Center and an associate research professor at Brigham Young University. She is the author of ten books and over one hundred articles dealing with Utah, Mormon, and western American history.

M<small>ATTHEW</small> C. G<small>ODFREY</small> is president of Historical Research Associates, Inc., a historical and archeological consulting firm headquartered in Missoula, Montana. He has a PhD in public history from Washington State University and is the author of *Religion, Politics, and Sugar: The Mormon Church, the Federal Government, and the Utah-Idaho Sugar Company, 1907–1921* (2007).

W<small>AYNE</small> K. H<small>INTON</small> retired from Southern Utah University in June 2006 after a thirty-eight-year teaching career, eighteen of which he served as department chair. He has published four books, several chapters in additional books, three encyclopedia articles, and over thirty articles in professional journals. He has degrees from Dixie College, Utah State University, and Brigham Young University and did a postdoctorate study at the University of California, Davis.

D<small>AVID</small> R<small>ICH</small> L<small>EWIS</small>, an Ogden, Utah, native, is professor of history at Utah State University and editor of the *Western Historical Quarterly*. His publications include *Neither Wolf Nor Dog: American Indians, Environment, and Agrarian Change* (1994), and most recently a chapter on Utah's Skull Valley Goshutes and nuclear waste storage in his co-edited book *Native Americans and the Environment: Perspectives on the Ecological Indian* (2007).

J<small>OHN</small> S. M<small>C</small>C<small>ORMICK</small> earned a PhD in intellectual history from the University of Iowa. He is dean of the School of Humanities and Social Sciences at Salt Lake Community College. One of his particular interests is the history of radical left movements in the United States

J<small>ACOB</small> W. O<small>LMSTEAD</small> is a PhD candidate studying American history at Texas Christian University. His writing has appeared in the *Journal of Mormon History* and the *Utah Historical Quarterly*. Examining Fort Worth's 1936 celebration of the Texas Frontier Centennial, his dissertation research explores the relationship of gender, morality, and boosterism in the development of a useable western past.

Stephen C. Roberds is associate professor of political science at Adams State College. His main research areas are scandals and congressional elections, voting behavior, and obscenity law. He has published articles and chapters in numerous books and journals including *Politics and Policy, Public Integrity,* and *NetSeXXX.*

Jedediah S. Rogers is a doctoral candidate in history at Arizona State University and a resident historian working for the Bureau of Reclamation in Denver, Colorado. His area of study is western American and environmental history, and his dissertation is a modern history of land-use and access conflicts in the West.

Kristen Rogers-Iversen is a writer who is the communication officer for the Utah Division of State History and a history columnist for the *Salt Lake Tribune.* Her goal is to make history meaningful and relevant to today's issues, in order to help create a more just, sustainable, and compassionate world.

Susan Sessions Rugh is associate professor of history at Brigham Young University and author of the book *Are We There Yet? The Golden Age of American Family Vacations* (2008).

Stephen C. Sturgeon is manuscript curator and associate librarian in Special Collections & Archives and adjunct associate professor in history at Utah State University. He received his PhD from the University of Colorado and is the author of *The Politics of Western Water* (2002).

John R. Sillito is professor of libraries at Weber State University, Ogden, Utah, where he was the Nye Honors Professor in 2002. His edited collection, *History's Apprentice: The Diaries of B. H. Roberts, 1880-1898* (2004), won the Mormon History Association's Steven F. Christensen Award for the best documentary work on Mormon history in 2005.

Index